# THE
# EGOTISTICAL SUBLIME

# THE EGOTISTICAL SUBLIME

*A History of*
WORDSWORTH'S
IMAGINATION

*By*
JOHN JONES
*Fellow of Merton College*
*Oxford*

1964
CHATTO & WINDUS
LONDON

Published by
Chatto and Windus Ltd
London

∗

Clarke, Irwin and Co. Ltd
Toronto

First Published 1954
Second Impression 1960
This Edition 1964

Printed in Great Britain
by NOVELLO & COMPANY LIMITED
LONDON W.1

For William Bell

1924-1948

## NOTE

I refer to *Wordsworth's Poetical Works*, edited by Professor Ernest de Selincourt and Dr Helen Darbishire, in the case of texts and variants of texts that will not be found in the Oxford Standard Authors Edition. References to *The Prelude* are, unless otherwise stated, to the text of 1805, which is published in a separate volume of the Oxford Standard Authors.

# PREFACE

THIS is a book of some pretension in its attempt to minister to truths that lie too often unregarded, bedridden in an outhouse of the soul.

The work of the Romantics, poets and novelists, celebrates the fact of love, at once marvellously evident and difficult beyond despair, and about which the age immediately preceding them had been less than honest. This is true also of Wordsworth's poetry, but in so peculiar a sense as to make us wonder how he can be called Romantic; for he begins with a vision of Sympathy that belongs, in so far as genius can belong anywhere, to the eighteenth century, and he ends with the Religion of Gratitude, tractarian and catholic in its associations.

While discussing these things I refer frequently to Coleridge, in the belief that his history and Wordsworth's continue to illuminate each other, by way of contrast, throughout their lives; and although I essay greater intellectual rigour than is usually thought necessary for interpretative criticism, I do so in the name of literature and not of philosophy. If, as seems the case with all philosophical thinking below the highest level of European achievement, clarity can be gained only at the cost of imaginative faintness, then we must persevere within that warm chaos which is critical tradition and in which the idea of poetry can be at least entertained. Even third-rate critics have touched a relevant humility and wonder.

An argument may be unphilosophical, arbitrary in its choice of route and its crossing of categorical frontiers, yet it need not be without its own kind of discipline. If there is no structural method, the way into the critical activity is unimportant. Thus Words-

worth made two suggestions to Coleridge for his
*Ancient Mariner*. One of these was the albatross, the
lonely bird which I relate to Wordsworth's preoccupation with solitude. The other was the navigation
of the ship by the dead men. Of this I make no use at
all, but only through an accident of inclination; for the
two poets might well be approached by way of their
attitudes to death. In early versions of the Immortality
Ode the child thinks of the grave, without horror or
disgust, as

> but a lonely bed without the sense or sight
> Of day or the warm light,
> A place of thought where we in waiting lie. . . .

Coleridge called this a "frightful notion", and persuaded Wordsworth to omit all reference to the child's
vision of life in death. Implicit in this clash of imaginations is a profound difference in understanding of the
life of thought and of sensation, of the Christian reality
of sin and judgment, of relationship with God and
Nature. The argument might have been quite other
than what it is, but directed towards the same conclusion.

If the study is unphilosophical, so is its subject.
Wordsworth, though no fool, was no philosopher; and
it were very perverse to seek a respectable metaphysical
home for his poetry. The most that we can say, which
may be everything or almost nothing, is that all apprehensions of truth support each other simply in their
humanity. Only through Wordsworth's sentiment of
the "one human heart" is it worth while to consider
his own ethical severity, his view of language as a mode
of Nature, and the commanding of expressive forms as
an exercise of practical reason pursued intuitively beyond the phenomenal limits of speculation. Only in this
spirit is his power of deep gazing upon objects to be
referred to that "change in the shading" of which

Husserl speaks, whereby a man may transform "a
pure psychology of the inner life into a self-styled
transcendental phenomenology". Thus, in striving for
final synthesis, the great movement of his life towards
solitude, then away, seems less a defeat than a discovery.
Aquinas had shown that singulars in the world are
infinite, but only potentially so. The moral may rest
here.

# CONTENTS

# I

## THE ARGUMENT

SINCE Wordsworth died, nothing has influenced the fortunes of his poetry so much as Matthew Arnold's *Golden Treasury Selection*. Nor is this hard to understand. Arnold's is a good Selection, and the path which he found through that vast extent of Pastoral and Patriotism is one which later explorers, critics and general readers alike, have been glad to follow. Also, and again because he selected well, Arnold made it impossible for those who came after him to ignore the fact that most of Wordsworth's best poetry was written within the single decade preceding the publication, in 1807, of his *Poems in Two Volumes*. This, more than anything else, has commanded the attention of writers on Wordsworth, and has produced a mass of speculation as to the cause of his decline.

But there is another and less obvious way in which Arnold's influence has been both widespread and enduring. He tells his readers, in the Preface to his Selection, to forget about Wordsworth's philosophy and to devote themselves to his poetry. Wordsworth the philosopher, says Arnold, is a sham; but Wordsworth the poet stands next to Shakespeare and Milton. And this judgment, apparently innocent in its Victorian largeness, is the beginning of our troubles.

Coleridge would have disagreed with Arnold. His knowledge of Wordsworth's poetry up to 1814—in particular, of the unpublished *Prelude*—led him to look forward to *The Recluse* as "the *first* and *only* true philosophical poem in existence".[1] In 1814 *The Excursion* was published, a poem of 10,000 lines, but still a mere instalment of the great *Recluse*, Words-

[1] *Letters of S. T. Coleridge* (ed. E. H. Coleridge), Vol. II. p. 648.

worth's intended life work. In *The Excursion* Coleridge expected to find a Christian Philosophy, and, as he admitted quite frankly,[1] he was disappointed. Now Arnold's attack on Wordsworth's philosophy was aimed primarily at *The Excursion*, which suggests that Coleridge came in the end to anticipate Arnold's view of Wordsworth. But this is not so. Arnold's quarrel with *The Excursion* was really a quarrel with his own generation, with the moral enthusiasm that confuses pietism and philosophy. *The Excursion* is certainly much more than pietism, but it is less than Christian apologetic: despite the doctrine strewn about its surface, it contains neither sustained defence nor clear affirmation of belief; and Arnold was not tempted by the ethical and undogmatic nature of his own Christianity to call *The Excursion* philosophical. Instead, he poked fun at earnest Wordsworthians, and their talk of the philosopher-poet. And here Arnold and Coleridge are never on common ground; for Coleridge continued, despite his disappointment, to maintain that "Wordsworth possessed more of the genius of a great philosophical poet than any man I ever knew, or, as I believe, has existed in England since Milton".[2] Both good critics, Coleridge and Arnold were both traffickers in generality. Coleridge believed that "no man was ever yet a great poet without being at the same time a profound philosopher"[3]; and Arnold dallied to little purpose with his distinguishing of philosopher and poet. To learn from them, we must ask direct questions.

Why did Arnold consider Wordsworth a great poet? That he discovered in Wordsworth's poetry a searching criticism of life, is no answer; for this was Arnold's universal measure of greatness. He has, as it turns out, something more to say. "In Wordsworth's case, the

[1] *Letters of S. T. Coleridge* (ed. E. H. Coleridge), Vol. II. pp. 645-6.
[2] *Table Talk*, July 31, 1832.
[3] *Biographia Literaria* (ed. J. Shawcross), Vol. II. p. 19.

accident, for so it may be called, of inspiration, is of peculiar importance." "He has no style." "Nature seems to take the pen out of his hand and to write for him with her own bare, sheer, penetrating power."[1] This is a graceful evasion; but not on that account to be ignored. Arnold strikes an attitude in which Wordsworthian criticism has for the most part persisted—less prettily, as the years pass, and with vague gestures towards the poetry of the Great Decade.

We must ask Arnold what sort of poetry it is that Nature writes for Wordsworth.

> He laid us as we lay at birth
> On the cool flowery lap of earth.[2]

Arnold's answer amounts to this: it is redemptive poetry. Its office is to deliver us from a stale, tired, doubt-ridden world, and restore us to a world fresh and undivided. This world is recognized at once as the home of the Scholar Gipsy; and although we cannot determine its limits exactly—Arnold had no clear sight of it himself, and in any case his invocation of the Oxford countryside diverts our attention—it is certainly less Christian than Pagan: it wears not the innocence of the Garden of Eden, but the brightness, the poetic immediacy of the Golden Age.

The Scholar Gipsy learnt a secret which enabled him to escape from this world and to find another. He promised, when he left, that he would return one day and divulge his secret; but even if he had kept this promise, he could not have helped Wordsworth to write The Recluse: Wordsworth's task was to make sense of this world, not to find a better and a timeless one. This is clearly brought out by Coleridge when, late in life, he reverts to the scheme of The Recluse:

> Then the plan laid out, and, I believe, partly suggested by me, was that Wordsworth should assume the station of a man

---

[1] Preface to Golden Treasury Selection.　　[2] Memorial Verses.

in mental repose, one whose principles were made up, and so prepared to deliver upon authority a system of philosophy. He was to treat man as man—a subject of eye, ear, touch, and taste, in contact with external nature, and informing the senses from the mind, and not compounding a mind out of the senses; then he was to describe the pastoral and other states of society, assuming something of the Juvenalian spirit as he approached the high civilization of cities and towns, and opening a melancholy picture of the present state of degeneracy and vice; thence he was to infer and reveal the proof of, and necessity for, the whole state of man and society being subject to, and illustrative of, a redemptive process in operation, showing how this idea reconciled all the anomalies, and promised future glory and restoration. Something of this sort was, I think, agreed on. It is, in substance, what I have been all my life doing in my system of philosophy.[1]

Unlike Arnold, Coleridge actually talks about redemption, intending that the word shall bear a Christian meaning. This brings in issue his own and Wordsworth's Christianity; and here we must be clear about dates. *The Recluse* was first thought of in the early months of 1798, at a time when Wordsworth and Coleridge were working together in close poetic partnership. Then, while the grand design was being evolved, Coleridge was still a disciple of Priestley and Frend in the Unitarian faith; his religion enthusiastic, but almost entirely innocent of doctrine. It is true that his attitude towards Wordsworth's Christianity was sometimes critical, but the criticism was aimed at his faint heart rather than his false opinions. He detected in Wordsworth a certain hesitancy, and was once or twice offended by his irreverent tone when speaking of religion.[2] Nevertheless, the measure of agreement

[1] *Table Talk*, July 31, 1832.
[2] *Letters* (ed. E. H. Coleridge), Vol. I. pp. 164, 246. *Anima Poetae* (ed. E. H. Coleridge), p. 35.

between them is of much greater importance than their differences: both, at this time, were trying to graft some sort of Christianity on to the dry and feeble stem of eighteenth-century deism; and Coleridge's account of *The Recluse*, in its confident, demonstrative tone, and its independence of revealed religion, catches the quality of this effort to study the world and to prove, as it were by internal evidence, both its need of a Redeemer and the fact of its redemption. But when he proceeds to say, of Wordsworth's aim in *The Recluse*, that "it is, in substance, what I have been all my life doing in my system of philosophy", he invites misunderstanding. Both Wordsworth and he moved a long way from the position which they held in 1798; and they did not travel together. They were in any case very different men.

Coleridge knew himself too well to suppose that he could live by philosophy alone, or yet to deny that philosophy nourished and supported him. "In certain waters," he said, "it may teach the exact depth and prevent a drowning."[1] When, in his discussion of the scheme of *The Recluse*, he speaks of the relationship between man and the external world, between the mind and the senses, we must place his remarks in the context of his reading in philosophy. Without some knowledge of philosophers there can be no understanding of Coleridge, for he lived with them and they helped to shape his world. He dealt instinctively in the currency of intellect, and the instinct was a deep one. In his own philosophizing one looks in vain for consistency of achievement; but there is a kind of consistency of intellectual effort, not to be passed over.

Coleridge wrote, in 1797: "My mind feels as if it ached to behold and know something *great*, something

[1] *Anima Poetae* (ed. E. H. Coleridge), p. 255.

*one* and *indivisible*. And it is only in the faith of that, that rocks or waterfalls, mountains or caverns, give me the sense of sublimity or majesty."[1] And in an autobiographical letter of the same year, he argued, in defence of his childhood reading of fairy stories and tales of adventure: "I know of no other way of giving the mind a love of the Great and the Whole."[2] The love of the great and the whole, and the struggle for its secure possession, is the story of Coleridge's life, both in thought and in art. Wherever we enter Coleridge's philosophy, we come upon Descartes' reduction of reality into the distinct kinds of thought and extension; a discovery which should not surprise us since the Cartesian Dichotomy has to a large extent determined the form of metaphysical thinking since the Renaissance. Perhaps reality is dualistic, constituted in this way of thinking things and extended things. And perhaps there can be no intercourse between the two kinds. But metaphysicians who admit the first nearly all deny the second, in the interest of knowledge and morality. They attempt to bridge the gulf between the self and the external world and thus to save philosophy; some, like Descartes himself, by means of scientific theories regarding mind and matter, and others by appealing to God as the Underwriter of appearance.

There is a second metaphysical tradition in which Descartes' initial dichotomy is denied, a tradition into which Coleridge eventually found his way. His theory of art serves to introduce us to this manner of thinking. "To make the external internal, the internal external, to make Nature thought and thought Nature—this is the mystery of genius in the Fine Arts."[3] Coleridge is on familiar ground: he is talking Idealism and

---

[1] *Letters* (ed. E. H. Coleridge), Vol. I. p. 228.
[2] *Ibid.*, p. 16.
[3] "Essay on Poesy or Art", *Biographia Literaria* (ed. J. Shawcross), Vol. II. p. 258.

he is heavily in debt to a German—in this case to Schelling.

The language of Idealism came naturally to Coleridge. He remained, throughout all his philosophical wanderings, a Platonist, and he saw the post-Kantian movement in which he took part as a return to Greek modes of thought. His own philosophy is dominated by the organic metaphor and by the dialectical method, and it can lay claim to more originality than Coleridge, by his widespread and usually unacknowledged borrowings, has led people to believe. The dialectic is itself in point. Coleridge is often assumed to be echoing Hegel; but this cannot be so, for he knew no Hegel when he evolved his own method, the true ancestry of which may be discovered in the references, scattered throughout his writings, to Heraclitus and his philosophy of flux, to Bruno's Polar Principle, and, more immediately, to the triadic form in which Kant disposed his categories, described by Coleridge as "the prominent excellence in Kant's *Critique of the Pure Reason*".[1] The weakness of his philosophy is not that it is derivative, but that it seeks to be Christian. He fails to perform the first, in a sense the impossible, task of Christian philosophy, which is to reconcile Greek thought with Hebrew faith.

At one time Coleridge seems to have been tempted to found his whole metaphysic, as Schelling did, upon a theory of creative imagination, which, in overcoming the opposition of subject and object, "enables art to compass the impossible, to resolve an infinite contradiction in a finite product".[2] But he resisted this temptation, and his reason for doing so is significant. Schelling and his followers, he says, are guilty of a "confusion of the creaturely spirit in the great moments

---

[1] MS. cited by Alice D. Snyder, *Coleridge on Logic and Learning*, p. 129 n
[2] Schelling, *Werke*, Vol. III. p. 349.

B

of its renascence with the deific energies in Deity itself".[1] The Jew and the Greek were both strong in Coleridge, and he could not keep the peace between them. This I believe to be the secret of the prodigious scope and energy of his thought, and of his lameness in formal exposition. He worshipped the Hebrew God, a God of righteousness and the world's creator, long before he reached anything that could be called Christian orthodoxy; and all his life he felt impelled in his own fashion to justify God's ways to men. But to talk of God and man is to consider personal relations; a thing Coleridge was ill equipped to do. For when he made alliance with his German contemporaries, he committed himself to a monistic philosophy dedicated to the overpassing of relation: a philosophy grounded in the unitary consciousness, and progressing in terms of the continual reconstitution and enlargement of consciousness. In deserting Spinoza, Coleridge rejected a philosophy of purely immanent deity; but he found nothing in German Idealism whereby to redress the balance through a philosophy of divine transcendence. He was not blind to his position: indeed his largest achievement was to anticipate, in part, both Hegel and Kierkegaard's criticism of Hegel. And so he found no rest, but wandered ceaselessly; in love with identity and haunted by relation; always, as Dorothy Wordsworth described him, "in search of something new", but returning again and again to the meeting-place of Jew and Greek in the Alexandrian schools.

With Wordsworth the case is different. Recently, and especially in America, there has been a reaction against Arnold's summary dismissal of his philosophy. Scarcely anyone has been so rash as to claim system for

[1] J. H. Muirhead, *Coleridge as Philosopher*, p. 56, citing C.'s MS. note on Jacob Boehme's *Aurora*.

the whole body of his writing, but it has become almost modish to argue that in a particular poem or period of his life Wordsworth was under the influence of this or that philosopher; and then to study the work of master and disciple in close relation. Wordsworth himself gives no encouragement to this tendency: his references to philosophy are few and usually disparaging. He read little, and showed no interest in contemporary thought. Towards Kant and his successors his attitude was one of ignorant defiance: when taxed, late in life, with the question of Coleridge's plagiarisms, he declared that he had "never read a word of German metaphysics, thank Heaven!"[1]

But the matter is not so easily disposed of; for it is always possible that what he failed to read in books he heard from Coleridge: and when a critic claims to discover echoes of Plato, of the hermetical books, of Spinoza, of Shaftesbury, of Hartley, of Stoic and Kantian morality, of all sorts of mystical writings, he can appeal with perfect confidence to Coleridge's conversation. No doubt Coleridge said it all. And there can be no general denial of such a claim, because Wordsworth's work abounds in verbal echoes. What must be denied is that the existence of these echoes is enough to establish the tracing of intellectual debts as a valid critical method.

Concerning Wordsworth's philosophical borrowings, the first of his prose works is the one most in point. In 1793 he made an essay in political theory, in the form of an open letter to the Bishop of Llandaff, "on the extraordinary avowal of his Political Principles, contained in the Appendix to his late Sermon: by a Republican". Men were being persecuted at this time for the expression of radical opinions, and Wordsworth prudently did not publish his letter. The Bishop's

---

[1] *Correspondence of Crabb Robinson with the Wordsworth Circle* (ed. Edith J. Morley), Vol. I. p. 401.

Appendix is a feeble performance. It is inordinately complacent:

> The greatest freedom that can be enjoyed by man in a state of civil society, the greatest security that can be given him with respect to the protection of his character, property, personal liberty, limb, and life, is afforded to every individual by our present constitution.[1]

And it presents, in as crude a form as one could find, the conservative argument for orders established and unchangeable:

> I do not mean to speak of peasants and mechanics with any degree of disrespect; I am not so ignorant of the importance, either of the natural or social chain by which all the individuals of the human race are connected together, as to think disrespectfully of any link of it. Peasants and mechanics are as useful to the State as any other order of men; but their utility consists in their discharging well the duties of their respective stations; it ceases when they affect to become legislators; when they intrude themselves into concerns for which their education has not fitted them.[2]

Wordsworth does better than this. Not long before his letter was written, as he relates in *The Prelude*, he had been in London, listening to the great parliamentary orators of the day. And not without profit, for his letter is a good debating performance. The bishop had declared: "The courts of British justice are impartial and incorrupt; they respect not the persons of men; the poor man's lamb is, in their estimation, as sacred as the monarch's crown. . . ."[3] Wordsworth replies: "I congratulate your Lordship upon your enthusiastic fondness for the judicial proceedings of this country. I am happy to find you have passed

---

[1] A. B. Grosart, *Prose Works of W. Wordsworth*, Vol. I. p. 26.
[2] Grosart, Vol. I. p. 28.
[3] *Ibid.*, p. 26.

through life without having your fleece torn from your back in the thorny labyrinth of litigation."[1] There is personal bitterness here, for at this date Wordsworth's family was still trying, without any success, to recover a large sum of money of which Lord Lonsdale had wrongfully deprived them ten years earlier.

Wordsworth follows the radical pamphleteers of the time in his argument for universal suffrage and in his attack on the powers of the Crown and all kinds of hereditary privilege. But what he has to say he says clearly, and with an impassioned dignity of style characteristic of his best prose. Moreover, there is something very personal to Wordsworth in his appreciating thus soon the economic evils of the Industrial Revolution: it is a standpoint which he never abandoned, and which explains the radicalism that stayed with him until he died. Our legislators, says Wordsworth, who profess to hold private property inviolable,

> have unjustly left unprotected that most important part of property, not less real because it has no material existence, that which ought to enable the labourer to provide food for himself and his family. I appeal to innumerable statutes, whose constant and professed object it is to lower the price of labour, to compel the workman to be *content* with arbitrary wages, evidently too small from the necessity of legal enforcement of the acceptance of them. Even from the astonishing amount of the sums raised for the support of one description of the poor may be concluded the extent and greatness of that oppression, whose effects have rendered it possible for the few to afford so much, and have shown us that such a multitude of our brothers exist in even helpless indigence.[2]

There is good sense and fine writing in Wordsworth's letter; but he is no more a political philosopher than his opponent. He meets the bishop's naïve affirma-

[1] Grosart, Vol. I. p. 20.      [2] *Ibid.*, p. 16.

tion of the *status quo* with an equally ingenuous plea for revolution. More than once in his letter Wordsworth refers to Rousseau's master concept, the General Will. Rousseau himself works the General Will very hard: it is the means by which he seeks to reconcile a democratic theory of government with the doctrine of natural rights. He argues, in the tradition of Locke, that every individual in the state is the bearer of certain fundamental rights of which he cannot be deprived by any other man or by the state itself; but, unlike Locke, he is a democrat and must explain why the natural rights of the minority are not at the mercy of the ruling majority. It has sometimes been said, and often implied, that the General Will is an elaborate device for proving that the majority can do no wrong. But this is misleading: the General Will has been an idea of enormous influence because it faces two ways—backwards, towards the eighteenth-century school of natural law; and forwards, towards corporate theories of the state in which the words "majority" and "minority" suffer a sea change.

Wordsworth shows no sign of having understood Rousseau: what is much more important, he makes it quite clear that he does not think like a philosopher. His argument is robustly practical; and, although decked out in the terms of political theory, it never moves among intellectual abstractions. He defines republican laws as "the expression of the general will"[1]; but then, instead of considering the General Will and the mode of its self-expression in terms of law, he reasons, like a sensible policeman, that "a Republic has a manifest advantage over a Monarchy, in as much as less force is requisite to compel obedience to its laws".[2] Wordsworth's political writing has moral passion and an intense though often incoherent humanity; but it has no theoretical merits.

[1] Grosart, Vol. I. p. 12.    [2] *Ibid.*, p. 12.

The General Will does not matter because Wordsworth's use of it scarcely extends beyond verbal echo. He knew the phrase, but did not see its point: nor, probably, did he try, for his interest in politics was not speculative. But there is another kind of indebtedness which Wordsworth admitted and which he believed to be important. He wrote to a friend, in March 1798, when he was beginning to think about *The Recluse*: "If you could collect for me any books of travels, you would render me an essential service, as without much of such reading my present labours cannot be brought to a conclusion."[1] Here we have the encouragement that is strikingly absent in the case of philosophy; and Wordsworth's poetry bears him out to this extent, that it shows wide and careful reading in the literature of travel.

There is, for example, a passage in *The Prelude* which, in its general tone of oriental delight and its reference to "Domes of Pleasure", invites comparison with *Kubla Khan*. We find in John Barrow's *Travels in China:* "The Emperor was pleased to give directions to his first minister to shew us his park or garden at Gehol. It is called in Chinese Van-shoo-yuen, or the Paradise of ten thousand trees. . . ."[2] And Wordsworth speaks of the country where he was born as a

> tract more exquisitely fair
> Than is that Paradise of ten thousand Trees,
> Or Gehol's famous Gardens, in a Clime
> Chosen from widest empire, for delight
> Of the Tartarian Dynasty composed;
> (Beyond that mighty Wall, not fabulous,
> China's stupendous mound!) by patient skill
> Of myriads, and boon Nature's lavish help;
> Scene link'd to scene, an evergrowing change,

1 *Early Letters of W. and Dorothy Wordsworth* (ed. de Selincourt), p. 188
2 *Wordsworth's "Prelude"* (ed. de Selincourt), p. 550.

> Soft, grand, or gay! with Palaces and Domes
> Of Pleasure spangled over, shady Dells
> For Eastern Monasteries, sunny Mounds
> With Temples crested, Bridges, Gondolas,
> Rocks, Dens, and Groves. . . .[1]

What can be said of this? No more, I think, than that Wordsworth read travel books for the good reason that they interested him, and when he came himself to describe strange or fabulous lands he drew upon his reading. A Wordsworthian equivalent to *The Road to Xanadu* would be dull indeed; for Wordsworth lacked the entireness of mind that makes Coleridge's borrowing revelant to his poetry. Travel books were sources of information, and he reproduced what he wanted, in loose verse paraphrase. The result is not always a failure: Wordsworth's description of tropical scenery in *Ruth*, for which he is indebted to Bartram's *Travels*, could hardly be improved upon in simple vividness. But Wordsworthian scholarship remains in this respect a negative discipline: it teaches the unimportance of his sources.

The story of Wordsworth's poetic debts has a similar beginning. At the age of fourteen he was set to write a poem in celebration of his school's second centenary. The result he later judged to be "but a tame imitation of Pope's versification".[2] And so it is: but to say no more is to deal harshly with a small boy's Heroics; for they have a certain alertness, and they catch the antithetical manner well enough to show that he had a quick ear for style:

> Oft have I said, the paths of Fame pursue,
> And all that Virtue dictates, dare to do;
> Go to the world, peruse the book of man,
> And learn from thence thy own defects to scan;

---

[1] Bk. VIII. 121.
[2] *Poetical Works* (ed. de Selincourt), Vol. I. p. 366.

Severely honest, break no plighted trust,
But coldly rest not here—be more than just. . . .[1]

In 1787, when he was sixteen, Wordsworth first published a poem, a sonnet *On seeing Miss Helen Maria
Williams weep at a tale of distress*. This also might be
called a tame imitation; but it differs from the centenary
poem in one important respect: Wordsworth has
abandoned the sense of Pope for the sensibility of Miss
Williams, a specialist in the poetry of feeling which
enjoyed a great vogue at this time and infested the
magazines with just such rubbish as Wordsworth's
sonnet:

She wept.—Life's purple tide began to flow
In languid streams through every thrilling vein;
Dim were my swimming eyes—my pulse beat slow,
And my full heart was swelled to dear delicious pain.

It is not at all extraordinary that a schoolboy should
imitate his elders. Wordsworth's early verse is none the
less remarkable in the extent to which it is pure copy—
much of it is direct translation or adaptation of Greek
and Latin originals—and in the diversity of its models.
Most of these were soon discarded; but Wordsworth
never outgrew the instinct to copy closely, as is
evidenced by his continuing interest in translation and
by the pains which he bestowed upon his modernized
versions of Chaucer.

This instinct, in itself a brute fact of which nothing
can be made, derives significance from its manifesting
the most vital quality of Wordsworth's mind—I mean
its literalness. Literalness is the necessary preface to his
genius. Everything, for him, was what it was, and it was
not anything else: the thing done or suffered, the thing
seen or heard or read, touched him because it was so.
In its being so he saw it as somehow self-guaranteeing

[1] *And Has the Sun . . .?*

—this was the heart of his naturalistic optimism; and yet to see things as they are he considered no easy matter, but the reward of vigilant devotion to the actual—and this was the burden of his greatest poetry. There is no escaping Wordsworth's literalness: it appears in the worst as well as in the best things he did. It betrays itself in his ill-considered appeal, when attacking poetic diction, to the "language really used by men", as more poetic than poetry; and much of his weakest verse stands as a monument to the delusion that he had done what was required of him if he stuck closely to the facts. Literalness is responsible for his profundity and narrowness alike. His obstinacy, his very limited powers of self-criticism, his feeble sense of humour, his plain dullness, are all attributable to it.

Because this literalness is everywhere, its kinds must be distinguished, and the difference made clear between what matters and what does not. The task is sometimes easy. Thus it would be patently absurd to explain the fair success of the poem *Stepping Westward* by the fact that it begins with the actual words of a greeting extended to Wordsworth when he was travelling in Scotland with Dorothy; or, on the other hand, to argue that *Simon Lee* is a failure because "the expression when the hounds were out, 'I dearly love their voices' was word for word from his own lips",[1] as Wordsworth tells us in his note to the poem. In both cases Wordsworth attached importance to the very words he heard, and he therefore held fast to them. In *Stepping Westward* he explains, effectively, why they mattered to him:

> The salutation had to me
> The very sound of courtesy:
> Its power was felt. . . .

[1] *P.W.*, Vol. IV. p. 413.

But in *Simon Lee* he is too intent upon an accurate recording of the facts to explain anything, and the result is a disaster:

> And he is lean and he is sick;
> His body, dwindled and awry,
> Rests upon ankles swoln and thick;
> His legs are thin and dry.
> One prop he has, and only one,
> His wife, an aged woman,
> Lives with him, near the waterfall,
> Upon the village Common.

But the utterances that caught Wordsworth's attention are both external to his poems: they are occasions for poetry, and everything depends on what is made of them.

This is simple enough. But when the sovereign quality of Wordsworth's mind reveals itself in purely literary debts, the distinction between relevant and irrelevant becomes much more subtle. There is a very early work, written probably when Wordsworth was sixteen, which I shall quote in full. By no means a good poem, it has things of interest in it; and the problem is made neat by the fact that we are concerned with indebtedness to a single poet, Milton, and a single poem, *Lycidas*. Wordsworth's elegy on a drowned dog opens thus:

> Where were ye, nymphs, when the remorseless deep
> Clos'd o'er your little favourite's hapless head?
> For neither did ye mark with solemn dread[1]
> In Derwent's rocky woods the white Moonbeam
> Pace like a Druid o'er the haunted steep;
> Nor in Winander's stream.[2]

---

[1] Professor de Selincourt's text has "dream", but the sense and the rhyme scheme seem to require "dread". In Wordsworth's MS. the page is torn and the last letter of this word is missing.

[2] *P.W.*, Vol. I. p. 264.

This looks like parody. Wordsworth, one might at once suppose, is warning us in the first two lines that he is being deliberately absurd at the expense of *Lycidas*; the absurdity heightened by the way Milton degenerates into the diction of eighteenth-century Miltonic as soon as the very words of *Lycidas* are abandoned, at "little favourite's hapless head". The skilfully managed short line and the echo of Milton's "steep Where your old bards, the famous Druids, lie", point to the same conclusion. But Wordsworth is not being funny: it was not in his nature to regard his own literalness as amusing or ridiculous. And there is more here than Milton. Let us isolate the simile:

> For neither did ye mark . . . the white Moonbeam
> Pace like a Druid. . . .

Milton's similes have an extended splendour: in their slow unfolding they enforce the relentless, even thrust of his verse. But this simile does not march. "White", which appears at first the conventional monosyllabic adjective needed for "moonbeam", gains suddenly in strength from its literal applicability to "Druid". And "pace", while plainly descriptive of "Druid", is startling in relation to its own subject. Wordsworth has so strengthened the second term of his comparison that it cannot be taken as in any way dependent on the first: the whole is instantly reread with the terms inverted, and because of this double movement, animate and inanimate are held in urgent and reciprocal relationship, the tension of which is accentuated by the line end pause and by the unexpected stress on "pace" which makes a fulcrum of the verb. There is an odd compactness by virtue of which Wordsworth's simile looks like a metaphor; and it has the same quality, although it is not so closely wrought, as

> The cataracts blow their trumpets from the steep

in the Immortality Ode. And yet this metaphor, in the deliberateness with which its relations are managed, itself looks curiously like a simile. This is the Wordsworthian middle air which must later be explored.

There follow, in Wordsworth's poem, four lines of eighteenth-century miltonizing, in the manner of *L'Allegro:*

> Then did ye swim with sportive smile
> From fairy-templed isle to isle,
> Which hear her far-off ditty sweet
> Yet feel not ev'n the milkmaid's feet.

And then:

> What tho' he still was at my side
> When, lurking near, I there have seen
> Your faces white, your tresses green,
> Like water lilies floating on the tide?

Wordsworth suddenly wrenches the poem from its remote mythological context by means of the visual appropriateness of the water lilies: he says "I there have seen"; and through the exactness of the simile he makes good his claim. Milton does not risk the ruin of *Lycidas* by pretending to see his nymphs, or anything else. His flowers are enamelled pageant-flowers, and their names are recited by a herald.

The poem continues:

> He saw not, bark'd not, he was still
> As the soft moonbeam sleeping on the hill,
> Or when ah! cruel maids, ye stretched him stiff and chill.

Again the simile is interesting; in the first place because of its connexion with Milton's line:

> And now the Sun had stretched out all the hills.

This is the only convincing visual image in *Lycidas*, and on that account likely to hold Wordsworth's attention. Furthermore, Milton manages the vowels of his line with extreme virtuosity—a skill which Wordsworth was quick to admire and to emulate, as in the famous *Prelude* lines on Spenser:

> Sweet Spenser, moving through his clouded heaven
> With the moon's beauty and the moon's soft pace. . . .[1]

Finally, the word "stretch'd" had a literal importance for Wordsworth. He wanted it, in perfect seriousness, for his dog, and he introduced it himself in the next line. As in the case of the druid and the moonbeam, Wordsworth is relating animate and inanimate; but here the relation is different. This simile is less highly organized than the other, and not so tense. "Soft" has no reference beyond "moonbeam", and in any case it is a careless choice, in its suggestion of relaxation and warmth, with "stiff and chill" following immediately. "Still" does nothing to the simile, because it is wide enough to cover both terms in a general and lazy way, without any stress. "Sleeping" appears at a glance to be playing a part in this simile like that of "pace" in the first. But this is not so. "Pace", lying between the two terms, is figurative and violent, and, helped by "white", compels them towards interaction. "Sleeping", on the other hand, succeeds both terms, which are referred simultaneously to it, as a fixed point equidistant from the dead dog and the motionless patch of light. The structure of the simile and the theme of stillness in death work together for a geometrical, not a dynamic relation.

Wordsworth ends his poem:

> If, while I gaz'd to Nature blind,
> In the calm Ocean of my mind
> Some new-created image rose

[1] Bk. III. 281.

In full-grown beauty at its birth
Lovely as Venus from the sea,
Then, while my glad hand sprung to thee,
We were the happiest pair on earth.

We noticed, regarding the nymphs and the water lilies, the opposition of an impossible, mythological world and an observed world of nature. Here the mind is a seascape, over against the mobile, earth-born relationship of boy and dog; and the sudden, perfect form of the mental image is emphasized by the classical allusion. This is a little grotesque, and it seems unlikely that Wordsworth had any clear idea of what he was doing. But he remembered the passage, and when he came in *The Prelude* to describe how he composed poetry while walking with his dog, he turned to it again:

this Dog was used
To watch me, an attendant and a friend
Obsequious to my steps, early and late,
Though often of such dilatory walk
Tired, and uneasy at the halts I made.
A hundred times when, in these wanderings,
I have been busy with the toil of verse,
Great pains and little progress, and at once
Some fair enchanting image in my mind
Rose up, full-form'd, like Venus from the sea
Have I sprung forth towards him, and let loose
My hand upon his back with stormy joy,
Caressing him again, and yet again.
And when, in the public roads at eventide
I saunter'd, like a river murmuring
And talking to itself, at such a season
It was his custom to jog on before;
But, duly, whensoever he had met
A passenger approaching, would he turn
To give me timely notice, and straitway,

> Punctual to such admonishment, I hush'd
> My voice, composed my gait, and shap'd myself
> To give and take a greeting that might save
> My name from piteous rumours, such as wait
> On men suspected to be craz'd in brain.[1]

The contrast between inner and outer, hurried and uncertain in the early poem, is now developed with entire success. Each world authenticates the other; and the dog, as he trots before the poet—a premonition, this, of Wordsworth's full power—mediates between them.

Within its very modest limits, this immature, patchwork poem foreshadows the kind of complexity in which Wordsworth's literalmindedness involves us. Direct verbal correspondences, even with poetry near to his heart, may mean very little. There is another phrase of Milton's, again from *Lycidas*, which is echoed three times in Wordsworth's work. Milton wrote:

> But, O the heavy change, now thou art gone,
> Now thou art gone, and never must return!

And in the 1805 text of *The Prelude* we find:

> To me [be] the grief confined that Thou art gone
> From this last spot of earth where Freedom now
> Stands single in her only sanctuary,
> A lonely wanderer, art gone, by pain
> Compell'd and sickness, at this latter day,
> This heavy time of change for all mankind. . . .[2]

This is almost certainly an accident, occasioned by the rhythm of the first line, with the phrase "thou art gone" at the end of it, and by the repetition of "art gone" three lines later. It may have been the realization of having unconsciously followed Milton that led Wordsworth to replace "this heavy time of change"

---

[1] *The Prelude*, Bk. IV. 96.     [2] Bk. X. 981.

by "this sorrowful reverse" when he revised *The Prelude*.

"Heavy change" also appears in the third book of *The Excursion*:

> with a holier love inspired, I looked
> On her—at once superior to my woes
> And partner of my loss—O heavy change!
> Dimness o'er this clear luminary crept
> Insensibly. . . .[1]

And again this is probably unintended: for language and context are very Miltonic, in fact directly suggestive of *Paradise Lost*.

The third occurrence is both unimportant and unhappy. Milton is interpolated in the midst of a tumbling Lyrical Ballad:

> But, oh the heavy change!—bereft
> Of health, strength, friends, and kindred, see!
> Old Simon to the world is left
> In liveried poverty![2]

This invoking of *Lycidas* in a purely external fashion defeats the declared purpose of Wordsworth's ballad, which is to be in the conventional sense unpoetic: it introduces exactly the wrong literary associations. Wordsworth is often attracted towards the words themselves in a way that prevents him from asking whether the present context is suitable: he is a magpie-poet, seizing any bright object that catches his eye, dropping it into his nest. In his maturity he borrows less frequently in this direct fashion, and with more discrimination; but he still resorts all too often to a set of well-worn devices, mainly rhetorical and Miltonic, with which to coax himself along.

---

[1] Bk. III. 667.       [2] *Simon Lee*.

Wordsworth's poem on the drowned dog shows him indulging his taste for quotation. It also shows him thinking as well as writing in the Miltonic mode—a submission to Milton's influence that runs very deep, and becomes as much a matter of entire attitude as of expression. Hence, often, the authority of his Miltonic blank verse:

> Sometimes, more sternly mov'd, I would relate
> How vanquish'd Mithridates northward pass'd,
> And, hidden in the cloud of years, became
> That Odin, Father of a Race, by whom
> Perish'd the Roman Empire. . . .[1]

This was how he felt about heroic themes; not less genuinely because Milton was in part responsible.

Wordsworth's poem also introduces the problem of originality. His way of comparing a moonbeam and a druid, then a moonbeam and a dead dog, I take for the sign of a most singular vision of the world, of its substantial ghostliness and its alliances in diversity. The mind's seascape and the Venus-Thoughts seem to me even more prophetic; for his understanding of the relationship of inner and outer is Wordsworth's principal claim to greatness. He had something new to say about mental and physical.

Even so, Wordsworth's originality is not easily approached. He enclosed his finest performance in a husk so tough and commonplace as to mislead bad critics and distress good ones. And although there is some sort of anthology agreement as to what is best, the rest is almost silence. Even Coleridge and Arnold could do little more than point, in their different ways, towards his best work, implying that it rises unaccountable from level wastes of mediocrity. Arnold thought Wordsworth was a kind of Scholar Gipsy, which I

---

[1] *The Prelude*, Bk. I. 185.

reckoned a mistake: while Coleridge regarded him as a philosophical poet who failed to realize his full powers.

Wondering what Coleridge meant, we are faced with his very liberal use of the word philosophy: he believed that all good poets must also be good philosophers. Nor is it clear what Coleridge understood by the philosophical character of poetry. He relates poetry in a very general way to his own variety of voluntaristic Idealism, as demonstrating both the primacy of will and the possibility of intuitive knowledge. Here and there, in his references to the "union and interpenetration of universal and particular"[1] in Shakespeare's characters, and to Shakespeare's dramatic presentation of "the *homo generalis* not as an abstraction from observation of a variety of men, but as a substance capable of endless modifications",[2] Coleridge hints at his reason for thinking Shakespeare the greatest of philosophers: he has in mind something like a poetic manifestation of the Hegelian Concrete Universal. But this is all much too vague. Fortunately he is more precise about Wordsworth. There is a remark which he repeats several times, with slight variation: Wordsworth is a philosophical poet because of "the contemplative position, which is peculiarly—perhaps I might say exclusively—fitted for him. His proper title is *Spectator ab extra*".[3] Although Wordsworth is capable of the most profound sympathy "with man as man", his is the sympathy of "a contemplator rather than a fellow-sufferer": he feels "for, never with" his subject.[4] There is, then, a detachment natural to Wordsworth which does not prevent him feeling strongly

[1] *The Friend* (4th ed.), Vol. III. p. 116.
[2] *Coleridge's Miscellaneous Criticism* (ed. T. M. Raysor), pp. 43-4.
[3] *Table Talk*, July 31, 1832.
[4] *Biographia Literaria* (ed. J. Shawcross), Vol. II. p. 122.

about his subject. This is the best of introductions to Wordsworth; and, since it is said by way of implied contrast with himself, to Coleridge also.

Coleridge's philosophy of the Great and the Whole is relevant to the entire man. His love of identity, of a speculative system through which the distinctness of his own individuality might be transcended, is no intellectual game, but the expression of a longing, born of great pain, to ease the burden of differentiated existence, to lose himself in higher synthesis, to be possessed by God. As in his approach to deity, so in his dealings with the world, Coleridge clung to his Idealism with more than intellectual loyalty. Wordsworth remarked of him that "he was not under the influence of natural objects"[1]; and Coleridge said the same thing of himself, in the form of an apparent paradox: "The further I ascend from animated Nature . . . the greater becomes in me the intensity of the feeling of life." The quality both of his imagination and his intelligence was determined by the force with which reality was borne in upon him as mind. He suffered terribly on that account in his dreams—"the very Substances", he called them, "and foot-thick calamities of my life"; and he defined Nightmare, with a pathetic pedantry, as "*terror corporeus sive materialis*".[2] His few great poems reflect the horror and the vivid completeness of the life which he lived within the mind: they reflect also his dread of isolation as a state of helplessness and vulnerability. Certainly Coleridge's proper title was not *Spectator ab extra*.

This dread of isolation is therefore both imaginative and intellectual. To be wholly conscious of one's distinctness, he said, is "to be betrayed into the wretchedness of *division*".[3] Division was intellectually wretched to him because it was unintelligible: he felt

---

[1] Grosart, Vol. III. p. 442.
[2] *Anima Poetae* (ed. E. H. Coleridge), p. 245.　　　[3] *Ibid.*, p. 184.

unable to talk about it without falling into a relational mode of thought which he recognized as the characteristic vice of eighteenth-century empiricism, and which he left behind him for ever when he set sail for a new philosophical world of rational synthesis.

Coleridge was not born a nineteenth-century Idealist: it was only after long hesitation that he finally turned his back on the British empirical tradition. A few months before Wordsworth and he became close friends, Coleridge named his eldest son after David Hartley, his acknowledged master in philosophy since his undergraduate days at Cambridge. Hartley was himself a disciple of Locke, an expounder of a fanciful physiology of mind and of a most intemperate version of the theory of association of ideas—a thinker small in talent who gained a short-lived celebrity by saying with vulgar emphasis the things that his generation wanted to hear. He combined, incongruously, a humdrum Christian orthodoxy with a show of scientific method directed to a deterministic, or a necessitarian interpretation of human nature. The young Coleridge was in search of a Christian philosophy, and he fell, as he continued all his life to fall, an easy victim to scientific quackery. It is because he wore the manners of his age with comic exaggeration that Hartley is an important figure in Coleridge's philosophical history: the abandonment of Hartley meant the abandonment of a way of thinking deeply entrenched in England since Bacon's *Advancement of Learning;* or, as Coleridge himself expressed it, viewing his crisis in even larger perspective, the return from Aristotle and the conceptionists to Plato and Idealism.

Hartley Coleridge was born in 1796; and Coleridge's disenchantment with David Hartley extended throughout 1797 and 1798, the years of his first and closest intimacy with Wordsworth. For Coleridge they were years of extreme unrest. He turned to Berkeley, after whom he named his second son; to Spinoza, to St Paul and the Fourth Gospel. Germany lay before him. Kant had not yet caught hold of him "with giant hands", nor Fichte and Schelling suggested the way beyond Kant. The shape of the new world was not clear to him, but the old was fast becoming uninhabitable. At this time he came to know Wordsworth and to think him capable of writing the "only true philosophical poem in existence". Wordsworth's poetry made an immediate and strong impression upon him because it referred directly to his own predicament: it revealed Wordsworth moving with obvious assurance through country in which he himself was losing all sense of direction; and thus it was that Wordsworth gained his greatest disciple. This is not to say that Coleridge supposed Wordsworth to be doing the same thing that Locke and Hartley had done, and to be doing it better. He knew very well that "when philosophy paints its grey monochrome some form of life has grown old, and it cannot by this grey in grey be made young again, but only known".[1] In the utterance of a great poet Coleridge witnessed not a world's illumination merely, but the palingenesis of its youth; for the work of Wordsworth's early maturity is the last and finest achievement of the eighteenth-century imagination. This important truth has not been appreciated, principally because Coleridge was at no time securely possessed of it himself; and the further he travelled into the nineteenth century the less able and willing he became to remember what had originally impelled him towards Wordsworth. As he grew unmindful of the other's sources of power he came, I shall argue, to demand impossibilities of him. But some things Coleridge always saw clearly, and the most vital of these was Wordsworth's isolation, his proper title of *Spectator ab extra.*

[1] Hegel, Preface to *Philosophie des Rechts.*

Coleridge himself discussed Wordsworth's isolation in terms of sexual psychology: "of all the men I ever knew, Wordsworth has the least femineity in his mind. He is *all* man. He is a man of whom it might have been said, 'It is good for him to be alone'."[1] The instinct to stand guard over its boundaries, to assert its distinctness, Coleridge considered the first indication of a masculine mind, and one supremely obvious in Wordsworth's. Certainly there was a self-centredness about him peculiarly masculine. This appears immediately as an aspect of weakness; of a narrow egotism betraying itself in his readiness to pontificate, in complacent moralizing, in a certain roughness in his dealings with others: all these accentuated by the retired life that he led, presiding over a household of attentive women.

Both Keats and Hazlitt made this egotism the ground of hostile criticism, but realized dimly, as did Coleridge, that it was merely a part of the much larger issue of Wordsworth's isolation. Keats suggested two basic types of poetic genius in his categories of the Wordsworthian or Egotistical Sublime and of Negative Capability. Hazlitt, in his review of *The Excursion*, wrote that "an intense intellectual egotism swallows up everything"; he noted the level tone, the quality of monologue in Wordsworth's verse, and he marvelled at the way Wordsworth turns inward for nourishment. "The power of his mind preys upon itself. It is as if there were nothing but himself and the universe. He lives in the busy solitude of his own heart; in the deep silence of thought." Hazlitt's account of his first meeting with Wordsworth still bears quotation:

> I think I see him now. He answered in some degree to his friend's description of him, but was more gaunt and Don Quixote-like. He was quaintly dressed (according to the

[1] *Table Talk and Omniana* (ed. T. Ashe), p. 339.

*costume* of that unconstrained period) in a brown fustian jacket and striped pantaloons. There was something of a roll, a lounge in his gait, not unlike his own Peter Bell. There was a severe, worn pressure of thought about his temples, a fire in his eye (as if he saw something in objects more than the outward appearance), an intense high narrow forehead. . . .[1]

The reference to Don Quixote, suggesting as it does the sublime absurdity of a self-appointed task pursued with utter singleness of purpose, beyond delusion to a kind of lonely sanity, is more appropriate than perhaps Hazlitt intended. But Hazlitt certainly did gain the impression of strenuous and solitary thought. So did Carlyle, when he met Wordsworth forty years later:

> His face bore marks of much, not always peaceful meditation, the look of it not bland or benevolent so much as close impregnable and hard. . . .[2]

And occasionally, in the correspondence of his later years, we catch a glimpse of the "desolate-minded" old man of local tradition, the silent walker with "no pleasure in his face",[3] much oppressed by the difficulty of communicating even with those he loved, and anxious to discover how he must appear to others:

> And now my dear Friend I should like to let loose my heart upon this scrap of paper—but it is folly to think of it. Mary has already told you how deeply we love you and how ardently we long for your return, though for my own part I must say that increasing years are I feel making me less and less of an interesting companion. Nothing however said or done to me for some time has in relation to myself given me so much pleasure as a casual word of Anna's that the expres-

[1] *My First Acquaintance with Poets.*
[2] *Reminiscences.*
[3] H. D. Rawnsley, *Reminiscences of Wordsworth among the Peasantry of Westmorland*, published in *Wordsworthiana* (ed. William Knight).

sion of my face was ever varying. I had begun to fear that it
had lately been much otherwise.[1]

Solitude is the theme of Wordsworth's long life. It
is also the preoccupation of his poetry. Long before he
reached old age, he came to accept his solitude as a
condition imposed upon him in the natural course of
things, an appointed burden to be borne uncomplain-
ingly. But it had not always been thus. In his youth he
sought solitude with his whole heart, and he makes it
quite clear, in *The Prelude* and elsewhere, that he
sought it as the means of poetic grace. The power to
write poetry, he says many times, depended for him
upon the power to be alone. This points to a truth that
is everywhere recognized: Wordsworth's best poetry
deals with lonely places and solitary people, whereas
he was easily daunted into silence by crowds. It also
suggests a more difficult conclusion of which Coleridge,
Hazlitt and Keats were all aware.

Wordsworth was not primarily concerned with solitude as physical isolation. Solitude in this limited sense
is not unimportant, but its significance lies in his use of
it as the token of a peculiarly Wordsworthian seriousness, an outward sign of a state of mind casting its
shadow over a whole poem.

> On Man on Nature, and on Human Life,
> Musing in solitude. . . .

In this, the opening phrase of the Preface to *The
Excursion*, which Wordsworth wished to be regarded
as a "kind of Prospectus" to the entire *Recluse*, the
word solitude plays the part of key signature in music:
and I am sure that Wordsworth is here acting with the
deliberation of a composer in his choice of key. Indeed,
in two famous studies of solitude—*The Leech-Gatherer*
and *I wandered lonely as a cloud*—he conceals the truth,

[1] *Letters* (ed. de Selincourt), 1841-50, p. 1132.

in defiance of his own principle of fidelity to fact, that
he was not alone.

Having introduced himself as "musing in solitude",
Wordsworth at once reveals his deeper purpose. He is
writing, he says,

> Of the individual Mind that keeps her own
> Inviolate retirement. . . .

The solitude of which he is speaking issues from an
attitude towards personality; from an eagerness to
accept the fact that I am myself just because I am not
anything else: to be me is to be always apart. The final
barrier which is differentiated existence, dreadful to
Coleridge, is embraced by Wordsworth as the source
of enlightenment and strength. "Inviolate retirement"
sounds a note of exultation because the poet believes
that the way to wisdom lies through the individual's
awareness of his individuality. When he considers his
fitness to undertake *The Recluse*, Wordsworth makes
this awareness his starting-point:

> Possessions have I that are solely mine,
> Something within which yet is shared by none,
> Not even the nearest to me and most dear,
> Something which power and effort may impart. . . .[1]

His discovery of himself in his solitude has universal
consequences: it leads him to the poetic and effective
understanding of all things:

> Points have we all of us within our souls,
> Where all stand single; this I feel, and make
> Breathings for incommunicable powers.[2]

In Wordsworth's poetry his own and his neighbour's private strength is developed into a philosophy
that can be expressed in terms both of solitude and of
relationship. The large and lazy assumption that the

---

[1] *P.W.*, Vol. V. p. 336.    [2] *The Prelude:* Bk. III. 186.

Romantic poets were all striving to express unity has obscured the structure of distinct but related things which is the world of Wordsworth. When he describes his education for poetry in the early books of *The Prelude*, he lays stress on the power to distinguish:

> I had an eye
> Which in my strongest workings, evermore
> Was looking for the shades of difference
> As they lie hid in all exterior forms. . . .[1]

The insight and joy of his childhood were derived

> From manifold distinctions, differences
> Perceived in things, where to the common eye,
> No difference is. . . .[2]

And elsewhere he states that the strength of the impression made by objects depends upon the distinctness with which they are individually imagined:

> While yet a child, and long before his time
> He had perceived the presence and the power
> Of greatness, and deep feelings had impressed
> Great objects on his mind, with portraiture
> And colour so distinct, that on his mind
> They lay like substances, and almost seemed
> To haunt the bodily sense.[3]

There is nothing of conventional romantic haze.

The *Spectator ab extra* does not move towards his object; he never clutches, he shows no eagerness to merge. "I gazed and gazed," "I looked and looked," "I stared and listened"—phrases of this kind, and they are many, at once suggests his authorship. In the poetry of the Great Decade Wordsworth is involved in a huge, sustained argument from solitude to relationship, from the points "where all stand single" to their connexions

---

[1] Bk. III. 156.          [2] Bk. II. 318.
[3] *P.W.*, Vol. V. p. 381. Compare *The Excursion:* Bk. I. 134.

with each other. And here there can be no substitute
for his poetry: the interdependence of true solitude and
true relationship was for Wordsworth a final issue
engaging his full powers and manageable only in poetic
terms. This interdependence makes an uncertain basis,
even for his own critical judgments:

> Having had the good fortune to be born and reared in a
> mountainous country, from my very childhood I have felt
> the falsehood that pervades the volumes imposed upon the
> world under the name of Ossian. From what I saw with my
> own eyes, I knew that the imagery was spurious. In nature
> everything is distinct, but nothing defined into absolute
> independent singleness. In Macpherson's work, it is exactly
> the reverse; everything (that is not stolen) is in this manner
> defined, insulated, dislocated, deadened—yet nothing
> distinct.[1]

Wordsworth must find another way of opposing the
thing single and the thing distinct.

What is a thing? How is one thing related to other
things? Wordsworth would not have framed his questions in quite the way he did, had he not grown up in
the eighteenth century; nor would his metaphysical
enquiry have been thus childlike in its unembarrass-
ment had he possessed the intellectual selfconsciousness
of a philosopher. This very innocence lends importance
to his inherited forms of thought: it allowed him to
give general assent to the assumptions of the age. He
accepted the problem as it had been stated by the
eighteenth century: in doubt or in extremity he did not,
like Coleridge, attempt restatement. Rather, he persisted in the old questions; and hence the monotony of
his genius.

There is thus a conservatism in the context of
Wordsworth's thought. He is not in revolt against the

[1] Essay Supplementary to the Preface to the 1815 Edition of Wordsworth's Poems.

Great Machine, the master-image of eighteenth-century science and philosophy. Only the phrase is un-wordsworthian (though there is enough of pure eighteenth-century poetic in him to allow a reference to his wife's spirit, in relation to her body, as "the very pulse of the machine"[1]): he would prefer something more supple, like "this universal frame of things". His complaint is that nobody has as yet observed its component parts with sufficiently devoted care, or experienced fully the power and beauty of its movement.

In *The Prelude* Wordsworth uses the word "things" with astonishing frequency. The Concordance reveals that the 1850 text alone accounts for about one-third of its occurrences in the entire bulk of his poetry. "I looked for universal things"; "I conversed with things that really are"; Wordsworth will make his verse "deal boldly with substantial things"—the word is clearly and consistently referred to the main theme of the poem.[2] His search for universal things is on one side a search for particularity: in his insistence upon constancy, boundedness, irreducibility, he betrays the imaginative impression of a traditional English materialism. But he is more than a materialist, in that he enquires not only for the particular but for the powerful. Here his resources are heavily taxed. In order to express essential energy, he is too often led to personify spirit, motion, power itself, in a context of vague declamation. But it is unfair to take this separation of effort at all seriously: Wordsworth is neither atomist nor animist, in any sense that matters. His problem comprehends both particularity and power; and it is pursued through a Wordsworthian royal line of solitary wanderers, from the Old Cumberland Beggar to the White Doe of Rylstone.

---

[1] *She Was a Phantom of Delight.* . . .
[2] Bk.III. 110. Bk. II. 412. Bk. XII. 234.

Because Wordsworth saw the world as an intelligible complex—"frame" is his favourite term—and yet was neither pure materialist nor pure idealist, it may fairly be argued that his closest philosophical link was with Spinoza. And this is an illuminating comparison, provided imaginative kinship be not confounded with formal allegiance. Both were possessed of intense ethical passion; both talked much of virtue and wisdom as a discipline (critics have noted the Judaic quality of *Michael* and other narrative poems); both had the same instinctive reaction to the Cartesian problem of matter and mind, admitting difference but denying opposition. Above all, both were monists. Wordsworth was nearer to Spinoza than he was to Locke and Hartley because, while not fundamentally at odds with the Great Machine, he could not accept the Great Mechanic. It is a significant point of emphasis that Wordsworth was not attracted towards any particular religion of divine immanence, but was repelled by the crude transcendence of eighteenth-century deity. The Great Mechanic, or Paley's Divine Watchmaker, could render a satisfactory account of creation, as he sat back and admired his craftsmanship. But Wordsworth was not curious about creation. In fact, even when he had become in most things orthodox, he still disliked talking about God as Creator. I do not, he says, in a letter written in 1814,

> consider the Supreme Being as bearing the same relation to the Universe, as a watch-maker bears to a watch. In fact, there is nothing in the course of the religious education adopted in this country, and in the use made by us of the Holy Scriptures, that appears to me so injurious as perpetually talking about *making* by God . . . for heaven's sake, in your religious talk with children, say as little as possible about *making*.[1]

[1] *Letters* (ed. de Selincourt), 1811-20, p. 619.

Wordsworth did not want a philosophical *deus ex machina* whereby to explain how the world was made: he was face to face with suffering and love, the vast consequences of will and passion. And so we find in Wordsworth's early work an eighteenth-century cosmology unassociated with eighteenth-century theology: the alliance which professional philosophers of the school of Locke were able to sustain was a lie in the soul, intolerable to him. A vague awareness of tension encouraged him in the anti-intellectualism of his early years; and, although he had no precise notion of the intellectual issues involved, there is sometimes audible in his poetry a kind of prose voice, insisting on the gulf between Creator and created:

> In such access of mind, in such high hour
> Of visitation from the living God,
> He did not feel the God; he felt his works. . . .[1]

This gulf his poetry denies; not positively, by argument for pantheism, but negatively, by showing that the world can give a good account of itself. In the 1805 *Prelude*, the phrase "God and Nature's single sovereignty"[2] is not Spinozistic: it constitutes Wordsworth's refusal to shift his gaze from the "here" of "this green earth" to the "there" of an eighteenth-century heaven. His eye was firmly on the object which, as he then believed, would yield its secret entire:

> the very world which is the world
> Of all of us—the place where in the end,
> We find our happiness, or not at all![3]

It needs to be said that Wordsworth is very little concerned with God in the early *Prelude*: in fact he suggests as much himself; for he explains more than once that his concern in *The Recluse* will be with man

---

[1] *P.W.*, Vol. V. p. 382.          [2] Bk.IX. 237.
[3] 1850; Bk. XI. 142.

and nature, but he makes no reference to God. "My object," he wrote in 1798, "is to give pictures of Nature, Man, and Society. Indeed I know not anything which will not come within the scope of my plan."[1] Divinity, we find, is invoked most sparingly, like an organ stop to be used only for sublime and terrible effect:

> And here, O Friend! have I retraced my life
> Up to an eminence, and told a tale
> Of matters which, not falsely, I may call
> The glory of my youth. Of Genius, Power,
> Creation and Divinity itself
> I have been speaking, for my theme has been
> What pass'd within me.[2]

The plan thus outlined in 1798 was partially executed in the 1805 text of *The Prelude*. How long Wordsworth himself continued to regard *The Prelude* as part of *The Recluse* is not certain. Coleridge still spoke of it as *The Recluse* in 1804, and when the 1805 text was read to him he composed a poem in praise of it[3] which is written with discrimination, in spite of its rapturous tone, and reflects Wordsworth's original design for *The Recluse*. Coleridge points to the central humanism of *The Prelude*, and to its presentation of man and nature as eternally engaged in some wholly meaningful dialogue. The success of *The Prelude*, he says—and this is a very revealing admission—, reminds him of the ways in which he himself had failed. He calls upon Wordsworth as

> my comforter and guide!
> Strong in thyself, and powerful to give strength!

and in an eye-taking phrase, "the dread watch-tower of man's absolute self", he refers to Wordsworth's dis-

---

1 *Early Letters* (ed. de Selincourt), p. 188.
2 *The Prelude*, Bk. III. 168.
3 *To William Wordsworth*.

covery of strength in solitude. Most striking, especially
in Coleridge, is the omission to make Christian claims
of any kind for *The Prelude;* or, indeed, to make Christian demands upon it. When he came, nine years later,
to criticize *The Excursion,* things were very different;
and Coleridge's dissatisfaction with *The Excursion*
makes a convenient approach to the problem of Wordsworth's decline.

In May 1815 Coleridge wrote Wordsworth a careful
letter in which he explained why *The Excursion* had
disappointed him. He states in this letter[1] that his poem
about *The Prelude* gives an accurate account of his
feelings at that time, and that he had hoped that *The
Prelude* and *The Excursion* would together form "one
complete whole", although "in matter, form, and
product to be different, each not only a distinct but a
different work". It is, however, clear, that if Coleridge's
expectations had been fulfilled, Wordsworth would
have written a poem at once different from *The Prelude*
and a contradiction of it. Coleridge hoped for a Christian poem treating of the Fall of Man and the Redemption. Wordsworth, he anticipated, was "to have
affirmed a Fall in some sense, as a fact, the possibility
of which cannot be understood from the nature of the
will, but the reality of which is attested by experience
and conscience". Such a poem would have denied not
merely the optimism of *The Prelude,* from a Christian
standpoint its Pelagianism, but the whole universe in
which it moves. Paradise is here, or it is nowhere; and
if it is here, there can have been no Fall: this imaginative monism at the heart of Wordsworth's poetry is
more important than either optimism or pessimism.
The world of Wordsworth's early tragedy, *The
Borderers,* is related in Suffering; that of *The Prelude,*
in Beauty and Fear; that of Wordsworth's Stoical
middle years, in Duty: his statement of the relational

[1] *Letters* (ed. E. H. Coleridge), Vol. II. pp. 643-50.

D

principle changes, but his view of reality as a single intelligible structure persists. While this is so, there can be no effective dealing with the supernatural, and Coleridge's demands must remain impossible to meet. Sometimes, as we shall see, Wordsworth asked the impossible of himself, in attempting to write Christian poetry before he had acquired the power to do so: this is an aspect of decline. Eighteenth-century cosmology had firm hold of him, and he lacked the agility of mind that would have helped him to shift his position. For a long time he was both a Christian and a man in search of a sovereign and internal principle, beyond Euclid and Newton, beyond the theory of Necessity and the Association of Ideas, wherein to relate the elements of his own version of the Great Machine.

Coleridge explains that his disappointment with *The Excursion* is due partly to Wordsworth's failure to write the Christian poem he had hoped for, and partly to his refusal to strive towards certain philosophical conclusions. He had expected Wordsworth

> to have laid a solid and immoveable foundation for the edifice by removing the sandy sophisms of Locke, and the mechanic dogmatists, and demonstrating that the senses were living growths and developments of the mind and spirit, in a much juster as well as higher sense, than the mind can be said to be formed by the senses.

This is sufficiently precise to show that Coleridge was unaware of the extent to which his path had diverged from Wordsworth's since the time of their early friendship. He assumed that Wordsworth will speak out, like a post-Kantian Idealist, bent on

> the substitution of life and intelligence . . . for the philosophy of mechanism, which, in everything that is most worthy of the human intellect, strikes *Death*, and cheats itself by mistaking clear images for distinct conceptions, and which

idly demands conceptions where intuitions alone are possible
or adequate to the majesty of the Truth.

But Coleridge could have discovered, in the Preface to
*The Excursion*, Wordsworth's own account of what he
intended to say:

> my voice proclaims
> How exquisitely the individual Mind
> (And the progressive powers perhaps no less
> Of the whole species) to the external World
> Is fitted:—and how exquisitely, too—
> Theme this but little heard of among men—
> The external World is fitted to the Mind. . . .

Wordsworth is arguing not for the primacy of mind,
but for a partnership between the mind and the external
world. The mind, he says in *The Prelude*, is

> creator and receiver both,
> Working but in alliance with the works
> Which it beholds.[1]

He does not rest his faith in "intuitions" as "alone
possible or adequate to the majesty of the Truth"—in
fact, he would not have understood what Coleridge was
talking about: his belief is in

> the discerning intellect of Man,
> When wedded to this goodly universe
> In love and holy passion. . . .[2]

Consistently with this, he regards the senses as
exercising a mediatory function between man and
nature. Hence his reference, in *Tintern Abbey* to "what
they half create, And what perceive".

Coleridge misinterprets Wordsworth's opinions
regarding the mind, the senses, and the external world.
He even forgets that Wordsworth had no philosophical
point of view at all, in the sense in which he here

---

[1] Bk. II. 273.    [2] Preface to *The Excursion*.

demands one of him. His feeling for the history of ideas led Coleridge to look upon eighteenth-century philosophy as moving inevitably towards Humeian scepticism; but Wordsworth, lacking both Coleridge's sense of history and his intellectual finesse, could not see things thus clearly: he was unselfconsciously living the pattern of ideas within which he had grown up.

Wordsworthian criticism is still suffering from this careless identification of attitudes, particularly in respect of his theory of poetry and of the imagination. It is very generally supposed that Wordsworth derived his opinions from Coleridge, and that he derived them ill, because viewed from the standpoint of Coleridge's own theory, they are largely unintelligible.

Poet, for Coleridge, meant Maker. In the tradition of Renaissance Platonism, he thought of the poet not as imitator of the world of appearance, but as creator of a better, because a truer, world. "Her world is brazen, the poets only deliver a golden": Coleridge elaborates Sidney's argument in one of his finest letters:

> The common end of all *narrative*, nay, of *all* Poems, is to convert a *series* into a *Whole*: to make those events, which in real or imagined History move on in a *strait* line, assume to our Understandings a *circular* motion—the snake with its tail in its mouth. Hence indeed the almost flattering and yet appropriate term—Poesy—i.e. poiesis=*making*. Doubtless, to His eye, which alone comprehends all Past and all Future in one eternal Present, what to our short sight appears strait is but a part of the great Cycle—just as the calm sea to us *appears* level, though it be indeed only a part of a *Globe*. Now what the Globe is in Geography, *miniaturing* in order to *manifest* the truth, such is a poem to that image of God, which we were created with. . . .[1]

*Kubla Khan* is a more compelling statement of the same conviction. The theme of creation with which the

---

[1] *Unpublished Letters of S. T. Coleridge* (ed. E. L. Griggs), Vol. II. p. 128.

poem opens becomes, in the frenzy of its ending, specifically poetic:

> Could I revive within me
> Her symphony and song,
> To such a deep delight 'twould win me,
> That with music loud and long,
> I would build that dome in air,
> That sunny dome. . . .

And Coleridge's theory of imagination, the "dim analogue of creation", is best understood as a rather forlorn commentary upon *Kubla Khan;* as an attempt to establish discursively that the poet does indeed deliver his golden world and build his dome in air.

For Wordsworth, Poet meant Observer. His theory, and, as he at least believed, his practice, were founded on an assumption inherited by the eighteenth century from Dryden and Ben Jonson, and from classical French criticism, to the effect that poetry is in some sense an imitation of nature. Wordsworth's condemnation of Macpherson's Ossian is typical: "From what I saw with my own eyes, I knew that the imagery was spurious."[1] The picture is such a poor likeness that it must be judged a fake.

This attitude is saved from obvious absurdity by Wordsworth's reliance on the refining and selective power of memory, and by the way he makes the poet's clearsightedness depend upon a disciplined shedding of artifice. Moreover, there is a serious discussion of its linguistic implications in the Preface to the 1815 edition of his poems. When he read this Preface, Coleridge told Byron[2] that it disclosed a wide difference of opinion between Wordsworth and himself as to the nature of the Fancy and the Imagination. Nor is this really surprising; for Coleridge was in complete earnest

[1] See p. 34.
[2] *Unpublished Letters* (ed. E. L. Griggs), Vol. II. p. 143.

about the creative function of the imagination, but had no interest in the Fancy, except as a relic of eighteenth-century theory; whereas Wordsworth thought of imaginative work primarily as the discovery of hitherto unapprehended relations, and argued that the Fancy was also, in this limited sense, a creative faculty. Hence, as between Fancy and Imagination, Coleridge accused Wordsworth of failure to distinguish, and Wordsworth Coleridge of distinguishing falsely. Coleridge required a dramatic contrast between mechanical juxtaposition and organic synthesis—or rather "prothesis"[1]; for he wanted a word that suggested identity rather than union, and so, characteristically, he contrived a monster. Wordsworth sought not contrast but the development of a received tradition: he wished to say something further about the faculty which, in open defiance of Coleridge, he continued to define as "the aggregative and associative power".[2]

Just as Coleridge's theory of imagination is a commentary on *Kubla Khan*, so is Wordsworth's a commentary on *The Recluse*,[3] on the fitting of the mind to the external world, and of the external world to the mind. The parenthetical line, "theme this but little heard of among men", indicates that Wordsworth believed the peculiar significance of *The Recluse* to lie in its raising of the external world into active and equal partnership with the mind. His treatment of the imagination in the 1815 Preface supports the same conclusion. The whole Preface illuminates Wordsworth's thinking about language and truth; and is immediately relevant in its concern with careful observation as the means of achieving a state of action and reaction between observer and observed. The mind, regarding objects, and "taking advantage of their appearance to the senses", endows them with properties

1 J. H. Muirhead, *Coleridge as Philosopher*, p. 87 n.
2 Preface to the Edition of 1815.              3 See p. 41.

that do not inhere in them, upon an incitement from properties and qualities the existence of which is inherent and obvious. These processes of imagination are carried on either by conferring additional properties upon an object, or abstracting from it some of those which it actually possesses, and thus enabling it to re-act upon the mind which hath performed the process, like a new existence.

Wordsworth's 1815 Preface opens, in the very manner of an eighteenth-century treatise, with a solemn account of "the powers requisite for the production of poetry", under the headings of Observation and Description, Sensibility, Reflexion, Imagination and Fancy, Invention, and Judgment; the which is followed by a catalogue of Kinds of Poetry: Narrative, Dramatic, Lyrical, The Idyllium, Didactic, and Philosophical Satire. The background to Wordsworth's thinking about poetry could not be more clearly indicated; and much of what he has to say only makes sense when held against it. In the Preface to the *Lyrical Ballads*, he states that poetry is in the purest and profoundest sense scientific. "Poetry is the breath and finer spirit of all knowledge; it is the impassioned expression which is in the countenance of all Science." This is not mere rant: it is the necessary consequence of his view of the poet as most faithful among students of appearance. But it *is* appearance that the poet studies. Wordsworth had little patience with any objective metaphysic of imagination:

> Imagination is a subjective term: it deals with objects not as they are, but as they appear to the mind of the poet.[1]

Coleridge refused to allow that philosophy can end in the opposition of subject and object. He therefore abandoned Locke and Hartley for Spinoza. But Spinoza was only able to overcome this opposition by

---

[1] Grosart, Vol. III. p. 464.

sacrificing personality: "did philosophy start with an
'it is' instead of an 'I am' Spinoza would be altogether
true".[1] So Coleridge left Spinoza, and eventually
found other masters. At the same time he saw that
neither Wordsworth's acceptance, nor his own rejection, of the condition of subject standing over against a
world of objects was a purely intellectual matter: in
fact, he achieved clearer understanding of Wordsworth's instinct to draw back and distance his object
than did Wordsworth of Coleridge's desire for union.
In his *Hymn before Sunrise in the Vale of Chamouny*,
Coleridge addresses Mont Blanc thus:

> Thou, the meantime, wast blending with my Thought,
> Yea with my Life, and Life's own secret joy:
> Till the dilating soul, enrapt, transfused,
> Into the mighty vision passing—there
> As in her natural form, swelled vast to Heaven.

And in a letter he records Wordsworth's criticism of
these lines:

> Mr Wordsworth, I remember, censured the passage as
> strained and unnatural, and condemned the Hymn *in toto*
> (which nevertheless I ventured to publish in the *Sibylline
> Leaves*) as a specimen of the Mock Sublime. It may be so for
> others, but it is impossible that I should find it myself un-
> natural.... For from my very childhood I have been accus-
> tomed to *abstract* and as it were unrealize whatever of more
> than common interest my eyes dwelt on; and then by a sort of
> transference and transmission of my consciousness to identify
> myself with the Object....[2]

But Wordsworth does not experience this urge towards
identity. Even at his most visionary, as when in *Tintern
Abbey* he speaks of

> A motion and a spirit that impels
> All thinking things, all objects of all thought,

[1] J. H. Muirhead, *Coleridge as Philosopher*, p. 47.
[2] *Unpublished Letters* (ed. E. L. Griggs), Vol. II. p. 261.

the instinct to place the thinking subject on his one hand and the object of his thought on the other does not desert him.

It will be remembered that Coleridge related Wordsworth's natural solitude to the fact that he was "all man".[1] Shelley, noticing the almost complete absence of the erotic in Wordsworth's verse, described him, in *Peter Bell the Third*, as "solemn and unsexual". But Coleridge's suggestion of a withdrawn and brooding masculinity is more profound, for it reckons not only with the absence of erotic,[2] but with Wordsworth's strange attachment at remove, which has a formalized sexual expression in the profuse family images of his poetry. Parent and child metaphors, brotherhood and sisterhood metaphors, household metaphors, are all abundant; and a remarkable number of his important poems have family themes—there is of course *The Brothers;* and also father and son in *Michael;* brother, sister and father, in *The White Doe;* father and daughter in *The Borderers;* mother and child in *The Prelude*, and at other decisive turns in his work. For Wordsworth the family is the universe in microcosm, a complex of individuals related in their independence. The totality which is the family is reflected in his attitude to his brother's death: "God keep the rest of us together! The set is now broken."[3] And again: "as the number of us is now broken, some more of the set will be following him".[4] His is an unusual blend of intelligence and passion; and passion needs emphasis. The certainty of his affection for Dorothy, and of his broken-heartedness at the death of his brother and daughter—the two events that shook his adult life to its founda-

---

[1] p. 29.
[2] Mr G. Wilson Knight (*The Starlit Dome*, p. 55) contrasts Wordsworth and Shelley in their use of "naked". In Wordsworth, "naked" is without erotic suggestion.
[3] *Early Letters* (ed. de Selincourt), p. 446.
[4] *Ibid.*, p. 476.

tions—is worth an infinity of speculation as to Wordsworth's feelings towards Annette Vallon.

Instead of dismissing Wordsworth as a sexless phenomenon, Coleridge distinguishes between love,[1] as the desire for union with the beloved and therefore able to comprehend only one object, and "long and deep affection", not necessarily less passionate than love, expressing itself as an "habitual attachment which may include many objects". Wordsworth, he argues, can experience only the latter: "thus Wordsworth is by nature incapable of being in love, though no man more tenderly attached". More than this it would be difficult to say, without building a tendentious thesis upon the undoubted oddness of Wordsworth's sexuality.

Solitude and attachment, the huge abstractions moving through Wordsworth's life and poetry, are in time joined by his Christianity, which makes its presence felt in opposition to them. After explaining that *The Excursion* had disappointed his hope of a poetic treatment of the Fall and the Redemption, Coleridge reaffirms that Wordsworth had a greater philosophical talent than any English poet since Milton, and states the following reason for his failure to exploit his gifts:

> it seems to me that he ought never to have abandoned the contemplative position, which is peculiarly—perhaps I might say exclusively—fitted for him. His proper title is *Spectator ab extra*.[2]

There is a fundamental confusion here. *The Excursion* is weaker than *The Prelude* because it lacks the relational and monistic coherence of the earlier poem: Coleridge has good reason to complain that *The Prelude's* imaginative strongholds have been surrendered. But Wordsworth has not capriciously

---

[1] *Unpublished Letters* (ed. E. L. Griggs), Vol. II. p. 46.
[2] *Table Talk*, July 31, 1832.

decided to put off him his proper title. He is trying to write a Christian poem; and Coleridge has failed to see that the birth of Christianity and the dying of attachment-in-solitude are inseparable issues.

Christianity reached Wordsworth neither through a sense of sin nor a sense of glory, but through wanhope, a colourless despair. As he begins *The Prelude*, he says:

> gleams of light
> Flash often from the East, then disappear
> And mock me with a sky that ripens not
> Into a steady morning. . . .[1]

Coleridge rightly insists on Wordsworth's extreme masculinity: he is a striking exception to the classical type of bi-sexual genius; and there is from the start something incomplete about his "self-sufficing power of solitude". Hence the restlessness of the early *Prelude:*

> the soul
> Remembering how she felt, but what she felt
> Remembering not, retains an obscure sense
> Of possible sublimity, to which
> With growing faculties she doth aspire,
> With faculties still growing, feeling still
> That whatsoever point they gain, they still
> Have something to pursue.[2]

And even the spiritual triumph which he experienced upon crossing the Alps dwells upon potentiality rather than present possession:

> in such visitings
> Of awful promise, when the light of sense
> Goes out in flashes that have shown to us
> The invisible world, doth Greatness make abode,
> There harbours whether we be young or old.

---

[1] Bk. I. 134.      [2] Bk. II. 334.

> Our destiny, our nature, and our home
> Is with infinitude, and only there;
> With hope it is, hope that can never die,
> Effort, and expectation, and desire,
> And something evermore about to be.[1]

Wordsworth's sense of "possible sublimity" sustained the terrible, vague urgency of this struggle from partial vision to partial vision. When he lost that sense, he ceased to tread "the very edge of vacancy". And this is more than failure of nerve, for the will is of very limited importance in the total involvement of the *Prelude* experience.

Wordsworth refers his great loss to two causes. The first, the gradual dulling of sensibility in the face of the natural world, is one of the themes of the Immortality Ode, and is hinted at in *The Prelude* itself:

> The days gone by
> Come back upon me from the dawn almost
> Of life: the hiding-places of my power
> Seem open; I approach, and then they close;
> I see by glimpses now; when age comes on,
> May scarcely see at all. . . .[2]

The second is a sudden accident. In February 1805, Wordsworth received news of his brother's death in shipwreck; and later in the same year he wrote his *Elegiac Stanzas suggested by a Picture of Peele Castle in a Storm*. Wordsworth recounts that he once lived within sight of Peele Castle during a long period of fine weather, so that had he then painted the castle, his picture would have been very different from that other which occasioned his poem:

> Ah! THEN, if mine had been the Painter's hand,
> To express what then I saw; and add the gleam,
> The light that never was, on sea or land,
> The consecration, and the Poet's dream;

[1] Bk. VI. 533.          [2] Bk. XI. 334.

> I would have painted thee, thou hoary Pile
> Amid a world how different from this!
> Beside a sea that could not cease to smile;
> On tranquil land, beneath a sky of bliss.

But such a picture is no longer possible:

> Not for a moment now could I behold
> A smiling sea, and be what I have been:
> The feeling of my loss will ne'er be old;
> This, which I know, I speak with mind serene.

His brother's death had brought about a universal change:

> So once it would have been—'tis now no more;
> I have submitted to a new control:
> A power is gone, which nothing can restore;
> A deep distress hath humanized my Soul.

It has destroyed his "sense of possible sublimity", or, in the present lovely paraphrase, it has quenched

> the gleam,
> The light that never was, on sea or land,
> The consecration, and the Poet's dream.

Wordsworth describes his crisis as an abandonment of solitude, thus inadvertently confirming Coleridge's statement of his case:

> Farewell, farewell the heart that lives alone,
> Housed in a dream, at distance from the Kind!

And in the place of solitude he speaks of a new humanity, and a "mind serene". This is a very large issue. Immediately, it touches the Stoicism of Wordsworth's middle years, the Roman severity foreshadowed in the final stanza:

> But welcome fortitude, and patient cheer,
> And frequent sights of what is to be borne!

And ultimately it concerns Wordsworth's Christianity. John Wordsworth's death set his brother to much heart-searching:

> A thousand times have I asked myself, as your tender sympathy led me to do, "why was he taken away?" and I have answered the question as you have done. In fact there is no other answer that can satisfy and lay the mind at rest. Why have we a choice and a will, and a notion of justice and injustice, enabling us to be moral agents? Why have we sympathies that make the best of us so afraid of inflicting pain and sorrow, which yet we see dealt about so lavishly by the supreme governor? Why should our notions of right towards each other, and to all sentient beings within our influence, differ so widely from what appears to be His notion and rule, if everything were to end here? Would it not be blasphemy to say that, upon the supposition of the thinking principle being destroyed by death, however inferior we may be to the great Cause and Ruler of things, we have *more of love* in our nature than he has? The thought is monstrous; and yet how to get rid of it, except on the supposition of *another* and a *better world*, I do not see.[1]

Wordsworth does not embrace Christianity: it is forced on him by the exclusion of alternatives. His admission, almost reluctant, that there must be "another and a better world" is followed by regular Christian observance; and this, I shall attempt to show, by a late and Christian maturity. He was still writing *The Prelude* when his brother died; his effort was directed elsewhere, and the first steps were taken with much hesitation. He was at all times a stubborn man, and, as Shelley said,

> he never could
> Fancy another situation,
> From which to dart his contemplation,
> Than that wherein he stood.[2]

---

[1] *Early Letters* (ed. de Selincourt), p. 460.   [2] *Peter Bell the Third*.

His masculinity is again pertinent. Only towards the
end of a very long life did he achieve that condition of
spirit, perhaps essentially feminine, in which intellectual paradox is resolved, and not merely opposed, in
faith.

Important also is his blindness to sin: the most
direct way to a Christian understanding of suffering
was thereby closed to him; and he was left to follow a
much longer path, determined by recurring patterns
of ceremonial, by the quiet influence of local and
ancient pieties, and of catholic association. Invincibly
Protestant only in his political hatred of the Roman
Church, he grew, in the course of time, into intelligent
sympathy with the Tractarian Movement. And he
came to look, for his religion's chief support, towards
the Incarnation, whereby the duality of earth and
Heaven, else to him intolerable, is taken upon unweary
shoulders.

Thus I persuade myself that I have seen three
things. There is the poetry of solitude and relationship.
There is the poetry of indecision, of glances behind and
before—the poetry, pre-eminently, of *The Excursion*
and *The White Doe*, long works of Wordsworth's
middle age. And then, though this has not yet been
touched on, there is the offering of a baptized imagination.

## II

## SOLITUDE AND RELATIONSHIP

WORDSWORTH'S tragedy, *The Borderers*, is the last work assigned by him to the class of "Poems written in Youth". Finished in 1797, and standing at the threshold of the Great Decade, the play has been a good deal noticed. It has been judged the unhappy result of Wordsworth's disillusionment with the French Revolution, or of a rash encounter with Godwin's *Enquiry concerning Political Justice;* and Annette Vallon has been held responsible for its consideration of remorse within a history of crime and punishment. Annette's influence must be a matter of conjecture, indeed of idle conjecture; for even if the thesis of her desertion by Wordsworth and of the gradual stifling of his genius in guilty contemplation of his act be wholly accepted, we still know nothing of his coming to be a poet, or of his achievement in poetry: we have discovered merely a reason for his falling off. Godwin's *Political Justice*, on the other hand, has certainly left its mark upon *The Borderers*, in the form of a plodding intellectualism that makes the play almost unreadable. Time and again the principles of Godwin's philosophy are stubbornly debated:

>                          I feel
> That you have shown, and by a signal instance,
> How they who would be just must seek the rule
> By diving for it into their own bosoms.
> To-day you have thrown off a tyranny
> That lives but in the torpid acquiescence
> Of the world's masters, with the musty rules
> By which they uphold their craft from age to age:
> You have obeyed the only law that sense

Submits to recognize; the immediate law,
From the clear light of circumstances, flashed
Upon an independent Intellect.[1]

Wordsworth may have been not entirely unaware of his desperate poverty in dramatic talent, for he makes the disarming admission that *The Borderers* was written "without any view to its exhibition upon the stage".[2] This is borne out by a reckless inattention to coherence of plot and consistency of character. No doubt Wordsworth was preoccupied with Godwin. But Godwin is of very transient importance in Wordsworth's poetry, whereas Shakespeare, whose shadow also lies across the play, is not. Wordsworth's parading of the externals of Shakespearean tragedy is merely tiresome: the thing that matters, and, perhaps, the thing that caused Coleridge to overpraise *The Borderers*, is its lively connexion with *Othello*, *Macbeth*, and *King Lear*.

*The Borderers* is about the doings of a band of philanthropic outlaws in the reign of Henry III. Marmaduke, their leader, is in love with Idonea, who is the joy and sole support of her father, the baron Herbert. Herbert has been cheated of his estates while crusading in Palestine, and wanders, old, blind, and helpless, through the play. Deceived by Oswald, a member of his band, Marmaduke causes the death of Herbert, and so loses Idonea.

Oswald is not a simple villain. Wordsworth refers, in his Preface, to Iago, and the correspondences between the two are clear. Oswald "nourishes a contempt for mankind the more dangerous because he has been led to it by reflection".[3] He regards "the world as a body which is in some sort of war with him"[4]; and this, coupled with a huge pride and love of power, leads him

---

[1] *l.* 1484.  
[2] Note to *The Borderers.*  
[3] *P.W.*, Vol. I. p. 346.  
[4] *Ibid.*, p. 346.

E

to a course of action purely destructive and indulged for its own sake. His character is a study in "the apparently *motiveless* actions of bad men"[1]; and Wordsworth, faithful to the spirit of Iago, draws him passionless and cynically regardant:

> *Idonea.* . . . if erring,
> Oh let me be forgiven!
> *Marmaduke.* I *do* forgive thee.
> *Id.* But take me to your arms—this breast, alas!
> It throbs, and you have a heart that does not feel it.
> *Marm (exultingly).* She is innocent. [*He embraces her.*
> *Oswald (aside).* Were I a Moralist
> I should make wondrous revolution here;
> It were a quaint experiment to show
> The beauty of truth. . . .[2]

Oswald raises the question not only of apparently motiveless wrongdoing, but of perseverence in crime. Wordsworth's Preface states it thus:

> We all know that the dissatisfaction accompanying the first impulses towards a criminal action, where the mind is familiar with guilt, acts as a stimulus to proceed in that action. . . . Besides, in a course of criminal conduct every fresh step that we make appears a justification of the one which preceded it, it seems to bring again the moment of liberty and choice; it banishes the idea of repentance, and seems to set remorse at defiance.[3]

Here Wordsworth turns to *Macbeth*, and into Oswald's character he works a distinct trace of the frantic hero, seeking action of any kind as a relief from guilty thoughts, and holding converse with Spirits. The scene of Oswald's incitement of Marmaduke to the murder is heavy with *Macbeth*. Marmaduke is unable to kill Herbert because he resembles Idonea in his sleep, and Oswald waits until Marmaduke "comes forth with

---

[1] *P.W.*, Vol. I. p. 343.  [2] *l.* 1617.  [3] *P.W.*, Vol. I. p. 347.

bloody hands",[1] arguing, in the version finished in 1797, that "a little water clears us of this deed":

> In the torrent hard by there is water enough
> to wash away all the blood in the universe.[2]

As in *Macbeth*, the image of bloody hands returns much later in the play:

> Here is my hand—The hue of a pure lily,
> A Lady hand—none of your crimson spots.[3]

The presence of *Lear* is much more strongly felt. Herbert, "meek and patient, feeble, old and blind", moves in the likeness of Shakespeare's king, against a background of desolation, storm, and human violence. Dispossessed and exposed in utter helplessness, he is *Lear's* realization of bare humanity; he is the "forked animal", the "thing itself". And beyond this affinity between characters there is the full savagery of setting:

> The storm beats hard—Mercy for poor or rich
> Whose heads are shelterless in such a night![4]

> We should deserve to wear a cap and bells
> Three good round years, for playing the fool here
> In such a night as this.[5]

> Howl, howl, poor dog! Thou'lt never find him more;
> Draggled with storm and wet, howl, howl amain. . . .[6]

> . . . perhaps
> He is not in his true and perfect mind.[7]

*The Borderers* recovers something of *Lear's* giant perplexity in the face of the primary forms of things; of naked suffering and endurance ranged against the

[1] *l.* 938.    [2] *P.W.*, Vol. I. p. 166.
[3] *Ibid.*, p. 221.    [4] *l.* 1882.
[5] *l.* 768.    [6] *P.W.*, Vol. I. p. 220.
[7] *Ibid.*, p. 353.

elemental cruelties of neighbour and neighbourhood.
Lear's all-embracing bewilderment is echoed here:

> I am perplexed, and cannot think it true
> That thus thou speak'st to me, and where I am
> I know not, nor if this be the same air
> And the same sun, and we are fellow beings,
> Or all is changed. . . .[1]

As between Lear and Cordelia, so between Herbert and
Idonea, there is the suggestion, in the midst of pain, of
a golden other-life of prayer and song:

> There is a psalm that speaks
> Of God's parental mercies—with Idonea
> I used to sing it.[2]

And Wordsworth, like Shakespeare, throws out abrupt
statements of vast and hazy significance, about
maturity, and patience, and the cyclical nature of
things:

> The dead have but one face. . . .[3]

> . . . . the grave
> Contains not all that perish. . . .[4]

> So meet extremes in this mysterious world. . . .[5]

But because they have not the massive structure of
*Lear* behind them, they sound in their context ghostly
thin. Herbert is a pale character, a mere sufferer, and
such strength as *The Borderers* possesses is not bent
towards his dying. In a scene which he later omitted,
but which contains the best verse of the play, Wordsworth introduces a Pilgrim who is a study in miniature
of Herbert, conforming perfectly to the type of lonely
and agonized wanderer. Those who watch as he passes

---

[1] *P.W.*, Vol. I. p. 355.      [2] l. 1266.
[3] l. 2162.                     [4] *P.W.*, Vol. I. p. 356.
[5] l. 1529.

by, try to tempt him from his destiny by offering as an alternative life a curious blend of Christian sanctity and pastoral sweetness:

> A holy man,
> We know you are heaven-favoured; freshest grass
> Shall strew your chamber and a candlestick
> And crucifix with picture of the virgin
> Stand at the right hand of your humble bed,
> And you shall feed my sheep, and the long day
> Their quiet shall be yours.[1]

But the Pilgrim, "on whose brow affliction's hand had left So little of earthly", rejects this resolution and proceeds on his way.

In the last two Acts of *The Borderers*, Wordsworth dwells upon the contrasted solitudes of Oswald and Marmaduke. Oswald, the Godwinian apologist, is set against the world by his individualistic rationalism. Rejecting traditional moralities, and holding "that merit has no surer test Than obloquy", he describes himself as "sounding on, Through words and things, a dim and perilous way".[2] Wordsworth repeats this phrase in *The Excursion*, with specific reference to intellect:

> By pain of heart—now checked—and now impelled—
> The intellectual power, through words and things,
> Went sounding on, a dim and perilous way![3]

And the isolation of intellectual genius is very well stated in *The Prelude* lines on Newton's statue:

> The marble index of a mind for ever
> Voyaging through strange seas of Thought, alone.[4]

Oswald has no successors, because Wordsworth's concern with the solitude of reason does not survive his

---

[1] *P.W.*, Vol. I. p. 354.  
[3] Bk. III. 699.  
[2] l. 1774.  
[4] 1850, Bk. III. 62.

loss of interest in Godwin. Marmaduke, on the other hand, takes upon himself at the end of the play the mantle of Herbert and the Pilgrim: he accepts his solitude as a condition imposed by the natural order of things, uncontrived and inescapable. This larger solitude dominates Wordsworth's poetry for the next ten years.

> No prayers, no tears, but hear my doom in silence.
> I will go forth a wanderer on the earth,
> A shadowy thing, and as I wander on
> No human ear shall ever hear me speak,
> No human dwelling ever give me food
> Or sleep or rest, and all the uncertain way
> Shall be as darkness to me, as a waste
> Unnamed by man![1]

As he sets out on his lonely course, Marmaduke asks why men should ever seek each other, even in extremity:

> Give me a reason why the wisest thing
> That the earth owns should never choose to die,
> But some one must be near to count his groans.
> The wounded deer retires to solitude,
> And dies in solitude: all things but man,
> All die in solitude.[2]

Wordsworth's hasty sketches in solitude are inspired by the bleakness of *Lear*, by its preoccupation with the elements of things natural and human ("Then let them anatomize Regan. . . ." "What is the cause of thunder?"), by the stumbling figure of the king. Regan tells her father: "Nature in you stands at the

---

[1] *P.W.*, Vol. I. p. 224. When he revised *The Borderers* in 1842 Wordsworth made Marmaduke wander abroad "in search of nothing, that this earth can give, But expiation" (ll. 2317-8). The idea of expiation is foreign to his original conception of the play.

[2] l. 2149.

very verge of her confine"; and for Wordsworth the total isolation of Lear ruined—forsaken, dispossessed, lunatic, immeasurably old—is the play's heart. In the final scenes of *Lear*, Shakespeare achieves the co-presence of great suffering and of a state beyond suffering, a state of peace embodied but not conceptualized, a substance walking shadowless upon the stage. Wordsworth also, at the end of *The Borderers*, points in suffering beyond suffering. Marmaduke is

> raised
> Above or sunk below, all further sense
> Of provocation.[1]

He counsels Idonea:

> Conflict must cease, and in thy frozen heart,
> The extremes of suffering meet in absolute peace.[2]

Both plays look beyond pain; but what is said slantingly and with the terrible weight of *Lear* behind it, becomes in *The Borderers* ineffectually direct. Wordsworth fails because he asks last questions first: he understands reconcilement in solitude, but he cannot present a world broken on the wheel. And it is impossible to believe in Wordsworth's resolution without first believing in his tragedy.

Wordsworth learnt from his failure in *The Borderers*. He did not attempt another play: he came, in fact, to see that his talent was not only undramatic in its kind, but in a positive sense the denial of drama. All his solitaries of the next few years are in their different ways at peace with their environment; and although they live on the other side of tragedy, there is no attempt to derive their situation from tragic conflict— they have always been where Wordsworth finds them,

[1] l. 2294.      [2] l. 2215.

and they remain there after he has gone. So it is with the Old Cumberland Beggar:

> Him from my childhood have I known; and then
> He was so old, he seems not older now;
> He travels on, a solitary man. . . .

And with the Leech-Gatherer:

> In my mind's eye I seemed to see him pace
> About the weary moors continually,
> Wandering about alone and silently.[1]

The impression is of eternal lonely wandering at a slow and even pace, and through a single boundless element. Silence is also important. Wordsworth's solitaries are often wholly inarticulate, like the Cumberland Beggar, or half articulate, with a mysterious private utterance, like the Discharged Soldier in *The Prelude:*

> From his lips meanwhile
> There issued murmuring sounds, as if of pain
> Or of uneasy thought . . . he remained
> Fix'd in his place, and still from time to time
> Sent forth a murmuring voice of dead complaint,
> Groans scarcely audible.[2]

Almost none of the Leech-Gatherer's conversation is reported in his own words, and so it does not obtrude itself upon the poem. By avoiding direct speech Wordsworth is able to indicate a power to overreach, in the Leech-Gatherer's presence, the huge dualism of word and voice, language and action:

> The old Man still stood talking by my side;
> But now his voice to me was like a stream
> Scarce heard; nor word from word could I divide;
> And the whole body of the Man did seem
> Like one whom I had met with in a dream;
> Or like a man from some far region sent,
> To give me human strength, by apt admonishment.

---

[1] *Resolution and Independence.*        [2] Bk. IV. 421.

In the first published version of *Old Man Travelling*, a poem short enough to quote in full, Wordsworth presents a solitary who is straightforwardly articulate:

The little hedgerow birds,
That peck along the road regard him not.
He travels on, and in his face, his step,
His gait, is one expression: every limb,
His look and bending figure, all bespeak
A man who does not move with pain, but moves
With thought—He is insensibly subdued
To settled quiet: he is one by whom
All effort seems forgotten; one to whom
Long patience hath such mild composure given,
That patience now doth seem a thing of which
He hath no need. He is by nature led
To peace so perfect that the young behold
With envy, what the Old Man hardly feels.
—I asked him whither he was bound, and what
The object of his journey; he replied
"Sir! I am going many miles to take
A last leave of my son, a mariner,
Who from a sea-fight hath been brought to Falmouth,
And there is dying in a hospital.[1]

Later, Wordsworth saw that the last six lines were a mistake, and he saved the poem by omitting them. The point is not that they are trite or prosaic, but that they do violence to the nature of the old man. Just as Wordsworth is admonished by "the whole body" of the Leech-Gatherer, of which his stream-like voice is one constituent, even so does the total aspect of the old man perfectly "bespeak" his condition. He does not need to do or say anything—he is. Like all the great solitaries, he has a primordial quality by virtue of which he stands anterior, in time or in logic, to a divorce in human understanding. Saying and doing, with all of

[1] *P.W.*, Vol. IV. p. 247.

them, are contained in what they are. Wordsworth tries to touch this mystery, in a comment on an early version of *The Leech-Gatherer:*

> A person reading this Poem with feelings like mine will have been awed and controuled, expecting almost something spiritual or supernatural—What is brought forward? "A lonely place, a Pond" "by which an old man *was*, far from all house or home"—not stood, not sat, but "*was*"—the figure presented in the most naked simplicity possible.[1]

Wordsworth's use of the verb "to be" in the poetry of this period is directly related, as he says, to the simplicity of his solitaries, which is as large as it is naked. By this means he calls upon the vast and the remote without reference to space, and upon the old and the enduring without reference to time. "To be", in Wordsworth, is the agent of primary meaning, not pointing forward in argument towards *ex post facto* synthesis, but bending back, like the growing child in the Immortality Ode, upon an entire experience. Under its influence,

> Our souls have sight of that immortal sea
> That brought us hither. . . .

In order to make one word do so much work, Wordsworth, like Humpty Dumpty, has to pay it extra. How hard it works we discover when we find ourselves, as we talk about these solitaries, groping among inert abstractions. Wordsworth does this himself. His alternative title for *Old Man Travelling* is *Animal Tranquillity and Decay.* The *Leech-Gatherer*, of course, is properly called *Resolution and Independence*, and in a letter about the poem Wordsworth contemplates "the fortitude, independence, persevering spirit, and the general moral dignity of this old man's character".[2] This is no substitute for the Leech-Gatherer, who is

[1] *Early Letters* (ed. de Selincourt), p. 306.
[2] *Ibid.*, p. 306.

what he is; and the question, "what is he?", can only
be answered by the poem.

Convinced of the uniqueness of the poetic activity
and of its power to comprehend experience, Wordsworth said some wild things about language and reality.
No poet has ever complained so much as he about the
medium of his art; and towards the close of the Great
Decade this complaint comes to wear a sinister aspect.
Repeatedly, and with a helpless shrug, Wordsworth
deplores the inadequacies of language: he says, of those
whom he places highest among men:

> Words are but under-agents in their souls;
> When they are grasping with their greatest strength
> They do not breathe among them. . . .[1]

These are signs of his flinching from poetry. But his
earlier dissatisfaction is not with language as in its
nature unable to meet his demands upon it, but with
the failure of himself and others before him to exploit
its full resources.

According to the Preface to the *Lyrical Ballads*,
poetry ought to be "the image of man and nature";
and in working towards this ideal, it appeals to the
language of rustic and humble life, as to a perfect
model. Even the language of the greatest poets

> must often, in liveliness and truth, fall short of that which is
> uttered by men in real life, under the actual pressure of those
> passions, certain shadows of which the Poet thus produces,
> or feels to be produced, in himself.

Inept in argument and conventional in expression, the
Preface reveals that conspiracy of faculties without
which great poetry has not been written. The possible
perfection towards which its theory is directed is not
the perfection of an autonomous linguistic world, a
treadmill from which no poet can escape, in success or
in failure, in abuse of poetic diction or in praise of

[1] *The Prelude*, Bk. XII. 272.

silence. Rather, it is an inclusive perfection, admitting no distinction between language and not-language. Language is an effective inhabitant of all possible worlds; it can "deal boldly with substantial things"; it can encompass the human predicament and make plain "what we are". "Is there not", Wordsworth asks in *The Recluse*, "a strain of words that shall be life?" At the time he started work on *The Recluse* and wrote the *Lyrical Ballads* Preface, the question was rhetorical. A refusal to allow any final separation of language and life lies behind his confused discussion of the poet's duty of fidelity to fact, and of his moral and scientific status. His entire devotion to poetry, and readiness to risk all in its profession, would otherwise have been impossible.

The Leech-Gatherer, "the whole body of the man", is presented in terms of an integration which, in the strength of the poem, is defined into neither synthesis nor identity: he is like a cloud, says Wordsworth, that "moveth all together, if it move at all". The point of focus of this integration is the eloquence by which Wordsworth is admonished, containing, as it does, the rival eloquencies of sound and sight. *Old Man Travelling* is also a study in integration, but of a different kind. The poem may be approached as a Cartesian essay on the relationship of thing and thought. On his journey, the old man keeps the company of abstractions: "in his face, his step, his gait, is one expression"; he is "a man who does not move with pain, but moves with thought"; he is "subdued to settled quiet"; "patience" has given him "mild composure"; he is led "to peace". In all this intercourse neither his nor their nature is denied: he is an old man, yet not reified into mere particularity, while they retain their universality in the poem, although strangely breathed upon. It is the power of Wordsworth's Roman imagination to move between abstract and concrete in a way that is now lost to men: he would have understood words like *mens* and *fides* which look to us sometimes like ordinary abstract nouns and sometimes like personifications.

In the large simplicity of these solitaries, the difference becomes clear which Wordsworth struggled to express in prose, between the thing poetically distinct and the thing reduced to singleness.[1] They earn their independence by their show of comprehension, of relational power; and this independence is accepted as genuine because it is not achieved at the expense of experienced differences, as, in the two cases just considered, of that between language and action and between thought and thing.

Their isolation has its external aspect, which Wordsworth states immediately. All of them are placed at the verge of life; in earliest childhood or extreme old age, in dispossession, in unemployment or in utter poverty, in lunacy or blindness, in pursuit of the lonely callings of mendicant or pedlar. The further consequences of their solitude are then made plain. Just as they are wanderers through space, so are they gatherers up of time. The Cumberland Beggar, "in that vast solitude to which The tide of things has borne him", seems no older than he did when Wordsworth first met him: his solitude is no less temporal than spatial. Of another solitary Wordsworth says that he had an eye

> that, under brows
> Shaggy and grey, had meanings which it brought
> From years of youth; which, like a Being made
> Of many Beings, he had wondrous skill
> To blend with knowledge of the years to come,
> Human, or such as lie beyond the grave.[2]

[1] See p. 34.
[2] *The Excursion*, Bk. I. 428. The passage is early, belonging to 1797, the year of *The Old Cumberland Beggar*. See *P.W.*, Vol. V. p. 387.

This encompassing of all modes of being, and of the conditions of life and death and sleep, is perfectly established in *The Leech-Gatherer:*

> As a huge stone is sometimes seen to lie
> Couched on the bald top of an eminence;
> Wonder to all who do the same espy,
> By what means it could thither come, and whence;
> So that it seemed a thing endued with sense:
> Like a sea-beast crawled forth, that on a shelf
> Of rock or sand reposeth, there to sun itself;
>
> Such seemed this Man, not all alive nor dead,
> Nor all asleep—in his extreme old age. . . .

These figures do not achieve their sovereign peace through any vulgar triumph of permanence over process. The Cumberland Beggar, in his vast solitude, still pursues the endless circuit of houses, in search of alms; and the Leech-Gatherer will always pace "about the weary moors", plying his trade from pool to pool. They understand, and this is a key to their true independence, that only the permanent can change. They have a stillness which does not deny movement, and movement which contains stillness; the whole self-sustaining in a final and heroic shedding of accident that foreshadows *The Excursion's*

> Authentic tidings of invisible things;
> Of ebb and flow, and everduring power;
> And central peace, subsisting at the heart
> Of endless agitation.[1]

The old man is consumed with the effort of his journey; yet "he is one to whom All effort seems forgotten". The discharged soldier[2] arrests Wordsworth with his "groans scarcely audible" and with "the ghastly mildness in his look"; but Wordsworth discovers that "in all he said There was a strange half-absence", and that

---

[1] Bk. IV. 1144.                    [2] See p. 62.

he speaks in the tone of one "Remembering the importance of his theme But feeling it no longer". The soldier is at peace, and he is fully acquainted with suffering. Here Wordsworth succeeds, where in *The Borderers* he failed, in penetrating to the other side of pain. There is no shirking the desperate personal issue: the soldier's personality is real, and so is his distress:

> He was of stature tall,
> A foot above man's common measure tall,
> Stiff in his form, and upright, lank and lean;
> A man more meagre, as it seem'd to me,
> Was never seen abroad by night or day.
> His arms were long, and bare his hands; his mouth
> Shew'd ghastly in the moonlight: from behind
> A milestone propp'd him, and his figure seem'd
> Half-sitting, and half-standing. I could mark
> That he was clad in military garb,
> Though faded, yet entire. He was alone,
> Had no attendant, neither Dog, nor Staff,
> Nor knapsack; in his very dress appear'd
> A desolation, a simplicity
> That seem'd akin to solitude.

And his immediate need of "food and lodgings for the night" is plainly stated. But somehow he has reached, through war, a peace that is not dependent upon the exclusion of strife, upon insensibility or oblivion.

We should be guided by Wordsworth's understanding of externals. The soldier is fully human, yet marvellously tall, and "ghastly in the moonlight". He is in the world, yet placed "half-sitting and half-standing", between the worlds. His soldier's dress, "though faded, yet entire". The last stroke is the most subtle. Nothing is lost to the soldier, but everything is changed: he is history at last become wholly meaningful. Thus when, after sustained concrete description, Wordsworth turns to three of his favourite abstractions

—"desolation", "simplicity", "solitude"—they are
ready to work very hard for him.

The soldier's faded uniform is beautifully relevant
to his story of violence and death, which he tells like
one "Remembering the importance of his theme But
feeling it no longer". In his case, the relational power
which he shares with the other solitaries is focused on
the opposition of war and peace; and the overcoming
of this opposition is referred to as an act of memory.
Memory, we shall see, is the vital centre of a theory
that poetry "takes its origin from emotion recollected
in tranquillity":[1] memory distinguishes the visionary
soul, described as

> Remembering how she felt, but what she felt
> Remembering not. . . .[2]

Here, memory commands the spiritual totality that is
Wordsworthian solitude.

Lucy must also be counted among the solitaries,
although clearly different from the others. All the Lucy
Poems, with one undistinguished exception,[3] were
written in Germany, in the winter of 1798-99. During
some of the coldest weather of the century, Wordsworth lodged with his sister in a provincial town,
separated from Coleridge, very short of money, dis-
liking the Germans and understanding little of their
language. This may have some bearing on the extraordinary quality of the Lucy Poems; on their remoteness, on their clarity and microcosmic perfection. They
touch the same issues as Wordsworth's other poetry of
solitude and relationship, but their extreme spirituality
of tone and lack of literal context is altogether un-
typical. Even the discharged soldier, the most ghostly

---

[1] Preface to the *Lyrical Ballads*.
[2] *The Prelude*, Bk. II. 335.
[3] *I travelled among unknown men.* . . .

of the relational solitaries, has about him enough of earthly matter of fact to be judged no ghost.

There are two poems, also written in Germany, which ought to be included in the Lucy canon. Of these, *The Danish Boy* is very close to Lucy. He is a spirit of eternal youth and solitude, in a paradisal setting:

> Between two sister moorland rills
> There is a spot that seems to lie
> Sacred to flowerets of the hills,
> And sacred to the sky.
> And in this smooth and open dell
> There is a tempest-stricken tree;
> A corner-stone by lightning cut,
> The last stone of a lonely hut;
> And in this dell you see
> A thing no storm can e'er destroy,
> The shadow of a Danish Boy.

This is the highly stylized Lucy setting; and in its midst,

> The Danish Boy walks here alone:
> This lovely dell is all his own.

He is the maker of music too fine for human ear, the expression of his perfect sympathy with the life surrounding him:

> A harp is from his shoulder slung;
> Resting the harp upon his knee,
> To words of a forgotten tongue
> He suits its melody.
> Of flocks upon the neighbouring hill
> He is the darling and the joy;
> And often, when no cause appears,
> The mountain-ponies prick their ears,
> —They hear the Danish Boy.
> While in the dell he sings alone
> Beside the tree and corner-stone.

F

And in the last stanza he holds war and peace, life and death, reconciled in his unearthly song:

> There sits he; in his face you spy
> No trace of a ferocious air,
> Nor ever was a cloudless sky
> So steady or so fair.
> The lovely Danish Boy is blest
> And happy in his flowery cove:
> From bloody deeds his thoughts are far;
> And yet he warbles songs of war,
> That seem like songs of love,
> For calm and gentle is his mien;
> Like a dead Boy he is serene.

Within its tiny compass, this poem succeeds in stating the Lucy theme.

*Lucy Gray*, the second of the poems outside the recognized canon, introduces in its opening stanzas the classical nature-solitary:

> Oft I had heard of Lucy Gray:
> And, when I crossed the wild,
> I chanced to see at break of day
> The solitary child.
>
> No mate, no comrade Lucy knew;
> She dwelt on the wide moor,
> —The sweetest thing that ever grew
> Beside a human door!

There follows a tale of death in sudden accident: and Lucy Gray finally returns, a singing child-ghost, to haunt the poem:

> —Yet some maintain that to this day
> She is a living child;
> That you may see sweet Lucy Gray
> Upon the lonesome wild.

O'er rough and smooth she trips along,
And never looks behind;
And sings a solitary song
That whistles in the wind.

The Lucy Poems share this preoccupation with perfect solitude discovered in perfect relationship with environment. *She Dwelt among Untrodden Ways* presents Lucy as a single jewel well set:

A violet by a mossy stone
Half hidden from the eye!
—Fair as a star, when only one
Is shining in the sky.

And *A Slumber Did My Spirit Seal* imagines her, much more sternly, as joined with the primary forms of nature in eternal cosmic movement:

Rolled round in earth's diurnal course
With rocks, and stones, and trees.

Of the remaining poems, *Strange Fits of Passion* is brilliantly and obliquely evocative of solitude. Lucy's cottage is the still point round which the poem is constructed; and the poet's journey towards it is described with a Coleridgean sense of foreboding:

My horse moved on; hoof after hoof
He raised, and never stopped:
When down behind the cottage roof,
At once, the bright moon dropped.

Lucy's ethereal remoteness is enforced by the way the poem ends with the poet still riding towards her cottage, struck by the sudden fear that she may be dead.

*Three Years She Grew*, the last of the group, considers the relationship between the solitary and her world as a thing of purity and finest eloquence, the lyrical delicacy of the verse scarcely equalled in Wordsworth:

> The floating clouds their state shall lend
> To her; for her the willow bend;
> Nor shall she fail to see
> Even in the motions of the Storm
> Grace that shall mould the Maiden's form
> By silent sympathy.
>
> The stars of midnight shall be dear
> To her; and she shall lean her ear
> In many a secret place
> Where rivulets dance their wayward round,
> And beauty born of murmuring sound
> Shall pass into her face.

Lucy's beauty is a universal thing, a Wordsworthian music of the spheres: the music of sight in the first stanza is joined by the music of sound in the second, which two beget a greater music that they both must recognize.

It is thus possible to see the Lucy Poems as consistent both with each other and with the rest of Wordsworth's poetry. There is evident, in everything that Wordsworth writes, a vision of reality as single, self-sustaining, and systematic. Hence, I have argued, his imaginative Spinozism; and, rather as Spinoza thought it possible, without relapsing into Cartesian dualism, to consider his Substance either under the aspect of Thought or of Extension, so Wordsworth moves from solitude to relationship and back again, without losing grip upon the fact of singleness. The one may only be reduced to the other, but the reduction may be perfect. Wordsworth can talk about Lucy's beauty in solitude, in the last quotation, only in terms of a relationship between visual and aural: both are present in her, because the beauty that "passed into her face" was "born of murmuring sound". But this, in Words-

worth's lyric, is entirely adequate. Nor does it matter
whether Wordsworth's poetry be approached through
the one or the other: only the simultaneity of the poetry
itself is unattainable. And the bungled studies of solitude in *The Borderers*, leading to success, have their
exact counterpart in relationship.

Lucy's "silent sympathy" with nature affords a
leading text. This sympathy is the obsession of Wordsworth's juvenile descriptive poetry, and passages like
the following from *An Evening Walk*, decked out in the
manners of eighteenth-century sentimental reflection,
are all too common:

> Last evening sight, the cottage smoke, no more,
> Lost in the thickened darkness, glimmers hoar;
> And, towering from the sullen, dark-brown mere,
> Like a black wall, the mountain-steeps appear.
> —Now o'er the soothed accordant heart we feel
> A sympathetic twilight slowly steal,
> And ever, as we fondly muse, we find
> The soft gloom deepening on the tranquil mind.[1]

At this early stage there is nothing to arrest the attention, beyond Wordsworth's persistence in this theme,
and the signs of his serious intellectual application to it.
In 1794, the year after he published *An Evening Walk*,
Wordsworth was engaged in its amendment. The 1794
corrections are of interest, for they develop a vitalistic
philosophy of nature in defence of these repeated
assertions of sympathy:

> A heart that vibrates evermore, awake
> To feeling for all forms that Life can take,
> That wider still its sympathy extends
> And sees not any line where being ends;

[1] l. 311. The edition of 1793 (*P.W.*, Vol. I. p. 34) does not differ in any
important respect from the shorter final version here quoted.

Sees sense, through Nature's rudest forms betrayed,
Tremble obscure through fountain, rock, and shade,
And while a secret power those forms endears
Their social accents never vainly hears.[1]

And a few lines later Wordsworth speaks of "those favoured souls" who

See common forms prolong the endless chain
Of joy and grief, of pleasure and of pain.[2]

The earliest surviving version of *Guilt and Sorrow*, a long narrative poem in Spenserian stanzas, also dates from 1794. Wordsworth is again deeply engrossed in the problem of sympathy; but however subtle his inward workings, he has made no headway in expression. Indeed, since *Guilt and Sorrow* lacks the varnished anonymity of his meditative heroics, there is more violent absurdity in the sight of man and nature walking hand in hand through the poem, in overt congruity of mood.

"O come," he cried, "come, after weary night
So ominous, far other scene to view."
So forth she came, and eastward looked; the sight
Over her brow like dawn of gladness threw,
That tinged with faint red smile her faded hue:
Not lovelier did the morning star appear,
Parting the lucid mist and bathed in dew:
The whilst her comrade to her pensive cheer
Tempered sweet words of hope; and the lark warbled near.[3]

Wordsworth said of *Guilt and Sorrow* that it was "addressed to coarse sympathies".[4] This is also true of *The Borderers*, which immediately succeeds it; but here, as in the history of the Wordsworthian solitaries, there are intimations of mature power. The pivot of the play,

---

[1] *P.W.*, Vol. I. p. 10.  [2] *Ibid.*, p. 13.
[3] *Ibid.*, p. 112.  [4] *Ibid.*, p. 334.

half obscured by the to and fro of Godwinian philosophizing, is a single star. Under the influence of Oswald's sophistry, Marmaduke is on the point of murdering Herbert, when he happens to raise his eyes:

> Upwards I cast my eyes, and, through a crevice,
> Beheld a star twinkling above my head,
> And, by the living God, I could not do it.[1]

Later in the play, when he is once more of Oswald's persuasion, Marmaduke reflects upon this moment:

> Last night, when moved to lift the avenging steel,
> I did believe all things were shadows—yea,
> Living or dead all things were bodiless,
> Or but the mutual mockeries of body,
> Till that same star summoned me back again.
> Now I could laugh till my ribs ached. Oh, Fool!
> To let a creed, built in the heart of things,
> Dissolve before a twinkling atom![2]

A star prevents a murder: this is the point towards which Wordsworth's prosings about the life of intellect and the life of sensation are vainly directed. Hitherto, sympathy has been simply a matter of external correspondence with environment. Wordsworth now tries to say something more difficult. Oswald, we have seen, stands for the isolation of intellect; and this isolation is false because it is achieved only through the denial of relationship. Wordsworth argues in his Preface that Oswald's world is determined by his intellectualism: he looks at things "through an optical glass of a peculiar tint": the colour of objects "is exclusively what he gives them; it is one, and it is his own". Since he can only see things in this intellectual monochrome, Oswald cannot see anything except himself. But Marmaduke saw a star, and in so doing he realized that Oswald's "creed" and the "twinkling atom" were

---

[1] l. 988. The early version is given in *P.W.*, Vol. I., p. 167.  [2] l. 1213.

at war. Wordsworth spends the next ten years showing what it means to see things: in *The Borderers* he makes a tentative beginning by contrasting Oswald's need, in false isolation, to

> turn perforce and seek for sympathy
> In dim relation to imagined Beings[1]

with Marmaduke's sudden wisdom in the presence of the star. This wisdom is the child of true sympathy, and true sympathy's other name is reciprocity, active relationship, or

> enobling interchange
> Of action from within and from without.[2]

Oswald's abstract creed made a ghost of the external world, "till that same star summoned me back again". *The Borderers* fails to impress the intervention of the star: it is merely suggested that the star showed Marmaduke that he had been wrong in supposing "all things were shadows". This association of the effectiveness of the world with its solidity is very characteristic of Wordsworth: he says of his Cumberland childhood:

> brought up in such a grand
> And lovely region, I had forms distinct
> To steady me . . . I still
> At all times had a real solid world
> Of images about me. . . .[3]

But of course this will not do by itself, and in *The Borderers* it goes unsupported.

The first book of *The Excursion* was conceived as an independent narrative poem. This poem, *The Ruined Cottage* or *The Pedlar*, was finished in the spring of

[1] l. 1454.  [2] *The Prelude*, Bk. XII. 376.
[3] *Ibid.*, Bk. VIII. 596.

1798, although there had once been a shorter version which Wordsworth read to Coleridge in the previous summer. As late as 1802, Wordsworth regarded *The Pedlar* as complete in itself, and was considering its publication. In date of composition it is close to *The Borderers*, but in little else; for *The Pedlar* takes a decisive step into maturity. Most of it is incorporated, with little change, in *The Excursion*, which shows that Wordsworth was prepared to stand by this early work in 1814, when he published *The Excursion*. The whole poem is charged with anticipation. Here, for example, is a foretaste of the 1800 Preface to the *Lyrical Ballads:*

> He from his native hills
> Had wandered far, much had he seen of men
> Their manners, their enjoyments and pursuits
> Their passions and their feelings, chiefly those
> Essential and eternal in the heart
> Which mid the simpler forms of rural life
> Exist more simple in their elements
> And speak a plainer language.[1]

This passage is taken from a long account of the Pedlar's early history which is itself autobiographical in spirit, and looks forward to *The Prelude*, where, in the 1805 text, much of it reappears unaltered.

The original *Pedlar* is thus a source poem of great importance. Furthermore, it has a personal merit easy to overlook in purely textual study. The first point of interest is its connexion with *The Old Cumberland Beggar*, written a few months before Wordsworth finished *The Pedlar*. In both these poems the relational power of the solitaries has a definite social aspect; but their roles are exactly opposed. The beggar binds the society through which he moves as recipient of elementary charities, his maintenance being accepted as a common duty; whereas the pedlar carries round with

[1] *P.W.*, Vol. V. p. 380. Compare *The Excursion*, Bk. I. 340.

him the means of satisfying the needs of a scattered, simple-living community, "all dependant", Wordsworth says, "upon the Pedlar's toil". And each of these cyclical wanderers is brought to his own "vast solitude".

The poem opens with Wordsworth's chance arrival at a ruined and deserted cottage where he meets an old pedlar, already well known to him. There follows a description of the pedlar's early childhood, which opens, feebly enough, with a few lines of gothic stage-setting:

> I loved to hear him talk of former days
> And tell how when a child, ere yet of age
> To be a shepherd, he had learned to read
> His bible in a school that stood alone,
> Sole building on a mountain's dreary edge,
> Far from the sight of city spire, or sound
> Of Minster clock.[1]

But the account of the child's education, with which Wordsworth continues, is of different quality. As in *The Prelude*, Wordsworth talks about the influence of nature and of books: in particular, he is attentive to the way in which the child relates his earliest understanding of mathematics to the natural objects around him:

> While yet he linger'd in the elements
> Of science, and among her simplest laws,
> His triangles, they were the stars of heaven,
> The *silent* stars; his altitudes the crag
> Which is the eagle's birthplace; or some peak
> Familiar with forgotten years, which shews,
> Inscribed, as with the silence of the thought,
> Upon its bleak and visionary sides,
> The history of many a winter storm,
> Or obscure records of the path of fire.[2]

[1] *P.W.*, Vol. V. p. 380.
[2] *Ibid.*, p. 384. Compare *The Excursion*, Bk. I. 270.

There is no passage in Wordsworth more important than this, for it makes the main argument of his poetry brilliantly clear. The juvenile and clumsy statements of sympathy, in terms of open correspondence between inner and outer, are in fact directed towards the experience which Wordsworth here describes. The child does not learn about one world of unchanging abstract types, of mental stuff, and about a second, shifting world of natural objects. He learns about a single world in which triangles march about the sky, in which *mountain-sides are suffering things, and also quietly, mathematically, eternal. The mountain with a history of violence "inscribed as with the silence of the thought" upon its sides is profoundly Wordsworthian in its command of mental and physical. And so my account of relationship, as of solitude, becomes a tale of dualisms ultimately daunting to intellect but mastered in poetry. Wordsworth remembered how the child had seen things when he came to write about the Danish Boy singing at once of love and war, Lucy in silent sympathy with wind and stars and perfectly alone, the discharged soldier, like the mountain, a living history, the old man walking with thought and towards peace, yet walking; the Leech-Gatherer, entirely eloquent.

*The Pedlar* deals thus with the visionary power of childhood:

> Ere his ninth summer he was sent abroad
> To tend his father's sheep, such was his task
> Henceforward to the later day of youth.
> Oh! then what soul was his when on the tops
> Of the high mountains he beheld the sun
> Rise up and bathe the world in light. He looked,
> The ocean and the earth beneath him lay
> In gladness and deep joy. The clouds were touched
> And in their silent faces did he read

Unutterable love. Sound needed none
Nor any voice of joy: his spirit drank
The spectacle. Sensation, soul and form
All melted into him. They swallowed up
His animal being; in them did he live
And by them did he live. They were his life.[1]

There are many passages, in *The Prelude* especially, very close to this in their manner of proceeding; nor is this by any means as good as the best, so that there is less to lose in using it roughly, to point a general moral. The opening is level-toned, the impression of quiet narrative conveyed by preliminary mention of age and occupation, and sustained by adherence to prose-order for nearly ten lines. In its ease and length of stride, Wordsworth's language wears its blank verse form very lightly. The vocabulary is characteristically limited, but of an elemental strength, building on the Wordsworthian bed-rock of earth, ocean, sun, cloud and mountain. As always, the spareness of texture that is not quite meanness is enforced by a profusion of monosyllables—two of the first six lines are entirely monosyllabic. Adjectives are few and carefully chosen: "high" and "deep" bind mathematical quantity to nature qualitative and sentient; and the faces of the clouds are "silent". "Unutterable", a sudden polysyllabic blaze, marks a decisive shift of mood. The change is at once apparent. In "sound needed none" there is both poetic omission and inversion. The periods become suddenly short and choppy, dragooned into blank verse. The vocabulary reaches out towards science and philosophy.

This is not altogether a success. The careful development towards "unutterable love" is marred by "Oh! then what soul was his. . . ."—an invitation to ecstasy delivered too soon and too crudely. But the real crux

[1] *P.W.*, Vol. V. p. 382. Compare *The Excursion*, Bk. I. 197.

rests in the second part of the passage, where Wordsworth addresses himself to the child's experience in two
different ways. On the one hand, he resorts to huge,
opaque technicalities—"sensation", "soul", "form"
—worn smooth in centuries of speculative use. On the
other, he describes the child's relation with his world
by means of a single metaphor. He "drank" the scene,
and the scene "swallowed" him; so that Wordsworth
concludes, emerging from the violent particularity of
this image, that the scene lived in him and he in it.
Here the two methods of approach consort a little un-
easily, and in consequence they both attract the wrong
sort of attention. "Sensation, soul and form" looks like
an intellectual smoke-screen, hastily laid to conceal a
false move in argument: we ask what it means, and find
it contorted and pretentiously obscure. This leaves the
metaphor exposed in a way it can ill afford. Isolated, it is
a blunt and conventional device; and, in its reciprocal
reference to child and scene, somewhat grotesque.

Even if unsuccessful, this passage from *The Pedlar*
is very instructive. Elsewhere Wordsworth uses a
vocabulary strong in intellectual associations: it is this
that has led critics to impose a formal philosophical
interpretation upon *The Prelude* which I do not think
it will bear. My discussion of solitude and relationship
is not intended to deny that Wordsworth was in some
sense influenced by Locke and Hartley; or even to
prefer Spinoza before them; but rather to show that
when he writes good poetry his language of intellect is
successfully directed to a further end. In *The Pedlar*
this language seems misty and unattached because
Wordsworth fails to refer it to the purpose sleeping in
his rough and very concrete metaphor. For a bald
summary of this purpose we must return to Wordsworth's statement of aims in the Prospectus to *The
Recluse*.[1] He hopes to reveal the exquisite fitting of

[1] See p. 41.

the mind and the external world, each to the other, and

> the creation (by no lower name
> Can it be called) which they with blended might
> Accomplish:—this is our high argument.[1]

This feeding on one another of the child and the visible scene is a typical statement of the fact of mutual fitting. The relationship is stable, both terms being wholly taken up in interaction whereby, through supporting each other they support themselves. Wordsworth develops this "interchange of action from within and from without" in a number of ways. The metaphor used in *The Pedlar* is a favourite. So is the silent dialogue in which each perfectly understands the other; and, close to this, the partnership in music-making—the Eolian Harp image in the first book of *The Prelude* is particularly fine.[2] Again, he talks of the mind as "wedded to this goodly universe",[3] and *The Prelude* is rich in images of communion and intercourse, though of sacramental rather than sexual quality. This concert of imagery lays stress on the difference between Wordsworth and Coleridge laboured in my first chapter. Both were natural monists, but the theme of the one was unity and of the other significant relation. Success meant for Coleridge the building of his dome in air, and failure the involuntary egotism of *The Dejection Ode:*

> O Lady! we receive but what we give,
> And in our life alone does Nature live.

Wordsworth could not have written this, as is evident even in his attempts to convey the whole truth in a phrase, in the largest of his reality-metaphors where he is driven as it were to reify relationship, so that in a general though unhelpful way one may talk about unity with reference to him as to anybody professing to make

---

[1] l. 69.     [2] ll. 101-7.     [3] Preface to *The Excursion*, l. 53.

sense of things. Reality in *The Prelude* is a building, a frame or a fabric—a complex of mutually sustaining elements. The word "unity", in all its forms, appears only twice in the entire poem,[1] and on the first of these occasions with direct reference to Coleridge, as one to whom "the unity of all has been revealed". On the other hand Wordsworth falls back three times in the first three books upon the various forms of "link"[2] in order to express his relational principle; and even the outlandish "collateral", with its adverb, is pressed twice in the first two books into the same service.[3] Only a fool would be guided by vocabulary alone, but it remains noteworthy that Wordsworth's concentration of effort is reflected at every level of seriousness.

Of Wordsworth's reality-metaphors, that of landscape is by far the most commanding. But since his landscapes do not reflect or represent or point towards absent realities, it were less confusing to talk about landscape than about metaphor, or about reality. There is an inclusive literalness about these landscapes to which we are introduced by *The Pedlar*. The child's stars are his triangles, and his mountain-peaks his altitudes—a blunt assertion at once justified in the strength of "inscribed as with the silence of the thought". Shelley spoke of Wordsworth as "wakening a sort of thought in sense"[4]; and he should be heeded. In the first book of *The Prelude* Wordsworth refers, with reference to earliest childhood, to

Those hallow'd and pure motions of the sense
Which seem in their simplicity to own
An intellectual charm, that calm delight
Which, if I err not, surely must belong

[1] Bk. II. 226; Bk. VIII. 826.
[2] Bk. I. 601; Bk. I. 639; Bk. III. 127.
[3] Bk. I. 621; Bk. II. 52.
[4] *Peter Bell the Third.*

> To those first-born affinities that fit
> Our new existence to existing things,
> And, in our dawn of being, constitute
> The bond of union betwixt life and joy.[1]

And, later on, he speaks of

> The gravitation and the filial bond
> Of nature, that connect him with the world.[2]

The child is "an inmate of this *active* universe" where he "creates, creator and receiver both":

> Such, verily, is the first
> Poetic spirit of our human life;
> By uniform control of after years
> In most abated or suppress'd, in some,
> Through every change of growth or of decay,
> Pre-eminent till death.

The child is wholly and unselfconsciously involved in this universal life of action and reaction. But the poet's participation cannot be in this manner complete, because he must reflect upon and express the condition of thought-in-sense which the child merely experiences. Hence the problem of poetry is for Wordsworth primarily one of self-awareness. The poet must experience thought-in-sense if he is to have anything to say, but if he is ever to say it, he must be aware of his experience. Experience without reflection means an inarticulate living of poetry—an idea near to Wordsworth's heart—and reflection on experience once past, poetic suicide. Thus the whole weight of Wordsworth's theory of poetry rests upon the poetic memory, in which the adult can return to his experience without bringing back with him, in any destructive way, the distinction between thought and sense which he has necessarily come to live by. And so "the first poetic spirit" is in some "pre-eminent till death".

[1] l. 578.        [2] Bk. II. 263.

Wordsworth's poetic memory is a sustained paradox. The poet loses himself and finds himself; he recovers the childish condition, yet he knows what he is doing when in poetry he wakens thought-in-sense. Once again, a general comparison with Spinoza is illuminating. Rather as the philosopher argues for an all-embracing Substance in which his reasoning self must somehow be contained, the poet is both experiencing, or re-experiencing, thought-in-sense, and telling the tale, at once inside and outside his "active universe".

This operation of memory, which Wordsworth more than once fails to expound in prose, is demonstrated in his poetry. *The Pedlar* makes a beginning, though still too expository for entire success: it is marred by an intellectual perseverance, sometimes shrill and heckling in tone, for the most part heavily didactic, which is the vice of Wordsworth's longer poems. The child instinctively held together abstract knowledge and natural appearance in one society.

> with her [Nature's] hues,
> Her forms, and with the spirit of her forms,
> He clothed the nakedness of austere truth.[1]

But as he grew up this "just equipoise" became harder to maintain: the state of thought-in-sense was giving place to a fearful tension:

> But now, before his twentieth year was pass'd,
> Accumulated feelings press'd his heart
> With an encreasing weight; he was o'er power'd
> By Nature, and his mind became disturbed,
> And many a time he wished the winds might rage
> When they were silent: from his intellect,
> And from the stillness of abstracted thought,
> In vain he sought repose, in vain he turned
> To science for a cure.

[1] *P.W.*, Vol. V. p. 384.

Even so, there could be no complete denial of his past;
for he retained the memory of what he had been, and
sometimes, in moments of insight, he returned to his
early peace:

> From Nature and her overflowing soul
> He had received so much, that all his thoughts
> Were steeped in feeling. He was only then
> Contented, when, with bliss ineffable
> He felt the sentiment of being, spread
> O'er all that moves, and all that seemeth still,
> O'er all which, lost beyond the reach of thought,
> And human knowledge, to the human eye
> Invisible, yet liveth to the heart,
> O'er all that leaps, and runs, and shouts, and sings,
> Or beats the gladsome air, o'er all that glides
> Beneath the wave, yea in the wave itself
> And mighty depth of waters. Wonder not
> If such his transports were; for in all things
> He saw one life, and felt that it was joy.
> One song they sang, and it was audible,
> Most audible then, when the fleshly ear
> O'ercome by grosser prelude of that strain,
> Forgot its functions, and slept undisturbed.

This passage, which appears almost unaltered in the
1805 *Prelude*,[1] is bent towards the poetic state of recovered integration. The "sentiment of being, spread
over all"; the universal sympathetic movement; the
"one life" and the "one song"—all reflect Wordsworthian permanence in process and the condition of
entire and urgent involvement:

> All things shall live in us and we shall live
> In all things that surround us.[2]

Wisely, Wordsworth avoids any exposition of the
working of thought and sense at the moment of insight:

[1] Bk. II. 416.          [2] *P.W.*, Vol. V. p. 402.

the poetic understanding touched things "lost beyond the reach of thought", and the poetic hearing was keenest when "the fleshly ear . . . forgot its functions, and slept undisturbed". Paradox had better be called paradox, though not too loudly. Later in *The Pedlar* Wordsworth returns to the problem, and achieves only a false explicitness:

> thus the senses and the intellect
> Shall each to each supply a mutual aid,
> Invigorate and sharpen and refine
> Each other with a power that knows no bound. . . .[1]

This sort of thing invites a specifically intellectual criticism that it cannot withstand.

Wordsworth describes the condition of insight as a kind of alert day-dream, an inclusive state, like that of the Leech-Gatherer, embracing waking life, and sleep, and death. Thus the famous account, in *Tintern Abbey*, of

> that blessed mood,
> In which the burthen of the mystery,
> In which the heavy and the weary weight
> Of all this unintelligible world,
> Is lightened:—that serene and blessed mood,
> In which the affections gently lead us on,—
> Until, the breath of this corporeal frame
> And even the motion of our human blood
> Almost suspended, we are laid asleep
> In body, and become a living soul:
> While with an eye made quiet by the power
> Of harmony, and the deep power of joy,
> We see into the life of things.

The "eye made quiet" is the key that opens all doors, the supreme poetic agent considered by nineteenth-century criticism in such terms as "meditative pathos" —with more sense of direction, I have tried to show,

[1] *P.W.*, Vol. V. p. 402.

than subsequent embroiderers of the theme of Wordsworth's mystical sense of unity with nature. The eye
made quiet is the relational principle in action, "looking
for the shades of difference As they lie hid in all
exterior forms", and at the same time observing
"affinities In objects where no brotherhood exists To
common minds".[1] In *Tintern Abbey* it is referred to the
beautiful and the intelligible: not frenziedly—no
"dying in a dance", no Keatsian rich urgency; but
with gentle insistence to record, in the *Prelude* phrase,
"a register of permanent relations".[2] The eye made
quiet is thought-in-sense reborn.

At the end of *The Pedlar* Wordsworth attempts to
state the terms of a private discipline through which the
regeneration of thought-in-sense may be achieved; and
again, in his *Letter to Mathetes*, published by Coleridge
in his journal, *The Friend*. What advice, Wordsworth
asks, can be offered to one who has recently lost his
childhood?

> He cannot recall past time; he cannot begin his journey
> afresh; he cannot untwist the links by which, in no undelight-
> ful harmony, images and sentiments are wedded in his mind.
> Granted that the sacred light of childhood is and must be for
> him no more than a remembrance. He may, notwithstanding,
> be remanded to Nature; and with trustworthy hopes; founded
> less upon his sentient than upon his intellectual being—to
> Nature, not as leading on insensibly to the society of Reason;
> but to Reason and Will, as leading back to the wisdom of
> Nature. A reunion, in this order accomplished, will bring
> reformation and timely support; and the two powers of
> Reason and Nature, thus reciprocally teacher and taught,
> may advance together in a track to which there is no limit.

This is a distinct echo of the mutual support of senses
and intellect for which Wordsworth argues in *The
Pedlar*. But there is an air of futility about discursive

---

[1] *The Prelude*, Bk. III. 158; Bk. II. 403.     [2] Bk. II. 311.

accounts of this kind: they lack the force of Wordsworth's open appeal to the poetic memory in his deriving of poetry from emotion recollected in tranquillity, and in his *Prelude* distinction between remembering *how* and remembering *what*[1] upon which he rests the "sense of possible sublimity".

While analysis of thought-in-sense is in the nature of the thing a hopeless venture, Wordsworth has left an interesting note of its psychology. Referring to the *Prelude* passage about the boy who hooted to the owls, which he published as a separate poem, he says:

> The Boy, there introduced, is listening with something of a feverish and restless anxiety for the recurrence of those riotous sounds which he had previously excited; and at the moment when the intenseness of his mind is beginning to remit, he is surprised into a perception of the solemn and tranquillizing images which the Poem describes.[2]

Now here are the relevant lines of the poem:

> And, when there came a pause
> Of silence such as baffled his best skill:
> Then, sometimes, in that silence, while he hung
> Listening, a gentle shock of mild surprise
> Has carried far into his heart the voice
> Of mountain-torrents; or the visible scene
> Would enter unawares into his mind
> With all its solemn imagery, its rocks,
> Its woods, and that uncertain heaven received
> Into the bosom of the steady lake.[3]

---

[1] See p. 70.

[2] Preface to the 1815 Edition of Wordsworth's Poems.

[3] *The Prelude*, Bk. V. 404. That the account is autobiographical is shown by the fact that Wordsworth's earliest draft is written in the first person (de Selincourt, p. 608 D). De Quincey has a story about Wordsworth that exactly corresponds to Wordsworth's own note to *There Was a Boy*. De Quincey's story is quoted, in different connexions, by Professor Beatty (*William Wordsworth*, p. 160), N. P. Stallknecht (*Strange Seas of Thought*, p. 60), and Dr Helen Darbishire (*The Poet Wordsworth*, p. 110).

The attention is entirely focused upon one object: then, as relaxation sets in, there is a moment of vulnerability. The child, or the poet, has trained all his conscious powers in one direction, and "he is surprised into a perception" before he can recover his normal balance. He is caught in mid-stride, as concentration fades, between one daylight condition and the next.

Wordsworth says, in *Tintern Abbey*, that once we have gained an eye made quiet, we "see into the life of things". The life of things he thought of primarily and to best effect as landscape. *There was a Boy* is in point: there thought-in-sense is presented as a state of exposure in which, because it has ceased to maintain the ordinary waking distinction between inner and outer, the mind is penetrated by the visible scene. This penetration, insisted on in "carried far into his heart" and "would enter unawares into his mind", is the very nerve of Wordsworth's literal genius; and the tendency to pass it by as weakly metaphorical results from inattention to his received modes of thought as to the nature of selfconsciousness. In the rationalist tradition, knowledge of the self is different in kind and superior in certainty to knowledge of the external world acquired through the senses; but an eighteenth-century empiricist regarded self-knowledge as the fruit of introspection, a sixth and inner sense, comparable in its working to the five external senses. Nor was this simply a matter between philosophers: it had, and still has, a profound effect on the assumptions of unreflective people. What distinguishes Wordsworth is the enormous importance which he attaches to introspection, or the inward eye. He believed in it with a seriousness attainable only by men of power.

The first consequence of Wordsworth's belief in the inward eye is a granting of extension to the inward world which it surveys. De Quincey makes a relevant comment on the poem which we have just been considering:

> The very expression "far" by which space and its infinities are attributed to the human heart, and its capacities of re-echoing the sublimities of nature, has always struck me as with a flash of sublime revelation.[1]

Wordsworth is as much in earnest about the inward world's extension as he is about the outward world's capacity to suffer. Here, where he emphasizes the heart's depth, his theme is penetration: in *Tintern Abbey* he speaks of sensations "felt along the heart", and the inward world is a wide coastline; for in that poem, as we shall see, the two face each other like sea and land.

In his dealings with the inward as with the outward world, Wordsworth depends upon landscape: he is constantly referring to the landscape of the mind, and he approaches his perennial problem of sympathy as one of apparent opposition between the two landscapes. *Tintern Abbey* is distinguished by its opening words from *There was a Boy* and from an even more famous poem about his earlier life: "There was a time when meadow, grove, and stream. . . ." Both of these are thrown—this use of the verb "to be" is quite characteristic—into a remote story-teller's past, larger than human, invested with the authority of myth; whereas *Tintern Abbey*, being concerned to relate two distinct points in time, begins: "Five years have past. . . ."

The occasion of *Tintern Abbey* is Wordsworth's return to a particular countryside, after an absence of five years. He thinks it important that the scene is outwardly unchanged, and that he stands in the very place where he then stood: "again" is reiterated four times in the first fifteen lines, and his own position pinpointed by "here, under this dark sycamore". Words-

---

[1] De Quincey, *Literary Reminiscences* (Boston, 1874). See p. 91 n.

worth's return leads him to reflect on the landscape
seen five years ago, on the landscape before him today,
and on the landscape which he has carried about with
him during his absence. The brutal contrast between
then and now is for a moment disquieting:

> And now, with gleams of half-extinguished thought,
> And many recognitions dim and faint,
> And somewhat of a sad perplexity,
> The picture of the mind revives again:
> While here I stand. . . .

But this is a fleeting shadow across a poem of steady
and shining optimism. As he stands before the familiar
scene, Wordsworth is convinced "that in this moment
there is life and food For future years" because this
same scene has proved its strength while he has been
away from it. In *The Pedlar* Wordsworth asks whether
it can have been meant that the natural world,

> the clouds,
> The ocean, and the firmament of heaven
> Should lie a barren picture on the mind?[1]

and he argues that when we have entered into a truly
reciprocal relationship, into

> quiet sympathies with things that hold
> An inarticulate language,

we

> shall discover what a power is theirs
> To stimulate our minds, and multiply
> The spiritual presences of absent things.[2]

*Tintern Abbey* is addressed to the fact of spiritual
presence enduring through physical absence. The
opposition of the landscape before him at this passing
moment and the landscape before him at another

[1] *P.W.*, Vol. V. p. 402.        [2] *Ibid.*, p. 400.

moment five years ago, "the picture of the mind" now suddenly recalled, is not final; for Wordsworth has knowledge of a third landscape.

> These beauteous forms,
> Through a long absence, have not been to me
> As is a landscape to a blind man's eye. . . .

And he proceeds to declare his indebtedness to absent things. His chief debt to this third landscape, a gift, he calls it, "of aspect more sublime", is the eye made quiet, which comprehends both the inward and the outward eye. By means of it he can gaze upon, and yet maintain his place and active function within, the larger landscape of Wordsworthian reality.

The Immortality Ode also has important things to say about the third landscape. The child lives naturally and wholeheartedly within it, for as yet he knows nothing of the other two. This Wordsworth has already explained, and at much greater length, in *The Pedlar* and *The Prelude*. Wordsworth's comment on the Ode[1] speaks of his own "absolute spirituality" and "all-soulness" in childhood; and its first two stanzas open with cascading images of splendour in which this condition is evoked as an inclusive natural grace—"innocent brightness" in the last stanza is a key—both ethical and aesthetic in quality; the stanzas ending, in each case, with an antiphonal lament for departed vision.

In the third stanza Wordsworth moves from the loss of childish integrity to its sudden recovery in poetic expression:

> Now, while the birds thus sing a joyous song,
> And while the young lambs bound
> As to the tabor's sound,
> To me alone there came a thought of grief:
> A timely utterance gave that thought relief,
> And I again am strong. . . .

[1] Grosart, Vol. III. p. 464.

He then states the meaning of this regained strength:

> The cataracts blow their trumpets from the steep;
> No more shall grief of mine the season wrong;
> I hear the Echoes through the mountains throng,
> The Winds come to me from the fields of sleep. . . .

And later in the Ode he has a few lines on the same subject:

> Hence in a season of calm weather
> Though inland far we be,
> Our souls have sight of that immortal sea
> Which brought us hither,
> Can in a moment travel thither,
> And see the Children sport upon the shore. . . .

About this treatment of recovered powers there is a supreme concentration and a finality: it bears a weight of poetic thought sustained through many years, and it regards Wordsworth's greater landscape with the steadiness and penetration of a dying gaze. Everything is here. The season of calm weather is the eye made quiet, the means of insight. The fields of sleep, not quite Elysian nor yet St Augustine's Fields of Memory, the home of insight, where, as again in "though inland far we be", the poet walks through time as he walks through space. The features of this greater landscape are wind, water, mountain, and echo. These bind the Ode to the poetry that precedes it.

Celebrating his escape from city life in the opening lines of *The Prelude*, Wordsworth turns first of all towards the wind.

> Oh there is blessing in this gentle breeze
> That blows from the green fields and from the clouds
> And from the sky: it beats against my cheek
> And seems half-conscious of the joy it gives.

For the wind brings with it the promise of life lived
with understanding:

> I breathe again;
> Trances of thought and mountings of the mind
> Come fast upon me. . . .

And it arouses a counterpart to itself within the poet:

> For I, methought, while the sweet breath of heaven
> Was blowing on my body, felt within
> A corresponding mild creative breeze,
> A vital breeze which travell'd gently on
> O'er things which it had made, and is become
> A tempest, a redundant energy
> Vexing its own creation.

Then, after recounting how for a time he gave "a
respite to this passion", Wordsworth again calls upon
the wind:

> It was a splendid evening; and my soul
> Did once again make trial of the strength
> Restored to her afresh; nor did she want
> Eolian visitations; but the harp
> Was soon defrauded, and the banded host
> Of harmony dispers'd in straggling sounds
> And, lastly, utter silence.

The wind that searches the *Prelude* landscape is from
the beginning of the world, aboriginal in its command
of the ideas, long since estranged, of breath, of vital
spirit, and of inspiration. In this wind's ebb and flow
Wordsworth demonstrates the fitting of mind and
external things, as in the Eolian harp image, or when
he finds himself in the face of nature

> obedient as a lute
> That waits upon the touches of the wind.[1]

----

[1] Bk. III. 137.

Thus he can speak at once of a partnership in harmony and of a single song resulting. As it passes freely between inward and outward, familiar with both and native to neither, the wind manifests universal coherence; so that with every breath we draw, according to the poet's childlike metaphysic, we say "Boo" to a philosophical goose over-anxious about the difference between himself and other things.

The wind is also important to Wordsworth because it comprehends vitality and movement, ideas finally inseparable to his understanding. In two passages, both written in Germany, he saw the world a cold star, wheeling through Galilean skies. Lucy, motionless in death, was

> Roll'd round in earth's diurnal course,
> With rocks, and stones, and trees.

And the skating adventures of *The Prelude* led him to a strangely severe vision:

> then at once
> Have I, reclining back upon my heels,
> Stopp'd short, yet still the solitary cliffs
> Wheeled by me, even as if the earth had roll'd
> With visible motion her diurnal round. . . .[1]

But much more characteristic of Wordsworth is a movement instinct with breath, as when he

> felt the sentiment of Being spread
> O'er all that moves and all that seemeth still.[2]

Or, in *Tintern Abbey* lines that compare with the German passages in vastness of conception and in which the cosmic "roll" appears for a third time, when he encountered

> A motion and a spirit, that impels
> All thinking things, all objects of all thought,
> And rolls through all things.

[1] Bk. I. 482.          [2] Bk. II. 420.

In *The Prelude* Wordsworth apostrophizes the "Wisdom and Spirit of the universe" as giving "to forms and images a breath And everlasting motion": but his frequent habit of entrusting movement to breath itself, without any personification, is much more effective. "All that I beheld," he says, "respired with inward meaning"; and the ceaseless to and fro of this universal breath is meaningful in its power to comprehend the moving and the vital. He speaks of "breathing sea", "breathing air", "breathing frame", and, many times, of "breathing world", to convey a surging life or a living surge, eternal and intelligible.

Breath is also closely associated with urgent spiritual presence. Thus he describes the thought of an absent person as being like "an *unseen* companionship, a breath"; and when in his childhood he stole game from another boy's snare, he says he

> heard among the solitary hills
> Low breathings coming after me, and sounds
> Of undistinguishable motion, steps
> Almost as silent as the turf they trod.[1]

Allied to this is the peculiar animation which he imparts to abstract nouns, among other means by coupling them with breath: things and persons in his poetry breath "life", "sweetness", "invitation", "tenderness", "intelligence", "immortality".

In *Michael*, written in 1800, the wind becomes the focus of an entire poetic attitude: the optimistic naturalism of the Great Decade stands or falls by it. Michael is a relational solitary in the classical tradition; a shepherd, a very old man who has reached perfect solitude through perfect sympathy with his environment. When Wordsworth introduces him he makes his understanding of the wind the measure of this perfection:

[1] *The Prelude*, Bk. I. 329.

in his shepherd's calling he was prompt
And watchful more than ordinary men.
Hence had he learnt the meaning of all winds,
And blasts of every tone; and oftentimes,
When others heeded not, He heard the South
Make subterraneous music, like the noise
Of bagpipers on distant Highland hills.
The Shepherd, at such warning, of his flock
Bethought him, and he to himself would say,
"The winds are now devising work for me!"
And, truly, at all times, the storm, that drives
The traveller to a shelter, summoned him
Up to the mountains: he had been alone
Amid the heart of many thousand mists,
That came to him, and left him, on the heights.

Michael has a son whom he brings up to succeed
him as a shepherd. But suddenly, and through no fault
of his own, he loses much of his money, and decides to
send Luke, the son, to seek his fortune in the town so
that the land, the family inheritance, may be saved.

Our Luke shall leave us, Isabel; the land
Shall not go from us, and it shall be free;
He shall possess it, free as is the wind
That passes over it.

For a time all goes well, and Luke sends home "loving
letters, full of wondrous news". Then disaster follows,
reported in an external, uncomprehending way that
makes Luke's new environment infinitely remote from
the one already described. This is typical of Wordsworth's use of the city as a pasteboard symbol of vice
and artifice, the home of the unintelligible, the wholly
random element in things:

Meantime Luke began
To slacken in his duty; and, at length,
He in the dissolute city gave himself

> To evil courses: ignominy and shame
> Fell on him, so that he was driven at last
> To seek a hiding-place beyond the seas.

And the poem at once returns to Michael and his
shepherding, its cyclical movement supported by the
exact repetition of several of its opening phrases, and
by "still" and "as before"; so that it ends as it began,
considering sun and cloud and eloquent wind—"in
truth", Wordsworth says, "an utter solitude".

> Among the rocks
> He went, and still looked up to sun and cloud,
> And listened to the wind; and, as before,
> Performed all kinds of labour for his sheep,
> And for the land, his small inheritance.

Although it lacks the clear design of *Michael*, *The
Prelude* also looks to the wind for a vindication of its
world. In the childhood adventures there is a strong
metaphysical undertow to the wind's working, as in the
way it supported and at the same time admonished
Wordsworth while he hung

> Above the raven's nest, by knots of grass
> And half-inch fissures in the slippery rock
> But ill-sustain'd, and almost, as it seem'd,
> Suspended by the blast that blew amain,
> Shouldering the naked crag; Oh! at that time,
> While on the perilous ridge I hung alone,
> With what strange utterance did the loud dry wind
> Blow through my ears![1]

As in *Michael*, the wind is the idea of a world bound
together in discourse with itself. "I would stand," he
says, again of his childhood,

> Beneath some rock, listening to sounds that are
> The ghostly language of the ancient earth,
> Or make their dim abode in distant winds.
> Thence did I drink the visionary power.[2]

[1] Bk. I. 342.                     [2] Bk. II. 327.

And this language is also spoken by the poet, for it is common to the entire universe of solitude in relationship, in which he lives "an equal among mighty energies". Wordsworth brings art and nature together in terms of a shared speech. He who "with living Nature hath been intimate" receives knowledge and joy, "in measure only dealt out to himself", from

> the great Nature that exists in works
> Of mighty Poets. Visionary Power
> Attends upon the motions of the winds
> Embodied in the mystery of words.[1]

The wind, Wordsworth repeats, is the means of visionary power; of effective understanding reached through movement and life, and the mind's marriage "to this goodly universe In love and holy passion".

This single element within Wordsworth's greater landscape is managed with extreme subtlety. Consider, again from *The Prelude*, a horseback expedition to a ruined abbey,

> which within the Vale
> Of Nightshade, to St Mary's honour built,
> Stands yet, a mouldering pile, with fractured Arch,
> Belfry, and Images, and living Trees,
> A holy Scene! Along the smoooth green turf
> Our horses grazed: to more than inland peace
> Left by the sea wind passing overhead
> (Though wind of roughest temper) trees and towers
> May in that Valley oftentimes be seen,
> Both silent and both motionless alike;
> Such is the shelter that is there, and such
> The safeguard for repose and quietness.

> Our steeds remounted, and the summons given,
> With whip and spur we by the Chauntry flew
> In uncouth race, and left the cross-legg'd Knight,

1 Bk. V. 618.

And the stone-Abbot, and that single Wren
Which one day sang so sweetly in the Nave
Of the old Church, that, though from recent showers
The earth was comfortless, and, touch'd by faint
Internal breezes, sobbings of the place,
And respirations, from the roofless walls
The shuddering ivy dripp'd large drops, yet still,
So sweetly 'mid the gloom the invisible Bird
Sang to itself, that there I could have made
My dwelling-place, and lived for ever there
To hear such music.[1]

Most of the vices of the 1805 *Prelude* are discovered in
this passage. It is so loose in grammatical construction
and so erratically punctuated[2] as to weary, almost to
confuse, the reader: wordy, here and there shambling
in its movement and in its diction disputably chaste.
At the same time it has a personal logic that recalls
Wordsworth's original intention, "to give pictures of
Nature, Man, and Society". Like the more famous
pictures of the *Prelude* Exhibition, it is a finished composition, hanging framed upon the wall.

Wordsworth is once more concerned with sympathy,
as he comes upon it in the "more than inland peace"
of the Nightshade valley. The valley is isolated, and the
bounds of Wordsworth's picture determined, by the
failure of the violent sea wind to break in upon it from
the outside world; and in coupling the abbey towers
with the living trees in their stillness and silence he
indicates that the subject of his study is a building that
has come in its old age to terms with its surroundings.
There is a striking imaginative consistency in the way
Wordsworth's lonely buildings (for this is one among
many) are placed, like his human solitaries, at the
extreme of life.

[1] Bk. II. 110.
[2] I have given "along" a capital letter where W. does not, in order to
make the sense clearer.

H

Within this old church, "the cross-legg'd Knight, and the stone-Abbot, and that single Wren", thus huddled together in apparent carelessness, form a single society to which the boy is admitted for a moment. If in fact Wordsworth had "lived for ever there", the knight and the abbot would always have stayed with him, and the bird would not have ceased to sing. The strength of the passage is its association of art and nature. The stone figures are the church's proper inhabitants, Wordsworthian "Presences", graven and alive like mountains; and about the invisible wren there is the suggestion of eternal artifact, of the bird "set upon a golden bough to sing" in Yeats's Byzantium. While still a thing made with hands, the church that contains them all has made acquaintance with the natural: open to the sky, ivy-clad, stirred by internal breezes, sobbing, gently breathing—without facile identification or analogy Wordsworth has resolved it into his greater landscape.

Echo is understood, rather like wind and breath, as a relational and binding force. In one of his *Poems on the Naming of Places*, Wordsworth describes how, while he was walking with Joanna Hutchinson, his eye was held by the beauty of the scene before him, and she, noticing his eager gaze, "laughed aloud":

> The Rock, like something starting from a sleep,
> Took up the Lady's voice, and laughed again;
> That ancient Woman seated on Helm-crag
> Was ready with her cavern; Hammar-scar,
> And the tall Steep of Silver-how, sent forth
> A noise of laughter; southern Loughrigg heard,
> And Fairfield answered with a mountain tone;
> Helvellyn far into the clear blue sky
> Carried the Lady's voice,—old Skiddaw blew
> His speaking-trumpet;—back out of the clouds
> Of Glaramara southward came the voice;

And Kirkstone tossed it from his misty head.
—Now whether . . . this were in simple truth
A work accomplished by the brotherhood
Of ancient mountains, or my ear was touched
With dreams and visionary impulses
To me alone imparted, sure I am
That there was a loud uproar in the hills.[1]

Wordsworth's use of echo is quite simply effective as a
roll-call, answered by the individual peaks when they
are identified by name: thus the surrounding hills are
enfolded into a single community, or "brotherhood";
for the work of echo is assisted by a characteristic
family-metaphor.

Reflection, especially water-reflection, is very near
to echo in the way it expounds Wordsworth's universe
by collating different modes of being. Being is a key
word: when Wordsworth sees "the sentiment of being
spread over all", he is affirming the relational monism
of his poetic faith and urging that the acknowledged
diversity of things has its issue in a single complex, or
"register of permanent relations". Reflection serves
this end through balance and a very peculiar stability.

Thus having reached a bridge, that overarched
The hasty rivulet where it lay becalmed
In a deep pool, by happy chance we saw
A twofold image; on a grassy bank
A snow-white ram, and in the crystal flood
Another and the same! Most beautiful,
On the green turf, with his imperial front
Shaggy and bold, and wreathèd horns superb,
The breathing creature stood; as beautiful,
Beneath him, showed his shadowy counterpart.
Each had his glowing mountains, each his sky,
And each seemed centre of his own fair world:

[1] *To Joanna.*

> Antipodes unconscious of each other,
> Yet, in partition, with their several spheres,
> Blended in perfect stillness, to our sight![1]

This is no ordinary reflection: the independence of the ram beneath the water is so insisted on throughout the passage that one cannot regard it as deriving its existence from the ram upon the bank. It is a distinct mode of being, self-sufficient in its nether world. Yet the two rams are not unconnected, for they are finally contained within a single picture, their connexion in distinctness beautifully foreshown in the antipodean image. Peculiar to Wordsworth is the way this single vision is achieved without sacrificing either of the rams. He does not reduce the second to a mere emanation from the living reality, nor the first to a gross and earthly instance of the ideal form shadowed in the water. The effect is of poise and comprehension—a literal grasp of all that is.

Wordsworth has been accused of taking refuge in a reckless magniloquence, mere dimness and fog, when faced with large issues. This is a just criticism, and it is for the most part Wordsworth's own fault that it has been too liberally applied; for he is overbold to assume an understanding of his poetry's general quality, and a further readiness in the reader to relate the particular to the general: he wrote too much and too badly for his claims as to the imaginative unity of his life's work to be taken entirely seriously. Thus in two much quoted lines from *The Brothers*, he says:

> The thought of death sits easy on the man
> Who has been born and dies among the mountains.

As it stands, this will not do; but it is not written in Wordsworth's later vein of pastoral bombast. The

---

[1] *The Excursion*, Bk. IX. 437. For an early version of this passage see *The Prelude* (ed. de Selincourt), p. 562.

immediate context is of little help. The priest of a mountain parish, when it is pointed out to him that the graves in his churchyard are unmarked, replies:

> We have no need of names and epitaphs;
> We talk about the dead by our fire-sides.
> And then, for our immortal part! *we* want
> No symbols, Sir, to tell us that plain tale:
> The thought of death sits easy on the man
> Who has been born and dies among the mountains.

Wordsworth cannot mean that mountains symbolize immortality because they are long lived: *The Brothers* is a poem about universal change and decay, applied to nature as to man. "Even among these rocks," he says, you "can trace the finger of mortality":

> On that tall pike
> (It is the loneliest place of all these hills)
> There were two springs which bubbled side by side,
> As if they had been made that they might be
> Companions for each other: the huge crag
> Was rent with lightning—one hath disappeared;
> The other, left behind, is flowing still.
> For accidents and changes such as these
> We want not store of them;—a waterspout
> Will bring down half a mountain. . . .

Wordsworth fails to give notice of his real intention, which is to refer to the mountain's place within his greater landscape. He describes in *The Pedlar* how the mountain appeared to his childhood both as an abiding logic and as a history of sentient nature; and in *The Prelude* he restates this as a double influence: he was affected at once by their "forms perennial" and by "the changeful language of their countenances".[1] The mountains of his greater landscape speak with authority

[1] Bk. VII. 725.

of the passing and the permanent. But what they say is what they are: hence Wordsworth's fearful struggle with words, and especially with the verb "to be", as if to reach a linguistic fourth dimension in which the mountain-quality of time and eternity can be realized. And sometimes, as here, he attempts no more than a gesture towards his poetry's battle-field.

Another mention of immortality, similar to that in *The Brothers*, occurs in *The Prelude*, where Wordsworth speaks of the "imaginative impulse" which he received in the Alps from

> These forests unapproachable by death,
> That shall endure as long as man endures
> To think, to hope, to worship and to feel,
> To struggle, to be lost within himself
> In trepidation, from the blank abyss
> To look with bodily eyes and be consoled.[1]

Again he is not concerned with mere longevity: but the opaqueness of the passage leaves one undecided whether to take it at its face value, as incantation or as tiresome rant, as the case may be; or yet to suspend judgment. Later in the same book, Wordsworth returns to the immortality of forests. He relates how, as he travelled down the Simplon Pass, the features of the landscape impressed him as "the types and symbols of eternity"; and he names first:

> The immeasurable height
> Of woods decaying, never to be decay'd,
> The stationary blasts of water-falls. . . .

Forests are unapproachable by death because the seeds of life are nourished in their dying: to the mortality of life they oppose the vitality of death, and so Wordsworth can call them a consolation, and a type of eter-

[1] 1850, Bk. VI. 466.

nity. His thought here is very compact. In "the stationary blasts of waterfalls" the eternity theme is maintained and extended. As the forest is the type of life in death, so moving water is that of changeless change. This is fully and perfectly said in the last of the River Duddon Sonnets.

> I thought of Thee, my partner and my guide,
> As being passed away.—Vain sympathies!
> For, backward, Duddon! as I cast my eyes,
> I see what was, and is, and will abide;
> Still glides the Stream, and shall for ever glide;
> The Form remains, the Function never dies. . . .

In the case of the *Prelude* waterfalls, stillness in movement has a double force. There is the question of form and function just considered, and there is the genuine ambiguity of sense-experience; for, as Wordsworth says of another "foaming flood", moving water is "frozen by distance".[1] Thus "stationary blasts" contains stillness to the eye, the idea of form persisting through change, and a subtle undersense of function resting in the waterfall's eternal voice: whereas, in the Immortality Ode's "the cataracts blow their trumpets from the steep", the song has become dominant, while stillness and enduring form are gently admitted in the statuesque image of the cataract-trumpeter.

Wordsworth's greater landscape is therefore great indeed. Certainly there is nothing allegorical about this landscape: Wordsworth is in the strictest sense a nature poet, in suit of the natural world, eager to converse "with things that really are". But the sense of nature poet, although strict, is not confining. He can say with the Pedlar, "I see around me here Things which you cannot see"; and the poetry of solitude and relationship is his witness. In the eighth book of *The Prelude*, which

[1] *Address to Kilchurn Castle.*

he entitled *Retrospect*, his eye returns for a moment, as in the Immortality Ode, to the childhood scene,

> the Wilds
> In which my early feelings had been nursed—
> Bare hills and valleys, full of caverns, rocks,
> And audible seclusions, dashing lakes,
> Echoes and waterfalls, and pointed crags
> That into music touch the passing wind.

Here again are the landscape's primary features— wind, water, mountain, echo; and the strange abstract-concrete quality of "audible seclusions", alive to eye and ear and understanding.

## III

## THE POETRY OF INDECISION

THERE is a kind of courage in Wordsworth's treatment of his solitaries within their landscape
setting: he dares to trust his poetry to do its own work
in its own way, without reliance upon an alien intellectualism or relapse into the primary romantic vice of
vagueness and the cult of feeling. The Romantics themselves discussed this courage. Keats thought it a mark
of high genius, and pre-eminently Shakespearean, that
a man should be in deadly earnest about life and death,
and yet "capable of being in uncertainties, mysteries,
doubts, without any irritable reaching after fact and
reason"; "content with half-knowledge",[1] but with a
contentment opposed altogether to complacency. And
Coleridge, aware of a personal destiny of thought and
of a longing to escape it, was quick to condemn any
offering of the indefinite in substitution for the infinite.
Both were thinking of a balance, a moral integration,
hard to achieve and harder to maintain; and so was
Shelley, when he spoke of Wordsworth's power to
awaken thought-in-sense: while Wordsworth himself
used the language of the poetic memory and of the eye
made quiet, to describe the condition of passionate
serenity in which his best poetry was written.

There is a much smaller critical courage which can
make a study worthy of its subject; a complementary
faith in the power native to poetry. No major poet has
suffered so severely as Wordsworth from the growth of
the anthology habit. His effort is slow and cumulative:
the idea of the representative poem is in his case
peculiarly damaging; and the temptation to escape

[1] *Letters* (ed. Maurice Buxton Forman), p. 72.

from his poetry to some easier construction is for this reason doubly hard to resist. The theme of Wordsworth's literalness is in fact a striving after critical courage; for it seems to me much more false to the quality of Wordsworth's imagination to brush aside the landscape of

> I hear the Echoes through the mountains throng,
> The Winds come to me from the fields of sleep

in search of absent realities than to suppose, in the most naïve way possible, that Wordsworth means what he says. For if this second attitude is informed with the devoted attention which Wordsworth asked for his poetry, it may grow into understanding of his meaning's unique immensity as it embraces an incarnate metaphysic of the natural world.

With characteristic bluntness Wordsworth asserted that poetry must be "at once real and ideal" if it is to achieve "truth in its largest sense"; an unremitting discipline in "exact and accurate detail" that subordinates itself "to the spirit of the whole".[1] But subordination is not sacrifice: there is no flight from literal to metaphorical; but rather an evolution from within of ampler, more inclusive, literalness. His poetry remains a chronicle of things seen, however great its burden of meaning, both with the solitary wanderers and the primary features of his landscape, and with the secondary figures: the cuckoo who is his own echo; the glow-worm whose pinpoint light is both particular and powerful; the rainbow-arch joining hope to memory; the river "going and never gone"; the fish "that moves And lives as in an element of death".

In one of his sonnets Wordsworth declares that "the universe is infinitely wide". With its peculiar alliance of narrowness and penetration his early poetry is saying

---

[1] Grosart, Vol. III. p. 488.

this all the time: in terms of an inspired monotony it finds within the world the answers to its questions, the realization of its potentialities, the passing of its limits. This concentration of effort to deny the finitude of nature is of course absent from Wordsworth's later poetry. There has been very general recognition of this change; and the traditional account of his decline from a healthy and confident religion of nature towards timid orthodoxy stands in loose relation to it—loose because it considers at once two issues that were better distinguished; that of poetry and joy and that of poetry and belief.

Wordsworth is partly responsible for the eagerness of critics to furnish a psychological explanation of his decline, for he was himself at pains to establish a necessary connexion between poetry and pleasure. This looms very large in the Preface to the *Lyrical Ballads*.

> The Poet writes under one restriction only, namely, the necessity of giving immediate pleasure to a human being. . . .

And if he is to give pleasure to others, the poet must himself be

> a man pleased with his own passions and volitions, and who rejoices more than other men in the spirit of life that is in him. . . .

In this respect Wordsworth never changed his mind. It remained a cardinal principle with him that only a happy man can write good poetry; and he attributed Coleridge's failure as a poet to his unhappiness, because of which "he could not afford to suffer with those whom he saw suffer".[1]

In speaking thus of Coleridge Wordsworth borrows from his own description of the Pedlar, which has about it a clear trace of autobiography:

---

[1] Barron Field's MS. *Memoirs.* Cited in *P.W.*, Vol. V. p. 413.

Unoccupied by sorrow or its own,
His heart lay open; and by nature tuned
And constant disposition of his thoughts
To sympathy with Man, he was alive
To all that was enjoyed where'er he went
And all that was endured; and in himself
Happy, and quiet in his cheerfulness,
He had no painful pressure from within[1]
Which made him turn away from wretchedness
With coward fears. He could afford to suffer
With those whom he saw suffer.[2]

At the end of *The Pedlar*, this theme of the poet's heart lying open in delight and of "the constant disposition of his thoughts To sympathy with man" is expanded into a comprehensive philosophy of optimism. On its own account a ramshackle affair, it is relevant to the early poetry and to the decline of Wordsworth's middle years.

In the form in which it was completed in 1798, *The Pedlar* is a story of unrelieved distress concerning the ruined cottage and its inhabitants. This story is subjected to a long reflective interpretation by the Pedlar, who is himself the teller of the tale, in order that Wordsworth, his audience, shall "no longer read The forms of things with an unworthy eye". The Pedlar's cheerful argument is based on the Wordsworthian fact of the mind's marriage to the natural world, its "quiet sympathies with things that hold An inarticulate language"; and it attempts to move from here to a further sympathy, likewise inevitable, with man. "Once taught to love such objects as excite No morbid passions", a man "needs must feel The joy of that pure principle of

---

[1] *The Excursion* (l. 368) has "without"; but I think this must be the mistake of Wordsworth and his editors, since "without" makes nonsense of the familiar argument from inner to outer. The earliest version reads "within" (*P.W.*, Vol. V. p. 387).

[2] *P.W.*, Vol. V. p. 386.

love So deeply" that "he cannot choose But seek for objects of a kindred love In fellow-natures".[1] By contemplating natural objects "in the relations which they bear to man", we shall find that "all things shall speak of man, and we shall read Our duties in all forms"; the whole passage culminating in an outburst of Necessitarian optimism:

> Thus deeply drinking in the soul of things
> We shall be wise perforce, and we shall move
> From strict necessity along the path
> Of order and of good.[2]

The most striking thing about the Pedlar's meditation is its finality for Wordsworth. It reappears in 1814, at a high point in *The Excursion's* argument,[3] substantially as it was written sixteen years before. And the reason that Wordsworth had no more to say on this subject cannot be that he had ceased to think about it in the meantime, for the eighth book of *The Prelude*, which cost him great effort and which he entitled *Love of Nature Leading to Love of Man*, is vitally concerned with it. *The Prelude* as a whole, with which must be reckoned hundreds of lines of rationalistic verse intended for *The Prelude* but finally not included, affords ample evidence of his application. So does *Peter Bell*, finished in 1798, but not published until 1819, after repeated and laborious revision.

The story of *Peter Bell* is simple, and in its method of proceeding very significant. Peter is in the tradition of wandering solitaries, but distinguished from the others by the wickedness of his ways: he is cruel to animals and to men—and, indeed, to women; for Wordsworth includes in a solemn catalogue of his vices the fact that "he had a dozen wedded wives". Now Peter is immoral because, although he lives in sight of nature,

---

[1] *P.W.*, Vol. V. p. 400.  [2] *Ibid.*, p. 402.
[3] Bk. IV. 1207-95.

there has not taken place the marriage of mind to the external world which is the source of morality:

> He roved among the vales and streams,
> In the green wood and hollow dell;
> They were his dwelling night and day,—
> But nature ne'er could find the way
> Into the heart of Peter Bell.

Wordsworth does not ask why nature should have failed in the particular case of Peter Bell: he simply records it as an unhappy accident that

> Nature could not touch his heart
> By lovely forms, and silent weather,
> And tender sounds. . . .

The point of this long and on the whole unsuccessful poem is that Peter becomes a moral man when nature finally manages to touch his heart. Wordsworth summarizes the issue thus, by means of a characteristic breath image:

> And now is Peter taught to feel
> That man's heart is a holy thing;
> And Nature, through a world of death,
> Breathes into him a second breath,
> More searching than the breath of spring.

There is a clear connexion between the morality of *Peter Bell* and the Pedlar's ragbag necessitarianism. In neither case are the intellectual outworks of Wordsworth's position in themselves important. He is day-labouring within a philosophical tradition of no consequence, and profoundly unchristian in its ignorance of sin and its lack of interest in the will as a moral instrument. But there is no question that Wordsworth earnestly believed that by "deeply drinking in the soul of things We shall be wise perforce"; and this belief is an effective presence within the poetic idea of sympathy which dominates the world of solitude and relationship. Peter Bell's coming to virtue is, as we have seen, a matter of the gradual increase of moral perception as nature begins to touch him: "his heart is opening more and more". And beyond the crude externality with which Peter's progress is described, this ruling and imaginative sympathy is just discernible.

Wordsworth's half-statement of his idea of sympathy is in the form of a paradox. If Peter can be brought into contact with the world about him, all will be well:

> Let good men feel the soul of nature,
> And see things as they are.

Yet in one sense he is seeing things as they are at the beginning of the poem.

> In vain, through every changeful year,
> Did Nature lead him as before;
> A primrose by a river's brim
> A yellow primrose was to him,
> And it was nothing more.

Thus there are two ways of seeing the same primrose, the second way no less literal than the first. Wordsworth's poetry is about this second way; and it is important to recognize that he believed in a necessary coincidence of the literal-poetic seeing of a primrose with morality and wisdom: for this belief nourished his poetry. He failed many times to prove that love of nature leads to love of man, but found a kind of poetic salvation in his striving. Much of Wordsworth's poetry, especially the pastoral and patriotic verse of his middle age, was written with a fatal facility—he admits somewhere that he threw off many a sonnet in an idle moment, and one may find a great deal of idleness among the 523 sonnets published by himself; but the poetry of sympathy made demands upon his personal resources which he could not meet simply by direction of the will. His letters during this period, Dorothy's *Journals*, the condition of his manuscripts: all point to intense conscious effort; and the poetry itself to an entire commitment in which strength of will is matched by keenness of appetite, and the creative spirit is both horse and horseman.

Love of neighbour and love of neighbourhood are inseparable issues: it was thus, through the idea of sympathy, that he expressed his belief in the relevance of poetry to life. Without this belief, his peculiar earnestness, the disposition of the whole man towards poetic effort, would not have been possible. For the quality of the response rested on the quality of the challenge: hence his hatred of mere aestheticism in poetic theory and his urgent concern with the morality of all great poetry, and especially of his own. He wished to be thought of "as a teacher or as nothing", to enter upon the scene of life and make men better. In some degree he was aware that his power to address himself to nature depended on his conviction as to the supreme importance of what was to be found there.

"Assent," Wordsworth wrote, "is power." But assent does not wait upon the will; and there is respect for its complexity in his awareness of present strength as a poet, no less than in his fear of future weakness. When he thought about these things, Wordsworth attended to childhood. His very newness to the world lends the child understanding. Nothing stays the same for him or happens twice: all experience is unique, and in appreciation of this he looks around him with unrelenting care. What Coleridge called "the film of familiarity", and Wordsworth "the regular action of the world", has not as yet blunted his perception or sated his appetite. The power to see, the clearsightedness granted, in *The Prelude* phrase, "to unaccustomed eyes", and the desire to see, are both present in the child. Childhood is the fact upon which Wordsworth's philosophy of natural good reclines, and childhood is the marriage in love of poetry and morals: for children live by the principle of sympathy, finding themselves while they search for their neighbours in nature, among all modes of being. Hence in *The Prelude* account of childhood, as in the *Lyrical Ballads* theorizing about art, the cardinal poetic-moral abstractions—Joy, Desire, Power, Belief—jostle one another ceaselessly.

Speaking of his own childhood, Wordsworth describes how he felt

> that calm delight
> Which, if I err not, surely must belong
> To those first-born affinities that fit
> Our new existence to existing things,
> And, in our dawn of being, constitute
> The bond of union betwixt life and joy.[1]

This partnership of relational appetite and relational achievement, as Wordsworth understands it, comes into being at the threshold of life and of poetry. It is founded upon joy, in accordance with the *Lyrical Ballads* doctrine that "we have no sympathy but what is propagated by pleasure"; and it yields to both child and poet the "sense of possible sublimity" without which a corresponding sense of creative urgency cannot be roused.

Wordsworth realized that the bond between his childhood and his poetry was unsafe, and that to rest his huge optimism upon it was to court disaster. "I see by glimpses now," he wrote, while still a young man, "when age comes on, May scarcely see at all"[2]: in the poetry of the Great Decade there is the foretaste of ruin to be encountered in a hopeless wasting war against the mustering forces of time. But Wordsworth had no other course. However false his generalizations about

---

[1] *The Prelude*, Bk. I. 580.
[2] *The Prelude*, Bk. XI. 338.

art and life, the derivation of his own poetry from a childhood state "that hath more power than all the elements" cannot be challenged. He reflects upon slow failure and the dwindling of his resources, as upon that assent which he calls power, with massive self-knowledge.

Much is said in *The Prelude* and the Immortality Ode about the difficulty of recovering childhood vision, of seeing the truth when increasingly beset with lies engendered by mere habit and the passing of years. It is a very large difficulty, because it embraces capacity and desire: Wordsworth's frequent talk of power in connexion with childhood has as much moral as poetic reference. In the Immortality Ode he is primarily concerned with the child as poet born, with an under-theme of natural morality—the "brightness", we have seen, is "innocent". In the *Ode to Duty*, written towards the close of the Great Decade, there is a significant shift of emphasis: Wordsworth's principal interest is moral, but with backward glancing towards "the genial sense of youth", and the state of poetic splendour in which

<blockquote>love is an unerring light,<br>
And joy its own security.</blockquote>

In these two odes he reviews his loss in both its aspects.

Wordsworth's final and most full discussion of this loss appears in the last book of *The Excursion*, which he doubtless intended to be the philosophical climax of the whole. The book opens with an abrupt statement of his doctrine of sympathy.

<blockquote>"To every Form of being is assigned,"<br>
Thus calmly spoke the venerable Sage,<br>
"An *active* principle. . . ."</blockquote>

This principle "subsists In all things, in all natures", and, because of it, "Whate'er exists hath properties

that spread Beyond itself"—a truth of particular force
in the case of

> the human Mind,
> Its most apparent home. The food of hope
> Is meditated action; robbed of this
> Her sole support, she languishes and dies.
> We perish also; for we live by hope
> And by desire; we see by the glad light
> And breathe the sweet air of futurity;
> And so we live, or else we have no life.

The active or sympathetic principle, the urge in
everything to "spread beyond itself", Wordsworth
describes in purely human terms as hope and desire;
and in the lines immediately following, he supports his
thesis by an appeal to childhood, to the condition of
two boys who have just appeared on *The Excursion's*
quasi-dramatic scene.

> Tomorrow—nay perchance this very hour
> (For every moment hath its own tomorrow!)
> Those blooming Boys, whose hearts are almost sick
> With present triumph, will be sure to find
> A field before them freshened with the dew
> Of other expectations;—in which course
> Their happy year spins round.

Because childhood is the living vindication of Wordsworth's principle, age seeks always to return. As so
often, this theme moves Wordsworth to the authentic
sublime: his verse starts out for a moment from the
wretched stuff surrounding it.

> Ah! why in age
> Do we revert so fondly to the walks
> Of childhood—but that there the Soul discerns
> The dear memorial footsteps unimpaired
> Of her own native vigour . . . ?

Now Wordsworth has reached the decisive step in his argument. He wishes next to show that despite its loss of childhood's relational power, age has virtues of its own. The querulous, fidgeting manner of his opening is ominous.

> Do not think
> That good and wise ever will be allowed,
> Though strength decay, to breathe in such estate
> As shall divide them wholly from the stir
> Of hopeful nature. Rightly it is said
> That Man descends into the VALE of years;
> Yet have I thought that we might also speak,
> And not presumptuously, I trust, of Age,
> As of a final EMINENCE; though bare
> In aspect and forbidding, yet a point
> On which 'tis not impossible to sit
> In awful sovereignty. . . .

Wordsworth calls age an eminence because he wishes to compare it with a mountain top. It is the experience of one who looks down upon the world from a high peak "in some placid day of summer" that

> the gross and visible frame of things
> Relinquishes its hold upon the sense,
> Yea almost on the Mind herself, and seems
> All unsubstantialized. . . . For on that superior height
> Who sits, is disencumbered from the press
> Of near obstructions, and is privileged
> To breathe in solitude, above the host
> Of ever-humming insects, 'mid thin air
> That suits not them. The murmur of the leaves
> Many and idle, visits not his ear:
> This he is freed from, and from thousand notes
> (Not less unceasing, not less vain than these)
> By which the finer passages of sense
> Are occupied; and the Soul, that would incline
> To listen, is prevented or deterred.

And may it not be hoped, that, placed by age
In like removal, tranquil though severe,
We are not so removed for utter loss;
But for some favour, suited to our need?
What more than that the severing should confer
Fresh power to commune with the invisible world,
And hear the mighty stream of tendency
Uttering, for elevation of our thought,
A clear sonorous voice, inaudible
To the vast multitude; whose doom it is
To run the giddy round of vain delight,
Or fret and labour on the Plain below.

This is bad poetry, and in its kind of badness quite
unlike the work of Wordsworth's first maturity. It
attempts the serene and total vision of spiritual detachment: it achieves a gathering up of its skirts and a tiresome snobbery. In Wordsworth's own unhappy phrase,
it breathes "thin air"—air too thin for the poetry of
his own past, which was bound to hear the ever-
humming insects and the murmur of the leaves, now
together classed as "near obstructions", or it must have
died. "The mighty stream of tendency", the only
memorable thing here, has been saved from a notebook
fragment written in 1798.[1] Otherwise there is poverty,
and a rejection of all that made his early poetry rich.
This is at once evident in its distaste for close observation, and its railing at the senses. But behind this, and
much more important, is the crude opposition of "the
gross and visible frame" and "the invisible world".
Wordsworth is trying to write a new kind of poetry.
He can assent no longer to the literalness of the natural
order and its moral-poetic power: he cannot strive, with
effort unparalleled in English poetry, to see things as
they are. He is trying to write transcendental poetry, to
tell tales of the invisible world. To him this does not

[1] *Wordsworth's Prelude* (ed. de Selincourt), p. 548.

appear a matter of choice. Age has come upon him as a "removal" and a "severing", and he has no other world to tell of. But the new discipline, which is no less severe than the old, gives him much pain in the learning.

Wordsworth's poetry was not suddenly invaded by the spiritual and the transcendent. *The Excursion* was published in 1814, but alteration is already to be seen in *The Prelude*, finished nine years earlier. When the childhood incidents of *The Prelude's* opening are held against the desperately obscure idea of spiritual love with which it concludes, the contrast is very striking: or when Wordsworth's description, in the first book, of his earliest intercourse

> Not with the mean and vulgar works of Man,
> But with high objects, with enduring things,
> With life and nature. . . .[1]

is compared with the final lines of the poem. "What we have loved," he says, speaking of Coleridge and himself,

> Others will love; and we may teach them how;
> Instruct them how the mind of man becomes
> A thousand times more beautiful than the earth
> On which he dwells, above this frame of things
> (Which, 'mid all revolution in the hopes
> And fears of men, doth still remain unchanged)
> In beauty exalted, as it is itself
> Of substance and of fabric more divine.

In this conclusion the mind's marriage "to this goodly universe In love and holy passion" has suffered an almost Platonic divorce.

*The Prelude* has a false continuity which obscures this great change. When Wordsworth said, at the out-

[1] l. 435.

set, that his object was to "give pictures of Nature, Man and Society", he chose his words advisedly; for *The Prelude* was not conceived as a poem of epic growth and movement. It is a selection of distinct incidents, and its superiority over *The Excursion* is partly due to the fact that the autobiographical thread on which they are strung is much more serviceable than the dramatic. Attentive reading of *The Prelude* reveals how an alien consecutiveness, both in chronology and logic, has been imposed upon it—a conclusion supported by the external facts of its composition.

Wordsworth's work at the poem falls into two periods. During 1798 and 1799 he wrote the first two books, substantially as they appear in the 1805 text; and much more that was finally incorporated in later books. There follows a long interval of about four years, during which he scarcely touched the poem. Early in 1804 he resumed work, and finished the whole in the early summer of 1805.

*The Prelude* of 1798-9 is in the high tradition of solitude and relationship. The Discharged Soldier, who finds his place eventually in Book IV, has already been considered with the Wordsworthian solitaries; and he is the greatest among many. And *The Prelude* incidents, by epic standards an inert pile, a mere addition, are related, in a way which makes it proper to talk of Wordsworth as a philosophical poet, to the master-thesis of the mind's marriage to the world. The child-hood episodes which crowd the first two books, and which are scattered throughout the rest of *The Prelude*, all expound the world's ministry through "intercourse with beauty" and "the impressive discipline of fear" (so that Wordsworth speaks of himself as "fostered alike by beauty and by fear"), and the mind's reciprocal action in human sympathy and appetite.

*The Prelude* of 1804-5 is a very different thing. Its quality cannot be caught at once because in the intervening years a vital concentration has been lost, and in its place there is dispersal of effort. Much of this later *Prelude* is mere joinery, and often none too neat. Thus in Book XI, two famous episodes, that of Wordsworth's coming upon a gibbet in a lonely valley and that of his waiting in a storm to be fetched home from school, are linked by a bridge-passage which betrays its modest function quite clearly:

> Yet another
> Of these to me affecting incidents
> With which we will conclude.[1]

The passages from the 1798-9 *Prelude* stand out in brilliant contrast to their drab surroundings in the later books.

The main task of the 1804-5 *Prelude* is to impress clearly the autobiographical form and martial into consequential argument "the history of a poet's mind". For when Wordsworth wrote the earliest of *The Prelude* episodes he had no thought of an independent poem about his own past: these were related in their distinctness to the scheme of the philosophical *Recluse*. Even when he returned to *The Prelude* in 1804, Wordsworth imagined it in nothing like its final state. By this time he had come to regard it as separate from *The Recluse*, but intended it to contain only five books as against the thirteen of the 1805 text. And so the later *Prelude* was both planned and written during the next eighteen months.

Change is perhaps most striking when the context remains familiar. In Book VIII there is a very typical solitary, a shepherd encountered in mountain mist.

> Seeking the raven's nest, and suddenly
> Surpriz'd with vapours, or on rainy days
> When I have angled up the lonely brooks
> Mine eyes have glanced upon him, few steps off,

[1] l. 343.

In size a giant, stalking through the fog,
His Sheep like Greenland Bears; at other times
When round some shady promontory turning,
His Form hath flash'd upon me, glorified
By the deep radiance of the setting sun:
Or him have I described in distant sky,
A solitary object and sublime,
Above all height! like an aerial Cross,
As it is stationed on some spiry Rock,
Of the Chartreuse, for worship.[1]

The shepherd is at first marked with obstinate peasant honesty, a "few steps off"—nobody can doubt it: and likewise his sheep. In the "Greenland bears" one discovers a gauche but convincing appeal to the unfamiliar the near-fabulous, to describe what was so strange and yet was clearly seen. About the shepherd looming gigantic in the mist there is a terrestrial sublimity worthy of the early *Prelude*. But after the sixth line Wordsworth loses his command. The description becomes rosily transcendental; the verse assumes the hazy, the golden, the remote, which is the conventional dress of otherness. Perhaps Wordsworth thought that he could make the shepherd "above all height" outshine the shepherd "few steps off". Or he may have mistrusted himself; so that his final unlucky reference to the Cross is a cry for help, in work which his poetry cannot do alone.

There is another solitary in the later *Prelude*, quite unlike the shepherd. In the midst of a London crowd, wholly occupied with his own thoughts, Wordsworth tells how
                                        lost
Amid the moving pageant, 'twas my chance
Abruptly to be smitten with the view
Of a blind Beggar, who, with upright face,

[1] l. 396.

Stood propp'd against a Wall, upon his Chest
Wearing a written paper, to explain
The story of the Man, and who he was.
My mind did at that spectacle turn round
As with the might of waters, and it seem'd
To me that in this Label was a type
And emblem, of the utmost that we know,
Both of ourselves and of the universe;
And, on the shape of the unmoving man,
His fixèd face and sightless eyes, I look'd
As if admonish'd from another world.[1]

In this case there is no descent into the mock sublime.
The passage falters for a moment in its unnecessary
explicitness as to the significance of the label; but with
"the shape of the unmoving man, His fixèd face and
sightless eyes", it recovers the characteristic spare
strength of its opening, reminiscent, in the details of
its phrasing—"upright face", "stood propp'd", "the
story of the man, and who he was"—, of the Discharged
Soldier himself. But it is distinguished from the early
*Prelude* by the air of profound unease that hangs over
it. All the great solitaries are ominous: none of them, as
this blind beggar, inauspicious. Wordsworth's encounter with him is instinct with defeat; and it
expresses well his entire attitude to the city, which is
very important in the later *Prelude* as an image of
sovereign chaos.

The London beggar illustrates a general truth, that
Wordsworth's achievement is most considerable when
he is entirely honest about the change he has experienced. This account is faithful to the personal tradition
—Wordsworth sees the beggar as he has always seen
his solitaries; but he cannot relate his vision, as once he
could, to the original scheme of *The Recluse*. The
optimism of the early *Prelude* is in the bone of the thing,

[1] Bk. VIII. 608.

inseparable from its conception and its execution. That of the late *Prelude* is a determined end towards which the poem must be manipulated, like the plot of a bad play. Wordsworth says, very near its conclusion, that *The Prelude* is a

> Song, which like a lark
> I have protracted, in the unwearied Heavens
> Singing, and often with more plaintive voice
> Attempted to the sorrows of the earth;
> Yet centring all in love, and in the end
> All gratulant if rightly understood.[1]

The last line gives itself the lie. One catches sight of Wordsworth already grown weary of his work, rushing through the last two books in a mere fortnight, with his brother three months dead and very much in mind. He records his feelings in a letter.

> I have the pleasure to say that I finished my poem about a fortnight ago. I had looked forward to the day as a most happy one; and I was indeed grateful to God for giving me life to complete the work, such as it is: but it was not a happy day for me; I was dejected on many accounts; when I looked back upon the performance it seemed to have a dead weight about it, the reality so far short of the expectation; it was the first long labour that I had finished, and the doubt whether I should ever live to write *The Recluse*, and the sense which I had of this poem being so far below what I seemed capable of executing, depressed me much; above all, many heavy thoughts of my poor departed Brother hung upon me, the joy which I should have had in showing him the Manuscript, and a thousand other vain fancies and dreams.[2]

At its best the late *Prelude* is urgently bewildered; torn between old certainties and new doubts, self-consuming in its efforts to deal justly with both. Only

[1] Bk. XIII. 380.
[2] *Early Letters* (ed. de Selincourt), p. 497.

once does it make its predicament entirely clear, and then, as seems to me significant, by way of nightmare. Wordsworth describes how he was reading Cervantes by the sea, and, having fallen asleep, dreamed strangely. In his dream Wordsworth was looking fearfully about him in a sandy desert, when there appeared a mysterious figure riding on a dromedary, half Bedouin Arab, half Don Quixote himself. The stranger was carrying a stone under one arm, and under the other a shell; and he explained that the stone was geometry and the shell, "something of more worth", poetry. Wordsworth put his ear to the shell and heard a voice, eloquent and passionate, "in an unknown tongue, Which yet I understood", foretelling the world's destruction by flood. The other then told him that the stone spoke certain truth, and that he himself was setting out to bury both stone and shell against the deluge:

> The one that held acquaintance with the stars,
> And wedded soul to soul in purest bond
> Of reason, undisturbed by space or time;
> The other that was a god, yea many gods,
> Had voices more than all the winds. . . .

Wordsworth sought to remain with his companion.

> Far stronger, now, grew the desire I felt
> To cleave unto this man; but when I prayed
> To share his enterprise, he hurried on
> Reckless of me. . . .

And the dream ends thus:

> His countenance, meanwhile, grew more disturbed;
> And, looking backwards when he looked, mine eyes
> Saw, over half the wilderness diffused,
> A bed of glittering light: I asked the cause:
> "It is," said he, "the waters of the deep
> Gathering upon us"; quickening then the pace
> Of the unwieldy creature he bestrode,

He left me: I called after him aloud;
He heeded not; but, with his twofold charge
Still in his grasp, before me, full in view,
Went hurrying o'er the illimitable waste,
With the fleet waters of a drowning world
In chase of him; whereat I waked in terror,
And saw the sea before me, and the book
In which I had been reading, at my side.[1]

Let no one be deceived by the Miltonic diction of this passage. Wordsworth's command of quickening pace, mounting terror, imminent eclipse, is altogether personal. He sustains magnificently the nightmare twilight of the scene: only "the unwieldy creature", a lapse very much in character, is false to it. And judgment as to diction may itself be overeasy; for neither Milton, nor any miltonizer, could have written "the fleet waters of a drowning world". But I quote Wordsworth's dream for its wider reference, for its dying upon an all-embracing question, with Wordsworth a mere spectator unable to influence the issue. The dream looks back across the Great Decade towards *The Pedlar*, in which Wordsworth first declared the alliance of mathematics and the natural world, of reason and experience. Mathematics and poetry are still related, and with the intensity of dream-conviction. How related, is now lost to waking sense; but they must be saved together, though the attempt prove vain and Wordsworth no party to it. Only in "the heroic attitudes of a dream" might a universal and an entirely private distress become thus identified.

Wordsworth reacts to this new perplexity by reducing the compass of *The Prelude*. He becomes much more attentive to the surface narrative: many hundreds of lines describing his residence in London

---

[1] 1850, Bk. V. 89. In the 1805 text Wordsworth gives the dream, quite unplausibly, to a friend.

or his part in the French Revolution have nothing but the sequence of events between themselves and complete destitution. The limiting of imaginative scope is betrayed by his persistent stating of his terms of reference, as if to avoid wider and undesired consequences. Thus there is a false and restricting finality in the later *Prelude's* attitude to the opposition of countryside and city, as the types of natural and artificial. But the first indication of this and of other changes is to be found in the work of the four years dividing the early from the late *Prelude*.

In *Michael*, as we have seen, Wordsworth opposes the country and the town. But the part played by the town is quite unimportant: it is the occasion of inexplicable ruin, serving only to emphasize the poem's cyclical movement, and the solitary's return, after disaster has struck him down, to the scene of its opening. *Michael* is a successful poem about solitude and relationship: the solitary and the natural scene are honestly regarded in the light of a structural optimism that seeks to contain suffering, and not to exclude or deny it. All that has passed is gathered up in the principle of sympathy, in "the strength of love" manifested in Michael's care for his sheep and attention to the wind. But this dichotomy of town and country is none the less menacing: it threatens the seriousness with which Wordsworth strove to make his poetry "the acknowledged voice of life". For as the writing of poetry became more difficult and painful, so the temptation to ease the burden grew harder to resist. And he had here the means at hand. The life of the city, described in *The Prelude* as "by nature an unmanageable sight", might be required, even though unconsciously, to contain all that poetic experience itself found most hard to manage. Wordsworth's attitude to the city

matters very little: it is of purely negative significance
that he found this the way to dispose silently of embarrassment. But the effect on the poetry of the country
is all-important. Thus opposed to the town, the greater
landscape is a thing of diminished urgency and comprehension. Wordsworth became able to say less, and
he had less to say—thus the complexity of decline.
Even when he addressed himself to poetry as to a total
activity, he was thinking, do what he might, of a
reduced totality. And often he was consciously satisfied
with less.

1800, the year of *Michael*, is also the year of *Home at
Grasmere*, the first book of *The Recluse* and the only
part of it that Wordsworth ever finished. The theme of
*Home at Grasmere* is Wordsworth's retirement to Dove
Cottage with Dorothy, to live the good life and to
write poetry. Town and country are once more contrasted, in terms of the first principles of Wordsworth's
poetic philosophy. Grasmere is the scene of solitude-in-
relationship sustained through sympathy; the city, of
false solitude or isolation, of meaningless difference and
meaningless identity, loveless and unintelligible.
Wordsworth describes the entire society of birds,
beasts and men, in their successive generations, and the
companionship of surrounding hills:

> Say boldly then that solitude is not
> Where these things are: he truly is alone,
> He of the multitude whose eyes are doomed
> To hold a vacant commerce day by day
> With objects wanting life, repelling love;
> He by the vast Metropolis immured,
> Where pity shrinks from unremitting calls,
> Where numbers overwhelm humanity,
> And neighbourhood serves rather to divide
> Then to unite.[1]

[1] *P.W.*, Vol. V. p. 333.

The argument of the later *Prelude* is here neatly epi-
tomized. And against the city stands Grasmere,

> A Whole without dependence or defect,
> Made for itself. . . .[1]

Much of *Home at Grasmere* is written with fine care;
and in its approach to "the calmest, fairest spot of
earth", shiningly gentle. But it is altogether smaller
poetry; restrictedly Paradisal, seeking Grasmere too
exclusively for retreat and shelter. One may observe
Wordsworth drawing his pencil round the manageable,
though still capable of greater range.

> What want we? have we not perpetual streams,
> Warm woods, and sunny hills, and fresh green fields,
> And mountains not less green, and flocks, and herds,
> And thickets full of songsters, and the voice
> Of lordly birds, an unexpected sound
> Heard now and then from morn till latest eve,
> Admonishing the man who walks below
> Of solitude, and silence in the sky?[2]

As if to admit the untruth of any circumscribed
perfection, Wordsworth says that he is forced, even in
Grasmere,

> To cast from time to time a painful look
> Upon unwelcome things, which unawares
> Reveal themselves. . . .[3]

But the poem's quality is not to be altered by a saving
clause. The circle of self-sufficiency is drawn in the
first place round the whole vale of Grasmere; then, in
case this outer defence should be surrendered to the
world, round the poet's own household at Dove
Cottage:

[1] *P.W.*, Vol. V. p. 318.
[2] *Ibid.*, p. 317.
[3] *Ibid.*, p. 329.

And if this
Were otherwise, we have within ourselves
Enough to fill the present day with joy,
And overspread the future years with hope,
Our beautiful and quiet home. . . .[1]

And finally round the poet's individual genius, by virtue of the "something within which yet is shared by none".[2] Despite its obvious accomplishment, *Home at Grasmere* points the way beyond Wordsworth's own decline, to an entire tradition of latter-day pastoral.

This change is sadly reflected in the disassociation of his poetry's landscape and his poetry's morality. Wordsworth always had a weakness for overt moralizing: even in *Tintern Abbey*, one of the greatest of the landscape poems, there is the Boy-Scoutishness of the "little, nameless, unremembered, acts Of kindness", unworthy of the theme of spiritual presences and their sustaining power. And as his early strength began to ebb, this tendency became ever more apparent, the landscape of his poetry being now too small to manifest the moral quality of life through its expression of life's physical context. Hence the opposition, blunt and confined like that of town and country, of human life and its natural setting. Already in *Home at Grasmere* Wordsworth shows an unwonted eagerness to establish an explicit moral connexion between the vale and those who live there. There is a mood, he says, of forgetfulness and pleasant self-deception, which can

bear us on
Without desire in full complacency,
Contemplating perfection absolute
And entertained as in a placid sleep.[3]

This is a state in which "the Soul becomes, Words cannot say, how beautiful"; and Wordsworth, once

---

[1] *P.W.*, Vol. V. p. 335.      [2] *Ibid.*, p. 336.      [3] *Ibid.*, p. 324.

K

caught up in it, attains the vision of Grasmere and its inhabitants in perfect harmony.

> They who are dwellers in this holy place
> Must needs themselves be hallowed, they require
> No benediction from the Stranger's lips,
> For they are blest already. None would give
> The greeting "peace be with you" unto them,
> For peace they have, it cannot but be theirs,
> And mercy and forbearance.

Aware that this dream-picture will not suffice, Wordsworth at once denies that he came to Grasmere "betrayed by tenderness of mind That feared, or wholly overlooked the truth". On the contrary:

> I came not dreaming of unruffled life,
> Untainted manners; born among the hills,
> Bred also there, I wanted not a scale
> To regulate my hopes. Pleased with the good,
> I shrink not from the evil with disgust,
> Or with immoderate pain.

He then proceeds to moderate his claims:

> Yet is it something gained, it is in truth
> A mighty gain, that Labour here preserves
> His rosy face, a Servant only here
> Of the fire-side, or of the open field,
> A Freeman, therefore, sound and unimpaired,
> That extreme penury is here unknown. . . .

And so on. But Wordsworth cannot leave the subject alone. He comes back to it, after a discreet interval, and restates the impossible perfection of his first vision, in scarcely milder terms.

> Take we at once this one sufficient hope,
>            . . . that, feeling as we do
> How goodly, how exceeding fair, how pure
> From all reproach is yon etherial vault,

And this deep Vale, its earthly counterpart,
By which, and under which, we are enclosed
To breathe in peace, we shall moreover find
(If sound, and what we ought to be ourselves,
If rightly we observe and justly weigh)
The Inmates not unworthy of their home
The Dwellers of their Dwelling.[1]

In this respect also, *Home at Grasmere* anticipates
decline. The particular small moral preoccupation, the
direct assault upon the understanding that advertises
its intention and excites resistance, are indications of
ill omen. Keats states the case against this kind of
poetry with force and with justice.

It may be said that we ought to read our contemporaries—
that Wordsworth &c. should have their due from us. But, for
the sake of a few fine imaginative or domestic passages, are
we to be bullied into a certain Philosophy engendered in the
whims of an Egotist—Every man has his own speculations,
but every man does not brood and peacock over them till he
makes a false coinage and deceives himself. Many a man can
travel to the very bourne of Heaven, and yet want confidence
to put down his half-seeing. Sancho will invent a Journey
heavenward as well as any body. We hate poetry that has a
palpable design upon us—and if we do not agree, seems to
put its hand in its breeches pocket. Poetry should be great and
unobtrusive, a thing which enters into one's soul, and does not
startle it or amaze it with itself, but with its subject.[2]

In one sense Wordsworth thought too much, and in
another sense he did not think enough. He ruined his
poetry in the effort to give it intellectual point and to
make it serve an immediate moral purpose: at the same
time he grew afraid of reasoning through to the end,
poetically. Keats has it again, when he remarks of a

---

[1] *P.W.*, Vol. V. p. 334.
[2] *Letters* (ed. Maurice Buxton Forman), p. 96.

particular poem, though with beautiful relevance to the wider issue, that "it is a kind of sketchy intellectual Landscape—not a search after Truth".[1] The fate that overtakes the landscape of Wordsworth's early poetry could not be better summarized: its loss of depth and width and detail, its sacrifice of the universal and the particular for the merely general.

Two more landscape poems, *Hart-Leap Well* and *The Brothers*, were written in the watershed year of 1800, while *The Prelude* slept. *Hart-Leap Well* is about the death of a hart who threw himself down from a cliff, in his great distress, after he had been hunted for many hours. Nothing will grow at the place he died, nor will animals come to drink there. This story of innocent suffering is treated in two ways. A shepherd who has just related it to Wordsworth does not ask why such things should happen under Heaven: instead, he wonders what made the hart choose this very place to die.

> For thirteen hours he ran a desperate race;
> And in my simple mind we cannot tell
> What cause the Hart might have to love this place,
> And come to make his death-bed near the well.

It may be that he died where he was born:

> And he perhaps, for aught we know, was born
> Not half a furlong from that self-same spring.

> Now, here is neither grass nor pleasant shade;
> The sun on drearier hollow never shone;
> So will it be, as I have often said,
> Till trees, and stones, and fountain, all are gone.

And Wordsworth then replies:

> Grey-headed Shepherd, thou hast spoken well;
> Small difference lies between thy creed and mine:

[1] *Letters* (ed. Maurice Buxton Forman), p. 56.

This Beast not unobserved by Nature fell;
His death was mourned by sympathy divine.

The Being, that is in the clouds and air,
That is in the green leaves among the groves,
Maintains a deep and reverential care
For the unoffending creatures whom he loves.

Wordsworth is wrong: there is a world of difference between the two creeds. The poet puts the direct
question which the shepherd left unasked, and tries to
meet the fact of suffering with an assertion of God's, or
Nature's, loving care. This may be the truth; but God's
love for the murdered creature is still too difficult a thing
to be stated thus. Another's love must be expressed to
be experienced, and, if from God, must enfold hart and
hound and horseman. There is a false neatness about
Wordsworth's implied question and answer—too much
and too little thought—which no banging the big Pantheistic drum can make acceptable. We resist it, as
poetry "that has a palpable design upon us".

The shepherd says something which cannot be called
a creed at all, in the sense of Wordsworth's own statement. He suggests that the hart suffered for thirteen
hours in order to meet his end at his beginning. Wordsworth looks for the solution to a puzzle: the shepherd is
halted by the fact of long pursuit and death at this place.
In wondering why the hart died *here*, he neither answers
nor evades what must seem the larger question: somehow he illuminates its circumstances, so that it looks
different, in a way bearable; yet is still a question. Perhaps, as he ran, the hart held a remembered landscape
before his eyes, and at the last, material and immaterial
came together. The idea of return in extremity to the
familiar scene reflects honestly the way in which
Wordsworth had been trying all his life to understand
the world. In the most serious of his schoolboy poems,
he says:

> Dear native regions, I foretell,
> From what I feel at this farewell,
> That, wheresoe'er my steps may tend,
> And whensoe'er my course shall end,
> If in that hour a single tie
> Survive of local sympathy,
> My soul will cast the backward view,
> The longing look alone on you.[1]

These blundering steps led him eventually to the poetry of solitude and relationship, to the powerful and familiar landscapes of *Tintern Abbey* and *Michael*. *Hart-Leap Well* does not explain suffering and death any more than *Tintern Abbey* explains absence and change; but what is unexplained by these poems does not remain unaffected.

*The Brothers*, like *Michael*, is a blank-verse dramatic poem of nearly five hundred lines. As in *Michael* and the other poems of 1800, a landscape is recovered. Once again it is a painful story, and painful with new emphasis; for the pain's insolubility becomes almost the theme of the poem. A man returns after many desperate years to his native valley, and finds his brother dead and even the mountains and rivers of his childhood altered by the violence of nature. The priest of the place, who now does not recognize him, urges that he should remain:

> The other thanked him with an earnest voice;
> But added, that, the evening being calm,
> He would pursue his journey. So they parted.
>
> It was not long ere Leonard reached a grove
> That overhung the road: he there stopped short,
> And, sitting down beneath the trees, reviewed
> All that the Priest had said: his early years
> Were with him:—his long absence, cherished hopes,

---

[1] *Dear Native Regions.* See *P.W.*, Vol. I. p. 281, for the early version.

And thoughts which had been his an hour before,
All pressed on him with such a weight, that now,
This vale, where he had been so happy, seemed
A place in which he could not bear to live:
So he relinquished all his purposes.

Wordsworth regarded his own brother's death, in
1805, as the cause of profound alteration in himself: it
is the "great distress", which, as he says in the poem
about Peele Castle, "hath humanized my soul"; and
which leads him to "welcome fortitude, and patient
cheer, And frequent sights of what is to be borne". The
crisis was real enough, but not unheralded, since
nothing is altogether new in imagination; and *The
Brothers*, humane, gently despairing, grave and un-
emphatic, is the forerunner of much in Wordsworth's
later poetry that is by no means meritless, although unlike what has gone before. This is the poetry of will,
as opposed to the poetry of intellect. It has no palpable
design upon us: indeed, but for a vision grown grey
with doubt, it would never have been written. It stands
out in welcome contrast to bad preaching and worse
philosophy because it remains true to the old and literal
way, in its endeavour to see things as they are. Certainly
it is much smaller poetry, lacking the metaphysical
passion that once directed Wordsworth in his search
for the second and revelatory sight of Peter Bell's
yellow primrose. But it is strong in its honesty: there
is no pretending that things make sense, and no pointing of a moral. The reader who wants a message must
extract it for himself from the unadvertised resolve and
discipline of its manner.

The other thanked him with an earnest voice;
But added, that, the evening being calm,
He would pursue his journey.

In the course of time Wordsworth grew more calcu-
lating in his attitude to the poetry of will. The *Ode to*

*Duty*, and his discussion of "the years that bring the philosophic mind" in the Immortality Ode, are quite consciously referred to the problem of decline: they ask what must be done when the light of childhood is extinguished. Wordsworth's answer betrays his own uncertainty. In the decade between the Immortality Ode and the publication of *The Excursion* he says a great deal about the need for Christian faith, and as much again about the human solution: about patient nursing of the will and husbanding of "what remains behind", about looking for relief precisely in one's humanity and in the "thoughts that spring Out of human suffering". Life is best undergone by him who does not ask too much of it. This is the period of Wordsworth's growing interest in Roman Stoicism: he came to know Seneca as he knew no philosopher, ancient or modern. And it is the period in which his own natural severity and detachment were much accentuated. The almost universal unkindness with which his early poetry was received only confirmed his belief in the fatal connexion of solitude and genius. He writes to a friend made anxious by the mockery and abuse showered on the *Poems in Two Volumes* published in 1807:

> Trouble not yourself upon their present reception; of what moment is that compared with what I trust is their destiny, to console the afflicted, to add sunshine to daylight by making the happy happier, to teach the young and the gracious of every age, to see, to think and feel, and therefore to become more actively and securely virtuous; this is their office, which I trust they will faithfully perform long after we (that is, all that is mortal of us) are mouldered in our graves.[1]

Two years later, in his open *Letter to Mathetes*, Wordsworth treats of present dishonour and isolation in

---

[1] *Letters*, 1806-11 (ed. de Selincourt), p. 126. Note the force of "therefore" in Wordsworth's argument.

wider terms, as the certain attendants of virtue. A man, he argues, must choose to follow the World or to follow Truth. The World entices him in many ways, but Truth

> does not venture to hold forth any of these allurements; she does not conceal from him whom she addresses the impediments, the disappointments, the ignorance and prejudice which her follower will have to encounter, if devoted, when duty calls, to active life; and if to contemplative, she lays nakedly before him a scheme of solitary and unremitting labour, a life of entire neglect perhaps, or assuredly a life exposed to scorn, insult, persecution, and hatred; but cheered by encouragement from a grateful few, by applauding conscience, and by a prophetic anticipation, perhaps, of fame—a late, though lasting consequence.

At its best this is a noble, if narrow, morality; a thing, as Wordsworth says in the same letter, of "passionate and pure choice", and sustained by "the inward sense of absolute and unchangeable devotion". Sometimes, it is true, he falls into a stiff-necked and very English stupidity, as in his *Character of the Happy Warrior*,

> Who, if he rise to station or command,
> Rises by open means, and there will stand
> On honourable terms, or else retire,
> And in himself possess his own desire;
> Who comprehends his trust, and to the same
> Keeps faithful with a singleness of aim;
> And therefore does not stoop, nor lie in wait
> For wealth, or honours, or for worldly state. . . .

*The Happy Warrior* is separated by whole continents from the *Ode to Duty*, next to which it stands in Wordsworth's own ordering of his poems. But they both illustrate, each according to its measure, the same aspect of Wordsworth's middle age.

I can therefore find no simple answer to the problem of Wordsworth's decline. What he says about the connexion between his childhood and his poetry is true, but still mysterious. I have tried to trace a dispersal of effort, in light pastoral, in the poetry of intellect and the poetry of will. To show what happened is not to give a reason; and I understand that my thesis must not be supposed to stand or fall by the loss of childhood and the advent of affliction. This would be an assumption as to the relation between literature and life no more warranted than that involved in any argument advancing, as the reason for decline, Wordsworth's love for Annette or for Dorothy, the failure of his eyesight or his political reaction. And yet it is a critic's business to show what happened. There was once an arrangement in Wordsworth's work, large and subtle enough to make him a very great poet. This was lost, and its place taken by the poetry of indecision. If the study of what happens in poetry were ever followed to a true conclusion, the reason for what happens—the critic no longer confusing natural causes and metaphysical reasons—would cease to perplex; not because it is a false question, but because it is here unaskable, as relating to a different order of the world.

Criticism of bad poetry has seldom saved itself from dullness, except through falsehood; and it would be a dishonest attempt to maintain interest, to pretend that the ways in which Wordsworth's early effort was dispersed can be precisely mapped. Much of his middle-aged poetry is bad just because it is unpredictable—random diversion-poetry that anybody might have written. But talk of tendencies is not quite idle.

The White Doe of Rylstone was written in 1807 and 1808, and published, by itself, in 1815. Except for The Excursion, it is the most ambitious work of Wordsworth's later life, a narrative poem of nearly two thousand lines, founded on a ballad in Percy's collection, *The Rising of The North*. It concerns the part played by a single family, the Nortons, in the northern revolt of 1569 against Queen Elizabeth, which had first among its aims the restoring of the old religion. Richard Norton is a fierce and aged squire, with nine strong sons and a single daughter, Emily. Emily, in the story's opening, is making a sacred banner at her father's command, against the day of open insurrection. She makes it unwillingly, because she has come, through her mother's teaching, to profess Christianity reformed. Francis, the eldest of Richard's sons, is also against taking part in the revolt, but he fails to persuade his father and brothers, who march off to war, bearing Emily's banner with them. Francis foresees that the whole family, and Rylstone Hall its home, are doomed to perish in this adventure; and he makes Emily promise to stay at Rylstone, doing—even hoping—nothing, while he follows the others, unarmed and unobserved, to see what happens. The revolt fails: the Nortons, except Francis, are captured and led off to execution. Just before he dies, old Richard Norton beseeches Francis to regain the banner if he can, and bring it to Bolton Priory, to rest for ever there on St Mary's shrine. Francis seizes the banner and escapes; but before he can reach Bolton he is discovered by a party of soldiers, and is killed.

Thus Emily survives alone, and the prophecy of Francis is fulfilled. But not entirely, for he had not reckoned with the white doe when, at the outset, he foretold universal ruin:

> "The blast will sweep us all away—
> One desolation, one decay!
> And even this Creature!" which words saying,
> He pointed to a lovely Doe,
> A few steps distant, feeding, straying;
> Fair creature, and more white than snow!

"Even she will to her peaceful woods
Return, and to her murmuring floods,
And be in heart and soul the same
She was before she hither came:
Ere she had learned to love us all,
Herself beloved in Rylstone-hall."[1]

In fact the white doe does not leave, but remains with
Emily at the end of the poem, her consolation in sorrow
and companion in lonely wandering. And when she
dies, the white doe watches over her grave.

The white doe is the strangest figure in this difficult
poem. She belongs to Wordsworth's past: reciprocally
loving and loved, she is the latest of the relational solitaries. Her direct ancestors are the Lucy solitaries,
immaculate and ghostly, the Danish Boy, and the albatross of *The Ancient Mariner*, which Wordsworth
suggested to Coleridge when they were working together at the scheme of the poem, long ago in 1797.[2]
In the end, Coleridge placed the albatross at the centre
of a very unwordsworthian story of sin and nightmare-
horror and contrition: the other poet would not have
dealt like this with the white and lonely bird, moving
between sky and ocean. What he might have done at
the height of his powers is faintly suggested by the
entry of the doe, described ten years later:

—When soft!—the dusky trees between,
And down the path through the open green,
Where is no living thing to be seen;
And through yon gateway, where is found,
Beneath the arch with ivy bound,
Free entrance to the church-yard ground—
Comes gliding in with lovely gleam,
Comes gliding in serene and slow,
Soft and silent as a dream,
A solitary Doe!

[1] l. 554.    [2] Note to *We are Seven*, *P.W.*, Vol. I. p. 361.

White she is as lily of June,
And beauteous as the silver moon
When out of sight the clouds are driven
And she is left alone in heaven;
Or like a ship some gentle day
In sunshine sailing far away,
A glittering ship, that hath the plain
Of ocean for her own domain.[1]

There are several reasons why *The White Doe* is not
one of Wordsworth's best poems. Like *The Lay of the
Last Minstrel*, and unlike *Christabel*, it makes little more
than period costume of the Antique Manner; and its
cultivation of a light Spenserian Faery, though skilful,
is too persistent. It is also overdeliberate in its following
of Wordsworth's old ways. The doe is painstakingly
white and solitary: whenever she appears, Wordsworth
insists on her distinctness and radiancy, to show her
"spotless, beautiful, innocent and loving",[2] in the language of his own comment on the poem. The emphasis
on her relational function is even more crude. Once
Emily and the doe are left alone, Wordsworth becomes
absurdly anxious to reveal how perfect is their companionship in solitude. Emily is resting, after Francis
has been killed, "with head reclined",

> When, with a noise like distant thunder,
> A troop of deer came sweeping by;
> And, suddenly, behold a wonder!
> For One, among those rushing deer,
> A single One, in mid career
> Hath stopped, and fixed her large full eye
> Upon the Lady Emily;
> A Doe most beautiful, clear-white,
> A radiant creature, silver-bright!

---

[1] l. 49.
[2] *Letters*, 1806-11 (ed. de Selincourt), p. 197.

Thus checked, a little while it stayed;
A little thoughtful pause it made;
And then advanced with stealth-like pace,
Drew softly near her, and more near—
Looked round—but saw no cause for fear;
So to her feet the creature came,
And laid its head upon her knee,
And looked into the Lady's face,
A look of pure benignity,
And fond unclouded memory.
It is, thought Emily, the same,
The very Doe of other years!—
The pleading look the Lady viewed,
And, by her gushing thoughts subdued,
She melted into tears—
A flood of tears that flowed apace
Upon the happy Creature's face.[1]

This day, says Wordsworth, was "the first of a re-
union Which was to teem with high communion", and
he continues, in much the same vein, to dwell upon
their love and understanding. Emily

hath ventured now to read
Of time, and place, and thought, and deed—
Endless history that lies
In her silent Follower's eyes;
Who with a power like human reason
Discerns the favourable season,
Skilled to approach or to retire,—
From looks conceiving her desire;
From look, deportment, voice, or mien,
That vary to the heart within.[2]

So that from this time until Emily's death, there might
the "kindliest intercourse ensue".

No theme could have been more attractive to Words-

[1] l. 1639.                    [2] l. 1714.

worth's young imagination than this one, of two different orders of nature perfectly alone and perfectly related. Nor is it handled, despite these damaging examples, without traces of his early mastery: the shining and unsexual quality of the relationship—light without heat—is reminiscent of the Lucy poems. To this extent Wordsworth still appears unselfconscious in his appreciation of the kind of poetry he writes; for he declines to versify the story of Beauty and the Beast, not long after he has written *The White Doe*, and with an interesting comment:

> I confess there is to me something disgusting in the notion of a human being consenting to mate with a beast, however amiable his qualities of heart. There is a line and a half in the *Paradise Lost* upon this subject which has always shocked me,—
>
> "for which cause
> Among the Beasts no Mate for thee was found."
>
> These are objects to which the mind ought not to be turned even as things in possibility.[1]

It can never have occurred to him, even "in possibility", that the love of Emily and the doe might be different from that which he imagines.

But *The White Doe* as a whole is all too self-aware: it manipulates solitude-in-relationship, as if to achieve the old result without expending the old effort. This very deliberation makes the poem strikingly intellectual; and Wordsworth himself stresses the mental nature of its tragedy. He believed that the poem would never be popular "because the main catastrophe was not a material but an intellectual one";[2] and he acknowledged that "the mere physical action was all unsuccessful",[3] averring at the same time that "the true

---

[1] *Letters*, 1806-11 (ed. de Selincourt), p. 427.    [2] *Ibid.*, p. 197.
[3] *P.W.*, Vol. III. p. 548.

action" took place in the realm of spirit and intellect. The intellectual catastrophe of *The White Doe* is worth closer study for its relevance to the poet's own position.

*The White Doe* presents four parties in conflict— Protestant, Catholic, Stoic, and Relational-Solitary. Emily is unwilling to make the Catholic banner, and must be compelled, because she remembers her mother

> Who with mild looks and language mild
> Instructed here her darling Child,
> While yet a prattler on the knee,
> To worship in simplicity
> The invisible God, and take for guide
> The faith reformed and purified.[1]

Opposed to her is her father and the rebel cause, stated but not argued by Wordsworth, with a force quite new to his poetry, and premonitory of his late achievement:

> Might this our enterprise have sped,
> Change wide and deep the Land had seen,
> A renovation from the dead,
> A spring-tide of immortal green:
> The darksome altars would have blazed
> Like stars when clouds have rolled away;
> Salvation to all eyes that gazed,
> Once more the Rood had been upraised
> To spread its arms, and stand for aye.[2]

There is a kind of victory in defeat, when the old man, about to die, asks Francis to take the banner, and

> Bear it to Bolton Priory,
> And lay it on Saint Mary's shrine;
> To wither in the sun and breeze
> 'Mid those decaying sanctities.[3]

[1] l. 1036.     [2] l. 1261.     [3] l. 1292.

Francis stands between these two parties, and is distinct from both. The speech in which he bids farewell to Emily stems from the poetry of will and from Wordsworth's reading in Stoicism. He speaks of the consolation to be found in "unmerited distress"—"in that thy very strength must lie"; of the need to play one's part exactly and without fear in the great drama which is the world:

> Farewell all wishes, all debate,
> All prayers for this cause, or for that!
> Weep, if that aids thee; but depend
> Upon no help of outward friend;
> Espouse thy doom at once, and cleave
> To fortitude without reprieve.[1]

He continues in praise of the human virtues of "forbearance and self-sacrifice"; and his speech ends thus:

> Be strong;—be worthy of the grace
> Of God, and fill thy destined place:
> A Soul, by force of sorrows high
> Uplifted to the purest sky
> Of undisturbed humanity.[2]

The argument of Francis, though not expressly directed against the Christian elements of *The White Doe*, is none the less very unchristian. Emily is in fact aware of the gulf between his attitude and her own, for she implores her mother's pious ghost to "descend on Francis", and bid him

> beware
> Of that most lamentable snare,
> The self-reliance of despair![3]

But it is upon the clash of a humanistic philosophy of reason, will, and duty, and the love shared by Emily and the doe, that the intellectual catastrophe and the

[1] l. 540.　　　[2] l. 583.　　　[3] l. 1054.

L

spirituality of the poem's action chiefly depend. Emily resists the desire to follow her family to the war because she regards her brother's injunction as an "insuperable bar". Reluctantly she admits, in a paraphrase of his own last words to her, that

> *Her duty is to stand and wait;*
> In resignation to abide
> The shock, AND FINALLY SECURE
> O'ER PAIN AND GRIEF A TRIUMPH PURE.[1]

Emily makes half-hearted assent to his argument, which is itself no more than half justified by events.

> Behold the prophecy fulfilled,
> Fulfilled, and she sustains her part!
> But here her Brother's words have failed;
> Here hath a milder doom prevailed;
> That she, of him and all bereft,
> Hath yet this faithful Partner left;
> This one Associate that disproves
> His words, remains for her, and loves.[2]

This is the point of the poem. Francis was right to fore-tell disaster, and Emily's final mastery of pain. But he was also wrong; for hers is not the kind of victory he had expected. It is a victory in love, that "disproves his words".

*The White Doe*, then, invokes the old against the new, and in doing so expresses the personal dilemma. Wordsworth's past stands over against his present, and is felt to refute it; but Emily's victory, which is this refutation, can have no poetic interest unless the past returns full-nerved, to confront later time: her life with the doe is otherwise a paper triumph. And it is partly because Wordsworth cannot recover solitude-in-relationship, except through intellectual definition, that *The White Doe* is a failure.

.1069.                              [2] l. 1783.

There is also the important difficulty that Wordsworth does not know—if he did, the poetry of indecision would not have been written—what he means by Emily's "triumph pure". If it were simply a matter of past confounding present, nature would finally be overcome by deeper nature. But there is a sudden loss of clarity at the end of *The White Doe*, when it becomes impossible to be certain whether Emily's victory is of earth or of heaven. Wordsworth echoes Francis, and lays the same stress on the natural, when he speaks of her as

> Uplifted to the purest sky
> Of undisturbed mortality.[1]

But this is a most equivocal mortality; for she is "by sorrow lifted toward her God", and she

> stood apart from human cares:
> But to the world returned no more. . . .[2]

She is stranger both to the mortal and immortal state, "faintly, faintly tied To earth", suspended and inert, the image of Wordsworth's impotence. Future is here involved, no less than past and present; and the movement towards a poetry of the supernatural.

[1] l. 1852.  [2] l. 1859.

## IV

## THE BAPTISED IMAGINATION

Wordsworth's high opinion of *The White Doe* and his insistence on its spirituality are closely connected. He thought the poem a complete failure in terms of its physical action, but made large claims for its other part, boasting, according to one story,[1] that he had published it in quarto "to show the world my own opinion of it", thus inviting comparison with the more fleshly romances of Scott and Byron which were also published in quarto. His own comments on *The White Doe* make it clear that he believed its spiritual success to lie in the relationship of Emily and the doe. He describes Emily as raised to "heights of heavenly serenity", as "ascending to pure etherial spirituality and forwarded in that ascent by communion with a creature not of her own species";[2] while the highest "point of imagination" in the poem is "nothing less than the Apotheosis of the Animal. . . ."[3] And again: "The anticipated beatification, if I may say so, of her mind, and the apotheosis of the companion of her solitude, are the points at which the Poem aims, and constitute its legitimate catastrophe, far too spiritual a one for instant or wide-spread sympathy. . . ."[4]

This talk of beatification and apotheosis, of the doe "raised from its mere animal nature into something mysterious and saint-like",[5] has a challenging novelty about it. Even the vocabulary would have been impossible ten years earlier. And Wordsworth's remarks

[1] Thomas Moore, *Memoirs*. Discussed by Miss Edith Batho, *The Later Wordsworth*, pp. 83-4 n.
[2] *Letters*, 1806-11 (ed. de Selincourt), p. 197.
[3] *Letters*, 1811-20 (ed. de Selincourt), p. 705.
[4] *P.W.*, Vol. III. p. 543.        [5] *Ibid.*, p. 548.

about his poem, agreeing too closely with each other for any possibility of accident, are accompanied by a more general observation which is also new and also deliberately made:

> Throughout, objects (the Banner, for instance) derive their influence not from properties inherent in them, not from what they are actually in themselves, but from such as are bestowed upon them by the minds of those who are conversant with or affected by those objects. Thus the Poetry, if there be any in the work, proceeds whence it ought to do, from the soul of Man, communicating its creative energies to the images of the external world.[1]

At one time Wordsworth believed that poetry and life were founded on the principle of reciprocity, on "ennobling interchange Of action from within and from without"; and in the giant *Recluse* he intended to demonstrate this truth. *The Recluse* was never finished, for a reason easier to confess than to comprehend: Wordsworth changed his mind. Already, in the last lines of *The Prelude*, the inner world is seen "above this frame of thing.... In beauty exalted". And now Wordsworth is urging that the interest of his poetry is spiritual, that the soul of man, instead of "working but in alliance with the works Which it beholds", is a single labourer.

As he suggests, the sacred banner is a key to this great change. Rivalling the doe herself in imaginative stature, the banner spans the action of the poem: bathed at its opening in Emily's tears, at its end in her brother's blood, throughout its central violence, the focus of Catholic effort. Francis, the hidden observer,

> following wheresoe'er he might,
> Hath watched the Banner from afar,
> As shepherds watch a lonely star,
> As mariners the distant light. . . .[2]

---

[1] *Letters*, 1811-20 (ed. de Selincourt), p. 705.  [2] l. 757.

and the banner becomes a guiding star not only for the Nortons but for the entire army. When old Richard Norton "took the Banner and unfurled The precious folds", the host rallied round him at once.

"Uplift the Standard!" was the cry
From all the listeners that stood round,
"Plant it,—by this we live or die."
The Norton ceased not from that sound,
But said; "The prayer which ye have heard,
Much injured Earls! by these preferred,
Is offered to the Saints, the sigh
Of tens of thousands, secretly."
"Uplift it!" cried once more the Band,
And then a thoughtful pause ensued:
"Uplift it!" said Northumberland—
Whereat, from all the multitude
Who saw the Banner reared on high
In all its dread emblazonry,
A voice of uttermost joy brake out. . . .[1]

What Wordsworth means by influence bestowed on objects as opposed to influence within them becomes clear from his treatment of the banner. He has an important use for the distinction between that which a thing is and that which it stands for. Furled, it is a banner: unfurled, it is "the ransom of a sinful world", a divine ambassador by virtue of the thing depicted on it. Its meaning is then understood. And the ritual shout, thrice repeated, makes the raising of the banner a sacramental gesture. This dualism runs through the poem's action. Emily objects not to her labour in making the banner but to its significance; and Francis, who at first opposed a cramped intellectual argument to the whole adventure, dies trying to bring the banner home, impelled by motives both in and out of the world, almost Shakespearean in their complexity and pathos.

[1] l. 670.

Quite new in Wordsworth is this show of emblematic power, this grasping of otherness through thing and act. And if the banner and the white doe worked together, instead of thwarting each other's purpose, the whole would not be a failure. As it is, the new poetry is an uncertain element in an unsuccessful poem, no more than an introduction to the problem of Wordsworth's Christianity.

Encouraged by the existence of the rival texts of 1805 and 1850, students of Wordsworth's religion have often concerned themselves with *The Prelude*. But his alterations to the 1805 text make a poor basis for generalization: as a whole, they are unimportant and even misleading. Wordsworth practised a kind of theological surgery on the body of his poem, grafting on to it pious digressions, and cutting away parts so distempered as to offend sound doctrine. Sometimes this is done with a simple-hearted dexterity entertaining to observe, as when

> I worshipped them among the depths of things
> As my soul bade me. . . .
> I felt and nothing else[1]

in the 1805 text becomes, in 1850,

> Worshipping then among the depths of things
> As piety ordained. . . .
> I felt, observed, and pondered;

and when

> God and nature's single sovereignty[2]

is saved for orthodoxy in this fashion:

> Presences of God's mysterious power
> Made manifest in Nature's sovereignty.

[1] Bk. XI. 234.          [2] Bk. IX. 237.

There is no denying the evidence of these changes. Wordsworth grew sensitive to accusations of heresy, especially pantheistic, levelled against his work; and he resorted to unworthy expedients in order to refute them. This was a sad mistake: he would have been better employed writing new poems than patching old ones. And it was doubly unfortunate in that it has lent colour to the belief that Wordsworth's Christianity was a timid afterthought, a false gesture of respectability comparable with his toryism or his taste for the nobility or his acceptance of the Laureateship. Thus the picture of an unlovely, frigescent character has been built up and generally accepted, which, although by no means wholly false, is least true in the things that matter most.

Wordsworth's alteration to poems already written went much further than the trimming of obnoxious details. *Peter Bell* and *The Pedlar* are both test cases, since they were written early and published late, with ample time for reflection. *Peter Bell* is also a very simple test case, because it is the most direct of Wordsworth's poems in its approach to the relationship between mind and nature.[1] As the result of a deficiency in Peter himself, "nature ne'er could find the way Into the heart of Peter Bell". Wordsworth views the problem from the standpoint of nature and asks what must be done by her when the opposite and human term of the relation has failed to play its part: this is the "theme but little heard of among men" to which he refers in the Prospectus to *The Recluse;* not how the mind is fitted to the world, but how "the external world is fitted to the mind".

The poem suffers on account of this directness; for Nature becomes absurdly purposeful in her assault on Peter's heart. "Potent spirits" and "dread beings" are invoked, together with terrible sights and sounds,

[1] See pp. 115-7.

which were the Gothic apparatus of Wordsworth's own schoolboy verse. Mindful of his present task, Wordsworth insists that none of these happenings are supernatural, thereby heightening their absurdity. A "rumbling sound" that made Peter believe "that earth was charged to quake And yawn for his unworthy sake" was in fact

> by a troop of miners made,
> Plying with gunpowder their trade,
> Some twenty fathoms under ground.

But the distinction between natural and supernatural agents of Peter's regeneration is not easily maintained. Even in the early versions of the poem Wordsworth has to call upon "a fervent methodist", encountered "preaching to no unheeding flock", to assist nature in her work. And many years later, shortly before he published *Peter Bell*, Wordsworth added two stanzas in which he described a further influence on Peter, effected through the donkey which he had stolen and ill-treated.

> 'Tis said, meek Beast! that, through Heaven's grace,
> He not unmoved did notice now
> The cross upon thy shoulder scored,
> For lasting impress, by the Lord
> To whom all human-kind shall bow;
>
> Memorial of his touch—that day
> When Jesus humbly deigned to ride,
> Entering the proud Jerusalem,
> By an immeasureable stream
> Of shouting people deified.[1]

It is almost as if Grace and Nature were consciously opposed, and the frailty of Nature admitted. These added stanzas, fine in themselves, do not improve *Peter Bell*: rather, they make matters worse by denying

[1] *P.W.*, Vol. II. pp. 377, 530.

momentarily and at a late stage the pagan optimism from which it proceeds. It is because they go to the root of Wordsworth's intention in a large and carefully constructed work that they must be taken for more than casual indulgence in self-regarding pietism or devotional sweetness.

In his changes to *The Pedlar* Wordsworth does not simply gainsay the past: he refashions it completely. Originally, we have seen, this was a narrative poem in which the Pedlar first told his tale of suffering and then subjected it to a cheerful necessitarian interpretation. These are the final lines of his lengthy argument:

> "My Friend, enough to sorrow have you given,
> The purposes of Wisdom asks no more,
> Be wise and cheerful, and no longer read
> The forms of things with an unworthy eye.
> She sleeps in the calm earth and peace is here.
> I well remember that those very plumes,
> Those weeds and the high spear-grass on that wall,
> By mist and silent rain-drops silvered o'er,
> As once I passed, did to my mind convey
> So still an image of tranquillity,
> So calm and still, and looked so beautiful,
> Amid the uneasy thoughts which filled my mind,
> That what we feel of sorrow and despair
> From ruin and from change, and all the grief
> The passing shews of being leave behind
> Appeared an idle dream that could not live
> Where meditation was. I turned away
> And walked along my road in happiness."
> He ceased. . . .[1]

"Meditation" comes at the end of the long and finely managed sentence that dominates this passage. It is the classical Wordsworthian abstract noun, referred to time and space through association with the verb "to

[1] *P.W.*, Vol. V. p. 403.

be", and so positioned, almost pointed at—"where meditation was"—as to gain the authority peculiar to the concrete and the evidence of things seen. It is one of Wordsworth's Presences, vast and yet precise in their encompassing of thing and thought. Wordsworth was wise to follow Humpty Dumpty's example and pay his word extra, for it has a great deal of work to do, gathering in the fruit of the Pedlar's prolonged philosophizing. The point of "meditation", in the Pedlar's own summary of his argument, is that by

> deeply drinking in the soul of things
> We shall be wise perforce, and we shall move
> From strict necessity along the path
> Of order and of good.[1]

And however shoddy the Pedlar's reasoning, there lies beyond it an entire poetry of joy and natural good. This is what makes a triumph of his great conclusion.

When it was published, *The Pedlar* became the first book of *The Excursion*. The story remains in substance the same, but its moral is profoundly altered; for the Pedlar's necessitarian argument, designed in the first place to counter the fact of suffering, is entirely omitted, and in the final text his conclusion is restated in Christian terms. Wordsworth's immediate response to his tale of Margaret's miserable death in the ruined cottage gives warning of change:

> I blessed her in the impotence of grief.[2]

And although the Pedlar still rebukes him, he does so for a different reason:

> My Friend! enough to sorrow you have given,
> The purposes of wisdom ask no more:
> Nor more would she have craved as due to One
> Who, in her worst distress, had ofttimes felt
> The unbounded might of prayer; and learned, with soul

[1] *P.W.*, Vol. V. p. 402.     [2] l. 924.

> Fixed on the Cross, that consolation springs,
> From sources deeper far than deepest pain,
> For the meek Sufferer. Why then should we read
> The forms of things with an unworthy eye?[1]

And so on, as before. But "meditation" has gone, and in its place is the assertion that grief

> Appeared an idle dream, that could maintain,
> Nowhere, dominion o'er the enlightened spirit
> Whose meditative sympathies repose
> Upon the breast of Faith.[2]

In *Peter Bell*, the entry of a concurrent Christian interest simply makes nonsense of the poem's naturalism. *The Pedlar*, on the other hand, still makes sense, but sense quite opposed to Wordsworth's original intention. Certainly it is of no immediate poetic interest that Hartleian philosophy has given way to a Christian statement of the problem of pain, clearly made and without compromise, but still with little imaginative force. We have nevertheless a preliminary advantage in knowing that Wordsworth's deliberate alteration of his poems cannot be dismissed as shamefaced tinkering with work that might displease the orthodox. There is no doubt that he was trying to write Christian poetry, and not merely to appear respectable.

It is also certain that Wordsworth's poetry was not changed by conscious application only, although what was meant and what was not are often hard to distinguish. Even in the 1850 *Prelude*, where his work is singularly deliberate, intentional and unintentional go hand in hand. At the beginning of the last book there is described a night ascent of Snowdon, which was written, like other great passages in the later books, certainly or probably during the marvellous years of 1798 and 1799. Wordsworth says, in the 1805 text of

---

[1] l. 932.                    [2] l. 952.

*The Prelude*, that the scene from the top of the mountain

> appear'd to me
> The perfect image of a mighty Mind,
> Of one that feeds upon infinity,
> That is exalted by an underpresence,
> The sense of God, or whatsoe'er is dim
> Or vast in its own being. . . .[1]

Out of its context this reads like muddy bombast, vaguely pantheistic in flavour. But I cannot believe that Wordsworth was much worried about its theological correctness when he altered and expanded it in this way:

> There I beheld the emblem of a mind
> That feeds upon infinity, that broods
> Over the dark abyss, intent to hear
> Its voices issuing forth to silent light
> In one continuous stream; a mind sustained
> By recognitions of transcendent power,
> In sense conducted to ideal form,
> In soul of more than mortal privilege.[2]

Now this is not much clearer than the 1805 account, but the impression that it leaves is utterly different. "Image" has become "emblem"—a significant change in Wordsworth—and everything conspires to set the mind over against the object of its attention. The mind "broods", "intent to hear" voices rising from below; and Wordsworth's picture is then generalized and given intellectual depth by reference to the Platonic vision of "ideal form" transcending the world of sense.

At this point it becomes profitless to talk about Wordsworth's intentions. His state of mind when he made these changes would probably, if it could be discovered, help us not at all. His earlier account felt

---

[1] Bk. XIII. 68.          [2] 1850, Bk. XIV. 70.

wrong to him: he could no longer say it like that. The
mood of cloudy exaltation which it recalled so effectively now embarrassed and perplexed him. This was
more what he meant. And so he undertook *The
Prelude's* revision, often very unclear what was the
matter with it, and unable for the most part to attempt
more than fragmentary restatement; but no doubt
consoled by the way in which the late *Prelude* of 1804
and 1805 had already worked deep change in the
poem's quality, with its doctrine of spiritual love and
its final rejoicing in the mind sovereign over nature.

Much more relevant than the question of intention
is that of alteration in the imaginative stuff of the Great
Decade. I have already mentioned two solitaries who
appear in the late *Prelude*.[1] The shepherd

> descried in distant sky,
> A solitary object and sublime,
> Above all height! like an aerial Cross. . . .

exemplifies the mock sublime and Wordsworth's
straining for a transcendental poetry, comparable with
his feeble defence of old age in *The Excursion*, as a
state of complete detachment. The blind beggar in
London, wearing a label that was for Wordsworth

> a type,
> Or emblem of the utmost that we know,
> Both of ourselves and of the universe. . . .

I have thought of as relevant to the poetry of indecision.
But "emblem" suggests that he may be important in a
different way; and this is borne out at the end of the
encounter:

> 'on the shape of the unmoving man,
> His fixèd face and sightless eyes, I look'd
> As if admonish'd from another world.

[1] See pp. 126-8.

The beggar is not a natural Presence, like the early
solitaries, but an intimation of otherness. He confirms
the change already discernible a year or two before, in
the figure of the Leech-Gatherer, who seemed

> like a man from some far region sent,
> To give me human strength, by apt admonishment.

These are signs of revolution in the primary
materials of Wordsworth's poetry; and the same can
be said of childhood as of solitude. It is upon childhood
that Wordsworth bases his idea of solitude-in-relationship in the early *Prelude;* for childhood is the great
natural fact which demonstrates the perfect working of
"those first-born affinities that fit Our new existence to
existing things". But when Wordsworth returns to
childhood in Book V, he has developed an interest that
extends beyond the natural order. "Our childhood,"
he says,

> Our simple childhood sits upon a throne
> That hath more power than all the elements.
> I guess not what this tells of Being past,
> Nor what it augurs of the life to come,
> But so it is. . . .[1]

And he goes on to describe childhood as "that dubious
hour, that twilight", making his meaning finally clear
by calling it an

> isthmus which we cross
> In progress from our native continent
> To earth and human life. . . .[2]

He is beginning to think of childhood as a bridge
between God and man.

Book V of *The Prelude* was written in the spring of
1804; and it has been argued, on the strength of
internal evidence, that the second part of the Im-

[1] Bk. V. 532.        [2] l. 560.

mortality Ode was written at the same time.[1] Comparison of the passage we have just considered with the opening lines of the fifth stanza suggests to me that this is true:

> Our birth is but a sleep and a forgetting:
> The Soul that rises with us, our life's Star,
> Hath had elsewhere its setting,
> And cometh from afar:
> Not in entire forgetfulness,
> And not in utter nakedness,
> But trailing clouds of glory do we come
> From God, who is our home:
> Heaven lies about us in our infancy!

In both cases Wordsworth is regarding childhood in the same way, but the mere sketch of *The Prelude* becomes in the Immortality Ode the pivot of his argument for the undying soul. Childhood is a revelation of "our native continent", or of "God, who is our home"; valued not for its solid and comprehensive hereness, but for its thereness, its power to illuminate the other.

At the outset I stressed Wordsworth's early monism because his late Christianity cannot be understood without it. In so far as he thought seriously about heaven and earth, it was as two aspects of the same thing. Now, in his treatment of solitude and childhood, we see him beginning to think of them as two different things. This is no play with words, with alternative means of expressing one idea: movement of this kind is the profoundest crisis that the life of the mind can suffer. In his own note to the Immortality Ode, Wordsworth defends his use of the doctrine of pre-existence in these words:

> Archimedes said that he could move the world if he had a point whereon to rest his machine. Who has not felt the same aspirations as regards the world of his own mind? Having to

wield some of its elements when I was impelled to write this poem on the *Immortality of the Soul*, I took hold of the notion of pre-existence as having sufficient foundation in humanity for authorizing me to make for my purpose the best use of it I could as a poet.[1]

Despite its bland tone, this is an admission of the first importance. Wordsworth had always intended, in entire seriousness, to "move the world" through his poetry; and he had once felt able, by sustained and Spinozistic paradox, to do so from within. But in the Immortality Ode he is preparing himself for the defeat of his imaginative monism: the answer to the world must be outside the world. Coleridge also acknowledged this, and left Spinoza for Christian orthodoxy. But in philosophy he thought his way back into the profounder monism of the German School: hence the tension of his thought and his confused utterance. Wordsworth escaped this dilemma because he was not the man to see the clash of old and new in speculative terms. But his own difficulties were no less real.

This work of 1804 anticipates Wordsworth's response to the death of his brother John which occurred a few months later. Under the immediate stress of pain and bewilderment he asserted an extreme religious dualism: the evils of earthly existence, he said, seemed to him inexplicable "except on the supposition of *another* and a *better world*"[2]; and he thought of his brother as going "to that God from whom I trust he will receive his reward".[3] Later, he consoled Southey in bereavement as he had consoled himself, with the expectation of "another and a more stable world",[4] venturing at another time the generalization that "all religions owe their origin or acceptance to the wish of

---

[1] *P.W.*, Vol. IV. p. 464.
[2] *Early Letters* (ed. de Selincourt), p. 460.
[3] *Ibid.*, p. 486.
[4] *Letters, 1811-20* (ed. de Selincourt), p. 736.

the human heart to supply in another state of existence the deficiences of this. . . ."[1]

The most certain thing about Wordsworth's religion is its initial poverty. Little more than an admission of defeat in a long war of which his brother's death was the last and decisive battle, it had at first no chance of engaging his finer powers. It lacked joy and creative interest and, in a sense, conviction, for a man is not entirely convinced of necessity: there is a difference between admitting and accepting the truth. Moreover, Wordsworth's imagination had certain natural limits which it never overstepped. His slender knowledge of sin is primarily responsible for the weak optimism of his late Christian Pastoral: he wanted Coleridge's lively sense of the enemy within, and an entire world of religious experience was thereby closed to him. Nor could he write about Christian doctrine. He had not the intellectual strength for sustained theological argument, nor the agility for metaphysical wit-writing. Wit-writing of every kind had always been foreign to his solemn and literal talent: if he had heard Coleridge declare that the stars appeared to him, one misty night, "like full stops on damp paper",[2] Wordsworth would have been almost shocked.

It is also true that Wordsworth's Christianity often made matters worse, as in *Peter Bell*, by augmenting chaos. I have taken *The White Doe* as the very type of indecision; but *The Excursion* would have done as well, were it not planned on a much larger and less manageable scale. The form of loose dialogue between persons of ill-defined character and opinion is exactly suited to the voicing of personal doubts, and the result is a scrapbook history of Wordsworth's imaginative life. The past is here: praise of solitude that "permits the mind to feel", and of relationship with the natural world in

---

[1] *Letters*, 1821-30 (ed. de Selincourt), p. 134.
[2] *Anima Poetae* (ed. E. H. Coleridge), p. 45.

which the "mind gives back the various forms of
things". There is rejoicing in the visionary innocence
of childhood, and lamentation over its departure
following "sad exclusion from decay of sense". The
Pedlar's Hartleian philosophy of long ago is now
transferred to the fourth book, where it rubs shoulders
with an invocation of the state in which

> the mind admits
> The law of duty; and can therefore move
> Through each vicissitude of loss and gain,
> Linked in entire complacence with her choice.[1]

One character asserts that the only "adequate support
For the calamities of mortal life" is "an assured belief"
in "a Being Of infinite benevolence and power"; and
then, fifty lines later in the same discourse, he asks himself, "what are things eternal?". and answers:

> subject neither to eclipse nor wane,
> Duty exists;—immutably survive,
> For our support, the measures and the forms,
> Which an abstract intelligence supplies. . . .[2]

And there is much transcendental yearning after "that
pure and unknown world of love Where injury cannot
come". *The Excursion* suffers for its large design.
Wordsworth devoted so much of his middle age to it
that it could not fail to commemorate the period of
flux, and often it gets the worst of all worlds. He felt
himself that the poem was inconclusive as he had
finished it, for he intended to continue the story with
an account of the sceptical Solitary witnessing "some
religious ceremony—a sacrament, say, in the open
fields, or a preaching among the mountains",[3] and this
was to have "done more towards restoring the Christian faith in which he had been educated, and, with
that, contentedness and even cheerfulness of mind,

---

[1] Bk. IV. 1035.    [2] *Ibid.*, 72.    [3] *P.W.*, Vol. V. p. 474.

than all that the Wanderer and Pastor, by their several effusions and addresses, had been able to effect. An issue like this was in my intentions". All this sounds ominous enough: religious-pastoral is one of the most tedious of his late manners. But at the same time it reveals an uncertainty of purpose too profound to be entirely conscious.

What is new and Christian in *The Excursion* is not always ineffectual. Wordsworth can still write persuasively of things that he has seen, though his gaze is now heavenward:

> homeward the shepherds moved
> Through the dull mist, I following—when a step,
> A single step that freed me from the skirts
> Of the blind vapour, opened to my view
> Glory beyond all glory ever seen
> By waking sense or by the dreaming soul!
> The appearance, instantaneously disclosed,
> Was of a mighty city—boldly say
> A wilderness of building, sinking far
> And self-withdrawn into a boundless depth,
> Far sinking into splendour—without end!
> Fabric it seemed of diamond and of gold,
> With alabaster domes, and silver spires,
> And blazing terrace upon terrace. . . .[1]

And while his eyes are raised to the Kingdom of Heaven, he still stands on earth; so that there is fugue-like movement of finite and infinite through the passage. The immediate occasion of the experience is clearly stated:

> By earthly nature had the effect been wrought
> Upon the dark materials of the storm
> Now pacified. . . .

[1] Bk. II. 828.

But no less clear, as he returns to it, is the sight of

> that marvellous array
> Of temple, palace, citadel, and huge
> Fantastic pomp of structure without name. . . .

Finally, the contrast of familiar valley and city that has suddenly usurped it, becomes explicit:

> This little Vale, a dwelling-place of Man,
> Lay low beneath my feet; 'twas visible—
> I saw not, but I felt that it was there.
> That which I *saw* was the revealed abode
> Of Spirits in beatitude. . . .
> . . . there I stood and gazed:
> The apparition faded not away,
> And I descended.

Wordsworth sees Paradise as a jewelled and holy city, as the New Jerusalem of Revelation. That the city should play this part is at once remarkable, since it has hitherto been very unimportant to him. The city of social and satirical poetry appears scarcely at all, because he was not this kind of poet. The city has no place within the greater landscape: if it has any poetic function, it is the negative one of circumscribing the unmanageable. This is not to say that all Wordsworth's poetry of the city is bad: sometimes, as in *The Prelude's* description of the "anarchy and din" of St Bartholomew's Fair, the countryman's wide-eyed stare, his fearful amazement, his almost unwilling fascination, are vividly conveyed. And once or twice, as when he saw London from Westminster Bridge "all bright and glittering" in the dress of early morning, or, in a fine poem which he left unpublished,

> white with winter's purest white, as fair,
> As fresh and spotless as he ever sheds
> On field or mountain,[1]

[1] *P.W.*, Vol. IV. p. 374.

the city is suddenly transmuted, and one can just understand how he came to see that other that has no need of sun or moon to shine upon it.

Even so, the *Excursion* city is a new thing—Paradise in an exact Christian and literary sense. It would be a tidy thesis that followed Wordsworth's imaginative course from the Garden of Eden in his greater landscape to the New Jerusalem in his late poetry. But it would not be true. The landscape is paradisal only in that difficult sense in which Wordsworth's early poetry is optimistic. Neither is it Christian nor is it the Never Never Land of Classical and Rousseauite myth: it is northern and severe, with a terrible simplicity that the pastoral Wordsworth of Arnold's tradition could not have compassed. And Wordsworth did not see his landscape as he now sees the holy city. Then, the point of his vision was the literalness that enabled him, as he insisted in a hundred different ways, to see things as they are. Now there is a duality which he openly admits. The valley "was visible", yet he did not see it. What he saw—and he italicizes the word so that there shall be no mistake—was "the revealed abode" of the blessed. "Revealed" emphasizes the divine gift of second-sight. We must believe that Wordsworth was in the spirit when he beheld this vision.

Nor does Wordsworth's spiritual eye report anything grey or ghostly: the picture is as brilliant and as substantial as that described in Revelation. This directness of visual appeal owes much to the philosophical innocence that allowed Wordsworth to write about the Kingdom of Heaven unalarmed by the huge difficulties at least as old as Plato's *Parmenides*, that attend belief in a transcendent order of reality. In this *Excursion* passage he is entirely concerned, like Blake, to report what he saw, in the faith that visions justify themselves; and, like Blake, he sees his problem as one of adequate description. Sustained prophetic frenzy is very rare in

Wordsworth, but he is clearly attracted to the lunatic state, as to childhood, for its privileged access to the supernatural. A late poem about a woman driven mad by the pain of bereavement ends thus:

> Nor of those maniacs is she one that kiss
> The air or laugh upon a precipice;
> No, passing through strange sufferings towards the tomb,
> She smiles as if a martyr's crown were won:
> Oft, when light breaks through clouds or waving trees,
> With outspread arms and fallen upon her knees
> The Mother hails in her descending Son
> An Angel, and in earthly ecstacies
> Her own angelic glory seems begun.[1]

The Christianity of this poetry is very unlike that which inspired the almost incredible final couplet of his *Address to a Skylark:*

> I, with my fate contented, will plod on,
> And hope for higher raptures, when life's day is done.

Anything but mean and pinched, its nature is already being unfolded in the architecture and jewelry of the holy city, and in the ceremonious action of lunacy— demoniac with those that "laugh upon a precipice" and adoring with the woman "fallen upon her knees": for art and symbolic action and eternity precious and unbreathing are the subject of his late poetry.

The Immortality Ode once more proves a turning-point. Arnold, and many since Arnold, have been offended by what they take for an unwordsworthian element in the ode's imagery and diction. The child comes earthward from an "imperial palace". The lambs that "bound As to the tabor's sound" discover the rhythm of their game in the Old Testament. The ode is suggestive of ritual form in "jubilee", "festival", "wedding", "funeral"; in "my head hath its coronal",

---

[1] *The Widow on Windermere Side.*

in "the gladness of the May", in "other palms are won". Critics are right to complain, but wrong to take no further interest in these discordancies.

The same thing happens in *The Prelude*, and is partly responsible for the discreteness of the later version.

> Witness, ye Solitudes! where I received
> My earliest visitations[1]

in the 1805 text becomes in 1850

> compassed round by mountain solitudes,
> Within whose solemn temple I received
> My earliest visitations. . . .[2]

Wordsworth is not simply indulging his taste for circumlocution. The God-graven temple of earth is one of the most persistent images in his late poetry, and one aspect of his changed attitude to the entire natural order. The idea of God as mere Creator is still repugnant to him: he follows his own advice, which was, we have seen, to "say as little as possible about *making*".[3] But God the loving and careful Artist—Wordsworth's theory of art, unlike Coleridge's, was not a theory of making—and God the Sustainer are both familiar.

Again, in the 1805 *Prelude*, he speaks of men of great soul who, in their dealings "with all the objects of the universe",

> for themselves create
> A like existence; and, whene'er it is
> Created for them, catch it by an instinct.[4]

In 1850, "all the objects" becomes "the whole compass", indicative of Wordsworth's loss of concentration upon particularity and the reciprocal principle; and the rest is much altered:

---

[1] Bk. XIII. 123.   [2] Bk. XIV. 139.
[3] Page 36.   [4] Bk. XIII. 94.

> for themselves create
> A like existence; and whene'er it dawns
> Created for them, catch it, or are caught
> By its inevitable mastery,
> Like angels stopped upon the wing by sound
> Of harmony from Heaven's remotest spheres.[1]

Clearly Wordsworth has come to dislike "instinct", with its natural and optimistic associations. In its place he introduces the equivocal "catch it, or are caught", and adds to this the angel simile. The simile is worth attention: it is more than a Miltonic flourish, just as the retreat from instinct is not mere cowardice or dishonesty. Wordsworth's movement from nature is also a movement towards art. There is an ever-increasing emphasis upon craftsmanship in his talk about poetry, and in his practice there is more of literary. Because of this, criticism that fails to use the criterion of Derivative with great tact may well go astray. Thus in the present case, the obvious Miltonism of the last line must not hide the sudden arrest of "angels stopped upon the wing", which is very effective and not quite Miltonic. And as for the general, angels work hard and successfully in Wordsworth's late poetry, speaking of heaven and earth as he requires them.

Angels live in heaven, but are sometimes seen by men. Thus they are persuaded by the beauty of spring on earth to "quit their mansions unsusceptible of change"[2] and walk abroad. Or a merciful errand may bring them here: Wordsworth tells how

> their own untroubled home
> They leave, and speed on nightly embassy
> To visit earthly chambers.[3]

They may have a purpose less specific than this comforting of sufferers. When attention seems wholly

[1] Bk. XIV. 94.        [2] *Vernal Ode.*        [3] *The Cuckoo Clock.*

directed towards earth they sometimes remind us un-
expectedly of the other order:

> In sunny glade,
> Or under leaves of thickest shade,
> Was such a stillness e'er diffused
> Since earth grew calm while angels mused ?[1]

This extreme delicacy with firmness of suggestion is
the angelic task. Their transcendentalism is often, as
here, a matter of being convincingly apart; or, like the
child, of coming from the courts of the holy city. And
they have their natural counterparts, in Wordsworth's
late poetry, in the heavenly bodies: in the moon,
looking down upon the earth's "unsettled atmosphere",[2] in order to "shield from harm the humblest
of the sleeping"; and the sun, "source inexhaustible
of life and joy", worshipped once as "a blazing intellectual deity".[3] *The Excursion* opens with the prayer
that the poem may shine "star-like", secure from
"those mutations that extend their sway Throughout
the nether sphere"[4]; and it closes[5] with the analogy,
too carefully developed, of the sun and the Deity. The
invisible sun, shedding light on evening clouds, is
called "this local transitory type Of thy paternal splen-
dours". And when Wordsworth hears the cuckoo, his
favourite among sky creatures,

> Wandering in solitude, and evermore
> Foretelling and proclaiming,[6]

---

[1] *The Triad.*

[2] *To the Moon.*

[3] *To the Clouds.*

[4] The very sharp contrast of Star-Poem and "nether sphere" only
appears in later versions of the Preface. In his first draft Wordsworth
merely expresses the hope

> that my song may live, and be
> Even as a light hung up in heaven to cheer
> The world in times to come.    (*P.W.*, Vol. V. p. 6).

[5] Bk. IX. 590-633.

[6] *The Cuckoo at Laverna.*

he is now put in mind of

> the great Prophet, styled *the Voice of One*
> *Crying amid the wilderness.*

Everything in nature speaks of its Original to one who
listens

> in the power, the faith,
> Of a baptized imagination.

Angels and shining things of earth serve Wordsworth's purpose in another way. Consider this glance
at the world through a magnifying glass:

> Glasses he had, that little things display,
> The beetle panoplied in gems and gold,
> A mailéd angel on a battle-day;
> The mysteries that cups of flowers enfold. . . .[1]

Unnatural in the way of art in its jewelled proportion,
the universe becomes a bright pageant that relates to
God with a fineness too elusive for the wide-meshed
vocabulary of symbol and analogy. Mastery of scale, in
the shift from beetle to angelic wars, is another aspect
of Wordsworth's understanding of God the Artist; and
later, in the great *Vernal Ode*, he exploits it to marvellous effect. He is resting his "tired lute", after a song
of time and immortality, when there steals upon his ear

> the soft murmur of the vagrant Bee.
> —A slender sound! Yet hoary Time
> Doth to the *Soul* exalt it with the chime
> Of all his years;—a company
> Of ages coming, ages gone;
> (Nations from before them sweeping,
> Regions in destruction steeping,)
> But every awful sound in unison
> With that faint utterance, which tells
> Of treasure sucked from buds and bells,
> For the pure keeping of those waxen cells.

[1] *Within our happy Castle* . . .

Then Wordsworth describes her pausing in flight, so that he can observe her parts:

> o'er this tempting flower
> Hovering, until the petals stay
> Her flight, and take its voice away!—
> Observe each wing!—a tiny van!
> The structure of her laden thigh,
> How fragile! yet of ancestry
> Mysteriously remote and high;
> High as the imperial front of man;
> The roseate bloom on woman's cheek;
> The soaring eagle's curvèd beak;
> The white plumes of the floating swan;
> Old as the tiger's paw. . . .

Scale is important for this reason, that by beating the bounds of creation, from the nature of time to the bee's humming and from her wing and thigh to tiger's paw, Wordsworth is able to suggest how God must see his own work. There is artistic love and justice in the handling of each element, none preferred before the rest since there is no small and no great within the work of art, but mutual support towards the end of coherence and beauty. Everything is intelligible in terms of everything else, as, by divine transposition, the temporal order in the voice of the bee; and the whole leans on the Artist's imaginative will. The idea of service directed to God's glory replaces the self-sustaining structure of the greater landscape: in terse little poems, not unlike those of Yeats's old age, Wordsworth sees the shadow of a daisy fulfil its nature by protecting a dew-drop from the sun,[1] or moon and planet together in the sky and wonders which is queen and which attendant.[2]

In natural things there is a new bright meaning: beak and plume and paw are the elements of a living

---

[1] *To a Child, Written in her Album.*
[2] *The Crescent-moon.*

heraldry, closely related to Wordsworth's jewelry and architecture, and adding to these the more urgent quality of ceremonious action. Only a poet grown old in wisdom would dare to use the conventions of "hoary time", "imperial front", "roseate bloom", because they exactly serve his purpose. The utterly conventional can thus approach the command of style proper to divinity.

Another aspect of heraldic nature is its anthropomorphism, mythical and heroic. Wordsworth at one time protested against the use of Classical mythology, as a kind of decadence. In a sonnet to a brook he said:

> If wish were mine some type of thee to view,
> Thee, and not thee thyself, I would not do
> Like Grecian Artists, give thee human cheeks,
> Channels for tears; no Naiad shouldst thou be. . . .[1]

The root of his objection is the offence that this sort of thing gives to his philosophy of inner and outer, the independence of each and the "ennobling interchange" between them. Nor in truth did he recant, for his late poetry is not in this sense anthropomorphic. Natural objects are not men in disguise; but there is a certain key, reached again through a kind of divine transposition, in which human inference may be drawn from all the music of the world. He speaks of trees that "tear The lingering remnant of their yellow hair",[2] of the eagle "shedding where he flew Loose fragments of wild wailing",[3] of waterfalls "white-robed"[4]— priestlike, perhaps, as Keats's "moving waters". The only Roman among the English Romantics, Wordsworth still went to Greece for his mythology, and he made of it something strong and personal. Because

---

[1] *Brook! whose society . . .*
[2] *One who was suffering tumult . . .*
[3] *A dark plume fetch me . . .*
[4] *The Excursion*, Bk. III. 48.

things are seen in God's eye, the anthropomorphism of nature is curiously without human prejudice or condescension.

The same bee of the *Vernal Ode* is called

> a warrior bold,
> Radiant all over with unburnished gold,
> And armed with living spear for mortal fight;
> A cunning forager
> That spreads no waste, a social builder; one
> In whom all busy offices unite
> With all fine functions that afford delight.

In his *Georgics*, Vergil compares bees to men, and later, in *The Æneid*, men to bees: a coming full circle that has been related to his poetry's development.[1] Wordsworth is doing neither—or both. Warrior, forager, social builder are impartial titles, above and between the bee-world and the man-world, which have both an equal claim to them. And again the angelic brightness of description marks a divine authenticity, the impress of the Just Artist's hands on all his creatures. Art in this way becomes the heart of Wordsworth's late poetry, and figures like the humming-bee its agents. Through the bee's embracing of all functions, warlike, peaceful, utilitarian, ornamental, art achieves the controlled boundlessness proper to itself. If the bee-world can be described in terms intelligible to men, but without reducing bees to men in miniature, we will know better how God sees us, and what it is like to be concerned in heaven for happenings on earth. Art helps in this because of its power to lay paradox to rest: it is at once the hardest work and the purest play; it matters finally and finally it does not matter, since love which is richness of art is not quite love which is richness of life— yet it is still love, and godlike in the artist's simultaneous detachment and participation; so that heat and

---

[1] W. F. J. Knight, *Roman Vergil*, pp. 167, 170.

light are undiminished, and he can escape, though only
in imagination, the precise human self-involvement
that makes divine compassion unattainable.

The flowers of Wordsworth's poetry are no longer
studied with literal passion, to discover what they are.
Already, in the Immortality Ode, the "pansy at my
feet" is completely formal, introduced with the barest
of gestures to confirm Wordsworth's story of lost childhood, and interesting only for its relevance to the
human predicament. Flowers, like the *Vernal Ode* bee,
supply a transcendental correlative for the root situations of men. "The flowers themselves," with

> all their glistening,
> Call to the heart for inward listening—
> And though for bridal wreaths and tokens true
> Welcomed wisely; though a growth
> Which the careless shepherd sleeps on,
> As fitly spring from turf the mourner weeps on—
> And without wrong are cropped the marble tomb to strew.[1]

Again there is convention and ceremony, and the
comprehension at remove peculiar to art.

In a very late poem, *Love Lies Bleeding*, the same
elements are present, and their organization is most
subtle. Wordsworth's theme is the red flower that is
always drooping, seems always to be dying, yet never
dies, its "life passing not away":

> A flower how rich in sadness! Even thus stoops,
> (Sentient by Grecian sculpture's marvellous power),
> Thus leans, with hanging brow and body bent
> Earthward in uncomplaining languishment,
> The dying Gladiator. So, sad Flower!
> ('Tis Fancy guides me willing to be led,
> Though by a slender thread,)
> So drooped Adonis, bathed in sanguine dew
> Of his death-wound, when he from innocent air

[1] *The Triad.*

The gentlest breath of resignation drew;
While Venus in a passion of despair
Rent, weeping over him, her golden hair
Spangled with drops of that celestial shower.
She suffered, as Immortals sometimes do. . . .

The flower is compared with the sculptured figure that
seems to be alive, and then with the mythical—the
fighter and the lover who were both killed in sport.
This is a large achievement in very small compass;
ranging from flesh to stone and from stone to story,
learning from each the same lesson which is also
different because of their varying conditions. The
passage has a great and almost anonymous distinction,
like the blue of sky, and seems to resolve the inexplicable
in its subject through some mystery of style. Wordsworth the unfanciful has reached an extreme of fancy
which before and since has been the province of old
imaginations.

This preoccupation with mere art is seen to be
nothing limited. The starlit dome, in Yeats's *Byzantium*,

> disdains
> All that man is,
> All mere complexities,
> The fury and the mire of human veins.

Wordsworth also moves towards art, but not in order
to oppose it to nature as Yeats does. His art is not in
this way disdainful: there is no parallel to Yeats's
rhetorical ascent towards his "artifice of eternity".
Wordsworth placed the same human limits on art as on
nature, but the difference between the two orders, as he
experienced it, helped him in his poetry. *Love Lies
Bleeding* has an added richness in its expression of
suffering through art. All the figures suffer, in the
modes of statuesque, literary and pictorial; until in the
end suffering and immortality are brought together.

It was the fact of suffering that first set Wordsworth thinking about the necessity of "another and a better world": struck down by his brother's death, he suggested an answer which may easily prove small and rigid; a philosophy of pain, of life to be undergone but not assented to. That he escaped such an issue is due to his taking firm hold of the fact that God too must suffer. We have already studied *Hart-Leap Well* as an essay in the problem of pain, in which Wordsworth is undecided whether he is writing a landscape poem about an animal that dies where it was born, or asserting God's love for "unoffending creatures" like the hart.[1] There is a third possibility, not hinted at in the poem, but clearly in Wordsworth's mind when he wrote some blank-verse lines a very short time before *Hart-Leap Well* itself. He says that a trance came over him when he stood at the well, thinking about the

> hunted beast, who there
> Had yielded up his breath, the awful trance,
> The vision of humanity, and of God
> The Mourner, God the Sufferer, when the heart
> Of his poor Creatures suffers wrongfully. . . .[2]

*Hart-Leap Well* was written too soon for Wordsworth to turn this experience to account. Later, in *Love Lies Bleeding* and in other poems, he is able to think of sadness as a kind of wealth, and suffering not without its divine likeness. And Wordsworth's Christianity also becomes rich, through acceptance of the consequences of the Incarnation. Eternal movement from heaven earthward, there manifested, justifies poetic effort; for although the poet must nourish his imagination at the "secondary founts" of time and space, he is still being "tutored for eternity".

In this there is a leaning on God, in His guarantee of the world for poets as for all men. Wordsworth

---

[1] Pages 138-40.    [2] *P.W.*, Vol. V. p. 319.

N

accepts Bradley's dramatic conclusion that appearance *is* reality, but the conclusion rests in the life of the Trinity, as a matter of faith. In his early poetry the star is an important feature of the greater landscape: it helps the Pedlar, in his childhood, to reach thought-in-sense, and is one of the types of eternity. Now it serves a general transcendental purpose, and is of particular interest for its power "to testify of Love and Grace divine". The stars appear

> to mortal eye,
> Blended in absolute serenity,
> And free from semblance of decline;[1]

and the certain mortality of stars does not gainsay this appearance:

> What if those bright fires
> Shine subject to decay,
> Sons haply of extinguished sires,
> Themselves to lose their light, or pass away
> Like clouds before the wind,
> Be thanks poured out to Him whose hand bestows,
> Nightly, on human kind
> That vision of endurance and repose.

Often, as here in the *Vernal Ode*, reliance on the hand that sustains through mortal change and gratitude to the hand that bestows, are found together. In *The Primrose of the Rock*, Wordsworth thinks of the flower as a "link in Nature's chain", and traces this chain, link by link, to God. His late lyrical verse, Christian and conventional rather in the manner of eighteenth-century hymns, has been underestimated by those anxious to see this much and to see no more. Originality has many kinds: Wordsworth, like Burke, his counsellor in politics, can handle received ideas with authority deriving from a serene largeness of scale and vital

[1] *Vernal Ode.*

control of emphasis. This primrose he sees, in its stem

> faithful to the root,
> That worketh out of view;
> And to the rock the root adheres
> In every fibre true.
>
> Close clings to earth the living rock,
> Though threatening still to fall;
> The earth is constant to her sphere;
> And God upholds them all:
> So blooms this lonely Plant, nor dreads
> Her annual funeral.

The immortality of succession becomes very dear to Wordsworth, as an earthly witness of eternal creative purpose. It also helps him in his personal struggle for humility and abatement of natural egotism: he is always trying to see himself a creature, to impress his finitude. In 1845 he instructed his printer to place a short passage of blank verse at the beginning of the volume, because, he said, "I mean it to serve as a sort of Preface".[1] This is not a good poem, but it catches this particular quality of his old age. He is once more watching the night sky, and the stars, some brilliant others dim, all owing their light to God. And he addresses himself thus:

> Then, to the measure of the light vouchsafed,
> Shine, Poet! in thy place, and be content.

His putting himself in his place has important consequences. Humility issues into thanks to God for all good things, and especially for the beauty of nature. Again perfectly conventional, his attitude is still worth consideration. What he calls "the religion of gratitude" can be seen at work in his poetry: gratitude is at the centre of his religious life because, as he declares,

[1] *P.W.*, Vol. I. p. 317.

"gratitude is the handmaid to hope, and hope the harbinger of faith".[1] It is as if he returned in different spirit to his first belief in the necessary connexion of poetry and pleasure. Pleasure that is coloured by gratitude to the giver is a sacrificial thing: the very taking joy becomes a handing back to God. As the motto of his Ecclesiastical Sonnets Wordsworth uses an adaptation of George Herbert's couplet:

> A verse may finde him, who a sermon flies
> And turn delight into a sacrifice:[2]

which makes the point entirely clear; and like other borrowings in thought and language, it shows how subtle is the question of originality.

Wordsworth's youth must not be set in judgment over his old age: nor, of course, must it be denied, as Wordsworth did when he pretended that he wrote the Preface to the *Lyrical Ballads* because "prevailed upon by Mr Coleridge".[3] When he was a young man he felt impelled to attack the accepted canons of poetic orthodoxy. When he was old, he became orthodox himself. Both states deserve serious regard; yet there is general willingness to forgive his youth ignorant and dogmatic theorising and much bad poetry, while age is scarcely listened to. Wordsworth found, as an honest man must, that orthodoxy is no easier than its opposite; and he could not achieve it without a partial recantation. In particular, there is his changed attitude to the conventional in diction and imagery, which at his best he makes the controlled means of serving new ends. But this change is itself enough to deny his poetry a hearing: the eye lights on "hoary time" and "roseate bloom" in the *Vernal Ode*, and a great poem goes unread.

Convention is thus on the circumference and at the centre of Wordsworth's late poetry: convention that is

---

[1] *Letters*, 1821-30 (ed. de Selincourt), p. 204.    [2] *The Church-porch*.
[3] *Letters*, 1831-40 (ed. de Selincourt), p. 910.

a plain matter of style leads to convention less plain and already approached through God's artistic manner, through the heraldry of nature and through action determined by accustomed forms—still a matter of style, or concern with the How of things. The last of these, style in ceremony, takes him furthest in his Christian poetry: indeed it proves to be almost the whole truth, since the religion of gratitude makes the imagination everywhere ceremonious, intent to cast experience into a form acceptable to God.

Small wonder, then, that Wordsworth has a lot to say about the ritual of belief. He likes to compare the incense that "curls in clouds Around angelic Forms" depicted on cathedral roof with the "flower-incense" of the fields and "unwearied canticles" of birds and streams.[1] In a more exact sense he is fascinated by the externals of worship. *Processions* is a study of Pagan and Christian within these terms. He recounts how

> mid the sacred grove
> Fed in the Libyan waste by gushing wells,
> The priests and damsels of Ammonian Jove
> Provoked responses with shrill canticles;
> While, in a ship begirt with silver bells,
> They round his altar bore the hornèd God,
> Old Cham, the solar Deity, who dwells
> Aloft, yet in a tilting vessel rode,
> When universal sea the mountains overflowed.

He then turns to "Roman Pomps":

> The feast of Neptune—and the Cereal Games,
> With images, and crowns, and empty cars;
> The dancing Salii—on the shields of Mars
> Smiting with fury; and a deeper dread
> Scattered on all sides by the hideous jars
> Of Corybantian cymbals, while the head
> Of Cybele was seen, sublimely turreted.

[1] *Devotional Incitements.*

And finally to "Christian pageantries": to

> The Cross, in calm procession, borne aloft
> Moved to the chant of sober litanies,

and his sight, one Sunday morning, of Swiss worshippers

> winding, between Alpine trees
> Spiry and dark, around their House of prayer.

This again is a small poem, but powerful in its dealing with ritual forms. Of all stylistic patterns, Wordsworth sees that of ritual as the most vital and comprehensive: within it he can blend sight and sound and movement in transcendental dedication. It is the favourite retreat of the baptized imagination; and while it serves perfectly the wish to touch all spiritual conditions, it can do so without the narrowness of judgment that seems unavoidable in any direct comparison of creeds. Thus in *Processions* the frenzy and compulsion of pagan rites are justly stated, but without prejudice to the poet's Christianity.

The finest achievement in this kind is the ode *On the Power of Sound;* and not in this kind only, for all the materials of his late poetry are here blended with supreme felicity. As physical eyesight failed, Wordsworth read few books, and he must have seen less as he walked abroad; but he still composed aloud, murmuring by the hour verses to himself. This too, I think, brought him to art in his old age, and a new love for the words themselves: unashamed delight in rhetorical utterance and much experimenting with the regular and the Pindaric ode, its fittest vehicles. Praise of sound, in the present poem, is also homage to poetry, as the thing that he was born to do.

Wordsworth approaches his subject, which is the divinity of sound, by way of the familiar road from nature to art. The voices of all natural things, streams and living creatures; echoes of voice

From rocky steep and rock-bestudded meadows
Flung back, and, in the sky's blue caves, reborn:

the voice that furthers action:

> the peasant's whistling breath that lightens
> His duteous toil of furrowing the green earth;

the voice that sustains patriot and martyr; the voice
that renders the lunatic

> aghast, as at the world
> Of reason partially let in—

all lead him to the conclusion stated at the exact middle
of the poem:

> Point not these mysteries to an Art
> Lodged above the starry pole. . . ?

In its second half the ode enquires more closely how
sound can be art, or "tutored passion". Working with
his favourite elements of story and ritual, Wordsworth
achieves an astonishing result:

The Gift to king Amphion
That walled a city with its melody
Was for belief no dream:—thy skill, Arion!
Could humanize the creatures of the sea,
Where men were monsters. A last grace he craves,
Leave for one chant;—the dulcet sound
Steals from the deck o'er willing waves,
And listening dolphins gather round.
Self-cast, as with a desperate course,
'Mid that strange audience, he bestrides
A proud One docile as a managed horse;
And singing, while the accordant hand
Sweeps his harp, the Master rides;
So shall he touch at length a friendly strand,
And he, with his preserver, shine starbright
In memory, through silent night.

The next stanza opens in heightened and frantic splendour:

> The pipe of Pan, to shepherds
> Couched in the shadow of Maenalian pines,
> Was passing sweet; the eyeballs of the leopards,
> That in high triumph drew the Lord of vines,
> How did they sparkle to the cymbal's clang!
> While Fauns and Satyrs beat the ground
> In cadence,—and Silenus swang
> This way and that, with wild-flowers crowned.

Myth, the kingship of story, a city walled with music; salvation in knowing what song to sing, and bright eternity reached through artistic action—the tale is of some great skill truly learnt, spiritual and gracious like the poetry itself, before it shifts to the terrible brilliance of the leopards' eyeballs and the beating on the ground.

Suddenly Wordsworth returns to the natural order, addressing those "who are longing to be rid Of fable", and bidding them

> hear
> The little sprinkling of cold earth that fell
> Echoed from the coffin-lid.

He then asks why Nature cannot achieve the artistic modulation of her own voices, adding, as a premonition of the truth, this fine Pythagorean comment:

> By one pervading spirit
> Of tones and numbers all things are controlled,
> As sages taught, where faith was found to merit
> Initiation in that mystery old.
> The heavens, whose aspect makes our minds as still
> As they themselves appear to be,
> Innumerable voices fill
> With everlasting harmony;
> The towering headlands, crowned with mist,
> Their feet among the billows, know
> That Ocean is a mighty harmonist. . . .

The Greek answer has already been anticipated by

> What more changeful than the sea?
> But over his great tides
> Fidelity presides,

from another of the late odes.[1] It prepares Wordsworth for his own conclusion. There is a kind of artistry, a meaningful ordering, in nature; in the ebb and flow of air and wash of sea. He had said so long ago, in the poetry of solitude and relationship, building thereon a magnificent and single structure. Glory is not now vanished, nor the affirmative, enfolding optimism of creative purpose: rather, delight becomes a sacrifice, and all this sounding movement confessional of the religion of gratitude:

> All worlds, all natures, mood and measure keep
> For praise and ceaseless gratulation, poured
> Into the ear of God, their Lord!

And so to the final stanza, telling how sound was before the beginning, and will survive the end:

> A Voice to Light gave Being;
> To Time, and Man his earth-born chronicler;
> A Voice shall finish doubt and dim foreseeing,
> And sweep away life's visionary stir;
> The trumpet (we, intoxicate with pride,
> Arm at its blast for deadly wars)
> To archangelic lips applied,
> The grave shall open, quench the stars.

Not sound exactly, but a Voice, which is also, in the poem's final line, "the word that shall not pass away". He is using a Semitic and European highroad in this language of the Word, a convention that becomes commandingly personal in his apocalyptic vision of Thought Self-Voiced, of divine Action-in-Utterance

[1] *The Triad.*

perfecting the Christian mystery of life. What can be
understood by the Word that was made flesh? For this
essay the answer must rest in the energy and coherence
of Wordsworth's transcendental symbolism.

I would not claim too much. There is no *Tempest*
lying unregarded in this late work, or even such poetry
as would reverse the universal judgment that the best
is early. Even so, it has been grossly underestimated,
too easily slipped into place to serve large theories of
Romantic defeat. The final privacy of greatness in style
has escaped notice. Wordsworth was not silenced by
the music of Christianity, nor stifled by Victorian
morals. He was profoundly changed. He writes now of
stories and strange ritual acts, of "doubt and dim fore-
seeing", of the witness of faith and the spiritual eye:
his waterfall-trumpeter is now the archangel.

## V

## EPILOGUE

THERE is an anxious problem of form in treating the work of sixty years within reasonable compass. The outline of a thesis must be clear—otherwise confusion and certain boredom; but it can scarcely be kept so without falling into the false simplicity of caricature: so that I ask help of all kinds, and especially belief in my questions. When, in his later poetry, Wordsworth tells of a noble shepherd, that

> both the undying fish that swim
> Through Bowscale-tarn did wait on him;
> The pair were servants of his eye
> In their immortality;[1]

and of men who

> in bells of crystal dive—
> Where winds and waters cease to strive—
> For no unholy visitings,
> Among the monsters of the Deep;
> And all the sad and precious things
> Which there in ghastly silence sleep;[2]

and of boulders strewn about a deserted mountain pass that appear

> Tents of a camp that never shall be raised:[3]

he is describing the natural world in a way that seems to me at once arresting and utterly foreign to his youth. This raises the largest of my initial questions—one that can be of no interest to him who thinks this verse

---

[1] *Song at the Feast of Brougham Castle.*  [2] *To Enterprise.*
[3] *The Pass of Kirkstone.*

undistinguished, or else close in imagination to Wordsworth's early work.

But if so much is granted, it becomes possible to walk more delicately. Solitude and childhood, once at the heart of his early poetry, do not entirely disappear: they play a different and smaller part, as agents of otherness; and between this beginning and this end lies the poetry of indecision. Consider *The Solitary Reaper*, written in 1805, the year of his brother's death, of *The Prelude's* conclusion, and of the poem about Peele Castle; and inviting comparison with Lucy and the Danish Boy, solitary singers of 1798 and 1799. The later poem is very successful; but in its quality of life size, in the precise humanity of its wistfulness— "Will no one tell me what she sings?"—the singer and her song are far removed from these others. Again it seems pertinent to wonder why; to consider where his middle age is weak, and where, within the limits of a smaller naturalism, it achieves a certain strength.

Such questions, even if well directed, do not establish universal criteria for literary judgment: they are personal to Wordsworth, and they serve other ends than that of judgment, which is but one aspect of the critical activity and which appears to good effect only when it attends the struggle to participate. Where I cannot share I feel most ill at ease. Thus I have been able to make almost nothing of Wordsworth's heroic manner, of the careful Miltonic sonnets and the patriotic odes; and am afraid not of simple blundering as to their merit, but of a deep failure of apprehension as to their bearing upon his mind's quality: for there can be no doubt that an element of the extrovert and brazen runs through its whole fabric, and works in hidden ways. The famous sonnets read like exercises, repellent often in their provincial self-importance and bourgeois noble enthusiasm. Wordsworth's use of the sonnet, as verse-paragraph, best shown in the River Duddon Sequence,

is a different matter: here the movement of his meaning
is so attempered to the limits of the medium as to give
a redeeming fluency to his slightest work, as to this,
published in a newspaper and not considered by the
poet to be worth reprinting:

> I find it written of Simonides
> That travelling in strange countries once he found
> A corpse that lay expos'd upon the ground,
> For which, with pains, he caused due obsequies
> To be performed, and paid all holy fees.
> Soon after, this man's Ghost unto him came
> And told him not to sail as was his aim,
> On board a ship then ready for the seas.
> Simonides, admonished by the ghost,
> Remained behind: the ship the following day
> Set sail, was wrecked, and all on board were lost.
> Thus was the tenderest Poet that could be,
> Who sang in ancient Greece his moving lay,
> Saved out of many by his piety.[1]

But his sonnets in the grand manner obtrude their box-
like form until I tire of witnessing so many storms in
so many teacups, and find comfort in the slender story
of Simonides. Even so, it is not enough to dislike this
poetry and to give a reason: I am still uncertain how to
fit it into my picture or how honestly to exclude it—
aware of being defeated by the individuality of consciousness, and not at all sure what it was to be Wordsworth.

Like all books, this is a public thing made for men
to stare at; and, while doubt and failure are in mind,
mention should be made of the attempt to say something of speculative interest about thought and language, something that sprang out of Wordsworth's
poetry and his scattered reflections upon poetry. When
he was confronted with the vulgar eighteenth-century

---

[1] *P.W.*, Vol. III. p. 408.

definition of language as the clothing of thought, Wordsworth replied that language is not thought's dress but its incarnation.[1] His more specific remarks about language are nearly always consistent with this statement of general principle, as, for example, his protest against the Augustan element in Byron's poetry:

> the sentiment by being expressed in an *antithetical* manner, is taken out of the Region of high and imaginative feeling, to be placed in that of point and epigram. To illustrate my meaning and for no other purpose I refer to my own Lines on the Wye [*Tintern Abbey*], where you will find the same sentiment not formally put as it is here, but ejaculated as it were fortuitously in the musical succession of preconceived feeling.[2]

Wordsworth rejects the notion that poets, or other men, think a thought and then look for an attractive way of presenting it. Language is not like that. What, then, of the distinction between knowing what you think and knowing how to say it? Implicit in his remarks about language, and especially in his reckless commendations of spontaneous utterance, is the will to free the activity of thinking from association with the concept thought. The abstract question is for men like Coleridge: he is concerned in a practical way, as an empirical psychologist, with an activity which is certainly polymorphous—he would not have denied musical or mathematical thinking—but which in one of its forms is linguistic; and his knowledge of this kind does not tally with conventional descriptions.

He dislikes the dress metaphor because it suggests that language is independent of other things in a way that is untrue. It goes wrong at the start by implying that there are naked thoughts. However importunate the hubbub of life below the level of expression, only

---

[1] Reported by De Quincey, Essay on Style, *Works*, Vol. X.
[2] *Letters*, 1811-20 (ed. de Selincourt), p. 790.

error can result from talking of thoughts arising, like Venus, from the sea of brute experience; for the false dichotomy of thought and word is immediately encouraged. This is partly a matter of chronology, of Wordsworth's testifying, as other artists have done, that although you cannot start work until you know what you want to do, it is equally the case that you do not know what you want to do until you have done it: so the thought has no priority in time. But more important is his objection to the analogy of the body and its dress. Even if Venus-Thoughts were described as emerging fully clothed, he would still have been unsatisfied. You can do what you like with clothes, tell any story you please, and if language is a kind of clothing, all use of language is a playing with words.

As always, Wordsworth's ultimate problem is a moral and aesthetic complex. Language is moral because of the way in which it is bound to life: it is poetic for the same reason. His quarrel with the dress metaphor affords an introduction to this complex since the status of language is endangered in both connexions when it is associated with adornment or even with working clothes. A moral-poetic responsibility is evaded by those who think of something ready made, waiting to be assumed. And so he challenged the divorce of language and life, the whole idea of poetic diction, the principles involved in Gray's famous statement that there is one language for art and another for nature. He believed in a single language, no further from the living heart of things than the breath that bears it.

> For the tired slave, Song lifts the languid oar,
> And bids it aptly fall:

the Sound Ode refuses to treat language as accessory to action: it is one of action's modes, and perhaps the most effective. The song that lifts the oar will also, in

his own poetry, "deal boldly with substantial things":
he speaks of "the intellectual power" that

> through words and things,
> Went sounding on, a dim and perilous way.[1]

Language is in the world, pushing and being pushed
against.

When he criticizes Byron's poetry for inhabiting the
region of point and epigram, having forsaken that of
imaginative feeling, Wordsworth is protesting against
a retirement from the world, encouraged by the dress
metaphor, which makes language unable to deal boldly
with things. Projected as the conceptual currency of
men, language becomes an abstract structure, impotent
because of its isolation, the external instrument of
analytic intelligence by means of which, the Lyrical
Ballad maintains, "we murder to dissect". How can
language be more than this? In his use of the incarnation metaphor Wordsworth strikes an attitude. There
is here no contrast of living and inorganic natures, or
of enduring form and its chance habit. Above all, there
is nothing to be made and mended, no independent
construction to be managed. The dress metaphor will
not do. Nor will that variation of the dress metaphor in
which we suppose our thoughts to be shrouded in a
diaphanous linguistic film. This is to reduce language
in a different way, by ignoring it. Wordsworth's own
solution is to abandon the idea of structure for that of
function, and in his poetry to embark on the activity of
language.

I once believed that this poetry held a lesson for the
modern philosophy of linguistic analysis. In Wordsworth's solitude and relationship and in the features of
his landscape there is a conspiracy of inner and outer
which might properly be called philosophical: one may
find a public context for this private effort in the tradi-

[1] *The Excursion*, Bk. III. 700.

tions of western thinking, and especially in the Cartesian dichotomy of thing and thought. Confidence in the relational power of language inspires his attempt, not to deny this dichotomy, but to make it metaphysically tolerable; while an extreme sensitiveness to the logical limits of language has led philosophy in this generation to turn its back on the possibility of metaphysics. But now, when the excitement that attends beginnings has died away, it seems to me that Wordsworth has nothing to teach modern philosophers which can be turned by them to philosophical advantage. Many of them take no pleasure in the estrangement of philosophy and wisdom, do not suppose that language is a symbolic structure, abstract and determined like that of mathematics, or even wish that it were so. But the logical distress is real: within the terms of a cognitive discipline there is very little they can find to say.

It is true that Wordsworth places over against the discursive intellect a higher and still rational faculty which he calls

> clearest insight, amplitude of mind,
> And reason in her most exalted mood:[1]

and in this thrusting beyond the logic of the understanding there is a genuine metaphysical passion, a thing tougher in its mental stuff than any cult of poetic sensibility. But this is not coincident with the profession of philosophy, and does not entitle us to throw him to very professional lions. With regard to his poetry of the supernatural, I think it would be misleading to speak of philosophy at all. Not that there is anything unclear about the visions which "appeared in presence of the spiritual eye": but visions are visions, whereas the early work is of a quite different order. Here I wish to have it both ways: to claim enough of system to justify the title of Philosopher-Poet first given him by Coleridge,

---

[1] *The Prelude*, Bk. XIII. 169.

o

and also to avoid any joining issue with contemporary thought, even though this has become in one sense a matter of language, of which Wordsworth had a larger knowledge than philosophers.

His attitude to language is consistent with the systematic whole which I have called solitude and relationship. Language serves the principle of action and reaction, of sympathy or reciprocity, through participation. Hence his curious theory of the imagination as a conferring or abstracting of properties so that the object may itself "react upon the mind";[1] and hence the personal ambition to celebrate the mind's marriage to the world, to

> chant, in lonely peace, the spousal verse
> Of this great consummation:—and, by words
> That speak of nothing more than what we are,
> Would I arouse the sensual from their sleep
> Of Death. . . .[2]

The poet is more than chronicler or commentator because his language is woven into the texture of this process, as a function of it, and not in the ordinary sense as a description. Reality and language are a going concern.

The linguistic activity is therefore central, and at the same time there is no problem of language, no *thing* about which to be perplexed. "Where meditation was," from *The Pedlar*, is one of Wordsworth's concretized abstractions; and this Roman secret is the whole secret. Wordsworth saw the world with a systematic eccentricity due to his being born out of time in attitude to mental and physical. This means, in respect of language, an instinctive grasp of history: he is no more concerned about the difference between language and not-language than the baby who uses his voice as the most effective way of procuring the presence of his

---

[1] See pp. 44-5.    [2] Preface to *The Excursion*.

mother. The infancy of the race may have been a little like that—the remote ancestor of the poet who wished to deal boldly with things.

Born into time, Wordsworth said that language is the incarnation of thought. Thought incarnate is not thought expressed, or there would be no need to distinguish the word and the mathematical symbol; but when he refuses to allow that thoughts are clothed in words, he fears not so much a direct confusion with mathematics as the reducing of language to a conceptual instrument, external to those who use it. Language must have a corresponding inwardness in order to enact the reciprocity of nature.

We begin, then, with the concretized abstractions: with the River Duddon which has

> No meaner Poet than the whistling Blast,
> And Desolation is thy Patron-saint;

and Toussaint L'Ouverture, imprisoned for defying Napoleon:

> There's not a breathing of the common wind
> That will forget thee; thou hast great allies;
> Thy friends are exultations, agonies,
> And love. . . .

In both cases the abstract nouns are associated with the action of the wind, which in its double movement is the most important feature of the Wordsworthian landscape. This is what they mean.

Four-syllable abstract nouns in "-ion" are very common in Wordsworth's poetry, and usually, as here with "exultations", they occupy the fourth to the seventh syllables of the decasyllabic line. *Tintern Abbey*, the supreme example of his blank-verse prosody, has three, all in this position. "Visitation", an important word in *The Prelude*, of the same kind as "Presence" and "Power", appears three times in the 1805 version

of Book I, and on each occasion it holds the middle of
the line, immense, bare, a windlike echoing. Wordsworth often uses these nouns at a decisive point in his
argument. This is true of

> the spousal verse
> Of this great consummation

which we have just noticed, and of the "authentic
tidings" of

> central peace, subsisting at the heart
> Of endless agitation

with which he concludes the account of the child
listening to the shell in *The Excursion*. For this and for
other reasons, Arnold should not have said that Wordsworth has no style.

The famous sonnet that begins:

> It is a beauteous evening, calm and free,
> The holy time is quiet as a Nun
> Breathless with adoration; . . .

betrays his authorship in several ways. "Adoration" is
one sign. The simile is another, and the strange un-
violence in which it relates very different natures, the
woman and the hour. "Holy" is certainly a kind of
bond between them, but the essence of the thing is his
unselfconscious movement from abstract to concrete.
In his Westminster Bridge sonnet he says that the city

> doth, like a garment, wear
> The beauty of the morning. . . .

To this a friend objected that he goes on to describe the
city as "silent, bare", thus contradicting himself.
Wordsworth admitted this fault, and in a letter he
altered the sonnet so as to omit the garment image.[1]

---

[1] *Letters*, 1831-40 (ed. de Selincourt), p. 812.

But the alteration was never adopted. He felt that the image was necessary, and we can see why:

> Earth has not anything to show more fair:
> Dull would he be of soul who could pass by
> A sight so touching in its majesty:
> This City now doth, like a garment, wear
> The beauty of the morning; silent, bare. . . .

It is needed to sustain, strengthen, and illuminate the "sight so touching in its majesty". The weak physical metaphor of "touching" gains sudden pathetic force through this association; and in the balancing of "touching . . . majesty" with "garment . . . beauty" the poem's nature is confirmed.

"Breathless", too, from the Holy Time sonnet, is characteristic of Wordsworth. There is unexpected tension and effort in the shift of stress to the first syllable, and the situation of the word allows its silent concentration to flood back through the line end pause. He makes a similar, though more obvious use of this pause in *The Prelude* account of the boy who hooted to the owls and then waited for them to answer him:

> Then sometimes, in that silence, while he hung
> Listening. . . .[1]

Language takes time—time backwards as well as time forwards.

This poet of many short words has a very careful use of the single long word. The best of the Ecclesiastical Sonnets compares the outward forms of truth with a ruined tower,

> which royally did wear
> Her crown of weeds, but could not even sustain
> Some casual shout that broke the silent air,
> Or the unimaginable touch of Time.[2]

---

[1] Bk. V. 406.                    [2] *Mutability*.

One of his many lonely women wonders what has become of her son: [Perhaps thou]

> hast been summoned to the deep,
> Thou, and all thy mates, to keep
> An incommunicable sleep.[1]

When he stole game from another boy's snare, Wordsworth heard, following him,

> sounds
> Of undistinguishable motion, steps
> Almost as silent as the turf they trod.[2]

In *Tintern Abbey* he speaks of the state

> In which the heavy and the weary weight
> Of all this unintelligible world
> Is lightened. . . .

All these words arrest the movement of the sense which is usually easy and swift, though in the last example laboriously slow; and while they are going on they give the means of new awareness through release from the poem's time scale. The murmured succession, the fearful patter, the prolonged striving, are different kinds of escape almost from language itself, to experience-worlds outside language.

These words are united in their negative form as well as in their length. Wordsworth carries his delight in negatives to the point of tiresome mannerism: there are too many double negatives, such as "not unnoticed"; too much rhetorical piling of adjective on adjective— "unchastened, unsubdued, unawed, unraised"—and pointless circumlocution—"not seldom" and "nor seldom" appear five times in the final text of *The Prelude*. But the roots of this practice run very deep: the balance of positive and negative is a mode of reciprocity, like echo and reflection in his landscape. It also

---

[1] *The Affliction of Margaret.*     [2] *The Prelude*, Bk. I. 330.

shows the unmathematical nature of language. If two
minuses make a plus, it is a special kind of plus: the
negative form can be on its own account heart-piercing.

> Six weeks beneath the moving sea
> He lay in slumber quietly;
> Unforced by wind or wave
> To quit the Ship for which he died. . . .[1]

Wordsworth believed that the problem of thought
issuing into language had been considered too much in
isolation, at the expense of language's impingement
upon the very mentality of mind. In this he felt no
logical embarrassment: the double movement was as
evident to him as the principle of sympathy in nature,
was in fact an aspect of that principle. We saw how, in
*The Borderers*, a star once held a man from murder.
Words have their corresponding authority; and it is
the moral-poetic duty of all who use them to command
attention of the precise quality required, and to command it for true ends. Sometimes language will fail:
here, as with Nature's unrequited love for Peter Bell,
Wordsworth's optimism was always precarious.

The poet's command of attention has often been
spoken of as an incantatory skill. This is peculiarly ill-
suited to Wordsworth's matter of fact and his reliance
on daylight powers. Nor is the idea of controlled
ambiguity in poetic statement much more serviceable;
for it must not imply, in his case, intellectual deliberation. Nor is the thing experienced as ambiguity. In *The
Prelude* he speaks of

> heights
> Clothed in the sunshine of the withering fern.[2]

This, the 1850 and final text, has no less than five fore-
runners.[3] The 1805 text speaks simply of "the moun-

---

[1] *Sweet Flower! belike* . . .                    [2] 1850, Bk. VI. 10.
[3] *Wordsworth's "Prelude"* (ed. de Selincourt), pp. 170-1.

tain pomp of Autumn", which is later expanded by
reference to the colour of the hills under autumn sun:

> the beauty and pomp
> Of Autumn, entering under azure skies
> To mountains clothed in yellow robe of fire.

He may have had the colour of the vegetation in mind,
as well as that of the sunlight, but he has not yet
succeeded in saying so. In the fourth version he gives
up the attempt to mention colour, and returns in effect
to 1805. The "golden fern" appears in his fifth version,
which paves the way for the final confluence of sun and
vegetation. Autumn is not mentioned because the
season is already known from the context.

"Clothed in sunshine" is easy: so is "clothed in the
withering fern". But "clothed in the sunshine of the
withering fern" is odd, its oddness resting in "of", and
the different kinds of work it has to do. One might say
that the word is ambiguous; but this would be a perverse way of expressing it, since the block-impression
of the phrase is clear, even without knowing its history.
We admit "of" as we admit others of Wordsworth's
busy prepositions: in their degree they are the stride
of his thought.

"Every great and original writer, in proportion as he
is great or original, must himself . . . teach the art by
which he is to be seen."[1] I have applied Wordsworth's
general rule to his own poetry, in the hope of showing
a *fait accompli*; the art well taught, the attention commanded. This is an achievement shared by the concretized abstractions, the mental-physical imagery, the
captive labours of the verb "to be"; by the short
words, the long words, and all the time and space of
language. Shared, too, by language's humblest parts.
"And", more frequent in Wordsworth than in any
poet, is the preserver of extreme structural simplicity

---

[1] *Letters*, 1806-11, x. (ed. de Selincourt), p. 130.

through hundreds of lines of *Prelude* narrative: if the ice is thin, the skating is light and swift. "And" helps to sustain the calm elevation of *Tintern Abbey:*

> And the round ocean and the living air,
> And the blue sky, and in the mind of man. . . .

By its monotony, its insistence on the particular, "and" develops Wordsworth's expository style, in common with other words of modest function—"but", "thus", "therefore". Notice, in *Tintern Abbey*, how the two cadences:

> Therefore am I still
> A lover of the meadows

and

> Therefore let the moon
> Shine on thee:

introduce a logical, knitted quality; cause the reader to glance behind and collect the poem for himself.

"Therefore" is a confidence trick and "of" an ambiguity only if Wordsworth's view of language is rejected for one more congenial because less fateful. Otherwise, following him to "the great Nature that exists in works Of mighty Poets", we can share what seems to be a divine joke—that this poet should bear the name he does.

# INDEX OF PERSONS

# INDEX OF WORDSWORTH'S POEMS

Printed in Great Britain
by NOVELLO & COMPANY LIMITED
LONDON W.I

achieved their most signal triumph. A swift ship, flying before the south-west monsoon, brought the evil tidings in few days to Calcutta. In twenty-four hours the Governor-General had framed a complete plan of policy adapted to the altered state of affairs. The struggle with Hyder was a struggle for life and death. All minor objects must be sacrificed to the preservation of the Carnatic. The disputes with the Mahrattas must be accommodated. A large military force and a supply of money must be instantly sent to Madras. But even these measures would be insufficient, unless the war, hitherto so grossly mismanaged, were placed under the direction of a vigorous mind. It was no time for trifling. Hastings determined to resort to an extreme exercise of power, to suspend the incapable governor of Fort St. George, to send Sir Eyre Coote to oppose Hyder, and to entrust that distinguished general with the whole administration of the war.

In spite of the sullen opposition of Francis, who had now recovered from his wound, and had returned to the Council, the Governor-General's wise and firm policy was approved by the majority of the board. The reinforcements were sent off with great expedition, and reached Madras before the French armament arrived in the Indian seas. Coote, broken by age and disease, was no longer the Coote of Wandewash; but he was still a resolute and skilful commander. The progress of Hyder was arrested; and in a few months the great victory of Porto Novo retrieved the honour of the English arms.

In the meantime Francis had returned to England, and Hastings was now left perfectly unfettered. Wheler had gradually been relaxing in his opposition, and, after the departure of his vehement and implacable colleague, cooperated heartily with the Governor-General, whose influence over the British in India, always great, had, by the vigour and success of his recent measures, been considerably increased.

But, though the difficulties arising from factions within the Council were at an end, another class of difficulties had become more pressing than ever. The financial embarrassment was extreme. Hastings had to find the means, not only of carrying on the government of Bengal, but of maintaining a most costly war against both Indian and European enemies in the Carnatic, and of making remittances to England. A few years before this time he had obtained relief by plundering the Mogul and enslaving the Rohillas; nor were the resources of his fruitful mind by any means exhausted.

His first design was on Benares, a city which in wealth, population, dignity, and sanctity, was among the foremost of Asia. It was commonly believed that half a million of human beings was crowded into that labyrinth of lofty alleys, rich with shrines, and minarets, and balconies, and carved oriels, to which the sacred apes clung by hundreds. The traveller could scarcely make his way through the press of holy mendicants and not less holy bulls. The broad and stately flights of steps which descended from these swarming haunts to the bathing-places along the Ganges were worn every day by the footsteps of an innumerable multitude of worshippers. The schools and temples drew crowds of pious Hindoos from every province where the Brahminical faith was known. Hundreds of devotees came thither every month to die: for it was believed that a peculiarly happy fate awaited the man who should pass from the sacred city into the sacred river. Nor was superstition the only motive which allured strangers to that great metropolis. Commerce had as many pilgrims as religion. All along the shores of the venerable stream lay great fleets of vessels laden with rich merchandize. From the looms of Benares went forth the most delicate silks that adorned the balls of St. James's and of the *Petit Trianon*; and, in the bazars, the muslins of Bengal and the sabres of Oude were mingled with the jewels of Golconda and the shawls of Cashmere. This rich capital, and the surrounding tract, had long been under the immediate rule of a Hindoo prince, who rendered homage to the Mogul emperors. During the great anarchy of India, the lords of Benares became independent of the court of Delhi, but were compelled to submit to the authority of the Nabob of Oude. Oppressed by this formidable neighbour, they invoked the protection of the English. The English protection was given; and at length the Nabob Vizier, by a solemn treaty, ceded all his rights over Benares to the Company. From that time the Rajah was the vassal of the government of Bengal, acknowledged its supremacy, and engaged to send an annual tribute to Fort William. This tribute Cheyte Sing, the reigning prince, had paid with strict punctuality.

Respecting the precise nature of the legal relation between the Company and the Rajah of Benares, there has been much warm and acute controversy. On the one side, it has been maintained that Cheyte Sing was merely a great subject on whom the superior power had a right to call for aid in the necessities of the empire. On the other side, it has been contended that he was an independent prince, that the only claim which the Company had upon him was for a fixed tribute, and that, while the fixed tribute was regularly paid, as it assuredly was, the English had no more right to exact any further contribution from him than to demand subsidies from

Holland or Denmark. Nothing is easier than to find precedents and analogies in favour of either view.

Our own impression is that neither view is correct. It was too much the habit of English politicians to take it for granted that there was in India a known and definite constitution by which questions of this kind were to be decided. The truth is that, during the interval which elapsed between the fall of the house of Tamerlane and the establishment of the British ascendency, there was no such constitution. The old order of things had passed away; the new order of things was not yet formed. All was transition, confusion, obscurity. Every body kept his head as he best might, and scrambled for whatever he could get. There have been similar seasons in Europe. The time of the dissolution of the Carlovingian empire is an instance. Who would think of seriously discussing the question, what extent of pecuniary aid and of obedience Hugh Capet had a constitutional right to demand from the Duke of Britanny or the Duke of Normandy? The words "constitutional right" had, in that state of society, no meaning. If Hugh Capet laid hands on all the possessions of the Duke of Normandy, this might be unjust and immoral; but it would not be illegal, in the sense in which the ordinances of Charles the Tenth were illegal. If, on the other hand, the Duke of Normandy made war on Hugh Capet, this might be unjust and immoral; but it would not be illegal in the sense in which the expedition of Prince Louis Buonaparte was illegal.

Very similar to this was the state of India sixty years ago. Of the existing governments not a single one could lay claim to legitimacy, or could plead any other title than recent occupation. There was scarcely a province in which the real sovereignty and the nominal sovereignty were not disjoined. Titles and forms were still retained which implied that the heir of Tamerlane was an absolute ruler, and that the Nabobs of the provinces were his lieutenants. In reality, he was a captive. The Nabobs were in some places independent princes. In other places, as in Bengal and the Carnatic, they had, like their master, become mere phantoms, and the Company was supreme. Among the Mahrattas again the heir of Sevajee still kept the title of Rajah; but he was a prisoner, and his prime minister, the Peshwa, had become the hereditary chief of the state. The Peshwa, in his turn, was fast sinking into the same degraded situation to which he had reduced the Rajah. It was, we believe, impossible to find, from the Himalayas to Mysore, a single government which was at once a government *de facto* and a government *de jure*, which possessed the physical means of making itself feared by its neighbours and subjects, and which had at the same time the authority derived from law and long prescription.

Hastings clearly discerned, what was hidden from most of his contemporaries, that such a state of things gave immense advantages to a ruler of great talents and few scruples. In every international question that could arise, he had his option between the *de facto* ground and the *de jure* ground; and the probability was that one of those grounds would sustain any claim that it might be convenient for him to make, and enable him to resist any claim made by others. In every controversy, accordingly, he resorted to the plea which suited his immediate purpose, without troubling himself in the least about consistency; and thus he scarcely ever failed to find what, to persons of short memories and scanty information, seemed to be a justification for what he wanted to do. Sometimes the nabob of Bengal is a shadow, sometimes a monarch. Sometimes the Vizier is a mere deputy, sometimes an independent potentate. If it is expedient for the Company to show some legal title to the revenues of Bengal, the grant under the seal of the Mogul is brought forward as an instrument of the highest authority. When the Mogul asks for the rents which were reserved to him by that very grant, he is told that he is a mere pageant, that the English power rests on a very different foundation from a charter given by him, that he is welcome to play at royalty as long as he likes, but that he must expect no tribute from the real masters of India.

It is true that it was in the power of others, as well as of Hastings, to practise this legerdemain; but in the controversies of governments, sophistry is of little use unless it be backed by power. There is a principle which Hastings was fond of asserting in the strongest terms, and on which he acted with undeviating steadiness. It is a principle which, we must own, though it may be grossly abused, can hardly be disputed in the present state of public law. It is this, that where an ambiguous question arises between two governments, there is, if they cannot agree, no appeal except to force, and that the opinion of the stronger must prevail. Almost every question was ambiguous in India. The English government was the strongest in India. The consequences are obvious. The English government might do exactly what it chose.

The English government now chose to wring money out of Cheyte Sing. It had formerly been convenient to treat him as a sovereign prince; it was now convenient to treat him as a subject. Dexterity inferior to that of Hastings could easily find, in the general chaos of laws and customs, arguments for either course. Hastings wanted a great supply. It was known that Cheyte Sing had a large revenue, and it was suspected that he had accumulated a treasure. Nor was he a favourite at Calcutta. He had, when the Governor-General was in great difficulties, courted the favour of Francis and Clavering. Hastings who, less we believe from evil passions than from policy, seldom left an injury unpunished, was not sorry that the fate of Cheyte Sing should teach neighbouring princes the same lesson which the fate of Nuncomar had already impressed on the inhabitants of Bengal.

In 1778, on the first breaking out of the war with France, Cheyte Sing was called upon to pay, in addition to his fixed tribute, an extraordinary contribution of fifty thousand pounds. In 1779, an equal sum was exacted. In 1780, the demand was renewed. Cheyte Sing, in the hope of obtaining some indulgence, secretly offered the Governor-General a bribe of twenty thousand pounds. Hastings took the money; and his enemies have maintained that he took it intending to keep it. He certainly concealed the transaction, for a time, both from the Council in Bengal and from the Directors at home; nor did he ever give any satisfactory reason for the concealment. Public spirit, or the fear of detection, however, determined him to withstand the temptation. He paid over the bribe to the Company's treasury, and insisted that the Rajah should instantly comply with the demands of the English government. The Rajah, after the fashion of his countrymen, shuffled, solicited, and pleaded poverty. The grasp of Hastings was not to be so eluded. He added to the requisition another ten thousand pounds as a fine for delay, and sent troops to exact the money.

The money was paid. But this was not enough. The late events in the south of India had increased the financial embarrassments of the Company. Hastings was determined to plunder Cheyte Sing, and, for that end, to fasten a quarrel on him. Accordingly, the Rajah was now required to keep a body of cavalry for the service of the British government. He objected and evaded. This was exactly what the Governor-General wanted. He had now a pretext for treating the wealthiest of his vassals as a criminal. "I resolved," —these are the words of Hastings himself,—"to draw from his guilt the means of relief to the Company's distresses, to make him pay largely for his pardon, or to exact a severe vengeance for past delinquency." The plan was simply this, to demand larger and larger contributions till the Rajah should be driven to remonstrate, then to call his remonstrance a crime, and to punish him by confiscating all his possessions.

Cheyte Sing was in the greatest dismay. He offered two hundred thousand pounds to propitiate the British government. But

M—14*

Hastings replied that nothing less than half a million would be accepted. Nay, he began to think of selling Benares to Oude, as he had formerly sold Allahabad and Rohilcund. The matter was one which could not be well managed at a distance; and Hastings resolved to visit Benares.

Cheyte Sing received his liege lord with every mark of reverence, came near sixty miles, with his guards, to meet and escort the illustrious visiter, and expressed his deep concern at the displeasure of the English. He even took off his turban, and laid it in the lap of Hastings, a gesture which in India marks the most profound submission and devotion. Hastings behaved with cold and repulsive severity. Having arrived at Benares, he sent to the Rajah a paper containing the demands of the government of Bengal. The Rajah, in reply, attempted to clear himself from the accusations brought against him. Hastings, who wanted money and not excuses, was not to be put off by the ordinary artifices of Eastern negotiation. He instantly ordered the Rajah to be arrested and placed under the custody of two companies of sepoys.

In taking these strong measures, Hastings scarcely showed his usual judgment. It is probable that, having had little opportunity of personally observing any part of the population of India, except the Bengalees, he was not fully aware of the difference between their character and that of the tribes which inhabit the upper provinces. He was now in a land far more favourable to the vigour of the human frame than the Delta of the Ganges; in a land fruitful of soldiers, who have been found worthy to follow English battalions to the charge and into the breach. The Rajah was popular among his subjects. His administration had been mild; and the prosperity of the district which he governed presented a striking contrast to the depressed state of Bahar under our rule, and a still more striking contrast to the misery of the provinces which were cursed by the tyranny of the Nabob Vizier. The national and religious prejudices with which the English were regarded throughout India were peculiarly intense in the metropolis of the Brahminical superstition. It can therefore scarcely be doubted that the Governor-General, before he outraged the dignity of Cheyte Sing by an arrest, ought to have assembled a force capable of bearing down all opposition. This had not been done. The handful of sepoys who attended Hastings would probably have been sufficient to overawe Moorshedabad, or the Black Town of Calcutta. But they were unequal to a conflict with the hardy rabble of Benares. The streets surrounding the palace were filled by an immense multitude, of whom a large proportion, as is usual in Upper India, wore arms. The tumult became a fight, and the fight a massacre. The English officers defended themselves with desperate courage against overwhelming numbers, and fell, as became them, sword in hand. The sepoys were butchered. The gates were forced. The captive prince, neglected by his gaolers during the confusion, discovered an outlet which opened on the precipitous bank of the Ganges, let himself down to the water by a string made of the turbans of his attendants, found a boat, and escaped to the opposite shore.

If Hastings had, by indiscreet violence, brought himself into a difficult and perilous situation, it is only just to acknowledge that he extricated himself with even more than his usual ability and presence of mind. He had only fifty men with him. The building in which he had taken up his residence was on every side blockaded by the insurgents. But his fortitude remained unshaken. The Rajah from the other side of the river sent apologies and liberal offers. They were not even answered. Some subtle and enterprizing men were found who undertook to pass through the throng of enemies, and to convey the intelligence of the late events to the English cantonments. It is the fashion of the natives of India to wear large earrings of gold. When they travel, the rings are laid aside, lest the precious metal should tempt some gang of robbers; and, in place of the ring, a quill or a roll of paper is inserted in the orifice to prevent it from closing. Hastings placed in the ears of his messengers letters rolled up in the smallest compass. Some of these letters were addressed to the commanders of the English troops. One was written to assure his wife of his safety. One was to the envoy whom he had sent to negotiate with the Mahrattas. Instructions for the negotiation were needed; and the Governor-General framed them in that situation of extreme danger, with as much composure as if he had been writing in his palace at Calcutta.

Things, however, were not yet at the worst. An English officer of more spirit than judgment, eager to distinguish himself, made a premature attack on the insurgents beyond the river. His troops were entangled in narrow streets, and assailed by a furious population. He fell, with many of his men; and the survivors were forced to retire.

This event produced the effect which has never failed to follow every check, however slight, sustained in India by the English arms. For hundreds of miles round, the whole country was in commotion. The entire population of the district of Benares took arms. The fields were abandoned by the husbandmen, who thronged to defend their prince. The infection spread to Oude. The oppressed people of that province rose up against the Nabob Vizier, refused to pay their imposts, and put the revenue officers to flight. Even Bahar was ripe for revolt. The hopes of Cheyte Sing began to rise. Instead of imploring mercy in the humble style of a vassal, he began to talk the language of a conqueror, and threatened, it was said, to sweep the white usurpers out of the land. But the English troops were now assembling fast. The officers, and even the private men, regarded the Governor-General with enthusiastic attachment, and flew to his aid with an alacrity which, as he boasted, had never been shown on any other occasion. Major Popham, a brave and skilful soldier who had highly distinguished himself in the Mahratta war, and in whom the Governor-General reposed the greatest confidence, took the command. The tumultuary army of the Rajah was put to rout. His fastnesses were stormed. In a few hours, above thirty thousand men left his standard, and returned to their ordinary avocations. The unhappy prince fled from his country for ever. His fair domain was added to the British dominions. One of his relations indeed was appointed rajah; but the Rajah of Benares was henceforth to be, like the Nabob of Bengal, a mere pensioner.

By this revolution, an addition of two hundred thousand pounds a-year was made to the revenues of the Company. But the immediate relief was not as great as had been expected. The treasure laid up by Cheyte Sing had been popularly estimated at a million sterling. It turned out to be about a fourth part of that sum; and, such as it was, it was seized by the army and divided as prize-money.

Disappointed in his expectations from Benares, Hastings was more violent than he would otherwise have been, in his dealings with Oude. Sujah Dowlah had long been dead. His son and successor, Asaph-ul-Dowlah, was one of the weakest and most vicious even of Eastern princes. His life was divided between torpid repose and the most odious forms of sensuality. In his court there was boundless waste, throughout his dominions wretchedness and disorder. He had been, under the skilful management of the English government, gradually sinking from the rank of an independent prince to that of a vassal of the Company. It was only by the help of a British brigade that he could be secure from the aggressions of neighbours who despised his weakness, and from the vengeance of subjects who detested his tyranny. A brigade was furnished; and he engaged to defray the charge of paying and maintaining it. From that time his independence was at an end. Hastings was not a man to lose the advantage which he had thus gained. The Nabob soon began to complain of the burden which he had undertaken to bear. His revenues, he said, were falling off;

his servants were unpaid; he could no longer support the expense of the arrangement which he had sanctioned. Hastings would not listen to these representations. The Vizier, he said, had invited the Government of Bengal to send him troops, and had promised to pay for them. The troops had been sent. How long the troops were to remain in Oude was a matter not settled by the treaty. It remained, therefore, to be settled between the contracting parties. But the contracting parties differed. Who then must decide? The stronger.

Hastings also argued that, if the English force was withdrawn, Oude would certainly become a prey to anarchy, and would probably be overrun by a Mahratta army. That the finances of Oude were embarrassed he admitted. But he contended, not without reason, that the embarrassment was to be attributed to the incapacity and vices of Asaph-ul-Dowlah himself, and that, if less were spent on the troops, the only effect would be that more would be squandered on worthless favourites.

Hastings had intended, after settling the affairs of Benares, to visit Lucknow, and there to confer with Asaph-ul-Dowlah. But the obsequious courtesy of the Nabob Vizier prevented this visit. With a small train he hastened to meet the Governor-General. An interview took place in the fortress which, from the crest of the precipitous rock of Chunar, looks down on the waters of the Ganges.

At first sight it might appear impossible that the negotiation should come to an amicable close. Hastings wanted an extraordinary supply of money. Asaph-ul-Dowlah wanted to obtain a remission of what he already owed. Such a difference seemed to admit of no compromise. There was, however, one course satisfactory to both sides, one course by which it was possible to relieve the finances both of Oude and of Bengal; and that course was adopted. It was simply this, that the Governor-General and the Nabob Vizier should join to rob a third party; and the third party whom they determined to rob was the parent of one of the robbers.

The mother of the late Nabob, and his wife, who was the mother of the present Nabob, were known as the Begums or Princesses of Oude. They had possessed great influence over Sujah Dowlah, and had, at his death, been left in possession of a splendid dotation. The domains of which they received the rents and administered the government were of wide extent. The treasure hoarded by the late Nabob, a treasure which was popularly estimated at near three millions sterling, was in their hands. They continued to occupy his favourite palace at Fyzabad, the Beautiful Dwelling; while Asaph-ul-Dowlah held his court in the stately Lucknow, which he had built for himself on the shores of the Goomti, and had adorned with noble mosques and colleges.

Asaph-ul-Dowlah had already extorted considerable sums from his mother. She had at length appealed to the English; and the English had interfered. A solemn compact had been made, by which she consented to give her son some pecuniary assistance, and he in his turn promised never to commit any further invasion of her rights. This compact was formerly guaranteed by the government of Bengal. But times had changed; money was wanted; and the power which had given the guarantee was not ashamed to instigate the spoiler to excesses such that even he shrank from them.

It was necessary to find some pretext for a confiscation inconsistent, not merely with plighted faith, not merely with the ordinary rules of humanity and justice, but also with that great law of filial piety which, even in the wildest tribes of savages, even in those more degraded communities which wither under the influence of a corrupt half-civilization, retains a certain authority over the human mind. A pretext was the last thing that Hastings was likely to want. The insurrection at Benares had produced disturbances in Oude. These disturbances it was convenient to impute to the Princesses. Evidence for the imputation there was scarcely any; unless reports wandering from one mouth to another, and gaining something by every transmission, may be called evidence. The accused were furnished with no charge; they were permitted to make no defence; for the Governor-General wisely considered that, if he tried them, he might not be able to find a ground for plundering them. It was agreed between him and the Nabob Vizier that the noble ladies should, by a sweeping measure of confiscation, be stripped of their domains and treasures for the benefit of the Company, and that the sums thus obtained should be accepted by the government of Bengal in satisfaction of its claims on the government of Oude.

While Asaph-ul-Dowlah was at Chunar, he was completely subjugated by the clear and commanding intellect of the English statesman. But, when they had separated, the Vizier began to reflect with uneasiness on the engagement into which he had entered. His mother and grandmother protested and implored. His heart, deeply corrupted by absolute power and licentious pleasures, yet not naturally unfeeling, failed him in this crisis. Even the English resident at Lucknow, though hitherto devoted to Hastings, shrank from extreme measures. But the Governor-General was inexorable. He wrote to the resident in terms of the greatest severity, and declared that, if the spoliation which had been agreed upon were not instantly carried into effect, he would himself go to Lucknow, and do that from which feebler minds recoil with dismay. The resident, thus menaced, waited on his Highness, and insisted that the treaty of Chunar should be carried into full and immediate effect. Asaph-ul-Dowlah yielded, making at the same time a solemn protestation that he yielded to compulsion. The lands were resumed; but the treasure was not so easily obtained. It was necessary to use violence. A body of the Company's troops marched to Fyzabad, and forced the gates of the palace. The Princesses were confined to their own apartments. But still they refused to submit. Some more stringent mode of coercion was to be found. A mode was found of which, even at this distance of time, we cannot speak without shame and sorrow.

There were at Fyzabad two ancient men, belonging to that unhappy class which a practice, of immemorial antiquity in the East, has excluded from the pleasures of love and from the hope of posterity. It has always been held in Asiatic courts that beings thus estranged from sympathy with their kind are those whom princes may most safely trust. Sujah Dowlah had been of this opinion. He had given his entire confidence to the two eunuchs; and after his death they remained at the head of the household of his widow.

These men were, by the orders of the British government, seized, imprisoned, ironed, starved almost to death, in order to extort money from the Princesses. After they had been two months in confinement, their health gave way. They implored permission to take a little exercise in the garden of their prison. The officer who was in charge of them stated that, if they were allowed this indulgence, there was not the smallest chance of their escaping, and that their irons really added nothing to the security of the custody in which they were kept. He did not understand the plan of his superiors. Their object in these inflictions was not security but torture; and all mitigation was refused. Yet this was not the worst. It was resolved by an English government that these two infirm old men should be delivered to the tormentors. For that purpose they were removed to Lucknow. What horrors their dungeon there witnessed can only be guessed. But there remains on the records of Parliament this letter, written by a British resident to a British soldier.

"Sir, the Nabob having determined to inflict corporal punishment upon the prisoners under your guard, this is to desire that his officers, when they shall come, may have free access to the prisoners, and be permitted to do with them as they shall see proper."

While these barbarities were perpetrated at Lucknow, the Princesses were still under duresse at Fyzabad. Food was allowed to enter their apartments only in such scanty quantities that their female attendants were in danger of perishing with hunger. Month after month this cruelty continued, till at length, after twelve hundred thousand pounds had been wrung out of the Princesses, Hastings began to think that he had really got to the bottom of their revenue, and that no rigour could extort more. Then at length the wretched men who were detained at Lucknow regained their liberty. When their irons were knocked off, and the doors of their prison opened, their quivering lips, the tears which ran down their cheeks, and the thanksgivings which they poured forth to the common Father of Mussulmans and Christians, melted even the stout hearts of the English warriors who stood by.

There is a man to whom the conduct of Hastings, through the whole of these proceedings, appears not only excusable but laudable. There is a man who tells us that he "must really be pardoned if he ventures to characterize as something preeminently ridiculous and wicked, the sensibility which would balance against the preservation of British India a little personal suffering, which was applied only so long as the sufferers refused to deliver up a portion of that wealth, the whole of which their own and their mistresses' treason had forfeited." We cannot, we must own, envy the reverend biographer, either his singular notion of what constitutes preeminent wickedness, or his equally singular perception of the preeminently ridiculous. Is this the generosity of an English soldier? Is this the charity of a Christian priest? Could neither Mr. Gleig's professions teach him the first rudiments of morality? Or is morality a thing which may be well enough in sermons, but which has nothing to do with biography?

But we must not forget to do justice to Sir Elijah Impey's conduct on this occasion. It was not indeed easy for him to intrude himself into a business so entirely alien from all his official duties. But there was something inexpressibly alluring, we must suppose, in the peculiar rankness of the infamy which was then to be got at Lucknow. He hurried thither as fast as relays of palankin-bearers could carry him. A crowd of people came before him with affidavits against the Begums, ready drawn in their hands. Those affidavits he did not read. Some of them, indeed, he could not read; for they were in the dialects of Northern India, and no interpreter was employed.[1] He administered the oath to the deponents, with all

[1] This passage has been slightly altered. As it originally stood, Sir Elijah Impey was described as ignorant of all the native languages in which the depositions were drawn. A writer who apparently has had access to some private source of information has contradicted this state-

possible expedition, and asked not a single question, not even whether they had perused the statements to which they swore. This work performed, he got again into his palankin, and posted back to Calcutta, to be in time for the opening of term. The cause was one which, by his own confession, lay altogether out of his jurisdiction. Under the charter of justice, he had no more right to inquire into crimes committed by natives in Oude than the Lord President of the Court of Session of Scotland to hold an assize at Exeter. He had no right to try the Begums, nor did he pretend to try them. With what object, then, did he undertake so long a journey? Evidently in order that he might give, in an irregular manner, that sanction which in a regular manner he could not give, to the crimes of those who had recently hired him; and in order that a confused mass of testimony which he did not sift, which he did not even read, might acquire an authority not properly belonging to it, from the signature of the highest judicial functionary in India.

The time was approaching, however, when he was to be stripped of that robe which has never, since the Revolution, been disgraced so foully as by him. The state of India had for some time occupied much of the attention of the British Parliament. Towards the close of the American war, two committees of the Commons sat on Eastern affairs. In one Edmund Burke took the lead. The other was under the presidency of the able and versatile Henry Dundas, then Lord Advocate of Scotland. Great as are the changes which, during the last sixty years, have taken place in our Asiatic dominions, the reports which those committees laid on the table of the House will still be found most interesting and instructive.

There was as yet no connexion between the Company and either of the great parties in the state. The ministers had no motive to defend Indian abuses. On the contrary, it was for their interest to show, if possible, that the government and patronage of our Oriental empire might, with advantage, be transferred to themselves. The votes therefore, which, in consequence of the reports made by the two committees, were passed by the Commons, breathed the spirit of stern and indignant justice. The severest epithets were applied

---

ment, and has asserted that Sir Elijah knew Persian and Bengalee. Some of the depositions were certainly in Persian. Those therefore Sir Elijah might have read if he had chosen to do so. But others were in the vernacular dialects of Upper India, with which it is not alleged that he had any acquaintance. Why the Bengalee is mentioned it is not easy to guess. Bengalee at Lucknow would have been as useless as Portuguese in Switzerland.

to several of the measures of Hastings, especially to the Rohilla war; and it was resolved, on the motion of Mr. Dundas, that the Company ought to recall a Governor-General who had brought such calamities on the Indian people, and such dishonour on the British name. An act was passed for limiting the jurisdiction of the Supreme Court. The bargain which Hastings had made with the Chief Justice was condemned in the strongest terms; and an address was presented to the king, praying that Impey might be ordered home to answer for his misdeeds.

Impey was recalled by a letter from the Secretary of State. But the proprietors of India Stock resolutely refused to dismiss Hastings from their service, and passed a resolution affirming, what was undeniably true, that they were entrusted by law with the right of naming and removing their Governor-General, and that they were not bound to obey the directions of a single branch of the legislature with respect to such nomination or removal.

Thus supported by his employers, Hastings remained at the head of the government of Bengal till the spring of 1785. His administration, so eventful and stormy, closed in almost perfect quiet. In the Council there was no regular opposition to his measures. Peace was restored to India. The Mahratta war had ceased. Hyder was no more. A treaty had been concluded with his son, Tippoo; and the Carnatic had been evacuated by the armies of Mysore. Since the termination of the American war, England had no European enemy or rival in the Eastern seas.

On a general review of the long administration of Hastings, it is impossible to deny that, against the great crimes by which it is blemished, we have to set off great public services. England had passed through a perilous crisis. She still, indeed, maintained her place in the foremost rank of European powers; and the manner in which she had defended herself against fearful odds had inspired surrounding nations with a high opinion both of her spirit and of her strength. Nevertheless, in every part of the world, except one, she had been a loser. Not only had she been compelled to acknowledge the independence of thirteen colonies peopled by her children, and to conciliate the Irish by giving up the right of legislating for them; but, in the Mediterranean, in the Gulf of Mexico, on the coast of Africa, on the continent of America, she had been compelled to cede the fruits of her victories in former wars. Spain regained Minorca and Florida; France regained Senegal, Goree, and several West Indian Islands. The only quarter of the world in which Britain had lost nothing was the quarter in which her interests had been committed to the care of Hastings. In spite of the utmost exertions both of European and Asiatic enemies, the power of our country in the East had been greatly augmented. Benares was subjected; the Nabob Vizier reduced to vassalage. That our influence had been thus extended, nay, that Fort William and Fort St. George had not been occupied by hostile armies, was owing, if we may trust the general voice of the English in India, to the skill and resolution of Hastings.

His internal administration, with all its blemishes, gives him a title to be considered as one of the most remarkable men in our history. He dissolved the double government. He transferred the direction of affairs to English hands. Out of a frightful anarchy, he educed at least a rude and imperfect order. The whole organization by which justice was dispensed, revenue collected, peace maintained, throughout a territory not inferior in population to the dominions of Louis the Sixteenth or of the Emperor Joseph, was formed and superintended by him. He boasted that every public office, without exception, which existed when he left Bengal was his creation. It is quite true that this system, after all the improvements suggested by the experience of sixty years, still needs improvement, and that it was at first far more defective than it now is. But whoever seriously considers what it is to construct from the beginning the whole of a machine so vast and complex as a government will allow that what Hastings effected deserves high admiration. To compare the most celebrated European ministers to him seems to us as unjust as it would be to compare the best baker in London with Robinson Crusoe, who, before he could bake a single loaf, had to make his plough and his harrow, his fences and his scarecrows, his sickle and his flail, his mill and his oven.

The just fame of Hastings rises still higher, when we reflect that he was not bred a statesman; that he was sent from school to a counting-house; and that he was employed during the prime of his manhood as a commercial agent, far from all intellectual society.

Nor must we forget that all, or almost all, to whom, when placed at the head of affairs, he could apply for assistance, were persons who owed as little as himself, or less than himself, to education. A minister in Europe finds himself, on the first day on which he commences his functions, surrounded by experienced public servants, the depositaries of official traditions. Hastings had no such help. His own reflection, his own energy, were to supply the place of all Downing Street and Somerset House. Having had no facilities for learning, he was forced to teach. He had first to form himself, and then to form his instruments; and this not in a single department, but in all the departments of the administration.

It must be added that, while engaged in this most arduous task, he was constantly trammelled by orders from home, and frequently borne down by a majority in council. The preservation of an Empire from a formidable combination of foreign enemies, the construction of a government in all its parts, were accomplished by him, while every ship brought out bales of censure from his employers, and while the records of every consultation were filled with acrimonious minutes by his colleagues. We believe that there never was a public man whose temper was so severely tried; not Marlborough, when thwarted by the Dutch Deputies; not Wellington, when he had to deal at once with the Portuguese Regency, the Spanish Juntas, and Mr. Percival. But the temper of Hastings was equal to almost any trial. It was not sweet; but it was calm. Quick and vigorous as his intellect was, the patience with which he endured the most cruel vexations, till a remedy could be found, resembled the patience of stupidity. He seems to have been capable of resentment, bitter and long-enduring; yet his resentment so seldom hurried him into any blunder that it may be doubted whether what appeared to be revenge was any thing but policy.

The effect of his singular equanimity was that he always had the full command of all the resources of one of the most fertile minds that ever existed. Accordingly, no complication of perils and embarrassments could perplex him. For every difficulty he had a contrivance ready; and, whatever may be thought of the justice and humanity of some of his contrivances, it is certain that they seldom failed to serve the purpose for which they were designed.

Together with this extraordinary talent for devising expedients, Hastings possessed, in a very high degree, another talent scarcely less necessary to a man in his situation; we mean the talent for conducting political controversy. It is as necessary to an English statesman in the East that he should be able to write, as it is to a minister in this country that he should be able to speak. It is chiefly by the oratory of a public man here that the nation judges of his powers. It is from the letters and reports of a public man in India that the dispensers of patronage form their estimate of him. In each case, the talent which receives peculiar encouragement is developed, perhaps at the expense of the other powers. In this country, we sometimes hear men speak above their abilities. It is not very unusual to find gentlemen in the Indian service who write above their abilities. The English politician is a little too much of a debater; the Indian politician a little too much of an essayist.

Of the numerous servants of the Company who have distinguished themselves as framers of minutes and despatches, Hastings stands at the head. He was indeed the person who gave to the official writing of the Indian governments the character which it still retains. He was matched against no common antagonist. But even Francis was forced to acknowledge, with sullen and resentful candour, that there was no contending against the pen of Hastings. And, in truth, the Governor-General's power of making out a case, of perplexing what it was inconvenient that people should understand, and of setting in the clearest point of view whatever would bear the light, was incomparable. His style must be praised with some reservation. It was in general forcible, pure, and polished; but it was sometimes, though not often, turgid, and, on one or two occasions, even bombastic. Perhaps the fondness of Hastings for Persian literature may have tended to corrupt his taste.

And, since we have referred to his literary tastes, it would be most unjust not to praise the judicious encouragement which, as a ruler, he gave to liberal studies and curious researches. His patronage was extended, with prudent generosity, to voyages, travels, experiments, publications. He did little, it is true, towards introducing into India the learning of the West. To make the young natives of Bengal familiar with Milton and Adam Smith, to substitute the geography, astronomy, and surgery of Europe for the dotages of the Brahminical superstition, or for the imperfect science of ancient Greece transfused through Arabian expositions, this was a scheme reserved to crown the beneficent administration of a far more virtuous ruler. Still, it is impossible to refuse high commendation to a man who, taken from a ledger to govern an empire, overwhelmed by public business, surrounded by people as busy as himself, and separated by thousands of leagues from almost all literary society, gave, both by his example and by his munificence, a great impulse to learning. In Persian and Arabic literature he was deeply skilled. With the Sanscrit he was not himself acquainted; but those who first brought that language to the knowledge of European students owed much to his encouragement. It was under his protection that the Asiatic Society commenced its honourable career. That distinguished body selected him to be its first president; but, with excellent taste and feeling, he declined the honour in favour of Sir William Jones. But the chief advantage which the students of Oriental letters derived from his patronage remains to be mentioned. The Pundits of Bengal had always looked with great jealousy on the attempts of foreigners to pry into those mysteries which were locked up in the sacred dialect. Their religion had been persecuted by the Mahommedans. What they knew of the spirit of the Portuguese government might warrant them in apprehending persecution from Christians. That apprehension, the wisdom and moderation of Hastings removed. He was the first foreign ruler who succeeded in gaining the confidence of the hereditary priests of India, and who induced them to lay open to English scholars the secrets of the old Brahminical theology and jurisprudence.

It is indeed impossible to deny that, in the great art of inspiring large masses of human beings with confidence and attachment, no ruler ever surpassed Hastings. If he had made himself popular with the English by giving up the Bengalees to extortion and oppression, or if, on the other hand, he had conciliated the Bengalees and alienated the English, there would have been no cause for wonder. What is peculiar to him is that, being the chief of a small band of strangers who exercised boundless power over a great indigenous population, he made himself beloved both by the subject many and by the dominant few. The affection felt for him by the civil service was singularly ardent and constant. Through all his disasters and perils, his brethren stood by him with steadfast loyalty. The army, at the same time, loved him as armies have seldom loved any but the greatest chiefs who have led them to victory. Even in his disputes with distinguished military men, he could always count on the support of the military profession. While such was his empire over the hearts of his countrymen, he enjoyed among the natives a popularity, such as other governors have perhaps better merited, but such as no other governor has been able to attain. He spoke their vernacular dialects with facility and precision. He was intimately acquainted with their feelings and usages. On one or two occasions, for great ends, he deliberately acted in defiance of their opinion; but on such occasions he gained more in their respect than he lost in their love. In general, he carefully avoided all that could shock their national or religious prejudices. His administration was indeed in many respects faulty; but the Bengalee standard of good government was not high. Under the Nabobs, the hurricane of Mahratta cavalry had passed annually over the rich alluvial plain. But even the Mahratta shrank from a conflict with the mighty children of the sea; and the immense rice-harvests of the Lower Ganges were safely gathered in, under the protection of the English sword. The first English conquerors had been more rapacious and merciless even than the Mahrattas; but that generation had passed away. Defective as was the police, heavy as were the public burdens, it is probable that the oldest man in Bengal could not recollect a season of equal security and prosperity. For the first time within living memory, the province was placed under a government strong enough to prevent others from robbing, and not inclined to play the robber itself. These things inspired good-will. At the same time, the constant success of Hastings and the manner in which he extricated himself from every difficulty made him an object of superstitious admiration; and the more than regal splendour which he sometimes displayed dazzled a people who have much in common with children. Even now, after the lapse of more than fifty years, the natives of India still talk of him as the greatest of the English; and nurses sing children to sleep with a jingling ballad about the fleet horses and richly caparisoned elephants of Sahib Warren Hostein.

The gravest offences of which Hastings was guilty did not affect his popularity with the people of Bengal; for those offences were committed against neighbouring states. Those offences, as our readers must have perceived, we are not disposed to vindicate; yet, in order that the censure may be justly apportioned to the transgression, it is fit that the motive of the criminal should be taken into consideration. The motive which prompted the worst acts of Hastings was misdirected and ill-regulated public spirit. The rules of justice, the sentiments of humanity, the plighted faith of treaties, were in his view as nothing, when opposed to the immediate interests of the state. This is no justification, according to the principles either of morality, or of what we believe to be identical with morality, namely, far-sighted policy. Nevertheless the common sense of mankind, which in questions of this sort seldom goes far wrong, will always recognise a distinction between crimes which originate in an inordinate zeal for the commonwealth, and crimes which originate in selfish cupidity. To the benefit of this distinction Hastings is fairly entitled. There is, we conceive, no reason to suspect that the Rohilla war, the revolution of Benares, or the spoliation of the Princesses of Oude, added a rupee to his fortune. We will not affirm that, in all pecuniary dealings, he showed that punctilious integrity, that dread of the faintest appearance of evil, which is now the glory of the Indian civil service. But when the school in which he had been trained and the temptations to which he was exposed are considered, we are more inclined to praise him for his general uprightness with respect to money, than rigidly to blame him for a few transactions which would now be called indelicate and irregular, but which even now would hardly be designated as corrupt. A rapacious man he certainly was not. Had he been so, he would infallibly have returned to his country the richest subject in Europe. We speak within compass, when we say that, without applying any extraordinary pressure, he might easily have obtained from the zemindars of the Company's provinces and from neighbouring princes, in the course of thirteen years, more than three millions sterling, and might have outshone the splendour of Carlton House and of the *Palais Royal*. He brought home a fortune such as a Governor-General, fond of state, and careless of thrift, might easily, during so long a tenure of office, save out of his legal salary. Mrs. Hastings, we are afraid, was less scrupulous. It was generally believed that she accepted presents with great alacrity, and that she thus formed, without the connivance of her husband, a private hoard amounting to several lacs of rupees. We are the more inclined to give credit to this story, because Mr. Gleig, who cannot but have heard it, does not, as far as we have observed, notice or contradict it.

The influence of Mrs. Hastings over her husband was indeed such that she might easily have obtained much larger sums than she was ever accused of receiving. At length her health began to give way; and the Governor-General, much against his will, was compelled to send her to England. He seems to have loved her with that love which is peculiar to men of strong minds, to men whose affection is not easily won or widely diffused. The talk of Calcutta ran for some time on the luxurious manner in which he fitted up the round-house of an Indiaman for her accommodation, on the profusion of sandal-wood and carved ivory which adorned her cabin, and on the thousands of rupees which had been expended in order to procure for her the society of an agreeable female companion during the voyage. We may remark here that the letters of Hastings to his wife are exceedingly characteristic. They are tender, and full of indications of esteem and confidence; but, at the same time, a little more ceremonious than is usual in so intimate a relation. The solemn courtesy with which he compliments "his elegant Marian" reminds us now and then of the dignified air with which Sir Charles Grandison bowed over Miss Byron's hand in the cedar parlour.

After some months Hastings prepared to follow his wife to England. When it was announced that he was about to quit his office, the feeling of the society which he had so long governed manifested itself by many signs. Addresses poured in from Europeans and Asiatics, from civil functionaries, soldiers, and traders. On the day on which he delivered up the keys of office, a crowd of friends and admirers formed a lane to the quay where he embarked. Several barges escorted him far down the river; and some attached friends refused to quit him till the low coast of Bengal was fading from the view, and till the pilot was leaving the ship.

Of his voyage little is known, except that he amused himself with books and with his pen; and that, among the compositions by which he beguiled the tediousness of that long leisure, was a pleasing imitation of Horace's *Otium Divos rogat*. This little poem was inscribed to Mr. Shore, afterwards Lord Teignmouth, a man of whose integrity, humanity, and honour, it is impossible to speak too highly; but who, like some other excellent members of the civil service, extended to the conduct of his friend Hastings an indulgence of which his own conduct never stood in need.

The voyage was, for those times, very speedy. Hastings was little more than four months on the sea. In June 1785, he landed at Plymouth, posted to London, appeared at Court, paid his respects in Leadenhall Street, and then retired with his wife to Cheltenham.

He was greatly pleased with his reception. The King treated him with marked distinction. The Queen, who had already incurred much censure on account of the favour which, in spite of the ordinary severity of her virtue, she had shown to the "elegant Marian," was not less gracious to Hastings. The Directors received him in a solemn sitting; and their chairman read to him a vote of thanks which they had passed without one dissentient voice. "I find myself," said Hastings, in a letter written about a quarter of a year after his arrival in England, "I find myself every where, and universally, treated with evidences, apparent even to my own observation, that I possess the good opinion of my country."

The confident and exulting tone of his correspondence about this time is the more remarkable, because he had already received ample notice of the attack which was in preparation. Within a week after he landed at Plymouth, Burke gave notice in the House of Commons of a motion seriously affecting a gentleman lately returned from India. The session, however, was then so far advanced, that it was impossible to enter on so extensive and important a subject.

Hastings, it is clear, was not sensible of the danger of his position. Indeed that sagacity, that judgment, that readiness in devising expedients, which had distinguished him in the East, seemed now to have forsaken him; not that his abilities were at all impaired; not that he was not still the same man who had triumphed over Francis and Nuncomar, who had made the Chief Justice and the Nabob Vizier his tools, who had deposed Cheyte Sing, and repelled Hyder Ali. But an oak, as Mr. Grattan finely said, should not be transplanted at fifty. A man who, having left England when a boy, returns to it after thirty or forty years passed in India, will find, be his talents what they may, that he has much both to learn and to unlearn before he can take a place among English statesmen. The working of a representative system, the war of parties, the arts of debate, the influence of the press, are startling novelties to him. Surrounded on every side by new machines and new tactics, he is as much bewildered as Hannibal would have been at Waterloo, or Themistocles at Trafalgar. His very acuteness deludes him. His very vigour causes him to stumble. The more correct his maxims, when applied to the state of society to which he is accustomed, the more certain they are to lead him astray. This was strikingly the case with Hastings. In India he had a bad hand; but he was master of the game, and he won every stake. In England he held excellent cards, if he had known how to play them; and it was chiefly by his own errors that he was brought to the verge of ruin.

Of all his errors the most serious was perhaps the choice of a champion. Clive, in similar circumstances, had made a singularly happy selection. He put himself into the hands of Wedderburn, afterwards Lord Loughborough, one of the few great advocates who have also been great in the House of Commons. To the defence of Clive, therefore, nothing was wanting, neither learning nor knowledge of the world, neither forensic acuteness nor that eloquence which charms political assemblies. Hastings entrusted his interests to a very different person, a major in the Bengal army, named Scott. This gentleman had been sent over from India some time before as the agent of the Governor-General. It was rumoured that his services were rewarded with Oriental munificence; and we believe that he received much more than Hastings could conveniently spare. The Major obtained a seat in Parliament, and was there regarded as the organ of his employer. It was evidently impossible that a gentleman so situated could speak with the authority which belongs to an independent position. Nor had the agent of Hastings the talents necessary for obtaining the ear of an assembly which, accustomed to listen to great orators, had naturally become fastidious. He was always on his legs; he was very tedious; and he had only one topic, the merits and wrongs of Hastings. Every body who knows the House of Commons will easily guess what followed. The Major was soon considered as the greatest bore of his time. His exertions were not confined to Parliament. There was hardly a day on which the newspapers did not contain some puff upon Hastings, signed *Asiaticus* or *Bengalensis*, but known to be written by the indefatigable Scott; and hardly a month in which some bulky pamphlet on the same subject, and from the same pen, did not pass to the trunk-makers and the pastry-cooks. As to this gentleman's capacity for conducting a delicate question through Parliament, our readers will want no evidence beyond that which they will find in letters preserved in these volumes. We will give a single specimen of his temper and judgment. He designated the greatest man then living as "that reptile Mr. Burke."

In spite, however, of this unfortunate choice, the general aspect of affairs was favourable to Hastings. The King was on his side. The Company and its servants were zealous in his cause. Among public men he had many ardent friends. Such were Lord Mansfield, who had outlived the vigour of his body, but not that of his mind; and Lord Lansdowne, who, though unconnected with any party, retained the importance which belongs to great talents and knowledge. The ministers were generally believed to be favourable to the late Governor-General. They owed their power to the clamour which had been raised against Mr. Fox's East India Bill. The authors of that bill, when accused of invading vested rights, and of setting up powers unknown to the constitution, had defended themselves by pointing to the crimes of Hastings, and by arguing that abuses so extraordinary justified extraordinary measures. Those who, by opposing that bill, had raised themselves to the head of affairs, would naturally be inclined to extenuate the evils which had been made the plea for administering so violent a remedy; and such, in fact, was their general disposition. The Lord Chancellor Thurlow, in particular, whose great place and force of intellect gave him a weight in the government inferior only to that of Mr. Pitt, espoused the cause of Hastings with indecorous violence. Mr. Pitt, though he had censured many parts of the Indian system, had studiously abstained from saying a word against the late chief of the Indian government. To Major Scott, indeed, the young minister had in private extolled Hastings as a great, a wonderful man, who had the highest claims on the government. There was only one objection to granting all that so eminent a servant of the public could ask. The resolution of censure still remained on the journals of the House of Commons. That resolution was, indeed, unjust; but, till it was rescinded, could the minister advise the King to bestow any mark of approbation on the person censured? If Major Scott is to be trusted, Mr. Pitt declared that this was the only reason which prevented the government from conferring a peerage on the late Governor-General. Mr. Dundas was the only important member of the administration who was deeply committed to a different view of the subject. He had moved the resolutions which created the difficulty; but even from him little was to be apprehended. Since he presided over the committee on Eastern affairs, great changes had taken place. He was surrounded by new allies; he had fixed his hopes on new objects; and whatever may have been his good qualities,—and he had many,—flattery itself never reckoned rigid consistency in the number.

From the ministry, therefore, Hastings had every reason to expect support; and the ministry was very powerful. The opposition was loud and vehement against him. But the opposition, though formidable from the wealth and influence of some of its members, and from the admirable talents and eloquence of others, was outnumbered in parliament, and odious throughout the country. Nor, as far as we can judge, was the opposition generally desirous to engage in so serious an undertaking as the impeachment of an Indian Governor. Such an impeachment must last for years. It must impose on the chiefs of the party an immense load of labour. Yet it could scarcely, in any manner, affect the event of the great political game. The followers of the coalition were therefore more inclined to revile Hastings than to prosecute him. They lost no opportunity of coupling his name with the names of the most hateful tyrants of whom history makes mention. The wits of Brookes's aimed their keenest sarcasms both at his public and at his domestic life. Some fine diamonds which he had presented, as it was rumoured, to the royal family, and a certain richly carved ivory bed which the Queen had done him the honour to accept from him, were favourite subjects of ridicule. One lively poet proposed, that the great acts of the fair Marian's present husband should be immortalized by the pencil of his predecessor; and that Imhoff should be employed to embellish the House of Commons with paintings of the bleeding Rohillas, of Nuncomar swinging, of Cheyte Sing letting himself down to the Ganges. Another, in an exquisitely humorous parody of Virgil's third eclogue, propounded the question, what that mineral could be of which the rays had power to make the most austere of princesses the friend of a wanton. A third described, with gay malevolence, the gorgeous appearance of Mrs. Hastings at St. James's, the galaxy of jewels, torn from Indian Begums, which adorned her head-dress, her necklace gleaming with future votes, and the depending questions that shone upon her ears. Satirical attacks of this description, and perhaps a motion for a vote of censure, would have satisfied the great body of the opposition. But there were two men whose indignation was not to be so appeased, Philip Francis and Edmund Burke.

Francis had recently entered the House of Commons, and had already established a character there for industry and talent. He laboured indeed under one most unfortunate defect, want of fluency. But he occasionally expressed himself with a dignity and energy worthy of the greatest orators. Before he had been many days in parliament, he incurred the bitter dislike of Pitt, who constantly treated him with as much asperity as the laws of debate would allow. Neither lapse of years nor change of scene had mitigated the enmities which Francis had brought back from the East. After his usual fashion, he mistook his malevolence for virtue, nursed it, as preachers tell us that we ought to nurse our good dispositions, and paraded it, on all occasions, with Pharisaical ostentation.

The zeal of Burke was still fiercer; but it was far purer. Men unable to understand the elevation of his mind have tried to find out some discreditable motive for the vehemence and pertinacity which he showed on this occasion. But they have altogether failed. The idle story that he had some private slight to revenge has long been given up, even by the advocates of Hastings. Mr. Gleig supposes that Burke was actuated by party spirit, that he retained a bitter remembrance of the fall of the coalition, that he attributed that fall to the exertions of the East India interest, and that he considered Hastings as the head and the representative of that interest. This explanation seems to be sufficiently refuted by a reference to dates. The hostility of Burke to Hastings commenced long before the coalition; and lasted long after Burke had become a strenuous supporter of those by whom the coalition had been defeated. It began when Burke and Fox, closely allied together, were attacking the influence of the crown, and calling for peace with the American republic. It continued till Burke, alienated from Fox, and loaded with the favours of the crown, died, preaching a crusade against the French republic. It seems absurd to attribute to the events of 1784 an enmity which began in 1781, and which retained undiminished force long after persons far more deeply implicated than Hastings in the events of 1784 had been cordially forgiven. And why should we look for any other explanation of Burke's conduct than that which we find on the surface? The plain truth is that Hastings had committed some great crimes, and that the thought of those crimes made the blood of Burke boil in his veins. For Burke was a man in whom compassion for suffering, and hatred of injustice and tyranny, were as strong as in Las Casas or Clarkson. And although in him, as in Las Casas and in Clarkson, these noble feelings were alloyed with the infirmity which belongs to human nature, he is, like them, entitled to this great praise, that he devoted years of intense labour to the service of a people with whom he had neither blood nor language, neither religion nor manners in common, and from whom no requital, no thanks, no applause could be expected.

His knowledge of India was such as few, even of those Europeans who have passed many years in that country, have attained, and such as certainly was never attained by any public man who had not quitted Europe. He had studied the history, the laws, and the usages of the East with an industry, such as is seldom found united to so much genius and so much sensibility. Others have perhaps been equally laborious, and have collected an equal mass of materials. But the manner in which Burke brought his higher powers of intellect to work on statements of facts, and on tables of figures, was peculiar to himself. In every part of those huge bales of Indian information which repelled almost all other readers, his mind, at once philosophical and poetical, found something to instruct or to delight. His reason analysed and digested those vast and shapeless masses; his imagination animated and coloured them. Out of darkness, and dulness, and confusion, he formed a multitude of ingenious theories and vivid pictures. He had, in the highest degree, that noble faculty whereby man is able to live in the past and in the future, in the distant and in the unreal. India and its inhabitants were not to him, as to most Englishmen, mere names and abstractions, but a real country and a real people. The burning sun, the strange vegetation of the palm and the cocoa-tree, the rice-field, the tank, the huge trees, older than the Mogul empire, under which the village crowds assemble, the thatched roof of the peasant's hut, the rich tracery of the mosque where the imaum prays with his face to Mecca, the drums, and banners, and gaudy idols, the devotee swinging in the air, the graceful maiden, with the pitcher on her head, descending the steps to the river-side, the black faces, the long beards, the yellow streaks of sect, the turbans and the flowing robes, the spears and the silver maces, the elephants with their canopies of state, the gorgeous palankin of the prince, and the close litter of the noble lady, all those things were to him as the objects amidst which his own life had been passed, as the objects which lay on the road between Beaconsfield and St. James's Street. All India was present to the eye of his mind, from the halls where suitors laid gold and perfumes at the feet of sovereigns to the wild moor where the gipsy camp was pitched, from the bazars, humming like bee-hives with the crowd of buyers and sellers, to the jungle where the lonely courier shakes his bunch of iron rings to scare away the hyænas. He had just as lively an idea of the insurrection at Benares as of Lord George Gordon's riots, and of the execution of Nuncomar as of the execution of Dr. Dodd. Oppression in Bengal was to him the same thing as oppression in the streets of London.

He saw that Hastings had been guilty of some most unjustifiable acts. All that followed was natural and necessary in a mind like Burke's. His imagination and his passions, once excited, hurried him beyond the bounds of justice and good sense. His reason, powerful as it was, became the slave of feelings which it should have controlled. His indignation, virtuous in its origin, acquired too much of the character of personal aversion. He could see no mitigating circumstance, no redeeming merit. His temper which, though generous and affectionate, had always been irritable, had now been made almost savage by bodily infirmities and mental vexations. Conscious of great powers and great virtues, he found himself, in age and poverty, a mark for the hatred of a perfidious court and a deluded people. In Parliament his eloquence was out of date. A young generation, which knew him not, had filled the House. Whenever he rose to speak, his voice was drowned by the unseemly interruptions of lads who were in their cradles when his orations on the Stamp Act called forth the applause of the great Earl of Chatham. These things had produced on his proud and sensitive spirit an effect at which we cannot wonder. He could no longer discuss any question with calmness, or make allowance for honest differences of opinion. Those who think that he was more violent and acrimonious in debates about India than on other occasions are ill informed respecting the last years of his life. In the discussions on the Commercial Treaty with the Court of Versailles, on the Regency, on the French Revolution, he showed even more virulence than in conducting the impeachment. Indeed it may be remarked that the very persons who called him a mischievous maniac, for condemning in burning words the Rohilla war and the spoliation of the Begums, exalted him into a prophet as soon as he began to declaim, with greater vehemence, and not with greater reason, against the taking of the Bastile and the insults offered to Marie Antoinette. To us he appears to have been neither a maniac in the former case, nor a prophet in the latter, but in both cases a great and good man, led into extravagance by a tempestuous sensibility which domineered over all his faculties.

It may be doubted whether the personal antipathy of Francis, or the nobler indignation of Burke, would have led their party to adopt extreme measures against Hastings, if his own conduct had been judicious. He should have felt that, great as his public services had been, he was not faultless; and should have been content to make his escape, without aspiring to the honours of a triumph. He and his agent took a different view. They were impatient for the rewards which, as they conceived, were deferred only till Burke's attack should be over. They accordingly resolved to force a decisive action with an enemy for whom, if they had been wise, they would have made a bridge of gold. On the first day of the session of 1786, Major Scott reminded Burke of the notice given in the preceding year, and asked whether it was seriously intended to bring any charge against the late Governor-General. This challenge left no course open to the Opposition, except to come forward as accusers, or to acknowledge themselves calumniators. The administration of Hastings had not been so blameless, nor was the great party of Fox and North so feeble, that it could be prudent to venture on so bold a defiance. The leaders of the Opposition instantly returned the only answer which they could with honour return; and the whole party was irrevocably pledged to a prosecution.

Burke began his operations by applying for Papers. Some of the documents for which he asked were refused by the ministers, who, in the debate, held language such as strongly confirmed the prevailing opinion, that they intended to support Hastings. In April, the charges were laid on the table. They had been drawn by Burke with great ability, though in a form too much resembling that of a pamphlet. Hastings was furnished with a copy of the accusation; and it was intimated to him that he might, if he thought fit, be heard in his own defence at the bar of the Commons.

Here again Hastings was pursued by the same fatality which had attended him ever since the day when he set foot on English ground. It seemed to be decreed that this man, so politic and so successful in the East, should commit nothing but blunders in Europe. Any judicious adviser would have told him that the best thing which he could do would be to make an eloquent, forcible, and affecting oration at the bar of the House; but that, if he could not trust himself to speak, and found it necessary to read, he ought to be as concise as possible. Audiences accustomed to extemporaneous debating of the highest excellence are always impatient of long written compositions. Hastings, however, sat down as he would have done at the Government-house in Bengal, and prepared a paper of immense length. That paper, if recorded on the consultations of an Indian administration, would have been justly praised as a very able minute. But it was now out of place. It fell flat, as the best written defence must have fallen flat, on an assembly accustomed to the animated and strenuous conflicts of Pitt and Fox. The members, as soon as their curiosity about the face and demeanour of so eminent a stranger was satisfied, walked away to dinner, and left Hastings to tell his story till midnight to the clerks and the sergeant-at-arms.

All preliminary steps having been duly taken, Burke, in the

beginning of June, brought forward the charge relating to the Rohilla war. He acted discreetly in placing this accusation in the van; for Dundas had formerly moved, and the House had adopted, a resolution condemning, in the most severe terms, the policy followed by Hastings with regard to Rohilcund. Dundas had little, or rather nothing, to say in defence of his own consistency; but he put a bold face on the matter, and opposed the motion. Among other things, he declared that, though he still thought the Rohilla war unjustifiable, he considered the services which Hastings had subsequently rendered to the state as sufficient to atone even for so great an offence. Pitt did not speak, but voted with Dundas; and Hastings was absolved by a hundred and nineteen votes against sixty-seven.

Hastings was now confident of victory. It seemed, indeed, that he had reason to be so. The Rohilla war was, of all his measures, that which his accusers might with greatest advantage assail. It had been condemned by the Court of Directors. It had been condemned by the House of Commons. It had been condemned by Mr. Dundas, who had since become the chief minister of the Crown for Indian affairs. Yet Burke, having chosen this strong ground, had been completely defeated on it. That, having failed here, he should succeed on any point, was generally thought impossible. It was rumoured at the clubs and coffee-houses that one or perhaps two more charges would be brought forward, that if, on those charges, the sense of the House of Commons should be against impeachment, the Opposition would let the matter drop, that Hastings would be immediately raised to the peerage, decorated with the star of the Bath, sworn of the privy council, and invited to lend the assistance of his talents and experience to the India board. Lord Thurlow indeed, some months before, had spoken with contempt of the scruples which prevented Pitt from calling Hastings to the House of Lords; and had even said, that if the Chancellor of the Exchequer was afraid of the Commons, there was nothing to prevent the Keeper of the Great Seal from taking the royal pleasure about a patent of peerage. The very title was chosen. Hastings was to be Lord Daylesford. For, through all changes of scene and changes of fortune, remained unchanged his attachment to the spot which had witnessed the greatness and the fall of his family, and which had borne so great a part in the first dreams of his young ambition.

But in a very few days these fair prospects were overcast. On the thirteenth of June, Mr. Fox brought forward, with great ability and eloquence, the charge respecting the treatment of Cheyte Sing.

Francis followed on the same side. The friends of Hastings were in high spirits when Pitt rose. With his usual abundance and felicity of language, the minister gave his opinion on the case. He maintained that the Governor-General was justified in calling on the Rajah of Benares for pecuniary assistance, and in imposing a fine when that assistance was contumaciously withheld. He also thought that the conduct of the Governor-General during the insurrection had been distinguished by ability and presence of mind. He censured, with great bitterness, the conduct of Francis, both in India and in Parliament, as most dishonest and malignant. The necessary inference from Pitt's arguments seemed to be that Hastings ought to be honourably acquitted; and both the friends and the opponents of the minister expected from him a declaration to that effect. To the astonishment of all parties, he concluded by saying that, though he thought it right in Hastings to fine Cheyte Sing for contumacy, yet the amount of the fine was too great for the occasion. On this ground, and on this ground alone, did Mr. Pitt, applauding every other part of the conduct of Hastings with regard to Benares, declare that he should vote in favour of Mr. Fox's motion.

The House was thunderstruck; and it well might be so. For the wrong done to Cheyte Sing, even had it been as flagitious as Fox and Francis contended, was a trifle when compared with the horrors which had been inflicted on Rohilcund. But if Mr. Pitt's view of the case of Cheyte Sing were correct, there was no ground for an impeachment, or even for a vote of censure. If the offence of Hastings was really no more than this, that, having a right to impose a mulct, the amount of which mulct was not defined, but was left to be settled by his discretion, he had, not for his own advantage, but for that of the state, demanded too much, was this an offence which required a criminal proceeding of the highest solemnity, a criminal proceeding, to which, during sixty years, no public functionary had been subjected? We can see, we think, in what way a man of sense and integrity might have been induced to take any course respecting Hastings, except the course which Mr. Pitt took. Such a man might have thought a great example necessary, for the preventing of injustice, and for the vindicating of the national honour, and might, on that ground, have voted for impeachment both on the Rohilla charge, and on the Benares charge. Such a man might have thought that the offences of Hastings had been atoned for by great services, and might, on that ground, have voted against the impeachment on both charges. With great diffidence, we give it as our opinion that the most correct course would, on the whole, have been to impeach on the Rohilla charge, and to acquit on the Benares charge. Had the Benares charge appeared to us in the same light in which it appeared to Mr. Pitt, we should, without hesitation, have voted for acquittal on that charge. The one course which it is inconceivable that any man of a tenth part of Mr. Pitt's abilities can have honestly taken was the course which he took. He acquitted Hastings on the Rohilla charge. He softened down the Benares charge till it became no charge at all; and then he pronounced that it contained matter for impeachment.

Nor must it be forgotten that the principal reason assigned by the ministry for not impeaching Hastings on account of the Rohilla war was this, that the delinquencies of the early part of his administration had been atoned for by the excellence of the later part. Was it not most extraordinary that men who had held this language could afterwards vote that the later part of his administration furnished matter for no less than twenty articles of impeachment? They first represented the conduct of Hastings in 1780 and 1781 as so highly meritorious that, like works of supererogation in the Catholic theology, it ought to be efficacious for the cancelling of former offences; and they then prosecuted him for his conduct in 1780 and 1781.

The general astonishment was the greater, because, only twenty-four hours before, the members on whom the minister could depend had received the usual notes from the treasury, begging them to be in their places and to vote against Mr. Fox's motion. It was asserted by Mr. Hastings that, early on the morning of the very day on which the debate took place, Dundas called on Pitt, woke him, and was closeted with him many hours. The result of this conference was a determination to give up the late Governor-General to the vengeance of the Opposition. It was impossible even for the most powerful minister to carry all his followers with him in so strange a course. Several persons high in office, the Attorney-General, Mr. Grenville, and Lord Mulgrave, divided against Mr. Pitt. But the devoted adherents who stood by the head of the government without asking questions, were sufficiently numerous to turn the scale. A hundred and nineteen members voted for Mr. Fox's motion; seventy-nine against it. Dundas silently followed Pitt.

That good and great man, the late William Wilberforce, often related the events of this remarkable night. He described the amazement of the House, and the bitter reflections which were muttered against the Prime Minister by some of the habitual supporters of government. Pitt himself appeared to feel that his conduct required some explanation. He left the treasury bench, sat for some time next to Mr. Wilberforce, and very earnestly declared that he had found it impossible, as a man of conscience, to stand any longer by Hastings. The business, he said, was too bad. Mr. Wilberforce, we are bound to add, fully believed that his friend was sincere, and that the suspicions to which this mysterious affair gave rise were altogether unfounded.

Those suspicions, indeed, were such as it is painful to mention. The friends of Hastings, most of whom, it is to be observed, generally supported the administration, affirmed that the motive of Pitt and Dundas was jealousy. Hastings was personally a favourite with the King. He was the idol of the East India Company and of its servants. If he were absolved by the Commons, seated among the Lords, admitted to the Board of Control, closely allied with the strong-minded and imperious Thurlow, was it not almost certain that he would soon draw to himself the entire management of Eastern affairs? Was it not possible that he might become a formidable rival in the cabinet? It had probably got abroad that very singular communications had taken place between Thurlow and Major Scott, and that, if the First Lord of the Treasury was afraid to recommend Hastings for a peerage, the Chancellor was ready to take the responsibility of that step on himself. Of all ministers, Pitt was the least likely to submit with patience to such an encroachment on his functions. If the Commons impeached Hastings, all danger was at an end. The proceeding, however it might terminate, would probably last some years. In the meantime, the accused person would be excluded from honours and public employments, and could scarcely venture even to pay his duty at court. Such were the motives attributed by a great part of the public to the young minister, whose ruling passion was generally believed to be avarice of power.

The prorogation soon interrupted the discussions respecting Hastings. In the following year, those discussions were resumed. The charge touching the spoliation of the Begums was brought forward by Sheridan, in a speech which was so imperfectly reported that it may be said to be wholly lost, but which was, without doubt, the most elaborately brilliant of all the productions of his ingenious mind. The impression which it produced was such as has never been equalled. He sat down, not merely amidst cheering, but amidst the loud clapping of hands, in which the Lords below the bar and the strangers in the gallery joined. The excitement of the House was such that no other speaker could obtain a hearing; and the debate was adjourned. The ferment spread fast through the town. Within four and twenty hours, Sheridan was offered a thousand pounds for the copyright of the speech, if he would himself correct it for the press. The impression made by this remarkable display of eloquence on severe and experienced critics, whose discernment may be supposed to have been quickened by emulation, was deep and permanent. Mr. Windham, twenty years later, said that the speech deserved all its fame, and was, in spite of some faults of taste, such as were seldom wanting either in the literary or in the parliamentary performances of Sheridan, the finest that had been delivered within the memory of man. Mr. Fox, about the same time, being asked by the late Lord Holland what was the best speech ever made in the House of Commons, assigned the first place, without hesitation, to the great oration of Sheridan on the Oude charge.

When the debate was resumed, the tide ran so strongly against the accused that his friends were coughed and scraped down. Pitt declared himself for Sheridan's motion; and the question was carried by a hundred and seventy-five votes against sixty-eight.

The Opposition, flushed with victory and strongly supported by the public sympathy, proceeded to bring forward a succession of charges relating chiefly to pecuniary transactions. The friends of Hastings were discouraged, and, having now no hope of being able to avert an impeachment, were not very strenuous in their exertions. At length the House, having agreed to twenty articles of charge, directed Burke to go before the Lords, and to impeach the late Governor-General of High Crimes and Misdemeanours. Hastings was at the same time arrested by the Sergeant-at-arms, and carried to the bar of the Peers.

The session was now within ten days of its close. It was, therefore, impossible that any progress could be made in the trial till the next year. Hastings was admitted to bail; and further proceedings were postponed till the Houses should re-assemble.

When Parliament met in the following winter, the Commons proceeded to elect a committee for managing the impeachment. Burke stood at the head; and with him were associated most of the leading members of the Opposition. But when the name of Francis was read a fierce contention arose. It was said that Francis and Hastings were notoriously on bad terms, that they had been at feud during many years, that on one occasion their mutual aversion had impelled them to seek each other's lives, and that it would be improper and indelicate to select a private enemy to be a public accuser. It was urged on the other side with great force, particularly by Mr. Windham, that impartiality, though the first duty of a judge, had never been reckoned among the qualities of an advocate; that in the ordinary administration of criminal justice among the English, the aggrieved party, the very last person who ought to be admitted into the jury-box, is the prosecutor; that what was wanted in a manager was, not that he should be free from bias, but that he should be able, well informed, energetic, and active. The ability and information of Francis were admitted; and the very animosity with which he was reproached, whether a virtue or a vice, was at least a pledge for his energy and activity. It seems difficult to refute these arguments. But the inveterate hatred borne by Francis to Hastings had excited general disgust. The House decided that Francis should not be a manager. Pitt voted with the majority, Dundas with the minority.

In the meantime, the preparations for the trial had proceeded rapidly; and on the thirteenth of February, 1788, the sittings of the Court commenced. There have been spectacles more dazzling to the eye, more gorgeous with jewellery and cloth of gold, more attractive to grown-up children, than that which was then exhibited at Westminster; but, perhaps, there never was a spectacle so well calculated to strike a highly cultivated, a reflecting, an imaginative mind. All the various kinds of interest which belong to the near and to the distant, to the present and to the past, were collected on one spot, and in one hour. All the talents and all the accomplishments which are developed by liberty and civilisation were now displayed, with every advantage that could be derived both from cooperation and from contrast. Every step in the proceedings carried the mind either backward, through many troubled centuries, to the days when the foundations of our constitution were laid; or far away, over boundless seas and deserts, to dusky nations living under strange stars, worshipping strange gods, and writing strange characters from right to left. The High Court of Parliament was to sit according to forms handed down from the days of the Plantagenets, on an Englishman accused of exercising tyranny over the lord of the holy city of Benares, and over the ladies of the princely house of Oude.

The place was worthy of such a trial. It was the great hall of William Rufus, the hall which had resounded with acclamations at the inauguration of thirty kings, the hall which had witnessed the just sentence of Bacon and the just absolution of Somers, the hall where the eloquence of Strafford had for a moment awed and melted a victorious party inflamed with just resentment, the hall where Charles had confronted the High Court of Justice with the placid courage which has half redeemed his fame. Neither military nor civil pomp was wanting. The avenues were lined with grenadiers. The streets were kept clear by cavalry. The peers, robed in gold and ermine, were marshalled by the heralds under Garter King-at-arms. The judges in their vestments of state attended to give advice on points of law. Near a hundred and seventy lords, three fourths of the Upper House as the Upper House then was, walked in solemn order from their usual place of assembling to the tribunal. The junior baron present led the way, George Eliott, Lord Heath-field, recently ennobled for his memorable defence of Gibraltar against the fleets and armies of France and Spain. The long procession was closed by the Duke of Norfolk, Earl Marshal of the realm, by the great dignitaries, and by the brothers and sons of the King. Last of all came the Prince of Wales, conspicuous by his fine person and noble bearing. The grey old walls were hung with scarlet. The long galleries were crowded by an audience such as has rarely excited the fears or the emulation of an orator. There were gathered together, from all parts of a great, free, enlightened, and prosperous empire, grace and female loveliness, wit and learning, the representatives of every science and of every art. There were seated round the Queen the fair-haired young daughters of the house of Brunswick. There the Ambassadors of great Kings and Commonwealths gazed with admiration on a spectacle which no other country in the world could present. There Siddons, in the prime of her majestic beauty, looked with emotion on a scene surpassing all the imitations of the stage. There the historian of the Roman Empire thought of the days when Cicero pleaded the cause of Sicily against Verres, and when, before a senate which still retained some show of freedom, Tacitus thundered against the oppressor of Africa. There were seen, side by side, the greatest painter and the greatest scholar of the age. The spectacle had allured Reynolds from that easel which has preserved to us the thoughtful foreheads of so many writers and statesmen, and the sweet smiles of so many noble matrons. It had induced Parr to suspend his labours in that dark and profound mine from which he had extracted a vast treasure of erudition, a treasure too often buried in the earth, too often paraded with injudicious and inelegant ostentation, but still precious, massive, and splendid. There appeared the voluptuous charms of her to whom the heir of the throne had in secret plighted his faith. There too was she, the beautiful mother of a beautiful race, the Saint Cecilia whose delicate features, lighted up by love and music, art has rescued from the common decay. There were the members of that brilliant society which quoted, criticized, and exchanged repartees, under the rich peacock-hangings of Mrs. Montague. And there the ladies whose lips, more persuasive than those of Fox himself, had carried the Westminster election against palace and treasury, shone round Georgiana Duchess of Devonshire.

The Sergeants made proclamation. Hastings advanced to the bar, and bent his knee. The culprit was indeed not unworthy of that great presence. He had ruled an extensive and populous country, had made laws and treaties, had sent forth armies, had set up and pulled down princes. And in his high place he had so borne himself, that all had feared him, that most had loved him, and that hatred itself could deny him no title to glory, except virtue. He looked like a great man, and not like a bad man. A person small and emaciated, yet deriving dignity from a carriage which, while it indicated deference to the court, indicated also habitual self-possession and self-respect, a high and intellectual forehead, a brow pensive, but not gloomy, a mouth of inflexible decision, a face pale and worn, but serene, on which was written, as legibly as under the picture in the council-chamber at Calcutta, *Mens æqua in arduis*; such was the aspect with which the great proconsul presented himself to his judges.

His counsel accompanied him, men all of whom were afterwards raised by their talents and learning to the highest posts in their profession, the bold and strong-minded Law, afterwards Chief Justice of the King's Bench; the more humane and eloquent Dallas, afterwards Chief Justice of the Common Pleas; and Plomer who, near twenty years later, successfully conducted in the same high court the defence of Lord Melville, and subsequently became Vice-chancellor and Master of the Rolls.

But neither the culprit nor his advocates attracted so much notice as the accusers. In the midst of the blaze of red drapery, a space had been fitted up with green benches and tables for the Commons. The managers, with Burke at their head, appeared in full dress. The collectors of gossip did not fail to remark that even Fox, generally so regardless of his appearance, had paid to the illustrious tribunal the compliment of wearing a bag and sword. Pitt had refused to be one of the conductors of the impeachment; and his commanding, copious, and sonorous eloquence was wanting to that great muster of various talents. Age and blindness had unfitted Lord North for the duties of a public prosecutor; and his friends were left without the help of his excellent sense, his tact, and his urbanity. But, in spite of the absence of these two distinguished members of the Lower House, the box in which the managers stood contained an array of speakers such as perhaps had not appeared together since the great age of Athenian eloquence. There were Fox and Sheridan, the English Demosthenes and the English Hyperides. There was Burke, ignorant, indeed, or negligent of the art of adapting his reasonings and his style to the capacity and taste of his hearers, but in amplitude of comprehension and richness of imagination superior to every orator, ancient or modern. There, with eyes reverentially fixed on Burke, appeared the finest gentleman of the age, his form developed by every manly exercise, his face beaming with intelligence and spirit, the ingenious, the chivalrous, the high-souled Windham. Nor, though surrounded by such men, did the youngest manager pass unnoticed. At an age when most of those who distinguish themselves in life are still contending for prizes and fellowships at college, he had won for himself a conspicuous place in parliament. No advantage of fortune or connexion was wanting that could set off to the height his splendid talents and his unblemished honour. At twenty-three he had been thought worthy to be ranked with the veteran statesmen who appeared as the delegates of the British Commons, at the bar of the British nobility. All who stood at that bar, save him alone, are gone, culprit, advocates, accusers. To the generation which is now in the vigour of life, he is the sole representative of a great age which has passed away. But those who, within the last ten years, have listened with delight, till the morning sun shone on the tapestries of the House of Lords, to the lofty and animated eloquence of Charles Earl Grey, are able to form some estimate of the powers of a race of men among whom he was not the foremost.

The charges and the answers of Hastings were first read. This ceremony occupied two whole days, and was rendered less tedious than it would otherwise have been by the silver voice and just emphasis of Cowper, the clerk of the court, a near relation of the amiable poet. On the third day Burke rose. Four sittings were occupied by his opening speech, which was intended to be a general introduction to all the charges. With an exuberance of thought and a splendour of diction which more than satisfied the highly raised expectation of the audience, he described the character and institutions of the natives of India, recounted the circumstances in which the Asiatic empire of Britain had originated, and set forth the constitution of the Company and of the English Presidencies. Having thus attempted to communicate to his hearers an idea of Eastern society, as vivid as that which existed in his own mind, he proceeded to arraign the administration of Hastings as systematically conducted in defiance of morality and public law. The energy and pathos of the great orator extorted expressions of un-

M—15*

wonted admiration from the stern and hostile Chancellor, and, for a moment, seemed to pierce even the resolute heart of the defendant. The ladies in the galleries, unaccustomed to such displays of eloquence, excited by the solemnity of the occasion, and perhaps not unwilling to display their taste and sensibility, were in a state of uncontrollable emotion. Handkerchiefs were pulled out; smelling-bottles were handed round; hysterical sobs and screams were heard; and Mrs. Sheridan was carried out in a fit. At length the orator concluded. Raising his voice till the old arches of Irish oak resounded, "Therefore," said he, "hath it with all confidence been ordered by the Commons of Great Britain, that I impeach Warren Hastings of high crimes and misdemeanours. I impeach him in the name of the Commons' House of Parliament whose trust he has betrayed. I impeach him in the name of the English nation, whose ancient honour he has sullied. I impeach him in the name of the people of India, whose rights he has trodden under foot, and whose country he has turned into a desert. Lastly, in the name of human nature itself, in the name of both sexes, in the name of every age, in the name of every rank, I impeach the common enemy and oppressor of all!"

When the deep murmur of various emotions had subsided, Mr. Fox rose to address the Lords respecting the course of proceeding to be followed. The wish of the accusers was that the Court would bring to a close the investigation of the first charge before the second was opened. The wish of Hastings and of his counsel was that the managers should open all the charges, and produce all the evidence for the prosecution, before the defence began. The Lords retired to their own House to consider the question. The Chancellor took the side of Hastings. Lord Loughborough, who was now in opposition, supported the demand of the managers. The division showed which way the inclination of the tribunal leaned. A majority of near three to one decided in favour of the course for which Hastings contended.

When the Court sat again, Mr. Fox, assisted by Mr. Grey, opened the charge respecting Cheyte Sing, and several days were spent in reading papers and hearing witnesses. The next article was that relating to the Princesses of Oude. The conduct of this part of the case was intrusted to Sheridan. The curiosity of the public to hear him was unbounded. His sparkling and highly finished declamation lasted two days; but the Hall was crowded to suffocation during the whole time. It was said that fifty guineas had been paid for a single ticket. Sheridan, when he concluded, contrived, with a knowledge of stage-effect which his father might have envied, to sink back, as if exhausted, into the arms of Burke, who hugged him with the energy of generous admiration.

June was now far advanced. The session could not last much longer; and the progress which had been made in the impeachment was not very satisfactory. There were twenty charges. On two only of these had even the case for the prosecution been heard: and it was now a year since Hastings had been admitted to bail.

The interest taken by the public in the trial was great when the Court began to sit, and rose to the height when Sheridan spoke on the charge relating to the Begums. From that time the excitement went down fast. The spectacle had lost the attraction of novelty. The great displays of rhetoric were over. What was behind was not of a nature to entice men of letters from their books in the morning, or to tempt ladies who had left the masquerade at two to be out of bed before eight. There remained examinations and cross-examinations. There remained statements of accounts. There remained the reading of papers, filled with words unintelligible to English ears, with lacs and crores, zemindars and aumils, sunnuds and perwannahs, jaghires and nuzzurs. There remained bickerings, not always carried on with the best taste or with the best temper, between the managers of the impeachment and the counsel for the defence, particularly between Mr. Burke and Mr. Law. There remained the endless marches and countermarches of the Peers between their house and the Hall: for as often as a point of law was to be discussed, their lordships retired to discuss it apart; and the consequence was, as a peer wittily said, that the judges walked and the trial stood still.

It is to be added that, in the spring of 1788 when the trial commenced, no important question, either of domestic or foreign policy, excited the public mind. The proceeding in Westminster Hall, therefore, naturally attracted most of the attention of Parliament and of the public. It was the one great event of that season. But in the following year the King's illness, the debates on the Regency, the expectation of a change of Ministry, completely diverted public attention from Indian affairs; and within a fortnight after George the Third had returned thanks in St. Paul's for his recovery, the States-General of France met at Versailles. In the midst of the agitation produced by these events, the impeachment was for a time almost forgotten.

The trial in the Hall went on languidly. In the session of 1788, when the proceedings had the interest of novelty, and when the Peers had little other business before them, only thirty-five days were given to the impeachment. In 1789, the Regency Bill occupied the Upper House till the session was far advanced. When the King recovered the circuits were beginning. The judges left town; the Lords waited for the return of the oracles of jurisprudence; and the consequence was that during the whole year only seventeen days were given to the case of Hastings. It was clear that the matter would be protracted to a length unprecedented in the annals of criminal law.

In truth, it is impossible to deny that impeachment, though it is a fine ceremony, and though it may have been useful in the seventeenth century, is not a proceeding from which much good can now be expected. Whatever confidence may be placed in the decisions of the Peers on an appeal arising out of ordinary litigation, it is certain that no man has the least confidence in their impartiality, when a great public functionary, charged with a great state crime, is brought to their bar. They are all politicians. There is hardly one among them whose vote on an impeachment may not be confidently predicted before a witness has been examined; and, even if it were possible to rely on their justice, they would still be quite unfit to try such a cause as that of Hastings. They sit only during half the year. They have to transact much legislative and much judicial business. The law-lords, whose advice is required to guide the unlearned majority, are employed daily in administering justice elsewhere. It is impossible, therefore, that during a busy session, the Upper House should give more than a few days to an impeachment. To expect that their Lordships would give up partridge-shooting, in order to bring the greatest delinquent to speedy justice, or to relieve accused innocence by speedy acquittal, would be unreasonable indeed. A well constituted tribunal, sitting regularly six days in the week, and nine hours in the day, would have brought the trial of Hastings to a close in less than three months. The Lords had not finished their work in seven years.

The result ceased to be matter of doubt, from the time when the Lords resolved that they would be guided by the rules of evidence which are received in the inferior courts of the realm. Those rules, it is well known, exclude much information which would be quite sufficient to determine the conduct of any reasonable man, in the most important transactions of private life. Those rules, at every assizes, save scores of culprits whom judges, jury, and spectators, firmly believe to be guilty. But when those rules were rigidly applied to offences committed many years before, at the distance of many thousand miles, conviction was, of course, out of the question. We do not blame the accused and his counsel for availing themselves of every legal advantage in order to obtain an acquittal. But it is clear that an acquittal so obtained cannot be pleaded in bar of the judgment of history.

Several attempts were made by the friends of Hastings to put a stop to the trial. In 1789 they proposed a vote of censure upon Burke, for some violent language which he had used respecting the death of Nuncomar and the connexion between Hastings and Impey. Burke was then unpopular in the last degree both with the House and with the country. The asperity and indecency of some expressions which he had used during the debates on the Regency had annoyed even his warmest friends. The vote of censure was carried; and those who had moved it hoped that the managers would resign in disgust. Burke was deeply hurt. But his zeal for what he considered as the cause of justice and mercy triumphed over his personal feelings. He received the censure of the house with dignity and meekness, and declared that no personal mortification or humiliation should induce him to flinch from the sacred duty which he had undertaken.

In the following year the Parliament was dissolved; and the friends of Hastings entertained a hope that the new House of Commons might not be disposed to go on with the impeachment. They began by maintaining that the whole proceeding was terminated by the dissolution. Defeated on this point, they made a direct motion that the impeachment should be dropped; but they were defeated by the combined forces of the Government and the Opposition. It was, however, resolved that, for the sake of expedition, many of the articles should be withdrawn. In truth, had not some such measure been adopted, the trial would have lasted till the defendant was in his grave.

At length, in the spring of 1795, the decision was pronounced, near eight years after Hastings had been brought by the Sergeant-at-arms of the Commons to the bar of the Lords. On the last day of this great procedure the public curiosity, long suspended, seemed to be revived. Anxiety about the judgment there could be none; for it had been fully ascertained that there was a great majority for the defendant. Nevertheless many wished to see the pageant, and the hall was as much crowded as on the first day. But those who, having been present on the first day, now bore a part in the proceedings of the last, were few; and most of those few were altered men.

As Hastings himself said, the arraignment had taken place before one generation, and the judgment was pronounced by another. The spectator could not look at the woolsack, or at the red benches of the Peers, or at the green benches of the Commons, without seeing something that reminded him of the instability of all human things, of the instability of power and fame and life, of the more lamentable instability of friendship. The great seal was borne before Lord Loughborough who, when the trial commenced, was a fierce opponent of Mr. Pitt's government, and who was now a member of that government, while Thurlow, who presided in the court when it first sat, estranged from all his old allies, sat scowling among the junior barons. Of about a hundred and sixty nobles who walked in the procession on the first day, sixty had been laid in their family vaults. Still more affecting must have been the sight of the managers' box. What had become of that fair fellowship, so closely bound together by public and private ties, so resplendent with every talent and accomplishment? It had been scattered by calamities more bitter than the bitterness of death. The great chiefs were still living, and still in the full vigour of their genius. But their friendship was at an end. It had been violently and publicly dissolved, with tears and stormy reproaches. If those men, once so dear to each other, were now compelled to meet for the purpose of managing the impeachment, they met as strangers whom public business had brought together, and behaved to each other with cold and distant civility. Burke had in his vortex whirled away Windham. Fox had been followed by Sheridan and Grey.

Only twenty-nine Peers voted. Of these only six found Hastings guilty on the charges relating to Cheyte Sing and to the Begums. On other charges, the majority in his favour was still greater. On some, he was unanimously absolved. He was then called to the bar, was informed from the woolsack that the Lords had acquitted him, and was solemnly discharged. He bowed respectfully, and retired.

We have said that the decision had been fully expected. It was also generally approved. At the commencement of the trial there had been a strong and indeed unreasonable feeling against Hastings. At the close of the trial, there was a feeling equally strong and equally unreasonable in his favour. One cause of the change was, no doubt, what is commonly called the fickleness of the multitude, but what seems to us to be merely the general law of human nature. Both in individuals and in masses violent excitement is always followed by remission, and often by reaction. We are all inclined to depreciate whatever we have overpraised, and, on the other hand, to show undue indulgence where we have shown undue rigour. It was thus in the case of Hastings. The length of his trial, moreover, made him an object of compassion. It was thought, and not without reason, that, even if he was guilty, he was still an ill-used man, and that an impeachment of eight years was more than a sufficient punishment. It was also felt that, though, in the ordinary course of criminal law, a defendant is not allowed to set off his good actions against his crimes, a great political cause should be tried on different principles, and that a man who had governed an empire during thirteen years might have done some very reprehensible things, and yet might be on the whole deserving of rewards and honours rather than of fine and imprisonment. The press, an instrument neglected by the prosecutors, was used by Hastings and his friends with great effect. Every ship, too, that arrived from Madras or Bengal brought a cuddy full of his admirers. Every gentleman from India spoke of the late Governor-General as having deserved better, and having been treated worse, than any man living. The effect of this testimony, unanimously given by all persons who knew the East, was naturally very great. Retired members of the Indian services, civil and military, were settled in all corners of the kingdom. Each of them was, of course, in his own little circle, regarded as an oracle on an Indian question; and they were, with scarcely one exception, the zealous advocates of Hastings. It is to be added, that the numerous addresses to the late Governor-General, which his friends in Bengal obtained from the natives and transmitted to England, made a considerable impression. To these addresses we attach little or no importance. That Hastings was beloved by the people whom he governed is true; but the eulogies of pundits, zemindars, Mahommedan doctors, do not prove it to be true. For an English collector or judge would have found it easy to induce any native who could write to sign a panegyric on the most odious ruler that ever was in India. It was said that at Benares, the very place at which the acts set forth in the first article of impeachment had been committed, the natives had erected a temple to Hastings; and this story excited a strong sensation in England. Burke's observations on the apotheosis were admirable. He saw no reason for astonishment, he said, in the incident which had been represented as so striking. He knew something of the mythology of the Brahmins. He knew that, as they worshipped some gods from love, so they worshipped others from fear. He knew that they erected shrines, not only to the benignant deities of light and plenty, but also to the fiends who preside over small-pox and murder. Nor did he at all dispute the claim of Mr. Hastings to be admitted into such a Pantheon. This reply has always struck us as one of the finest that ever was made in Parliament. It is a grave and forcible argument, decorated by the most brilliant wit and fancy.

Hastings was, however, safe. But in every thing except character he would have been far better off if, when first impeached, he had at once pleaded guilty, and paid a fine of fifty thousand pounds. He was a ruined man. The legal expenses of his defence had been enormous. The expenses which did not appear in his attorney's bill were perhaps larger still. Great sums had been paid to Major Scott. Great sums had been laid out in bribing newspapers, rewarding pamphleteers, and circulating tracts. Burke, so early as 1790, declared in the House of Commons that twenty thousand pounds had been employed in corrupting the press. It is certain that no controversial weapon, from the gravest reasoning to the coarsest ribaldry, was left unemployed. Logan defended the accused governor with great ability in prose. For the lovers of verse, the speeches of the managers were burlesqued in Simpkin's letters. It is, we are afraid, indisputable that Hastings stooped so low as to court the aid of that malignant and filthy baboon John Williams, who called himself Anthony Pasquin. It was necessary to subsidise such allies largely. The private hoards of Mrs. Hastings had disappeared. It is said that the banker to whom they had been intrusted had failed. Still, if Hastings had practised strict economy, he would, after all his losses, have had a moderate competence; but in the management of his private affairs he was imprudent. The dearest wish of his heart had always been to regain Daylesford. At length, in the very year in which his trial commenced, the wish was accomplished; and the domain, alienated more than seventy years before, returned to the descendant of its old lords. But the manor-house was a ruin; and the grounds round it had, during many years, been utterly neglected. Hastings proceeded to build, to plant, to form a sheet of water, to excavate a grotto; and, before he was dismissed from the bar of the House of Lords, he had expended more than forty thousand pounds in adorning his seat.

The general feeling both of the directors and of the proprietors of the East India Company was that he had great claims on them, that his services to them had been eminent, and that his misfortunes had been the effect of his zeal for their interest. His friends in Leadenhall Street proposed to reimburse him for the costs of his trial, and to settle on him an annuity of five thousand pounds a-year. But the consent of the Board of Control was necessary; and at the head of the Board of Control was Mr. Dundas, who had himself been a party to the impeachment, who had, on that account, been reviled with great bitterness by the adherents of Hastings, and who, therefore, was not in a very complying mood. He refused to consent to what the Directors suggested. The Directors remonstrated. A long controversy followed. Hastings, in the mean time, was reduced to such distress, that he could hardly pay his weekly bills.

At length a compromise was made. An annuity of four thousand a-year was settled on Hastings; and, in order to enable him to meet pressing demands, he was to receive ten years' annuity in advance. The Company was also permitted to lend him fifty thousand pounds, to be repaid by instalments, without interest. This relief, though given in the most absurd manner, was sufficient to enable the retired governor to live in comfort, and even in luxury, if he had been a skilful manager. But he was careless and profuse, and was more than once under the necessity of applying to the Company for assistance, which was liberally given.

He had security and affluence, but not the power and dignity which, when he landed from India, he had reason to expect. He had then looked forward to a coronet, a red riband, a seat at the Council Board, an office at Whitehall. He was then only fifty-two, and might hope for many years of bodily and mental vigour. The case was widely different when he left the bar of the Lords. He was now too old a man to turn his mind to a new class of studies and duties. He had no chance of receiving any mark of royal favour while Mr. Pitt remained in power; and, when Mr. Pitt retired, Hastings was approaching his seventieth year.

Once, and only once, after his acquittal, he interfered in politics; and that interference was not much to his honour. In 1804 he exerted himself strenuously to prevent Mr. Addington, against whom Fox and Pitt had combined, from resigning the Treasury. It is difficult to believe that a man so able and energetic as Hastings can have thought that, when Bonaparte was at Boulogne with a great army, the defence of our island could safely be entrusted to a ministry which did not contain a single person whom flattery could describe as a great statesman. It is also certain that, on the important question which had raised Mr. Addington to power, and on which he differed from both Fox and Pitt, Hastings, as might have been expected, agreed with Fox and Pitt, and was decidedly opposed to Addington. Religious intolerance has never been the vice of the Indian service, and certainly was not the vice of Hastings. But Mr. Addington had treated him with marked favour. Fox had been a principal manager of the impeachment. To Pitt it was owing that there had been an impeachment; and Hastings, we fear, was on this occasion guided by personal considerations, rather than by a regard to the public interest.

The last twenty-four years of his life were chiefly passed at Daylesford. He amused himself with embellishing his grounds, riding fine Arab horses, fattening prize-cattle, and trying to rear Indian animals and vegetables in England. He sent for seeds of a very fine custard-apple, from the garden of what had once been his own villa, among the green hedgerows of Allipore. He tried also to naturalise in Worcestershire the delicious leechee, almost the only fruit of Bengal which deserves to be regretted even amidst the plenty of Covent Garden. The Mogul emperors, in the time of their greatness, had in vain attempted to introduce into Hindostan the goat of the table-land of Thibet, whose down supplies the looms of Cashmere with the materials of the finest shawls. Hastings tried, with no better fortune, to rear a breed at Daylesford; nor does he seem to have succeeded better with the cattle of Bootan, whose tails are in high esteem as the best fans for brushing away the mosquitoes.

Literature divided his attention with his conservatories and his menagerie. He had always loved books, and they were now necessary to him. Though not a poet, in any high sense of the word, he wrote neat and polished lines with great facility, and was fond of exercising this talent. Indeed, if we must speak out, he seems to have been more of a Trissotin than was to be expected from the powers of his mind, and from the great part which he had played in life. We are assured in these Memoirs that the first thing which he did in the morning was to compose a copy of verses. When the family and guests assembled, the poem made its appearance as regularly as the eggs and rolls; and Mr. Gleig requires us to believe that, if from any accident Hastings came to the breakfast-table without one of his charming performances in his hand, the omission was felt by all as a grievous disappointment. Tastes differ widely. For ourselves, we must say that, however good the breakfasts at Daylesford may have been,—and we are assured that the tea was of the most aromatic flavour, and that neither tongue nor venison-pasty was wanting,—we should have thought the reckoning high if we had been forced to earn our repast by listening every day to a new madrigal or sonnet composed by our host. We are glad, however, that Mr. Gleig has preserved this little feature of character, though we think it by no means a beauty. It is good to be often reminded of the inconsistency of human nature, and to learn to look without wonder or disgust on the weaknesses which are found in the strongest minds. Dionysius in old times, Frederic in the last century, with capacity and vigour equal to the conduct of the greatest affairs, united all the little vanities and affectations of provincial blue-stockings. These great examples may console the admirers of Hastings for the affliction of seeing him reduced to the level of the Hayleys and Sewards.

When Hastings had passed many years in retirement, and had

long outlived the common age of men, he again became for a short time an object of general attention. In 1813 the charter of the East India Company was renewed; and much discussion about Indian affairs took place in Parliament. It was determined to examine witnesses at the bar of the Commons; and Hastings was ordered to attend. He had appeared at that bar once before. It was when he read his answer to the charges which Burke had laid on the table. Since that time twenty-seven years had elapsed; public feeling had undergone a complete change; the nation had now forgotten his faults, and remembered only his services. The reappearance, too, of a man who had been among the most distinguished of a generation that had passed away, who now belonged to history, and who seemed to have risen from the dead, could not but produce a solemn and pathetic effect. The Commons received him with acclamations, ordered a chair to be set for him, and, when he retired, rose and uncovered. There were, indeed, a few who did not sympathize with the general feeling. One or two of the managers of the impeachment were present. They sate in the same seats which they had occupied when they had been thanked for the services which they had rendered in Westminster Hall: for, by the courtesy of the House, a member who has been thanked in his place is considered as having a right always to occupy that place. These gentlemen were not disposed to admit that they had employed several of the best years of their lives in persecuting an innocent man. They accordingly kept their seats, and pulled their hats over their brows; but the exceptions only made the prevailing enthusiasm more remarkable. The Lords received the old man with similar tokens of respect. The University of Oxford conferred on him the degree of Doctor of Laws; and, in the Sheldonian theatre, the undergraduates welcomed him with tumultuous cheering.

These marks of public esteem were soon followed by marks of royal favour. Hastings was sworn of the Privy Council, and was admitted to a long private audience of the Prince Regent, who treated him very graciously. When the Emperor of Russia and the King of Prussia visited England, Hastings appeared in their train both at Oxford and in the Guildhall of London, and, though surrounded by a crowd of princes and great warriors, was every where received by the public with marks of respect and admiration. He was presented by the Prince Regent both to Alexander and to Frederick William; and his Royal Highness went so far as to declare in public that honours far higher than a seat in the Privy Council were due, and would soon be paid, to the man who had saved the British dominions in Asia. Hastings now confidently expected a peerage; but, from some unexplained cause, he was again disappointed.

He lived about four years longer, in the enjoyment of good spirits, of faculties not impaired to any painful or degrading extent, and of health such as is rarely enjoyed by those who attain such an age. At length, on the twenty-second of August 1818, in the eighty-sixth year of his age, he met death with the same tranquil and decorous fortitude which he had opposed to all the trials of his various and eventful life.

With all his faults,—and they were neither few nor small,—only one cemetery was worthy to contain his remains. In that temple of silence and reconciliation where the enmities of twenty generations lie buried, in the Great Abbey which has during many ages afforded a quiet resting-place to those whose minds and bodies have been shattered by the contentions of the Great Hall, the dust of the illustrious accused should have mingled with the dust of the illustrious accusers. This was not to be. Yet the place of interment was not ill chosen. Behind the chancel of the parish-church of Daylesford, in earth which already held the bones of many chiefs of the house of Hastings, was laid the coffin of the greatest man who has ever borne that ancient and widely extended name. On that very spot probably, fourscore years before, the little Warren, meanly clad and scantily fed, had played with the children of ploughmen. Even then his young mind had revolved plans which might be called romantic. Yet, however romantic, it is not likely that they had been so strange as the truth. Not only had the poor orphan retrieved the fallen fortunes of his line. Not only had he repurchased the old lands, and rebuilt the old dwelling. He had preserved and extended an empire. He had founded a polity. He had administered government and war with more than the capacity of Richelieu. He had patronised learning with the judicious liberality of Cosmo. He had been attacked by the most formidable combination of enemies that ever sought the destruction of a single victim; and over that combination, after a struggle of ten years, he had triumphed. He had at length gone down to his grave in the fulness of age, in peace, after so many troubles, in honour, after so much obloquy.

Those who look on his character without favour or malevolence will pronounce that, in the two great elements of all social virtue, in respect for the rights of others, and in sympathy for the sufferings of others, he was deficient. His principles were somewhat lax. His heart was somewhat hard. But while we cannot with truth describe him either as a righteous or as a merciful ruler, we cannot regard without admiration the amplitude and fertility of his intellect, his rare talents for command, for administration, and for controversy, his dauntless courage, his honourable poverty, his fervent zeal for the interests of the state, his noble equanimity, tried by both extremes of fortune, and never disturbed by either.

## WILLIAM PITT

### (JANUARY 1859)

WILLIAM PITT, the second son of William Pitt, Earl of Chatham, and of Lady Hester Grenville, daughter of Hester, Countess Temple, was born on the 28th of May 1759. The child inherited a name which, at the time of his birth, was the most illustrious in the civilised world, and was pronounced by every Englishman with pride, and by every enemy of England with mingled admiration and terror. During the first year of his life, every month had its illuminations and bonfires, and every wind brought some messenger charged with joyful tidings and hostile standards. In Westphalia the English infantry won a great battle which arrested the armies of Louis the Fifteenth in the midst of a career of conquest: Boscawen defeated one French fleet on the coast of Portugal: Hawke put to flight another in the Bay of Biscay: Johnson took Niagara: Amherst took Ticonderoga: Wolfe died by the most enviable of deaths under the walls of Quebec: Clive destroyed a Dutch armament in the Hooghley, and established the English supremacy in Bengal: Coote routed Lally at Wandewash, and established the English supremacy in the Carnatic. The nation, while loudly applauding the successful warriors, considered them all, on sea and on land, in Europe, in America, and in Asia, merely as instruments which received their direction from one superior mind. It was the great William Pitt, the great commoner, who had vanquished French marshals in Germany, and French admirals on the Atlantic; who had conquered for his country one great empire on the frozen shores of Ontario, and another under the tropical sun near the mouths of the Ganges. It was not in the nature of things that popularity such as he at this time enjoyed should be permanent. That popularity had lost its gloss before his children were old enough to understand that their father was a great man. He was at length placed in situations in which neither his talents for administration nor his talents for debate appeared to the best advantage. The energy and decision which had eminently fitted him for the direction of war were not needed in time of peace. The lofty and spirit-stirring eloquence which had made him supreme in the House of Commons, often fell dead on the House of Lords. A cruel malady racked his joints, and left his joints only to fall on his nerves and on his brain. During the closing years of his life, he was odious to the court, and yet was not on cordial terms with the great body of the opposition. Chatham was only the ruin of Pitt, but an awful and majestic ruin, not to be contemplated by any man of sense and feeling without emotions resembling those which are excited by the remains of the Parthenon and of the Coliseum. In one respect the old statesman was eminently happy. Whatever might be the vicissitudes of his public life, he never failed to find peace and love by his own hearth. He loved all his children, and was loved by them; and, of all his children, the one of whom he was fondest and proudest was his second son.

The child's genius and ambition displayed themselves with a rare and almost unnatural precocity. At seven, the interest which he took in grave subjects, the ardour with which he pursued his studies, and the sense and vivacity of his remarks on books and on events, amazed his parents and instructors. One of his sayings of this date was reported to his mother by his tutor. In August 1766, when the world was agitated by the news that Mr. Pitt had become Earl of Chatham, little William exclaimed, "I am glad that I am not the eldest son. I want to speak in the House of Commons like papa." A letter is extant in which Lady Chatham, a woman of considerable abilities, remarked to her lord, that their younger son at twelve had left far behind him his elder brother, who was fifteen. "The fineness," she wrote, "of William's mind makes him enjoy with the greatest pleasure what would be above the reach of any other creature of his small age." At fourteen the lad was in intellect a man. Hayley, who met him at Lyme in the summer of 1773, was astonished, delighted, and somewhat overawed, by hearing wit and wisdom from so young a mouth. The poet, indeed, was afterwards sorry that his shyness had prevented him from submitting the plan of an extensive literary work, which he was then meditating, to the judgment of this extraordinary boy. The boy, indeed, had already written a tragedy, bad of course, but not worse than the tragedies of his friend. This piece is still preserved at Chevening, and is in some respects highly curious. There is no love. The whole plot is political; and it is remarkable that the interest, such as it is, turns on a contest about a regency. On one side is a faithful servant of the Crown, on the other an ambitious and unprincipled conspirator. At length the king, who had been missing, reappears, resumes his power, and rewards the faithful defender of his rights. A reader who should judge only by internal evidence would have no hesitation in pronouncing that the play was written by some Pittite poetaster at the time of the rejoicings for the recovery of George the Third in 1789.

The pleasure with which William's parents observed the rapid development of his intellectual powers was alloyed by apprehensions about his health. He shot up alarmingly fast; he was often ill, and always weak; and it was feared that it would be impossible to rear a stripling so tall, so slender, and so feeble. Port wine was prescribed by his medical advisers; and it is said that he was, at fourteen, accustomed to take this agreeable physic in quantities which would, in our abstemious age, be thought much more than sufficient for any full-grown man. This regimen, though it would probably have killed ninety-nine boys out of a hundred, seems to have been well suited to the peculiarities of William's constitution; for at fifteen he ceased to be molested by disease, and, though never a strong man, continued, during many years of labour and anxiety, of nights passed in debate and of summers passed in London, to be a tolerably healthy one. It was probably on account of the delicacy of his frame that he was not educated like other boys of the same rank. Almost all the eminent English statesmen and orators to whom he was afterwards opposed or allied, North, Fox, Shelburne, Windham, Grey, Wellesley, Grenville, Sheridan, Canning, went through the training of great public schools. Lord Chatham had himself been a distinguished Etonian; and it is seldom that a distinguished Etonian forgets his obligations to Eton. But William's infirmities required a vigilance and tenderness such as could be found only at home. He was therefore bred under the paternal roof. His studies were superintended by a clergyman named Wilson; and those studies, though often interrupted by illness, were prosecuted with extraordinary success. Before the lad had completed his fifteenth year, his knowledge both of the ancient languages and of mathematics was such as very few men of eighteen then carried up to college. He was therefore sent, towards the close of the year 1773, to Pembroke Hall, in the university of Cambridge. So young a student required much more than the ordinary care which a college tutor bestows on undergraduates. The governor, to whom the direction of William's academical life was confided, was a bachelor of arts named Pretyman, who had been senior wrangler in the preceding year, and who, though not a man of prepossessing appearance or brilliant parts, was eminently acute and laborious, a sound scholar, and an excellent geometrician. At Cambridge, Pretyman was, during more than two years, the inseparable companion, and indeed almost the only companion, of his pupil. A close and lasting friendship sprang up between the pair. The disciple was able, before he completed his twenty-eighth year, to make his preceptor bishop of Lincoln and dean of St. Paul's; and the preceptor showed his gratitude by writing a Life of the disciple, which enjoys the distinction of being the worst biographical work of its size in the world.

Pitt, till he graduated, had scarcely one acquaintance, attended chapel regularly morning and evening, dined every day in hall, and never went to a single evening party. At seventeen, he was admitted, after the bad fashion of those times, by right of birth, without any examination, to the degree of Master of Arts. But he continued during some years to reside at college, and to apply himself vigorously, under Pretyman's direction, to the studies of the place, while mixing freely in the best academic society.

The stock of learning which Pitt laid in during this part of his life was certainly very extraordinary. In fact, it was all that he ever possessed; for he very early became too busy to have any spare time for books. The work in which he took the greatest delight was Newton's Principia. His liking for mathematics, indeed, amounted to a passion, which, in the opinion of his instructors, themselves distinguished mathematicians, required to be checked rather than encouraged. The acuteness and readiness with which he solved problems was pronounced by one of the ablest of the moderators, who in those days presided over the disputations in the schools, and conducted the examinations of the Senate-House, to be unrivalled in the university. Nor was the youth's proficiency in classical learning less remarkable. In one respect, indeed, he appeared to disadvantage when compared with even second-rate and third-rate men from public schools. He had never, while under Wilson's care, been in the habit of composing in the ancient languages; and he therefore never acquired that knack of versification which is sometimes possessed by clever boys whose knowledge of the language and literature of Greece and Rome is very superficial. It would have been utterly out of his power to produce such charming elegiac lines as those in which Wellesley bade farewell to Eton, or such Virgilian hexameters as those in which Canning described the pilgrimage to Mecca. But it may be doubted whether any scholar has ever, at twenty, had a more solid and profound knowledge of the two great tongues of the old civilised world. The facility with which he penetrated the meaning of the most intricate sentences in the Attic writers astonished veteran critics. He had set his heart on being intimately acquainted with all the extant poetry of Greece, and was not satisfied till he had mastered Lycophron's Cassandra, the most obscure work in the whole range of ancient literature. This strange rhapsody, the difficulties of which have perplexed and repelled many excellent scholars, "he read," says his preceptor, "with an ease at first sight, which, if I had not witnessed it, I should have thought beyond the compass of human intellect."

To modern literature Pitt paid comparatively little attention. He knew no living language except French; and French he knew very imperfectly. With a few of the best English writers he was intimate, particularly with Shakespeare and Milton. The debate in Pandemonium was, as it well deserved to be, one of his favourite passages; and his early friends used to talk, long after his death, of the just emphasis and the melodious cadence with which they had heard him recite the incomparable speech of Belial. He had indeed been carefully trained from infancy in the art of managing his voice, a voice naturally clear and deep-toned. His father, whose oratory owed no small part of its effect to that art, had been a most skilful and judicious instructor. At a later period, the wits of Brookes's, irritated by observing, night after night, how powerfully Pitt's sonorous elocution fascinated the rows of country gentlemen, reproached him with having been "taught by his dad on a stool."

His education, indeed, was well adapted to form a great parliamentary speaker. One argument often urged against those classical studies which occupy so large a part of the early life of every gentleman bred in the south of our island is, that they prevent him from acquiring a command of his mother tongue, and that it is not unusual to meet with a youth of excellent parts, who writes Ciceronian Latin prose and Horatian Latin Alcaics, but who would find it impossible to express his thoughts in pure, perspicuous, and forcible English. There may perhaps be some truth in this observation. But the classical studies of Pitt were carried on in a peculiar manner, and had the effect of enriching his English vocabulary, and of making him wonderfully expert in the art of constructing correct English sentences. His practice was to look over a page or two of a Greek or Latin author, to make himself master of the meaning, and then to read the passage straight forward into his own language. This practice, begun under his first teacher Wilson, was continued under Pretyman. It is not strange that a young man of great abilities, who had been exercised daily in this way during ten years, should have acquired an almost unrivalled power of putting his thoughts, without premeditation, into words well selected and well arranged.

Of all the remains of antiquity, the orations were those on which he bestowed the most minute examination. His favourite employment was to compare harangues on opposite sides of the same question, to analyse them, and to observe which of the arguments of the first speaker were refuted by the second, which were evaded, and which were left untouched. Nor was it only in books that he at this time studied the art of parliamentary fencing. When he was at home, he had frequent opportunities of hearing important debates at Westminster; and he heard them, not only with interest and enjoyment, but with a close scientific attention resembling that with which a diligent pupil at Guy's Hospital watches every turn of the hand of a great surgeon through a difficult operation. On one of these occasions, Pitt, a youth whose abilities were as yet known only to his own family and to a small knot of college friends, was introduced on the steps of the throne in the House of Lords to Fox, who was his senior by eleven years, and who was already the greatest debater, and one of the greatest orators, that had appeared in England. Fox used afterwards to relate that, as the discussion proceeded, Pitt repeatedly turned to him, and said, "But surely, Mr. Fox, that might be met thus;" or, "Yes; but he lays himself open to this retort." What the particular criticisms were Fox had forgotten; but he said that he was much struck at the time by the precocity of a lad who, through the whole sitting, seemed to be thinking only how all the speeches on both sides could be answered.

One of the young man's visits to the House of Lords was a sad and memorable era in his life. He had not quite completed his nineteenth year, when, on the 7th of April, 1778, he attended his father to Westminster. A great debate was expected. It was known that France had recognised the independence of the United States. The Duke of Richmond was about to declare his opinion that all thought of subjugating those states ought to be relinquished. Chatham had always maintained that the resistance of the colonies to the mother country was justifiable. But he conceived, very erroneously, that on the day on which their independence should be acknowledged the greatness of England would be at an end. Though sinking under the weight of years and infirmities, he determined, in spite of the entreaties of his family, to be in his place. His son supported him to a seat. The excitement and exertion were too much for the old man. In the very act of addressing the peers, he fell back in convulsions. A few weeks later his corpse was borne, with gloomy pomp, from the Painted Chamber to the Abbey. The favourite child and namesake of the deceased statesman followed the coffin as chief mourner, and saw it deposited in the transept where his own was destined to lie.

His elder brother, now Earl of Chatham, had means sufficient, and barely sufficient, to support the dignity of the peerage. The other members of the family were poorly provided for. William had little more than three hundred a year. It was necessary for him to follow a profession. He had already begun to eat his terms. In the spring of 1780 he came of age. He then quitted Cambridge, was called to the bar, took chambers in Lincoln's Inn, and joined the western circuit. In the autumn of that year a general election took place; and he offered himself as a candidate for the university; but he was at the bottom of the poll. It is said that the grave doctors, who then sate, robed in scarlet, on the benches of Golgotha, thought it great presumption in so young a man to solicit so high a distinction. He was, however, at the request of a hereditary friend, the Duke of Rutland, brought into Parliament by Sir James Lowther for the borough of Appleby.

The dangers of the country were at that time such as might well have disturbed even a constant mind. Army after army had been sent in vain against the rebellious colonists of North America. On pitched fields of battle the advantage had been with the disciplined troops of the mother country. But it was not on pitched fields of battle that the event of such a contest could be decided. An armed nation, with hunger and the Atlantic for auxiliaries, was not to be subjugated. Meanwhile the House of Bourbon, humbled to the dust a few years before by the genius and vigour of Chatham, had seized the opportunity of revenge. France and Spain were united against us, and had recently been joined by Holland. The command of the Mediterranean had been for a time lost. The British flag had been scarcely able to maintain itself in the British Channel. The northern powers professed neutrality; but their neutrality had a menacing aspect. In the East, Hyder had descended on the Carnatic, had destroyed the little army of Baillie, and had spread terror even to the ramparts of Fort Saint George. The discontents of Ireland threatened nothing less than civil war. In England the authority of the government had sunk to the lowest point. The King and the House of Commons were alike unpopular. The cry for parliamentary reform was scarcely less loud and vehement than in the autumn of 1830. Formidable associations, headed, not by ordinary demagogues, but by men of high rank, stainless character, and distinguished ability, demanded a revision of the representative system. The populace, emboldened by the impotence and irresolution of the government, had recently broken loose from all restraint, besieged the chambers of the legislature, hustled peers, hunted bishops, attacked the residences of ambassadors, opened prisons, burned and pulled down houses. London had presented during some days the aspect of a city taken by storm; and it had been necessary to form a camp among the trees of Saint James's Park.

In spite of dangers and difficulties abroad and at home, George the Third, with a firmness which had little affinity with virtue or with wisdom, persisted in his determination to put down the American rebels by force of arms; and his ministers submitted their judgment to his. Some of them were probably actuated merely by selfish cupidity; but their chief, Lord North, a man of high honour, amiable temper, winning manners, lively wit, and excellent talents both for business and for debate, must be acquitted of all sordid motives. He remained at a post from which he had long wished and had repeatedly tried to escape, only because he had not sufficient fortitude to resist the entreaties and reproaches of the King, who silenced all arguments by passionately asking whether any gentleman, any man of spirit, could have the heart to desert a kind master in the hour of extremity.

The opposition consisted of two parties which had once been hostile to each other, and which had been very slowly, and, as it soon appeared, very imperfectly reconciled, but which at this conjuncture seemed to act together with cordiality. The larger of these parties consisted of the great body of the Whig aristocracy. Its head was Charles, Marquess of Rockingham, a man of sense and virtue, and in wealth and parliamentary interest equalled by very few of the English nobles, but afflicted with a nervous timidity which prevented him from taking a prominent part in debate. In the House of Commons, the adherents of Rockingham were led by Fox, whose dissipated habits and ruined fortunes were the talk of the whole town, but whose commanding genius, and whose sweet, generous, and affectionate disposition, extorted the admiration and love of those who most lamented the errors of his private life. Burke, superior to Fox in largeness of comprehension, in extent of knowledge, and in splendour of imagination, but less skilled in that kind of logic and in that kind of rhetoric which convince and persuade great assemblies, was willing to be the lieutenant of a young chief who might have been his son.

A smaller section of the opposition was composed of the old followers of Chatham. At their head was William, Earl of Shelburne, distinguished both as a statesman and as a lover of science and letters. With him were leagued Lord Camden, who had formerly held the Great Seal, and whose integrity, ability, and constitutional knowledge commanded the public respect; Barré, an eloquent and acrimonious declaimer; and Dunning, who had long held the first place at the English bar. It was to this party that Pitt was naturally attracted.

On the 26th of February 1781 he made his first speech in favour of Burke's plan of economical reform. Fox stood up at the same moment, but instantly gave way. The lofty yet animated deportment of the young member, his perfect self-possession, the readiness with which he replied to the orators who had preceded him, the silver tones of his voice, the perfect structure of his unpremeditated sentences, astonished and delighted his hearers. Burke, moved even to tears, exclaimed, "It is not a chip of the old block; it is the old block itself." "Pitt will be one of the first men in Parliament," said a member of the opposition to Fox. "He is so already," answered Fox, in whose nature envy had no place. It is a curious fact, well remembered by some who were very recently living, that soon after this debate Pitt's name was put up by Fox at Brookes's.

On two subsequent occasions during that session Pitt addressed the House, and on both fully sustained the reputation which he had acquired on his first appearance. In the summer, after the prorogation, he again went the western circuit, held several briefs, and acquitted himself in such a manner that he was highly complimented by Buller from the bench, and by Dunning at the bar.

On the 27th of November the Parliament reassembled. Only forty-eight hours before had arrived tidings of the surrender of Cornwallis and his army; and it had consequently been necessary to rewrite the royal speech. Every man in the kingdom, except the King, was now convinced that it was mere madness to think of conquering the United States. In the debate on the report of the address, Pitt spoke with even more energy and brilliancy than on any former occasion. He was warmly applauded by his allies; but it was remarked that no person on his own side of the house was so loud in eulogy as Henry Dundas, the Lord Advocate of Scotland, who spoke from the ministerial ranks. That able and versatile politician distinctly foresaw the approaching downfall of the government with which he was connected, and was preparing to make his own escape from the ruin. From that night dates his connection with Pitt, a connection which soon became a close intimacy, and which lasted till it was dissolved by death.

About a fortnight later, Pitt spoke in the committee of supply on the army estimates. Symptoms of dissension had begun to appear on the Treasury bench. Lord George Germaine, the Secretary of State who was especially charged with the direction of the war in America, had held language not easily to be reconciled with declarations made by the First Lord of the Treasury. Pitt noticed the discrepancy with much force and keenness. Lord George and Lord North began to whisper together; and Welbore Ellis, an ancient placeman who had been drawing salary almost every quarter since the days of Henry Pelham, bent down between them to put in a word. Such interruptions sometimes discompose veteran speakers. Pitt stopped, and, looking at the group, said, with admirable readiness, "I shall wait till Nestor has composed the dispute between Agamemnon and Achilles."

After several defeats, or victories hardly to be distinguished from defeats, the ministry resigned. The King, reluctantly and ungraciously, consented to accept Rockingham as first minister. Fox and Shelburne became Secretaries of State. Lord John Cavendish, one of the most upright and honourable of men, was made Chancellor of the Exchequer. Thurlow, whose abilities and force of character had made him the dictator of the House of Lords, continued to hold the great seal.

To Pitt was offered, through Shelburne, the Vice-Treasurership of Ireland, one of the easiest and most highly paid places in the gift of the Crown; but the offer was, without hesitation, declined. The young statesman had resolved to accept no post which did not entitle him to a seat in the cabinet: and a few days later, he announced that resolution in the House of Commons. It must be remembered that the cabinet was then a much smaller and more select body than at present. We have seen cabinets of sixteen. In the time of our grandfathers a cabinet of ten or eleven was thought inconveniently large. Seven was an usual number. Even Burke, who had taken the lucrative office of Paymaster, was not in the cabinet. Many therefore thought Pitt's declaration indecent. He himself was sorry that he had made it. The words, he said in private, had escaped him in the heat of speaking; and he had no sooner uttered them than he would have given the world to recall them. They, however, did him no harm with the public. The second William Pitt, it was said, had shown that he had inherited the spirit, as well as the genius, of the first. In the son, as in the father, there might perhaps be too much pride; but there was nothing low or sordid. It might be called arrogance in a young barrister, living in chambers on three hundred a year, to refuse a salary of five thousand a year, merely because he did not choose to bind himself to speak or vote for plans which he had no share in framing; but surely such arrogance was not very far removed from virtue.

Pitt gave a general support to the administration of Rockingham, but omitted, in the meantime, no opportunity of courting that

Ultra-Whig party which the persecution of Wilkes and the Middle-sex election had called into existence, and which the disastrous events of the war, and the triumph of republican principles in America, had made formidable both in numbers and in temper. He supported a motion for shortening the duration of Parliaments. He made a motion for a committee to examine into the state of the representation, and, in the speech by which that motion was intro-duced, avowed himself the enemy of the close boroughs, the strong-holds of that corruption to which he attributed all the calamities of the nation, and which, as he phrased it in one of those exact and sonorous sentences of which he had a boundless command, had grown with the growth of England and strengthened with her strength, but had not diminished with her diminution or decayed with her decay. On this occasion he was supported by Fox. The motion was lost by only twenty votes in a house of more than three hundred members. The reformers never again had so good a division till the year 1831.

The new administration was strong in abilities, and was more popular than any administration which had held office since the first year of George the Third, but was hated by the King, hesita-tingly supported by the Parliament, and torn by internal dissensions. The Chancellor was disliked and distrusted by almost all his colleagues. The two Secretaries of State regarded each other with no friendly feeling. The line between their departments had not been traced with precision; and there were consequently jealousies, encroachments, and complaints. It was all that Rockingham could do to keep the peace in his cabinet; and, before the cabinet had existed three months, Rockingham died.

In an instant all was confusion. The adherents of the deceased statesman looked on the Duke of Portland as their chief. The King placed Shelburne at the head of the Treasury. Fox, Lord John Cavendish, and Burke, immediately resigned their offices; and the new prime minister was left to constitute a government out of very defective materials. His own parliamentary talents were great; but he could not be in the place where parliamentary talents were most needed. It was necessary to find some member of the House of Commons who could confront the great orators of the opposition; and Pitt alone had the eloquence and the courage which were required. He was offered the great place of Chancellor of the Exchequer, and he accepted it. He had scarcely completed his twenty-third year.

The Parliament was speedily prorogued. During the recess, a negotiation for peace which had been commenced under Rocking-

ham was brought to a successful termination. England acknowledged the independence of her revolted colonies; and she ceded to
her European enemies some places in the Mediterranean and in the
Gulf of Mexico. But the terms which she obtained were quite as
advantageous and honourable as the events of the war entitled her
to expect, or as she was likely to obtain by persevering in a contest
against immense odds. All her vital parts, all the real sources of her
power, remained uninjured. She preserved even her dignity; for
she ceded to the House of Bourbon only part of what she had won
from that House in previous wars. She retained her Indian empire
undiminished; and, in spite of the mightiest efforts of two great
monarchies, her flag still waved on the rock of Gibraltar. There is
not the slightest reason to believe that Fox, if he had remained in
office, would have hesitated one moment about concluding a treaty
on such conditions. Unhappily that great and most amiable man
was, at this crisis, hurried by his passions into an error which made
his genius and his virtues, during a long course of years, almost
useless to his country.

He saw that the great body of the House of Commons was divided
into three parties, his own, that of North, and that of Shelburne;
that none of those three parties was large enough to stand alone;
that, therefore, unless two of them united, there must be a miserably
feeble administration, or, more probably, a rapid succession of
miserably feeble administrations, and this at a time when a strong
government was essential to the prosperity and respectability of the
nation. It was then necessary and right that there should be a
coalition. To every possible coalition there were objections. But,
of all possible coalitions, that to which there were the fewest objections was undoubtedly a coalition between Shelburne and Fox. It
would have been generally applauded by the followers of both. It
might have been made without any sacrifice of public principle on
the part of either. Unhappily, recent bickerings had left in the
mind of Fox a profound dislike and distrust of Shelburne. Pitt
attempted to mediate, and was authorised to invite Fox to return
to the service of the Crown. "Is Lord Shelburne," said Fox, "to
remain prime minister?" Pitt answered in the affirmative. "It is
impossible that I can act under him," said Fox. "Then negotiation is at an end," said Pitt; "for I cannot betray him." Thus the
two statesmen parted. They were never again in a private room
together.

As Fox and his friends would not treat with Shelburne, nothing
remained to them but to treat with North. That fatal coalition
which is emphatically called "The Coalition" was formed. Not

three quarters of a year had elapsed since Fox and Burke had threatened North with impeachment, and had described him, night after night, as the most arbitrary, the most corrupt, the most incapable of ministers. They now allied themselves with him for the purpose of driving from office a statesman with whom they cannot be said to have differed as to any important question. Nor had they even the prudence and the patience to wait for some occasion on which they might, without inconsistency, have combined with their old enemies in opposition to the government. That nothing might be wanting to the scandal, the great orators, who had, during seven years, thundered against the war, determined to join with the authors of that war in passing a vote of censure on the peace.

The Parliament met before Christmas 1782. But it was not till January 1783 that the preliminary treaties were signed. On the 17th of February they were taken into consideration by the House of Commons. There had been, during some days, floating rumours that Fox and North had coalesced; and the debate indicated but too clearly that those rumours were not unfounded. Pitt was suffering from indisposition: he did not rise till his own strength and that of his hearers were exhausted; and he was consequently less successful than on any former occasion. His admirers owned that his speech was feeble and petulant. He so far forgot himself as to advise Sheridan to confine himself to amusing theatrical audiences. This ignoble sarcasm gave Sheridan an opportunity of retorting with great felicity. "After what I have seen and heard to-night," he said, "I really feel strongly tempted to venture on a competition with so great an artist as Ben Jonson, and to bring on the stage a second Angry Boy." On a division, the address proposed by the supporters of the government was rejected by a majority of sixteen.

But Pitt was not a man to be disheartened by a single failure, or to be put down by the most lively repartee. When, a few days later, the opposition proposed a resolution directly censuring the treaties, he spoke with an eloquence, energy, and dignity, which raised his fame and popularity higher than ever. To the coalition of Fox and North he alluded in language which drew forth tumultuous applause from his followers. "If," he said, "this ill-omened and unnatural marriage be not yet consummated, I know of a just and lawful impediment; and, in the name of the public weal, I forbid the banns."

The ministers were again left in a minority; and Shelburne consequently tendered his resignation. It was accepted; but the King struggled long and hard before he submitted to the terms

M—16

dictated by Fox, whose faults he detested, and whose high spirit and powerful intellect he detested still more. The first place at the board of Treasury was repeatedly offered to Pitt: but the offer, though tempting, was steadfastly declined. The young man, whose judgment was as precocious as his eloquence, saw that his time was coming, but was not come, and was deaf to royal importunities and reproaches. His Majesty, bitterly complaining of Pitt's faint-heartedness, tried to break the coalition. Every art of seduction was practised on North, but in vain. During several weeks the country remained without a government. It was not till all devices had failed, and till the aspect of the House of Commons became threatening, that the King gave way. The Duke of Portland was declared First Lord of the Treasury. Thurlow was dismissed. Fox and North became Secretaries of State, with power ostensibly equal. But Fox was the real prime minister.

The year was far advanced before the new arrangements were completed; and nothing very important was done during the remainder of the session. Pitt, now seated on the opposition bench, brought the question of parliamentary reform a second time under the consideration of the Commons. He proposed to add to the House at once a hundred county members and several members for metropolitan districts, and to enact that every borough of which an election committee should report that the majority of voters appeared to be corrupt should lose the franchise. The motion was rejected by 293 votes to 149.

After the prorogation, Pitt visited the Continent for the first and last time. His travelling companion was one of his most intimate friends, a young man of his own age, who had already distinguished himself in Parliament by an engaging natural eloquence, set off by the sweetest and most exquisitely modulated of human voices, and whose affectionate heart, caressing manners, and brilliant wit, made him the most delightful of companions, William Wilberforce. That was the time of Anglomania in France; and at Paris the son of the great Chatham was absolutely hunted by men of letters and women of fashion, and forced, much against his will, into political disputation. One remarkable saying which dropped from him during this tour has been preserved. A French gentleman expressed some surprise at the immense influence which Fox, a man of pleasure, ruined by the dice-box and the turf, exercised over the English nation. "You have not," said Pitt, "been under the wand of the magician."

In November 1783 the Parliament met again. The government had irresistible strength in the House of Commons, and seemed to be scarcely less strong in the House of Lords, but was, in truth, surrounded on every side by dangers. The King was impatiently waiting for the moment at which he could emancipate himself from a yoke which galled him so severely that he had more than once seriously thought of retiring to Hanover; and the King was scarcely more eager for a change than the nation. Fox and North had committed a fatal error. They ought to have known that coalitions between parties which have long been hostile can succeed only when the wish for coalition pervades the lower ranks of both. If the leaders unite before there is any disposition to union among the followers, the probability is that there will be a mutiny in both camps, and that the two revolted armies will make a truce with each other, in order to be revenged on those by whom they think that they have been betrayed. Thus it was in 1783. At the beginning of that eventful year, North had been the recognised head of the old Tory party, which, though for a moment prostrated by the disastrous issue of the American war, was still a great power in the state. To him the clergy, the universities, and that large body of country gentlemen whose rallying cry was "Church and King," had long looked up with respect and confidence. Fox had, on the other hand, been the idol of the Whigs, and of the whole body of Protestant dissenters. The coalition at once alienated the most zealous Tories from North, and the most zealous Whigs from Fox. The University of Oxford, which had marked its approbation of North's orthodoxy by electing him chancellor, the city of London, which had been during two and twenty years at war with the Court, were equally disgusted. Squires and rectors, who had inherited the principles of the cavaliers of the preceding century, could not forgive their old leader for combining with disloyal subjects in order to put a force on the sovereign. The members of the Bill of Rights Society and of the Reform Associations were enraged by learning that their favourite orator now called the great champion of tyranny and corruption his noble friend. Two great multitudes were at once left without any head, and both at once turned their eyes on Pitt. One party saw in him the only man who could rescue the King; the other saw in him the only man who could purify the Parliament. He was supported on one side by Archbishop Markham, the preacher of divine right, and by Jenkinson, the captain of the Prætorian band of the King's friends; on the other side by Jebb and Priestley, Sawbridge and Cartwright, Jack Wilkes and Horne Tooke. On the benches of the House of Commons, however, the ranks of the ministerial majority were unbroken; and that any statesman would venture to brave such a majority was thought impossible. No prince of the Hanoverian line had ever, under any provocation, ventured to appeal from the representative body to the constituent body. The ministers, therefore, notwithstanding the sullen looks and muttered words of displeasure with which their suggestions were received in the closet, notwithstanding the roar of obloquy which was rising louder and louder every day from every corner of the island, thought themselves secure.

Such was their confidence in their strength that, as soon as the Parliament had met, they brought forward a singularly bold and original plan for the government of the British territories in India. What was proposed was that the whole authority, which till that time had been exercised over those territories by the East India Company, should be transferred to seven commissioners who were to be named by Parliament, and were not to be removable at the pleasure of the Crown. Earl Fitzwilliam, the most intimate personal friend of Fox, was to be chairman of this board; and the eldest son of North was to be one of the members.

As soon as the outlines of the scheme were known, all the hatred which the coalition had excited burst forth with an astounding explosion. The question which ought undoubtedly to have been considered as paramount to every other was, whether the proposed change was likely to be beneficial or injurious to the thirty millions of people who were subject to the Company. But that question cannot be said to have been even seriously discussed. Burke, who, whether right or wrong in the conclusions to which he came, had at least the merit of looking at the subject in the right point of view, vainly reminded his hearers of that mighty population whose daily rice might depend on a vote of the British Parliament. He spoke, with even more than his wonted power of thought and language, about the desolation of Rohilcund, about the spoliation of Benares, about the evil policy which had suffered the tanks of the Carnatic to go to ruin; but he could scarcely obtain a hearing. The contending parties, to their shame it must be said, would listen to none but English topics. Out of doors the cry against the ministry was almost universal. Town and country were united. Corporations exclaimed against the violation of the charter of the greatest corporation in the realm. Tories and democrats joined in pronouncing the proposed board an unconstitutional body. It was to consist of Fox's nominees. The effect of his bill was to give, not to the Crown, but to him personally, whether in office or in opposition, an enormous power, a patronage sufficient to counterbalance the patronage of the Treasury and of the Admiralty, and to decide the elections for fifty boroughs. He knew, it was said, that he was hateful alike to King and people; and he had devised a plan which would make him independent of both. Some nicknamed him Cromwell, and some Carlo Khan. Wilberforce, with his usual felicity of expression, and with very unusual bitterness of feeling, described the scheme as the genuine offspring of the coalition, as marked with the features of both its parents, the corruption of one and the violence of the other. In spite of all opposition, however, the bill was supported in every stage by great majorities, was rapidly passed, and was sent up to the Lords. To the general astonishment, when the second reading was moved in the Upper House, the opposition proposed an adjournment, and carried it by eighty-seven votes to seventy-nine. The cause of this strange turn of fortune was soon known. Pitt's cousin, Earl Temple, had been in the royal closet, and had there been authorised to let it be known that His Majesty would consider all who voted for the bill as his enemies. The ignominious commission was performed, and instantly a troop of Lords of the Bedchamber, of Bishops who wished to be translated, and of Scotch peers who wished to be re-elected, made haste to change sides. On a later day, the Lords rejected the bill. Fox and North were immediately directed to send their seals to the palace by their Under Secretaries; and Pitt was appointed First Lord of the Treasury and Chancellor of the Exchequer.

The general opinion was, that there would be an immediate dissolution. But Pitt wisely determined to give the public feeling time to gather strength. On this point he differed from his kinsman Temple. The consequence was, that Temple, who had been appointed one of the Secretaries of State, resigned his office forty-eight hours after he had accepted it, and thus relieved the new government from a great load of unpopularity: for all men of sense and honour, however strong might be their dislike of the India Bill, disapproved of the manner in which that bill had been thrown out. Temple carried away with him the scandal which the best friends of the new government could not but lament. The fame of the young prime minister preserved its whiteness. He could declare with perfect truth that, if unconstitutional machinations had been employed, he had been no party to them.

He was, however, surrounded by difficulties and dangers. In the House of Lords, indeed, he had a majority; nor could any orator of the opposition in that assembly be considered as a match for Thurlow, who was now again Chancellor, or for Camden, who cordially supported the son of his old friend Chatham. But in the other House there was not a single eminent speaker among the official men who sate round Pitt. His most useful assistant was Dundas, who, though he had not eloquence, had sense, knowledge, readiness, and boldness. On the opposite benches was a powerful majority, led by Fox, who was supported by Burke, North, and Sheridan. The heart of the young minister, stout as it was, almost died within him. He could not once close his eyes on the night which followed Temple's resignation. But, whatever his internal emotions might be, his language and deportment indicated nothing but unconquerable firmness and haughty confidence in his own powers. His contest against the House of Commons lasted from the 17th of December 1783 to the 8th of March 1784. In sixteen divisions the opposition triumphed. Again and again the King was requested to dismiss his ministers. But he was determined to go to Germany rather than yield. Pitt's resolution never wavered. The cry of the nation in his favour became vehement and almost furious. Addresses assuring him of public support came up daily from every part of the kingdom. The freedom of the city of London was presented to him in a gold box. He went in state to receive this mark of distinction. He was sumptuously feasted in Grocers' Hall; and the shopkeepers of the Strand and Fleet Street illuminated their houses in his honour. These things could not but produce an effect within the walls of Parliament. The ranks of the majority began to waver; a few passed over to the enemy; some skulked away; many were for capitulating while it was still possible to capitulate with the honours of war. Negotiations were opened with the view of forming an administration on a wide basis; but they had scarcely been opened when they were closed. The opposition demanded, as a preliminary article of the treaty, that Pitt should resign the Treasury; and with this demand Pitt steadfastly refused to comply. While the contest was raging, the Clerkship of the Pells, a sinecure place for life, worth three thousand a year, and tenable with a seat in the House of Commons, became vacant. The appointment was with the Chancellor of the Exchequer: nobody doubted that he would appoint himself; and nobody could have blamed him if he had done so: for such sinecure offices had always been defended on the ground that they enabled a few men of eminent abilities and small incomes to live without any profession, and to devote themselves to the service of the state. Pitt, in spite of the remonstrances of his friends, gave the Pells to his father's old adherent, Colonel Barré, a man distinguished by talent and eloquence, but poor and afflicted with blindness. By this arrangement a pension which the Rockingham administration had granted to Barré was saved to the public. Never was there a happier stroke of policy. About treaties, wars, expeditions, tariffs, budgets, there will always be room for dispute. The policy which is applauded by half the nation may be condemned by the other half. But pecuniary disinterestedness everybody comprehends. It is a great thing for a man who has only three hundred a year to be able to show that he considers three thousand a year as mere dirt beneath his feet, when compared with the public interest and the public esteem. Pitt had his reward. No minister was ever more rancorously libelled; but, even when he was known to be overwhelmed with debt, when millions were passing through his hands, when the wealthiest magnates of the realm were soliciting him for marquisates and garters, his bitterest enemies did not dare to accuse him of touching unlawful gain.

At length the hard fought fight ended. A final remonstrance, drawn up by Burke with admirable skill, was carried on the 8th of March by a single vote in a full House. Had the experiment been repeated, the supporters of the coalition would probably have been in a minority. But the supplies had been voted; the Mutiny Bill had been passed; and the Parliament was dissolved.

The popular constituent bodies all over the country were in general enthusiastic on the side of the new government. A hundred and sixty of the supporters of the coalition lost their seats. The First Lord of the Treasury himself came in at the head of the poll for the University of Cambridge. His young friend, Wilberforce, was elected Knight of the great shire of York, in opposition to the whole influence of the Fitzwilliams, Cavendishes, Dundases, and Saviles. In the midst of such triumphs Pitt completed his twenty-fifth year. He was now the greatest subject that England had seen during many generations. He domineered absolutely over the cabinet, and was the favourite at once of the Sovereign, of the Parliament, and of the nation. His father had never been so powerful, nor Walpole, nor Marlborough.

This narrative has now reached a point, beyond which a full history of the life of Pitt would be a history of England, or rather of the whole civilised world; and for such a history this is not the proper place. Here a very slight sketch must suffice; and in that sketch prominence will be given to such points as may enable a reader who is already acquainted with the general course of events to form a just notion of the character of the man on whom so much depended.

It we wish to arrive at a correct judgment of Pitt's merits and defects, we must never forget that he belonged to a peculiar class of statesmen, and that he must be tried by a peculiar standard. It is not easy to compare him fairly with such men as Ximenes and Sully, Richelieu and Oxenstiern, John de Witt and Warren Hastings. The means by which those politicians governed great communities were of quite a different kind from those which Pitt was under the necessity of employing. Some talents, which they never had any opportunity of showing that they possessed, were developed in him to an extraordinary degree. In some qualities, on the other hand, to which they owe a large part of their fame, he was decidedly their inferior. They transacted business in their closets, or at boards where a few confidential councillors sate. It was his lot to be born in an age and in a country in which parliamentary government was completely established; his whole training from infancy was such as fitted him to bear a part in parliamentary government; and, from the prime of his manhood to his death, all the powers of his vigorous mind were almost constantly exerted in the work of parliamentary government. He accordingly became the greatest master of the whole art of parliamentary government that has ever existed, a greater than Montague or Walpole, a greater than his father Chatham or his rival Fox, a greater than either of his illustrious successors Canning and Peel.

Parliamentary government, like every other contrivance of man, has its advantages and its disadvantages. On the advantages there is no need to dilate. The history of England during the hundred and seventy years which have elapsed since the House of Commons became the most powerful body in the state, her immense and still growing prosperity, her freedom, her tranquillity, her greatness in arts, in sciences, and in arms, her maritime ascendency, the marvels of her public credit, her American, her African, her Australian, her Asiatic empires, sufficiently prove the excellence of her institutions. But those institutions, though excellent, are assuredly not perfect. Parliamentary government is government by speaking. In such a government, the power of speaking is the most highly prized of all the qualities which a politician can possess; and that power may exist, in the highest degree, without judgment, without fortitude, without skill in reading the characters of men or the signs of the times, without any knowledge of the principles of legislation or of political economy, and without any skill in diplomacy or in the administration of war. Nay, it may well happen that those very intellectual qualities which give a peculiar charm to the speeches of a public man may be incompatible with the qualities which would fit him to meet a pressing emergency with promptitude and firmness. It was thus with Charles Townshend. It was thus with Windham. It was a privilege to listen to those accomplished and ingenious orators. But in a perilous crisis they would have been found far inferior in all the qualities of rulers to such a man as Oliver Cromwell, who talked nonsense, or as William the Silent, who did not talk at all. When parliamentary government is established, a Charles Townshend or a Windham will almost always exercise much greater influence than such men as the great Protector of England, or as the founder of the Batavian commonwealth. In such a government, parliamentary talent, though quite distinct from the talents of a good executive or judicial officer, will be a chief qualification for executive and judicial office. From the Book of Dignities a curious list might be made out of Chancellors ignorant of the principles of equity, and First Lords of the Admiralty ignorant of the principles of navigation, of Colonial ministers who could not repeat the names of the Colonies, of Lords of the Treasury who did not know the difference between funded and unfunded debt, and of Secretaries of the India Board who did not know whether the Mahrattas were Mahometans or Hindoos. On these grounds, some persons, incapable of seeing more than one side of a question, have pronounced parliamentary government a positive evil, and have maintained that the administration would be greatly improved if the power, now exercised by a large assembly, were transferred to a single person. Men of sense will probably think the remedy very much worse than the disease, and will be of opinion that there would be small gain in exchanging Charles Townshend and Windham for the Prince of the Peace, or the poor slave and the dog Steenie.

Pitt was emphatically the man of parliamentary government, the type of his class, the minion, the child, the spoiled child, of the House of Commons. For the House of Commons he had a hereditary, an infantine love. Through his whole boyhood, the House of Commons was never out of his thoughts, or out of the thoughts of his instructors. Reciting at his father's knee, reading Thucydides and Cicero into English, analysing the great Attic speeches on the Embassy and on the Crown, he was constantly in training for the conflicts of the House of Commons. He was a distinguished member of the House of Commons at twenty-one. The ability which he had displayed in the House of Commons made him the most powerful subject in Europe before he was twenty-five. It would have been happy for himself and for his country if his elevation had been deferred. Eight or ten years, during which he would have had leisure and opportunity for reading and reflection, for foreign travel, for social intercourse and free exchange of thought on equal terms with a great variety of companions, would have supplied what, without any fault on his part, was wanting to

M—16*

his powerful intellect. He had all the knowledge that he could be expected to have; that is to say, all the knowledge that a man can acquire while he is a student at Cambridge, and all the knowledge that a man can acquire when he is First Lord of the Treasury and Chancellor of the Exchequer. But the stock of general information which he brought from college, extraordinary for a boy, was far inferior to what Fox possessed, and beggarly when compared with the massy, the splendid, the various treasures laid up in the large mind of Burke. After Pitt became minister, he had no leisure to learn more than was necessary for the purposes of the day which was passing over him. What was necessary for those purposes such a man could learn with little difficulty. He was surrounded by experienced and able public servants. He could at any moment command their best assistance. From the stores which they produced his vigorous mind rapidly collected the materials for a good parliamentary case: and that was enough. Legislation and administration were with him secondary matters. To the work of framing statutes, of negotiating treaties, of organising fleets and armies, of sending forth expeditions, he gave only the leavings of his time and the dregs of his fine intellect. The strength and sap of his mind were all drawn in a different direction. It was when the House of Commons was to be convinced and persuaded that he put forth all his powers.

Of those powers we must form our estimate chiefly from tradition; for of all the eminent speakers of the last age Pitt has suffered most from the reporters. Even while he was still living, critics remarked that his eloquence could not be preserved, that he must be heard to be appreciated. They more than once applied to him the sentence in which Tacitus describes the fate of a senator whose rhetoric was admired in the Augustan age: "Haterii canorum illud et profluens cum ipso simul exstinctum est." There is, however, abundant evidence that nature had bestowed on Pitt the talents of a great orator; and those talents had been developed in a very peculiar manner, first by his education, and secondly by the high official position to which he rose early, and in which he passed the greater part of his public life.

At his first appearance in Parliament he showed himself superior to all his contemporaries in command of language. He could pour forth a long succession of round and stately periods, without premeditation, without ever pausing for a word, without ever repeating a word, in a voice of silver clearness, and with a pronunciation so articulate that not a letter was slurred over. He had less amplitude of mind and less richness of imagination than Burke, less ingenuity than Windham, less wit than Sheridan, less perfect mastery of dialectical fence, and less of that highest sort of eloquence which consists of reason and passion fused together, than Fox. Yet the almost unanimous judgment of those who were in the habit of listening to that remarkable race of men placed Pitt, as a speaker, above Burke, above Windham, above Sheridan, and not below Fox. His declamation was copious, polished, and splendid. In power of sarcasm he was probably not surpassed by any speaker, ancient or modern; and of this formidable weapon he made merciless use. In two parts of the oratorical art which are of the highest value to a minister of state he was singularly expert. No man knew better how to be luminous or how to be obscure. When he wished to be understood, he never failed to make himself understood. He could with ease present to his audience, not perhaps an exact or profound, but a clear, popular, and plausible view of the most extensive and complicated subject. Nothing was out of place; nothing was forgotten; minute details, dates, sums of money, were all faithfully preserved in his memory. Even intricate questions of finance, when explained by him, seemed clear to the plainest man among his hearers. On the other hand, when he did not wish to be explicit,—and no man who is at the head of affairs always wishes to be explicit,—he had a marvellous power of saying nothing in language which left on his audience the impression that he had said a great deal. He was at once the only man who could open a budget without notes, and the only man who, as Windham said, could speak that most elaborately evasive and unmeaning of human compositions, a King's speech, without premeditation.

The effect of oratory will always to a great extent depend on the character of the orator. There perhaps never were two speakers whose eloquence had more of what may be called the race, more of the flavour imparted by moral qualities, than Fox and Pitt. The speeches of Fox owe a great part of their charm to that warmth and softness of heart, that sympathy with human suffering, that admiration for everything great and beautiful, and that hatred of cruelty and injustice, which interest and delight us even in the most defective reports. No person, on the other hand, could hear Pitt without perceiving him to be a man of high, intrepid, and commanding spirit, proudly conscious of his own rectitude and of his own intellectual superiority, incapable of the low vices of fear and envy, but too prone to feel and to show disdain. Pride, indeed, pervaded the whole man, was written in the harsh, rigid lines of his face, was marked by the way in which he walked, in which he sate, in which he stood, and, above all, in which he bowed. Such pride, of course, inflicted many wounds. It may confidently be affirmed that there cannot be found, in all the ten thousand invectives written against Fox, a word indicating that his demeanour had ever made a single personal enemy. On the other hand, several men of note who had been partial to Pitt, and who to the last continued to approve his public conduct and to support his administration, Cumberland, for example, Boswell, and Matthias, were so much irritated by the contempt with which he treated them, that they complained in print of their wrongs. But his pride, though it made him bitterly disliked by individuals, inspired the great body of his followers in Parliament and throughout the country with respect and confidence. They took him at his own valuation. They saw that his self-esteem was not that of an upstart, who was drunk with good luck and with applause, and who, if fortune turned, would sink from arrogance into abject humility. It was that of the magnanimous man so finely described by Aristotle in the Ethics, of the man who thinks himself worthy of great things, being in truth worthy. It sprang from a consciousness of great powers and great virtues, and was never so conspicuously displayed as in the midst of difficulties and dangers which would have unnerved and bowed down any ordinary mind. It was closely connected, too, with an ambition which had no mixture of low cupidity. There was something noble in the cynical disdain with which the mighty minister scattered riches and titles to right and left among those who valued them, while he spurned them out of his own way. Poor himself, he was surrounded by friends on whom he had bestowed three thousand, six thousand, ten thousand a year. Plain Mister himself, he had made more lords than any three ministers that had preceded him. The garter, for which the first dukes in the kingdom were contending, was repeatedly offered to him, and offered in vain.

The correctness of his private life added much to the dignity of his public character. In the relations of son, brother, uncle, master, friend, his conduct was exemplary. In the small circle of his intimate associates, he was amiable, affectionate, even playful. They loved him sincerely; they regretted him long; and they would hardly admit that he who was so kind and gentle with them could be stern and haughty with others. He indulged, indeed, somewhat too freely in wine, which he had early been directed to take as a medicine, and which use had made a necessary of life to him. But it was very seldom that any indication of undue excess could be detected in his tones or gestures; and, in truth, two bottles of port were little more to him than two dishes of tea. He had, when he was first introduced into the clubs of Saint James's Street, shown a strong taste for play; but he had the prudence and the resolution to stop before this taste had acquired the strength of habit. From the passion which generally exercises the most tyrannical dominion over the young he possessed an immunity, which is probably to be ascribed partly to his temperament and partly to his situation. His constitution was feeble: he was very shy; and he was very busy. The strictness of his morals furnished such buffoons as Peter Pindar and Captain Morris with an inexhaustible theme for merriment of no very delicate kind. But the great body of the middle class of Englishmen could not see the joke. They warmly praised the young statesman for commanding his passions, and for covering his frailties, if he had frailties, with decorous obscurity, and would have been very far indeed from thinking better of him if he had vindicated himself from the taunts of his enemies by taking under his protection a Nancy Parsons or a Marianne Clark.

No part of the immense popularity which Pitt long enjoyed is to be attributed to the eulogies of wits and poets. It might have been naturally expected that a man of genius, of learning, of taste, an orator whose diction was often compared to that of Tully, the representative, too, of a great university, would have taken a peculiar pleasure in befriending eminent writers, to whatever political party they might have belonged. The love of literature had induced Augustus to heap benefits on Pompeians, Somers to be the protector of nonjurors, Harley to make the fortunes of Whigs. But it could not move Pitt to show any favour even to Pittites. He was doubtless right in thinking that, in general, poetry, history and philosophy ought to be suffered, like calico and cutlery, to find their proper price in the market, and that to teach men of letters to look habitually to the state for their recompense is bad for the state and bad for letters. Assuredly nothing can be more absurd or mischievous than to waste the public money in bounties for the purpose of inducing people who ought to be weighing out grocery or measuring out drapery to write bad or middling books. But, though the sound rule is that authors should be left to be remunerated by their readers, there will, in every generation, be a few exceptions to this rule. To distinguish these special cases from the mass is an employment well worthy of the faculties of a great and accomplished ruler; and Pitt would assuredly have had little difficulty in finding such cases. While he was in power, the greatest philologist of the age, his own contemporary at Cambridge, was reduced to earn a livelihood by the lowest literary drudgery, and to spend in writing squibs for the Morning Chronicle years to which we might have owed an all but perfect text of the whole tragic and comic drama of Athens. The greatest historian of the age, forced by poverty to leave his country, completed his immortal work on the shores of Lake Leman. The political heterodoxy of Porson, and the religious heterodoxy of Gibbon, may perhaps be pleaded in defence of the minister by whom those eminent men were neglected. But there were other cases in which no such excuse could be set up. Scarcely had Pitt obtained possession of unbounded power when an aged writer of the highest eminence, who had made very little by his writings, and who was sinking into the grave under a load of infirmities and sorrows, wanted five or six hundred pounds to enable him, during the winter or two which might still remain to him, to draw his breath more easily in the soft climate of Italy. Not a farthing was to be obtained; and before Christmas the author of the English Dictionary and of the Lives of the Poets had gasped his last in the river fog and coal smoke of Fleet Street. A few months after the death of Johnson appeared the Task, incomparably the best poem that any Englishman then living had produced—a poem, too, which could hardly fail to excite in a well constituted mind a feeling of esteem and compassion for the poet, a man of genius and virtue, whose means were scanty, and whom the most cruel of all the calamities incident to humanity had made incapable of supporting himself by vigorous and sustained exertion. Nowhere had Chatham been praised with more enthusiasm, or in verse more worthy of the subject, than in the Task. The son of Chatham, however, contented himself with reading and admiring the book, and left the author to starve. The pension which, long after, enabled poor Cowper to close his melancholy life, unmolested by duns and bailiffs, was obtained for him by the strenuous kindness of Lord Spencer. What a contrast between the way in which Pitt acted towards Johnson and the way in which Lord Grey acted towards his political enemy Scott, when Scott, worn out by misfortune and disease, was advised to try the effect of the Italian air! What a contrast between the way in which Pitt acted towards Cowper and the way in which Burke, a poor man and out of place, acted towards Crabbe! Even Dundas, who made no pretensions to literary taste, and was content to be considered as a hard-headed and somewhat coarse man of business, was, when compared with his eloquent and classically educated friend, a Mæcenas or a Leo. Dundas made Burns an exciseman, with seventy pounds a year; and this was more than Pitt, during his long tenure of power, did for the encouragement of letters. Even those who may think that

is, in general, no part of the duty of a government to reward literary merit will hardly deny that a government, which has much lucrative church preferment in its gift, is bound, in distributing that preferment, not to overlook divines whose writings have rendered great service to the cause of religion. But it seems never to have occurred to Pitt that he lay under any such obligation. All the theological works of all the numerous bishops whom he made and translated are not, when put together, worth fifty pages of the Horæ Paulinæ, of the Natural Theology, or of the View of the Evidences of Christianity. But on Paley the all-powerful minister never bestowed the smallest benefice. Artists Pitt treated as contemptuously as writers. For painting he did simply nothing. Sculptors, who had been selected to execute monuments voted by Parliament, had to haunt the ante-chambers of the Treasury during many years before they could obtain a farthing from him. One of them, after vainly soliciting the minister for payment during fourteen years, had the courage to present a memorial to the King, and thus obtained tardy and ungracious justice. Architects it was absolutely necessary to employ; and the worst that could be found seem to have been employed. Not a single fine public building of any kind or in any style was erected during his long administration. It may be confidently affirmed that no ruler whose abilities and attainments would bear any comparison with his has ever shown such cold disdain for what is excellent in arts and letters.

His first administration lasted seventeen years. That long period is divided by a strongly marked line into two almost exactly equal parts. The first part ended and the second began in the autumn of 1792. Throughout both parts Pitt displayed in the highest degree the talents of a parliamentary leader. During the first part he was a fortunate and, in many respects, a skilful administrator. With the difficulties which he had to encounter during the second part he was altogether incapable of contending: but his eloquence and his perfect mastery of the tactics of the House of Commons concealed his incapacity from the multitude.

The eight years which followed the general election of 1784 were as tranquil and prosperous as any eight years in the whole history of England. Neighbouring nations which had lately been in arms against her, and which had flattered themselves that, in losing her American colonies, she had lost a chief source of her wealth and of her power, saw, with wonder and vexation, that she was more wealthy and more powerful than ever. Her trade increased. Her manufactures flourished. Her exchequer was full to overflowing. Very idle apprehensions were generally entertained, that the public debt, though much less than a third of the debt which we now bear with ease, would be found too heavy for the strength of the nation. Those apprehensions might not perhaps have been easily quieted by reason. But Pitt quieted them by a juggle. He succeeded in persuading first himself, and then the whole nation, his opponents included, that a new sinking fund, which, so far as it differed from former sinking funds, differed for the worse, would, by virtue of some mysterious power of propagation belonging to money, put into the pocket of the public creditor great sums not taken out of the pocket of the tax-payer. The country, terrified by a danger which was no danger, hailed with delight and boundless confidence a remedy which was no remedy. The minister was almost universally extolled as the greatest of financiers. Meanwhile both the branches of the House of Bourbon found that England was as formidable an antagonist as she had ever been. France had formed a plan for reducing Holland to vassalage. But England interposed; and France receded. Spain interrupted by violence the trade of our merchants with the regions near the Oregon. But England armed, and Spain receded. Within the island there was profound tranquillity. The King was, for the first time, popular. During the twenty-three years which had followed his accession he had not been loved by his subjects. His domestic virtues were acknowledged. But it was generally thought that the good qualities by which he was distinguished in private life were wanting to his political character. As a Sovereign, he was resentful, unforgiving, stubborn, cunning. Under his rule the country had sustained cruel disgraces and disasters; and every one of those disgraces and disasters was imputed to his strong antipathies, and to his perverse obstinacy in the wrong. One statesman after another complained that he had been induced by royal caresses, entreaties, and promises, to undertake the direction of affairs at a difficult conjuncture, and that, as soon as he had, not without sullying his fame and alienating his best friends, served the turn for which he was wanted, his ungrateful master began to intrigue against him, and to canvass against him. Grenville, Rockingham, Chatham, men of widely different characters, but all three upright and high-spirited, agreed in thinking that the Prince under whom they had successively held the highest place in the government was one of the most insincere of mankind. His confidence was reposed, they said, not in those known and responsible counsellors to whom he had delivered the seals of office, but in secret advisers who stole up the back stairs into his closet. In Parliament, his ministers, while defending themselves against the attacks of the opposition in front, were perpetually, at his instigation, assailed on the flank or in the rear by a vile band of mercenaries who called themselves his friends. These men constantly, while in possession of lucrative places in his service, spoke and voted against bills which he had authorised the First Lord of the Treasury or the Secretary of State to bring in. But from the day on which Pitt was placed at the head of affairs there was an end of secret influence. His haughty and aspiring spirit was not to be satisfied with the mere show of power. Any attempt to undermine him at Court, any mutinous movement among his followers in the House of Commons, was certain to be at once put down. He had only to tender his resignation; and he could dictate his own terms. For he, and he alone, stood between the King and the Coalition. He was therefore little less than Mayor of the Palace. The nation loudly applauded the King for having the wisdom to repose entire confidence in so excellent a minister. His Majesty's private virtues now began to produce their full effect. He was generally regarded as the model of a respectable country gentleman, honest, goodnatured, sober, religious. He rose early: he dined temperately: he was strictly faithful to his wife: he never missed church; and at church he never missed a response. His people heartily prayed that he might long reign over them; and they prayed the more heartily because his virtues were set off to the best advantage by the vices and follies of the Prince of Wales, who lived in close intimacy with the chiefs of the opposition.

How strong this feeling was in the public mind appeared signally on one great occasion. In the autumn of 1788 the King became insane. The opposition, eager for office, committed the great indiscretion of asserting that the heir apparent had, by the fundamental laws of England, a right to be Regent with the full powers of royalty. Pitt, on the other hand, maintained it to be the constitutional doctrine that, when a Sovereign is, by reason of infancy, disease, or absence, incapable of exercising the regal functions, it belongs to the estates of the realm to determine who shall be the vicegerent, and with what portion of the executive authority such vicegerent shall be entrusted. A long and violent contest followed, in which Pitt was supported by the great body of the people with as much enthusiasm as during the first months of his administration. Tories with one voice applauded him for defending the sick-bed of a virtuous and unhappy Sovereign against a disloyal faction and an undutiful son. Not a few Whigs applauded him for asserting the authority of Parliaments and the principles of the Revolution, in opposition to a doctrine which seemed to have too much affinity with the servile theory of indefeasible hereditary right. The middle class, always zealous on the side of decency and the domestic virtues, looked forward with dismay to a reign resembling that of Charles II. The palace, which had now been, during thirty years, the pattern of an English home, would be a public nuisance, a school of profligacy. To the good King's repast of mutton and lemonade, despatched at three o'clock, would succeed midnight banquets, from which the guests would be carried home speechless. To the backgammon board at which the good King played for a little silver with his equerries, would succeed faro tables from which young patricians who had sate down rich would rise up beggars. The drawing-room, from which the frown of the Queen had repelled a whole generation of frail beauties, would now be again what it had been in the days of Barbara Palmer and Louisa de Querouaille. Nay, severely as the public reprobated the Prince's many illicit attachments, his one virtuous attachment was reprobated more severely still. Even in grave and pious circles his Protestant mistresses gave less scandal than his Popish wife. That he must be Regent nobody ventured to deny. But he and his friends were so unpopular that Pitt could, with general approbation, propose to limit the powers of the Regent by restrictions to which it would have been impossible to subject a Prince beloved and trusted by the country. Some interested men, fully expecting a change of administration, went over to the opposition. But the majority, purified by these desertions, closed its ranks, and presented a more firm array than ever to the enemy. In every division Pitt was victorious. When at length, after a stormy interregnum of three months, it was announced, on the very eve of the inauguration of the Regent, that the King was himself again, the nation was wild with delight. On the evening of the day on which His Majesty resumed his functions, a spontaneous illumination, the most general that had ever been seen in England, brightened the whole vast space from Highgate to Tooting, and from Hammersmith to Greenwich. On the day on which he returned thanks in the cathedral of his capital, all the horses and carriages within a hundred miles of London were too few for the multitudes which flocked to see him pass through the streets. A second illumination followed, which was even superior to the first in magnificence. Pitt with difficulty escaped from the tumultuous kindness of an innumerable multitude which insisted on drawing his coach from Saint Paul's Churchyard to Downing Street. This was the moment at which his fame and fortune may be said to have reached the zenith. His influence in the closet was as great as that of Carr or Villiers had been. His dominion over the Parliament was more absolute than that of Walpole or Pelham had been. He was at the same time as high in the favour of the populace as ever Wilkes or Sacheverell had been. Nothing did more to raise his character than his noble poverty. It was well known that, if he had been dismissed from office after more than five years of boundless power, he would hardly have carried out with him a sum sufficient to furnish the set of chambers in which, as he cheerfully declared, he meant to resume the practice of the law. His admirers, however, were by no means disposed to suffer him to depend on daily toil for his daily bread. The voluntary contributions which were awaiting his acceptance in the city of London alone would have sufficed to make him a rich man. But it may be doubted whether his haughty spirit would have stooped to accept a provision so honourably earned and so honourably bestowed.

To such a height of power and glory had this extraordinary man risen at twenty-nine years of age. And now the tide was on the turn. Only ten days after the triumphant procession to Saint Paul's, the States-General of France, after an interval of a hundred and seventy-four years, met at Versailles.

The nature of the great Revolution which followed was long very imperfectly understood in this country. Burke saw much further than any of his contemporaries: but whatever his sagacity descried was refracted and discoloured by his passions and his imagination. More than three years elapsed before the principles of the English administration underwent any material change. Nothing could as yet be milder or more strictly constitutional than the minister's domestic policy. Not a single act indicating an arbitrary temper or a jealousy of the people could be imputed to him. He had never applied to Parliament for any extraordinary powers. He had never used with harshness the ordinary powers entrusted by the constitution to the executive government. Not a single state prosecution which would even now be called oppressive had been instituted by him. Indeed, the only oppressive state prosecution instituted during the first eight years of his administration was that of Stockdale, which is to be attributed, not to the government, but to the chiefs of the opposition. In office, Pitt had redeemed the pledges which he had, at his entrance into public life, given to the supporters of parliamentary reform. He had, in 1785, brought forward a judicious plan for the improvement of the representative system, and had prevailed on the King, not only to refrain from talking against that plan, but to recommend it to the Houses in a speech from the throne.[1] This attempt failed; but there can be little doubt

---

[1] The speech with which the King opened the session of 1785, concluded with an assurance that His Majesty would heartily concur in every measure which could tend to secure the true principles of the constitution. These words were at the time understood to refer to Pitt's Reform Bill.

that, if the French Revolution had not produced a violent reaction of public feeling, Pitt would have performed, with little difficulty and no danger, that great work which, at a later period, Lord Grey could accomplish only by means which for a time loosened the very foundations of the commonwealth. When the atrocities of the slave trade were first brought under the consideration of Parliament, no abolitionist was more zealous than Pitt. When sickness prevented Wilberforce from appearing in public, his place was most efficiently supplied by his friend the minister. A humane bill, which mitigated the horrors of the middle passage, was, in 1788, carried by the eloquence and determined spirit of Pitt, in spite of the opposition of some of his own colleagues; and it ought always to be remembered to his honour that, in order to carry that bill, he kept the Houses sitting, in spite of many murmurs, long after the business of the government had been done, and the Appropriation Act passed. In 1791 he cordially concurred with Fox in maintaining the sound constitutional doctrine, that an impeachment is not terminated by a dissolution. In the course of the same year the two great rivals contended side by side in a far more important cause. They are fairly entitled to divide the high honour of having added to our statute-book the inestimable law which places the liberty of the press under the protection of juries. On one occasion, and one alone, Pitt, during the first half of his long administration, acted in a manner unworthy of an enlightened Whig. In the debate on the Test Act, he stooped to gratify the master whom he served, the university which he represented, and the great body of clergymen and country gentlemen on whose support he rested, by talking, with little heartiness, indeed, and with no asperity, the language of a Tory. With this single exception, his conduct from the end of 1783 to the middle of 1792 was that of an honest friend of civil and religious liberty.

Nor did anything, during that period, indicate that he loved war, or harboured any malevolent feelings against any neighbouring nation. Those French writers who have represented him as a Hannibal sworn in childhood by his father to bear eternal hatred to France, as having, by mysterious intrigues and lavish bribes, instigated the leading Jacobins to commit those excesses which dishonoured the Revolution, as having been the real author of the first coalition, know nothing of his character or of his history. So far was he from being a deadly enemy to France, that his laudable attempts to bring about a closer connection with that country by means of a wise and liberal treaty of commerce brought on him the severe censure of the opposition. He was told in the House of Commons that he was a degenerate son, and that his partiality for the hereditary foes of our island was enough to make his great father's bones stir under the pavement of the Abbey.

And this man, whose name, if he had been so fortunate as to die in 1792, would now have been associated with peace, with freedom, with philanthropy, with temperate reform, with mild and constitutional administration, lived to associate his name with arbitrary government, with harsh laws harshly executed, with alien bills, with gagging bills, with suspensions of the Habeas Corpus Act, with cruel punishments inflicted on some political agitators, with unjustifiable prosecutions instituted against others, and with the most costly and most sanguinary wars of modern times. He lived to be held up to obloquy as the stern oppressor of England, and the indefatigable disturber of Europe. Poets, contrasting his earlier with his later years, likened him sometimes to the apostle who kissed in order to betray, and sometimes to the evil angels who kept not their first estate. A satirist of great genius introduced the fiends of Famine, Slaughter, and Fire, proclaiming that they had received their commission from One whose name was formed of four letters, and promising to give their employer ample proofs of gratitude. Famine would gnaw the multitude till they should rise up against him in madness. The demon of Slaughter would impel them to tear him from limb to limb. But Fire boasted that she alone could reward him as he deserved, and that she would cling round him to all eternity. By the French press and the French tribune every crime that disgraced and every calamity that afflicted France was ascribed to the monster Pitt and his guineas. While the Jacobins were dominant, it was he who had corrupted the Gironde, who had raised Lyons and Bordeaux against the Convention, who had suborned Paris to assassinate Lepelletier, and Cecilia Regnault to assassinate Robespierre. When the Thermidorian reaction came, all the atrocities of the Reign of Terror were imputed to him. Collot D'Herbois and Fouquier Tinville had been his pensioners. It was he who had hired the murderers of September, who had dictated the pamphlets of Marat and the Carmagnoles of Barrere, who had paid Lebon to deluge Arras with blood, and Carrier to choke the Loire with corpses.

The truth is, that he liked neither war nor arbitrary government. He was a lover of peace and freedom, driven, by a stress against which it was hardly possible for any will or any intellect to struggle, out of the course to which his inclinations pointed, and for which his abilities and acquirements fitted him, and forced into a policy repugnant to his feelings and unsuited to his talents.

The charge of apostasy is grossly unjust. A man ought no more to be called an apostate because his opinions alter with the opinions of the great body of his contemporaries than he ought to be called an oriental traveller because he is always going round from west to east with the globe and everything that is upon it. Between the spring of 1789 and the close of 1792, the public mind of England underwent a great change. If the change of Pitt's sentiments attracted peculiar notice, it was not because he changed more than his neighbours; for in fact he changed less than most of them; but because his position was far more conspicuous than theirs, because he was, till Bonaparte appeared, the individual who filled the greatest space in the eyes of the inhabitants of the civilised world. During a short time the nation, and Pitt, as one of the nation, looked with interest and approbation on the French Revolution. But soon vast confiscations, the violent sweeping away of ancient institutions, the domination of clubs, the barbarities of mobs maddened by famine and hatred, produced a reaction here. The court, the nobility, the gentry, the clergy, the manufacturers, the merchants, in short, nineteen twentieths of those who had good roofs over their heads and good coats on their backs, became eager and intolerant Antijacobins. This feeling was at least as strong among the minister's adversaries as among his supporters. Fox in vain attempted to restrain his followers. All his genius, all his vast personal influence, could not prevent them from rising up against him in general mutiny. Burke set the example of revolt; and Burke was in no long time joined by Portland, Spencer, Fitzwilliam, Loughborough, Carlisle, Malmesbury, Windham, Elliot. In the House of Commons, the followers of the great Whig statesman and orator diminished from about a hundred and sixty to fifty. In the House of Lords he had but ten or twelve adherents left. There can be no doubt that there would have been a similar mutiny on the ministerial benches if Pitt had obstinately resisted the general wish. Pressed at once by his master and by his colleagues, by old friends and by old opponents, he abandoned, slowly and reluctantly, the policy which was dear to his heart. He laboured hard to avert the European war. When the European war broke out, he still flattered himself that it would not be necessary for this country to take either side. In the spring of 1792 he congratulated the Parliament on the prospect of long and profound peace, and proved his sincerity by proposing large remissions of taxation. Down to the end of that year he continued to cherish the hope that England might be able to preserve neutrality. But the passions which raged on both sides of the Channel were not to be restrained. The republicans who ruled France were inflamed by a fanaticism resembling that of the

Mussulmans who, with the Koran in one hand and the sword in the other, went forth, conquering and converting, eastward to the Bay of Bengal, and westward to the Pillars of Hercules. The higher and middle classes of England were animated by zeal not less fiery than that of the Crusaders who raised the cry of *Deus vult* at Clermont. The impulse which drove the two nations to a collision was not to be arrested by the abilities or by the authority of any single man. As Pitt was in front of his fellows, and towered high above them, he seemed to lead them. But in fact he was violently pushed on by them, and, had he held back but a little more than he did, would have been thrust out of their way or trampled under their feet.

He yielded to the current: and from that day his misfortunes began. The truth is that there were only two consistent courses before him. Since he did not choose to oppose himself, side by side with Fox, to the public feeling, he should have taken the advice of Burke, and should have availed himself of that feeling to the full extent. If it was impossible to preserve peace, he should have adopted the only policy which could lead to victory. He should have proclaimed a Holy War for religion, morality, property, order, public law, and should have thus opposed to the Jacobins an energy equal to their own. Unhappily he tried to find a middle path; and he found one which united all that was worst in both extremes. He went to war: but he would not understand the peculiar character of that war. He was obstinately blind to the plain fact, that he was contending against a state which was also a sect, and that the new quarrel between England and France was of quite a different kind from the old quarrel about colonies in America and fortresses in the Netherlands. He had to combat frantic enthusiasm, boundless ambition, restless activity, the wildest and most audacious spirit of innovation; and he acted as if he had to deal with the harlots and fops of the old Court of Versailles, with Madame de Pompadour and the Abbé de Bernis. It was pitiable to hear him, year after year, proving to an admiring audience that the wicked Republic was exhausted, that she could not hold out, that her credit was gone, and her assignats were not worth more than the paper of which they were made; as if credit was necessary to a government of which the principle was rapine, as if Alboin could not turn Italy into a desert till he had negotiated a loan at five per cent., as if the exchequer bills of Attila had been at par. It was impossible that a man who so completely mistook the nature of a contest could carry on that contest successfully. Great as Pitt's abilities were, his military administration was that of a driveller. He was at the head of a nation engaged in a struggle for life and death, of a nation eminently distinguished by all the physica and all the moral qualities which make excellent soldiers. The resources at his command were unlimited. The Parliament was even more ready to grant him men and money than he was to ask for them. In such an emergency, and with such means, such a statesman as Richelieu, as Louvois, as Chatham, as Wellesley, would have created in a few months one of the finest armies in the world, and would soon have discovered and brought forward generals worthy to command such an army. Germany might have been saved by another Blenheim; Flanders recovered by another Ramilies; another Poitiers might have delivered the Royalist and Catholic provinces of France from a yoke which they abhorred, and might have spread terror even to the barriers of Paris. But the fact is, that, after eight years of war, after a vast destruction of life, after an expenditure of wealth far exceeding the expenditure of the American war, of the Seven Years' War, of the war of the Austrian Succession, and of the war of the Spanish Succession united, the English army, under Pitt, was the laughing-stock of all Europe. It could not boast of one single brilliant exploit. It had never shown itself on the Continent but to be beaten, chased, forced to reembark, or forced to capitulate. To take some sugar island in the West Indies, to scatter some mob of half naked Irish peasants, such were the most splendid victories won by the British troops under Pitt's auspices.

The English navy no mismanagement could ruin. But during a long period whatever mismanagement could do was done. The Earl of Chatham, without a single qualification for high public trust, was made, by fraternal partiality, First Lord of the Admiralty, and was kept in that great post during two years of a war in which the very existence of the state depended on the efficiency of the fleet. He continued to doze away and trifle away the time which ought to have been devoted to the public service, till the whole mercantile body, though generally disposed to support the government, complained bitterly that our flag gave no protection to our trade. Fortunately he was succeeded by George Earl Spencer, one of those chiefs of the Whig party who, in the great schism caused by the French Revolution, had followed Burke. Lord Spencer, though inferior to many of his colleagues as an orator, was decidedly the best administrator among them. To him it was owing that a long and gloomy succession of days of fasting, and, most emphatically, of humiliation, was interrupted, twice in the short space of eleven months, by days of thanksgiving for great victories.

It may seem paradoxical to say that the incapacity which Pitt showed in all that related to the conduct of the war is, in some sense, the most decisive proof that he was a man o₁ very extra-ordinary abilities. Yet this is the simple truth. For assuredly one-tenth part of his errors and disasters would have been fatal to the power and influence of any minister who had not possessed, in the highest degree, the talents of a parliamentary leader. While his schemes were confounded, while his predictions were falsified, while the coalitions which he had laboured to form were falling to pieces, while the expeditions which he had sent forth at enormous cost were ending in rout and disgrace, while the enemy against whom he was feebly contending was subjugating Flanders and Brabant, the Electorate of Mentz, the Electorate of Treves, Holland, Piedmont, Liguria, Lombardy, his authority over the House of Commons was constantly becoming more and more absolute. There was his empire. There were his victories, his Lodi and his Arcola, his Rivoli and his Marengo. If some great misfortune, a pitched battle lost by the allies, the annexation of a new department to the French Republic, a sanguinary insurrection in Ireland, a mutiny in the fleet, a panic in the city, a run on the bank, had spread dismay through the ranks of his majority, that dismay lasted only till he rose from the Treasury bench, drew up his haughty head, stretched his arm with commanding gesture, and poured forth, in deep and sonorous tones, the lofty language of inextinguishable hope and inflexible resolution. Thus, through a long and calamitous period, every disaster that happened without the walls of Parliament was regularly followed by a triumph within them. At length he had no longer an opposition to encounter. Of the great party which had contended against him during the first eight years of his administration more than one half now marched under his standard, with his old competitor the Duke of Portland at their head; and the rest had, after many vain struggles, quitted the field in despair. Fox had retired to the shades of St. Anne's Hill, and had there found, in the society of friends whom no vicissitude could estrange from him, of a woman whom he tenderly loved, and of the illustrious dead of Athens, of Rome, and of Florence, ample compensation for all the misfortunes of his public life. Session followed session with scarcely a single division. In the eventful year 1799, the largest minority that could be mustered against the government was twenty-five.

In Pitt's domestic policy there was at this time assuredly no want of vigour. While he offered to French Jacobinism a resistance so feeble that it only encouraged the evil which he wished to suppress, he put down English Jacobinism with a strong hand. The Habeas Corpus Act was repeatedly suspended. Public meetings were placed under severe restraints. The government obtained from

Parliament power to send out of the country aliens who were suspected of evil designs; and that power was not suffered to be idle. Writers who propounded doctrines adverse to monarchy and aristocracy were proscribed and punished without mercy. It was hardly safe for a republican to avow his political creed over his beefsteak and his bottle of port at a chop-house. The old laws of Scotland against sedition, laws which were considered by Englishmen as barbarous, and which a succession of governments had suffered to rust, were now furbished up and sharpened anew. Men of cultivated minds and polished manners were, for offences which at Westminster would have been treated as mere misdemeanours, sent to herd with felons at Botany Bay. Some reformers, whose opinions were extravagant, and whose language was intemperate, but who had never dreamed of subverting the government by physical force, were indicted for high treason, and were saved from the gallows only by the righteous verdicts of juries. This severity was at the time loudly applauded by alarmists whom fear had made cruel, but will be seen in a very different light by posterity. The truth is, that the Englishmen who wished for a revolution were, even in number, not formidable, and, in everything but number, a faction utterly contemptible, without arms, or funds, or plans, or organisation, or leader. There can be no doubt that Pitt, strong as he was in the support of the great body of the nation, might easily have repressed the turbulence of the discontented minority by firmly yet temperately enforcing the ordinary law. Whatever vigour he showed during this unfortunate part of his life was vigour out of place and season. He was all feebleness and languor in his conflict with the foreign enemy who was really to be dreaded, and reserved all his energy and resolution for the domestic enemy who might safely have been despised.

One part only of Pitt's conduct during the last eight years of the eighteenth century deserves high praise. He was the first English minister who formed great designs for the benefit of Ireland. The manner in which the Roman Catholic population of that unfortunate country had been kept down during many generations seemed to him unjust and cruel; and it was scarcely possible for a man of his abilities not to perceive that, in a contest against the Jacobins, the Roman Catholics were his natural allies. Had he been able to do all that he wished, it is probable that a wise and liberal policy would have averted the rebellion of 1798. But the difficulties which he encountered were great, perhaps insurmountable; and the Roman Catholics were, rather by his misfortune than by his fault, thrown into the hands of the Jacobins. There was a third great rising of the Irishry against the Englishry, a rising not less formidable than the risings of 1641 and 1689. The Englishry remained victorious; and it was necessary for Pitt, as it had been necessary for Oliver Cromwell and William of Orange before him, to consider how the victory should be used. It is only just to his memory to say that he formed a scheme of policy, so grand and so simple, so righteous and so humane, that it would alone entitle him to a high place among statesmen. He determined to make Ireland one kingdom with England, and, at the same time, to relieve the Roman Catholic laity from civil disabilities, and to grant a public maintenance to the Roman Catholic clergy. Had he been able to carry these noble designs into effect, the Union would have been an Union indeed. It would have been inseparably associated in the minds of the great majority of Irishmen with civil and religious freedom; and the old Parliament in College Green would have been regretted only by a small knot of discarded jobbers and oppressors, and would have been remembered by the body of the nation with the loathing and contempt due to the most tyrannical and the most corrupt assembly that had ever sate in Europe. But Pitt could execute only one half of what he had projected. He succeeded in obtaining the consent of the Parliaments of both kingdoms to the Union; but that reconciliation of races and sects, without which the Union could exist only in name, was not accomplished. He was well aware that he was likely to find difficulties in the closet. But he flattered himself that, by cautious and dexterous management, those difficulties might be overcome. Unhappily, there were traitors and sycophants in high place who did not suffer him to take his own time and his own way, but prematurely disclosed his scheme to the King, and disclosed it in the manner most likely to irritate and alarm a weak and diseased mind. His Majesty absurdly imagined that his Coronation oath bound him to refuse his assent to any bill for relieving Roman Catholics from civil disabilities. To argue with him was impossible. Dundas tried to explain the matter, but was told to keep his Scotch metaphysics to himself. Pitt, and Pitt's ablest colleagues, resigned their offices. It was necessary that the King should make a new arrangement. But by this time his anger and distress had brought back the malady which had, many years before, incapacitated him for the discharge of his functions. He actually assembled his family, read the Coronation oath to them, and told them that, if he broke it, the Crown would immediately pass to the House of Savoy. It was not until after an interregnum of several weeks that he regained the full use of his small faculties, and that a ministry after his own heart was at length formed.

The materials out of which he had to construct a government were neither solid nor splendid. To that party, weak in numbers, but strong in every kind of talent, which was hostile to the domestic and foreign policy of his late advisers, he could not have recourse. For that party, while it differed from his late advisers on every point on which they had been honoured with his approbation, cordially agreed with them as to the single matter which had brought on them his displeasure. All that was left to him was to call up the rear ranks of the old ministry to form the front rank of a new ministry. In an age pre-eminently fruitful of parliamentary talents, a cabinet was formed containing hardly a single man who, in parliamentary talents, could be considered as even of the second rate. The most important offices in the state were bestowed on decorous and laborious mediocrity. Henry Addington was at the head of the Treasury. He had been an early, indeed a hereditary, friend of Pitt, and had by Pitt's influence been placed, while still a young man, in the chair of the House of Commons. He was universally admitted to have been the best speaker that had sate in that chair since the retirement of Onslow. But nature had not bestowed on him very vigorous faculties; and the highly respectable situation which he had long occupied with honour had rather un-fitted than fitted him for the discharge of his new duties. His business had been to bear himself evenly between contending factions. He had taken no part in the war of words; and he had always been addressed with marked deference by the great orators who thundered against each other from his right and from his left. It was not strange that, when, for the first time, he had to encounter keen and vigorous antagonists, who dealt hard blows without the smallest ceremony, he should have been awkward and unready, or that the air of dignity and authority which he had acquired in his former post, and of which he had not divested himself, should have made his helplessness laughable and pitiable. Nevertheless, during many months, his power seemed to stand firm. He was a favourite with the King, whom he resembled in narrowness of mind, and to whom he was more obsequious than Pitt had ever been. The nation was put into high good humour by a peace with France. The enthusiasm with which the upper and middle classes had rushed into the war had spent itself. Jacobinism was no longer formidable. Everywhere there was a strong reaction against what was called the atheistical and anarchical philosophy of the eighteenth century. Bonaparte, now First Consul, was busied in constructing out of the ruins of old institutions a new ecclesiastical establishment and a new order of knighthood. That nothing less than the dominion of the whole civilised world would satisfy his selfish ambition was not yet suspected; nor did even wise men see any reason to doubt that he might be as safe a neighbour as any prince of the House of Bourbon had been. The treaty of Amiens was therefore hailed by the great body of the English people with extravagant joy. The popularity of the minister was for the moment immense. His want of parliamentary ability was, as yet, of little consequence: for he had scarcely any adversary to encounter. The old opposition, delighted by the peace, regarded him with favour. A new opposition had indeed been formed by some of the late ministers, and was led by Grenville in the House of Lords, and by Windham in the House of Commons. But the new opposition could scarcely muster ten votes, and was regarded with no favour by the country. On Pitt the ministers relied as on their firmest support. He had not, like some of his colleagues, retired in anger. He had expressed the greatest respect for the conscientious scruple which had taken possession of the royal mind; and he had promised his successors all the help in his power. In private his advice was at their service. In Parliament he took his seat on the bench behind them; and, in more than one debate, defended them with powers far superior to their own. The King perfectly understood the value of such assistance. On one occasion, at the palace, he took the old minister and the new minister aside. "If we three," he said, "keep together, all will go well."

But it was hardly possible, human nature being what it is, and, more especially, Pitt and Addington being what they were, that this union should be durable. Pitt, conscious of superior powers, imagined that the place which he had quitted was now occupied by a mere puppet which he had set up, which he was to govern while he suffered it to remain, and which he was to fling aside as soon as he wished to resume his old position. Nor was it long before he began to pine for the power which he had relinquished. He had been so early raised to supreme authority in the state, and had enjoyed that authority so long, that it had become necessary to him. In retirement his days passed heavily. He could not, like Fox, forget the pleasures and cares of ambition in the company of Euripides or Herodotus. Pride restrained him from intimating, even to his dearest friends, that he wished to be again minister. But he thought it strange, almost ungrateful, that his wish had not been divined, that it had not been anticipated, by one whom he regarded as his deputy.

Addington, on the other hand, was by no means inclined to descend from his high position. He was, indeed, under a delusion much resembling that of Abon Hassan in the Arabian tale. His brain was turned by his short and unreal Caliphate. He took his elevation quite seriously, attributed it to his own merit, and considered himself as one of the great triumvirate of English statesmen, as worthy to make a third with Pitt and Fox.

Such being the feelings of the late minister and of the present minister, a rupture was inevitable; and there was no want of persons bent on making that rupture speedy and violent. Some of these persons wounded Addington's pride by representing him as a lacquey, sent to keep a place on the Treasury bench till his master should find it convenient to come. Others took every opportunity of praising him at Pitt's expense. Pitt had waged a long, a bloody, a costly, an unsuccessful war. Addington had made peace. Pitt had suspended the constitutional liberties of Englishmen. Under Addington those liberties were again enjoyed. Pitt had wasted the public resources. Addington was carefully nursing them. It was sometimes but too evident that these compliments were not unpleasing to Addington. Pitt became cold and reserved. During many months he remained at a distance from London. Meanwhile his most intimate friends, in spite of his declarations that he made no complaint, and that he had no wish for office, exerted themselves to effect a change of ministry. His favourite disciple, George Canning, young, ardent, ambitious, with great powers and great virtues, but with a temper too restless and a wit too satirical for his own happiness, was indefatigable. He spoke; he wrote; he intrigued; he tried to induce a large number of the supporters of the government to sign a round robin desiring a change; he made game of Addington and of Addington's relations in a succession of lively pasquinades. The minister's partisans retorted with equal acrimony, if not with equal vivacity. Pitt could keep out of the affray only by keeping out of politics altogether; and this it soon became impossible for him to do. Had Napoleon, content with the first place among the sovereigns of the Continent, and with a military reputation surpassing that of Marlborough or of Turenne, devoted himself to the noble task of making France happy by mild administration and wise legislation, our country might have long continued to tolerate a government of fair intentions and feeble abilities. Unhappily, the treaty of Amiens had scarcely been signed, when the restless ambition and the insupportable insolence of the First Consul convinced the great body of the English people that the peace, so eagerly welcomed, was only a precarious armistice. As it became clearer and clearer that a war for the dignity, the independence, the very existence of the nation was at hand, men looked with increasing uneasiness on the weak and languid cabinet which would have to contend against an enemy who united more than the power of Lewis the Great to more than the genius of Frederick the Great. It is true that Addington might easily have been a better war minister than Pitt, and could not possibly have been a worse. But Pitt had cast a spell on the public mind. The eloquence, the judgment, the calm and disdainful firmness, which he had, during many years, displayed in Parliament, deluded the world into the belief that he must be eminently qualified to super-intend every department of politics; and they imagined, even after the miserable failures of Dunkirk, of Quiberon, and of the Helder, that he was the only statesman who could cope with Bonaparte. This feeling was nowhere stronger than among Addington's own colleagues. The pressure put on him was so strong that he could not help yielding to it: yet, even in yielding, he showed how far he was from knowing his own place. His first proposition was, that some insignificant nobleman should be First Lord of the Treasury and nominal head of the administration, and that the real power should be divided between Pitt and himself, who were to be secretaries of state. Pitt, as might have been expected, refused even to discuss such a scheme, and talked of it with bitter mirth. "Which secretaryship was offered to you?" his friend Wilberforce asked. "Really," said Pitt, "I had not the curiosity to inquire." Addington was frightened into bidding higher. He offered to resign the Treasury to Pitt, on condition that there should be no extensive change in the Government. But Pitt would listen to no such terms. Then came a dispute such as often arises after negotiations orally conducted, even when the negotiators are men of strict honour. Pitt gave one account of what had passed; Addington gave another: and, though the discrepancies were not such as necessarily implied any intentional violation of truth on either side, both were greatly exasperated.

Meanwhile the quarrel with the First Consul had come to a crisis. On the 16th of May 1803, the King sent a message calling on the House of Commons to support him in withstanding the ambitious and encroaching policy of France; and, on the 22nd, the House took the message into consideration.

Pitt had now been living many months in retirement. There had been a general election since he had spoken in Parliament, and there were two hundred members who had never heard him. It was known that on this occasion he would be in his place, and curiosity was wound up to the highest point. Unfortunately, the short-hand writers were, in consequence of some mistake, shut out on that day from the gallery, so that the newspapers contained only a very meagre report of the proceedings. But several accounts of what passed are extant; and of those accounts the most interesting is contained in an unpublished letter, written by a very young member, John William Ward, afterwards Earl of Dudley. When Pitt rose, he was received with loud cheering. At every pause in his speech there was a burst of applause. The peroration is said to have been one of the most animated and magnificent ever heard in Parliament. "Pitt's speech," Fox wrote a few days later, "was admired very much, and very justly. I think it was the best he ever made in that style." The debate was adjourned; and on the second night Fox replied in an oration which, as the most zealous Pittites were forced to acknowledge, left the palm of eloquence doubtful. Addington made a pitiable appearance between the two great rivals; and it was observed that Pitt, while exhorting the Commons to stand resolutely by the executive government against France, said not a word indicating esteem or friendship for the prime minister.

War was speedily declared. The First Consul threatened to invade England at the head of the conquerors of Belgium and Italy, and formed a great camp near the Straits of Dover. On the other side of those Straits the whole population of our island was ready to rise up as one man in defence of the soil. At this conjuncture, as at some other great conjunctures in our history, the conjuncture of 1660, for example, and the conjuncture of 1688, there was a general disposition among honest and patriotic men to forget old quarrels, and to regard as a friend every person who was ready, in the existing emergency, to do his part towards the saving of the state. A coalition of all the first men in the country would, at that moment, have been as popular as the coalition of 1783 had been unpopular. Alone in the kingdom the King looked with perfect complacency on a cabinet in which no man superior to himself in genius was to be found, and was so far from being willing to admit all his ablest subjects to office that he was bent on excluding them all.

A few months passed before the different parties which agreed in regarding the government with dislike and contempt came to an understanding with each other. But in the spring of 1804 it became evident that the weakest of ministries would have to defend itself against the strongest of oppositions, an opposition made up of three oppositions, each of which would, separately, have been formidable from ability, and which, when united, were also formidable from number. The party which had opposed the peace, headed by Grenville and Windham, and the party which had opposed the renewal of the war, headed by Fox, concurred in thinking that the men now in power were incapable of either making a good peace or waging a vigorous war. Pitt had, in 1802, spoken for peace against the party of Grenville, and had, in 1803, spoken for war against the party of Fox. But of the capacity of the cabinet, and especially of its chief, for the conduct of great affairs, he thought as meanly as either Fox or Grenville. Questions were easily found on which all the enemies of the government could act cordially together. The unfortunate First Lord of the Treasury, who had, during the earlier months of his administration, been supported by Pitt on one side, and by Fox on the other, now had to answer Pitt, and to be answered by Fox. Two sharp debates, followed by close divisions, made him weary of his post. It was known, too, that the Upper House was even more hostile to him than the Lower, that the Scotch representative peers wavered, that there were signs of mutiny among the Bishops. In the cabinet itself there was discord, and, worse than discord, treachery. It was necessary to give way: the ministry was dissolved; and the task of forming a government was entrusted to Pitt.

Pitt was of opinion that there was now an opportunity, such as had never before offered itself, and such as might never offer itself again, of uniting in the public service, on honourable terms, all the eminent talents of the kingdom. The passions to which the French Revolution had given birth were extinct. The madness of the innovator and the madness of the alarmist had alike had their day. Jacobinism and Antijacobinism had gone out of fashion together. The most liberal statesman did not think that season propitious for schemes of parliamentary reform; and the most conservative statesman could not pretend that there was any occasion for gagging bills and suspensions of the Habeas Corpus Act. The great struggle for independence and national honour occupied all minds; and those who were agreed as to the duty of maintaining that struggle with vigour might well postpone to a more convenient time all disputes about matters comparatively unimportant. Strongly impressed by these considerations, Pitt wished to form a ministry including all the first men in the country. The Treasury he reserved for himself; and to Fox he proposed to assign a share of power little inferior to his own.

The plan was excellent: but the King would not hear of it. Dull, obstinate, unforgiving, and, at that time, half mad, he positively refused to admit Fox into his service. Anybody else, even men who had gone as far as Fox, or further than Fox, in what His Majesty considered as Jacobinism, Sheridan, Grey, Erskine, should be graciously received; but Fox never. During several hours Pitt laboured in vain to reason down this senseless antipathy. That he was perfectly sincere there can be no doubt; but it was not enough to be sincere; he should have been resolute. Had he declared himself determined not to take office without Fox, the royal obstinacy would have given way, as it gave way, a few months later, when opposed to the immutable resolution of Lord Grenville. In an evil hour Pitt yielded. He flattered himself with the hope that, though he consented to forego the aid of his illustrious rival, there would still remain ample materials for the formation of an efficient ministry. That hope was cruelly disappointed. Fox entreated his friends to leave personal considerations out of the question, and declared that he would support, with the utmost cordiality, an efficient and patriotic ministry from which he should be himself excluded. Not only his friends, however, but Grenville and Grenville's adherents, answered, with one voice, that the question was not personal, that a great constitutional principle was at stake, and that they would not take office while a man eminently qualified to render service to the commonwealth was placed under a ban merely because he was disliked at Court. All that was left to Pitt was to construct a government out of the wreck of Addington's feeble administration. The small circle of his personal retainers furnished him with a very few useful assistants, particularly Dundas, who had been created Viscount Melville, Lord Harrowby, and Canning.

Such was the inauspicious manner in which Pitt entered on his second administration. The whole history of that administration was of a piece with the commencement. Almost every month brought some new disaster or disgrace. To the war with France was soon added a war with Spain. The opponents of the minister were numerous, able, and active. His most useful coadjutors he soon lost. Sickness deprived him of the help of Lord Harrowby. It was discovered that Lord Melville had been guilty of highly culpable laxity in transactions relating to public money. He was censured by the House of Commons, driven from office, ejected from the Privy Council, and impeached of high crimes and misdemeanours. The blow fell heavy on Pitt. It gave him, he said in Parliament, a deep pang; and, as he uttered the word pang, his lip quivered, his voice shook; he paused, and his hearers thought that he was about to burst into tears. Such tears shed by Eldon would have moved nothing but laughter. Shed by the warm-hearted and open-hearted Fox, they would have moved sympathy, but would have caused no surprise. But a tear from Pitt would have been something portentous. He suppressed his emotion, however, and proceeded with his usual majestic self-possession.

His difficulties compelled him to resort to various expedients. At one time Addington was persuaded to accept office with a peerage; but he brought no additional strength to the government. Though he went through the form of reconciliation, it was impossible for him to forget the past. While he remained in place he was jealous and punctilious; and he soon retired again. At another time Pitt renewed his efforts to overcome his master's aversion to Fox; and it was rumoured that the King's obstinacy was gradually giving way. But, meanwhile, it was impossible for the minister to conceal from the public eye the decay of his health, and the constant anxiety which gnawed at his heart. His sleep was broken. His food ceased to nourish him. All who passed him in the Park, all who had interviews with him in Downing Street, saw misery written in his face. The peculiar look which he wore during the last months of his life was often pathetically described by Wilberforce, who used to call it the Austerlitz look.

Still the vigour of Pitt's intellectual faculties, and the intrepid haughtiness of his spirit, remained unaltered. He had staked everything on a great venture. He had succeeded in forming another mighty coalition against the French ascendency. The united forces of Austria, Russia and England might, he hoped, oppose an insurmountable barrier to the ambition of the common enemy. But the genius and energy of Napoleon prevailed. While the English troops were preparing to embark for Germany, while the Russian troops were slowly coming up from Poland, he, with rapidity unprecedented in modern war, moved a hundred thousand men from the shores of the Ocean to the Black Forest, and compelled a great Austrian army to surrender at Ulm. To the first faint rumours of this calamity Pitt would give no credit. He was irritated by the alarms of those around him. "Do not believe a word of it," he said: "it is all a fiction." The next day he received a Dutch newspaper containing the capitulation. He knew no Dutch. It was Sunday; and the public offices were shut. He carried the paper to Lord Malmesbury, who had been Minister in Holland; and Lord Malmesbury translated it. Pitt tried to bear up; but the shock was too great; and he went away with death in his face.

The news of the battle of Trafalgar arrived four days later, and seemed for a moment to revive him. Forty-eight hours after that most glorious and most mournful of victories had been announced to the country came the Lord Mayor's day; and Pitt dined at Guildhall. His popularity had declined. But on this occasion the multitude, greatly excited by the recent tidings, welcomed him enthusiastically, took off his horses in Cheapside, and drew his carriage up King Street. When his health was drunk, he returned thanks in two or three of those stately sentences of which he had a boundless command. Several of those who heard him laid up his words in their hearts; for they were the last words that he ever uttered in public: "Let us hope that England, having saved herself by her energy, may save Europe by her example."

This was but a momentary rally. Austerlitz soon completed what Ulm had begun. Early in December Pitt had retired to Bath, in the hope that he might there gather strength for the approaching session. While he was languishing there on his sofa arrived the news that a decisive battle had been fought and lost in Moravia, that the coalition was dissolved, that the Continent was at the feet of France. He sank down under the blow. Ten days later, he was so emaciated that his most intimate friends hardly knew him. He came up from Bath by slow journeys, and, on the 11th of January 1806, reached his villa at Putney. Parliament was to meet on the 21st. On the 20th was to be the parliamentary dinner at the house of the First Lord of the Treasury in Downing Street; and the cards were already issued. But the days of the great minister were numbered. The only chance for his life, and that a very slight chance, was, that he should resign his office, and pass some months in profound repose. His colleagues paid him very short visits, and carefully avoided political conversation. But his spirit, long accustomed to dominion, could not, even in that extremity, relinquish hopes which everybody but himself perceived to be vain. On the day on which he was carried into his bedroom at Putney, the Marquess Wellesley, whom he had long loved, whom he had sent to govern India, and whose administration had been eminently able, energetic, and successful, arrived in London after an absence of eight years. The friends saw each other once more. There was an affectionate meeting, and a last parting. That it was a last parting Pitt did not seem to be aware. He fancied himself to be recovering, talked on various subjects cheerfully, and with an unclouded mind, and pronounced a warm and discerning eulogium on the Marquess's brother Arthur. "I never," he said, "met with any military man with whom it was so satisfactory to converse." The excitement and exertion of this interview were too much for the sick man. He fainted away; and Lord Wellesley left the house, convinced that the close was fast approaching.

And now members of Parliament were fast coming up to London. The chiefs of the opposition met for the purpose of considering the course to be taken on the first day of the session. It was easy to guess what would be the language of the King's speech, and of the address which would be moved in answer to that speech. An amendment condemning the policy of the government had been prepared, and was to have been proposed in the House of Commons by Lord Henry Petty, a young nobleman who had already won for himself that place in the esteem of his country which, after the lapse of more than half a century, he still retains. He was unwilling, however, to come forward as the accuser of one who was incapable of defending himself. Lord Grenville, who had been informed of Pitt's state by Lord Wellesley, and had been deeply affected by it, earnestly recommended forbearance; and Fox, with characteristic generosity and good nature, gave his voice against attacking his now helpless rival. "Sunt lacrymæ rerum," he said, "et mentem mortalia tangunt." On the first day, therefore, there was no debate. It was rumoured that evening that Pitt was better. But on the following morning his physicians pronounced that there were no hopes. The commanding faculties of which he had been too proud were beginning to fail. His old tutor and friend, the Bishop of Lincoln, informed him of his danger, and gave such religious advice and consolation as a confused and obscured mind could receive. Stories were told of devout sentiments fervently uttered by the dying man. But these stories found no credit with anybody who knew him. Wilberforce pronounced it impossible that they could be true. "Pitt," he added, "was a man who always said less than he thought on such topics." It was asserted in many after-dinner speeches, Grub Street elegies, and academic prize poems and prize declamations, that the great minister died exclaiming, "Oh my country!" This is a fable; but it is true that the last words which he uttered, while he knew what he said, were broken exclamations about the alarming state of public affairs. He ceased to breathe on the morning of the 23rd of January 1806, the twenty-fifth anniversary of the day on which he first took his seat in Parliament. He was in his forty-seventh year, and had been, during near nineteen years, First Lord of the Treasury, and undisputed chief of the administration. Since parliamentary government was established in England, no English statesman has held supreme power so long. Walpole, it is true, was First Lord of the Treasury during more than twenty years, but it was not till Walpole had been some time First Lord of the Treasury that he could be properly called Prime Minister.

It was moved in the House of Commons that Pitt should be honoured with a public funeral and a monument. The motion was opposed by Fox in a speech which deserves to be studied as a model of good taste and good feeling. The task was the most invidious that ever an orator undertook: but it was performed with a humanity and delicacy which were warmly acknowledged by the mourning friends of him who was gone. The motion was carried by 288 votes to 89.

The 22nd of February was fixed for the funeral. The corpse, having lain in state during two days in the Painted Chamber, was borne with great pomp to the northern transept of the Abbey. A splendid train of princes, nobles, bishops, and privy councillors followed. The grave of Pitt had been made near to the spot where his great father lay, near also the spot where his great rival was soon to lie. The sadness of the assistants was beyond that of ordinary mourners. For he whom they were committing to the dust had died of sorrows and anxieties of which none of the survivors could be altogether without a share. Wilberforce, who carried the banner before the hearse, described the awful ceremony with deep feeling. As the coffin descended into the earth, he said, the eagle face of Chatham from above seemed to look down with consternation into the dark house which was receiving all that remained of so much power and glory.

All parties in the House of Commons readily concurred in voting forty thousand pounds to satisfy the demands of Pitt's creditors. Some of his admirers seemed to consider the magnitude of his embarrassments as a circumstance highly honourable to him; but men of sense will probably be of a different opinion. It is far better, no doubt, that a great minister should carry his contempt of money to excess than that he should contaminate his hands with unlawful gain. But it is neither right nor becoming in a man to whom the public has given an income more than sufficient for his comfort and dignity to bequeath to that public a great debt, the effect of mere negligence and profusion. As First Lord of the Treasury and Chancellor of the Exchequer, Pitt never had less than six thousand a year, besides an excellent house. In 1792 he was forced by his royal master's friendly importunity to accept for life the office of Warden of the Cinque Ports, with near four thousand a year more. He had neither wife nor child: he had no needy relations: he had no expensive tastes: he had no long election bills. Had he given but a quarter of an hour a week to the regulation of his household, he would have kept his expenditure within bounds. Or, if he could not spare even a quarter of an hour a week for that purpose, he had numerous friends, excellent men of business, who would have been proud to act as his stewards. One of those friends, the chief of a great commercial house in the city, made an attempt to put the establishment in Downing Street to rights; but in vain. He found that the waste of the servants' hall was almost fabulous. The quantity of butcher's meat charged in the bills was nine hundred-weight a week. The consumption of poultry, of fish, and of tea was in proportion. The character of Pitt would have stood higher if, with the disinterestedness of Pericles and of De Witt, he had united their dignified frugality.

The memory of Pitt has been assailed, times innumerable, often justly, often unjustly; but it has suffered much less from his assailants than from his eulogists. For, during many years, his name was the rallying cry of a class of men with whom, at one of those terrible conjunctures which confound all ordinary distinctions, he was accidentally and temporarily connected, but to whom, on almost all great questions of principle, he was diametrically opposed. The haters of parliamentary reform called themselves Pittites, not choosing to remember that Pitt made three motions for parliamentary reform, and that, though he thought that such a reform could not safely be made while the passions excited by the French revolution were raging, he never uttered a word indicating that he should not be prepared at a more convenient season to bring the question forward a fourth time. The toast of Protestant ascendency was drunk on Pitt's birthday by a set of Pittites who could not but be aware that Pitt had resigned his office because he could not carry Catholic emancipation. The defenders of the Test Act called themselves Pittites, though they could not be ignorant that Pitt had laid before George the Third unanswerable reasons for abolishing the Test Act. The enemies of free trade called themselves Pittites, though Pitt was far more deeply imbued with the doctrines of Adam Smith than either Fox or Grey. The very negro-drivers invoked the name of Pitt, whose eloquence was never more conspicuously displayed than when he spoke of the wrongs of the negro. This mythical Pitt, who resembles the genuine Pitt as little as the Charlemagne of Ariosto resembles the Charlemagne of Eginhard, has had his day. History will vindicate the real man from calumny disguised under the semblance of adulation, and will exhibit him as what he was, a minister of great talents, honest intentions, and liberal opinions, pre-eminently qualified, intellectually and morally, for the part of a parliamentary leader, and capable of administering, with prudence and moderation, the government of a prosperous and tranquil country, but unequal to surprising and terrible emergencies, and liable, in such emergencies, to err grievously, both on the side of weakness and on the side of violence.

# II. *Literary Essays*

## MOORE'S LIFE OF LORD BYRON

### (JUNE 1830)

*Letters and Journals of Lord Byron; with Notices of his Life.* By THOMAS MOORE, Esq. 2 vols. 4to. London: 1830.

WE have read this book with the greatest pleasure. Considered merely as a composition, it deserves to be classed among the best specimens of English prose which our age has produced. It contains, indeed, no single passage equal to two or three which we could select from the Life of Sheridan. But, as a whole, it is immeasurably superior to that work. The style is agreeable, clear, and manly, and, when it rises into eloquence, rises without effort or ostentation. Nor is the matter inferior to the manner. It would be difficult to name a book which exhibits more kindness, fairness, and modesty. It has evidently been written, not for the purpose of showing, what, however, it often shows, how well its author can write, but for the purpose of vindicating, as far as truth will permit, the memory of a celebrated man who can no longer vindicate himself. Mr. Moore never thrusts himself between Lord Byron and the public. With the strongest temptations to egotism, he has said no more about himself than the subject absolutely required.

A great part, indeed the greater part, of these volumes, consists of extracts from the Letters and Journals of Lord Byron; and it is difficult to speak too highly of the skill which has been shown in the selection and arrangement. We will not say that we have not occasionally remarked in these two large quartos an anecdote which should have been omitted, a letter which should have been suppressed, a name which should have been concealed by asterisks, or asterisks which do not answer the purpose of concealing the name. But it is impossible, on a general survey, to deny that the task has been executed with great judgment and great humanity. When we consider the life which Lord Byron had led, his petulance, his irritability, and his communicativeness, we cannot but admire the dexterity with which Mr. Moore has contrived to exhibit so much of the character and opinions of his friend, with so little pain to the feelings of the living.

The extracts from the journals and correspondence of Lord Byron are in the highest degree valuable, not merely on account of the information which they contain respecting the distinguished man by whom they were written, but on account also of their rare merit as compositions. The Letters, at least those which were sent from Italy, are among the best in our language. They are less affected than those of Pope and Walpole; they have more matter in them than those of Cowper. Knowing that many of them were not written merely for the person to whom they were directed, but were general epistles, meant to be read by a large circle, we expected to find them clever and spirited, but deficient in ease. We looked with vigilance for instances of stiffness in the language and awkwardness in the transitions. We have been agreeably disappointed; and we must confess that, if the epistolary style of Lord Byron was artificial, it was a rare and admirable instance of that highest art which cannot be distinguished from nature.

Of the deep and painful interest which this book excites no abstract can give a just notion. So sad and dark a story is scarcely to be found in any work of fiction; and we are little disposed to envy the moralist who can read it without being softened.

The pretty fable by which the Duchess of Orleans illustrated the character of her son the Regent might, with little change, be applied to Byron. All the fairies, save one, had been bidden to his cradle. All the gossips had been profuse of their gifts. One had bestowed nobility, another genius, a third beauty. The malignant elf who had been uninvited came last, and, unable to reverse what her sisters had done for their favourite, had mixed up a curse with every blessing. In the rank of Lord Byron, in his understanding, in his character, in his very person, there was a strange union of opposite extremes. He was born to all that men covet and admire. But in every one of those eminent advantages which he possessed over others was mingled something of misery and debasement. He was sprung from a house, ancient indeed and noble, but degraded and impoverished by a series of crimes and follies which had attained a scandalous publicity. The kinsman whom he succeeded had died poor, and, but for merciful judges, would have died upon the gallows. The young peer had great intellectual powers; yet there was an unsound part in his mind. He had naturally a generous and feeling heart; but his temper was wayward and irritable. He had a head which statuaries loved to copy, and a foot the deformity of which the beggars in the streets mimicked. Distinguished at once by the strength and by the weakness of his intellect, affectionate yet perverse, a poor lord, and a handsome cripple, he required, if ever man required, the firmest and the most judicious training. But, capriciously as nature had dealt with him, the parent to whom the office of forming his character was intrusted was more capricious

M—17*

still. She passed from paroxysms of rage to paroxysms of tenderness. At one time she stifled him with her caresses: at another time she insulted his deformity. He came into the world; and the world treated him as his mother had treated him, sometimes with fondness, sometimes with cruelty, never with justice. It indulged him without discrimination, and punished him without discrimination. He was truly a spoiled child, not merely the spoiled child of his parent, but the spoiled child of nature, the spoiled child of fortune, the spoiled child of fame, the spoiled child of society. His first poems were received with a contempt which, feeble as they were, they did not absolutely deserve. The poem which he published on his return from his travels was, on the other hand, extolled far above its merit. At twenty-four he found himself on the highest pinnacle of literary fame, with Scott, Wordsworth, Southey, and a crowd of other distinguished writers beneath his feet. There is scarcely an instance in history of so sudden a rise to so dizzy an eminence.

Every thing that could stimulate, and every thing that could gratify the strongest propensities of our nature, the gaze of a hundred drawing-rooms, the acclamations of the whole nation, the applause of applauded men, the love of lovely women, all this world and all the glory of it were at once offered to a youth to whom nature had given violent passions, and whom education had never taught to control them. He lived as many men live who have no similar excuse to plead for their faults. But his countrymen and his countrywomen would love him and admire him. They were resolved to see in his excesses only the flash and outbreak of that same fiery mind which glowed in his poetry. He attacked religion; yet in religious circles his name was mentioned with fondness, and in many religious publications his works were censured with singular tenderness. He lampooned the Prince Regent; yet he could not alienate the Tories. Every thing, it seemed, was to be forgiven to youth, rank, and genius.

Then came the reaction. Society, capricious in its indignation as it had been capricious in its fondness, flew into a rage with its froward and petted darling. He had been worshipped with an irrational idolatry. He was persecuted with an irrational fury. Much has been written about those unhappy domestic occurrences which decided the fate of his life. Yet nothing is, nothing ever was, positively known to the public, but this, that he quarrelled with his lady, and that she refused to live with him. There have been hints in abundance, and shrugs and shakings of the head, and "Well, well, we know," and "We could an if we would," and "If we list to speak," and "There be that might an they list." But we are not aware that there is before the world, substantiated by credible, or even by tangible evidence, a single fact indicating that Lord Byron was more to blame than any other man who is on bad terms with his wife. The professional men whom Lady Byron consulted were undoubtedly of opinion that she ought not to live with her husband. But it is to be remembered that they formed that opinion without hearing both sides. We do not say, we do not mean to insinuate, that Lady Byron was in any respect to blame. We think that those who condemn her on the evidence which is now before the public are as rash as those who condemn her husband. We will not pronounce any judgment, we cannot, even in our own minds, form any judgment, on a transaction which is so imperfectly known to us. It would have been well if, at the time of the separation, all those who knew as little about the matter then as we know about it now had shown that forbearance which, under such circumstances, is but common justice.

We know no spectacle so ridiculous as the British public in one of its periodical fits of morality. In general, elopements, divorces, and family quarrels, pass with little notice. We read the scandal, talk about it for a day, and forget it. But once in six or seven years our virtue becomes outrageous. We cannot suffer the laws of religion and decency to be violated. We must make a stand against vice. We must teach libertines that the English people appreciate the importance of domestic ties. Accordingly some unfortunate man, in no respect more depraved than hundreds whose offences have been treated with lenity, is singled out as an expiatory sacrifice. If he has children, they are to be taken from him. If he has a profession, he is to be driven from it. He is cut by the higher orders, and hissed by the lower. He is, in truth, a sort of whipping-boy, by whose vicarious agonies all the other transgressors of the same class are, it is supposed, sufficiently chastised. We reflect very complacently on our own severity, and compare with great pride the high standard of morals established in England with the Parisian laxity. At length our anger is satiated. Our victim is ruined and heart-broken. And our virtue goes quietly to sleep for seven years more.

It is clear that those vices which destroy domestic happiness ought to be as much as possible repressed. It is equally clear that they cannot be repressed by penal legislation. It is therefore right and desirable that public opinion should be directed against them. But it should be directed against them uniformly, steadily, and temperately, not by sudden fits and starts. There should be one weight and one measure. Decimation is always an objectionable mode of punishment. It is the resource of judges too indolent and hasty to investigate facts and to discriminate nicely between shades of guilt. It is an irrational practice, even when adopted by military tribunals. When adopted by the tribunal of public opinion, it is infinitely more irrational. It is good that a certain portion of disgrace should constantly attend on certain bad actions. But it is not good that the offenders should merely have to stand the risks of a lottery of infamy, that ninety-nine out of every hundred should escape, and that the hundredth, perhaps the most innocent of the hundred, should pay for all. We remember to have seen a mob assembled in Lincoln's Inn to hoot a gentleman against whom the most oppressive proceeding known to the English law was then in progress. He was hooted because he had been an indifferent and unfaithful husband, as if some of the most popular men of the age, Lord Nelson for example, had not been indifferent and unfaithful husbands. We remember a still stronger case. Will posterity believe that, in an age in which men whose gallantries were universally known, and had been legally proved, filled some of the highest offices in the state and in the army, presided at the meetings of religious and benevolent institutions, were the delight of every society, and the favourites of the multitude, a crowd of moralists went to the theatre, in order to pelt a poor actor for disturbing the conjugal felicity of an alderman? What there was in the circumstances either of the offender or of the sufferer to vindicate the zeal of the audience, we could never conceive. It has never been supposed that the situation of an actor is peculiarly favourable to the rigid virtues, or that an alderman enjoys any special immunity from injuries such as that which on this occasion roused the anger of the public. But such is the justice of mankind.

In these cases the punishment was excessive; but the offence was known and proved. The case of Lord Byron was harder. True Jedwood justice was dealt out to him. First came the execution, then the investigation, and last of all, or rather not at all, the accusation. The public, without knowing any thing whatever about the transactions in his family, flew into a violent passion with him, and proceeded to invent stories which might justify its anger. Ten or twenty different accounts of the separation, inconsistent with each other, with themselves, and with common sense, circulated at the same time. What evidence there might be for any one of these, the virtuous people who repeated them neither knew nor cared. For in fact these stories were not the causes, but the effects of the public indignation. They resembled those loathsome slanders which Lewis Goldsmith, and other abject libellers of the same class, were in the habit of publishing about Bonaparte; such as that he poisoned a girl with arsenic when he was at the military school, that he hired a grenadier to shoot Dessaix at Marengo, that he filled St. Cloud with all the pollutions of Capreæ. There was a time when anecdotes like these obtained some credence from persons who, hating the French emperor without knowing why, were eager to believe any thing which might justify their hatred. Lord Byron fared in the same way. His countrymen were in a bad humour with him. His writings and his character had lost the charm of novelty. He had been guilty of the offence which, of all offences, is punished most severely; he had been over-praised; he had excited too warm an interest; and the public, with its usual justice, chastised him for its own folly. The attachments of the multitude bear no small resemblance to those of the wanton enchantress in the Arabian Tales, who, when the forty days of her fondness were over, was not content with dismissing her lovers, but condemned them to expiate, in loathsome shapes, and under cruel penances, the crime of having once pleased her too well.

The obloquy which Byron had to endure was such as might well have shaken a more constant mind. The newspapers were filled with lampoons. The theatres shook with execrations. He was excluded from circles where he had lately been the observed of all observers. All those creeping things that riot in the decay of nobler natures hastened to their repast; and they were right; they did after their kind. It is not every day that the savage envy of aspiring dunces is gratified by the agonies of such a spirit, and the degradation of such a name.

The unhappy man left his country for ever. The howl of contumely followed him across the sea, up the Rhine, over the Alps; it gradually waxed fainter; it died away; those who had raised it began to ask each other, what, after all, was the matter about which they had been so clamorous, and wished to invite back the criminal whom they had just chased from them. His poetry became more popular than it had ever been; and his complaints were read with tears by thousands and tens of thousands who had never seen his face.

He had fixed his home on the shores of the Adriatic, in the most picturesque and interesting of cities, beneath the brightest of skies, and by the brightest of seas. Censoriousness was not the vice of the neighbours whom he had chosen. They were a race corrupted by a bad government and a bad religion, long renowned for skill in the arts of voluptuousness, and tolerant of all the caprices of sensuality. From the public opinion of the country of his adoption, he had nothing to dread. With the public opinion of the country of his birth, he was at open war. He plunged into wild and desperate excesses, ennobled by no generous or tender sentiment. From his Venetian haram he sent forth volume after volume, full of eloquence, of wit, of pathos, of ribaldry, and of bitter disdain. His health sank under the effects of his intemperance. His hair turned grey. His food ceased to nourish him. A hectic fever withered him up. It seemed that his body and mind were about to perish together.

From this wretched degradation he was in some measure rescued by a connexion, culpable indeed, yet such as, if it were judged by the standard of morality established in the country where he lived, might be called virtuous. But an imagination polluted by vice, a temper embittered by misfortune, and a frame habituated to the fatal excitement of intoxication, prevented him from fully enjoying the happiness which he might have derived from the purest and most tranquil of his many attachments. Midnight draughts of ardent spirits and Rhenish wines had begun to work the ruin of his fine intellect. His verse lost much of the energy and condensation which had distinguished it. But he would not resign, without a struggle, the empire which he had exercised over the men of his generation. A new dream of ambition arose before him; to be the chief of a literary party; to be the great mover of an intellectual revolution; to guide the public mind of England from his Italian retreat, as Voltaire had guided the public mind of France from the villa of Ferney. With this hope, as it should seem, he established The Liberal. But, powerfully as he had affected the imaginations of his contemporaries, he mistook his own powers if he hoped to direct their opinions; and he still more grossly mistook his own disposition, if he thought that he could long act in concert with other men of letters. The plan failed, and failed ignominiously. Angry with himself, angry with his coadjutors, he relinquished it, and turned to another project, the last and noblest of his life.

A nation, once the first among the nations, preeminent in knowledge, preeminent in military glory, the cradle of philosophy, of eloquence, and of the fine arts, had been for ages bowed down under a cruel yoke. All the vices which oppression generates, the abject vices which it generates in those who submit to it, the ferocious vices which it generates in those who struggle against it, had deformed the character of that miserable race. The valour which had won the great battle of human civilisation, which had saved Europe, which had subjugated Asia, lingered only among pirates and robbers. The ingenuity, once so conspicuously displayed in every department of physical and moral science, had been depraved into a timid and servile cunning. On a sudden this degraded people had risen on their oppressors. Discountenanced or betrayed by the surrounding potentates, they had found in themselves something of that which might well supply the place of all foreign assistance, something of the energy of their fathers.

As a man of letters, Lord Byron could not but be interested in the event of this contest. His political opinions, though, like all his opinions, unsettled, leaned strongly towards the side of liberty. He had assisted the Italian insurgents with his purse, and, if their struggle against the Austrian government had been prolonged, would probably have assisted them with his sword. But to Greece he was attached by peculiar ties. He had when young resided in that country. Much of his most splendid and popular poetry had been inspired by its scenery and by its history. Sick of inaction, degraded in his own eyes by his private vices and by his literary failures, pining for untried excitement and honourable distinction, he carried his exhausted body and his wounded spirit to the Grecian camp.

His conduct in his new situation showed so much vigour and good sense as to justify us in believing that, if his life had been prolonged, he might have distinguished himself as a soldier and a politician. But pleasure and sorrow had done the work of seventy years upon his delicate frame. The hand of death was upon him: he knew it; and the only wish which he uttered was that he might die sword in hand.

This was denied to him. Anxiety, exertion, exposure, and those fatal stimulants which had become indispensable to him, soon stretched him on a sick bed, in a strange land, amidst strange faces, without one human being that he loved near him. There, at thirty-six, the most celebrated Englishman of the nineteenth century closed his brilliant and miserable career.

We cannot even now retrace those events without feeling something of what was felt by the nation, when it was first known that the grave had closed over so much sorrow and so much glory; something of what was felt by those who saw the hearse, with its long train of coaches, turn slowly northward, leaving behind it that cemetery which had been consecrated by the dust of so many great poets, but of which the doors were closed against all that remained of Byron. We well remember that, on that day, rigid moralists could not refrain from weeping for one so young, so illustrious, so unhappy, gifted with such rare gifts, and tried by such strong temptations. It is unnecessary to make any reflections. The history carries its moral with it. Our age has indeed been fruitful of warnings to the eminent, and of consolations to the obscure. Two men have died within our recollection, who, at a time of life at which many people have hardly completed their education, had raised themselves, each in his own department, to the height of glory. One of them died at Longwood; the other at Missolonghi.

It is always difficult to separate the literary character of a man who lives in our own time from his personal character. It is peculiarly difficult to make this separation in the case of Lord Byron. For it is scarcely too much to say, that Lord Byron never wrote without some reference, direct or indirect, to himself. The interest excited by the events of his life mingles itself in our minds, and probably in the minds of almost all our readers, with the interest which properly belongs to his works. A generation must pass away before it will be possible to form a fair judgment of his books, considered merely as books. At present they are not only books, but relics. We will however venture, though with unfeigned diffidence, to offer some desultory remarks on his poetry.

His lot was cast in the time of a great literary revolution. That poetical dynasty which had dethroned the successors of Shakspeare and Spenser was, in its turn, dethroned by a race who represented themselves as heirs of the ancient line, so long dispossessed by usurpers. The real nature of this revolution has not, we think, been comprehended by the great majority of those who concurred it it.

Wherein especially does the poetry of our times differ from that of the last century? Ninety-nine persons out of a hundred would answer that the poetry of the last century was correct, but cold and mechanical, and that the poetry of our time, though wild and irregular, presented far more vivid images, and excited the passions far more strongly than that of Parnell, of Addison, or of Pope. In the same manner we constantly hear it said, that the poets of the age of Elizabeth had far more genius, but far less correctness, than those of the age of Anne. It seems to be taken for granted, that there is some incompatibility, some antithesis between correctness and creative power. We rather suspect that this notion arises merely from an abuse of words, and that it has been the parent of many of the fallacies which perplex the science of criticism.

What is meant by correctness in poetry? If by correctness be meant the conforming to rules which have their foundation in truth and in the principles of human nature, then correctness is only another name for excellence. If by correctness be meant the conforming to rules purely arbitrary, correctness may be another name for dulness and absurdity.

A writer who describes visible objects falsely and violates the propriety of character, a writer who makes the mountains "nod their drowsy heads" at night, or a dying man take leave of the world with a rant like that of Maximin, may be said, in the high and just sense of the phrase, to write incorrectly. He violates the first great law of his art. His imitation is altogether unlike the thing imitated. The four poets who are most eminently free from incorrectness of this description are Homer, Dante, Shakspeare, and Milton. They are, therefore, in one sense, and that the best sense, the most correct of poets.

When it is said that Virgil, though he had less genius than Homer, was a more correct writer, what sense is attached to the word correctness? Is it meant that the story of the Æneid is developed more skilfully than that of the Odyssey? that the Roman describes the face of the external world, or the emotions of the mind, more accurately than the Greek? that the characters of Achates and Mnestheus are more nicely discriminated, and more consistently supported, than those of Achilles, of Nestor, and of Ulysses? The fact incontestably is that, for every violation of the fundamental laws of poetry which can be found in Homer, it would be easy to find twenty in Virgil.

Troilus and Cressida is perhaps of all the plays of Shakspeare that which is commonly considered as the most incorrect. Yet it seems to us infinitely more correct, in the sound sense of the term, than what are called the most correct plays of the most correct dramatists. Compare it, for example, with the Iphigénie of Racine. We are sure that the Greeks of Shakspeare bear a far greater resemblance than the Greeks of Racine to the real Greeks who besieged Troy; and for this reason, that the Greeks of Shakspeare are human beings, and the Greeks of Racine mere names, mere words printed in capitals at the head of paragraphs of declamation. Racine, it is true, would have shuddered at the thought of making a warrior at the siege of Troy quote Aristotle. But of what use is it to avoid a single anachronism, when the whole play is one anachronism, the sentiments and phrases of Versailles in the camp of Aulis?

In the sense in which we are now using the word correctness, we think that Sir Walter Scott, Mr. Wordsworth, Mr. Coleridge, are far more correct poets than those who are commonly extolled as the models of correctness, Pope, for example, and Addison. The single description of a moonlight night in Pope's Iliad contains more inaccuracies than can be found in all the Excursion. There is not a single scene in Cato, in which all that conduces to poetical illusion, all the propriety of character, of language, of situation, is not more grossly violated than in any part of the Lay of the Last Minstrel. No man can possibly think that the Romans of Addison resemble the real Romans so closely as the moss-troopers of Scott resemble the real moss-troopers. Watt Tinlinn and William of Deloraine are not, it is true, persons of so much dignity as Cato. But the dignity of the persons represented has as little to do with the correctness of poetry as with the correctness of painting. We prefer a gipsy by Reynolds to his Majesty's head on a signpost, and a Borderer by Scott to a Senator by Addison.

In what sense, then, is the word correctness used by those who say, with the author of the Pursuits of Literature, that Pope was the most correct of English Poets, and that next to Pope came the late Mr. Gifford? What is the nature and value of that correctness, the praise of which is denied to Macbeth, to Lear, and to Othello, and given to Hoole's translations and to all the Seatonian prize-poems? We can discover no eternal rule, no rule founded in reason and in the nature of things, which Shakspeare does not observe much more strictly than Pope. But if by correctness be meant the conforming to a narrow legislation which, while lenient to the *mala in se*, multiplies, without the shadow of a reason, the *mala prohibita*, if by correctness be meant a strict attention to certain ceremonious observances, which are no more essential to poetry than etiquette to good government, or than the washings of a Pharisee to devotion, then, assuredly, Pope may be a more correct poet than Shakspeare; and, if the code were a little altered, Colley Cibber might be a more correct poet than Pope. But it may well be doubted whether this kind of correctness be a merit, nay, whether it be not an absolute fault.

It would be amusing to make a digest of the irrational laws which bad critics have framed for the government of poets. First in celebrity and in absurdity stand the dramatic unities of place and time. No human being has ever been able to find any thing that could, even by courtesy, be called an argument for these unities, except that they have been deduced from the general practice of the Greeks. It requires no very profound examination to discover that the Greek dramas, often admirable as compositions, are, as exhibitions of human character and human life, far inferior to the English plays of the age of Elizabeth. Every scholar knows that the dramatic part of the Athenian tragedies was at first subordinate to the lyrical part. It would, therefore, have been little less than a miracle if the laws of the Athenian stage had been found to suit plays in which there was no chorus. All the greatest masterpieces of the dramatic art have been composed in direct violation of the unities, and could never have been composed if the unities had not been violated. It is clear, for example, that such a character as that of Hamlet could never have been developed within the limits to which Alfieri confined himself. Yet such was the reverence of literary men during the last century for these unities that Johnson who, much to his honour, took the opposite side, was, as he says, "frightened at his own temerity," and "afraid to stand against the authorities which might be produced against him."

There are other rules of the same kind without end. "Shakspeare," says Rymer, "ought not to have made Othello black; for the hero of a tragedy ought always to be white." "Milton," says another critic, "ought not to have taken Adam for his hero; for the hero of an epic poem ought always to be victorious." "Milton," says another, "ought not to have put so many similes into his first book; for the first book of an epic poem ought always to be the most unadorned. There are no similes in the first book of the Iliad." "Milton," says another, "ought not to have placed in an epic poem such lines as these:—

" 'While thus I called, and strayed I knew not whither.' "

And why not? The critic is ready with a reason, a lady's reason. "Such lines," says he, "are not, it must be allowed, unpleasing to the ear; but the redundant syllable ought to be confined to the drama, and not admitted into epic poetry." As to the redundant syllable in heroic rhyme on serious subjects, it has been, from the time of Pope downward, proscribed by the general consent of all the correct school. No magazine would have admitted so incorrect a couplet as that of Drayton;

"As when we lived untouch'd with these disgraces,
When as our kingdom was our dear embraces."

Another law of heroic rhyme, which, fifty years ago, was considered as fundamental, was, that there should be a pause, a comma at least, at the end of every couplet. It was also provided that there should never be a full stop except at the end of a line. Well do we remember to have heard a most correct judge of poetry revile Mr. Rogers for the incorrectness of that most sweet and graceful passage,

"Such grief was ours,—it seems but yesterday,—
When in thy prime, wishing so much to stay,
'Twas thine, Maria, thine without a sigh
At midnight in a sister's arms to die.
Oh thou wert lovely; lovely was thy frame,
And pure thy spirit as from heaven it came:
And when recalled to join the blest above
Thou diedst a victim to exceeding love,
Nursing the young to health. In happier hours,
When idle Fancy wove luxuriant flowers,
Once in thy mirth thou bad'st me write on thee;
And now I write what thou shalt never see."

Sir Roger Newdigate is fairly entitled, we think, to be ranked among the great critics of this school. He made a law that none of the poems written for the prize which he established at Oxford should exceed fifty lines. This law seems to us to have at least as much foundation in reason as any of those which we have mentioned; nay, much more, for the world, we believe, is pretty well agreed in thinking that the shorter a prize-poem is, the better.

We do not see why we should not make a few more rules of the same kind; why we should not enact that the number of scenes in every act shall be three or some multiple of three, that the number of lines in every scene shall be an exact square, that the *dramatis personæ* shall never be more or fewer than sixteen, and that, in heroic rhymes, every thirty-sixth line shall have twelve syllables. If we were to lay down these canons, and to call Pope, Goldsmith, and Addison incorrect writers for not having complied with our whims, we should act precisely as those critics act who find incorrectness in the magnificent imagery and the varied music of Coleridge and Shelley.

The correctness which the last century prized so much resembles the correctness of those pictures of the garden of Eden which we see in old Bibles. We have an exact square, enclosed by the rivers Pison, Gihon, Hiddekel, and Euphrates, each with a convenient bridge in the centre, rectangular beds of flowers, a long canal, neatly bricked and railed in, the tree of knowledge, clipped like one of the limes behind the Tuilleries, standing in the centre of the grand alley, the snake twined round it, the man on the right hand, the woman on the left, and the beasts drawn up in an exact circle round them. In one sense the picture is correct enough. That is to say, the squares are correct; the circles are correct: the man and the woman are in a most correct line with the tree; and the snake forms a most correct spiral.

But if there were a painter so gifted that he could place on the canvass that glorious paradise, seen by the interior eye of him whose outward sight had failed with long watching and labouring for liberty and truth, if there were a painter who could set before us the mazes of the sapphire brook, the lake with its fringe of myrtles, the flowery meadows, the grottoes overhung by vines, the forests shining with Hesperian fruit and with the plumage of gorgeous birds, the massy shade of that nuptial bower which showered down roses on the sleeping lovers, what should we think of a connoisseur who should tell us that this painting, though finer than the absurd picture in the old Bible, was not so correct? Surely we should answer, It is both finer and more correct; and it is finer because it is more correct. It is not made up of correctly drawn diagrams; but it is a correct painting, a worthy representation of that which it is intended to represent.

It is not in the fine arts alone that this false correctness is prized by narrow-minded men, by men who cannot distinguish means from ends, or what is accidental from what is essential. M. Jourdain admired correctness in fencing. "You had no business to hit me then. You must never thrust in quart till you have thrust in tierce." M. Tomès liked correctness in medical practice. "I stand up for Artemius. That he killed his patient is plain enough. But still he acted quite according to rule. A man dead is a man dead; and there is an end of the matter. But if rules are to be broken, there is no saying what consequences may follow." We have heard of an old German officer, who was a great admirer of correctness in military operations. He used to revile Bonaparte for spoiling the science of war, which had been carried to such exquisite perfection by Marshal Daun. "In my youth we used to march and countermarch all the summer without gaining or losing a square league, and then we went into winter quarters. And now comes an ignorant, hotheaded young man, who flies about from Boulogne to Ulm, and from Ulm to the middle of Moravia, and fights battles in December. The whole system of his tactics is monstrously incorrect." The world is of opinion, in spite of critics like these, that the end of fencing is to hit, that the end of medicine is to cure, that the end of war is to conquer, and that those means are the most correct which best accomplish the ends.

And has poetry no end, no eternal and immutable principles? Is poetry, like heraldry, mere matter of arbitrary regulation? The heralds tell us that certain scutcheons and bearings denote certain conditions, and that to put colours on colours, or metals on metals, is false blazonry. If all this were reversed, if every coat of arms in

Europe were new fashioned, if it were decreed that or should never be placed but on argent, or argent but on or, that illegitimacy should be denoted by a lozenge, and widowhood by a bend, the new science would be just as good as the old science, because both the new and the old would be good for nothing. The mummery of Portcullis and Rouge Dragon, as it has no other value than that which caprice has assigned to it, may well submit to any laws which caprice may impose on it. But it is not so with that great imitative art, to the power of which all ages, the rudest and the most enlightened, bear witness. Since its first great masterpieces were produced, every thing that is changeable in this world has been changed. Civilisation has been gained, lost, gained again. Religions, and languages, and forms of government, and usages of private life, and modes of thinking, all have undergone a succession of revolutions. Every thing has passed away but the great features of nature, and the heart of man, and the miracles of that art of which it is the office to reflect back the heart of man and the features of nature. Those two strange old poems, the wonder of ninety generations, still retain all their freshness. They still command the veneration of minds enriched by the literature of many nations and ages. They are still, even in wretched translations, the delight of schoolboys. Having survived ten thousand capricious fashions, having seen successive codes of criticism become obsolete, they still remain to us, immortal with the immortality of truth, the same when perused in the study of an English scholar as when they were first chanted at the banquets of the Ionian princes.

Poetry is, as was said more than two thousand years ago, imitation. It is an art analogous in many respects to the art of painting, sculpture, and acting. The imitations of the painter, the sculptor, and the actor, are, indeed, within certain limits, more perfect than those of the poet. The machinery which the poet employs consists merely of words; and words cannot, even when employed by such an artist as Homer or Dante, present to the mind images of visible objects quite so lively and exact as those which we carry away from looking on the works of the brush and the chisel. But, on the other hand, the range of poetry is infinitely wider than that of any other imitative art, or than that of all the other imitative arts together. The sculptor can imitate only form; the painter only form and colour; the actor, until the poet supplies him with words, only form, colour, and motion. Poetry holds the outer world in common with the other arts. The heart of man is the province of poetry, and of poetry alone. The painter, the sculptor, and the actor can exhibit no more of human passion and character than that small portion which overflows into the gesture and the face, always an imperfect, often a deceitful, sign of that which is within. The deeper and more complex parts of human nature can be exhibited by means of words alone. Thus the objects of the imitation of poetry are the whole external and the whole internal universe, the face of nature, the vicissitudes of fortune, man as he is in himself, man as he appears in society, all things which really exist, all things of which we can form an image in our minds by combining together parts of things which really exist. The domain of this imperial art is commensurate with the imaginative faculty.

An art essentially imitative ought not surely to be subjected to rules which tend to make its imitations less perfect than they otherwise would be; and those who obey such rules ought to be called, not correct, but incorrect artists. The true way to judge of the rules by which English poetry was governed during the last century is to look at the effects which they produced.

It was in 1780 that Johnson completed his Lives of the Poets. He tells us in that work that, since the time of Dryden, English poetry had shown no tendency to relapse into its original savageness, that its language had been refined, its numbers tuned, and its sentiments improved. It may perhaps be doubted whether the nation had any great reason to exult in the refinements and improvements which gave it Douglas for Othello, and the Triumphs of Temper for the Fairy Queen.

It was during the thirty years which preceded the appearance of Johnson's Lives that the diction and versification of English poetry were, in the sense in which the word is commonly used, most correct. Those thirty years are, as respects poetry, the most deplorable part of our literary history. They have indeed bequeathed to us scarcely any poetry which deserves to be remembered. Two or three hundred lines of Gray, twice as many of Goldsmith, a few stanzas of Beattie and Collins, a few strophes of Mason, and a few clever prologues and satires, were the masterpieces of this age of consummate excellence. They may all be printed in one volume, and that volume would be by no means a volume of extraordinary merit. It would contain no poetry of the very highest class, and little which could be placed very high in the second class. The Paradise Regained or Comus would outweigh it all.

At last, when poetry had fallen into such utter decay that Mr. Hayley was thought a great poet, it began to appear that the excess of the evil was about to work the cure. Men became tired of an insipid conformity to a standard which derived no authority from nature or reason. A shallow criticism had taught them to ascribe a superstitious value to the spurious correctness of poetasters. A deeper criticism brought them back to the true correctness of the first great masters. The eternal laws of poetry regained their power, and the temporary passions which had superseded those laws went after the wig of Lovelace and the hoop of Clarissa.

It was in a cold and barren season that the seeds of that rich harvest which we have reaped were first sown. While poetry was every year becoming more feeble and more mechanical, while the monotonous versification which Pope had introduced, no longer redeemed by his brilliant wit and his compactness of expression, palled on the ear of the public, the great works of the old masters were every day attracting more and more of the admiration which they deserved. The plays of Shakspeare were better acted, better edited, and better known than they had ever been. Our fine ancient ballads were again read with pleasure, and it became a fashion to imitate them. Many of the imitations were altogether contemptible. But they showed that men had at least begun to admire the excellence which they could not rival. A literary revolution was evidently at hand. There was a ferment in the minds of men, a vague craving for something new, a disposition to hail with delight any thing which might at first sight wear the appearance of originality. A reforming age is always fertile of impostors. The same excited state of public feeling which produced the great separation from the see of Rome produced also the excesses of the Anabaptists. The same stir in the public mind of Europe which overthrew the abuses of the old French government, produced the Jacobins and Theophilanthropists. Macpherson and Della Crusca were to the true reformers of English poetry what Knipperdoling was to Luther, or Clootz to Turgot. The success of Chatterton's forgeries and of the far more contemptible forgeries of Ireland showed that people had begun to love the old poetry well, though not wisely. The public was never more disposed to believe stories without evidence, and to admire books without merit. Any thing which could break the dull monotony of the correct school was acceptable.

The forerunner of the great restoration of our literature was Cowper. His literary career began and ended at nearly the same time with that of Alfieri. A comparison between Alfieri and Cowper may, at first sight, appear as strange as that which a loyal Presbyterian minister is said to have made in 1745 between George the Second and Enoch. It may seem that the gentle, shy, melancholy Calvinist, whose spirit had been broken by fagging at school, who had not courage to earn a livelihood by reading the titles of bills in the House of Lords, and whose favourite associates were a blind old lady and an evangelical divine, could have nothing in common with the haughty, ardent, and voluptuous nobleman, the horse-jockey, the libertine, who fought Lord Ligonier in Hyde Park, and robbed the Pretender of his queen. But though the private lives of these remarkable men present scarcely any points of resemblance, their literary lives bear a close analogy to each other. They both found poetry in its lowest state of degradation, feeble, artificial, and altogether nerveless. They both possessed precisely the talents which fitted them for the task of raising it from that deep abasement. They cannot, in strictness, be called great poets. They had not in any very high degree the creative power,

"The vision and the faculty divine;"

but they had great vigour of thought, great warmth of feeling, and what, in their circumstances, was above all things important, a manliness of taste which approached to roughness. They did not deal in mechanical versification and conventional phrases. They wrote concerning things the thought of which set their hearts on fire; and thus what they wrote, even when it wanted every other grace, had that inimitable grace which sincerity and strong passion impart to the rudest and most homely compositions. Each of them sought for inspiration in a noble and affecting subject, fertile of images which had not yet been hackneyed. Liberty was the muse of Alfieri, Religion was the muse of Cowper. The same truth is found in their lighter pieces. They were not among those who deprecated the severity, or deplored the absence, of an unreal mistress in melodious commonplaces. Instead of raving about imaginary Chloes and Sylvias, Cowper wrote of Mrs. Unwin's knitting-needles. The only love verses of Alfieri were addressed to one whom he truly and passionately loved. "Tutte le rime amorose che seguono," says he, "tutte sono per essa, e ben sue, e di lei solamente; poichè mai d' altra donna per certo non canterò."

These great men were not free from affectation. But their affectation was directly opposed to the affectation which generally prevailed. Each of them expressed, in strong and bitter language, the contempt which he felt for the effeminate poetasters who were in fashion both in England and in Italy. Cowper complains that

"Manner is all in all, whate'er is writ,
    The substitute for genius, taste, and wit."

He praised Pope; yet he regretted that Pope had

> "Made poetry a mere mechanic art,
>  And every warbler had his tune by heart."

Alfieri speaks with similar scorn of the tragedies of his predecessors. "Mi cadevano dalle mani per la languidezza, trivialità e prolissità dei modi e del verso, senza parlare poi della snervatezza dei pensieri· Or perchè mai questa nostra divina lingua, sì maschia anco, ed energica, e feroce, in bocca di Dante, dovra ella farsi così sbiadata ed eunuca nel dialogo tragico?"

To men thus sick of the languid manner of their contemporaries ruggedness seemed a venial fault, or rather a positive merit. In their hatred of meretricious ornament, and of what Cowper calls "creamy smoothness," they erred on the opposite side. Their style was too austere, their versification too harsh. It is not easy, however, to overrate the service which they rendered to literature. The intrinsic value of their poems is considerable. But the example which they set of mutiny against an absurd system was invaluable. The part which they performed was rather that of Moses than that of Joshua. They opened the house of bondage; but they did not enter the promised land.

During the twenty years which followed the death of Cowper, the revolution in English poetry was fully consummated. None of the writers of this period, not even Sir Walter Scott, contributed so much to the consummation as Lord Byron. Yet Lord Byron contributed to it unwillingly, and with constant self-reproach and shame. All his tastes and inclinations led him to take part with the school of poetry which was going out against the school which was coming in. Of Pope himself he spoke with extravagant admiration. He did not venture directly to say that the little man of Twickenham was a greater poet than Shakspeare or Milton: but he hinted pretty clearly that he thought so. Of his contemporaries, scarcely any had so much of his admiration as Mr. Gifford who, considered as a poet, was merely Pope, without Pope's wit and fancy, and whose satires are decidedly inferior in vigour and poignancy to the very imperfect juvenile performance of Lord Byron himself. He now and then praised Mr. Wordsworth and Mr. Coleridge, but ungraciously and without cordiality. When he attacked them, he brought his whole soul to the work. Of the most elaborate of Mr. Wordsworth's poems he could find nothing to say, but that it was "clumsy, and frowsy, and his aversion." Peter Bell excited his spleen to such a degree that he evoked the shades of Pope and Dryden, and demanded of them whether it were possible that such trash could evade contempt? In his heart he thought his own Pilgrimage of Harold inferior to his Imitation of Horace's Art of Poetry, a feeble echo of Pope and Johnson. This insipid performance he repeatedly designed to publish, and was withheld only by the solicitations of his friends. He has distinctly declared his approbation of the unities, the most absurd laws by which genius was ever held in servitude. In one of his works, we think in his Letter to Mr. Bowles, he compares the poetry of the eighteenth century to the Parthenon, and that of the nineteenth to a Turkish mosque, and boasts that, though he had assisted his contemporaries in building their grotesque and barbarous edifice, he had never joined them in defacing the remains of a chaster and more graceful architecture. In another letter, he compares the change which had recently passed on English poetry to the decay of Latin poetry after the Augustan age. In the time of Pope, he tells his friends, it was all Horace with us. It is all Claudian now.

For the great old masters of the art he had no very enthusiastic veneration. In his letter to Mr. Bowles he uses expressions which clearly indicate that he preferred Pope's Iliad to the original. Mr. Moore confesses that his friend was no very fervent admirer of Shakspeare. Of all the poets of the first class, Lord Byron seems to have admired Dante and Milton most. Yet in the fourth canto of Childe Harold he places Tasso, a writer not merely inferior to them, but of quite a different order of mind, on at least a footing of equality with them. Mr. Hunt is, we suspect, quite correct in saying that Lord Byron could see little or no merit in Spenser.

But Byron the critic and Byron the poet were two very different men. The effects of the noble writer's theory may indeed often be traced in his practice. But his disposition led him to accommodate himself to the literary taste of the age in which he lived; and his talents would have enabled him to accommodate himself to the taste of any age. Though he said much of his contempt for mankind, and though he boasted that amidst the inconstancy of fortune and of fame he was all-sufficient to himself, his literary career indicated nothing of that lonely and unsocial pride which he affected. We cannot conceive him, like Milton or Wordsworth, defying the criticism of his contemporaries, retorting their scorn, and labouring on a poem in the full assurance that it would be unpopular, and in the full assurance that it would be immortal. He has said, by the mouth of one of his heroes, in speaking of political greatness, that "he must serve who fain would sway;" and this he assigns as a reason for not entering into political life. He did not consider that the sway which he had exercised in literature had been purchased by servitude, by the sacrifice of his own taste to the taste of the public.

He was the creature of his age; and whenever he had lived he would have been the creature of his age. Under Charles the First Byron would have been more quaint than Donne. Under Charles the Second the rants of Byron's rhyming plays would have pitted it, boxed it, and galleried it, with those of any Bayes or Bilboa. Under George the First the monotonous smoothness of Byron's versification and the terseness of his expression would have made Pope himself envious.

As it was, he was the man of the last thirteen years of the eighteenth century, and of the first twenty-three years of the nineteenth century. He belonged half to the old, and half to the new school of poetry. His personal taste led him to the former; his thirst of praise to the latter; his talents were equally suited to both. His fame was a common ground on which the zealots of both sides, Gifford, for example, and Shelley, might meet. He was the representative, not of either literary party, but of both at once, and of their conflict, and of the victory by which that conflict was terminated. His poetry fills and measures the whole of the vast interval through which our literature has moved since the time of Johnson. It touches the Essay on Man at the one extremity, and the Excursion at the other.

There are several parallel instances in literary history. Voltaire, for example, was the connecting link between the France of Louis the Fourteenth and the France of Louis the Sixteenth, between Racine and Boileau on the one side, and Condorcet and Beaumarchais on the other. He, like Lord Byron, put himself at the head of an intellectual revolution, dreading it all the time, murmuring at it, sneering at it, yet choosing rather to move before his age in any direction than to be left behind and forgotten. Dryden was the connecting link between the literature of the age of James the First, and the literature of the age of Anne. Oromasdes and Arimanes fought for him. Arimanes carried him off. But his heart was to the last with Oromasdes. Lord Byron was, in the same manner, the mediator between two generations, between two hostile poetical sects. Though always sneering at Mr. Wordsworth, he was yet, though perhaps unconsciously, the interpreter between Mr. Wordsworth and the multitude. In the Lyrical Ballads and the Excursion Mr. Wordsworth appeared as the high priest of a worship of which Nature was the idol. No poems have ever indicated a more exquisite perception of the beauty of the outer world, or a more passionate love and reverence for that beauty. Yet they were not popular; and it is not likely that they ever will be popular as the poetry of Sir Walter Scott is popular. The feeling which pervaded them was too deep for general sympathy. Their style was often too mysterious for general comprehension. They made a few esoteric disciples, and many scoffers. Lord Byron founded what may be called an exoteric Lake school; and all the readers of verse in England, we might say in Europe, hastened to sit at his feet. What Mr. Wordsworth had said like a recluse, Lord Byron said like a man of the world, with less profound feeling, but with more perspicuity, energy, and conciseness. We would refer our readers to the last two cantos of Childe Harold and to Manfred, in proof of these observations.

Lord Byron, like Mr. Wordsworth, had nothing dramatic in his genius. He was indeed the reverse of a great dramatist, the very antithesis to a great dramatist. All his characters, Harold looking on the sky, from which his country and the sun are disappearing together, the Giaour, standing apart in the gloom of the side-aisle, and casting a haggard scowl from under his long hood at the crucifix and the censer, Conrad leaning on his sword by the watch-tower, Lara smiling on the dancers, Alp gazing steadily on the fatal cloud as it passes before the moon, Manfred wandering among the precipices of Berne, Azzo on the judgment seat, Ugo at the bar, Lambro frowning on the siesta of his daughter and Juan, Cain presenting his unacceptable offering, are essentially the same. The varieties are varieties merely of age, situation, and outward show. If ever Lord Byron attempted to exhibit men of a different kind, he always made them either insipid or unnatural. Selim is nothing. Bonnivart is nothing. Don Juan, in the first and best cantos, is a feeble copy of the Page in the Marriage of Figaro. Johnson, the man whom Juan meets in the slave-market, is a most striking failure. How differently would Sir Walter Scott have drawn a bluff, fearless Englishman, in such a situation! The portrait would have seemed to walk out of the canvass.

Sardanapalus is more coarsely drawn than any dramatic personage that we can remember. His heroism and his effeminacy, his contempt of death, and his dread of a weighty helmet, his kingly resolution to be seen in the foremost ranks, and the anxiety with which he calls for a looking-glass, that he may be seen to advantage, are contrasted, it is true, with all the point of Juvenal. Indeed the hint of the character seems to have been taken from what Juvenal says of Otho:

"Speculum civilis sarcina belli.
Nimirum summi ducis est occidere Galbam,
Et curare cutem summi constantia civis,
Bedriaci in campo spolium affectare Palati,
Et pressum in faciem digitis extendere panem."

These are excellent lines in a satire. But it is not the business of the dramatist to exhibit characters in this sharp antithetical way. It is not thus that Shakspeare makes Prince Hal rise from the rake of Eastcheap into the hero of Shrewsbury, and sink again into the rake of Eastcheap. It is not thus that Shakspeare has exhibited the union of effeminacy and valour in Antony. A dramatist cannot commit a greater error than that of following those pointed descriptions of character, in which satirists and historians indulge so much. It is by rejecting what is natural that satirists and historians produce these striking characters. Their great object generally is to ascribe to every man as many contradictory qualities as possible: and this is an object easily attained. By judicious selection and judicious exaggeration, the intellect and the disposition of any human being might be described as being made up of nothing but startling contrasts. If the dramatist attempts to create a being answering to one of these descriptions, he fails, because he reverses an imperfect analytical process. He produces, not a man, but a personified epigram. Very eminent writers have fallen into this snare. Ben Jonson has given us a Hermogenes, taken from the lively lines of Horace; but the inconsistency which is so amusing in the satire appears unnatural and disgusts us in the play. Sir Walter Scott has committed a far more glaring error of the same kind in the novel of Peveril. Admiring, as every judicious reader must admire, the keen and vigorous lines in which Dryden satirised the Duke of Buckingham, Sir Walter attempted to make a Duke of Buckingham to suit them, a real living Zimri; and he made, not a man, but the most grotesque of all monsters. A writer who should attempt to introduce into a play or a novel such a Wharton as the Wharton of Pope, or a Lord Hervey answering to Sporus, would fail in the same manner.

But to return to Lord Byron; his women, like his men, are all of one breed. Haidee is a half-savage and girlish Julia; Julia is a civilised and matronly Haidee. Leila is a wedded Zuleika, Zuleika a virgin Leila. Gulnare and Medora appear to have been intentionally opposed to each other. Yet the difference is a difference of situation only. A slight change of circumstances would, it should seem, have sent Gulnare to the lute of Medora, and armed Medora with the dagger of Gulnare.

It is hardly too much to say, that Lord Byron could exhibit only one man and only one woman, a man proud, moody, cynical, with defiance on his brow, and misery in his heart, a scorner of his kind, implacable in revenge, yet capable of deep and strong affection; a woman all softness and gentleness, loving to caress and to be caressed, but capable of being transformed by passion into a tigress.

Even these two characters, his only two characters, he could not exhibit dramatically. He exhibited them in the manner, not of Shakspeare, but of Clarendon. He analysed them; he made them analyse themselves; but he did not make them show themselves. We are told, for example, in many lines of great force and spirit, that the speech of Lara was bitterly sarcastic, that he talked little of his travels, that, if he was much questioned about them, his answers became short, and his brow gloomy. But we have none of Lara's sarcastic speeches or short answers. It is not thus that the great masters of human nature have portrayed human beings. Homer never tells us that Nestor loved to relate long stories about his youth. Shakspeare never tells us that in the mind of Iago every thing that is beautiful and endearing was associated with some filthy and debasing idea.

It is curious to observe the tendency which the dialogue of Lord Byron always has to lose its character of dialogue, and to become soliloquy. The scenes between Manfred and the Chamois-hunter, between Manfred and the Witch of the Alps, between Manfred and the Abbot, are instances of this tendency. Manfred, after a few unimportant speeches, has all the talk to himself. The other interlocutors are nothing more than good listeners. They drop an occasional question or ejaculation which sets Manfred off again on the inexhaustible topic of his personal feelings. If we examine the fine passages in Lord Byron's dramas, the description of Rome, for example, in Manfred, the description of a Venetian revel in Marino Faliero, the concluding invective which the old doge pronounces against Venice, we shall find that there is nothing dramatic in these speeches, that they derive none of their effect from the character or situation of the speaker, and that they would have been as fine, or finer, if they had been published as fragments of blank verse by Lord Byron. There is scarcely a speech in Shakspeare of which the same could be said. No skilful reader of the plays of Shakspeare can endure to see what are called the fine things taken out, under the name of "Beauties" or of "Elegant Extracts," or to hear any single passage, "To be or not to be," for example, quoted as a sample of the great poet. "To be or not to be" has merit undoubtedly as a composition. It would have merit if put into the mouth of a chorus. But its merit as a composition vanishes when compared with its merit as belonging to Hamlet. It is not too much to say that the great plays of Shakspeare would lose less by being deprived of all the passages which are commonly called the fine passages, than those passages lose by being read separately from the play. This is perhaps the highest praise which can be given to a dramatist.

On the other hand, it may be doubted whether there is, in all Lord Byron's plays, a single remarkable passage which owes any portion of its interest or effect to its connexion with the characters or the action. He has written only one scene, as far as we can re-collect, which is dramatic even in manner, the scene between Lucifer and Cain. The conference is animated, and each of the interlocutors has a fair share of it. But this scene, when examined, will be found to be a confirmation of our remarks. It is a dialogue only in form. It is a soliloquy in essence. It is in reality a debate carried on within one single unquiet and sceptical mind. The questions and the answers, the objections and the solutions, all belong to the same character.

A writer who showed so little dramatic skill in works professedly dramatic was not likely to write narrative with dramatic effect. Nothing could indeed be more rude and careless than the structure of his narrative poems. He seems to have thought, with the hero of the Rehearsal, that the plot was good for nothing but to bring in fine things. His two longest works, Childe Harold and Don Juan, have no plan whatever. Either of them might have been extended to any length, or cut short at any point. The state in which the Giaour appears illustrates the manner in which all Byron's poems were constructed. They are all, like the Giaour, collections of fragments; and, though there may be no empty spaces marked by asterisks, it is still easy to perceive, by the clumsiness of the joining, where the parts for the sake of which the whole was composed end and begin.

It was in description and meditation that Byron excelled. "Description," as he said in Don Juan, "was his forte." His manner is indeed peculiar, and is almost unequalled; rapid, sketchy, full of vigour; the selection happy; the strokes few and bold. In spite of the reverence which we feel for the genius of Mr. Wordsworth, we cannot but think that the minuteness of his descriptions often diminishes their effect. He has accustomed him-self to gaze on nature with the eye of a lover, to dwell on every feature, and to mark every change of aspect. Those beauties which strike the most negligent observer, and those which only a close attention discovers, are equally familiar to him and are equally prominent in his poetry. The proverb of old Hesiod, that half is often more than the whole, is eminently applicable to description. The policy of the Dutch, who cut down most of the precious trees in the Spice Islands, in order to raise the value of what remained, was a policy which poets would do well to imitate. It was a policy which no poet understood better than Lord Byron. Whatever his faults might be, he was never, while his mind retained its vigour, accused of prolixity.

His descriptions, great as was their intrinsic merit, derived their principal interest from the feeling which always mingled with them. He was himself the beginning, the middle, and the end, of all his own poetry, the hero of every tale, the chief object in every landscape. Harold, Lara, Manfred, and a crowd of other characters, were universally considered merely as loose incognitos of Byron; and there is every reason to believe that he meant them to be so considered. The wonders of the outer world, the Tagus, with the mighty fleets of England riding on its bosom, the towers of Cintra overhanging the shaggy forest of cork-trees and willows, the glaring marble of Pentelicus, the banks of the Rhine, the glaciers of Clarens, the sweet Lake of Leman, the dell of Egeria with its summer-birds and rustling lizards, the shapeless ruins of Rome overgrown with ivy and wall-flowers, the stars, the sea, the mountains, all were mere accessaries, the background to one dark and melancholy figure.

Never had any writer so vast a command of the whole eloquence of scorn, misanthropy, and despair. That Marah was never dry. No art could sweeten, no draughts could exhaust, its perennial waters of bitterness. Never was there such variety in monotony as that of Byron. From maniac laughter to piercing lamentation, there was not a single note of human anguish of which he was not master. Year after year, and month after month, he continued to repeat that to be wretched is the destiny of all; that to be eminently wretched is the destiny of the eminent; that all the desires by which we are cursed lead alike to misery, if they are not gratified, to the misery of disappointment, if they are gratified, to the misery of satiety. His heroes are men who have arrived by different roads at the same goal of despair, who are sick of life, who are at war with society, who are supported in their anguish only by an unconquerable pride resembling that of Prometheus on the rock or of Satan in the burning marl, who can master their agonies by the force of their will, and who, to the last, defy the whole power of earth and heaven. He always described himself as a man of the same kind with his favourite creations, as a man whose heart had been withered, whose capacity for happiness was gone and could not be restored, but whose invincible spirit dared the worst that could befall him here or hereafter.

How much of this morbid feeling sprang from an original disease of the mind, how much from real misfortune, how much from the nervousness of dissipation, how much was fanciful, how much was merely affected, it is impossible for us, and would probably have been impossible for the most intimate friends of Lord Byron, to decide. Whether there ever existed, or can ever exist, a person answering to the description which he gave of himself, may be doubted: but that he was not such a person is beyond all doubt. It is ridiculous to imagine that a man whose mind was really imbued with scorn of his fellow-creatures would have published three or four books every year in order to tell them so; or that a man who could say with truth that he neither sought sympathy nor needed it would have admitted all Europe to hear his farewell to his wife, and his blessings on his child. In the second canto of Childe Harold, he tells us that he is insensible to fame and obloquy.

> "Ill may such contest now the spirit move,
> Which heeds nor keen reproof nor partial praise."

Yet we know on the best evidence that, a day or two before he published these lines, he was greatly, indeed childishly, elated by the compliments paid to his maiden speech in the House of Lords.

We are far, however, from thinking that his sadness was altogether feigned. He was naturally a man of great sensibility; he had been ill educated; his feelings had been early exposed to sharp trials; he had been crossed in his boyish love; he had been mortified by the failure of his first literary efforts; he was straitened in pecuniary circumstances; he was unfortunate in his domestic relations; the public treated him with cruel injustice; his health and spirits suffered from his dissipated habits of life; he was, on the whole, an unhappy man. He early discovered that, by parading his unhappiness before the multitude, he produced an immense sensation. The world gave him every encouragement to talk about his mental sufferings. The interest which his first confessions excited induced him to affect much that he did not feel; and the affectation probably reacted on his feelings. How far the character in which he exhibited himself was genuine, and how far theatrical, it would probably have puzzled himself to say.

There can be no doubt that this remarkable man owed the vast influence which he exercised over his contemporaries at least as much to his gloomy egotism as to the real power of his poetry. We never could very clearly understand how it is that egotism, so unpopular in conversation, should be so popular in writing; or how it is that men who affect in their compositions qualities and feelings which they have not impose so much more easily on their contemporaries than on posterity. The interest which the loves of Petrarch excited in his own time, and the pitying fondness with which half Europe looked upon Rousseau, are well known. To readers of our age, the love of Petrarch seems to have been love of that kind which breaks no hearts, and the sufferings of Rousseau to have deserved laughter rather than pity, to have been partly counterfeited, and partly the consequences of his own perverseness and vanity.

What our grandchildren may think of the character of Lord Byron, as exhibited in his poetry, we will not pretend to guess. It is certain, that the interest which he excited during his life is without a parallel in literary history. The feeling with which young readers of poetry regarded him can be conceived only by those who have experienced it. To people who are unacquainted with real calamity, "nothing is so dainty sweet as lovely melancholy." This faint image of sorrow has in all ages been considered by young gentlemen as an agreeable excitement. Old gentlemen and middle-aged gentlemen have so many real causes of sadness that they are rarely inclined "to be as sad as night only for wantonness." Indeed they want the power almost as much as the inclination. We know very few persons engaged in active life who, even if they were to procure stools to be melancholy upon, and were to sit down with all the premeditation of Master Stephen, would be able to enjoy much of what somebody calls the "ecstasy of woe."

Among that large class of young persons whose reading is almost entirely confined to works of imagination, the popularity of Lord Byron was unbounded. They bought pictures of him; they treasured up the smallest relics of him; they learned his poems by heart, and did their best to write like him, and to look like him. Many of them practised at the glass, in the hope of catching the curl of the upper lip, and the scowl of the brow, which appear in some of his portraits. A few discarded their neckcloths in imitation of their great leader. For some years the Minerva press sent forth no novel without a mysterious, unhappy, Lara-like peer. The number of hopeful under-graduates and medical students who became things of dark imaginings, on whom the freshness of the heart ceased to fall like dew, whose passions had consumed themselves to dust, and to whom the relief of tears was denied, passes all calculation. This was not the worst. There was created in the minds of many of these enthusiasts, a pernicious and absurd association between intellectual power and moral depravity. From the poetry of Lord Byron they drew a system of ethics, compounded of misanthropy and voluptuousness, a system in which the two great commandments were, to hate your neighbour, and to love your neighbour's wife.

This affectation has passed away; and a few more years will destroy whatever yet remains of that magical potency which once belonged to the name of Byron. To us he is still a man, young, noble, and unhappy. To our children he will be merely a writer; and their impartial judgment will appoint his place among writers, without regard to his rank or to his private history. That his poetry will undergo a severe sifting, that much of what has been admired by his contemporaries will be rejected as worthless, we have little doubt. But we have as little doubt that, after the closest scrutiny, there will still remain much that can only perish with the English language.

# SAMUEL JOHNSON

## (DECEMBER 1856)

SAMUEL JOHNSON, one of the most eminent English writers of the eighteenth century, was the son of Michael Johnson, who was, at the beginning of that century, a magistrate of Lichfield, and a bookseller of great note in the midland counties. Michael's abilities and attainments seem to have been considerable. He was so well acquainted with the contents of the volumes which he exposed to sale, that the country rectors of Staffordshire and Worcestershire thought him an oracle on points of learning. Between him and the clergy, indeed, there was a strong religious and political sympathy. He was a zealous churchman, and, though he had qualified himself for municipal office by taking the oaths to the sovereigns in possession, was to the last a Jacobite in heart. At his house, a house which is still pointed out to every traveller who visits Lichfield, Samuel was born on the 18th of September 1709. In the child, the physical, intellectual, and moral peculiarities which afterwards distinguished the man were plainly discernible; great muscular strength accompanied by much awkwardness and many infirmities; great quickness of parts, with a morbid propensity to sloth and procrastination; a kind and generous heart, with a gloomy and irritable temper. He had inherited from his ancestors a scrofulous taint, which it was beyond the power of medicine to remove. His parents were weak enough to believe that the royal touch was a specific for this malady. In his third year he was taken up to London, inspected by the court surgeon, prayed over by the court chaplains, and stroked and presented with a piece of gold by Queen Anne. One of his earliest recollections was that of a stately lady in a diamond stomacher and a long black hood. Her hand was applied in vain. The boy's features, which were originally noble and not irregular, were distorted by his malady. His cheeks were deeply scarred. He lost for a time the sight of one eye; and he saw but very imperfectly with the other. But the force of his mind overcame every impediment. Indolent as he was, he acquired knowledge with such ease and rapidity, that at every school to which he was sent he was soon the best scholar. From sixteen to eighteen he resided at home, and was left to his own devices. He learned much at this time, though his studies were without guidance and without plan. He ransacked his father's shelves, dipped into a multitude of books, read what was interesting, and passed over what was dull. An ordinary lad would have acquired little or no useful knowledge in such a way: but much that was dull to ordinary lads was interesting to Samuel. He read little Greek; for his proficiency in that language was not such that he could take much pleasure in the masters of Attic poetry and eloquence. But he had left school a good Latinist, and he soon acquired, in the large and miscellaneous library of which he now had the command, an extensive knowledge of Latin literature. That Augustan delicacy of taste, which is the boast of the great public schools of England, he never possessed. But he was early familiar with some classical writers, who were quite unknown to the best scholars in the sixth form at Eton. He was peculiarly attracted by the works of the great restorers of learning. Once, while searching for some apples, he found a huge folio volume of Petrarch's works. The name excited his curiosity, and he eagerly devoured hundreds of pages. Indeed, the diction and versification of his own Latin compositions show that he had paid at least as much attention to modern copies from the antique as to the original models.

While he was thus irregularly educating himself, his family was sinking into hopeless poverty. Old Michael Johnson was much better qualified to pore upon books, and to talk about them, than to trade in them. His business declined: his debts increased: it was with difficulty that the daily expenses of his household were defrayed. It was out of his power to support his son at either university; but a wealthy neighbour offered assistance; and, in reliance on promises which proved to be of very little value, Samuel was entered at Pembroke College, Oxford. When the young scholar presented himself to the rulers of that society, they were amazed not more by his ungainly figure and eccentric manners than by the quantity of extensive and curious information which he had picked up during many months of desultory, but not unprofitable study. On the first day of his residence he surprised his teachers by quoting Macrobius; and one of the most learned among them declared, that he had never known a freshman of equal attainments.

At Oxford, Johnson resided during about three years. He was poor, even to raggedness; and his appearance excited a mirth and a pity, which were equally intolerable to his haughty spirit. He was driven from the quadrangle of Christ Church by the sneering looks which the members of that aristocratical society cast at the holes in his shoes. Some charitable person placed a new pair at his door; but he spurned them away in a fury. Distress made him, not servile, but reckless and ungovernable. No opulent gentleman commoner, panting for one-and-twenty, could have treated the academical authorities with more gross disrespect. The needy scholar was generally to be seen under the gate of Pembroke, a gate now adorned with his effigy, haranguing a circle of lads, over whom, in spite of his tattered gown and dirty linen, his wit and audacity gave him an undisputed ascendency. In every mutiny against the discipline of the college he was the ringleader. Much was pardoned, however, to a youth so highly distinguished by abilities and acquirements. He had early made himself known by turning Pope's Messiah into Latin verse. The style and rhythm, indeed, were not exactly Virgilian; but the translation found many admirers, and was read with pleasure by Pope himself.

The time drew near at which Johnson would, in the ordinary course of things, have become a Bachelor of Arts: but he was at the end of his resources. Those promises of support on which he had relied had not been kept. His family could do nothing for him. His debts to Oxford tradesmen were small indeed, yet larger than he could pay. In the autumn of 1731, he was under the necessity of quitting the university without a degree. In the following winter his father died. The old man left but a pittance; and of that pittance almost the whole was appropriated to the support of his widow. The property to which Samuel succeeded amounted to no more than twenty pounds.

His life, during the thirty years which followed, was one hard struggle with poverty. The misery of that struggle needed no aggravation, but was aggravated by the sufferings of an unsound body and an unsound mind. Before the young man left the university, his hereditary malady had broken forth in a singularly cruel form. He had become an incurable hypochondriac. He said long after that he had been mad all his life, or at least not perfectly sane; and, in truth, eccentricities less strange than his have often been thought grounds sufficient for absolving felons, and for setting aside wills. His grimaces, his gestures, his mutterings, sometimes diverted and sometimes terrified people who did not know him. At a dinner table he would, in a fit of absence, stoop down and twitch off a lady's shoe. He would amaze a drawing room by suddenly ejaculating a clause of the Lord's Prayer. He would conceive an unintelligible aversion to a particular alley, and perform a great circuit rather than see the hateful place. He would set his heart on touching every post in the streets through which he walked. If by any chance he missed a post, he would go back a hundred yards and repair the omission. Under the influence of his disease, his senses became morbidly torpid, and his imagination morbidly active. At one time he would stand poring on the town clock without being able to tell the hour. At another, he would distinctly hear his mother, who was many miles off, calling him by his name. But this was not the worst. A deep melancholy took possession of him, and gave a dark tinge to all his views of human nature and of human destiny. Such wretchedness as he endured has driven many men to shoot themselves or drown themselves. But he was under no temptation to commit suicide. He was sick of life; but he was afraid of death; and he shuddered at every sight or sound which reminded him of the inevitable hour. In religion he found but little comfort during his long and frequent fits of dejection; for his religion partook of his own character. The light from heaven shone on him indeed, but not in a direct line, or with its own pure splendour. The rays had to struggle through a disturbing medium; they reached him refracted, dulled and discoloured by the thick gloom which had settled on his soul; and, though they might be sufficiently clear to guide him, were too dim to cheer him.

With such infirmities of body and of mind, this celebrated man was left, at two-and-twenty, to fight his way through the world. He remained during about five years in the midland counties. At Lichfield, his birth-place and his early home, he had inherited some friends and acquired others. He was kindly noticed by Henry Hervey, a gay officer of noble family, who happened to be quartered there. Gilbert Walmesley, registrar of the ecclesiastical court of the diocese, a man of distinguished parts, learning, and knowledge of the world, did himself honour by patronising the young adventurer, whose repulsive person, unpolished manners, and squalid garb moved many of the petty aristocracy of the neighbourhood to laughter or to disgust. At Lichfield, however, Johnson could find no way of earning a livelihood. He became usher of a grammar school in Leicestershire; he resided as a humble companion in the house of a country gentleman; but a life of dependence was insupportable to his haughty spirit. He repaired to Birmingham, and there earned a few guineas by literary drudgery. In that town he printed a translation, little noticed at the time, and long forgotten, of a Latin book about Abyssinia. He then put forth proposals for publishing by subscription the poems of Politian, with notes containing a history of modern Latin verse; but subscriptions did not come in; and the volume never appeared.

While leading this vagrant and miserable life, Johnson fell in love. The object of his passion was Mrs. Elizabeth Porter, a widow who had children as old as himself. To ordinary spectators, the lady appeared to be a short, fat, coarse woman, painted half an inch thick, dressed in gaudy colours, and fond of exhibiting provincial airs and graces which were not exactly those of the Queensberrys and Lepels. To Johnson, however, whose passions were strong, whose eyesight was too weak to distinguish ceruse from natural bloom, and who had seldom or never been in the same room with a woman of real fashion, his Titty, as he called her, was the most beautiful, graceful and accomplished of her sex. That his admiration was unfeigned cannot be doubted; for she was as poor as himself. She accepted, with a readiness which did her little honour, the addresses of a suitor who might have been her son. The marriage, however, in spite of occasional wranglings, proved happier than might have been expected. The lover continued to be under the illusions of the wedding-day till the lady died in her sixty-fourth year. On her monument he placed an inscription extolling the charms of her person and of her manners; and, when long after her decease, he had occasion to mention her, he exclaimed, with a tenderness half ludicrous, half pathetic, "Pretty creature!"

His marriage made it necessary for him to exert himself more strenuously than he had hitherto done. He took a house in the neighbourhood of his native town, and advertised for pupils. But eighteen months passed away; and only three pupils came to his academy. Indeed, his appearance was so strange, and his temper so violent, that his schoolroom must have resembled an ogre's den. Nor was the tawdry painted grandmother whom he called his Titty well qualified to make provision for the comfort of young gentlemen. David Garrick, who was one of the pupils, used, many years later, to throw the best company of London into convulsions of laughter by mimicking the endearments of this extraordinary pair.

At length Johnson, in the twenty-eighth year of his age, determined to seek his fortune in the capital as a literary adventurer. He set out with a few guineas, three acts of the tragedy of Irene in manuscript, and two or three letters of introduction from his friend Walmesley.

Never since literature became a calling in England had it been a less gainful calling than at the time when Johnson took up his residence in London. In the preceding generation a writer of eminent merit was sure to be munificently rewarded by the government. The least that he could expect was a pension or a sinecure place; and, if he showed any aptitude for politics, he might hope to be a member of parliament, a lord of the treasury, an ambassador, a secretary of state. It would be easy, on the other hand, to name several writers of the nineteenth century of whom the least successful has received forty thousand pounds from the booksellers. But Johnson entered on his vocation in the most dreary part of the dreary interval which separated two ages of prosperity. Literature had ceased to flourish under the patronage of the great, and had not begun to flourish under the patronage of the public. One man of letters, indeed, Pope, had acquired by his pen what was then considered as a handsome fortune, and lived on a footing of equality with nobles and ministers of state. But this was a solitary exception. Even an author whose reputation was established, and whose works were popular, such an author as Thomson, whose Seasons were in every library, such an author as Fielding, whose Pasquin had had a greater run than any drama since The Beggar's Opera, was sometimes glad to obtain, by pawning his best coat, the means of dining on tripe at a cookshop underground, where he could wipe his hands, after his greasy meal, on the back of a Newfoundland dog. It is easy, therefore, to imagine what humiliations and privations must have awaited the novice who had still to earn a name. One of the publishers to whom Johnson applied for employment measured with a scornful eye that athletic though uncouth frame, and exclaimed, "You had better get a porter's knot, and carry trunks." Nor was the advice bad; for a porter was likely to be as plentifully fed, and as comfortably lodged, as a poet.

Some time appears to have elapsed before Johnson was able to form any literary connection from which he could expect more than bread for the day which was passing over him. He never forgot the generosity with which Hervey, who was now residing in London,

M—18*

relieved his wants during this time of trial. "Harry Hervey," said the old philosopher many years later, "was a vicious man; but he was very kind to me. If you call a dog Hervey, I shall love him." At Hervey's table Johnson sometimes enjoyed feasts which were made more agreeable by contrast. But in general he dined, and thought that he dined well, on sixpenny worth of meat, and a pennyworth of bread, at an alehouse near Drury Lane.

The effect of the privations and sufferings which he endured at this time was discernible to the last in his temper and his deportment. His manners had never been courtly. They now became almost savage. Being frequently under the necessity of wearing shabby coats and dirty shirts, he became a confirmed sloven. Being often very hungry when he sat down to his meals, he contracted a habit of eating with ravenous greediness. Even to the end of his life, and even at the tables of the great, the sight of food affected him as it affects wild beasts and birds of prey. His taste in cookery, formed in subterranean ordinaries and *Alamode* beefshops, was far from delicate. Whenever he was so fortunate as to have near him a hare that had been kept too long, or a meat pie made with rancid butter, he gorged himself with such violence that his veins swelled, and the moisture broke out on his forehead. The affronts which his poverty emboldened stupid and low-minded men to offer to him would have broken a mean spirit into sycophancy, but made him rude even to ferocity. Unhappily the insolence which, while it was defensive, was pardonable, and in some sense respectable, accompanied him into societies where he was treated with courtesy and kindness. He was repeatedly provoked into striking those who had taken liberties with him. All the sufferers, however, were wise enough to abstain from talking about their beatings, except Osborne, the most rapacious and brutal of booksellers, who proclaimed everywhere that he had been knocked down by the huge fellow whom he had hired to puff the Harleian Library.

About a year after Johnson had begun to reside in London, he was fortunate enough to obtain regular employment from Cave, an enterprising and intelligent bookseller, who was proprietor and editor of the Gentleman's Magazine. That journal, just entering on the ninth year of its long existence, was the only periodical work in the kingdom which then had what would now be called a large circulation. It was indeed, the chief source of parliamentary intelligence. It was not then safe, even during a recess, to publish an account of the proceedings of either House without some disguise. Cave, however, ventured to entertain his readers with what he called Reports of the Debates of the Senate of Lilliput.

France was Blefuscu; London was Mildendo: pounds were sprugs: the Duke of Newcastle was the Nardac secretary of state: Lord Hardwicke was the Hurgo Hickrad; and William Pulteney was Wingul Pulnub. To write the speeches was, during several years, the business of Johnson. He was generally furnished with notes, meagre indeed, and inaccurate, of what had been said; but sometimes he had to find arguments and eloquence both for the ministry and for the opposition. He was himself a Tory, not from rational conviction—for his serious opinion was that one form of government was just as good or as bad as another—but from mere passion, such as inflamed the Capulets against the Montagues, or the Blues of the Roman circus against the Greens. In his infancy he had heard so much talk about the villanies of the Whigs, and the dangers of the Church, that he had become a furious partisan when he could scarcely speak. Before he was three he had insisted on being taken to hear Sacheverell preach at Lichfield Cathedral, and had listened to the sermon with as much respect, and probably with as much intelligence, as any Staffordshire squire in the congregation. The work which had been begun in the nursery had been completed by the university. Oxford, when Johnson resided there, was the most Jacobitical place in England; and Pembroke was one of the most Jacobitical colleges in Oxford. The prejudices which he brought up to London were scarcely less absurd than those of his own Tom Tempest. Charles II. and James II. were two of the best kings that ever reigned. Laud, a poor creature who never did, said, or wrote any thing indicating more than the ordinary capacity of an old woman, was a prodigy of parts and learning over whose tomb Art and Genius still continued to weep. Hampden deserved no more honourable name than that of "the zealot of rebellion." Even the ship money, condemned not less decidedly by Falkland and Clarendon than by the bitterest Roundheads, Johnson would not pronounce to have been an unconstitutional impost. Under a government the mildest that had ever been known in the world under a government which allowed to the people an unprecedented liberty of speech and action, he fancied that he was a slave; he assailed the ministry with obloquy which refuted itself, and regretted the lost freedom and happiness of those golden days in which a writer who had taken but one-tenth part of the license allowed to him would have been pilloried, mangled with the shears, whipped at the cart's tail, and flung into a noisome dungeon to die. He hated dissenters and stock-jobbers, the excise and the army, septennial parliaments, and continental connections. He long had an aversion to the Scotch, an aversion of which he could not remember the commencement, but which, he owned, had probably originated in his abhorrence of the conduct of the nation during the Great Rebellion. It is easy to guess in what manner debates on great party questions were likely to be reported by a man whose judgment was so much disordered by party spirit. A show of fairness was indeed necessary to the prosperity of the Magazine. But Johnson long afterwards owned that, though he had saved appearances, he had taken care that the Whig dogs should not have the best of it; and, in fact, every passage which has lived, every passage which bears the marks of his higher faculties, is put into the mouth of some member of the opposition.

A few weeks after Johnson had entered on these obscure labours, he published a work which at once placed him high among the writers of his age. It is probable that what he had suffered during his first year in London had often reminded him of some parts of that noble poem in which Juvenal had described the misery and degradation of a needy man of letters, lodged among the pigeons' nests in the tottering garrets which overhung the streets of Rome. Pope's admirable imitations of Horace's Satires and Epistles had recently appeared, were in every hand, and were by many readers thought superior to the originals. What Pope had done for Horace, Johnson aspired to do for Juvenal. The enterprise was bold, and yet judicious. For between Johnson and Juvenal there was much in common, much more certainly than between Pope and Horace.

Johnson's London appeared without his name in May 1738. He received only ten guineas for this stately and vigorous poem: but the sale was rapid, and the success complete. A second edition was required within a week. Those small critics who are always desirous to lower established reputations ran about proclaiming that the anonymous satirist was superior to Pope in Pope's own peculiar department of literature. It ought to be remembered, to the honour of Pope, that he joined heartily in the applause with which the appearance of a rival genius was welcomed. He made inquiries about the author of London. Such a man, he said, could not long be concealed. The name was soon discovered; and Pope, with great kindness, exerted himself to obtain an academical degree and the mastership of a grammar school for the poor young poet. The attempt failed, and Johnson remained a bookseller's hack.

It does not appear that these two men, the most eminent writer of the generation which was going out, and the most eminent writer of the generation which was coming in, ever saw each other. They lived in very different circles, one surrounded by dukes and earls, the other by starving pamphleteers and indexmakers. Among

Johnson's associates at this time may be mentioned Boyse, who, when his shirts were pledged, scrawled Latin verses sitting up in bed with his arms through two holes in his blanket, who composed very respectable sacred poetry when he was sober, and who was at last run over by a hackney coach when he was drunk; Hoole, surnamed the metaphysical tailor, who, instead of attending to his measures, used to trace geometrical diagrams on the board where he sate cross-legged; and the penitent impostor, George Psalmanazar, who, after poring all day, in a humble lodging, on the folios of Jewish rabbis and Christian fathers, indulged himself at night with literary and theological conversation at an alehouse in the city. But the most remarkable of the persons with whom at this time Johnson consorted, was Richard Savage, an earl's son, a shoemaker's apprentice, who had seen life in all its forms, who had feasted among blue ribands in Saint James's Square, and had lain with fifty pounds weight of irons on his legs in the condemned ward of Newgate. This man had, after many vicissitudes of fortune, sunk at last into abject and hopeless poverty. His pen had failed him. His patrons had been taken away by death, or estranged by the riotous profusion with which he squandered their bounty, and the ungrateful insolence with which he rejected their advice. He now lived by begging. He dined on venison and Champagne whenever he had been so fortunate as to borrow a guinea. If his questing had been unsuccessful, he appeased the rage of hunger with some scraps of broken meat, and lay down to rest under the Piazza of Covent Garden in warm weather, and, in cold weather, as near as he could get to the furnace of a glass house. Yet, in his misery, he was still an agreeable companion. He had an inexhaustible store of anecdotes about that gay and brilliant world from which he was now an outcast. He had observed the great men of both parties in hours of careless relaxation, had seen the leaders of opposition without the mask of patriotism, and had heard the prime minister roar with laughter and tell stories not over decent. During some months Savage lived in the closest familiarity with Johnson; and then the friends parted, not without tears. Johnson remained in London to drudge for Cave. Savage went to the West of England, lived there as he had lived everywhere, and, in 1743, died, penniless and heartbroken, in Bristol gaol.

Soon after his death, while the public curiosity was strongly excited about his extraordinary character, and his not less extraordinary adventures, a life of him appeared widely different from the catchpenny lives of eminent men which were then a staple article of manufacture in Grub Street. The style was indeed deficient in ease and variety; and the writer was evidently too partial to the Latin element of our language. But the little work, with all its faults, was a masterpiece. No finer specimen of literary biography existed in any language, living or dead; and a discerning critic might have confidently predicted that the author was destined to be the founder of a new school of English eloquence.

The Life of Savage was anonymous; but it was well known in literary circles that Johnson was the writer. During the three years which followed, he produced no important work; but he was not, and indeed could not be, idle. The fame of his abilities and learning continued to grow. Warburton pronounced him a man of parts and genius; and the praise of Warburton was then no light thing. Such was Johnson's reputation that, in 1747, several eminent booksellers combined to employ him in the arduous work of preparing a Dictionary of the English Language, in two folio volumes. The sum which they agreed to pay him was only fifteen hundred guineas; and out of this sum he had to pay several poor men of letters who assisted him in the humbler parts of his task.

The Prospectus of the Dictionary he addressed to the Earl of Chesterfield. Chesterfield had long been celebrated for the politeness of his manners, the brilliancy of his wit, and the delicacy of his taste. He was acknowledged to be the finest speaker in the House of Lords. He had recently governed Ireland, at a momentous conjuncture, with eminent firmness, wisdom, and humanity; and he had since become Secretary of State. He received Johnson's homage with the most winning affability, and requited it with a few guineas, bestowed doubtless in a very graceful manner, but was by no means desirous to see all his carpets blackened with the London mud, and his soups and wines thrown to right and left over the gowns of fine ladies and the waistcoats of fine gentlemen, by an absent, awkward scholar, who gave strange starts and uttered strange growls, who dressed like a scarecrow, and ate like a cormorant. During some time Johnson continued to call on his patron, but, after being repeatedly told by the porter that his lordship was not at home, took the hint, and ceased to present himself at the inhospitable door.

Johnson had flattered himself that he should have completed his Dictionary by the end of 1750; but it was not till 1755 that he at length gave his huge volumes to the world. During the seven years which he passed in the drudgery of penning definitions and marking quotations for transcriptions, he sought for relaxation in literary labour of a more agreeable kind. In 1749 he published the Vanity of Human Wishes, an excellent imitation of the Tenth Satire of

Juvenal. It is in truth not easy to say whether the palm belongs to the ancient or to the modern poet. The couplets in which the fall of Wolsey is described, though lofty and sonorous, are feeble when compared with the wonderful lines which bring before us all Rome in tumult on the day of the fall of Sejanus, the laurels on the door-posts, the white bull stalking towards the Capitol, the statues rolling down from their pedestals, the flatterers of the disgraced minister running to see him dragged with a hook through the streets, and to have a kick at his carcase before it is hurled into the Tiber. It must be owned too that in the concluding passage the Christian moralist has not made the most of his advantages, and has fallen decidedly short of the sublimity of his Pagan model. On the other hand, Juvenal's Hannibal must yield to Johnson's Charles; and Johnson's vigorous and pathetic enumeration of the miseries of a literary life must be allowed to be superior to Juvenal's lamentation over the fate of Demosthenes and Cicero.

For the copyright of the Vanity of Human Wishes Johnson received only fifteen guineas.

A few days after the publication of this poem, his tragedy, begun many years before, was brought on the stage. His pupil, David Garrick, had, in 1741, made his appearance on a humble stage in Goodman's Fields, had at once risen to the first place among actors, and was now, after several years of almost uninterrupted success, manager of the Drury Lane Theatre. The relation between him and his old preceptor was of a very singular kind. They repelled each other strongly, and yet attracted each other strongly. Nature had made them of very different clay; and circumstances had fully brought out the natural peculiarities of both. Sudden prosperity had turned Garrick's head. Continued adversity had soured Johnson's temper. Johnson saw with more envy than became so great a man the villa, the plate, the china, the Brussels carpet, which the little mimic had got by repeating, with grimaces and gesticulations, what wiser men had written; and the exquisitely sensitive vanity of Garrick was galled by the thought that, while all the rest of the world was applauding him, he could obtain from one morose cynic, whose opinion it was impossible to despise, scarcely any compliment not acidulated with scorn. Yet the two Lichfield men had so many early recollections in common, and sympathized with each other on so many points on which they sympathized with nobody else in the vast population of the capital, that, though the master was often provoked by the monkey-like impertinence of the pupil, and the pupil by the bearish rudeness of the master, they remained friends till they were parted by death. Garrick now brought Irene out, with alterations sufficient to displease the author, yet not sufficient to make the piece pleasing to the audience. The public, however, listened with little emotion, but with much civility, to five acts of monotonous declamation. After nine representations the play was withdrawn. It is, indeed, altogether unsuited to the stage, and, even when perused in the closet, will be found hardly worthy of the author. He had not the slightest notion of what blank verse should be. A change in the last syllable of every other line would make the versification of the Vanity of Human Wishes closely resemble the versification of Irene. The poet, however, cleared, by his benefit nights, and by the sale of the copyright of his tragedy, about three hundred pounds, then a great sum in his estimation.

About a year after the representation of Irene, he began to publish a series of short essays on morals, manners, and literature. This species of composition had been brought into fashion by the success of the Tatler, and by the still more brilliant success of the Spectator. A crowd of small writers had vainly attempted to rival Addison. The Lay Monastery, the Censor, the Freethinker, the Plain Dealer, the Champion, and other works of the same kind, had had their short day. None of them had obtained a permanent place in our literature; and they are now to be found only in the libraries of the curious. At length Johnson undertook the adventure in which so many aspirants had failed. In the thirty-sixth year after the appearance of the last number of the Spectator appeared the first number of the Rambler. From March 1750 to March 1752, this paper continued to come out every Tuesday and Saturday.

From the first the Rambler was enthusiastically admired by a few eminent men. Richardson, when only five numbers had appeared, pronounced it equal, if not superior, to the Spectator. Young and Hartley expressed their approbation not less warmly. Bubb Dodington, among whose many faults indifference to the claims of genius and learning cannot be reckoned, solicited the acquaintance of the writer. In consequence probably of the good offices of Dodington, who was then the confidential adviser of Prince Frederic, two of his Royal Highness's gentlemen carried a gracious message to the printing office, and ordered seven copies for Leicester House. But these overtures seem to have been very coldly received. Johnson had had enough of the patronage of the great to last him all his life, and was not disposed to haunt any other door as he had haunted the door of Chesterfield.

By the public the Rambler was at first very coldly received. Though the price of a number was only twopence, the sale did not amount to five hundred. The profits were therefore very small.

But as soon as the flying leaves were collected and reprinted they became popular. The author lived to see thirteen thousand copies spread over England alone. Separate editions were published for the Scotch and Irish markets. A large party pronounced the style perfect, so absolutely perfect that in some essays it would be impossible for the writer himself to alter a single word for the better. Another party, not less numerous, vehemently accused him of having corrupted the purity of the English tongue. The best critics admitted that his diction was too monotonous, too obviously artificial, and now and then turgid even to absurdity. But they did justice to the acuteness of his observations on morals and manners, to the constant precision and frequent brilliancy of his language, to the weighty and magnificent eloquence of many serious passages, and to the solemn yet pleasing humour of some of the lighter papers. On the question of precedence between Addison and Johnson, a question which, seventy years ago, was much disputed, posterity has pronounced a decision from which there is no appeal. Sir Roger, his chaplain and his butler, Will Wimble and Will Honeycomb, the Vision of Mirza, the Journal of the Retired Citizen, the Everlasting Club, the Dunmow Flitch, the Loves of Hilpah and Shalum, the Visit to the Exchange, and the Visit to the Abbey, are known to everybody. But many men and women, even of highly cultivated minds, are unacquainted with Squire Bluster and Mrs. Busy, Quisquilius and Venustulus, the Allegory of Wit and Learning, the Chronicle of the Revolutions of a Garret, and the sad fate of Aningait and Ajut.

The last Rambler was written in a sad and gloomy hour. Mrs. Johnson had been given over by the physicians. Three days later she died. She left her husband almost broken-hearted. Many people had been surprised to see a man of his genius and learning stooping to every drudgery, and denying himself almost every comfort, for the purpose of supplying a silly, affected old woman with superfluities, which she accepted with but little gratitude. But all his affection had been concentrated on her. He had neither brother nor sister, neither son nor daughter. To him she was beautiful as the Gunnings, and witty as Lady Mary. Her opinion of his writings was more important to him than the voice of the pit of Drury Lane Theatre or the judgment of the Monthly Review. The chief support which had sustained him through the most arduous labour of his life was the hope that she would enjoy the fame and the profit which he anticipated from his Dictionary. She was gone; and in that vast labyrinth of streets, peopled by eight hundred thousand human beings, he was alone. Yet it was necessary for him to set himself, as he expressed it, doggedly to work. After three more laborious years, the Dictionary was at length complete.

It had been generally supposed that this great work would be dedicated to the eloquent and accomplished nobleman to whom the Prospectus had been addressed. He well knew the value of such a compliment; and therefore, when the day of publication drew near, he exerted himself to sooth, by a show of zealous and at the same time of delicate and judicious kindness, the pride which he had so cruelly wounded. Since the Ramblers had ceased to appear, the town had been entertained by a journal called The World, to which many men of high rank and fashion contributed. In two successive numbers of The World, the Dictionary was, to use the modern phrase, puffed with wonderful skill. The writings of Johnson were warmly praised. It was proposed that he should be invested with the authority of a Dictator, nay, of a Pope, over our language, and that his decisions about the meaning and the spelling of words should be received as final. His two folios, it was said, would of course be bought by everybody who could afford to buy them. It was soon known that these papers were written by Chesterfield. But the just resentment of Johnson was not to be so appeased. In a letter written with singular energy and dignity of thought and language, he repelled the tardy advances of his patron. The Dictionary came forth without a dedication. In the preface the author truly declared that he owed nothing to the great, and described the difficulties with which he had been left to struggle so forcibly and pathetically that the ablest and most malevolent of all the enemies of his fame, Horne Tooke, never could read that passage without tears.

The public, on this occasion, did Johnson full justice, and something more than justice. The best lexicographer may well be content if his productions are received by the world with cold esteem. But Johnson's Dictionary was hailed with an enthusiasm such as no similar work has ever excited. It was indeed the first dictionary which could be read with pleasure. The definitions show so much acuteness of thought and command of language, and the passages quoted from poets, divines, and philosophers, are so skilfully selected, that a leisure hour may always be very agreeably spent in turning over the pages. The faults of the book resolve themselves, for the most part, into one great fault. Johnson was a wretched etymologist. He knew little or nothing of any Teutonic language except English, which indeed, as he wrote it, was scarcely a Teutonic language; and thus he was absolutely at the mercy of Junius and Skinner.

The Dictionary, though it raised Johnson's fame, added nothing to his pecuniary means. The fifteen hundred guineas which the booksellers had agreed to pay him had been advanced and spent before the last sheets issued from the press. It is painful to relate that, twice in the course of the year which followed the publication of this great work, he was arrested and carried to spunging-houses, and that he was twice indebted for his liberty to his excellent friend Richardson. It was still necessary for the man who had been formally saluted by the highest authority as Dictator of the English language to supply his wants by constant toil. He abridged his Dictionary. He proposed to bring out an edition of Shakspeare by subscription; and many subscribers sent in their names, and laid down their money; but he soon found the task so little to his taste that he turned to more attractive employments. He contributed many papers to a new monthly journal, which was called the Literary Magazine. Few of these papers have much interest; but among them was the very best thing that he ever wrote, a master-piece both of reasoning and of satirical pleasantry, the review of Jenyns's Inquiry into the Nature and Origin of Evil.

In the spring of 1758 Johnson put forth the first of a series of essays, entitled The Idler. During two years these essays continued to appear weekly. They were eagerly read, widely circulated, and, indeed, impudently pirated while they were still in the original form, and had a large sale when collected into volumes. The Idler may be described as a second part of the Rambler, somewhat livelier and somewhat weaker than the first part.

While Johnson was busied with his Idlers, his mother, who had accomplished her ninetieth year, died at Lichfield. It was long since he had seen her; but he had not failed to contribute largely, out of his small means, to her comfort. In order to defray the charges of her funeral, and to pay some debts which she had left, he wrote a little book in a single week, and sent off the sheets to the press without reading them over. A hundred pounds were paid to him for the copyright; and the purchasers had great cause to be pleased with their bargain; for the book was Rasselas.

The success of Rasselas was great, though such ladies as Miss Lydia Languish must have been grievously disappointed when they found that the new volume from the circulating library was little more than a dissertation on the author's favourite theme, the Vanity of Human Wishes; that the Prince of Abyssinia was without a mistress, and the Princess without a lover; and that the story set the hero and the heroine down exactly where it had taken them up. The style was the subject of much eager controversy. The Monthly

Review and the Critical Review took different sides. Many readers pronounced the writer a pompous pedant, who would never use a word of two syllables where it was possible to use a word of six, and who could not make a waiting woman relate her adventures without balancing every noun with another noun, and every epithet with another epithet. Another party, not less zealous, cited with delight numerous passages in which weighty meaning was expressed with accuracy and illustrated with splendour. And both the censure and the praise were merited.

About the plan of Rasselas little was said by the critics; and yet the faults of the plan might seem to invite severe criticism. Johnson has frequently blamed Shakspeare for neglecting the proprieties of time and place, and for ascribing to one age or nation the manners and opinions of another. Yet Shakspeare has not sinned in this way more grievously than Johnson. Rasselas and Imlac, Nekayah and Pekuah, are evidently meant to be Abyssinians of the eighteenth century: for the Europe which Imlac describes is the Europe of the eighteenth century; and the inmates of the Happy Valley talk familiarly of that law of gravitation which Newton discovered, and which was not fully received even at Cambridge till the eighteenth century. What a real company of Abyssinians would have been may be learned from Bruce's Travels. But Johnson, not content with turning filthy savages, ignorant of their letters, and gorged with raw steaks cut from living cows, into philosophers as eloquent and enlightened as himself or his friend Burke, and into ladies as highly accomplished as Mrs. Lennox or Mrs. Sheridan, transferred the whole domestic system of England to Egypt. Into a land of harems, a land of polygamy, a land where women are married without ever being seen, he introduced the flirtations and jealousies of our ball-rooms. In a land where there is boundless liberty of divorce, wedlock is described as the indissoluble compact. "A youth and maiden meeting by chance, or brought together by artifice, exchange glances, reciprocate civilities, go home, and dream of each other. Such," says Rasselas, "is the common process of marriage." Such it may have been, and may still be, in London, but assuredly not at Cairo. A writer who was guilty of such improprieties had little right to blame the poet who made Hector quote Aristotle, and represented Julio Romano as flourishing in the days of the oracle of Delphi.

By such exertions as have been described, Johnson supported himself till the year 1762. In that year a great change in his circumstances took place. He had from a child been an enemy of the reigning dynasty. His Jacobite prejudices had been exhibited with little disguise both in his works and in his conversation. Even in his massy and elaborate Dictionary, he had, with a strange want of taste and judgment, inserted bitter and contumelious reflections on the Whig party. The excise, which was a favourite resource of Whig financiers, he had designated as a hateful tax. He had railed against the commissioners of excise in language so coarse that they had seriously thought of prosecuting him. He had with difficulty been prevented from holding up the Lord Privy Seal by name as an example of the meaning of the word "renegade." A pension he had defined as pay given to a state hireling to betray his country; a pensioner as a slave of state hired by a stipend to obey a master. It seemed unlikely that the author of these definitions would himself be pensioned. But that was a time of wonders. George the Third had ascended the throne; and had, in the course of a few months, disgusted many of the old friends and conciliated many of the old enemies of his house. The city was becoming mutinous. Oxford was becoming loyal. Cavendishes and Bentincks were murmuring. Somersets and Wyndhams were hastening to kiss hands. The head of the treasury was now Lord Bute, who was a Tory, and could have no objection to Johnson's Toryism. Bute wished to be thought a patron of men of letters; and Johnson was one of the most eminent and one of the most needy men of letters in Europe. A pension of three hundred a year was graciously offered, and with very little hesitation accepted.

This event produced a change in Johnson's whole way of life. For the first time since his boyhood he no longer felt the daily goad urging him to the daily toil. He was at liberty, after thirty years of anxiety and drudgery, to indulge his constitutional indolence, to lie in bed till two in the afternoon, and to sit up talking till four in the morning, without fearing either the printer's devil or the sheriff's officer.

One laborious task indeed he had bound himself to perform. He had received large subscriptions for his promised edition of Shakspeare; he had lived on those subscriptions during some years; and he could not without disgrace omit to perform his part of the contract. His friends repeatedly exhorted him to make an effort; and he repeatedly resolved to do so. But, notwithstanding their exhortations and his resolutions, month followed month, year followed year, and nothing was done. He prayed fervently against his idleness; he determined, as often as he received the sacrament, that he would no longer doze away and trifle away his time; but the spell under which he lay resisted prayer and sacrament. His private notes at this time are made up of self-reproaches. "My indolence," he wrote on Easter eve in 1764, "has sunk into grosser sluggishness. A kind of strange oblivion has overspread me, so that I know not what has become of the last year." Easter 1765 came, and found him still in the same state. "My time," he wrote, "has been unprofitably spent, and seems as a dream that has left nothing behind. My memory grows confused, and I know not how the days pass over me." Happily for his honour, the charm which held him captive was at length broken by no gentle or friendly hand. He had been weak enough to pay serious attention to a story about a ghost which haunted a house in Cock Lane, and had actually gone himself, with some of his friends, at one in the morning, to St. John's Church, Clerkenwell, in the hope of receiving a communication from the perturbed spirit. But the spirit, though adjured with all solemnity, remained obstinately silent; and it soon appeared that a naughty girl of eleven had been amusing herself by making fools of so many philosophers. Churchill, who, confident in his powers, drunk with popularity, and burning with party spirit, was looking for some man of established fame and Tory politics to insult, celebrated the Cock Lane Ghost in three cantos, nicknamed Johnson Pomposo, asked where the book was which had been so long promised and so liberally paid for, and directly accused the great moralist of cheating. This terrible word proved effectual; and in October 1765 appeared, after a delay of nine years, the new edition of Shakspeare.

This publication saved Johnson's character for honesty, but added nothing to the fame of his abilities and learning. The preface, though it contains some good passages, is not in his best manner. The most valuable notes are those in which he had an opportunity of showing how attentively he had during many years observed human life and human nature. The best specimen is the note on the character of Polonius. Nothing so good is to be found even in Wilhelm Meister's admirable examination of Hamlet. But here praise must end. It would be difficult to name a more slovenly, a more worthless, edition of any great classic. The reader may turn over play after play without finding one happy conjectural emendation, or one ingenious and satisfactory explanation of a passage which had baffled preceding commentators. Johnson had, in his Prospectus, told the world that he was peculiarly fitted for the task which he had undertaken, because he had, as a lexicographer, been under the necessity of taking a wider view of the English language than any of his predecessors. That his knowledge of our literature was extensive is indisputable. But, unfortunately, he had altogether neglected that very part of our literature with which it is especially desirable that an editor of Shakspeare should be conversant. It is dangerous to assert a negative. Yet little will be risked by the assertion, that in the two folio volumes of the English Dictionary there is not a single passage quoted from any dramatist of the Elizabethan age, except Shakspeare and Ben. Even from Ben the quotations are few. Johnson might easily, in a few months, have made himself well acquainted with every old play that was extant. But it never seems to have occurred to him that this was a necessary preparation for the work which he had undertaken. He would doubtless have admitted that it would be the height of absurdity in a man who was not familiar with the works of Æschylus and Euripides to publish an edition of Sophocles. Yet he ventured to publish an edition of Shakspeare, without having ever in his life, as far as can be discovered, read a single scene of Massinger, Ford, Decker, Webster, Marlow, Beaumont, or Fletcher. His detractors were noisy and scurrilous. Those who most loved and honoured him had little to say in praise of the manner in which he had discharged the duty of a commentator. He had, however, acquitted himself of a debt which had long lain heavy on his conscience, and he sank back into the repose from which the sting of satire had roused him. He long continued to live upon the fame which he had already won. He was honoured by the University of Oxford with a Doctor's degree, by the Royal Academy with a professorship, and by the King with an interview, in which his Majesty most graciously expressed a hope that so excellent a writer would not cease to write. In the interval, however, between 1765 and 1775 Johnson published only two or three political tracts, the longest of which he could have produced in forty-eight hours, if he had worked as he worked on the Life of Savage and on Rasselas.

But, though his pen was now idle, his tongue was active. The influence exercised by his conversation, directly upon those with whom he lived, and indirectly on the whole literary world, was altogether without a parallel. His colloquial talents were indeed of the highest order. He had a strong sense, quick discernment, wit, humour, immense knowledge of literature and of life, and an infinite store of curious anecdotes. As respected style, he spoke far better than he wrote. Every sentence which dropped from his lips was as correct in structure as the most nicely balanced period of the Rambler. But in his talk there were no pompous triads, and little more than a fair proportion of words in *osity* and *ation*. All was simplicity, ease, and vigour. He uttered his short, weighty, and pointed sentences with a power of voice, and a justness and energy of emphasis, of which the effect was rather increased than diminished by the rollings of his huge form, and by the asthmatic gaspings and puffings in which the peals of his eloquence generally ended. Nor did the laziness which made him unwilling to sit down to his desk prevent him from giving instruction or entertainment orally. To discuss questions of taste, of learning, of casuistry, in language so exact and so forcible that it might have been printed without the alteration of a word, was to him no exertion, but a pleasure. He loved, as he said, to fold his legs and have his talk out. He was ready to bestow the overflowings of his full mind on anybody who would start a subject, on a fellow-passenger in a stage coach, or on the person who sate at the same table with him in an eating house. But his conversation was nowhere so brilliant and striking as when he was surrounded by a few friends, whose abilities and knowledge enabled them, as he once expressed it, to send him back every ball that he threw. Some of these, in 1764, formed themselves into a club, which gradually became a formidable power in the commonwealth of letters. The verdicts pronounced by this conclave on new books were speedily known over all London, and were sufficient to sell off a whole edition in a day, or to condemn the sheets to the service of the trunk-maker and the pastrycook. Nor shall we think this strange when we consider what great and various talents and acquirements met in the little fraternity. Goldsmith was the representative of poetry and light literature, Reynolds of the arts, Burke of political eloquence and political philosophy. There, too, were Gibbon, the greatest historian, and Jones, the greatest linguist, of the age. Garrick brought to the meetings his inexhaustible pleasantry, his incomparable mimicry, and his consummate knowledge of stage effect. Among the most constant attendants were two high-born and high-bred gentlemen, closely bound together by friendship, but of widely different characters and habits; Bennet Langton, distinguished by his skill in Greek literature, by the orthodoxy of his opinions, and by the sanctity of his life; and Topham Beauclerk, renowned for his amours, his knowledge of the gay world, his fastidious taste, and his sarcastic wit. To predominate over such a society was not easy. Yet even over such a society Johnson predominated. Burke might indeed have disputed the supremacy to which others were under the necessity of submitting. But Burke, though not generally a very patient listener, was content to take the second part when Johnson was present; and the club itself, consisting of so many eminent men, is to this day popularly designated as Johnson's Club.

Among the members of this celebrated body was one to whom it has owed the greater part of its celebrity, yet who was regarded with little respect by his brethren, and had not without difficulty obtained a seat among them. This was James Boswell, a young Scotch lawyer, heir to an honourable name and a fair estate. That he was a coxcomb and a bore, weak, vain, pushing, curious, garrulous, was obvious to all who were acquainted with him. That he could not reason, that he had no wit, no humour, no eloquence, is apparent from his writings. And yet his writings are read beyond the Mississippi, and under the Southern Cross, and are likely to be read as long as the English exists, either as a living or as a dead language. Nature had made him a slave and an idolater. His mind resembled those creepers which the botanists call parasites, and which can subsist only by clinging round the stems and imbibing the juices of stronger plants. He must have fastened himself on somebody. He might have fastened himself on Wilkes, and have become the fiercest patriot in the Bill of Rights Society. He might have fastened himself on Whitfield, and have become the loudest field preacher among the Calvinistic Methodists. In a happy hour he fastened himself on Johnson. The pair might seem ill matched. For Johnson had early been prejudiced against Boswell's country. To a man of Johnson's strong understanding and irritable temper, the silly egotism and adulation of Boswell must have been as teasing as the constant buzz of a fly. Johnson hated to be questioned; and Boswell was eternally catechizing him on all kinds of subjects, and sometimes propounded such questions as, "What would you do, sir, if you were locked up in a tower with a baby?" Johnson was a water drinker; and Boswell was a winebibber, and indeed little better than a habitual sot. It was impossible that there should be perfect harmony between two such companions. Indeed, the great man was sometimes provoked into fits of passion in which he said things which the small man, during a few hours, seriously resented. Every quarrel, however, was soon made up. During twenty years the disciple continued to worship the master: the master continued to scold the disciple, to sneer at him, and to love him. The two friends ordinarily resided at a great distance from each other. Boswell practised in the Parliament House of Edinburgh, and could pay only occasional visits to London. During those visits his chief business was to watch Johnson, to discover all Johnson's habits, to turn the conversation to subjects about which Johnson was likely to say something remarkable, and to fill quarto note books with minutes of what Johnson had said. In this way were gathered the materials, out of which was afterwards constructed the most interesting biographical work in the world.

Soon after the club began to exist, Johnson formed a connection less important indeed to his fame, but much more important to his happiness, than his connection with Boswell. Henry Thrale, one of the most opulent brewers in the kingdom, a man of sound and cultivated understanding, rigid principles, and liberal spirit, was married to one of those clever, kind-hearted, engaging, vain, pert young women, who are perpetually doing or saying what is not exactly right, but who, do or say what they may, are always agreeable. In 1765 the Thrales became acquainted with Johnson, and the acquaintance ripened fast into friendship. They were astonished and delighted by the brilliancy of his conversation. They were flattered by finding that a man so widely celebrated preferred their house to any other in London. Even the peculiarities which seemed to unfit him for civilised society, his gesticulations, his rollings, his puffings, his mutterings, the strange way in which he put on his clothes, the ravenous eagerness with which he devoured his dinner, his fits of melancholy, his fits of anger, his frequent rudeness, his occasional ferocity, increased the interest which his new associates took in him. For these things were the cruel marks left behind by a life which had been one long conflict with disease and with adversity. In a vulgar hack writer such oddities would have excited only disgust. But in a man of genius, learning, and virtue, their effect was to add pity to admiration and esteem. Johnson soon had an apartment at the brewery in Southwark, and a still more pleasant apartment at the villa of his friends on Streatham Common. A large part of every year he passed in those abodes, abodes which must have seemed magnificent and luxurious indeed, when compared with the dens in which he had generally been lodged. But his chief pleasures were derived from what the astronomer of his Abyssinian tale called "the endearing elegance of female friendship." Mrs. Thrale rallied him, soothed him, coaxed him, and, if she sometimes provoked him by her flippancy, made ample amends by listening to his reproofs with angelic sweetness of temper. When he was diseased in body and in mind, she was the most tender of nurses. No comfort that wealth could purchase, no contrivance that womanly ingenuity, set to work by womanly compassion, could devise, was wanting to his sick room. He requited her kindness by an affection pure as the affection of a father, yet delicately tinged with a gallantry, which, though awkward, must have been more flattering than the attentions of a crowd of the fools who gloried in the names, now obsolete, of Buck and Maccaroni. It should seem that a full half of Johnson's life, during about sixteen years, was passed under the roof of the Thrales. He accompanied the family sometimes to Bath, and sometimes to Brighton, once to Wales, and once to Paris. But he had at the same time a house in one of the narrow and gloomy courts on the north of Fleet Street. In the garrets was his library, a large and miscellaneous collection of books, falling to pieces and begrimed with dust. On a lower floor he sometimes, but very rarely, regaled a friend with a plain dinner, a veal pie, or a leg of lamb and spinage, and a rice pudding. Nor was the dwelling uninhabited during his long absences. It was the home of the most extraordinary assemblage of inmates that ever was brought together. At the head of the establishment Johnson had placed an old lady named Williams, whose chief recommendations were her blindness and her poverty. But, in spite of her murmurs and reproaches, he gave an asylum to another lady who was as poor as herself, Mrs. Desmoulins, whose family he had known many years before in Staffordshire. Room was found for the daughter of Mrs. Desmoulins, and for another destitute damsel, who was generally addressed as Miss Carmichael, but whom her generous host called Polly. An old quack doctor named Levett, who bled and dosed coal-heavers and hackney coachmen, and received for fees crusts of bread, bits of bacon, glasses of gin, and sometimes a little copper, completed this strange menagerie. All these poor creatures were at constant war with each other, and with Johnson's negro servant Frank. Sometimes, indeed, they transferred their hostilities from the servant to the master, complained that a better table was not kept for them, and railed or maundered till their benefactor was glad to make his escape to Streatham, or to the Mitre Tavern. And yet he, who was generally the haughtiest and most irritable of mankind, who was but too prompt to resent anything which looked like a slight on the part of a purse-proud bookseller, or of a noble and powerful patron, bore patiently from mendicants, who, but for his bounty, must have gone to the workhouse, insults more provoking than those for which he had knocked down Osborne and bidden defiance to Chesterfield. Year after year Mrs. Williams and Mrs. Desmoulins, Polly and Levett, continued to torment him and to live upon him.

The course of life which has been described was interrupted in Johnson's sixty-fourth year by an important event. He had early read an account of the Hebrides, and had been much interested by learning that there was so near him a land peopled by a race which was still as rude and simple as in the middle ages. A wish to become intimately acquainted with a state of society so utterly unlike all that he had ever seen frequently crossed his mind. But it is not probable that his curiosity would have overcome his habitual sluggishness, and his love of the smoke, the mud, and the cries of

London, had not Boswell importuned him to attempt the adventure, and offered to be his squire. At length, in August 1773, Johnson crossed the Highland line, and plunged courageously into what was then considered, by most Englishmen, as a dreary and perilous wilderness. After wandering about two months through the Celtic region, sometimes in rude boats which did not protect him from the rain, and sometimes on small shaggy poneys which could hardly bear his weight, he returned to his old haunts with a mind full of new images and new theories. During the following year he employed himself in recording his adventures. About the beginning of 1775, his Journey to the Hebrides was published, and was, during some weeks, the chief subject of conversation in all circles in which any attention was paid to literature. The book is still read with pleasure. The narrative is entertaining; the speculations, whether sound or unsound, are always ingenious; and the style, though too stiff and pompous, is somewhat easier and more graceful than that of his early writings. His prejudice against the Scotch had at length become little more than matter of jest; and whatever remained of the old feeling had been effectually removed by the kind and respectful hospitality with which he had been received in every part of Scotland. It was, of course, not to be expected that an Oxonian Tory should praise the Presbyterian polity and ritual, or that an eye accustomed to the hedgerows and parks of England should not be struck by the bareness of Berwickshire and East Lothian. But even in censure Johnson's tone is not unfriendly. The most enlightened Scotchmen, with Lord Mansfield at their head, were well pleased. But some foolish and ignorant Scotchmen were moved to anger by a little unpalatable truth which was mingled with much eulogy, and assailed him whom they chose to consider as the enemy of their country with libels much more dishonourable to their country than anything that he had ever said or written. They published paragraphs in the newspapers, articles in the magazines, sixpenny pamphlets, five shilling books. One scribbler abused Johnson for being blear-eyed; another for being a pensioner: a third informed the world that one of the Doctor's uncles had been convicted of felony in Scotland, and had found that there was in that country one tree capable of supporting the weight of an Englishman. Macpherson, whose Fingal had been proved in the Journey to be an impudent forgery, threatened to take vengeance with a cane. The only effect of this threat was that Johnson reiterated the charge of forgery in the most contemptuous terms, and walked about, during some time, with a cudgel, which, if the impostor had not been too wise to encounter it, would assuredly have descended upon him, to borrow the sublime language of his own epic poem, "like a hammer on the red son of the furnace."

Of other assailants Johnson took no notice whatever. He had early resolved never to be drawn into controversy; and he adhered to his resolution with a steadfastness which is the more extra-ordinary, because he was, both intellectually and morally, of the stuff of which controversialists are made. In conversation, he was a singularly eager, acute, and pertinacious disputant. When at a loss for good reasons, he had recourse to sophistry; and when heated by altercation, he made unsparing use of sarcasm and invective. But when he took his pen in his hand, his whole character seemed to be changed. A hundred bad writers misrepresented him and reviled him; but not one of the hundred could boast of having been thought by him worthy of a refutation, or even of a retort. The Kenricks, Campbells, MacNicols, and Hendersons, did their best to annoy him, in the hope that he would give them importance by answering them. But the reader will in vain search his works for any allusion to Kenrick or Campbell, to MacNicol or Henderson. One Scotchman, bent on vindicating the fame of Scotch learning, defied him to the combat in a detestable Latin hexameter.

"Maxime, si tu vis, cupio contendere tecum."

But Johnson took no notice of the challenge. He had learned, both from his own observation and from literary history, in which he was deeply read, that the place of books in the public estimation is fixed, not by what is written about them, but by what is written in them; and that an author whose works are likely to live is very unwise if he stoops to wrangle with detractors whose works are certain to die. He always maintained that fame was a shuttlecock which could be kept up only by being beaten back, as well as beaten forward, and which would soon fall if there were only one battle-dore. No saying was oftener in his mouth than that fine apophthegm of Bentley, that no man was ever written down but by himself.

Unhappily, a few months after the appearance of the Journey to the Hebrides, Johnson did what none of his envious assailants could have done, and to a certain extent succeeded in writing himself down. The disputes between England and her American colonies had reached a point at which no amicable adjustment was possible. Civil war was evidently impending; and the ministers seem to have thought that the eloquence of Johnson might with advantage be employed to inflame the nation against the opposition here, and against the rebels beyond the Atlantic. He had already written two or three tracts in defence of the foreign and domestic policy of the government; and those tracts, though hardly worthy of him, were much superior to the crowd of pamphlets which lay on the counters of Almon and Stockdale. But his Taxation No Tyranny was a pitiable failure. The very title was a silly phrase, which can have been recommended to his choice by nothing but a jingling alliteration which he ought to have despised. The arguments were such as boys use in debating societies. The pleasantry was as awkward as the gambols of a hippopotamus. Even Boswell was forced to own that, in this unfortunate piece, he could detect no trace of his master's powers. The general opinion was that the strong faculties which had produced the Dictionary and the Rambler were beginning to feel the effect of time and of disease, and that the old man would best consult his credit by writing no more.

But this was a great mistake. Johnson had failed, not because his mind was less vigorous than when he wrote Rasselas in the evenings of a week, but because he had foolishly chosen, or suffered others to choose for him, a subject such as he would at no time have been competent to treat. He was in no sense a statesman. He never willingly read or thought or talked about affairs of state. He loved biography, literary history, the history of manners; but political history was positively distasteful to him. The question at issue between the colonies and the mother country was a question about which he had really nothing to say. He failed, therefore, as the greatest men must fail when they attempt to do that for which they are unfit; as Burke would have failed if Burke had tried to write comedies like those of Sheridan; as Reynolds would have failed if Reynolds had tried to paint landscapes like those of Wilson. Happily, Johnson soon had an opportunity of proving most signally that his failure was not to be ascribed to intellectual decay.

On Easter eve 1777, some persons, deputed by a meeting which consisted of forty of the first booksellers in London, called upon him. Though he had some scruples about doing business at that season, he received his visitors with much civility. They came to inform him that a new edition of the English poets, from Cowley downwards, was in contemplation, and to ask him to furnish short biographical prefaces. He readily undertook the task, a task for which he was pre-eminently qualified. His knowledge of the literary history of England since the Restoration was unrivalled. That knowledge he had derived partly from books, and partly from sources which had long been closed; from old Grub Street traditions; from the talk of forgotten poetasters and pamphleteers who had long been lying in parish vaults; from the recollections of such men as Gilbert Walmesley, who had conversed with the wits of Button; Cibber, who had mutilated the plays of two generations of dramatists; Orrery, who had been admitted to the society of Swift; and Savage, who had rendered services of no very honourable kind to Pope. The biographer therefore sate down to his task with a mind full of matter. He had at first intended to give only a paragraph to every minor poet, and only four or five pages to the greatest name. But the flood of anecdote and criticism overflowed the narrow channel. The work, which was originally meant to consist only of a few sheets, swelled into ten volumes, small volumes, it is true, and not closely printed. The first four appeared in 1779, the remaining six in 1781.

The Lives of the Poets are, on the whole, the best of Johnson's works. The narratives are as entertaining as any novel. The remarks on life and on human nature are eminently shrewd and profound. The criticisms are often excellent, and, even when grossly and provokingly unjust, well deserve to be studied. For, however erroneous they may be, they are never silly. They are the judgments of a mind trammelled by prejudice and deficient in sensibility, but vigorous and acute. They therefore generally contain a portion of valuable truth which deserves to be separated from the alloy; and, at the very worst, they mean something, a praise to which much of what is called criticism in our time has no pretensions.

Savage's Life Johnson reprinted nearly as it had appeared in 1744. Whoever, after reading that life, will turn to the other lives will be struck by the difference of style. Since Johnson had been at ease in his circumstances he had written little and had talked much. When, therefore, he, after the lapse of years, resumed his pen, the mannerism which he had contracted while he was in the constant habit of elaborate composition was less perceptible than formerly; and his diction frequently had a colloquial ease which it had formerly wanted. The improvement may be discerned by a skilful critic in the Journey to the Hebrides, and in the Lives of the Poets is so obvious that it cannot escape the notice of the most careless reader.

Among the lives the best are perhaps those of Cowley, Dryden, and Pope. The very worst is, beyond all doubt, that of Gray.

This great work at once became popular. There was, indeed, much just and much unjust censure: but even those who were loudest in blame were attracted by the book in spite of themselves. Malone computed the gains of the publishers at five or six thousand pounds. But the writer was very poorly remunerated. Intending at first to write very short prefaces, he had stipulated for only two hundred guineas. The booksellers, when they saw how far his performance had surpassed his promise, added only another hundred. Indeed, Johnson, though he did not despise, or affect to despise money, and though his strong sense and long experience ought to have qualified him to protect his own interests, seems to have been singularly unskilful and unlucky in his literary bargains. He was generally reputed the first English writer of his time. Yet several writers of his time sold their copyrights for sums such as he never ventured to ask. To give a single instance, Robertson received four thousand five hundred pounds for the History of Charles V.; and it is no disrespect to the memory of Robertson to say that the History of Charles V. is both a less valuable and a less amusing book than the Lives of the Poets.

Johnson was now in his seventy-second year. The infirmities of age were coming fast upon him. That inevitable event of which he never thought without horror was brought near to him; and his whole life was darkened by the shadow of death. He had often to pay the cruel price of longevity. Every year he lost what could never be replaced. The strange dependents to whom he had given shelter, and to whom, in spite of their faults, he was strongly attached by habit, dropped off one by one; and, in the silence of his home, he regretted even the noise of their scolding matches. The kind and generous Thrale was no more; and it would have been well if his wife had been laid beside him. But she survived to be the laughing-stock of those who had envied her, and to draw from the eyes of the old man who had loved her beyond anything in the world tears far more bitter than he would have shed over her grave. With some estimable and many agreeable qualities, she was not made to be independent. The control of a mind more steadfast than her own was necessary to her respectability. While she was restrained by her husband, a man of sense and firmness, indulgent to her taste in trifles, but always the undisputed master of his house, her worst offences had been impertinent jokes, white lies, and short fits of pettishness ending in sunny good humour. But he was gone; and she was left an opulent widow of forty, with strong sensibility, volatile fancy, and slender judgment. She soon fell in love with a music-master from Brescia, in whom nobody but herself could discover anything to admire. Her pride, and perhaps some better feelings, struggled hard against this degrading passion. But the struggle irritated her nerves, soured her temper, and at length endangered her health. Conscious that her choice was one which Johnson could not approve, she became desirous to escape from his inspection. Her manner towards him changed. She was sometimes cold and sometimes petulant. She did not conceal her joy when he left Streatham; she never pressed him to return; and, if he came unbidden, she received him in a manner which convinced him that he was no longer a welcome guest. He took the very intelligible hints which she gave. He read, for the last time, a chapter of the Greek Testament in the library which had been formed by himself. In a solemn and tender prayer he commended the house and its inmates to the Divine protection, and, with emotions which choked his voice and convulsed his powerful frame, left for ever that beloved home for the gloomy and desolate house behind Fleet Street, where the few and evil days which still remained to him were to run out. Here, in June 1783, he had a paralytic stroke, from which, however, he recovered, and which does not appear to have at all impaired his intellectual faculties. But other maladies came thick upon him. His asthma tormented him day and night. Dropsical symptoms made their appearance. While sinking under a complication of diseases, he heard that the woman whose friend-ship had been the chief happiness of sixteen years of his life had married an Italian fiddler; that all London was crying shame upon her; and that the newspapers and magazines were filled with allusions to the Ephesian matron, and the two pictures in Hamlet. He vehemently said that he would try to forget her existence. He never uttered her name. Every memorial of her which met his eye he flung into the fire. She meanwhile fled from the laughter and hisses of her countrymen and countrywomen to a land where she was unknown, hastened across Mount Cenis, and learned, while passing a merry Christmas of concerts and lemonade parties at Milan, that the great man with whose name hers is inseparably associated had ceased to exist.

He had, in spite of much mental and much bodily affliction, clung vehemently to life. The feeling described in that fine but gloomy paper which closes the series of his Idlers seemed to grow stronger in him as his last hour drew near. He fancied that he should be able to draw his breath more easily in a southern climate, and would probably have set out for Rome and Naples, but for his fear of the expense of the journey. That expense, indeed, he had the means of defraying; for he had laid up about two thousand pounds, the fruit of labours which had made the fortune of several publishers. But he was unwilling to break in upon this hoard, and he seems to have wished even to keep its existence a secret. Some of his friends hoped that the government might be induced to increase his pension to six hundred pounds a-year: but this hope was disappointed; and he resolved to stand one English winter more. That winter was his last. His legs grew weaker; his breath grew shorter; the fatal water gathered fast, in spite of incisions which he, courageous against pain, but timid against death, urged his surgeons to make deeper and deeper. Though the tender care which had mitigated his sufferings during months of sickness at Streatham was withdrawn, he was not left desolate. The ablest physicians and surgeons attended him, and refused to accept fees from him. Burke parted from him with deep emotion. Windham sate much in the sick room, arranged the pillows, and sent his own servant to watch a night by the bed. Frances Burney, whom the old man had cherished with fatherly kindness, stood weeping at the door; while Langton, whose piety eminently qualified him to be an adviser and comforter at such a time, received the last pressure of his friend's hand within. When at length the moment, dreaded through so many years, came close, the dark cloud passed away from Johnson's mind. His temper became unusually patient and gentle; he ceased to think with terror of death, and of that which lies beyond death; and he spoke much of the mercy of God, and of the propitiation of Christ. In this serene frame of mind he died on the 13th of December, 1784. He was laid, a week later, in Westminster Abbey, among the eminent men of whom he had been the historian,—Cowley and Denham, Dryden and Congreve, Gay, Prior, and Addison.

Since his death the popularity of his works—the Lives of the Poets, and perhaps, the Vanity of Human Wishes, excepted—has greatly diminished. His Dictionary has been altered by editors till it can scarcely be called his. An allusion to his Rambler or his Idler is not readily apprehended in literary circles. The fame even of Rasselas has grown somewhat dim. But though the celebrity of the writings may have declined, the celebrity of the writer, strange to say, is as great as ever. Boswell's book has done for him more than the best of his own books could do. The memory of other authors is kept alive by their works. But the memory of Johnson keeps many of his works alive. The old philosopher is still among us in the brown coat with the metal buttons and the shirt which ought to be at wash, blinking, puffing, rolling his head, drumming with his fingers, tearing his meat like a tiger, and swallowing his tea in oceans. No human being who has been more than seventy years in the grave is so well known to us. And it is but just to say that our intimate acquaintance with what he himself would have called the anfractuosities of his intellect and of his temper serves only to strengthen our conviction that he was both a great and a good man.

# III. *Controversial Essays*

## MILL ON GOVERNMENT

(MARCH 1829)

*Essays on Government, Jurisprudence, the Liberty of the Press, Prisons and Prison Discipline, Colonies, the Law of Nations, and Education.* By JAMES MILL, Esq. author of the History of British India. Reprinted by permission from the Supplement to the Encyclopædia Britannica. (Not for sale.) London, 1828.

OF those philosophers who call themselves Utilitarians, and whom others generally call Benthamites, Mr. Mill is, with the exception of the illustrious founder of the sect, by far the most distinguished. The little work now before us contains a summary of the opinions held by this gentleman and his brethren on several subjects most important to society. All the seven Essays, of which it consists, abound in curious matter. But at present we intend to confine our remarks to the Treatise on Government, which stands first in the volume. On some future occasion, we may perhaps attempt to do justice to the rest.

It must be owned, that, to do justice to any composition of Mr. Mill is not, in the opinion of his admirers, a very easy task. They do not, indeed, place him in the same rank with Mr. Bentham; but the terms in which they extol the disciple, though feeble when compared with the hyperboles of adoration employed by them in speaking of the master, are as strong as any sober man would allow himself to use concerning Locke or Bacon. The Essay before us is perhaps the most remarkable of the works to which Mr. Mill owes his fame. By the members of his sect, it is considered as perfect and unanswerable. Every part of it is an article of their faith; and the damnatory clauses, in which their creed abounds far beyond any theological symbol with which we are acquainted, are strong and full against all who reject any portion of what is so irrefragably established. No man, they maintain, who has understanding sufficient to carry him through the first proposition of Euclid, can read this master-piece of demonstration, and honestly declare that he remains unconvinced.

We have formed a very different opinion of this work. We think that the theory of Mr. Mill rests altogether on false principles, and that even on those false principles he does not reason logically. Nevertheless, we do not think it strange that his speculations should have filled the Utilitarians with admiration. We have been for some time past inclined to suspect that these people, whom some regard as the lights of the world, and others as incarnate demons, are in general ordinary men, with narrow understandings, and little information. The contempt which they express for elegant literature, is evidently the contempt of ignorance. We apprehend that many of them are persons who, having read little or nothing, are delighted to be rescued from the sense of their own inferiority by some teacher, who assures them that the studies which they have neglected are of no value, puts five or six phrases into their mouths, lends them an odd number of the Westminster Review, and in a month transforms them into philosophers. Mingled with these smatterers, whose attainments just suffice to elevate them from the insignificance of dunces to the dignity of bores, and to spread dismay among their pious aunts and grandmothers, there are, we well know, many well-meaning men, who have really read and thought much; but whose reading and meditation have been almost exclusively confined to one class of subjects; and who, consequently, though they possess much valuable knowledge respecting those subjects, are by no means so well qualified to judge of a great system as if they had taken a more enlarged view of literature and society.

Nothing is more amusing or instructive than to observe the manner in which people, who think themselves wiser than all the rest of the world, fall into snares which the simple good sense of their neighbours detects and avoids. It is one of the principal tenets of the Utilitarians, that sentiment and eloquence serve only to impede the pursuit of truth. They therefore affect a quakerly plainness, or rather a cynical negligence and impurity of style. The strongest arguments, when clothed in brilliant language, seem to them so much wordy nonsense. In the mean time they surrender their understandings, with a facility found in no other party, to the meanest and most abject sophisms, provided those sophisms come before them disguised with the externals of demonstration. They do not seem to know that logic has its illusions as well as rhetoric,— that a fallacy may lurk in a syllogism as well as in a metaphor.

Mr. Mill is exactly the writer to please people of this description. His arguments are stated with the utmost affectation of precision; his divisions are awfully formal; and his style is generally as dry as that of Euclid's Elements. Whether this be a merit, we must be permitted to doubt. Thus much is certain, that the ages in which the true principles of philosophy were least understood, were those in which the ceremonial of logic was most strictly observed, and that the time from which we date the rapid progress of the experimental sciences was also the time at which a less exact and formal way of writing came into use.

The style which the Utilitarians admire, suits only those subjects on which it is possible to reason *a priori*. It grew up with the verbal sophistry which flourished during the dark ages. With that sophistry it fell before the Baconian philosophy, in the day of the great deliverance of the human mind. The inductive method not only endured, but required greater freedom of diction. It was impossible to reason from phenomena up to principles, to mark slight shades of difference in quality, or to estimate the comparative effect of two opposite considerations between which there was no common measure, by means of the naked and meagre jargon of the schoolmen. Of those schoolmen Mr. Mill has inherited both the spirit and the style. He is an Aristotelian of the fifteenth century, born out of due season. We have here an elaborate treatise on Government, from which, but for two or three passing allusions, it would not appear that the author was aware that any governments actually existed among men. Certain propensities of Human Nature are assumed; and from these premises the whole science of Politics is synthetically deduced! We can scarcely persuade ourselves that we are not reading a book written before the time of Bacon and Galileo,—a book written in those days in which physicians reasoned from the nature of heat to the treatment of fever, and astronomers proved syllogistically that the planets could have no independent motion,—because the heavens were incorruptible, and nature abhorred a vacuum!

The reason, too, which Mr. Mill has assigned for taking this course strikes us as most extraordinary.

"Experience," says he, "if we look only at the outside of the facts, appears to be *divided* on this subject. Absolute monarchy, under Neros and Caligulas, under such men as the Emperors of Morocco and Sultans of Turkey, is the scourge of human nature. On the other side, the people of Denmark, tired out with the oppression of an aristocracy, resolved that their king should be absolute; and, under their absolute monarch, are as well governed as any people in Europe."

This Mr. Mill actually gives as a reason for pursuing the *a priori* method. But, in our judgment, the very circumstances which he mentions, irresistibly prove that the *a priori* method is altogether unfit for investigations of this kind, and that the only way to arrive at the truth is by induction. *Experience* can never be divided, or even appear to be divided, except with reference to some hypothesis.

When we say that one fact is inconsistent with another fact, we mean only that it is inconsistent with *the theory* which we have founded on that other fact. But, if the fact be certain, the unavoidable conclusion is that our theory is false; and, in order to correct it, we must reason back from an enlarged collection of facts to principles.

Now here we have two governments which, by Mr. Mill's own account, come under the same head in his *theoretical* classification. It is evident, therefore, that, by reasoning on that theoretical classification, we shall be brought to the conclusion that these two forms of government must produce the same effects. But Mr. Mill himself tells us that they do not produce the same effects. Hence he infers that the only way to get at truth is to place implicit confidence in that chain of proof *a priori*, from which it appears that they must produce the same effects! To believe at once in a theory, and in a fact which contradicts it, is an exercise of faith sufficiently hard: But, to believe in a theory *because* a fact contradicts it, is what neither philosopher nor pope ever before required. This, however, is what Mr. Mill demands of us. He seems to think that if all despots, without exception, governed ill, it would be unnecessary to prove, by a synthetical argument, what would then be sufficiently clear from experience. But as some despots will be so perverse as to govern well, he finds himself compelled to prove the impossibility of their governing well, by that synthetical argument, which would have been superfluous had not the facts contradicted it. He reasons *a priori*, because the phenomena are not what, by reasoning *a priori*, he will prove them to be. In other words, he reasons *a priori*, because, by so reasoning, he is certain to arrive at a false conclusion!

In the course of the examination to which we propose to subject the speculations of Mr. Mill, we shall have to notice many other curious instances of that turn of mind which the passage above quoted indicates.

The first chapter of his Essay relates to the ends of government. The conception on this subject, he tell us, which exists in the minds of most men is vague and undistinguishing. He first assumes, justly enough, that the end of government is "to increase to the utmost the pleasures, and diminish to the utmost the pains, which men derive from each other." He then proceeds to show, with great form, that "the greatest possible happiness of society is attained by insuring to every man the greatest possible quantity of the produce of his labour." To effect this is, in his opinion, the end of government. It is remarkable that Mr. Mill, with all his affected display of precision, has here given a description of the ends of government far less precise than that which is in the mouths of the vulgar. The first man with whom Mr. Mill may travel in a stage-coach, will tell him that government exists for the protection of the *persons* and property of men. But Mr. Mill seems to think that the preservation of property is the first and only object. It is true, doubtless, that many of the injuries which are offered to the persons of men, proceed from a desire to possess their property. But the practice of vindictive assassination as it has existed in some parts of Europe—the practice of fighting wanton and sanguinary duels, like those of the sixteenth and seventeenth centuries, in which bands of seconds risked their lives as well as the principals;—these practices, and many others which might be named, are evidently injurious to society; and we do not see how a government which tolerated them could be said "to diminish to the utmost the pains which men derive from each other." Therefore, according to Mr. Mill's very correct assumption, such a government would not perfectly accomplish the end of its institution. Yet such a government might, as far as we can perceive, "insure to every man the greatest possible quantity of the produce of his labour." Therefore such a government might, according to Mr. Mill's subsequent doctrine, perfectly accomplish the end of its institution. The matter is not of much consequence, except as an instance of that slovenliness of thinking which is often concealed beneath a peculiar ostentation of logical neatness.

Having determined the ends, Mr. Mill proceeds to consider the means. For the preservation of property, some portion of the community must be intrusted with power. This is Government; and the question is, how are those to whom the necessary power is intrusted to be prevented from abusing it?

Mr. Mill first passes in review the simple forms of government. He allows that it would be inconvenient, if not physically impossible, that the whole community should meet in a mass; it follows, therefore, that the powers of government cannot be directly exercised by the people. But he sees no objection to pure and direct Democracy, except the difficulty which we have mentioned.

"The community," says he, "cannot have an interest opposite to its interests. To affirm this would be a contradiction in terms. The community within itself, and with respect to itself, can have no sinister interest. One community may intend the evil of another; never its own. This is an indubitable proposition, and one of great importance."

Mr. Mill then proceeds to demonstrate, that a purely Aristocratical form of government is necessarily bad.

"The reason for which government exists, is, that one man, if stronger than another, will take from him whatever that other possesses and he desires. But if one man will do this, so will several. And if powers are put into the hands of a comparatively small number, called an aristocracy,—powers which make them stronger than the rest of the community, they will take from the rest of the community as much as they please of the objects of desire. They will thus defeat the very end for which government was instituted. The unfitness, therefore, of an aristocracy to be intrusted with the powers of government, rests on demonstration."

In exactly the same manner Mr. Mill proves absolute monarchy to be a bad form of government.

"If government is founded upon this as a law of human nature, that a man, if able, will take from others any thing which they have and he desires, it is sufficiently evident, that when a man is called a king he does not change his nature; so that when he has got power to enable him to take from every man what he pleases, he will take whatever he pleases. To suppose that he will not, is to affirm that government is unnecessary, and that human beings will abstain from injuring one another of their own accord.

"It is very evident that this reasoning extends to every modification of the smaller number. Whenever the powers of government are placed in any hands other than those of the community, whether those of one man, of a few, or of several, those principles of human nature which imply that government is at all necessary, imply that those persons will make use of them to defeat the very end for which government exists."

But is it not possible that a king or an aristocracy may soon be saturated with the objects of their desires, and may then protect the community in the enjoyment of the rest? Mr. Mill answers in the negative. He proves, with great pomp, that every man desires to have the actions of every other correspondent to his will. Others can be induced to conform to our will only by motives derived from pleasure or from pain. The infliction of pain is of course direct injury; and even if it take the milder course, in order to produce obedience by motives derived from pleasure, the government must confer favours. But, as there is no limit to its desire of obedience, there will be no limit to its disposition to confer favours; and, as it can confer favours only by plundering the people, there will be no limit to its disposition to plunder the people. "It is therefore not true, that there is in the mind of a king, or in the minds of an aristocracy, any point of saturation with the objects of desire."

Mr. Mill then proceeds to show, that as monarchical and oligarchical governments can influence men by motives drawn from pain, as well as by motives drawn from pleasure, they will carry their cruelty, as well as their rapacity, to a frightful extent. As he seems greatly to admire his own reasonings on this subject, we think it but fair to let him speak for himself.

"The chain of inference in this case is close and strong to a most unusual degree. A man desires that the actions of other men shall be instantly and accurately correspondent to his will. He desires that the actions of the greatest possible number shall be so. Terror is the grand instrument. Terror can work only through assurance that evil will follow any failure of conformity between the will and the actions willed. Every failure must therefore be punished. As there are no bounds to the mind's desire of its pleasure, there are, of course, no bounds to its desire of perfection in the instruments of that pleasure. There are, therefore, no bounds to its desire of exactness in the conformity between its will and the actions willed; and by consequence to the strength of that terror which is its procuring cause. Every the most minute failure must be visited with the heaviest infliction; and as failure in extreme exactness must frequently happen, the occasions of cruelty must be incessant.

"We have thus arrived at several conclusions of the highest possible importance. We have seen that the principle of human nature, upon which the necessity of government is founded, the propensity of one man to possess himself of the objects of desire at the cost of another, leads on, by infallible sequence, where power over a community is attained, and nothing checks, not only to that degree of plunder which leaves the members (excepting always the recipients and instruments of the plunder) the bare means of subsistence, but to that degree of cruelty which is necessary to keep in existence the most intense terrors."

Now, no man who has the least knowledge of the real state of the world, either in former ages or at the present moment, can possibly be convinced, though he may perhaps be bewildered, by arguments like these. During the last two centuries, some hundreds of absolute princes have reigned in Europe. Is it true, that their cruelty has kept in existence the most intense degree of terror, that their rapacity has left no more than the bare means of subsistence to any of their subjects, their ministers and soldiers excepted? Is this true of all of them? Of one half of them? Of one tenth part of them? Of a single one? Is it true, in the full extent, even of Philip the Second, of Lewis the Fifteenth, or of the Emperor Paul? But it is scarcely necessary to quote history. No man of common sense, however ignorant he may be of books, can be imposed on by Mr. Mill's argument; because no man of common sense can live among his fellow-creatures for a day without seeing innumerable

M—19*

facts which contradict it. It is our business, however, to point out its fallacy; and happily the fallacy is not very recondite.

We grant that rulers will take as much as they can of the objects of their desires; and that, when the agency of other men is necessary to that end, they will attempt by all means in their power to enforce the prompt obedience of such men. But what are the objects of human desire? Physical pleasure, no doubt, in part. But the mere appetites which we have in common with the animals, would be gratified almost as cheaply and easily as those of the animals are gratified, if nothing were given to taste, to ostentation, or to the affections. How small a portion of the income of a gentleman in easy circumstances is laid out merely in giving pleasurable sensations to the body of the possessor! The greater part even of what is spent on his kitchen and his cellar, goes not to titillate his palate, but to keep up his character for hospitality, to save him from the reproach of meanness in housekeeping, and to cement the ties of good neighbourhood. It is clear, that a king or an aristocracy may be supplied to satiety with mere corporal pleasures, at an expense which the rudest and poorest community would scarcely feel.

Those tastes and propensities which belong to us as reasoning and imaginative beings are not indeed so easily gratified. There is, we admit, no point of saturation with objects of desire which come under this head. And therefore the argument of Mr. Mill will be just, unless there be something in the nature of the objects of desire themselves which is inconsistent with it. Now, of these objects there is none which men in general seem to desire more than the good opinion of others. The hatred and contempt of the public are generally felt to be intolerable. It is probable, that our regard for the sentiments of our fellow-creatures springs by association from a sense of their ability to hurt or to serve us. But be this as it may, it is notorious, that when the habit of mind of which we speak has once been formed, men feel extremely solicitous about the opinions of those by whom it is most improbable, nay, absolutely impossible, that they should ever be in the slightest degree injured or benefited. The desire of posthumous fame, and the dread of posthumous reproach and execration, are feelings from the influence of which scarcely any man is perfectly free, and which in many men are powerful and constant motives of action. As we are afraid that, if we handle this part of the argument after our own manner, we shall incur the reproach of sentimentality, a word which, in the sacred language of the Benthamites, is synonymous with idiocy, we will quote what Mr. Mill himself says on the subject, in his Treatise on Jurisprudence.

"Pains from the moral source are the pains derived from the unfavourable sentiments of mankind. . . . . These pains are capable of rising to a height with which hardly any other pains incident to our nature can be compared. There is a certain degree of unfavourableness in the sentiments of his fellow-creatures, under which hardly any man, not below the standard of humanity, can endure to live.

"The importance of this powerful agency, for the prevention of injurious acts, is too obvious to need to be illustrated. If sufficiently at command, it would almost supersede the use of other means. . . . .

"To know how to direct the unfavourable sentiments of mankind, it is necessary to know in as complete, that is, in as comprehensive, a way as possible, what it is which gives them birth. Without entering into the metaphysics of the question, it is a sufficient practical answer, for the present purpose, to say that the unfavourable sentiments of man are excited by every thing which hurts them."

It is strange that a writer who considers the pain derived from the unfavourable sentiments of others as so acute, that, if sufficiently at command, it would supersede the use of the gallows and the tread-mill, should take no notice of this most important restraint, when discussing the question of Government. We will attempt to deduce a theory of politics in the mathematical form, in which Mr. Mill delights, from the premises with which he has himself furnished us.

PROPOSITION I. THEOREM.

No rulers will do any thing which may hurt the people.

This is the thesis to be maintained; and the following we humbly offer to Mr. Mill, as its syllogistic demonstration.

No rulers will do that which produces pain to themselves.

But the unfavourable sentiments of the people will give pain to them.

Therefore no rulers will do any thing which may excite the unfavourable sentiments of the people.

But the unfavourable sentiments of the people are excited by every thing which hurts them.

Therefore no rulers will do any thing which may hurt the people, which was the thing to be proved.

Having thus, as we think, not unsuccessfully imitated Mr. Mill's logic, we do not see why we should not imitate, what is at least equally perfect in its kind, his self-complacency, and proclaim our Ἔυρηκα in his own words: "The chain of inference, in this case, is close and strong to a most unusual degree."

The fact is, that, when men, in treating of things which cannot be circumscribed by precise definitions, adopt this mode of reasoning, when once they begin to talk of power, happiness, misery, pain, pleasure, motives, objects of desire, as they talk of lines and numbers, there is no end to the contradictions and absurdities into which they fall. There is no proposition so monstrously untrue in morals or politics that we will not undertake to prove it, by something which shall sound like a logical demonstration, from admitted principles.

Mr. Mill argues, that if men are not inclined to plunder each other, government is unnecessary; and that, if they are so inclined, the powers of government, when intrusted to a small number of them, will necessarily be abused. Surely it is not by propounding dilemmas of this sort, that we are likely to arrive at sound conclusions in any moral science. The whole question is a question of degree. If all men preferred the moderate approbation of their neighbours, to any degree of wealth or grandeur, or sensual pleasure, government would be unnecessary. If all men desired wealth so intensely as to be willing to brave the hatred of their fellow-creatures for sixpence, Mr. Mill's argument against monarchies and aristocracies would be true to the full extent. But the fact is, that all men have some desires which impel them to injure their neighbours, and some desires which impel them to benefit their neighbours. Now, if there were a community consisting of two classes of men, one of which should be principally influenced by the one set of motives and the other by the other, government would clearly be necessary to restrain the class which was eager for plunder, and careless of reputation: and yet the powers of government might be safely intrusted to the class which was chiefly actuated by the love of approbation. Now, it might, with no small plausibility be maintained, that, in many countries, *there are* two classes which, in some degree, answer to this description; that the poor compose the class which government is established to restrain; and the people of some property the class to which the powers of government may without danger be confided. It might be said that a man who can barely earn a livelihood by severe labour, is under stronger temptations to pillage others than a man who enjoys many luxuries. It might be said that a man who is lost in the crowd is less likely to have the fear of public opinion before his eyes, than a man whose station and mode of living render him conspicuous. We do not assert all this. We only say, that it was Mr. Mill's business to prove the contrary; and that, not having proved the contrary, he is not entitled to say, "that those principles which imply that government is at all necessary, imply that an aristocracy will make use of its power to defeat the end for which governments exist." This is not true, unless it be true that a rich man is as likely to covet the goods of his neighbours as a poor man; and that a poor man is as likely to be solicitous about the opinions of his neighbours as a rich man.

But we do not see that, by reasoning *a priori* on such subjects as these, it is possible to advance one single step. We know that every man has some desires which he can gratify only by hurting his neighbours, and some which he can gratify only by pleasing them. Mr. Mill has chosen to look only at one-half of human nature, and to reason on the motives which impel men to oppress and despoil others, as if they were the only motives by which men could possibly be influenced. We have already shown that, by taking the other half of the human character, and reasoning on it as if it were the whole, we can bring out a result diametrically opposite to that at which Mr. Mill has arrived. We can, by such a process, easily prove that any form of government is good, or that all government is superfluous.

We must now accompany Mr. Mill on the next stage of his argument. Does any combination of the three simple forms of government afford the requisite securities against the abuse of power? Mr. Mill complains that those who maintain the affirmative generally beg the question, and proceeds to settle the point by proving, after his fashion, that no combination of the three simple forms, or of any two of them, can possibly exist.

"From the principles which we have already laid down it follows that, of the objects of human desire, and, speaking more definitely, of the means to the ends of human desire, namely, wealth and power, each party will endeavour to obtain as much as possible.

"If any expedient presents itself to any of the supposed parties effectual to this end, and not opposed to any preferred object of pursuit, we may infer, with certainty, that it will be adopted.    One effectual expedient is not more effectual than obvious. Any two of the parties, by combining may swallow up the third. That such combination will take place appears to be as certain as any thing which depends upon human will; because there are strong motives in favour of it, and none that can be conceived in opposition to it. . . . . The mixture of three of the kinds of government, it is thus evident, cannot possibly exist. . . . . It may be proper to enquire, whether an union may not be possible of two of them. . . .

"Let us first suppose, that monarchy is united with aristocracy. Their power is equal or not equal. If it is not equal, it follows, as a necessary consequence, from the principles which we have already established, that the stronger will take from the weaker till it engrosses the whole. The only question therefore is, What will happen when the power is equal?

"In the first place, it seems impossible that such equality should ever exist. How is it to be established? or, By what criterion is it to be ascertained? If there is no such criterion, it must, in all cases, be the result of chance. If so, the chances against it are as infinity to one. The idea, therefore, is wholly chimerical and absurd. . . .

"In this doctrine of the mixture of the simple forms of government is included the celebrated theory of the balance among the component parts of a government. By this it is supposed that, when a government is composed of monarchy, aristocracy, and democracy, they balance one another, and by mutual checks produce good government. A few words will suffice to show that, if any theory deserves the epithets of 'wild, visionary, and chimerical,' it is that of the balance. If there are three powers, How is it possible to prevent two of them from combining to swallow up the third?

"The analysis which we have already performed will enable us to trace rapidly the concatenation of causes and effects in this imagined case.

"We have already seen that the interest of the community, considered in the aggregate, or in the democratical point of view, is, that each individual should receive protection; and that the powers which are constituted for that purpose should be employed exclusively for that purpose. . . . . We have also seen that the interest of the king and of the governing aristocracy is directly the reverse. It is to have unlimited power over the rest of the community, and to use it for their own advantage. In the supposed case of the balance of the monarchical, aristocratical, and democratical powers, it cannot be for the interest of either the monarchy or the aristocracy to combine with the democracy; because it is the interest of the democracy, or community at large, that neither the king nor the aristocracy should have one particle of power, or one particle of the wealth of the community, for their own advantage.

"The democracy or community have all possible motives to endeavour to prevent the monarchy and aristocracy from exercising power, or obtaining the wealth of the community for their own advantage. The monarchy and aristocracy have all possible motives for endeavouring to obtain unlimited power over the persons and property of the community. The consequence is inevitable: they have all possible motives for combining to obtain that power."

If any part of this passage be more eminently absurd than another, it is, we think, the argument by which Mr. Mill proves that there cannot be an union of monarchy and aristocracy. Their power, he says, must be equal or not equal. But of equality there is no criterion. Therefore the chances against its existence are as infinity to one. If the power be not equal, then it follows, from the principles of human nature, that the stronger will take from the weaker, till it has engrossed the whole.

Now, if there be no criterion of equality between two portions of power, there can be no common measure of portions of power. Therefore it is utterly impossible to compare them together. But where two portions of power are of the same kind, there is no difficulty in ascertaining, sufficiently for all practical purposes, whether they are equal or unequal. It is easy to judge whether two men run equally fast, or can lift equal weights. Two arbitrators, whose joint decision is to be final, and neither of whom can do any thing without the assent of the other, possess equal power. Two electors, each of whom has a vote for a borough, possess, in that respect, equal power. If not, all Mr. Mill's political theories fall to the ground at once. For, if it be impossible to ascertain whether two portions of power are equal, he never can show that, even under a system of universal suffrage, a minority might not carry every thing their own way, against the wishes and interests of the majority.

Where there are two portions of power differing in kind, there is, we admit, no criterion of equality. But then, in such a case, it is absurd to talk, as Mr. Mill does, about the stronger and the weaker. Popularly, indeed, and with reference to some particular objects, these words may very fairly be used. But to use them mathematically is altogether improper. If we are speaking of a boxing-match, we may say that some famous bruiser has greater bodily power than any man in England. If we are speaking of a pantomime, we may say the same of some very agile Harlequin. But it would be talking nonsense to say, in general, that the power of Harlequin either exceeded that of the pugilist, or fell short of it.

If Mr. Mill's argument be good as between different branches of a legislature, it is equally good as between sovereign powers. Every government, it may be said, will, if it can, take the objects of its desires from every other. If the French government can subdue England, it will do so. If the English government can subdue France, it will do so. But the power of England and France is either equal or not equal. The chance that it is not exactly equal is as infinity to one, and may safely be left out of the account; and then the stronger will infallibly take from the weaker till the weaker is altogether enslaved.

Surely the answer to all this hubbub of unmeaning words is the plainest possible. For some purposes, France is stronger than England. For some purposes, England is stronger than France. For some, neither has any power at all. France has the greater population, England the greater capital; France has the greater army, England the greater fleet. For an expedition to Rio Janeiro or the

Philippines, England has the greater power. For a war on the Po or the Danube, France has the greater power. But neither has power sufficient to keep the other in quiet subjection for a month. Invasion would be very perilous; the idea of complete conquest on either side utterly ridiculous. This is the manly and sensible way of discussing such questions. The *ergo*, or rather the *argal*, of Mr. Mill cannot impose on a child. Yet we ought scarcely to say this; for we remember to have heard *a child* ask whether Bonaparte was stronger than an elephant!

Mr. Mill reminds us of those philosophers of the sixteenth century, who, having satisfied themselves *a priori* that the rapidity with which bodies descended to the earth varied exactly as their weights, refused to believe the contrary on the evidence of their own eyes and ears. The British constitution, according to Mr. Mill's classification, is a mixture of monarchy and aristocracy; one House of Parliament being composed of hereditary nobles, and the other almost entirely chosen by a privileged class, who possess the elective franchise on account of their property, or their connexion with certain corporations. Mr. Mill's argument proves that, from the time that these two powers were mingled in our government, that is, from the very first dawn of our history, one or the other must have been constantly encroaching. According to him, moreover, all the encroachments must have been on one side. For the first encroachment could only have been made by the stronger; and that first encroachment would have made the stronger stronger still. It is, therefore, matter of absolute demonstration, that either the Parliament was stronger than the Crown in the reign of Henry VIII., or that the Crown was stronger than the Parliament in 1641. "Hippocrate dira ce que lui plaira," says the girl in Moliere; "mais le cocher est mort." Mr. Mill may say what he pleases; but the English constitution is still alive. That, since the Revolution the Parliament has possessed great power in the state, is what nobody will dispute. The King, on the other hand, can create new peers, and can dissolve Parliaments. William sustained severe mortifications from the House of Commons, and was, indeed, unjustifiably oppressed. Anne was desirous to change a ministry which had a majority in both Houses. She watched her moment for a dissolution, created twelve Tory peers, and succeeded. Thirty years later, the House of Commons drove Walpole from his seat. In 1784, George III. was able to keep Mr. Pitt in office in the face of a majority of the House of Commons. In 1804, the apprehension of a defeat in Parliament compelled the same King to part from his most favoured minister. But, in 1807, he was able to do exactly what Anne had done nearly a hundred years before. Now, had the power of the King increased during the intervening century, or had it remained stationary? Is it possible that the one lot among the infinite number should have fallen to us? If not, Mr. Mill has proved that one of the two parties must have been constantly taking from the other. Many of the ablest men in England think that the influence of the Crown has, on the whole, increased since the reign of Anne. Others think that the Parliament has been growing in strength. But of this there is no doubt, that both sides possessed great power then, and possess great power now. Surely, if there were the least truth in the argument of Mr. Mill, it could not possibly be a matter of doubt, at the end of a hundred and twenty years, whether the one side or the other had been the gainer.

But we ask pardon. We forgot that a fact, irreconcilable with Mr. Mill's theory, furnishes, in his opinion, the strongest reason for adhering to the theory. To take up the question in another manner, is it not plain that there may be two bodies, each possessing a perfect and entire power, which cannot be taken from it without its own concurrence? What is the meaning of the words stronger and weaker, when applied to such bodies as these? The one may, indeed, by physical force, altogether destroy the other. But this is not the question. A third party, a general of their own, for example, may, by physical force, subjugate them both: Nor is there any form of government, Mr. Mill's Utopian democracy not excepted, secure from such an occurrence. We are speaking of the powers with which the constitution invests the two branches of the legislature; and we ask Mr. Mill how, on his own principles, he can maintain that one of them will be able to encroach on the other, if the consent of the other be necessary to such encroachment?

Mr. Mill tells us that, if a government be composed of the three simple forms, which he will not admit the British constitution to be, two of the component parts will inevitably join against the third. Now, if two of them combine and act as one, this case evidently resolves itself into the last; and all the observations which we have just made will fully apply to it. Mr. Mill says, that "any two of the parties, by combining, may swallow up the third;" and afterwards asks, "How it is possible to prevent two of them from combining to swallow up the third?" Surely Mr. Mill must be aware that in politics two is not always the double of one. If the concurrence of all the three branches of the legislature be necessary to every law, each branch will possess constitutional power sufficient to protect it against any thing but that physical force, from which no form of government is secure. Mr. Mill reminds us of the Irishman, who could not be brought to understand how one juryman could possibly starve out eleven others.

But is it certain that two of the branches of the legislature will combine against the third? "It appears to be as certain," says Mr. Mill, "as any thing which depends upon human will; because there are strong motives in favour of it, and none that can be conceived in opposition to it." He subsequently sets forth what these motives are. The interest of the democracy is, that each individual should receive protection. The interest of the King and the aristocracy is, to have all the power that they can obtain, and to use it for their own ends. Therefore the King and the aristocracy have all possible motives for combining against the people. If our readers will look back to the passage quoted above, they will see that we represent Mr. Mill's argument quite fairly.

Now we should have thought that, without the help of either history or experience, Mr. Mill would have discovered, by the light of his own logic, the fallacy which lurks, and indeed scarcely lurks, under this pretended demonstration. The interest of the King may be opposed to that of the people. But is it identical with that of the aristocracy? In the very page which contains this argument, intended to prove that the King and the aristocracy will coalesce against the people, Mr. Mill attempts to show that there is so strong an opposition of interest between the King and the aristocracy, that if the powers of government are divided between them, the one will inevitably usurp the power of the other. If so, he is not entitled to conclude that they will combine to destroy the power of the people, merely because their interests may be at variance with those of the people. He is bound to show, not merely that in all communities the interest of a king must be opposed to that of the people, but also that, in all communities, it must be more directly opposed to the interest of the people than to the interest of the aristocracy. But he has not shown this. Therefore he has not proved his proposition on his own principles. To quote history would be a mere waste of time. Every schoolboy, whose studies have gone so far as the Abridgements of Goldsmith, can mention instances in which sovereigns have allied themselves with the people against the aristocracy, and in which the nobles have allied themselves with the people against the sovereign. In general, when there are three parties, every one of which has much to fear from the others, it is not found that two of them combine to plunder the third. If such a combination be formed, it scarcely ever effects its purpose. It soon becomes evident which member of the coalition is likely to be the greater gainer by the transaction. He becomes an object of jealousy to his ally, who, in all probability, changes sides, and compels him to restore what he has taken. Everybody knows how Henry VIII. trimmed between Francis and the Emperor Charles. But it is idle to cite examples of the operation of a principle which is illustrated in almost every page of history, ancient or modern, and to which almost every state in Europe has, at one time or another, been indebted for its independence.

Mr. Mill has now, as he conceives, demonstrated that the simple forms of government are bad, and that the mixed forms cannot possibly exist. There is still, however, it seems, a hope for mankind.

"In the grand discovery of modern times, the system of representation, the solution of all the difficulties, both speculative and practical, will perhaps be found. If it cannot, we seem to be forced upon the extraordinary conclusion, that good government is impossible. For, as there is no individual or combination of individuals, except the community itself, who would not have an interest in bad government, if intrusted with its powers, and as the community itself is incapable of exercising those powers, and must intrust them to certain individuals, the conclusion is obvious: the community itself must check those individuals; else they will follow their interest, and produce bad government. But how is it the community can check? The community can act only when assembled; and when assembled, it is incapable of acting. The community, however, can choose representatives."

The next question is—How must the representative body be constituted? Mr. Mill lays down two principles, about which, he says, "it is unlikely that there will be any dispute."

"First, The checking body must have a degree of power sufficient for the business of checking.

"Secondly, It must have an identity of interest with the community. Otherwise, it will make a mischievous use of its power."

The first of these propositions certainly admits of no dispute. As to the second, we shall hereafter take occasion to make some remarks on the sense in which Mr. Mill understands the words, "interest of the community."

It does not appear very easy, on Mr. Mill's principles, to find out any mode of making the interest of the representative body identical with that of the constituent body. The plan proposed by Mr. Mill is simply that of very frequent election. "As it appears," says he, "that limiting the duration of their power is a security against the sinister interest of the people's representatives, so it appears that it is the only security of which the nature of the case admits." But all the arguments by which Mr. Mill has proved monarchy and aristocracy to be pernicious, will, as it appears to us, equally prove this security to be no security at all. Is it not clear that the representatives, as soon as they are elected, are an aristocracy, with an interest opposed to the interest of the community? Why should they not pass a law for extending the term of their power from one year to ten years, or declare themselves senators for life? If the whole legislative power is given to them, they will be constitutionally competent to do this. If part of the legislative power is withheld from them, to whom is that part given? Is the people to retain it, and to express its assent or dissent in primary assemblies? Mr. Mill himself tells us that the community can only act when assembled, and that, when assembled, it is incapable of acting. Or is it to be provided, as in some of the American republics, that no change in the fundamental laws shall be made without the consent of a convention, specially elected for the purpose? Still the difficulty recurs: Why may not the members of the convention betray their trust, as well as the members of the ordinary legislature? When private men, they may have been zealous for the interests of the community. When candidates, they may have pledged themselves to the cause of the constitution. But as soon as they are a convention, as soon as they are separated from the people, as soon as the supreme power is put into their hands, commences that interest opposite to the interest of the community, which must, according to Mr. Mill, produce measures opposite to the interests of the community. We must find some other means, therefore, of checking this check upon a check; some other prop to carry the tortoise, that carries the elephant, that carries the world.

We know well that there is no real danger in such a case. But there is no danger, only because there is no truth in Mr. Mill's principles. If men were what he represents them to be, the letter of the very constitution which he recommends would afford no safeguard against bad government. The real security is this, that legislators will be deterred by the fear of resistance and of infamy, from acting in the manner which we have described. But restraints, exactly the same in kind, and differing only in degree, exist in all forms of government. That broad line of distinction which Mr. Mill tries to point out between monarchies and aristocracies on the one side, and democracies on the other, has in fact no existence. In no form of government is there an absolute identity of interest between the people and their rulers. In every form of government, the rulers stand in some awe of the people. The fear of resistance and the sense of shame operate, in a certain degree, on the most absolute kings and the most illiberal oligarchies. And nothing but the fear of resistance and the sense of shame preserves the freedom of the most democratic communities from the encroachments of their annual and biennial delegates.

We have seen how Mr. Mill proposes to render the interest of the representative body identical with that of the constituent body. The next question is, in what manner the interest of the constituent body is to be rendered identical with that of the community. Mr. Mill shows that a minority of the community, consisting even of many thousands, would be a bad constituent body, and, indeed, merely a numerous aristocracy.

"The benefits of the representative system," says he, "are lost, in all cases in which the interests of the choosing body are not the same with those of the community. It is very evident, that if the community itself were the choosing body, the interest of the community and that of the choosing body would be the same."

On these grounds Mr. Mill recommends that all males of mature age, rich and poor, educated and ignorant, shall have votes. But why not the women too? This question has often been asked in parliamentary debate, and has never, to our knowledge, received a plausible answer. Mr. Mill escapes from it as fast as he can. But we shall take the liberty to dwell a little on the words of the oracle. "One thing," says he, "is pretty clear, that all those individuals whose interests are involved in those of other individuals, may be struck off without inconvenience. . . . . In this light Women may be regarded, the interest of almost all of whom is involved either in that of their fathers, or in that of their husbands."

If we were to content ourselves with saying, in answer to all the arguments in Mr. Mill's Essay, that the interest of a king is involved in that of the community, we should be accused, and justly, of talking nonsense. Yet such an assertion would not, as far as we can perceive, be more unreasonable than that which Mr. Mill has here ventured to make. Without adducing one fact, without taking the trouble to perplex the question by one sophism, he placidly dogmatizes away the interest of one half of the human race. If there be a word of truth in history, women have always been, and still are, over the greater part of the globe, humble companions, play-things, captives, menials, beasts of burden. Except in a few happy and highly civilized communities, they are strictly in a state of personal slavery. Even in those countries where they are best treated, the laws are generally unfavourable to them, with respect to almost all the points in which they are most deeply interested.

Mr. Mill is not legislating for England or the United States; but for mankind. Is then the interest of a Turk the same with that of the girls who compose his haram? Is the interest of a Chinese the same with that of the woman whom he harnesses to his plough? Is the interest of an Italian the same with that of the daughter whom he devotes to God? The interest of a respectable Englishman may be said, without any impropriety, to be identical with that of his wife. But why is it so? Because human nature is *not* what Mr. Mill conceives it to be; because civilized men, pursuing their own happiness in a social state, are not Yahoos fighting for carrion; because there is a pleasure in being loved and esteemed, as well as in being feared and servilely obeyed. Why does not a gentleman restrict his wife to the bare maintenance which the law would compel him to allow her, that he may have more to spend on his personal pleasures? Because, if he loves her, he has pleasure in seeing her pleased; and because, even if he dislikes her, he is unwilling that the whole neighbourhood should cry shame on his meanness and ill-nature. Why does not the legislature, altogether composed of males, pass a law to deprive women of all civil privileges whatever, and reduce them to the state of slaves? By passing such a law, they would gratify what Mr. Mill tells us is an inseparable part of human nature, the desire to possess unlimited power of inflicting pain upon others. That they do not pass such a law, though they have the power to pass it, and that no man in England wishes to see such a law passed, proves that the desire to possess unlimited power of inflicting pain is not inseparable from human nature.

If there be in this country an identity of interest between the two sexes, it cannot possibly arise from any thing but the pleasure of being loved, and of communicating happiness. For, that it does not spring from the mere instinct of sex, the treatment which women experience over the greater part of the world abundantly proves. And if it be said that our laws of marriage have produced it, this only removes the argument a step further; for those laws have been made by males. Now, if the kind feelings of one half of the species be a sufficient security for the happiness of the other, why may not the kind feelings of a monarch or an aristocracy be sufficient at least to prevent them from grinding the people to the very utmost of their power?

If Mr. Mill will examine why it is that women are better treated in England than in Persia, he may perhaps find out, in the course of his enquiries, why it is that the Danes are better governed than the subjects of Caligula.

We now come to the most important practical question in the whole Essay. Is it desirable that all males arrived at years of discretion should vote for representatives, or should a pecuniary qualification be required? Mr. Mill's opinion is, that the lower the qualification the better; and that the best system is that in which there is none at all.

"The qualification," says he, "must either be such as to embrace the majority of the population, or something less than the majority. Suppose, in the first place, that it embraces the majority, the question is, whether the majority would have an interest in oppressing those who, upon this supposition, would be deprived of political power? If we reduce the calculation to its elements, we shall see that the interest which they would have of this deplorable kind, though it would be something, would not be very great. Each man of the majority, if the majority were constituted the governing body, would have something less than the benefit of oppressing a single man. If the majority were twice as great as the minority, each man of the majority would only have one half the benefit of oppressing a single man. . . . . Suppose, in the second place, that the qualification did not admit a body of electors so large as the majority, in that case, taking again the calculation in its elements, we shall see that each man would have a benefit equal to that derived from the oppression of more than one man; and that, in proportion as the elective body constituted a smaller and smaller minority, the benefit of misrule to the elective body would be increased, and bad government would be insured."

The first remark which we have to make on this argument is, that, by Mr. Mill's own account, even a government in which every human being should vote would still be defective. For, under a system of universal suffrage, the majority of the electors return the representative, and the majority of the representatives make the law. The whole people may vote, therefore, but only the majority govern. So that, by Mr. Mill's own confession, the most perfect system of government conceivable is one in which the interest of the ruling body to oppress, though not great, is something.

But is Mr. Mill in the right, when he says that such an interest could not be very great? We think not. If, indeed, every man in the community possessed an equal share of what Mr. Mill calls the objects of desire, the majority would probably abstain from plundering the minority. A large minority would offer a vigorous resistance; and the property of a small minority would not repay the other members of the community for the trouble of dividing it. But it happens that in all civilized communities there is a small minority of rich men, and a great majority of poor men. If there were a thousand men with ten pounds a-piece, it would not be worth while for nine hundred and ninety of them to rob ten, and it would be a bold attempt for six hundred of them to rob four hundred.

But if ten of them had a hundred thousand pounds a-piece, the case would be very different. There would then be much to be got, and nothing to be feared.

"That one human being will desire to render the person and property of another subservient to his pleasures, notwithstanding the pain or loss of pleasure which it may occasion to that other individual, is," according to Mr. Mill, "the foundation of government." That the property of the rich minority can be made subservient to the pleasures of the poor majority, will scarcely be denied. But Mr. Mill proposes to give the poor majority power over the rich minority. Is it possible to doubt to what, on his own principles, such an arrangement must lead?

It may perhaps be said that, in the long run, it is for the interest of the people that property should be secure, and that therefore they will respect it. We answer thus:—It cannot be pretended that it is not for the immediate interest of the people to plunder the rich. Therefore, even if it were quite certain that, in the long run, the people would, as a body, lose by doing so, it would not necessarily follow that the fear of remote ill consequences would overcome the desire of immediate acquisitions. Every individual might flatter himself that the punishment would not fall on him. Mr. Mill himself tell us, in his Essay on Jurisprudence, that no quantity of evil which is remote and uncertain will suffice to prevent crime.

But we are rather inclined to think that it would, on the whole, be for the interest of the majority to plunder the rich. If so, the Utilitarians will say, that the rich *ought* to be plundered. We deny the inference. For, in the first place, if the object of government be the greatest happiness of the greatest number, the intensity of the suffering which a measure inflicts must be taken into consideration, as well as the number of the sufferers. In the next place, we have to notice one most important distinction which Mr. Mill has altogether overlooked. Throughout his Essay, he confounds the community with the species. He talks of the greatest happiness of the greatest number: but when we examine his reasonings, we find that he thinks only of the greatest number of a single generation.

Therefore, even if we were to concede, that all those arguments of which we have exposed the fallacy, are unanswerable, we might still deny the conclusion at which the essayist arrives. Even if we were to grant that he had found out the form of government which is best for the majority of the people now living on the face of the earth, we might still without inconsistency maintain that form of government to be pernicious to mankind. It would still be incumbent on Mr. Mill to prove that the interest of every generation is identical with the interest of all succeeding generations. And how on his own principles he could do this we are at a loss to conceive.

The case, indeed, is strictly analogous to that of an aristocratic government. In an aristocracy, says Mr. Mill, the few, being invested with the powers of government, can take the objects of their desires from the people. In the same manner, every generation in turn can gratify itself at the expense of posterity,—priority of time, in the latter case, giving an advantage exactly corresponding to that which superiority of station gives in the former. That an aristocracy will abuse its advantage, is, according to Mr. Mill, matter of demonstration. Is it not equally certain, that the whole people will do the same; that, if they have the power, they will commit waste of every sort on the estate of mankind, and transmit it to posterity impoverished and desolated?

How is it possible for any person who holds the doctrines of Mr. Mill to doubt that the rich, in a democracy such as that which he recommends, would be pillaged as unmercifully as under a Turkish Pacha? It is no doubt for the interest of the next generation, and it may be for the remote interest of the present generation, that property should be held sacred. And so no doubt it will be for the interest of the next Pacha, and even for that of the present Pacha, if he should hold office long, that the inhabitants of his Pachalik should be encouraged to accumulate wealth. Scarcely any despotic sovereign has plundered his subjects to a large extent, without having reason before the end of his reign to regret it. Every body knows how bitterly Louis the Fourteenth, towards the close of his life, lamented his former extravagance. If that magnificent prince had not expended millions on Marli and Versailles, and tens of millions on the aggrandizement of his grandson, he would not have been compelled at last to pay servile court to low-born money-lenders, to humble himself before men on whom, in the days of his pride, he would not have vouchsafed to look, for the means of supporting even his own household. Examples to the same effect might easily be multiplied. But despots, we see, do plunder their subjects, though history and experience tell them, that by prematurely exacting the means of profusion, they are in fact devouring the seed-corn, from which the future harvest of revenue is to spring. Why then should we suppose that the people will be deterred from procuring immediate relief and enjoyment by the fear of distant calamities, of calamities which perhaps may not be fully felt till the times of their grand-children?

These conclusions are strictly drawn from Mr. Mill's own principles: and, unlike most of the conclusions which he has himself drawn from those principles, they are not, as far as we know, contradicted by facts. The case of the United States is not in point. In a country where the necessaries of life are cheap and the wages of labour high, where a man who has no capital but his legs and arms may expect to become rich by industry and frugality, it is not very decidedly even for the immediate advantage of the poor to plunder the rich; and the punishment of doing so would very speedily follow the offence. But in countries in which the great majority live from hand to mouth, and in which vast masses of wealth have been accumulated by a comparatively small number, the case is widely different. The immediate want is, at particular seasons, craving, imperious, irresistible. In our own time it has steeled men to the fear of the gallows, and urged them on the point of the bayonet. And, if these men had at their command that gallows, and those bayonets, which now scarcely restrain them, what is to be expected? Nor is this state of things one which can exist only under a bad government. If there be the least truth in the doctrines of the school to which Mr. Mill belongs, the increase of population will necessarily produce it every where. The increase of population is accelerated by good and cheap government. Therefore, the better the government, the greater is the inequality of conditions: and the greater the inequality of conditions, the stronger are the motives which impel the populace to spoliation. As for America, we appeal to the twentieth century.

It is scarcely necessary to discuss the effects which a general spoliation of the rich would produce. It may indeed happen, that where a legal and political system full of abuses is inseparably bound up with the institution of property, a nation may gain by a single convulsion, in which both perish together. The price is fearful: But if, when the shock is over, a new order of things should arise under which property may enjoy security, the industry of individuals will soon repair the devastation. Thus we entertain no doubt that the revolution was, on the whole, a most salutary event for France. But would France have gained if, ever since the year 1793, she had been governed by a democratic convention? If Mr. Mill's principles be sound, we say that almost her whole capital would by this time have been annihilated. As soon as the first explosion was beginning to be forgotten, as soon as wealth again began to germinate, as soon as the poor again began to compare their cottages and sallads with the hotels and banquets of the rich, there would have been another scramble for property, another maximum, another general confiscation, another reign of terror.

Four or five such convulsions following each other, at intervals of ten or twelve years, would reduce the most flourishing countries of Europe to the state of Barbary or the Morea.

The civilized part of the world has now nothing to fear from the hostility of savage nations. Once the deluge of barbarism has passed over it, to destroy and to fertilize; and in the present state of mankind we enjoy a full security against that calamity. That flood will no more return to cover the earth. But is it possible that, in the bosom of civilization itself, may be engendered the malady which shall destroy it? Is it possible that institutions may be established which, without the help of earthquake, of famine, of pestilence, or of the foreign sword, may undo the work of so many ages of wisdom and glory, and gradually sweep away taste, literature, science, commerce, manufactures, everything but the rude arts necessary to the support of animal life? Is it possible that, in two or three hundred years, a few lean and half-naked fishermen may divide with owls and foxes the ruins of the greatest European cities—may wash their nets amidst the relics of her gigantic docks, and build their huts out of the capitals of her stately cathedrals? If the principles of Mr. Mill be sound, we say, without hesitation, that the form of government which he recommends will assuredly produce all this. But if these principles be unsound, if the reasonings by which we have opposed them be just, the higher and middling orders are the natural representatives of the human race. Their interest may be opposed, in some things, to that of their poorer contemporaries, but it is identical with that of the innumerable generations which are to follow.

Mr. Mill concludes his Essay, by answering an objection often made to the project of universal suffrage—that the people do not understand their own interests. We shall not go through his arguments on this subject, because, till he has proved, that it is for the interest of the people to respect property, he only makes matters worse, by proving that they understand their interests. But we cannot refrain from treating our readers with a delicious *bonne bouche* of wisdom, which he has kept for the last moment.

"The opinions of that class of the people who are below the middle rank are formed, and their minds are directed, by that intelligent, that virtuous rank, who come the most immediately in contact with them, who are in the constant habit of intimate communication with them, to whom they fly for advice and assistance in all their numerous difficulties, upon whom they feel an immediate and daily dependence in health and in sickness, in infancy and in old age, to whom their children look up as models for their imitation, whose opinions they hear daily repeated, and account it their honour to adopt. There can be no doubt that the middle rank, which gives to science, to art, and to legislation itself, their most distinguished ornaments, and is the chief source of all that has exalted and refined human nature, is that portion of the community, of which, if the basis of representation were ever so far extended, the opinion would ultimately decide. Of the people beneath them, a vast majority would be sure to be guided by their advice and example."

This single paragraph is sufficient to upset Mr. Mill's theory. Will the people act against their own interest? Or will the middle rank act against its own interest? Or is the interest of the middle rank identical with the interest of the people? If the people act according to the directions of the middle rank, as Mr. Mill says that they assuredly will, one of these three questions must be answered in the affirmative. But if any one of the three be answered in the affirmative, his whole system falls to the ground. If the interest of the middle rank be identical with that of the people, why should not the powers of government be intrusted to that rank? If the powers of government were intrusted to that rank, there would evidently be an aristocracy of wealth; and "to constitute an aristocracy of wealth, though it were a very numerous one, would," according to Mr. Mill, "leave the community without protection, and exposed to all the evils of unbridled power." Will not the same motives which induce the middle classes to abuse one kind of power, induce them to abuse another? If their interest be the same with that of the people, they will govern the people well. If it be opposite to that of the people, they will advise the people ill. The system of universal suffrage, therefore, according to Mr. Mill's own account, is only a device for doing circuitously, what a representative system, with a pretty high qualification, would do directly.

So ends this celebrated Essay. And such is this philosophy, for which the experience of three thousand years is to be discarded; this philosophy, the professors of which speak as if it had guided the world to the knowledge of navigation and alphabetical writing; as if, before its dawn, the inhabitants of Europe had lived in caverns and eaten each other! We are sick, it seems, like the children of Israel, of the objects of our old and legitimate worship. We pine for a new idolatry. All that is costly and all that is ornamental in our intellectual treasures must be delivered up, and cast into the furnace—and there comes out this Calf!

Our readers can scarcely mistake our object in writing this

article. They will not suspect us of any disposition to advocate the cause of absolute monarchy, or of any narrow form of oligarchy, or to exaggerate the evils of popular government. Our object at present is, not so much to attack or defend any particular system of polity, as to expose the vices of a kind of reasoning utterly unfit for moral and political discussions; of a kind of reasoning which may so readily be turned to purposes of falsehood that it ought to receive no quarter, even when by accident it may be employed on the side of truth.

Our objection to the Essay of Mr. Mill is fundamental. We believe that it is utterly impossible to deduce the science of government from the principles of human nature.

What proposition is there respecting human nature which is absolutely and universally true? We know of only one: and that is not only true, but identical; that men always act from self-interest. This truism the Utilitarians proclaim with as much pride as if it were new, and as much zeal as if it were important. But in fact, when explained, it means only that men, if they can, will do as they choose. When we see the actions of a man, we know with certainty what he thinks his interest to be. But it is impossible to reason with certainty from what *we* take to be his interest to his actions. One man goes without a dinner, that he may add a shilling to a hundred thousand pounds: another runs in debt to give balls and masquerades. One man cuts his father's throat to get possession of his old clothes: another hazards his own life to save that of an enemy. One man volunteers on a forlorn hope: another is drummed out of a regiment for cowardice. Each of these men has, no doubt, acted from self-interest. But we gain nothing by knowing this, except the pleasure, if it be one, of multiplying useless words. In fact, this principle is just as recondite, and just as important, as the great truth that whatever is, is. If a philosopher were always to state facts in the following form—"There is a shower: but whatever is, is; therefore, there is a shower," his reasoning would be perfectly sound; but we do not apprehend that it would materially enlarge the circle of human knowledge. And it is equally idle to attribute any importance to a proposition which, when interpreted, means only that a man had rather do what he had rather do.

If the doctrine, that men always act from self-interest, be laid down in any other sense than this—if the meaning of the word self-interest be narrowed so as to exclude any one of the motives which may by possibility act on any human being,—the proposition ceases to be identical; but at the same time it ceases to be true.

What we have said of the word self-interest applies to all the synonymes and circumlocutions which are employed to convey the same meaning; pain and pleasure, happiness and misery, objects of desire, and so forth.

The whole art of Mr. Mill's Essay consists in one simple trick of legerdemain. It consists in using words of the sort which we have been describing, first in one sense and then in another. Men will take the objects of their desire if they can. Unquestionably:— but this is an identical proposition: For an object of desire means merely a thing which a man will procure if he can. Nothing can possibly be inferred from a maxim of this kind. When we see a man take something, we shall know that it was an object of his desire. But till then, we have no means of judging with certainty what he desires, or what he will take. The general proposition, however, having been admitted, Mr. Mill proceeds to reason as if men had no desires but those which can be gratified only by spoliation and oppression. It then becomes easy to deduce doctrines of vast importance from the original axiom. The only misfortune is, that by thus narrowing the meaning of the word desire, the axiom becomes false, and all the doctrines consequent upon it are false likewise.

When we pass beyond those maxims which it is impossible to deny without a contradiction in terms, and which, therefore, do not enable us to advance a single step in practical knowledge, we do not believe that it is possible to lay down a single general rule respecting the motives which influence human actions. There is nothing which may not, by association or by comparison, become an object either of desire or of aversion. The fear of death is generally considered as one of the strongest of our feelings. It is the most formidable sanction which legislators have been able to devise. Yet it is notorious that, as Lord Bacon has observed, there is no passion by which that fear has not been often overcome. Physical pain is indisputably an evil: yet it has been often endured, and even welcomed. Innumerable martyrs have exulted in torments which made the spectators shudder; and, to use a more homely illustration, there are few wives who do not long to be mothers.

Is the love of approbation a stronger motive than the love of wealth? It is impossible to answer this question generally, even in the case of an individual with whom we are very intimate. We often say, indeed, that a man loves fame more than money, or money more than fame. But this is said in a loose and popular sense; for there is scarcely a man who would not endure a few sneers for a great sum of money, if he were in pecuniary distress; and scarcely a man, on the other hand, who, if he were in flourishing circumstances, would expose himself to the hatred and contempt of the public for a trifle. In order, therefore, to return a precise answer even about a single human being, we must know what is the amount of the sacrifice of reputation demanded, and of the pecuniary advantage offered, and in what situation the person to whom the temptation is proposed stands at the time. But when the question is propounded generally about the whole species, the impossibility of answering is still more evident. Man differs from man; generation from generation; nation from nation. Education, station, sex, age, accidental associations, produce infinite shades of variety.

Now, the only mode in which we can conceive it possible to deduce a theory of government from the principles of human nature, is this. We must find out what are the motives which, in a particular form of government, impel rulers to bad measures, and what are those which impel them to good measures. We must then compare the effect of the two classes of motives; and according as we find the one or the other to prevail, we must pronounce the form of government in question good or bad.

Now let it be supposed that, in aristocratical and monarchical states, the desire of wealth and other desires of the same class always tend to produce misgovernment, and that the love of approbation and other kindred feelings always tend to produce good government. Then, if it be impossible, as we have shown that it is, to pronounce generally which of the two classes of motives is the more influential, it is impossible to find out, *a priori*, whether a monarchical or aristocratical form of government be good or bad.

Mr. Mill has avoided the difficulty of making the comparison, by very coolly putting all the weights into one of the scales,—by reasoning as if no human being had ever sympathized with the feelings, been gratified by the thanks, or been galled by the execrations, of another.

The case, as we have put it, is decisive against Mr. Mill; and yet we have put it in a manner far too favourable to him. For, in fact, it is impossible to lay it down as a general rule that the love of wealth in a sovereign always produces misgovernment, or the love of approbation good government. A patient and far-sighted ruler, for example, who is less desirous of raising a great sum immediately than of securing an unencumbered and progressive revenue, will, by taking off restraints from trade and giving perfect security to property, encourage accumulation and entice capital from foreign countries. The commercial policy of Prussia, which is perhaps superior to that of any country in the world, and which puts to shame the absurdities of our republican brethren on the other side of the Atlantic, has probably sprung from the desire of an absolute ruler to enrich himself. On the other hand, when the popular estimate of virtues and vices is erroneous, which is too often the case, the love of approbation leads sovereigns to spend the wealth of the nation on useless shows, or to engage in wanton and destructive wars. If then we can neither compare the strength of two motives, nor determine with certainty to what description of actions either motive will lead, how can we possibly deduce a theory of government from the nature of man?

How, then, are we to arrive at just conclusions on a subject so important to the happiness of mankind? Surely by that method, which, in every experimental science to which it has been applied, has signally increased the power and knowledge of our species,—by that method for which our new philosophers would substitute quibbles scarcely worthy of the barbarous respondents and opponents of the middle ages,—by the method of Induction;—by observing the present state of the world,—by assiduously studying the history of past ages,—by sifting the evidence of facts,—by carefully combining and contrasting those which are authentic,—by generalizing with judgment and diffidence,—by perpetually bringing the theory which we have constructed to the test of new facts,—by correcting, or altogether abandoning it, according as those new facts prove it to be partially or fundamentally unsound. Proceeding thus,—patiently,—diligently,—candidly,—we may hope to form a system as far inferior in pretension to that which we have been examining and as far superior to it in real utility, as the prescriptions of a great physician, varying with every stage of every malady, and with the constitution of every patient, to the pill of the advertising quack which is to cure all human beings, in all climates, of all diseases.

This is that noble Science of Politics, which is equally removed from the barren theories of the Utilitarian sophists, and from the petty craft, so often mistaken for statesmanship by minds grown narrow in habits of intrigue, jobbing, and official etiquette;—which, of all sciences, is the most important to the welfare of nations, —which of all sciences most tends to expand and invigorate the mind,—which draws nutriment and ornament from every part of philosophy and literature, and dispenses, in return, nutriment and ornament to all. We are sorry and surprised when we see men of good intentions and good natural abilities abandon this healthful and generous study to pore over speculations like those which we have been examining. And we should heartily rejoice to find that our remarks had induced any person of this description to employ, in researches of real utility, the talents and industry which are now wasted on verbal sophisms, wretched of their wretched kind.

As to the greater part of the sect, it is, we apprehend, of little consequence, what they study, or under whom. It would be more amusing, to be sure, and more reputable, if they would take up the old republican cant, and declaim about Brutus and Timoleon, the duty of killing tyrants, and the blessedness of dying for liberty. But, on the whole, they might have chosen worse. They may as well be Utilitarians as jockeys or dandies. And though quibbling about self-interest and motives, and objects of desire, and the greatest happiness of the greatest number, is but a poor employment for a grown man, it certainly hurts the health less than hard drinking, and the fortune less than high play: it is not much more laughable than phrenology, and is immeasurably more humane than cock-fighting.

# GLADSTONE ON CHURCH AND STATE

## (APRIL 1839)

*The State in its Relations with the Church.* By W. E. GLADSTONE, Esq., Student of Christ Church, and M.P. for Newark. 8vo. Second Edition. London: 1839.

THE author of this volume is a young man of unblemished character, and of distinguished parliamentary talents, the rising hope of those stern and unbending Tories, who follow, reluctantly and mutinously, a leader, whose experience and eloquence are indispensable to them, but whose cautious temper and moderate opinions they abhor. It would not be at all strange if Mr. Gladstone were one of the most unpopular men in England. But we believe that we do him no more than justice when we say that his abilities and his demeanour have obtained for him the respect and good will of all parties. His first appearance in the character of an author is therefore an interesting event; and it is natural that the gentle wishes of the public should go with him to his trial.

We are much pleased, without any reference to the soundness or unsoundness of Mr. Gladstone's theories, to see a grave and elaborate treatise on an important part of the Philosophy of Government proceed from the pen of a young man who is rising to eminence in the House of Commons. There is little danger that people engaged in the conflicts of active life will be too much addicted to general speculation. The opposite vice is that which most easily besets them. The times and tides of business and debate tarry for no man. A politician must often talk and act before he has thought and read. He may be very ill-informed respecting a question; all his notions about it may be vague and inaccurate; but speak he must; and if he is a man of talents, of tact, and of intrepidity, he soon finds that, even under such circumstances, it is possible to speak successfully. He finds that there is a great difference between the effect of written words, which are perused and reperused in the stillness of the closet, and the effect of spoken words which, set off by the graces of utterance and gesture, vibrate for a single moment on the ear. He finds that he may blunder without much chance of being detected, that he may reason sophistically, and escape unrefuted. He finds that, even on knotty questions of trade and legislation, he can, without reading ten pages, or thinking ten minutes, draw forth loud plaudits, and sit down with the credit of having made an excellent speech. Lysias, says Plutarch, wrote a defence for a man who was to be tried before one of the Athenian tribunals. Long before the defendant had learned the speech by heart, he became so much dissatisfied with it that he went in great distress to the author. "I was delighted with your speech the first time I read it; but I liked it less the second time, and still less the third time; and now it seems to me to be no defence at all." "My good friend," said Lysias, "you quite forget that the judges are to hear it only once." The case is the same in the English parliament. It would be as idle in an orator to waste deep meditation and long research on his speeches, as it would be in the manager of a theatre to adorn all the crowd of courtiers and ladies who cross over the stage in a procession with real pearls and diamonds. It is not by accuracy or profundity that men become the masters of great assemblies. And why be at the charge of providing logic of the best quality, when a very inferior article will be equally acceptable? Why go as deep into a question as Burke, only in order to be, like Burke, coughed down, or left speaking to green benches and red boxes? This has long appeared to us to be the most serious of the evils which are to be set off against the many blessings of popular government. It is a fine and true saying of Bacon, that reading makes a full man, talking a ready man, and writing an exact man. The tendency of institutions like those of England is to encourage readiness in public men, at the expense both of fulness and of exactness. The keenest and most vigorous minds of every generation, minds often admirably fitted for the investigation of truth, are habitually employed in producing arguments, such as no man of sense would ever put into a treatise intended for publication, arguments which are just good enough to be used once, when aided by fluent delivery and pointed language. The habit of discussing questions in this way necessarily reacts on the intellects of our ablest men; particularly of those who are introduced into parliament at a very early age, before their minds have expanded to full maturity. The talent for debate is developed in such men to a degree which, to the multitude, seems as marvellous as the performances of an Italian *improvisatore*. But they are fortunate indeed if they retain unimpaired the faculties which are required for close reasoning or for enlarged speculation. Indeed we should sooner expect a great original work on political science, such a work, for example, as the Wealth of Nations, from an apothecary in a country town, or from a minister in the Hebrides, than from a statesman who, ever since he was one-and-twenty, had been a distinguished debater in the House of Commons.

We therefore hail with pleasure, though assuredly not with unmixed pleasure, the appearance of this work. That a young politician should, in the intervals afforded by his parliamentary avocations, have constructed and propounded, with much study and mental toil, an original theory on a great problem in politics, is a circumstance which, abstracted from all consideration of the soundness or unsoundness of his opinions, must be considered as highly creditable to him. We certainly cannot wish that Mr. Gladstone's doctrines may become fashionable among public men. But we heartily wish that his laudable desire to penetrate beneath the surface of questions, and to arrive, by long and intent meditation, at the knowledge of great general laws, were much more fashionable than we at all expect it to become.

Mr. Gladstone seems to us to be, in many respects, exceedingly well qualified for philosophical investigation. His mind is of large grasp; nor is he deficient in dialectical skill. But he does not give his intellect fair play. There is no want of light, but a great want of what Bacon would have called dry light. Whatever Mr. Gladstone sees is refracted and distorted by a false medium of passions and prejudices. His style bears a remarkable analogy to his mode of thinking, and indeed exercises great influence on his mode of thinking. His rhetoric, though often good of its kind, darkens and perplexes the logic which it should illustrate. Half his acuteness and diligence, with a barren imagination and a scanty vocabulary, would have saved him from almost all his mistakes. He has one gift most dangerous to a speculator, a vast command of a kind of language, grave and majestic, but of vague and uncertain import; of a kind of language which affects us much in the same way in which the lofty diction of the chorus of Clouds affected the simple-hearted Athenian.

ᾧ γῆ τοῦ φθέγματος, ὡς ἱερὸν, καὶ σεμνὸν, καὶ τερατῶδες.

When propositions have been established, and nothing remains but to amplify and decorate them, this dim magnificence may be in place. But if it is admitted into a demonstration, it is very much worse than absolute nonsense; just as that transparent haze, through which the sailor sees capes and mountains of false sizes and in false bearings, is more dangerous than utter darkness. Now, Mr. Gladstone is fond of employing the phraseology of which we speak in those parts of his work which require the utmost perspicuity and precision of which human language is capable; and in this way, he deludes first himself, and then his readers. The foundations of his theory, which ought to be buttresses of adamant, are made out of the flimsy materials which are fit only for perorations. This fault is one which no subsequent care or industry can correct. The more strictly Mr. Gladstone reasons on his premises, the more absurd are the conclusions which he brings out; and, when at last his good sense and good nature recoil from the horrible practical inferences to which his theory leads, he is reduced sometimes to take refuge in arguments inconsistent with his fundamental doctrines, and sometimes to escape from the legitimate consequences of his false principles, under cover of equally false history.

It would be unjust not to say that this book, though not a good book, shows more talent than many good books. It abounds with eloquent and ingenious passages. It bears the signs of much patient thought. It is written throughout with excellent taste and excellent temper; nor does it, so far as we have observed, contain one expression unworthy of a gentleman, a scholar, or a Christian. But the doctrines which are put forth in it appear to us, after full and calm consideration, to be false, to be in the highest degree pernicious, and to be such as, if followed out in practice to their legitimate consequences, would inevitably produce the dissolution of society: and for this opinion we shall proceed to give our reasons with that freedom which the importance of the subject requires, and which Mr. Gladstone, both by precept and by example, invites us to use, but, we hope, without rudeness, and, we are sure, without malevolence.

Before we enter on an examination of this theory, we wish to guard ourselves against one misconception. It is possible that some persons who have read Mr. Gladstone's book carelessly, and others who have merely heard in conversation, or seen in a newspaper, that the member for Newark has written in defence of the Church of England against the supporters of the voluntary system, may imagine that we are writing in defence of the voluntary system, and that we desire the abolition of the Established Church. This is not the case. It would be as unjust to accuse us of attacking the Church, because we attack Mr. Gladstone's doctrines, as it would be to accuse Locke of wishing for anarchy, because he refuted Filmer's patriarchal theory of government, or to accuse Blackstone of recommending the confiscation of ecclesiastical property, because he denied that the right of the rector to tithe was derived from the Levitical law. It is to be observed, that Mr. Gladstone rests his case on entirely new grounds, and does not differ more widely from us than from some of those who have hitherto been considered as the most illustrious champions of the Church. He is not content with the Ecclesiastical Polity, and rejoices that the latter part of that celebrated work "does not carry with it the weight of Hooker's plenary authority." He is not content with Bishop Warburton's Alliance of Church and State. "The propositions of that work generally," he says, "are to be received with qualification;" and he agrees with Bolingbroke in thinking that Warburton's whole theory rests on a fiction. He is still less satisfied with Paley's defence of the Church, which he pronounces to be "tainted by the original vice of false ethical principles," and "full of the seeds of evil." He conceives that Dr. Chalmers has taken a partial view of the subject, and "put forth much questionable matter." In truth, on almost every point on which we are opposed to Mr. Gladstone, we have on our side the authority of some divine, eminent as a defender of existing establishments.

Mr. Gladstone's whole theory rests on this great fundamental proposition, that the propagation of religious truth is one of the principal ends of government, as government. If Mr. Gladstone has not proved this proposition, his system vanishes at once.

We are desirous, before we enter on the discussion of this important question, to point out clearly a distinction which, though very obvious, seems to be overlooked by many excellent people. In their opinion, to say that the ends of government are temporal and not spiritual is tantamount to saying that the temporal welfare of man is of more importance than his spiritual welfare. But this is an entire mistake. The question is not whether spiritual interests be or be not superior in importance to temporal interests; but whether the machinery which happens at any moment to be employed for the purpose of protecting certain temporal interests of a society be necessarily such a machinery as is fitted to promote the spiritual interests of that society. Without a division of labour the world could not go on. It is of very much more importance that men should have food than that they should have pianofortes. Yet it by no means follows that every pianoforte-maker ought to add the business of a baker to his own; for, if he did so, we should have both much worse music and much worse bread. It is of much more importance that the knowledge of religious truth should be wisely diffused than that the art of sculpture should flourish among us. Yet it by no means follows that the Royal Academy ought to unite with its present functions those of the Society for promoting Christian Knowledge, to distribute theological tracts, to send forth missionaries, to turn out Nollekens for being a Catholic, Bacon for being a Methodist, and Flaxman for being a Swedenborgian. For the effect of such folly would be that we should have the worst possible academy of arts, and the worst possible society for the promotion of Christian knowledge. The community, it is plain, would be thrown into universal confusion, if it were supposed to be the duty of every association which is formed for one good object to promote every other good object.

As to some of the ends of civil government, all people are agreed. That it is designed to protect our persons and our property, that it is designed to compel us to satisfy our wants, not by rapine, but by industry, that it is designed to compel us to decide our differences, not by the strong hand, but by arbitration, that it is designed to direct our whole force, as that of one man, against any other society which may offer us injury, these are propositions which will hardly be disputed.

Now these are matters in which man, without any reference to any higher being or to any future state, is very deeply interested. Every human being, be he idolater, Mahometan, Jew, Papist, Socinian, Deist, or Atheist, naturally loves life, shrinks from pain, desires comforts which can be enjoyed only in communities where property is secure. To be murdered, to be tortured, to be robbed, to be sold into slavery, to be exposed to the outrages of gangs of foreign banditti calling themselves patriots, these are evidently evils from which men of every religion, and men of no religion, wish to be protected; and therefore it will hardly be disputed that men of every religion, and of no religion, have thus far a common interest in being well governed.

But the hopes and fears of man are not limited to this short life and to this visible world. He finds himself surrounded by the signs of a power and wisdom higher than his own; and, in all ages and nations, men of all orders of intellect, from Bacon and Newton down to the rudest tribes of cannibals, have believed in the existence of some superior mind. Thus far the voice of mankind is almost unanimous. But whether there be one God or many, what may be his natural and what his moral attributes, in what relation his creatures stand to him, whether he have ever disclosed himself to us by any other revelation than that which is written in all the parts of the glorious and well-ordered world which he has made, whether his revelation be contained in any permanent record, how that record should be interpreted, and whether it have pleased him to appoint any unerring interpreter on earth, these are questions respecting which there exists the widest diversity of opinion, and respecting which a large part of our race has, ever since the dawn of regular history, been deplorably in error.

Now here are two great objects: one is the protection of the persons and estates of citizens from injury; the other is the propagation of religious truth. No two objects more entirely distinct can well be imagined. The former belongs wholly to the visible and tangible world in which we live; the latter belongs to that higher world which is beyond the reach of our senses. The former belongs to this life; the latter to that which is to come. Men who are perfectly agreed as to the importance of the former object, and as to the way of attaining it, differ as widely as possible respecting the latter object. We must, therefore, pause before we admit that the persons, be they who they may, who are intrusted with power for the promotion of the former object, ought always to use that power for the promotion of the latter object.

Mr. Gladstone conceives that the duties of governments are paternal; a doctrine which we shall not believe till he can show us some government which loves its subjects as a father loves a child, and which is as superior in intelligence to its subjects as a father is to a child. He tells us, in lofty though somewhat indistinct language, that "Government occupies in moral the place of τὸ πᾶν in physical science." If government be indeed τὸ πᾶν in moral science, we do not understand why rulers should not assume all the functions which Plato assigned to them. Why should they not take away the child from the mother, select the nurse, regulate the school, overlook the playground, fix the hours of labour and of recreation, prescribe what ballads shall be sung, what tunes shall be played, what books shall be read, what physic shall be swallowed? Why should not they choose our wives, limit our expenses, and stint us to a certain number of dishes of meat, of glasses of wine, and of cups of tea? Plato, whose hardihood in speculation was perhaps more wonderful than any other peculiarity of his extraordinary mind, and who shrank from nothing to which his principles led, went this whole length. Mr. Gladstone is not so intrepid. He contents himself with laying down this proposition, that, whatever be the body which in any community is employed to protect the persons and property of men, that body ought also, in its corporate capacity, to profess a religion, to employ its power for the propagation of that religion, and to require conformity to that religion, as an indispensable qualification for all civil office. He distinctly declares that he does not in this proposition confine his view to orthodox governments, or even to Christian governments. The circumstance that a religion is false does not, he tells us, diminish the obligation of governors, as such, to uphold it. If they neglect to do so, "we cannot," he says, "but regard the fact as aggravating the case of the holders of such creed." "I do not scruple to affirm," he adds, "that, if a Mahometan conscientiously believes his religion to come from God, and to teach divine truth, he must believe that truth to be beneficial, and beneficial beyond all other things to the soul of man; and he must, therefore, and ought to desire its extension, and to use for its extension all proper and legitimate means; and that, if such Mahometan be a prince, he ought to count among those means the application of whatever influence or funds he may lawfully have at his disposal for such purposes."

Surely this is a hard saying. Before we admit that the Emperor Julian, in employing the influence and the funds at his disposal for the extinction of Christianity, was doing no more than his duty, before we admit that the Arian, Theodoric, would have committed a crime if he had suffered a single believer in the divinity of Christ to hold any civil employment in Italy, before we admit that the Dutch Government is bound to exclude from office all members of the Church of England, the King of Bavaria to exclude from office all Protestants, the Great Turk to exclude from office all Christians, the King of Ava to exclude from office all who hold the unity of God, we think ourselves entitled to demand very full and accurate demonstration. When the consequences of a doctrine are so startling, we may well require that its foundations shall be very solid.

The following paragraph is a specimen of the arguments by which Mr. Gladstone has, as he conceives, established his great fundamental proposition:—

"We may state the same proposition in a more general form, in which it surely must command universal assent. Wherever there is power in the universe, that power is the property of God, the King of that universe—his property of right, however for a time withholden or abused. Now this property is, as it were, realized, is used according to the will of the owner, when it is used for the purposes he has ordained, and in the temper of mercy, justice, truth, and faith, which he has taught us. But those principles never can be truly, never can be permanently, entertained in the human breast, except by a continual reference to their source, and the supply of the Divine grace. The powers, therefore, that dwell in individuals acting as a government, as well as those that dwell in individuals acting for themselves, can only be secured for right uses by applying to them a religion."

Here are propositions of vast and indefinite extent, conveyed in language which has a certain obscure dignity and sanctity, attractive, we doubt not, to many minds. But the moment that we examine these propositions closely, the moment that we bring them to the test by running over but a very few of the particulars which are included in them, we find them to be false and extravagant. The doctrine which "must surely command universal assent" is this, that every association of human beings which exercises any power whatever, that is to say, every association of human beings, is bound, as such association, to profess a religion. Imagine the effect which would follow if this principle were really in force during four-and-twenty hours. Take one instance out of a million. A stage-coach company has power over its horses. This power is the property of God. It is used according to the will of God when it is used with mercy. But the principle of mercy can never be truly or permanently entertained in the human breast without continual reference to God. The powers, therefore, that dwell in individuals, acting as a stage-coach company, can only be secured for right uses by applying to them a religion. Every stage-coach company ought, therefore, in its collective capacity, to profess some one faith, to have its articles, and its public worship, and its tests. That this conclusion, and an infinite number of other conclusions equally strange, follow of necessity from Mr. Gladstone's principle, is as certain as it is that two and two make four. And, if the legitimate conclusions be so absurd, there must be something unsound in the principle.

We will quote another passage of the same sort:—

"Why, then, we now come to ask, should the governing body in a state profess a religion? First, because it is composed of individual *men;* and they, being appointed to act in a definite moral capacity, must sanctify their acts done in that capacity by the offices of

M—20*

religion; inasmuch as the acts cannot otherwise be acceptable to God, or anything but sinful and punishable in themselves. And whenever we turn our face away from God in our conduct, we are living atheistically. . . . . . . . In fulfilment, then, of his obligations as an individual, the statesman must be a worshipping man. But his acts are public—the powers and instruments with which he works are public—acting under and by the authority of the law, he moves at his word ten thousand subject arms; and because such energies are thus essentially public, and wholly out of the range of mere individual agency; they must be sanctified not only by the private personal prayers and piety of those who fill public situations, but also by public acts of the men composing the public body. They must offer prayer and praise in their public and collective character—in that character wherein they constitute the organ of the nation, and wield its collective force. Wherever there is a reasoning agency, there is a moral duty and responsibility involved in it. The governors are reasoning agents for the nation, in their conjoint acts as such. And therefore there must be attached to this agency, as that without which none of our responsibilities can be met, a religion. And this religion must be that of the conscience of the governor, or none."

Here again we find propositions of vast sweep, and of sound so orthodox and solemn, that many good people, we doubt not, have been greatly edified by it. But let us examine the words closely; and it will immediately become plain that, if these principles be once admitted, there is an end of all society. No combination can be formed for any purpose of mutual help, for trade, for public works, for the relief of the sick or the poor, for the promotion of art or science, unless the members of the combination agree in their theological opinions. Take any such combination at random, the London and Birmingham Railway Company, for example, and observe to what consequences Mr. Gladstone's arguments inevitably lead. "Why should the Directors of the Railway Company, in their collective capacity, profess a religion? First, because the direction is composed of individual men appointed to act in a definite moral capacity, bound to look carefully to the property, the limbs, and the lives of their fellow-creatures, bound to act diligently for their constituents, bound to govern their servants with humanity and justice, bound to fulfil with fidelity many important contracts. They must, therefore, sanctify their acts by the offices of religion, or these acts will be sinful and punishable in themselves. In fulfilment, then, of his obligations as an individual, the Director of the London and Birmingham Railway Company must be a worshipping man. But his acts are public. He acts for a body. He moves at his word ten thousand subject arms. And because these energies are out of the range of his mere individual agency, they must be sanctified by public acts of devotion. The Railway Directors must offer prayer and praise in their public and collective character, in that character wherewith they constitute the organ of the Company, and wield its collected power. Wherever there is reasoning agency, there is moral responsibility. The Directors are reasoning agents for the Company. And therefore there must be attached to this agency, as that without which none of our responsibilities can be met, a religion. And this religion must be that of the conscience of the Director himself, or none. There must be public worship and a test. No Jew, no Socinian, no Presbyterian, no Catholic, no Quaker, must be permitted to be the organ of the Company, and to wield its collected force." Would Mr. Gladstone really defend this proposition? We are sure that he would not; but we are sure that to this proposition, and to innumerable similar propositions, his reasoning inevitably leads.

Again,—

"National will and agency are indisputably one, binding either a dissentient minority or the subject body, in a manner that nothing but the recognition of the doctrine of national personality can justify. National honour and good faith are words in every one's mouth. How do they less imply a personality in nations than the duty towards God, for which we now contend? They are strictly and essentially distinct from the honour and good faith of the individuals composing the nation. France is a person to us, and we to her. A wilful injury done to her is a moral act, and a moral act quite distinct from the acts of all the individuals composing the nation. Upon broad facts like these we may rest, without resorting to the more technical proof which the laws afford in their manner of dealing with corporations. If, then, a nation have unity of will, have pervading sympathies, have capability of reward and suffering contingent upon its acts, shall we deny its responsibility; its need of a religion to meet that responsibility? . . . . A nation, then, having a personality, lies under the obligation, like the individuals composing its governing body, of sanctifying the acts of that personality by the offices of religion, and thus we have a new and imperative ground for the existence of a state religion."

A new ground we have here, certainly, but whether very imperative may be doubted. Is it not perfectly clear, that this argument applies with exactly as much force to every combination of human beings for a common purpose, as to governments? Is there any such combination in the world, whether technically a corporation or not, which has not this collective personality from which Mr. Gladstone deduces such extraordinary consequences? Look at banks, insurance offices, dock companies, canal companies, gas companies, hospitals, dispensaries, associations for the relief of the poor, associations for apprehending malefactors, associations of medical pupils for procuring subjects, associations of country gentlemen for keeping fox-hounds, book societies, benefit societies, clubs of all ranks, from those which have lined Pall-Mall and St. James's Street with their palaces, down to the Free-and-easy which meets in the shabby parlour of a village inn. Is there a single one of these combinations to which Mr. Gladstone's argument will not apply as well as to the State? In all these combinations, in the Bank of England, for example, or in the Athenæum club, the will and agency of the society are one, and bind the dissentient minority. The Bank and the Athenæum have a good faith and a justice different from the good faith and justice of the individual members. The Bank is a person to those who deposit bullion with it. The Athenæum is a person to the butcher and the wine-merchant. If the Athenæum keeps money at the Bank, the two societies are as much persons to each other as England and France. Either society may pay its debts honestly; either may try to defraud its creditors; either may increase in prosperity; either may fall into difficulties. If, then, they have this unity of will; if they are capable of doing and suffering good and evil, can we, to use Mr. Gladstone's words, "deny their responsibility, or their need of a religion to meet that responsibility?" Joint-stock banks, therefore, and clubs, "having a personality, lie under the necessity of sanctifying that personality by the offices of religion;" and thus we have "a new and imperative ground" for requiring all the directors and clerks of joint-stock banks, and all the officers of clubs, to qualify by taking the sacrament.

The truth is that Mr. Gladstone has fallen into an error very common among men of less talents than his own. It is not unusual for a person who is eager to prove a particular proposition to assume a *major* of huge extent, which includes that particular proposition, without ever reflecting that it includes a great deal more. The fatal facility with which Mr. Gladstone multiplies expressions stately and sonorous, but of indeterminate meaning, eminently qualifies him to practise this sleight on himself and on his readers. He lays down broad general doctrines about power, when the only power of which he is thinking is the power of governments, and about conjoint action, when the only conjoint action of which he is thinking is the conjoint action of citizens in a state. He first resolves on his conclusion. He then makes a *major* of most comprehensive dimensions, and, having satisfied himself that it contains his conclusion, never troubles himself about what else it may contain: and, as soon as we examine it, we find that it contains an infinite number of conclusions, every one of which is a monstrous absurdity.

It is perfectly true that it would be a very good thing if all the members of all the associations in the world were men of sound religious views. We have no doubt that a good Christian will be under the guidance of Christian principles, in his conduct as director of a canal company or steward of a charity dinner. If he were, to recur to a case which we before put, a member of a stage-coach company, he would, in that capacity, remember that "a righteous man regardeth the life of his beast." But it does not follow that every association of men must therefore, as such association, profess a religion. It is evident that many great and useful objects can be attained in this world only by cooperation. It is equally evident that there cannot be efficient cooperation, if men proceed on the principle that they must not cooperate for one object unless they agree about other objects. Nothing seems to us more beautiful or admirable in our social system than the facility with which thousands of people, who perhaps agree only on a single point, can combine their energies for the purpose of carrying that single point. We see daily instances of this. Two men, one of them obstinately prejudiced against missions, the other president of a missionary society, sit together at the board of a hospital, and heartily concur in measures for the health and comfort of the patients. Two men, one of whom is a zealous supporter and the other a zealous opponent of the system pursued in Lancaster's schools, meet at the Mendicity Society, and act together with the utmost cordiality. The general rule we take to be undoubtedly this, that it is lawful and expedient for men to unite in an association for the promotion of a good object, though they may differ with respect to other objects of still higher importance.

It will hardly be denied that the security of the persons and property of men is a good object, and that the best way, indeed the only way, of promoting that object is to combine men together in certain great corporations which are called States. These corporations are very variously, and, for the most part, very imperfectly organized. Many of them abound with frightful abuses. But it seems reasonable to believe that the worst that ever existed was, on the whole, preferable to complete anarchy.

Now, reasoning from analogy, we should say that these great corporations would, like all other associations, be likely to attain their end most perfectly if that end were kept singly in view; and that to refuse the services of those who are admirably qualified to promote that end, because they are not also qualified to promote some other end, however excellent, seems at first sight as unreasonable as it would be to provide that nobody who was not a fellow of the Society of Antiquaries should be a governor of the Eye Infirmary; or that nobody who was not a member of the Society for promoting Christianity among the Jews should be a trustee of the Literary Fund.

It is impossible to name any collection of human beings to which Mr. Gladstone's reasonings would apply more strongly than to an army. Where shall we find more complete unity of action than in an army? Where else do so many human beings implicitly obey one ruling mind? What other mass is there which moves so much like one man? Where is such tremendous power intrusted to those who command? Where is so awful a responsibility laid upon them? If Mr. Gladstone has made out, as he conceives, an imperative necessity for a State Religion, much more has he made it out to be imperatively necessary that every army should, in its collective capacity, profess a religion. Is he prepared to adopt this consequence?

On the morning of the thirteenth of August, in the year 1704, two great captains, equal in authority, united by close private and public ties, but of different creeds, prepared for a battle, on the event of which were staked the liberties of Europe. Marlborough had passed a part of the night in prayer, and before daybreak received the sacrament according to the rites of the Church of England. He then hastened to join Eugene, who had probably just confessed himself to a Popish priest. The generals consulted together, formed their plan in concert, and repaired each to his own post. Marlborough gave orders for public prayers. The English chaplains read the service at the head of the English regiments. The Calvinistic chaplains of the Dutch army, with heads on which hand of Bishop had never been laid, poured forth their supplications in front of their countrymen. In the mean time, the Danes might listen to their Lutheran ministers; and Capuchins might encourage the Austrian squadrons, and pray to the Virgin for a blessing on the arms of the Holy Roman Empire. The battle commences, and these men of various religions all act like members of one body. The Catholic and the Protestant general exert themselves to assist and to surpass each other. Before sunset the Empire is saved. France has lost in a day the fruits of eighty years of intrigue and of victory. And the allies, after conquering together, return thanks to God separately, each after his own form of worship. Now, is this practical atheism? Would any man in his senses say, that, because the allied army had unity of action and a common interest, and because a heavy responsibility lay on its Chiefs, it was therefore imperatively necessary that the Army should, as an Army, have one established religion, that Eugene should be deprived of his command for being a Catholic, that all the Dutch and Austrian colonels should be broken for not subscribing the Thirty-nine Articles? Certainly not. The most ignorant grenadier on the field of battle would have seen the absurdity of such a proposition. "I know," he would have said, "that the Prince of Savoy goes to mass, and that our Corporal John cannot abide it; but what has the mass to do with the taking of the village of Blenheim? The prince wants to beat the French, and so does Corporal John. If we stand by each other we shall most likely beat them. If we send all the Papists and Dutch away, Tallard will have every man of us." Mr. Gladstone himself, we imagine, would admit that our honest grenadier would have the best of the argument; and if so, what follows? Even this: that all Mr. Gladstone's general principles about power, and responsibility, and personality, and conjoint action, must be given up; and that, if his theory is to stand at all, it must stand on some other foundation.

We have now, we conceive, shown that it may be proper to form men into combinations for important purposes, which combinations shall have unity and common interests, and shall be under the direction of rulers intrusted with great power and lying under solemn responsibility; and yet that it may be highly improper that these combinations should, as such, profess any one system of religious beliefs, or perform any joint act of religious worship. How, then, is it proved that this may not be the case with some of those great combinations which we call States? We firmly believe that it is the case with some states. We firmly believe that there are communities in which it would be as absurd to mix up theology with government, as it would have been in the right wing of the allied army at Blenheim to commence a controversy with the left wing, in the middle of the battle, about purgatory and the worship of images.

It is the duty, Mr. Gladstone tell us, of the persons, be they who they may, who hold supreme power in the state, to employ that power in order to promote whatever they may deem to be theological truth. Now surely, before he can call on us to admit this proposition, he is bound to prove that these persons are likely to do more good than harm by so employing their power. The first question is, whether a government, proposing to itself the propagation of religious truth, as one of its principal ends, is more likely to lead the people right than to lead them wrong? Mr. Gladstone evades this question; and perhaps it was his wisest course to do so.

"If," says he, "the government be good, let it have its natural duties and powers at its command; but, if not good, let it be made so. . . . We follow, therefore, the true course in looking first for the true ἰδέα, or abstract conception of a government, of course with allowance for the evil and frailty that are in man, and then in examining whether there be comprised in that ἰδέα a capacity and consequent duty on the part of a government to lay down any laws, or devote any means for the purposes of religion,—in short, to exercise a choice upon religion."

Of course, Mr. Gladstone has a perfect right to argue any abstract question, provided he will constantly bear in mind that it is only an abstract question that he is arguing. Whether a perfect government would or would not be a good machinery for the propagation of religious truth is certainly a harmless, and may, for aught we know, be an edifying subject of enquiry. But it is very important that we should remember that there is not, and never has been, any such government in the world. There is no harm at all in enquiring what course a stone thrown into the air would take, if the law of gravitation did not operate. But the consequences would be unpleasant, if the enquirer, as soon as he had finished his calculation, were to begin to throw stones about in all directions, without considering that his conclusion rests on a false hypothesis, and that his projectiles, instead of flying away through infinite space, will speedily return in parabolas, and break the windows and heads of his neighbours.

It is very easy to say that governments are good, or, if not good, ought to be made so. But what is meant by good government? And how are all the bad governments in the world to be made good? And of what value is a theory which is true only on a supposition in the highest degree extravagant?

We do not, however, admit that, if a government were, for all its temporal ends, as perfect as human frailty allows, such government would, therefore, be necessarily qualified to propagate true religion. For we see that the fitness of governments to propagate true religion is by no means proportioned to their fitness for the temporal ends of their institution. Looking at individuals, we see that the princes under whose rule nations have been most ably protected from foreign and domestic disturbance, and have made the most rapid advances in civilisation, have been by no means good teachers of divinity. Take, for example, the best French sovereign, Henry the Fourth, a king who restored order, terminated a terrible civil war, brought the finances into an excellent condition, made his country respected throughout Europe, and endeared himself to the great body of the people whom he ruled. Yet this man was twice a Huguenot, and twice a Papist. He was, as Davila hints, strongly suspected of having no religion at all in theory; and was certainly not much under religious restraints in his practice. Take the Czar Peter, the Empress Catharine, Frederick the Great. It will surely not be disputed that these sovereigns, with all their faults, were, if we consider them with reference merely to the temporal ends of government, above the average of merit. Considered as theological guides, Mr. Gladstone would probably put them below the most abject drivellers of the Spanish branch of the house of Bourbon. Again, when we pass from individuals to systems, we by no means find that the aptitude of governments for propagating religious truth is proportioned to their aptitude for secular functions. Without being blind admirers either of the French or of the American institutions, we think it clear that the persons and property of citizens are better protected in France and in New England than in almost any society that now exists, or that has ever existed; very much better, certainly, than in the Roman empire under the orthodox rule of Constantine and Theodosius. But neither the government of France, nor that of New England, is so organized as to be fit for the propagation of theological doctrines. Nor do we think it improbable that the most serious religious errors might prevail in a state which, considered merely with reference to temporal objects, might approach far nearer than any that has ever been known to the ἰδέα of what a state should be.

But we shall leave this abstract question, and look at the world as we find it. Does, then, the way in which governments generally obtain their power make it at all probable that they will be more favourable to orthodoxy than to heterodoxy? A nation of barbarians pours down on a rich and unwarlike empire, enslaves the people, portions out the land, and blends the institutions which it finds in the cities with those which it has brought from the woods. A handful of daring adventurers from a civilised nation wander to some savage country, and reduce the aboriginal race to bondage. A successful general turns his arms against the state which he serves. A society, made brutal by oppression, rises madly on its masters, sweeps away all old laws and usages, and, when its first paroxysm of rage is over, sinks down passively under any form of polity which may spring out of the chaos. A chief of a party, as at Florence, becomes imperceptibly a sovereign and the founder of a dynasty. A captain of mercenaries, as at Milan, seizes on a city, and by the sword makes himself its ruler. An elective senate, as at Venice, usurps permanent and hereditary power. It is in events such as these that governments have generally originated; and we can see nothing in such events to warrant us in believing that the governments thus called into existence will be peculiarly well fitted to distinguish between religious truth and heresy.

When, again, we look at the constitutions of governments which have become settled, we find no great security for the orthodoxy of rulers. One magistrate holds power because his name was drawn out of a purse; another, because his father held it before him. There are representative systems of all sorts, large constituent bodies, small constituent bodies, universal suffrage, high pecuniary qualifications. We see that, for the temporal ends of government, some of these constitutions are very skilfully constructed, and that the very worst of them is preferable to anarchy. We see some sort of connexion between the very worst of them, and the temporal well-being of society. But it passes our understanding to comprehend what connexion any one of them has with theological truth.

And how stands the fact? Have not almost all the governments in the world always been in the wrong on religious subjects? Mr. Gladstone, we imagine, would say that, except in the time of Constantine, of Jovian, and of a very few of their successors, and occasionally in England since the Reformation, no government has ever been sincerely friendly to the pure and apostolical Church of Christ. If, therefore, it be true that every ruler is bound in conscience to use his power for the propagation of his own religion, it will follow that, for one ruler who has been bound in conscience to use his power for the propagation of truth, a thousand have been bound in conscience to use their power for the propagation of falsehood. Surely this is a conclusion from which common sense recoils. Surely, if experience shows that a certain machine, when used to produce a certain effect, does not produce that effect once in a thousand times, but produces, in the vast majority of cases, an effect directly contrary, we cannot be wrong in saying that it is not a machine of which the principal end is to be so used.

If, indeed, the magistrate would content himself with laying his opinions and reasons before the people, and would leave the people, uncorrupted by hope or fear, to judge for themselves, we should see little reason to apprehend that his interference in favour of error would be seriously prejudicial to the interests of truth. Nor do we, as will hereafter be seen, object to his taking this course, when it is compatible with the efficient discharge of his more especial duties. But this will not satisfy Mr. Gladstone. He would have the magistrate resort to means which have a great tendency to make malcontents, to make hypocrites, to make careless nominal conformists, but no tendency whatever to produce honest and rational conviction. It seems to us quite clear that an enquirer who has no wish, except to know the truth, is more likely to arrive at the truth than an enquirer who knows that, if he decides one way, he shall be rewarded, and that, if he decides the other way, he shall be punished. Now, Mr. Gladstone would have governments propagate their opinions by excluding all dissenters from all civil offices. That is to say, he would have governments propagate their opinions by a process which has no reference whatever to the truth or falsehood of those opinions, by arbitrarily uniting certain worldly advantages with one set of doctrines, and certain worldly inconveniences with another set. It is of the very nature of argument to serve the interest of truth; but if rewards and punishments serve the interest of truth, it is by mere accident. It is very much easier to find arguments for the Divine authority of the Gospel than for the Divine authority of the Koran. But it is just as easy to bribe or rack a Jew into Mahometanism as into Christianity.

From racks, indeed, and from all penalties directed against the persons, the property, and the liberty of heretics, the humane spirit of Mr. Gladstone shrinks with horror. He only maintains that conformity to the religion of the state ought to be an indispensable qualification for office; and he would, unless we have greatly misunderstood him, think it his duty, if he had the power, to revive the Test Act, to enforce it rigorously, and to extend it to important classes who were formerly exempt from its operation.

This is indeed a legitimate consequence of his principles. But why stop here? Why not roast dissenters at slow fires? All the general reasonings on which this theory rests evidently lead to sanguinary persecution. If the propagation of religious truth be a principal end of government, as government; if it be the duty of a government to employ for that end its constitutional power; if the constitutional power of governments extends, as it most unquestionably does, to the making of laws for the burning of heretics; if burning be, as it most assuredly is, in many cases, a most effectual mode of suppressing opinions; why should we not burn? If the relation in which government ought to stand to the people be, as Mr. Gladstone tell us, a paternal relation, we are irresistibly led to the conclusion that persecution is justifiable. For the right of propagating opinions by punishment is one which belongs to parents as clearly as the right to give instruction. A boy is compelled to attend family worship: he is forbidden to read irreligious books: if he will not learn his catechism, he is sent to bed without his supper: if he plays truant at church-time, a task is set him. If he should display the precocity of his talents by expressing impious opinions before his brothers and sisters, we should not much blame his father for cutting short the controversy with a horsewhip. All the reasons which lead us to think that parents are peculiarly fitted to conduct the education of their children, and that education is a principal end of the parental relation, lead us also to think, that parents ought to be allowed to use punishment, if necessary, for the purpose of forcing children, who are incapable of judging for themselves, to receive religious instruction and to attend religious worship. Why, then, is this prerogative of punishment, so eminently paternal, to be withheld from a paternal government? It seems to us, also, to be the height of absurdity to employ civil disabilities for the propagation of an opinion, and then to shrink from employing other punishments for the same purpose. For nothing can be clearer than that, if you punish at all, you ought to punish enough. The pain caused by punishment is pure unmixed evil, and never ought to be inflicted, except for the sake of some good. It is mere foolish cruelty to provide penalties which torment the criminal without preventing the crime. Now it is possible, by sanguinary persecution unrelentingly inflicted, to suppress opinions. In this way the Albigenses were put down. In this way the Lollards were put down. In this way the fair promise of the Reformation was blighted in Italy and Spain. But we may safely defy Mr. Gladstone to point out a single instance in which the system which he recommends has succeeded.

And why should he be so tender-hearted? What reason can he give for hanging a murderer, and suffering a heresiarch to escape without even a pecuniary mulct? Is the heresiarch a less pernicious member of society than the murderer? Is not the loss of one soul a greater evil than the extinction of many lives? And the number of murders committed by the most profligate bravo that ever let out his poniard to hire in Italy, or by the most savage buccaneer that ever prowled on the Windward Station, is small indeed, when compared with the number of souls which have been caught in the snares of one dexterous heresiarch. If, then, the heresiarch causes infinitely greater evils than the murderer, why is he not as proper an object of penal legislation as the murderer? We can give a reason, a reason, short, simple, decisive, and consistent. We do not extenuate the evil which the heresiarch produces; but we say that it is not evil of that sort against which it is the end of government to guard. But how Mr. Gladstone, who considers the evil which the heresiarch produces as evil of the sort against which it is the end of government to guard, can escape from the obvious consequence of his doctrine, we do not understand. The world is full of parallel cases. An orange-woman stops up the pavement with her wheel-barrow; and a policeman takes her into custody. A miser who has amassed a million suffers an old friend and benefactor to die in a work-house, and cannot be questioned before any tribunal for his baseness and ingratitude. Is this because legislators think the orange-woman's conduct worse than the miser's? Not at all. It is because the stopping up of the pathway is one of the evils against which it is the business of the public authorities to protect society, and heartlessness is not one of those evils. It would be the height of folly to say that the miser ought, indeed, to be punished, but that he ought to be punished less severely than the orange-woman.

The heretical Constantius persecutes Athanasius; and why not? Shall Cæsar punish the robber who has taken one purse, and spare the wretch who has taught millions to rob the Creator of his honour, and to bestow it on the creature? The orthodox Theodosius persecutes the Arians, and with equal reason. Shall an insult offered to the Cæsarean majesty be expiated by death; and shall there be no penalty for him who degrades to the rank of a creature the almighty, the infinite Creator? We have a short answer for both: "To Cæsar the things which are Cæsar's. Cæsar is appointed for the punishment of robbers and rebels. He is not appointed for the purpose of either propagating or exterminating the doctrine of the consubstantiality of the Father and the Son." "Not so," says Mr. Gladstone. "Cæsar is bound in conscience to propagate whatever he thinks to be the truth as to this question. Constantius is bound to establish the Arian worship throughout the empire, and to displace the bravest captains of his legions, and the ablest ministers of his treasury, if they hold the Nicene faith. Theodosius is equally bound to turn out every public servant whom his Arian predecessors have put in. But if Constantius lays on Athanasius a fine of a single *aureus*, if Theodosius imprisons an Arian presbyter for a week, this is most unjustifiable oppression." Our readers will be curious to know how this distinction is made out.

The reasons which Mr. Gladstone gives against persecution affecting life, limb, and property, may be divided into two classes; first, reasons which can be called reasons only by extreme courtesy, and which nothing but the most deplorable necessity would ever have induced a man of his abilities to use; and, secondly, reasons which are really reasons, and which have so much force that they not only completely prove his exception, but completely upset his general rule. His artillery on this occasion is composed of two sorts of pieces, pieces which will not go off at all, and pieces which go off with a vengeance, and recoil with most crushing effect upon himself.

"We, as fallible creatures," says Mr. Gladstone, "have no right, from any bare speculations of our own, to administer pains and penalties to our fellow-creatures, whether on social or religious grounds. We have the right to enforce the laws of the land by such pains and penalties, because it is expressly given by Him who has declared that the civil rulers are to bear the sword for the punishment of evil-doers, and for the encouragement of them that do well. And so, in things spiritual, had it pleased God to give to the Church or the State this power, to be permanently exercised over their members, or mankind at large, we should have the right to use it; but it does not appear to have been so received, and, consequently, it should not be exercised."

We should be sorry to think that the security of our lives and property from persecution rested on no better ground than this. Is not a teacher of heresy an evil-doer? Has not heresy been condemned in many countries, and in our own among them, by the laws of the land, which, as Mr. Gladstone says, it is justifiable to enforce by penal sanctions? If a heretic is not specially mentioned in the text to which Mr. Gladstone refers, neither is an assassin, a kidnapper, or a highwayman: and if the silence of the New Testament as to all interference of governments to stop the progress of heresy be a reason for not fining or imprisoning heretics, it is surely just as good a reason for not excluding them from office.

"God," says Mr. Gladstone, "has seen fit to authorize the employment of force in the one case and not in the other; for it was with regard to chastisement inflicted by the sword for an insult offered to himself, that the Redeemer declared his kingdom not to be of this world;—meaning, apparently in an especial manner, that it should be otherwise than after this world's fashion, in respect to the sanctions by which its laws should be maintained."

Now here Mr. Gladstone, quoting from memory, has fallen into an error. The very remarkable words which he cites do not appear to have had any reference to the wound inflicted by Peter on Malchus. They were addressed to Pilate, in answer to the question, "Art thou the King of the Jews?" We cannot help saying that we are surprised that Mr. Gladstone should not have more accurately verified a quotation on which, according to him, principally depends the right of a hundred millions of his fellow-subjects, idolaters, Mussulmans, Catholics, and dissenters, to their property, their liberty, and their lives.

Mr. Gladstone's humane interpretations of Scripture are lamentably destitute of one recommendation, which he considers as of the highest value: they are by no means in accordance with the general precepts or practice of the Church, from the time when the Christians became strong enough to persecute down to a very recent period. A dogma favourable to toleration is certainly not a dogma *quod semper, quod ubique, quod omnibus*. Bossuet was able to say, we fear with too much truth, that on one point all Christians had long been unanimous, the right of the civil magistrate to propagate truth by the sword; that even heretics had been orthodox as to this right, and that the Anabaptists and Socinians were the first who called it in question. We will not pretend to say what is the best explanation of the text under consideration; but we are sure that Mr. Gladstone's is the worst. According to him, government ought to exclude dissenters from office, but not to fine them, because Christ's kingdom is not of this world. We do not see why the line may not be drawn at a hundred other places as well as at that which he has chosen. We do not see why Lord Clarendon, in recommending the act of 1664 against conventicles, might not have said, "It hath been thought by some that this *classis* of men might with advantage be not only imprisoned, but pilloried. But methinks, my Lords, we are inhibited from the punishment of the pillory by that Scripture, 'My kingdom is not of this world.' " Archbishop Laud, when he sate on Burton in the Star-Chamber, might have said, "I pronounce for the pillory; and, indeed, I could wish that all such wretches were delivered to the fire, but that our Lord hath said that his kingdom is not of this world." And Gardiner might have written to the Sheriff of Oxfordshire: "See that execution be done without fail on Master Ridley and Master Latimer, as you will answer the same to the Queen's grace at your peril. But if they shall desire to have some gunpowder for the shortening of their torment, I see not but you may grant it, as it is written, *Regnum meum non est de hoc mundo*; that is to say, My kingdom is not of this world."

But Mr. Gladstone has other arguments against persecution, arguments which are of so much weight, that they are decisive not only against persecution, but against his whole theory. "The government," he says, "is incompetent to exercise minute and constant supervision over religious opinion." And hence he infers, that "a government exceeds its province when it comes to adapt a scale of punishments to variations in religious opinion, according to their respective degrees of variation from the established creed. To decline affording countenance to sects is a single and simple rule. To punish their professors, according to their several errors, even were there no other objection, is one for which the state must assume functions wholly ecclesiastical, and for which it is not intrinsically fitted."

This is, in our opinion, quite true. But how does it agree with Mr. Gladstone's theory? What! The government incompetent to exercise even such a degree of supervision over religious opinion as is implied by the punishment of the most deadly heresy! The government incompetent to measure even the grossest deviations from the standard of truth! The government not intrinsically qualified to judge of the comparative enormity of any theological errors! The government so ignorant on these subjects that it is compelled to leave, not merely subtle heresies, discernible only by the eye of a Cyril or a Bucer, but Socinianism, Deism, Mahometanism, Idolatry, Atheism, unpunished! To whom does Mr. Gladstone assign the office of selecting a religion for the state, from among hundreds of religions, every one of which lays claim to truth? Even to this same government, which he now pronounces to be so unfit for theological investigations that it cannot venture to punish a man for worshipping a lump of stone with a score of heads and hands! We do not remember ever to have fallen in with a more extraordinary instance of inconsistency. When Mr. Gladstone wishes to prove that the government ought to establish and endow a religion, and to fence it with a test act, government is τὸ πᾶν in the moral world. Those who would confine it to secular ends take a low view of its nature. A religion must be attached to its agency; and this religion must be that of the conscience of the governor, or none. It is for the Governor to decide between

Papists and Protestants, Jansenists and Molinists, Arminians and Calvinists, Episcopalians and Presbyterians, Sabellians and Tritheists, Homoousians and Homoiousians, Nestorian sand Eutychians, Monothelites and Monophysites, Pædobaptists and Anabaptists. It is for him to rejudge the Acts of Nice and Rimini, of Ephesus and Chalcedon, of Constantinople and St. John Lateran, of Trent and Dort. It is for him to arbitrate between the Greek and the Latin procession, and to determine whether that mysterious *filioque* shall or shall not have a place in the national creed. When he has made up his mind, he is to tax the whole community in order to pay people to teach his opinion, whatever it may be. He is to rely on his own judgment, though it may be opposed to that of nine tenths of the society. He is to act on his own judgment, at the risk of exciting the most formidable discontents. He is to inflict, perhaps on a great majority of the population, what, whether Mr. Gladstone may choose to call it persecution or not, will always be felt as persecution by those who suffer it. He is, on account of differences often too slight for vulgar comprehension, to deprive the state of the services of the ablest men. He is to debase and enfeeble the community which he governs, from a nation into a sect. In our own country, for example, millions of Catholics, millions of Protestant Dissenters, are to be excluded from all power and honours. A great hostile fleet is on the sea; but Nelson is not to command in the Channel if in the mystery of the Trinity he confounds the persons. An invading army has landed in Kent; but the Duke of Wellington is not to be at the head of our forces if he divides the substance. And, after all this, Mr. Gladstone tells us, that it would be wrong to imprison a Jew, a Mussulman, or a Budhist, for a day; because really a government cannot understand these matters, and ought not to meddle with questions which belong to the Church. A singular theologian, indeed, this government! So learned that it is competent to exclude Grotius from office for being a Semi-Pelagian, so unlearned that it is incompetent to fine a Hindoo peasant a rupee for going on a pilgrimage to Juggernaut!

"To solicit and persuade one another," says Mr. Gladstone, "are privileges which belong to us all; and the wiser and better man is bound to advise the less wise and good: but he is not only not bound, he is not allowed, speaking generally, to coerce him. It is untrue, then, that the same considerations which bind a government to submit a religion to the free choice of the people would therefore justify their enforcing its adoption."

Granted. But it is true that all the same considerations which would justify a government in propagating a religion by means of civil disabilities would justify the propagating of that religion by penal laws. To solicit! Is it solicitation to tell a Catholic Duke, that he must abjure his religion or walk out of the House of Lords? To persuade! Is it persuasion to tell a barrister of distinguished eloquence and learning that he shall grow old in his stuff gown, while his pupils are seated above him in ermine, because he cannot digest the damnatory clauses of the Athanasian creed? Would Mr. Gladstone think that a religious system which he considers as false, Socinianism for example, was submitted to his free choice, if it were submitted in these terms. "If you obstinately adhere to the faith of the Nicene fathers, you shall not be burned in Smithfield; you shall not be sent to Dorchester gaol; you shall not even pay double land-tax. But you shall be shut out from all situations in which you might exercise your talents with honour to yourself and advantage to the country. The House of Commons, the bench of magistracy, are not for such as you. You shall see younger men, your inferiors in station and talents, rise to the highest dignities and attract the gaze of nations, while you are doomed to neglect and obscurity. If you have a son of the highest promise, a son such as other fathers would contemplate with delight, the development of his fine talents and of his generous ambition shall be a torture to you. You shall look on him as a being doomed to lead, as you have led, the abject life of a Roman or a Neapolitan in the midst of the great English people. All those high honours, so much more precious than the most costly gifts of despots, with which a free country decorates its illustrious citizens, shall be to him, as they have been to you, objects not of hope and virtuous emulation, but of hopeless, envious pining. Educate him, if you wish him to feel his degradation. Educate him, if you wish to stimulate his craving for what he never must enjoy. Educate him, if you would imitate the barbarity of that Celtic tyrant who fed his prisoners on salted food till they called eagerly for drink, and then let down an empty cup into the dungeon and left them to die of thirst." Is this to solicit, to persuade, to submit religion to the free choice of man? Would a fine of a thousand pounds, would imprisonment in Newgate for six months, under circumstances not disgraceful, give Mr. Gladstone the pain which he would feel, if he were to be told that he was to be dealt with in the way in which he would himself deal with more than one half of his countrymen?

We are not at all surprised to find such inconsistency even in a man of Mr. Gladstone's talents. The truth is, that every man is, to a great extent, the creature of the age. It is to no purpose that he resists the influence which the vast mass, in which he is but an atom, must exercise on him. He may try to be a man of the tenth century: but he cannot. Whether he will or no, he must be a man of the nineteenth century. He shares in the motion of the moral as well as in that of the physical world. He can no more be as intolerant as he would have been in the days of the Tudors than he can stand in the evening exactly where he stood in the morning. The globe goes round from west to east; and he must go round with it. When he says that he is where he was, he means only that he has moved at the same rate with all around him. When he says that he has gone a good way to the westward, he means only that he has not gone to the eastward quite so rapidly as his neighbours. Mr. Gladstone's book is, in this respect, a very gratifying performance. It is the measure of what a man can do to be left behind by the world. It is the strenuous effort of a very vigorous mind to keep as far in the rear of the general progress as possible. And yet, with the most intense exertion, Mr. Gladstone cannot help being, on some important points, greatly in advance of Locke himself: and, with whatever admiration he may regard Laud, it is well for him, we can tell him, that he did not write in the days of that zealous primate, who would certainly have refuted the expositions of Scripture which we have quoted by one of the keenest arguments that can be addressed to human ears.

This is not the only instance in which Mr. Gladstone has shrunk in a very remarkable manner from the consequences of his own theory. If there be in the whole world a state to which this theory is applicable, that state is the British Empire in India. Even we, who detest paternal governments in general, shall admit that the duties of the government of India are, to a considerable extent, paternal. There, the superiority of the governors to the governed in moral science is unquestionable. The conversion of the whole people to the worst form that Christianity ever wore in the darkest ages would be a most happy event. It is not necessary that a man should be a Christian to wish for the propagation of Christianity in India. It is sufficient that he should be an European not much below the ordinary European level of good sense and humanity. Compared with the importance of the interests at stake, all those Scotch and Irish questions which occupy so large a portion of Mr. Gladstone's book sink into insignificance. In no part of the world, since the days of Theodosius, has so large a heathen population been subject to a Christian government. In no part of the world is heathenism more cruel, more licentious, more fruitful of absurd rites and pernicious laws. Surely, if it be the duty of government to use its power and its revenue in order to bring seven millions of Irish Catholics over to the Protestant Church, it is *a fortiori* the duty of the government to use its power and its revenue in order to make seventy millions of idolaters Christians. If it be a sin to suffer John Howard or William Penn to hold any office in England, because they are not in communion with the Established Church, it must be a crying sin indeed to admit to high situations men who bow down, in temples covered with emblems of vice, to the hideous images of sensual or malevolent gods.

But no. Orthodoxy, it seems, is more shocked by the priests of Rome than by the priests of Kalee. The plain red-brick building, the Cave of Adullam, or Ebenezer Chapel, where uneducated men hear a half educated man talk of the Christian law of love and the Christian hope of glory, is unworthy of the indulgence which is reserved for the shrine where the Thug suspends a portion of the spoils of murdered travellers, and for the car which grinds its way through the bones of self-immolated pilgrims. "It would be," says Mr. Gladstone, "an absurd exaggeration to maintain it as the part of such a government as that of the British in India to bring home to the door of every subject at once the ministrations of a new and totally unknown religion." The government ought indeed to desire to propagate Christianity. But the extent to which they must do so must be "limited by the degree in which the people are found willing to receive it." He proposes no such limitation in the case of Ireland. He would give the Irish a Protestant Church whether they like it or not. "We believe," says he, "that that which we place before them is, whether they know it or not, calculated to be beneficial to them; and that, if they know it not now, they will know it when it is presented to them fairly. Shall we, then, purchase their applause at the expense of their substantial, nay, their spiritual interests?"

And why does Mr. Gladstone allow to the Hindoo a privilege which he denies to the Irishman? Why does he reserve his greatest liberality for the most monstrous errors? Why does he pay most respect to the opinion of the least enlightened people? Why does he withhold the right to exercise paternal authority from that one government which is fitter to exercise paternal authority than any government that ever existed in the world? We will give the reason in his own words.

"In British India," he says, "a small number of persons advanced to a higher grade of civilisation, exercise the powers of government over an immensely greater number of less cultivated persons, not by coercion, but under free stipulation with the governed. Now, the rights of a government, in circumstances thus peculiar, obviously depend neither upon the unrestricted theory of paternal principles, nor upon any primordial or fictitious contract of indefinite powers, but upon an express and known treaty, matter of positive agreement, not of natural ordinance."

Where Mr. Gladstone has seen this treaty we cannot guess; for, though he calls it a "known treaty," we will stake our credit that it is quite unknown both at Calcutta and Madras, both in Leadenhall Street and Cannon Row, that it is not to be found in any of the enormous folios of papers relating to India which fill the book-cases of members of Parliament, that it has utterly escaped the researches of all the historians of our Eastern empire, that, in the long and interesting debates of 1813 on the admission of missionaries to India, debates of which the most valuable part has been excellently preserved by the care of the speakers, no allusion to this important instrument is to be found. The truth is that this treaty is a nonentity. It is by coercion, it is by the sword, and not by free stipulation with the governed, that England rules India; nor is England bound by any contract whatever not to deal with Bengal as she deals with Ireland. She may set up a Bishop of Patna, and a Dean of Hoogley; she may grant away the public revenue for the maintenance of prebendaries of Benares and canons of Moorshedabad; she may divide the country into parishes, and place a rector with a stipend in every one of them; and all this without infringing any positive agreement. If there be such a treaty, Mr. Gladstone can have no difficulty in making known its date, its terms, and, above all, the precise extent of the territory within which we have sinfully bound ourselves to be guilty of practical atheism. The last point is of great importance. For, as the provinces of our Indian empire were acquired at different times, and in very different ways, no single treaty, indeed no ten treaties, will justify the system pursued by our government there.

The plain state of the case is this. No man in his senses would dream of applying Mr. Gladstone's theory to India, because, if so applied, it would inevitably destroy our empire, and, with our empire, the best chance of spreading Christianity among the natives. This Mr. Gladstone felt. In some way or other his theory was to be saved, and the monstrous consequences avoided.

Of intentional misrepresentation we are quite sure that he is incapable. But we cannot acquit him of that unconscious disingenuousness from which the most upright man, when strongly attached to an opinion, is seldom wholly free. We believe that he recoiled from the ruinous consequences which his system would produce, if tried in India; but that he did not like to say so, lest he should lay himself open to the charge of sacrificing principle to expediency, a word which is held in the utmost abhorrence by all his school. Accordingly, he caught at the notion of a treaty, a notion which must, we think, have originated in some rhetorical expression which he has imperfectly understood. There is one excellent way of avoiding the drawing of a false conclusion from a false *major*; and that is by having a false *minor*. Inaccurate history is an admirable corrective of unreasonable theory. And thus it is in the present case. A bad general rule is laid down, and obstinately maintained, wherever the consequences are not too monstrous for human bigotry. But when they become so horrible that even Christ Church shrinks, that even Oriel stands aghast, the rule is evaded by means of a fictitious contract. One imaginary obligation is set up against another. Mr. Gladstone first preaches to governments the duty of undertaking an enterprise just as rational as the Crusades, and then dispenses them from it on the ground of a treaty which is just as authentic as the donation of Constantine to Pope Sylvester. His system resembles nothing so much as a forged bond with a forged release indorsed on the back of it.

With more show of reason he rests the claims of the Scotch Church on a contract. He considers that contract, however, as most unjustifiable, and speaks of the setting up of the Kirk as a disgraceful blot on the reign of William the Third. Surely it would be amusing, if it were not melancholy, to see a man of virtue and abilities unsatisfied with the calamities which one Church, constituted on false principles, has brought upon the empire, and repining that Scotland is not in the same state with Ireland, that no Scottish agitator is raising rent and putting county members in and out, that no Presbyterian association is dividing supreme power with the government, that no meetings of precursors and repealers are covering the side of the Calton Hill, that twenty-five thousand troops are not required to maintain order on the north of the Tweed, that the anniversary of the Battle of Bothwell Bridge is not regularly celebrated by insult, riot, and murder. We could hardly find a stronger argument against Mr. Gladstone's system than that which Scotland furnishes. The policy which has been followed in that country has been directly opposed to the policy which he recommends. And the consequence is that Scotland, having been one of the rudest, one of the poorest, one of the most turbulent countries in Europe, has become one of the most highly civilised, one of the most flourishing, one of the most tranquil. The atrocities which were of common occurrence while an unpopular church was dominant are unknown. In spite of a mutual aversion as bitter as ever separated one people from another, the two kingdoms which compose our island have been indissolubly joined together. Of the ancient national feeling there remains just enough to be ornamental and useful; just enough to inspire the poet, and to kindle a generous and friendly emulation in the bosom of the soldier. But for all the ends of government the nations are one. And why are they so? The answer is simple. The nations are one for all the ends of government, because in their union the true ends of government alone were kept in sight. The nations are one, because the Churches are two.

Such is the union of England with Scotland, an union which resembles the union of the limbs of one healthful and vigorous body, all moved by one will, all cooperating for common ends. The system of Mr. Gladstone would have produced an union which can be compared only to that which is the subject of a wild Persian fable. King Zohak,—we tell the story as Mr. Southey tells it to us,—gave the devil leave to kiss his shoulders. Instantly two serpents sprang out, who, in the fury of hunger, attacked his head, and attempted to get at his brain. Zohak pulled them away, and tore them with his nails. But he found that they were inseparable parts of himself, and that what he was lacerating was his own flesh. Perhaps we might be able to find, if we looked round the world, some political union like this, some hideous monster of a state, cursed with one principle of sensation and two principles of volition, self-loathing and self-torturing, made up of parts which are driven by a frantic impulse to inflict mutual pain, yet are doomed to feel whatever they inflict, which are divided by an irreconcileable hatred, yet are blended in an indissoluble identity. Mr. Gladstone, from his tender concern for Zohak, is unsatisfied because the devil has as yet kissed only one shoulder, because there is not a snake mangling and mangled on the left to keep in countenance his brother on the right.

But we must proceed in our examination of his theory. Having, as he conceives, proved that it is the duty of every government to profess some religion or other, right or wrong, and to establish that religion, he then comes to the question what religion a government ought to prefer, and he decides this question in favour of the form of Christianity established in England. The Church of England is, according to him, the pure Catholic Church of Christ, which possesses the apostolical succession of ministers, and within whose pale is to be found that unity which is essential to truth. For her decisions he claims a degree of reverence far beyond what she has ever, in any of her formularies, claimed for herself; far beyond what the moderate school of Bossuet demands for the Pope; and scarcely short of what that school would ascribe to Pope and General Council together. To separate from her communion is schism. To reject her traditions or interpretations of Scripture is sinful presumption.

Mr. Gladstone pronounces the right of private judgment, as it is generally understood throughout Protestant Europe, to be a monstrous abuse. He declares himself favourable, indeed, to the exercise of private judgment, after a fashion of his own. We have, according to him, a right to judge all the doctrines of the Church of England to be sound, but not to judge any of them to be unsound. He has no objection, he assures us, to active enquiry into religious questions. On the contrary, he thinks such enquiry highly desirable, as long as it does not lead to diversity of opinion; which is much the same thing as if he were to recommend the use of fire that will not burn down houses, or of brandy that will not make men drunk. He conceives it to be perfectly possible for mankind to exercise their intellects vigorously and freely on theological subjects, and yet to come to exactly the same conclusions with each other and with the Church of England. And for this opinion he gives, as far as we have been able to discover, no reason whatever, except that every body who vigorously and freely exercises his understanding on Euclid's Theorems assents to them. "The activity of private judgment," he truly observes, "and the unity and strength of conviction in mathematics vary directly as each other." On this unquestionable fact he constructs a somewhat questionable argument. Every body who freely inquires agrees, he says, with Euclid. But the Church is as much in the right as Euclid. Why, then, should not every free inquirer agree with the Church? We could put many similar questions. Either the affirmative or the negative of the proposition that King Charles wrote the *Icon Basilike* is as true as that two sides of a triangle are greater than the third side. Why, then, do Dr. Wordsworth and Mr. Hallam agree in thinking two sides of a triangle greater than the third side, and yet differ about the genuineness of the *Icon Basilike*? The state of the exact sciences proves, says Mr. Gladstone, that, as respects religion, "the association of these two ideas, activity of enquiry, and variety of conclusion, is a fallacious one." We might just as well turn the argument the other way, and infer from the variety of religious opinions that there must necessarily be hostile mathematical sects, some affirming, and some denying, that the square of the hypothenuse is equal to the squares of the sides. But we do not think either the one analogy or the other of the smallest value. Our way of ascertaining the tendency of free enquiry is simply to open our eyes and look at the world in which we live; and there we see that free enquiry on mathematical subjects produces unity, and that free enquiry on moral subjects produces discrepancy. There would undoubtedly be less discrepancy if enquirers were more diligent and candid. But discrepancy there will be among the most diligent and candid, as long as the constitution of the human mind, and the nature of moral evidence, continue unchanged. That we have not freedom and unity together is a very sad thing; and so it is that we have not wings. But we are just as likely to see the one defect removed as the other. It is not only in religion that this discrepancy is found. It is the same with all matters which depend on moral evidence, with judicial questions, for example, and with political questions. All the judges will work a sum in the rule of three on the same principle, and bring out the same conclusion. But it does not follow that, however honest and laborious they may be, they will all be of one mind on the Douglas case. So it is vain to hope that there may be a free constitution under which every representative will be unanimously elected, and every law unanimously passed; and it would be ridiculous for a statesman to stand wondering and bemoaning himself, because people who agree in thinking that two and two make four cannot agree about the new poor law, or the administration of Canada.

There are two intelligible and consistent courses which may be followed with respect to the exercise of private judgment; the course of the Romanist, who interdicts private judgment because of its inevitable inconveniences; and the course of the Protestant, who permits private judgment in spite of its inevitable inconveniences. Both are more reasonable than Mr. Gladstone, who would have private judgment without its inevitable inconveniences. The Romanist produces repose by means of stupefaction. The Protestant encourages activity, though he knows that, where there is much activity, there will be some aberration. Mr. Gladstone wishes for the unity of the fifteenth century with the active and searching spirit of the sixteenth. He might as well wish to be in two places at once.

When Mr. Gladstone says that we "actually require discrepancy of opinion—require and demand error, falsehood, blindness, and plume ourselves on such discrepancy as attesting a freedom which is only valuable when used for unity in the truth," he expresses himself with more energy than precision. Nobody loves discrepancy for the sake of discrepancy. But a person who conscientiously believes that free enquiry is, on the whole, beneficial to the interests of truth, and that, from the imperfection of the human faculties, wherever there is much free enquiry there will be some discrepancy, may, without impropriety, consider such discrepancy, though in itself an evil, as a sign of good. That there are ten thousand thieves in London is a very melancholy fact. But, looked at in one point of view, it is a reason for exultation. For what other city could maintain ten thousand thieves? What must be the mass of wealth, where the fragments gleaned by lawless pilfering rise to so large an amount? St. Kilda would not support a single pickpocket. The quantity of theft is, to a certain extent, an index of the quantity of useful industry and judicious speculation. And just as we may, from the great number of rogues in a town, infer that much honest gain is made there; so may we often, from the quantity of error in a community, draw a cheering inference as to the degree in which the public mind is turned to those enquiries which alone can lead to rational convictions of truth.

Mr. Gladstone seems to imagine that most Protestants think it possible for the same doctrine to be at once true and false; or that they think it immaterial whether, on a religious question, a man comes to a true or a false conclusion. If there be any Protestants who hold notions so absurd, we abandon them to his censure.

The Protestant doctrine touching the right of private judgment, that doctrine, which is the common foundation of the Anglican, the Lutheran, and the Calvinistic Churches, that doctrine by which every sect of dissenters vindicates its separation, we conceive not to be this, that opposite opinions may both be true; nor this, that truth and falsehood are both equally good; nor yet this, that all speculative error is necessarily innocent; but this, that there is on the face of the earth no visible body to whose decrees men are bound to submit their private judgment on points of faith.

Is there always such a visible body? Was there such a visible body in the year 1500? If not, why are we to believe that there is such a body in the year 1839? If there was such a body in the year 1500, what was it? Was it the Church of Rome? And how can the Church of England be orthodox now, if the Church of Rome was orthodox then?

"In England," says Mr. Gladstone, "the case was widely different from that of the Continent. Her reformation did not destroy, but successfully maintained, the unity and succession of the Church in her apostolical ministry. We have, therefore, still among us the ordained hereditary witnesses of the truth, conveying it to us through an unbroken series from our Lord Jesus Christ and his apostles. This is to us the ordinary voice of authority; of authority equally reasonable and equally true, whether we will hear, or whether we will forbear."

Mr. Gladstone's reasoning is not so clear as might be desired. We have among us, he says, ordained hereditary witnesses of the truth, and their voice is to us the voice of authority. Undoubtedly, if they are witnesses of the truth, their voice is the voice of authority. But this is little more than saying that the truth is the truth. Nor is truth more true because it comes in an unbroken series from the apostles. The Nicene faith is not more true in the mouth of the Archbishop of Canterbury, than in that of a Moderator of the General Assembly. If our respect for the authority of the Church is to be only consequent upon our conviction of the truth of her doctrines, we come at once to that monstrous abuse, the Protestant exercise of private judgment. But if Mr. Gladstone means that we ought to believe that the Church of England speaks the truth, because she has the apostolical succession, we greatly doubt whether such a doctrine can be maintained. In the first place, what proof have we of the fact? We have, indeed, heard it said that Providence would certainly have interfered to preserve the apostolical succession in the true Church. But this is an argument fitted for understandings of a different kind from Mr. Gladstone's. He will hardly tell us that the Church of England is the true Church because she has the succession; and that she has the succession because she is the true Church.

What evidence, then, have we for the fact of the apostolical succession? And here we may easily defend the truth against Oxford with the same arguments with which, in old times, the truth was defended by Oxford against Rome. In this stage of our combat with Mr. Gladstone, we need few weapons except those which we find in the well furnished and well ordered armoury of Chillingworth.

The transmission of orders from the Apostles to an English clergyman of the present day must have been through a very great number of intermediate persons. Now, it is probable that no clergyman in the Church of England can trace up his spiritual genealogy from bishop to bishop, so far back as the time of the Conquest. There remain many centuries during which the history of the transmission of his orders is buried in utter darkness. And whether he be a priest by succession from the Apostles depends on the question, whether, during that long period, some thousands of events took place, any one of which may, without any gross improbability, be supposed not to have taken place. We have not a tittle of evidence for any one of these events. We do not even know the names or countries of the men to whom it is taken for granted that these events happened. We do not know whether the spiritual ancestors of any one of our contemporaries were Spanish or Armenian, Arian or Orthodox. In the utter absence of all particular evidence, we are surely entitled to require that there should be very strong evidence indeed that the strictest regularity was observed in every generation, and that episcopal functions were exercised by none who were not bishops by succession from the Apostles. But we have no such evidence. In the first place, we have not full and accurate information touching the polity of the Church during the century which followed the persecution of Nero. That, during this period, the overseers of all the little Christian societies scattered through the Roman empire held their spiritual authority by virtue of holy orders derived from the Apostles, cannot be proved by contemporary testimony, or by any testimony which can be regarded as decisive. The question, whether the primitive ecclesiastical constitution bore a greater resemblance to the Anglican or to the Calvinistic model has been fiercely disputed. It is a question on which men of eminent parts, learning, and piety, have differed, and do to this day differ very widely. It is a question on which at least a full half of the ability and erudition of Protestant Europe has, ever since the Reformation, been opposed to the Anglican pretensions. Mr. Gladstone himself, we are persuaded, would have the candour to allow that, if no evidence were admitted but that which is furnished by the genuine Christian literature of the first two centuries, judgment would not go in favour of prelacy. And if he looked at the subject as calmly as he would look at a controversy respecting the Roman *Comitia* or the Anglo-Saxon Wittenagemote, he would probably think that the absence of contemporary evidence during so long a period was a defect which later attestations, however numerous, could but very imperfectly supply. It is surely impolitic to rest the doctrines of the English Church on a historical theory which, to ninety-nine Protestants out of a hundred, would seem much more questionable than any of those doctrines. Nor is this all. Extreme obscurity overhangs the history of the middle ages; and the facts which are discernible through that obscurity prove that the Church was exceedingly ill regulated. We read of sees of the highest dignity openly sold, transferred backwards and forwards by popular tumult, bestowed sometimes by a profligate woman on her paramour, sometimes by a warlike baron on a kinsman still a stripling. We read of bishops of ten years old, of bishops of five years old, of many popes who were mere boys, and who rivalled the frantic dissoluteness of Caligula, nay, of a female pope. And though this last story, once believed throughout all Europe, has been disproved by the strict researches of modern criticism, the most discerning of those who reject it have admitted that it is not intrinsically improbable. In our own island, it was the complaint of Alfred that not a single priest, south of the Thames, and very few on the north, could read either Latin or English. And this illiterate clergy exercised their ministry amidst a rude and half heathen population, in which Danish pirates, unchristened, or christened by the hundred on a field of battle, were mingled with a Saxon peasantry scarcely better instructed in religion. The state of Ireland was still worse. "Tota illa per universam Hiberniam dissolutio ecclesiasticæ disciplinæ, illa ubique pro consuetudine Christiana sæva subintroducta barbaries," are the expressions of St. Bernard. We are, therefore, at a loss to conceive how any clergyman can feel confident that his orders have come down correctly. Whether he be really a successor of the Apostles depends on an immense number of such contingencies as these; whether, under King Ethelwolf, a stupid priest might not, while baptizing several scores of Danish prisoners who had just made their option between the font and the gallows, inadvertently omit to perform the rite on one of these graceless proselytes; whether, in the seventh century, an impostor, who had never received consecration, might not have passed himself off as a bishop on a rude tribe of Scots; whether a lad of twelve did really, by a ceremony huddled over when he was too drunk to know what he was about, convey the episcopal character to a lad of ten.

Since the first century, not less, in all probability, than a hundred thousand persons have exercised the functions of bishops. That many of these have not been bishops by apostolical succession is quite certain. Hooker admits that deviations from the general rule have been frequent, and, with a boldness worthy of his high and statesman-like intellect, pronounces them to have been often justifiable. "There may be," says he, "sometimes very just and sufficient reason to allow ordination made without a bishop. Where the Church must needs have some ordained, and neither hath nor can have possibly a bishop to ordain, in case of such necessity the ordinary institution of God hath given *oftentimes*, and may give place. And therefore we are not simply without exception to urge a lineal descent of power from the Apostles by continued succession of bishops in every effectual ordination." There can be little doubt, we think, that the succession, if it ever existed, has often been interruped in ways much less respectable. For example, let us suppose, and we are sure that no well informed person will think the supposition by any means improbable, that, in the third century, a man of no principle and some parts, who has, in the course of a roving and discreditable life, been a catechumen at Antioch, and has there become familiar with Christian usages and doctrines, afterwards rambles to Marseilles, where he finds a Christian society, rich, liberal, and simple-hearted. He pretends to be a Christian, attracts notice by his abilities and affected zeal, and is raised to the episcopal dignity without having ever been baptized. That such an event might happen, nay, was very likely to happen, cannot well be disputed by any one who has read the Life of Peregrinus. The very virtues, indeed, which distinguished the early Christians, seem to have laid them open to those arts which deceived

> "Uriel, though Regent of the Sun, and held
> The sharpest-sighted spirit of all in Heaven."

Now, this unbaptized impostor is evidently no successor of the Apostles. He is not even a Christian; and all orders derived through such a pretended bishop are altogether invalid. Do we know enough of the state of the world and of the Church in the third century to be able to say with confidence that there were not at that time twenty such pretended bishops? Every such case makes a break in the apostolical succession.

Now, suppose that a break, such as Hooker admits to have been both common and justifiable, or such as we have supposed to be produced by hypocrisy and cupidity, were found in the chain which connected the Apostles with any of the missionaries who first spread Christianity in the wilder parts of Europe, who can say how extensive the effect of this single break may be? Suppose that St. Patrick, for example, if ever there was such a man, or Theodore of Tarsus, who is said to have consecrated in the seventh century the first bishops of many English sees, had not the true apostolical orders, is it not conceivable that such a circumstance may affect the orders of many clergymen now living? Even if it were possible, which it assuredly is not, to prove that the Church had the apostolical orders in the third century, it would be impossible to prove that those orders were not in the twelfth century so far lost that no ecclesiastic could be certain of the legitimate descent of his own spiritual character. And if this were so, no subsequent precautions could repair the evil.

Chillingworth states the conclusion at which he had arrived on this subject in these very remarkable words: "That of ten thousand probables no one should be false; that of ten thousand requisites, whereof any one may fail, not one should be wanting, this to me is extremely improbable, and even cousin-german to impossible. So that the assurance hereof is like a machine composed of an innumerable multitude of pieces, of which it is strangely unlikely but some will be out of order; and yet, if any one be so, the whole fabric falls of necessity to the ground: and he that shall put them together, and maturely consider all the possible ways of lapsing and nullifying a priesthood in the Church of Rome, will be very inclinable to think that it is a hundred to one, that among a hundred seeming priests, there is not one true one; nay, that it is not a thing very improbable that, amongst those many millions which make up the Romish hierarchy, there are not twenty true." We do not pretend to know to what precise extent the canonists of Oxford agree with those of Rome as to the circumstances which nullify orders. We will not, therefore, go so far as Chillingworth. We only say that we see no satisfactory proof of the fact, that the Church of England possesses the apostolical succession. And, after all, if Mr. Gladstone could prove the apostolical succession, what would the apostolical succession prove? He says that "we have among us the ordained hereditary witnesses of the truth, conveying it to us through an *unbroken* series from our Lord Jesus Christ and his Apostles." Is this the fact? Is there any doubt that the orders of the Church of England are generally derived from the Church of Rome? Does not the Church of England declare, does not Mr. Gladstone himself admit, that the Church of Rome teaches much error and condemns much truth? And is it not quite clear, that as far as the doctrines of the Church of England differ from those of the Church of Rome, so far the Church of England conveys the truth through a broken series?

That the founders, lay and clerical, of the Church of England, corrected all that required correction in the doctrines of the

Church of Rome, and nothing more, may be quite true. But we never can admit the circumstance that the Church of England possesses the apostolical succession as a proof that she is thus perfect. No stream can rise higher than its fountain. The succession of ministers in the Church of England, derived as it is through the Church of Rome, can never prove more for the Church of England than it proves for the Church of Rome. But this is not all. The Arian Churches which once predominated in the kingdoms of the Ostrogoths, the Visigoths, the Burgundians, the Vandals, and the Lombards, were all episcopal churches, and all had a fairer claim than that of England to the apostolical succession, as being much nearer to the apostolical times. In the East, the Greek Church, which is at variance on points of faith with all the Western Churches, has an equal claim to this succession. The Nestorian, the Eutychian, the Jacobite Churches, all heretical, all condemned by councils, of which even Protestant divines have generally spoken with respect, had an equal claim to the apostolical succession. Now if, of teachers having apostolical orders, a vast majority have taught much error, if a large proportion have taught deadly heresy, if, on the other hand, as Mr. Gladstone himself admits, churches not having apostolical orders, that of Scotland for example, have been nearer to the standard of orthodoxy than the majority of teachers who have had apostolical orders, how can he possibly call upon us to submit our private judgment to the authority of a Church, on the ground that she has these orders?

Mr. Gladstone dwells much on the importance of unity in doctrine. Unity, he tells us, is essential to truth. And this is most unquestionable. But when he goes on to tell us that this unity is the characteristic of the Church of England, that she is one in body and in spirit, we are compelled to differ from him widely. The apostolical succession she may or may not have. But unity she most certainly has not, and never has had. It is matter of perfect notoriety, that her formularies are framed in such a manner as to admit to her highest offices men who differ from each other more widely than a very high Churchman differs from a Catholic, or a very low Churchman from a Presbyterian; and that the general leaning of the Church, with respect to some important questions, has been sometimes one way and sometimes another. Take, for example, the questions agitated between the Calvinists and the Arminians. Do we find in the Church of England, with respect to those questions, that unity which is essential to truth? Was it ever found in the Church? Is it not certain that, at the end of the sixteenth century, the rulers of the Church held doctrines as Calvinistic as ever were held by any Cameronian, and not only held them, but persecuted every body who did not hold them? And is it not equally certain, that the rulers of the Church have, in very recent times, considered Calvinism as a disqualification for high preferment, if not for holy orders? Look at the questions which Archbishop Whitgift propounded to Barret, questions framed in the very spirit of William Huntington, S.S.[1] And then look at the eighty-seven questions which Bishop Marsh, within our own memory, propounded to candidates for ordination. We should be loth to say that either of these celebrated prelates had intruded himself into a Church whose doctrines he abhorred, and that he deserved to be stripped of his gown. Yet it is quite certain, that one or other of them must have been very greatly in error. John Wesley again, and Cowper's friend, John Newton, were both presbyters of this Church. Both were men of talents. Both we believe to have been men of rigid integrity, men who would not have subscribed a Confession of Faith which they disbelieved for the richest bishopric in the empire. Yet, on the subject of predestination, Newton was strongly attached to doctrines which Wesley designated as "blasphemy, which might make the ears of a Christian to tingle." Indeed, it will not be disputed that the clergy of the Established Church are divided as to these questions, and that her formularies are not found practically to exclude even scrupulously honest men of both sides from her altars. It is notorious that some of her most distinguished rulers think this latitude a good thing, and would be sorry to see it restricted in favour of either opinion. And herein we most cordially agree with them. But what becomes of the unity of the Church, and of that truth to which unity is essential? Mr. Gladstone tells us that the *Regium Donum* was given originally to orthodox Presbyterian ministers, but that part of it is now received by their heterodox successors. "This," he says, "serves to illustrate the difficulty in which governments entangle themselves, when they covenant with arbitrary systems of opinion, and not with the Church alone. The opinion passes away, but the gift remains." But is it not clear, that if a strong Supralapsarian had, under Whitgift's primacy, left a large estate at the disposal of the bishops for ecclesiastical purposes, in the hope that the rulers of the Church would abide by Whitgift's theology, he would really have been giving his substance

[1] One question was, whether God had from eternity reprobated certain; and why. The answer which contented the Archbishop was, "Affirmative, et quia voluit."

M—21*

for the support of doctrines which he detested? The opinion would have passed away, and the gift would have remained.

This is only a single instance. What wide differences of opinion respecting the operation of the sacraments are held by bishops, doctors, presbyters of the Church of England, all men who have conscientiously declared their assent to her articles, all men who are, according to Mr. Gladstone, ordained hereditary witnesses of the truth, all men whose voices make up, what he tells us, is the voice of true and reasonable authority! Here, again, the Church has not unity; and as unity is the essential condition of truth, the Church has not the truth.

Nay, take the very question which we are discussing with Mr. Gladstone. To what extent does the Church of England allow of the right of private judgment? What degree of authority does she claim for herself in virtue of the apostolical succession of her ministers? Mr. Gladstone, a very able and a very honest man, takes a view of this matter widely differing from the view taken by others whom he will admit to be as able and as honest as himself. People who altogether dissent from him on this subject eat the bread of the Church, preach in her pulpits, dispense her sacraments, confer her orders, and carry on that apostolical succession, the nature and importance of which, according to him, they do not comprehend. Is this unity? Is this truth?

It will be observed that we are not putting cases of dishonest men who, for the sake of lucre, falsely pretend to believe in the doctrines of an establishment. We are putting cases of men as upright as ever lived, who, differing on theological questions of the highest importance, and avowing that difference, are yet priests and prelates of the same Church. We therefore say that, on some points which Mr. Gladstone himself thinks of vital importance, the Church has either not spoken at all, or, what is for all practical purposes the same thing, has not spoken in language to be understood even by honest and sagacious divines. The religion of the Church of England is so far from exhibiting that unity of doctrine which Mr. Gladstone represents as her distinguishing glory that it is, in fact, a bundle of religious systems without number. It comprises the religious system of Bishop Tomline, and the religious system of John Newton, and all the religious systems which lie between them. It comprises the religious system of Mr. Newman, and the religious system of the Archbishop of Dublin, and all the religious systems which lie between them. All these different opinions are held, avowed, preached, printed, within the pale of the Church, by men of unquestioned integrity and understanding.

Do we make this diversity a topic of reproach to the Church of England? Far from it. We would oppose with all our power every attempt to narrow her basis. Would to God that, a hundred and fifty years ago, a good king and a good primate had possessed the power as well as the will to widen it! It was a noble enterprise, worthy of William and of Tillotson. But what becomes of all Mr. Gladstone's eloquent exhortations to unity? Is it not mere mockery to attach so much importance to unity in form and name, where there is so little in substance, to shudder at the thought of two churches in alliance with one state, and to endure with patience the spectacle of a hundred sects battling within one church? And is it not clear that Mr. Gladstone is bound, on all his own principles, to abandon the defence of a church in which unity is not found? Is it not clear that he is bound to divide the House of Commons against every grant of money which may be proposed for the clergy of the Established Church in the colonies? He objects to the vote for Maynooth, because it is monstrous to pay one man to teach truth, and another to denounce that truth as falsehood. But it is a mere chance whether any sum which he votes for the English Church in any colony will go to the maintenance of an Arminian or a Calvinist, of a man like Mr. Froude, or of a man like Dr. Arnold. It is a mere chance, therefore, whether it will go to support a teacher of truth, or one who will denounce that truth as falsehood.

This argument seems to us at once to dispose of all that part of Mr. Gladstone's book which respects grants of public money to dissenting bodies. All such grants he condemns. But surely, if it be wrong to give the money of the public for the support of those who teach any false doctrine, it is wrong to give that money for the support of the ministers of the Established Church. For it is quite certain that, whether Calvin or Arminius be in the right, whether Laud or Burnet be in the right, a great deal of false doctrine is taught by the ministers of the Established Church. If it be said that the points on which the clergy of the Church of England differ ought to be passed over, for the sake of the many important points on which they agree, why may not the same argument be maintained with respect to other sects which hold in common with the Church of England the fundamental doctrines of Christianity? The principle, that a ruler is bound in conscience to propagate religious truth, and to propagate no religious doctrine which is untrue, is abandoned as soon as it is admitted that a gentleman of Mr. Gladstone's opinions may lawfully vote the public money to a chaplain whose opinions are those of Paley or of Simeon. The whole question then becomes one of degree. Of course no individual and no government can justifiably propagate error for the sake of propagating error. But both individuals and governments must work with such machinery as they have; and no human machinery is to be found which will impart truth without some alloy of error. We have shown irrefragably, as we think, that the Church of England does not afford such a machinery. The question then is this; with what degree of imperfection in our machinery must we put up? And to this question we do not see how any general answer can be given. We must be guided by circumstances. It would, for example, be very criminal in a Protestant to contribute to the sending of Jesuit missionaries among a Protestant population. But we do not conceive that a Protestant would be to blame for giving assistance to Jesuit missionaries who might be engaged in converting the Siamese to Christianity. That tares are mixed with the wheat is matter of regret; but it is better that wheat and tares should grow together than that the promise of the year should be blighted.

Mr. Gladstone, we see with deep regret, censures the British Government in India for distributing a small sum among the Catholic priests who minister to the spiritual wants of our Irish soldiers. Now, let us put a case to him. A Protestant gentleman is attended by a Catholic servant, in a part of the country where there is no Catholic congregation within many miles. The servant is taken ill, and is given over. He desires, in great trouble of mind, to receive the last sacraments of his Church. His master sends off a messenger in a chaise and four, with orders to bring a confessor from a town at a considerable distance. Here a Protestant lays out money for the purpose of causing religious instruction and consolation to be given by a Catholic priest. Has he committed a sin? Has he not acted like a good master and a good Christian? Would Mr. Gladstone accuse him of "laxity of religious principle," of "confounding truth with falsehood," of "considering the support of religion as a boon to an individual, not as a homage to truth?" But how if this servant had, for the sake of his master, undertaken a journey which removed him from the place where he might easily have obtained religious attendance? How if his death were occasioned by a wound received in defending his master? Should we not then say that the master had only fulfilled a sacred obligation of duty? Now, Mr. Gladstone himself owns that "nobody can think that the personality of the state is more stringent, or entails stronger obligations, than that of the individual." How then stands the case of the Indian Government? Here is a poor fellow, enlisted in Clare or Kerry, sent over fifteen thousand miles of sea, quartered in a depressing and pestilential climate. He fights for the Government; he conquers for it; he is wounded; he is laid on his pallet, withering away with fever, under that terrible sun, without a friend near him. He pines for the consolations of that religion which, neglected perhaps in the season of health and vigour, now comes back to his mind, associated with all the overpowering recollections of his earlier days, and of the home which he is never to see again. And because the state for which he dies sends a priest of his own faith to stand at his bedside, and to tell him, in language which at once commands his love and confidence, of the common Father, of the common Redeemer, of the common hope of immortality, because the state for which he dies does not abandon him in his last moments to the care of heathen attendants, or employ a chaplain of a different creed to vex his departing spirit with a controversy about the Council of Trent, Mr. Gladstone finds that India presents "a melancholy picture," and that there is "a large allowance of false principle" in the system pursued there. Most earnestly do we hope that our remarks may induce Mr. Gladstone to reconsider this part of his work, and may prevent him from expressing in that high assembly, in which he must always be heard with attention, opinions so unworthy of his character.

We have now said almost all that we think it necessary to say respecting Mr. Gladstone's theory. And perhaps it would be safest for us to stop here. It is much easier to pull down than to build up. Yet, that we may give Mr. Gladstone his revenge, we will state concisely our own views respecting the alliance of Church and State.

We set out in company with Warburton, and remain with him pretty sociably till we come to his contract; a contract which Mr. Gladstone very properly designates as a fiction. We consider the primary end of government as a purely temporal end, the protection of the persons and property of men.

We think that government, like every other contrivance of human wisdom, from the highest to the lowest, is likely to answer its main end best when it is constructed with a single view to that end. Mr. Gladstone, who loves Plato, will not quarrel with us for illustrating our proposition, after Plato's fashion, from the most familiar objects. Take cutlery, for example. A blade which is designed both to shave and to carve will certainly not shave so well as a razor, or carve so well as a carving-knife. An academy of painting, which should also be a bank, would, in all probability, exhibit very bad pictures and discount very bad bills. A gas company, which should also be an infant school society, would, we apprehend, light the streets ill, and teach the children ill. On this principle, we think that government should be organized solely with a view to its main end; and that no part of its efficiency for that end should be sacrificed in order to promote any other end however excellent.

But does it follow from hence that governments ought never to pursue any end other than their main end? In no wise. Though it is desirable that every institution should have a main end, and should be so formed as to be in the highest degree efficient for that main end; yet if, without any sacrifice of its efficiency for that end, it can pursue any other good end, it ought to do so. Thus, the end for which a hospital is built is the relief of the sick, not the beautifying of the street. To sacrifice the health of the sick to splendour of architectural effect, to place the building in a bad air only that it may present a more commanding front to a great public place, to make the wards hotter or cooler than they ought to be, in order that the columns and windows of the exterior may please the passers-by, would be monstrous. But if, without any sacrifice of the chief object, the hospital can be made an ornament to the metropolis, it would be absurd not to make it so.

In the same manner, if a government can, without any sacrifice of its main end, promote any other good work, it ought to do so. The encouragement of the fine arts, for example, is by no means the main end of government; and it would be absurd, in constituting a government, to bestow a thought on the question, whether it would be a government likely to train Raphaels and Domenichinos. But it by no means follows that it is improper for a government to form a national gallery of pictures. The same may be said of patronage bestowed on learned men, of the publication of archives, of the collecting of libraries, menageries, plants, fossils, antiques, of journeys and voyages for purposes of geographical discovery or astronomical observation. It is not for these ends that government is constituted. But it may well happen that a government may have at its command resources which will enable it, without any injury to its main end, to pursue these collateral ends far more effectually than any individual or any voluntary association could do. If so, government ought to pursue these collateral ends.

It is still more evidently the duty of government to promote, always in subordination to its main end, every thing which is useful as a means for the attaining of that main end. The improvement of steam navigation, for example, is by no means a primary object of government. But as steam vessels are useful for the purpose of national defence, and for the purpose of facilitating intercourse between distant provinces, and of thereby consolidating the force of the empire, it may be the bounden duty of government to encourage ingenious men to perfect an invention which so directly tends to make the state more efficient for its great primary end.

Now, on both these grounds, the instruction of the people may with propriety engage the care of the government. That the people should be well educated is in itself a good thing; and the state ought therefore to promote this object, if it can do so without any sacrifice of its primary object. The education of the people, conducted on those principles of morality which are common to all the forms of Christianity, is highly valuable as a means of promoting the main object for which government exists, and is on this ground well deserving the attention of rulers. We will not at present go into the general question of education; but will confine our remarks to the subject which is more immediately before us, namely, the religious instruction of the people.

We may illustrate our view of the policy which governments ought to pursue with respect to religious instruction, by recurring to the analogy of a hospital. Religious instruction is not the main end for which a hospital is built; and to introduce into a hospital any regulations prejudicial to the health of the patients, on the plea of promoting their spiritual improvement, to send a ranting preacher to a man who has just been ordered by the physician to lie quiet and try to get a little sleep, to impose a strict observance of Lent on a convalescent who has been advised to eat heartily of nourishing food, to direct, as the bigoted Pius the Fifth actually did, that no medical assistance should be given to any person who declined spiritual attendance, would be the most extravagant folly. Yet it by no means follows that it would not be right to have a chaplain to attend the sick, and to pay such a chaplain out of the hospital funds. Whether it will be proper to have such a chaplain at all, and of what religious persuasion such a chaplain ought to be, must depend on circumstances. There may be a town in which it would be impossible to set up a good hospital without the help of people of different opinions: and religious parties may run so high that, though people of different opinions are willing to contribute for the relief of the sick, they will not concur in the choice of any one chaplain. The high Churchmen insist that, if there is a paid chaplain, he shall be a high Churchman. The Evangelicals stickle for an Evangelical. Here it would evidently be absurd and cruel to let an useful and humane design, about which all are agreed, fall to the ground, because all cannot agree about something else. The governors must either appoint two chaplains, and pay them both; or they must appoint none; and every one of them must, in his individual capacity, do what he can for the purpose of providing the sick with such religious instruction and consolation as will, in his opinion, be most useful to them.

We should say the same of government. Government is not an institution for the propagation of religion, any more than St. George's Hospital is an institution for the propagation of religion: and the most absurd and pernicious consequences would follow, if Government should pursue, as its primary end, that which can never be more than its secondary end, though intrinsically more important than its primary end. But a government which considers the religious instruction of the people as a secondary end, and follows out that principle faithfully, will, we think, be likely to do much good and little harm.

We will rapidly run over some of the consequences to which this principle leads, and point out how it solves some problems which, on Mr. Gladstone's hypothesis, admit of no satisfactory solution.

All persecution directed against the persons or property of men is, on our principle, obviously indefensible. For the protection of the persons and property of men being the primary end of government, and religious instruction only a secondary end, to secure the people from heresy by making their lives, their limbs, or their estates insecure, would be to sacrifice the primary end to the secondary end. It would be as absurd as it would be in the governors of a hospital to direct that the wounds of all Arian and Socinian patients should be dressed in such a way as to make them fester.

Again, on our principles, all civil disabilities on account of religious opinions are indefensible. For all such disabilities make government less efficient for its main end: they limit its choice of able men for the administration and defence of the state; they alienate from it the hearts of the sufferers; they deprive it of a part of its effective strength in all contests with foreign nations. Such a course is as absurd as it would be in the governors of an hospital to reject an able surgeon because he is an universal Restitutionist, and to send a bungler to operate because he is perfectly orthodox.

Again, on our principles, no government ought to press on the people religious instruction, however sound, in such a manner as to excite among them discontents dangerous to public order. For here again government would sacrifice its primary end to an end intrinsically indeed of the highest importance, but still only a secondary end of government, as government. This rule at once disposes of the difficulty about India, a difficulty of which Mr. Gladstone can get rid only by putting in an imaginary discharge in order to set aside an imaginary obligation. There is assuredly no country where it is more desirable that Christianity should be propagated. But there is no country in which the government is so completely disqualified for the task. By using our power in order to make proselytes, we should produce the dissolution of society, and bring utter ruin on all those interests for the protection of which government exists. Here the secondary end is, at present, inconsistent with the primary end, and must therefore be abandoned. Christian instruction given by individuals and voluntary societies may do much good. Given by the Government it would do unmixed harm. At the same time, we quite agree with Mr. Gladstone in thinking that the English authorities in India ought not to participate in any idolatrous rite; and indeed we are fully satisfied that all such participation is not only unchristian, but also unwise and most undignified.

Supposing the circumstances of a country to be such, that the government may with propriety, on our principles, give religious instruction to a people; we have next to inquire, what religion shall be taught. Bishop Warburton answers, the religion of the majority. And we so far agree with him, that we can scarcely conceive any circumstances in which it would be proper to establish, as the one exclusive religion of the state, the religion of the minority. Such a preference could hardly be given without exciting most serious discontent, and endangering those interests, the protection of which is the first object of government. But we never can admit that a ruler can be justified in helping to spread a system of opinions solely because that system is pleasing to the majority. On the other hand, we cannot agree with Mr. Gladstone, who would of course answer that the only religion which a ruler ought to propagate is the religion of his own conscience. In truth, this is an impossibility. And, as we have shown, Mr. Gladstone himself, whenever he supports a grant of money to the Church of England, is really assisting to propagate, not the precise religion of his own conscience, but some one or more, he knows not how many or which, of the innumerable religions which lie between the confines of Pelagianism and those of Antinomianism, and between the confines of Popery and those of Presbyterianism. In our opinion, that religious instruction which the ruler ought, in his public capacity, to patronise, is the instruction from which he, in his conscience, believes that the people will learn most good with the smallest mixture of evil. And thus it is not necessarily his own religion that he will select. He will, of course, believe that his own religion is unmixedly good. But the question which he has to consider is, not how much good his religion contains, but how much good the people will learn, if instruction is given them in that religion. He may prefer the doctrines and government of the Church of England to those of the Church of Scotland. But if he knows that a Scotch congregation will listen with deep attention and respect while an Erskine or a Chalmers sets before them the fundamental doctrines of Christianity, and that a glimpse of a surplice or a single line of a liturgy would be the signal for hooting and riot, and would probably bring stools and brick-bats about the ears of the minister, he acts wisely if he conveys religious knowledge to the Scotch rather by means of that imperfect Church, as he may think it, from which they will learn much, than by means of that perfect Church from which they will learn nothing. The only end of teaching is, that men may learn; and it is idle to talk of the duty of teaching truth in ways which only cause men to cling more firmly to falsehood.

On these principles we conceive that a statesman, who might be far indeed from regarding the Church of England with the reverence which Mr. Gladstone feels for her, might yet firmly oppose all attempts to destroy her. Such a statesman may be too well acquainted with her origin to look upon her with superstitious awe. He may know that she sprang from a compromise huddled up between the eager zeal of reformers and the selfishness of greedy, ambitious, and time-serving politicians. He may find in every page of her annals ample cause for censure. He may feel that he could not, with ease to his conscience, subscribe all her articles. He may regret that all the attempts which have been made to open her gates to large classes of non-conformists should have failed. Her episcopal polity he may consider as of purely human institution. He cannot defend her on the ground that she possesses the apostolical succession; for he does not know whether that succession may not be altogether a fable. He cannot defend her on the ground of her unity: for he knows that her frontier sects are much more remote from each other, than one frontier is from the Church of Rome, or the other from the Church of Geneva. But he may think that she teaches more truth with less alloy of error than would be taught by those who, if she were swept away, would occupy the vacant space. He may think that the effect produced by her beautiful services and by her pulpits on the national mind, is, on the whole, highly beneficial. He may think that her civilising influence is usefully felt in remote districts. He may think that, if she were destroyed, a large portion of those who now compose her congregations would neglect all religious duties; and that a still larger portion would fall under the influence of spiritual mountebanks, hungry for gain, or drunk with fanaticism. While he would with pleasure admit that all the qualities of Christian pastors are to be found in large measure within the existing body of Dissenting ministers, he would perhaps be inclined to think that the standard of intellectual and moral character among that exemplary class of men may have been raised to its present high point and maintained there by the indirect influence of the Establishment. And he may be by no means satisfied that, if the Church were at once swept away, the place of our Sumners and Whateleys would be supplied by Doddridges and Halls. He may think that the advantages which we have described are obtained, or might, if the existing system were slightly modified, be obtained, without any sacrifice of the paramount objects which all governments ought to have chiefly in view. Nay, he may be of opinion that an institution, so deeply fixed in the hearts and minds of millions, could not be subverted without loosening and shaking all the foundations of civil society. With at least equal ease he would find reasons for supporting the Church of Scotland. Nor would he be under the necessity of resorting to any contract to justify the connection of two religious establishments with one government. He would think scruples on that head frivolous in any person who is zealous for a Church, of which both Dr. Herbert Marsh and Dr. Daniel Wilson are bishops. Indeed he would gladly follow out his principles much further. He would have been willing to vote in 1825 for Lord Francis Egerton's resolution, that it is expedient to give a public maintenance to the Catholic clergy of Ireland; and he would deeply regret that no such measure was adopted in 1829.

In this way, we conceive, a statesman might, on our principles, satisfy himself that it would be in the highest degree inexpedient to abolish the Church, either of England or of Scotland.

But if there were, in any part of the world, a national church regarded as heretical by four-fifths of the nation committed to its care, a church established and maintained by the sword, a church producing twice as many riots as conversions, a church which, though possessing great wealth and power, and though long backed by persecuting laws, had, in the course of many generations, been found unable to propagate its doctrines, and barely able to maintain its ground, a church so odious, that fraud and violence, when used against its clear rights of property, were generally regarded as fair play, a church, whose ministers were preaching to desolate walls, and with difficulty obtaining their lawful subsistence by the help of bayonets, such a church, on our principles, could not, we must own, be defended. We should say that the state which allied itself with such a church postponed the primary end of government to the secondary; and that the consequences had been such as any sagacious observer would have predicted. Neither the primary nor the secondary end is attained. The temporal and spiritual interests of the people suffer alike. The minds of men, instead of being drawn to the church, are alienated from the state. The magistrate, after sacrificing order, peace, union, all the interests which it is his first duty to protect, for the purpose of promoting pure religion, is forced, after the experience of centuries, to admit that he has really been promoting error. The sounder the doctrines of such a church, the more absurd and noxious the superstition by which those doctrines are opposed, the stronger are the arguments against the policy which has deprived a good cause of its natural advantages. Those who preach to rulers the duty of employing power to propagate truth would do well to remember that falsehood, though no match for truth alone, has often been found more than a match for truth and power together.

A statesman, judging on our principles, would pronounce without hesitation that a church, such as we have last described, never ought to have been set up. Further than this we will not venture to speak for him. He would doubtless remember that the world is full of institutions which, though they never ought to have been set up, yet, having been set up, ought not to be rudely pulled down; and that it is often wise in practice to be content with the mitigation of an abuse which, looking at it in the abstract, we might feel impatient to destroy.

We have done; and nothing remains but that we part from Mr. Gladstone with the courtesy of antagonists who bear no malice. We dissent from his opinions; but we admire his talents; we respect his integrity and benevolence; and we hope that he will not suffer political avocations so entirely to engross him, as to leave him no leisure for literature and philosophy.

# SPEECHES

## AND

## THE MINUTE ON INDIAN EDUCATION

MACAULAY'S collected speeches first appeared in an unauthorised and inaccurate edition published in 1853 by Henry Vizetelly in two volumes, which were also issued simultaneously in New York. This was quite legal; Hansard had given his licence and most of the speeches had already been printed in newspapers, but Macaulay pronounced it "a gross injury to me and a gross fraud on the public," and hastened to bring out his own: *Speeches of the Right Honorable T. B. Macaulay, M.P. Corrected by Himself,* which was published in one volume by Longman in 1854 and is the text used here.

The Minute on Indian Education follows the text of the Cambridge University Library copy of *Macaulay's Minutes on Education in India . . . now first collected from Records in the Department of Public Instruction,* Calcutta, 1862. This is an extremely rare book of which there is no copy in the British Museum, and the Minute has so far been generally available only in Sir George Otto Trevelyan's *The Competition Wallah,* 1864, and in the present editor's selection of the Speeches in the World's Classics, 1935, from which the editorial notes are here reprinted by kind permission of the Oxford University Press.

All Macaulay's own notes have been retained.

# SPEECHES

AND THE MINUTE ON INDIAN EDUCATION

## PARLIAMENTARY REFORM. I

A SPEECH DELIVERED IN THE HOUSE OF COMMONS ON THE 2ND OF MARCH, 1831

On Tuesday, the first of March, 1831, Lord John Russell moved the House of Commons for leave to bring in a Bill to amend the representation of the people in England and Wales. The discussion occupied seven nights. At length, on the morning of Thursday, the tenth of March, the motion was carried without a division. The following Speech was made on the second night of the debate.

It is a circumstance, Sir, of happy augury for the motion before the House, that almost all those who have opposed it have declared themselves hostile on principle to Parliamentary Reform. Two Members, I think, have confessed that, though they disapprove of the plan now submitted to us, they are forced to admit the necessity of a change in the Representative system. Yet even those gentlemen have used, as far as I have observed, no arguments which would not apply as strongly to the most moderate change as to that which has been proposed by His Majesty's Government. I say, Sir, that I consider this as a circumstance of happy augury. For what I feared was, not the opposition of those who are averse to all Reform, but the disunion of reformers. I knew that, during three months, every reformer had been employed in conjecuring what the plan of the Government would be. I knew that every reformer had imagined in his own mind a scheme differing doubtless in some points from that which my noble friend, the Paymaster of the Forces, has developed. I felt therefore great apprehension that one person would be dissatisfied with one part of the bill, that another person would be dissatisfied with another part, and that thus our whole strength would be wasted in internal dissensions. That apprehension is now at an end. I have seen with delight the perfect concord which prevails among all who deserve the name of reformers in this House; and I trust that I may consider it as an omen of the concord which

663

will prevail among reformers throughout the country. I will not, Sir, at present express any opinion as to the details of the bill; but, having during the last twenty-four hours given the most diligent consideration to its general principles, I have no hesitation in pronouncing it a wise, noble, and comprehensive measure, skilfully framed for the healing of great distempers, for the securing at once of the public liberties and of the public repose, and for the reconciling and knitting together of all the orders of the State.

The honorable Baronet who has just sate down[1] has told us, that the Ministers have attempted to unite two inconsistent principles in one abortive measure. Those were his very words. He thinks, if I understand him rightly, that we ought either to leave the representative system such as it is, or to make it perfectly symmetrical. I think, Sir, that the Ministers would have acted unwisely if they had taken either course. Their principle is plain, rational, and consistent. It is this, to admit the middle class to a large and direct share in the representation, without any violent shock to the institutions of our country. I understand those cheers: but surely the gentlemen who utter them will allow that the change which will be made in our institutions by this bill is far less violent than that which, according to the honorable Baronet, ought to be made if we make any Reform at all. I praise the Ministers for not attempting, at the present time, to make the representation uniform. I praise them for not effacing the old distinction between the towns and the counties, and for not assigning Members to districts, according to the American practice, by the Rule of Three. The Government has, in my opinion, done all that was necessary for the removing of a great practical evil, and no more than was necessary.

I consider this, Sir, as a practical question. I rest my opinion on no general theory of government. I distrust all general theories of government. I will not positively say, that there is any form of polity which may not, in some conceivable circumstances, be the best possible. I believe that there are societies in which every man may safely be admitted to vote. Gentlemen may cheer, but such is my opinion. I say, Sir, that there are countries in which the condition of the labouring classes is such that they may safely be intrusted with the right of electing Members of the Legislature. If the labourers of England were in that state in which I, from my soul, wish to see them, if employment were always plentiful, wages always high, food always cheap, if a large family were considered not as an encumbrance but as a blessing, the principal objections to Universal Suffrage would, I think, be removed. Universal

[1] Sir John Walsh.

Suffrage exists in the United States without producing any very frightful consequences; and I do not believe, that the people of those States, or of any part of the world, are in any good quality naturally superior to our own countrymen. But, unhappily, the labouring classes in England, and in all old countries, are occasionally in a state of great distress. Some of the causes of this distress are, I fear, beyond the control of the Government. We know what effect distress produces, even on people more intelligent than the great body of the labouring classes can possibly be. We know that it makes even wise men irritable, unreasonable, credulous, eager for immediate relief, heedless of remote consequences. There is no quackery in medicine, religion, or politics, which may not impose even on a powerful mind, when that mind has been disordered by pain or fear. It is therefore no reflection on the poorer class of Englishmen, who are not, and who cannot in the nature of things be, highly educated, to say that distress produces on them its natural effects, those effects which it would produce on the Americans, or on any other people, that it blinds their judgment, that it inflames their passions, that it makes them prone to believe those who flatter them, and to distrust those who would serve them. For the sake, therefore, of the whole society, for the sake of the labouring classes themselves, I hold it to be clearly expedient that, in a country like this, the right of suffrage should depend on a pecuniary qualification.

But, Sir, every argument which would induce me to oppose Universal Suffrage, induces me to support the plan which is now before us. I am opposed to Universal Suffrage, because I think that it would produce a destructive revolution. I support this plan, because I am sure that it is our best security against a revolution. The noble Paymaster of the Forces hinted, delicately indeed and remotely, at this subject. He spoke of the danger of disappointing the expectations of the nation; and for this he was charged with threatening the House. Sir, in the year 1817, the late Lord Londonderry proposed a suspension of the Habeas Corpus Act. On that occasion he told the House that, unless the measures which he recommended were adopted, the public peace could not be preserved. Was he accused of threatening the House? Again, in the year 1819, he proposed the laws known by the name of the Six Acts. He then told the House that, unless the executive power were reinforced, all the institutions of the country would be overturned by popular violence. Was he then accused of threatening the House? Will any gentleman say that it is parliamentary and decorous to urge the danger arising from popular discontent as an argument for severity; but that it is unparliamentary and indecorous to urge that same danger as an argument for conciliation? I, Sir, do entertain great apprehension for the fate of my country. I do in my conscience believe that, unless the plan proposed, or some similar plan, be speedily adopted, great and terrible calamities will befal us. Entertaining this opinion, I think myself bound to state it, not as a threat, but as a reason. I support this bill because it will improve our institutions; but I support it also because it tends to preserve them. That we may exclude those whom it is necessary to exclude, we must admit those whom it may be safe to admit. At present we oppose the schemes of revolutionists with only one half, with only one quarter of our proper force. We say, and we say justly, that it is not by mere numbers, but by property and intelligence, that the nation ought to be governed. Yet, saying this, we exclude from all share in the government great masses of property and intelligence, great numbers of those who are most interested in preserving tranquillity, and who know best how to preserve it. We do more. We drive over to the side of revolution those whom we shut out from power. Is this a time when the cause of law and order can spare one of its natural allies?

My noble friend, the Paymaster of the Forces, happily described the effect which some parts of our representative system would produce on the mind of a foreigner, who had heard much of our freedom and greatness. If, Sir, I wished to make such a foreigner clearly understand what I consider as the great defects of our system, I would conduct him through that immense city which lies to the north of Great Russell Street and Oxford Street, a city superior in size and in population to the capitals of many mighty kingdoms; and probably superior in opulence, intelligence, and general respectability, to any city in the world. I would conduct him through that interminable succession of streets and squares, all consisting of well built and well furnished houses. I would make him observe the brilliancy of the shops, and the crowd of well appointed equipages. I would show him that magnificent circle of palaces which surrounds the Regent's Park. I would tell him, that the rental of this district was far greater than that of the whole kingdom of Scotland, at the time of the Union. And then I would tell him, that this was an unrepresented district. It is needless to give any more instances. It is needless to speak of Manchester, Birmingham, Leeds, Sheffield, with no representation, or of Edinburgh and Glasgow with a mock representation. If a property tax were now imposed on the principle that no person who had less than a hundred and fifty pounds a year should contribute, I should not be surprised to find that one half in number and value of the contributors had no votes at all; and it would, beyond all doubt, be found that one fiftieth part in number and value of the contributors had a larger share of the representation than the other forty nine fiftieths. This is not government by property. It is government by certain detached portions and fragments of property, selected from the rest, and preferred to the rest, on no rational principle whatever.

To say that such a system is ancient is no defence. My honorable friend, the Member for the University of Oxford,[1] challenges us to show, that the Constitution was ever better than it is. Sir, we are legislators, not antiquaries. The question for us is, not whether the Constitution was better formerly, but whether we can make it better now. In fact, however, the system was not in ancient times by any means so absurd as it is in our age. One noble Lord[2] has to-night told us that the town of Aldborough, which he represents, was not larger in the time of Edward the First than it is at present. The line of its walls, he assures us, may still be traced. It is now built up to that line. He argues, therefore, that as the founders of our representative institutions gave Members to Aldborough when it was as small as it now is, those who would disfranchise it on account of its smallness have no right to say that they are recurring to the original principle of our representative institutions. But does the noble Lord remember the change which has taken place in the country during the last five centuries? Does he remember how much England has grown in population, while Aldborough has been standing still? Does he consider, that in the time of Edward the First the kingdom did not contain two millions of inhabitants? It now contains nearly fourteen millions. A hamlet of the present day would have been a town of some importance in the time of our early Parliaments. Aldborough may be absolutely as considerable a place as ever. But compared with the kingdom, it is much less considerable, by the noble Lord's own showing, than when it first elected burgesses. My honorable friend, the Member for the University of Oxford, has collected numerous instances of the tyranny which the kings and nobles anciently exercised, both over this House and over the electors. It is not strange that, in times when nothing was held sacred, the rights of the people, and of the representatives of the people, should not have been held sacred. The proceedings which my honorable friend has mentioned, no more prove that, by the

[1] Sir Robert Harry Inglis.          [2] Lord Stormont.

ancient constitution of the realm, this House ought to be a tool of the king and of the aristocracy, than the Benevolences and the Shipmoney prove their own legality, or than those unjustifiable arrests, which took place long after the ratification of the great Charter, and even after the Petition of Right, prove that the subject was not anciently entitled to his personal liberty. We talk of the wisdom of our ancestors: and in one respect at least they were wiser than we. They legislated for their own times. They looked at the England which was before them. They did not think it necessary to give twice as many Members to York as they gave to London, because York had been the capital of Britain in the time of Constantius Chlorus; and they would have been amazed indeed if they had foreseen, that a city of more than a hundred thousand inhabitants would be left without Representatives in the nineteenth century, merely because it stood on ground which, in the thirteenth century, had been occupied by a few huts. They framed a representative system, which, though not without defects and irregularities, was well adapted to the state of England in their time. But a great revolution took place. The character of the old corporations changed. New forms of property came into existence. New portions of society rose into importance. There were in our rural districts rich cultivators, who were not freeholders. There were in our capital rich traders, who were not liverymen. Towns shrank into villages. Villages swelled into cities larger than the London of the Plantagenets. Unhappily, while the natural growth of society went on, the artificial polity continued unchanged. The ancient form of the representation remained; and precisely because the form remained, the spirit departed. Then came that pressure almost to bursting, the new wine in the old bottles, the new society under the old institutions. It is now time for us to pay a decent, a rational, a manly reverence to our ancestors, not by superstitiously adhering to what they, in other circumstances, did, but by doing what they, in our circumstances, would have done. All history is full of revolutions, produced by causes similar to those which are now operating in England. A portion of the community which had been of no account expands and becomes strong. It demands a place in the system, suited, not to its former weakness, but to its present power. If this is granted, all is well. If this is refused, then comes the struggle between the young energy of one class and the ancient privileges of another. Such was the struggle between the Plebeians and the Patricians of Rome. Such was the struggle of the Italian allies for admission to the full rights of Roman citizens. Such was the struggle of our North American colonies against the mother country. Such was the struggle which the Third Estate of France maintained against the aristocracy of birth. Such was the struggle which the Roman Catholics of Ireland maintained against the aristocracy of creed. Such is the struggle which the free people of colour in Jamaica are now maintaining against the aristocracy of skin. Such, finally, is the struggle which the middle classes in England are maintaining against an aristocracy of mere locality, against an aristocracy the principle of which is to invest a hundred drunken potwallopers in one place, or the owner of a ruined hovel in another, with powers which are withheld from cities renowned to the furthest ends of the earth, for the marvels of their wealth and of their industry.

But these great cities, says my honorable friend, the Member for the University of Oxford, are virtually, though not directly, represented. Are not the wishes of Manchester, he asks, as much consulted as those of any town which sends Members to Parliament? Now, Sir, I do not understand how a power which is salutary when exercised virtually can be noxious when exercised directly. If the wishes of Manchester have as much weight with us as they would have under a system which should give Representation to Manchester, how can there be any danger in giving Representatives to Manchester? A virtual Representative is, I presume, a man who acts as a direct Representative would act: for surely it would be absurd to say that a man virtually represents the people of Manchester, who is in the habit of saying No, when a man directly representing the people of Manchester would say Aye. The utmost that can be expected from virtual Representation is that it may be as good as direct Representation. If so, why not grant direct Representation to places which, as every body allows, ought, by some process or other, to be represented?

If it be said that there is an evil in change as change, I answer that there is also an evil in discontent as discontent. This, indeed, is the strongest part of our case. It is said that the system works well. I deny it. I deny that a system works well, which the people regard with aversion. We may say here, that it is a good system and a perfect system. But if any man were to say so to any six hundred and fifty-eight respectable farmers or shopkeepers, chosen by lot in any part of England, he would be hooted down, and laughed to scorn. Are these the feelings with which any part of the government ought to be regarded? Above all, are these the feelings with which the popular branch of the legislature ought to be regarded? It is almost as essential to the utility of a House of Commons, that it should possess the confidence of the people, as that it should deserve that confidence. Unfortunately, that which is in theory the popular part of our government, is in practice the unpopular part. Who wishes to dethrone the King? Who wishes to turn the Lords out of their House? Here and there a crazy radical, whom the boys in the street point at as he walks along. Who wishes to alter the constitution of this House? The whole people. It is natural that it should be so. The House of Commons is, in the language of Mr. Burke, a check, not on the people, but for the people. While that check is efficient, there is no reason to fear that the King or the nobles will oppress the people. But if that check requires checking, how is it to be checked? If the salt shall lose its savour, wherewith shall we season it? The distrust with which the nation regards this House may be unjust. But what then? Can you remove that distrust? That it exists cannot be denied. That it is an evil cannot be denied. That it is an increasing evil cannot be denied. One gentleman tells us that it has been produced by the late events in France and Belgium; another, that it is the effect of seditious works which have lately been published. If this feeling be of origin so recent, I have read history to little purpose. Sir, this alarming discontent is not the growth of a day or of a year. If there be any symptoms by which it is possible to distinguish the chronic diseases of the body politic from its passing inflammations, all those symptoms exist in the present case. The taint has been gradually becoming more extensive and more malignant, through the whole lifetime of two generations. We have tried anodynes. We have tried cruel operations. What are we to try now? Who flatters himself that he can turn this feeling back? Does there remain any argument which escaped the comprehensive intellect of Mr. Burke, or the subtlety of Mr. Windham? Does there remain any species of coercion which was not tried by Mr. Pitt and by Lord Londonderry? We have had laws. We have had blood. New treasons have been created. The Press has been shackled. The Habeas Corpus Act has been suspended. Public meetings have been prohibited. The event has proved that these expedients were mere palliatives. You are at the end of your palliatives. The evil remains. It is more formidable than ever. What is to be done?

Under such circumstances, a great plan of reconciliation, prepared by the Ministers of the Crown, has been brought before us in a manner which gives additional lustre to a noble name, inseparably associated during two centuries with the dearest liberties of the English people. I will not say, that this plan is in all its details precisely such as I might wish it to be; but it is founded on a great and a sound principle. It takes away a vast power from a few. It distributes that power through the great mass of the middle order. Every man, therefore, who thinks as I think is bound to stand firmly by Ministers who are resolved to stand or fall with this measure. Were I one of them, I would sooner, infinitely sooner, fall with such a measure than stand by any other means that ever supported a Cabinet.

My honorable friend, the Member for the University of Oxford, tells us, that if we pass this law, England will soon be a republic. The reformed House of Commons will, according to him, before it has sate ten years, depose the King, and expel the Lords from their House. Sir, if my honorable friend could prove this, he would have succeeded in bringing an argument for democracy, infinitely stronger than any that is to be found in the works of Paine. My honorable friend's proposition is in fact this; that our monarchical and aristocratical institutions have no hold on the public mind of England; that these institutions are regarded with aversion by a decided majority of the middle class. This, Sir, I say, is plainly deducible from his proposition; for he tells us that the Representatives of the middle class will inevitably abolish royalty and nobility within ten years: and there is surely no reason to think that the Representatives of the middle class will be more inclined to a democratic revolution than their constituents. Now, Sir, if I were convinced that the great body of the middle class in England look with aversion on monarchy and aristocracy, I should be forced, much against my will, to come to this conclusion, that monarchical and aristocratical institutions are unsuited to my country. Monarchy and aristocracy, valuable and useful as I think them, are still valuable and useful as means, and not as ends. The end of government is the happiness of the people: and I do not conceive that, in a country like this, the happiness of the people can be promoted by a form of government in which the middle classes place no confidence, and which exists only because the middle classes have no organ by which to make their sentiments known. But, Sir, I am fully convinced that the middle classes sincerely wish to uphold the Royal prerogatives and the constitutional rights of the Peers. What facts does my honorable friend produce in support of his opinion? One fact only; and that a fact which has absolutely nothing to do with the question. The effect of this Reform, he tells us, would be to make the House of Commons allpowerful. It was allpowerful once before, in the beginning of 1649. Then it cut off the head of the King, and abolished the House of Peers. Therefore, if it again has the supreme power, it will act in the same manner. Now, Sir, it was not the House of Commons that cut off the head of Charles the First; nor was the House of Commons then allpowerful. It had been greatly reduced in numbers by successive expulsions. It was under the absolute dominion of the army. A majority of the House was willing to take the terms offered by the King. The soldiers turned out the majority; and the minority, not a sixth part of the whole House, passed those votes of which my honorable friend speaks, votes of which the middle classes disapproved then, and of which they disapprove still.

My honorable friend, and almost all the gentlemen who have taken the same side with him in this Debate, have dwelt much on the utility of close and rotten boroughs. It is by means of such boroughs, they tell us, that the ablest men have been introduced into Parliament. It is true that many distinguished persons have represented places of this description. But, Sir, we must judge of a form of government by its general tendency, not by happy accidents. Every form of government has its happy accidents. Despotism has its happy accidents. Yet we are not disposed to abolish all constitutional checks, to place an absolute master over us, and to take our chance whether he may be a Caligula or a Marcus Aurelius. In whatever way the House of Commons may be chosen, some able men will be chosen in that way who would not be chosen in any other way. If there were a law that the hundred tallest men in England should be Members of Parliament, there would probably be some able men among those who would come into the House by virtue of this law. If the hundred persons whose names stand first in the alphabetical list of the Court Guide were made Members of Parliament, there would probably be able men among them. We read in ancient history, that a very able king was elected by the neighing of his horse: but we shall scarcely, I think, adopt this mode of election. In one of the most celebrated republics of antiquity, Athens, Senators and Magistrates were chosen by lot; and sometimes the lot fell fortunately. Once, for example, Socrates was in office. A cruel and unjust proposition was made by a demagogue. Socrates resisted it at the hazard of his own life. There is no event in Grecian history more interesting than that memorable resistance. Yet who would have officers appointed by lot, because the accident of the lot may have given to a great and good man a power which he would probably never have attained in any other way? We must judge, as I said, by the general tendency of a system. No person can doubt that a House of Commons, chosen freely by the middle classes, will contain many very able men. I do not say, that precisely the same able men who would find their way into the present House of Commons will find their way into the reformed House: but that is not the question. No particular man is necessary to the State. We may depend on it that, if we provide the country with popular institutions, those institutions will provide it with great men.

There is another objection, which, I think, was first raised by the honorable and learned Member for Newport.[1] He tells us that the elective franchise is property; that to take it away from a man who has not been judicially convicted of malpractices is robbery; that no crime is proved against the voters in the close boroughs; that no crime is even imputed to them in the preamble of the bill; and that therefore to disfranchise them without compensation would be an act of revolutionary tyranny. The honorable and learned gentleman has compared the conduct of the present Ministers to that of those odious tools of power, who, towards the close of the reign of Charles the Second, seized the charters of the Whig Corporations. Now, there was another precedent, which I wonder that he did not recollect, both because it is much more nearly in point than that to which he referred, and because my noble friend, the Paymaster of the Forces, had previously alluded to it. If the elective franchise is property, if to disfranchise voters without a crime proved, or a compensation given, be robbery, was there ever such an act of robbery as the disfranchising of the Irish forty shilling freeholders? Was any pecuniary compensation given to them? Is it declared in the preamble of the bill which took away their franchise, that they had been convicted of any offence? Was any judicial inquiry instituted into their conduct? Were they even accused of any crime? Or if you say that it was a crime in the electors of Clare to vote for the honorable and learned gentleman[2] who now represents the county of Waterford, was a Protestant freeholder in Louth to be punished for the crime of a Catholic freeholder in Clare? If the principle of the honorable and learned Member for Newport be sound, the franchise of the Irish peasant was property. That franchise the Ministers under whom the honorable and learned Member held office did not scruple to take away. Will he accuse those Ministers of robbery? If not, how can he bring such an accusation against their successors?

Every gentleman, I think, who has spoken from the other side of the House, has alluded to the opinions which some of His Majesty's Ministers formerly entertained on the subject of Reform.

[1] Mr. Horace Twiss.        [2] [Daniel O'Connell.]

M—22

It would be officious in me, Sir, to undertake the defence of gentlemen who are so well able to defend themselves. I will only say that, in my opinion, the country will not think worse either of their capacity or of their patriotism, because they have shown that they can profit by experience, because they have learned to see the folly of delaying inevitable changes. There are others who ought to have learned the same lesson. I say, Sir, that there are those who, I should have thought, must have had enough to last them all their lives of that humiliation which follows obstinate and boastful resistance to changes rendered necessary by the progress of society, and by the development of the human mind. Is it possible that those persons can wish again to occupy a position which can neither be defended nor surrendered with honour? I well remember, Sir, a certain evening in the month of May, 1827. I had not then the honour of a seat in this House; but I was an attentive observer of its proceedings. The right honorable Baronet opposite,[1] of whom personally I desire to speak with that high respect which I feel for his talents and his character, but of whose public conduct I must speak with the sincerity required by my public duty, was then, as he is now, out of office. He had just resigned the seals of the Home Department, because he conceived that the recent ministerial arrangements had been too favourable to the Catholic claims. He rose to ask whether it was the intention of the new Cabinet to repeal the Test and Corporation Acts, and to reform the Parliament. He bound up, I well remember, those two questions together; and he declared that, if the Ministers should either attempt to repeal the Test and Corporation Acts, or bring forward a measure of Parliamentary Reform, he should think it his duty to oppose them to the utmost. Since that declaration was made four years have elapsed; and what is now the state of the three questions which then chiefly agitated the minds of men? What is become of the Test and Corporation Acts? They are repealed. By whom? By the right honorable Baronet. What has become of the Catholic disabilities? They are removed. By whom? By the right honorable Baronet. The question of Parliamentary Reform is still behind. But signs, of which it is impossible to misconceive the import, do most clearly indicate that, unless that question also be speedily settled, property, and order, and all the institutions of this great monarchy, will be exposed to fearful peril. Is it possible that gentlemen long versed in high political affairs cannot read these signs? Is it possible that they can really believe that the Representative system of England, such as it

[1] Sir Robert Peel.

now is, will last till the year 1860? If not, for what would they have us wait? Would they have us wait merely that we may show to all the world how little we have profited by our own recent experience? Would they have us wait, that we may once again hit the exact point where we can neither refuse with authority, nor concede with grace? Would they have us wait, that the numbers of the discontented party may become larger, its demands higher, its feelings more acrimonious, its organisation more complete? Would they have us wait till the whole tragicomedy of 1827 has been acted over again; till they have been brought into office by a cry of "No Reform," to be reformers, as they were once before brought into office by a cry of "No Popery," to be emancipators? Have they obliterated from their minds—gladly, perhaps, would some among them obliterate from their minds—the transactions of that year? And have they forgotten all the transactions of the succeeding year? Have they forgotten how the spirit of liberty in Ireland, debarred from its natural outlet, found a vent by forbidden passages? Have they forgotten how we were forced to indulge the Catholics in all the licence of rebels, merely because we chose to withhold from them the liberties of subjects? Do they wait for associations more formidable than that of the Corn Exchange, for contributions larger than the Rent, for agitators more violent than those who, three years ago, divided with the King and the Parliament the sovereignty of Ireland? Do they wait for that last and most dreadful paroxysm of popular rage, for that last and most cruel test of military fidelity? Let them wait, if their past experience shall induce them to think that any high honor or any exquisite pleasure is to be obtained by a policy like this. Let them wait, if this strange and fearful infatuation be indeed upon them, that they should not see with their eyes, or hear with their ears, or understand with their heart. But let us know our interest and our duty better. Turn where we may, within, around, the voice of great events is proclaiming to us, Reform, that you may preserve. Now, therefore, while every thing at home and abroad forebodes ruin to those who persist in a hopeless struggle against the spirit of the age, now, while the crash of the proudest throne of the continent is still resounding in our ears, now, while the roof of a British palace affords an ignominious shelter to the exiled heir of forty kings, now, while we see on every side ancient institutions subverted, and great societies dissolved, now, while the heart of England is still sound, now, while old feelings and old associations retain a power and a charm which may too soon pass away, now, in this your accepted time, now, in this your day of salvation, take counsel, not of prejudice, not of party spirit, not of the ignominious pride of a fatal consistency, but of history, of reason, of the ages which are past, of the signs of this most portentous time. Pronounce in a manner worthy of the expectation with which this great debate has been anticipated, and of the long remembrance which it will leave behind. Renew the youth of the State. Save property, divided against itself. Save the multitude, endangered by its own ungovernable passions. Save the aristocracy, endangered by its own unpopular power. Save the greatest, and fairest, and most highly civilised community that ever existed, from calamities which may in a few days sweep away all the rich heritage of so many ages of wisdom and glory. The danger is terrible. The time is short. If this bill should be rejected, I pray to God that none of those who concur in rejecting it may ever remember their votes with unavailing remorse, amidst the wreck of laws, the confusion of ranks, the spoliation of property, and the dissolution of social order.

# PARLIAMENTARY REFORM. II

### A SPEECH DELIVERED IN THE HOUSE OF COMMONS ON THE 20TH OF SEPTEMBER, 1831

On Monday, the nineteenth of September, 1831, the Bill to amend the representation of the people in England and Wales was read a third time, at an early hour and in a thin house, without any debate. But on the question whether the Bill should pass a discussion arose which lasted three nights. On the morning of the twenty-second of September the House divided; and the Bill passed by 345 votes to 236. The following Speech was made on the second night of the debate.

IT is not without great diffidence, Sir, that I rise to address you on a subject which has been nearly exhausted. Indeed, I should not have risen had I not thought that, though the arguments on this question are for the most part old, our situation at present is in a great measure new. At length the Reform Bill, having passed without vital injury through all the dangers which threatened it, during a long and minute discussion, from the attacks of its enemies and from the dissensions of its friends, comes before us for our final ratification, altered, indeed, in some of its details for the better, and in some for the worse, but in its great principles still the same bill which, on the first of March, was proposed to the late Parliament, the same bill which was received with joy and gratitude by the whole nation, the same bill which, in an instant, took away the power of interested agitators, and united in one firm body all the sects of sincere Reformers, the same bill which, at the late election, received the approbation of almost every great constituent body in the empire. With a confidence which discussion has only strengthened, with an assured hope of great public blessings if the wish of the nation shall be gratified, with a deep and solemn apprehension of great public calamities if that wish shall be disappointed, I, for the last time, give my most hearty assent to this noble law, destined, I trust, to be the parent of many good laws, and, through a long series of years, to secure the repose and promote the prosperity of my country.

When I say that I expect this bill to promote the prosperity of the country, I by no means intend to encourage those chimerical hopes which the honorable and learned Member for Rye,[1] who has so much distinguished himself in this debate, has imputed to the Reformers. The people, he says, are for the bill, because they expect that it will immediately relieve all their distresses. Sir, I believe that very few of that large and respectable class which we are now about to admit to a share of political power entertain any such absurd expectation. They expect relief, I doubt not; and I doubt not that they will find it; but sudden relief they are far too wise to expect. The bill, says the honorable and learned gentleman, is good for nothing: it is merely theoretical: it removes no real and sensible evil: it will not give the people more work, or higher wages, or cheaper bread. Undoubtedly, Sir, the bill will not immediately give all those things to the people. But will any institutions give them all those things? Do the present institutions of the country secure to them those advantages? If we are to pronounce the Reform Bill good for nothing, because it will not at once raise the nation from distress to prosperity, what are we to say of that system under which the nation has been of late sinking from prosperity into distress? The defect is not in the Reform Bill, but in the very nature of government. On the physical condition of the great body of the people, government acts not as a specific, but as an alterative. Its operation is powerful, indeed, and certain, but gradual and indirect. The business of government is not directly to make the people rich, but to protect them in making themselves rich; and a government which attempts more than this is precisely the government which is likely to perform less. Governments do not and cannot support the people. We have no miraculous powers: we have not the rod of the Hebrew lawgiver: we cannot rain down bread on the multitude from Heaven: we

[1] Mr. Pemberton.

cannot smite the rock and give them to drink. We can give them only freedom to employ their industry to the best advantage, and security in the enjoyment of what their industry has acquired. These advantages it is our duty to give at the smallest possible cost. The diligence and forethought of individuals will thus have fair play; and it is only by the diligence and forethought of individuals that the community can become prosperous. I am not aware that His Majesty's Ministers, or any of the supporters of this bill, have encouraged the people to hope, that Reform will remove distress, in any other way than by this indirect process. By this indirect process the bill will, I feel assured, conduce to the national prosperity. If it had been passed fifteen years ago, it would have saved us from our present embarrassments. If we pass it now, it will gradually extricate us from them. It will secure to us a House of Commons, which, by preserving peace, by destroying monopolies, by taking away unnecessary public burthens, by judiciously distributing necessary public burthens, will, in the progress of time, greatly improve our condition. This it will do; and those who blame it for not doing more blame it for not doing what no Constitution, no code of laws, ever did or ever will do; what no legislator, who was not an ignorant and unprincipled quack, ever ventured to promise.

But chimerical as are the hopes which the honorable and learned Member for Rye imputes to the people, they are not, I think, more chimerical than the fears which he has himself avowed. Indeed, those very gentlemen who are constantly telling us that we are taking a leap in the dark, that we pay no attention to the lessons of experience, that we are mere theorists, are themselves the despisers of experience, are themselves the mere theorists. They are terrified at the thought of admitting into Parliament members elected by ten pound householders. They have formed in their own imaginations a most frightful idea of these members. My honorable and learned friend, the Member for Cockermouth,[1] is certain that these members will take every opportunity of promoting the interests of the journeyman in opposition to those of the capitalist. The honorable and learned Member for Rye is convinced that none but persons who have strong local connections, will ever be returned for such constituent bodies. My honorable friend, the Member for Thetford,[2] tells us, that none but mob orators, men who are willing to pay the basest court to the multitude, will have any chance. Other speakers have gone still further, and have described to us the future borough members as so many

[1] Sir James Scarlett.        [2] Mr. Alexander Baring.

Marats and Santerres, low, fierce, desperate men, who will turn the House into a bear garden, and who will try to turn the monarchy into a republic, mere agitators, without honor, without sense, without education, without the feelings or the manners of gentlemen. Whenever, during the course of the fatiguing discussions by which we have been so long occupied, there has been a cry of "question," or a noise at the bar, the orator who has been interrupted has remarked, that such proceedings will be quite in place in the Reformed Parliament, but that we ought to remember that the House of Commons is still an assembly of gentlemen. This, I say, is to set up mere theory, or rather mere prejudice, in opposition to long and ample experience. Are the gentlemen who talk thus ignorant that we have already the means of judging what kind of men the ten pound householders will send up to Parliament? Are they ignorant that there are even now large towns with very popular franchises, with franchises even more democratic than those which will be bestowed by the present bill? Ought they not, on their own principles, to look at the results of the experiments which have already been made, instead of predicting frightful calamities at random? How do the facts which are before us agree with their theories? Nottingham is a city with a franchise even more democratic than that which this bill establishes. Does Nottingham send hither mere vulgar demagogues? It returns two distinguished men, one an advocate, the other a soldier, both unconnected with the town. Every man paying scot and lot has a vote at Leicester. This is a lower franchise than the ten pound franchise. Do we find that the Members for Leicester are the mere tools of the journeymen? I was at Leicester during the contest of 1826; and I recollect that the suffrages of the scot and lot voters were pretty equally divided between two candidates, neither of them connected with the place, neither of them a slave of the mob, one a Tory Baronet from Derbyshire, the other a most respectable and excellent friend of mine, connected with the manufacturing interest, and also an inhabitant of Derbyshire. Look at Norwich. Look at Northampton, with a franchise more democratic than even the scot and lot franchise. Northampton formerly returned Mr. Perceval, and now returns gentlemen of high respectability, gentlemen who have a great stake in the prosperity and tranquillity of the country. Look at the metropolitan districts. This is an *a fortiori* case. Nay it is—the expression, I fear, is awkward—an *a fortiori* case at two removes. The ten pound householders of the metropolis are persons in a lower station of life than the ten pound householders of other towns.

The scot and lot franchise in the metropolis is again lower than the ten pound franchise. Yet have Westminster and Southwark been in the habit of sending us members of whom we have had reason to be ashamed, of whom we have not had reason to be proud? I do not say that the inhabitants of Westminster and Southwark have always expressed their political sentiments with proper moderation. That is not the question. The question is this: what kind of men have they elected? The very principle of all Representative government is, that men who do not judge well of public affairs may be quite competent to choose others who will judge better. Whom, then, have Westminster and Southwark sent us during the last fifty years, years full of great events, years of intense popular excitement? Take any one of those nomination boroughs, the patrons of which have conscientiously endeavoured to send fit men into this House. Compare the Members for that borough with the Members for Westminster and Southwark; and you will have no doubt to which the preference is due. It is needless to mention Mr. Fox, Mr. Sheridan, Mr. Tierney, Sir Samuel Romilly. Yet I must pause at the name of Sir Samuel Romilly. Was he a mob orator? Was he a servile flatterer of the multitude? Sir, if he had any fault, if there was any blemish on that most serene and spotless character, that character which every public man, and especially every professional man engaged in politics, ought to propose to himself as a model, it was this, that he despised popularity too much and too visibly. The honorable Member for Thetford told us that the honorable and learned Member for Rye, with all his talents, would have no chance of a seat in the Reformed Parliament, for want of the qualifications which succeed on the hustings. Did Sir Samuel Romilly ever appear on the hustings of Westminster? He never solicited one vote; he never showed himself to the electors, till he had been returned at the head of the poll. Even then, as I have heard from one of his nearest relatives, it was with reluctance that he submitted to be chaired. He shrank from being made a show. He loved the people, and he served them; but Coriolanus himself was not less fit to canvass them. I will mention one other name, that of a man of whom I have only a childish recollection, but who must have been intimately known to many of those who hear me, Mr. Henry Thornton. He was a man eminently upright, honorable, and religious, a man of strong understanding, a man of great political knowledge; but, in all respects, the very reverse of a mob orator. He was a man who would not have yielded to what he considered as unreasonable clamour, I will not say to save his seat, but to save his life. Yet he continued to represent South-wark, Parliament after Parliament, for many years. Such has been the conduct of the scot and lot voters of the metropolis; and there is clearly less reason to expect democratic violence from ten pound householders than from scot and lot householders; and from ten pound householders in the country towns than from ten pound householders in London. Experience, I say, therefore, is on our side; and on the side of our opponents nothing but mere conjecture and mere assertion.

Sir, when this bill was first brought forward, I supported it, not only on the ground of its intrinsic merits, but, also, because I was convinced that to reject it would be a course full of danger. I believe that the danger of that course is in no respect diminished. I believe, on the contrary, that it is increased. We are told that there is a reaction. The warmth of the public feeling, it seems, has abated. In this story both the sections of the party opposed to Reform are agreed; those who hate Reform, because it will remove abuses, and those who hate it, because it will avert anarchy; those who wish to see the electing body controlled by ejectments, and those who wish to see it controlled by riots. They must now, I think, be undeceived. They must have already discovered that the surest way to prevent a reaction is to talk about it, and that the enthusiasm of the people is at once rekindled by any indiscreet mention of their seeming coolness. This, Sir, is not the first reaction which the sagacity of the Opposition has discovered since the Reform Bill was brought in. Every gentleman who sat in the late Parliament, every gentleman who, during the sitting of the late Parliament, paid attention to political speeches and publications, must remember how, for some time before the debate on General Gascoyne's motion, and during the debate on that motion, and down to the very day of the dissolution, we were told that public feeling had cooled. The right honorable Baronet, the Member for Tamworth, told us so. All the literary organs of the Opposition, from the Quarterly Review down to the Morning Post, told us so. All the Members of the Opposition with whom we conversed in private told us so. I have in my eye a noble friend of mine, who assured me, on the very night which preceded the dissolution, that the people had ceased to be zealous for the Ministerial plan, and that we were more likely to lose than to gain by the elections. The appeal was made to the people; and what was the result? What sign of a reaction appeared among the Livery of London? What sign of a reaction did the honorable Baronet who now represents Okehampton find among the freeholders of Cornwall?[1] How was it with the large represented towns? Had Liverpool cooled? or Bristol? or Leicester? or Coventry? or Nottingham? or Norwich? How was it with the great seats of manufacturing industry, Yorkshire, and Lancashire, and Staffordshire, and Warwickshire, and Cheshire? How was it with the agricultural districts, Northumberland and Cumberland, Leicestershire and Lincolnshire, Kent and Essex, Oxfordshire, Hampshire, Somersetshire, Dorsetshire, Devonshire? How was it with the strongholds of aristocratical influence, Newark, and Stamford, and Hertford, and St. Alban's? Never did any people display, within the limits prescribed by law, so generous a fervour, or so steadfast a determination, as that very people whose apparent languor had just before inspired the enemies of Reform with a delusive hope.

Such was the end of the reaction of April; and, if that lesson shall not profit those to whom it was given, such and yet more signal will be the end of the reaction of September. The two cases are strictly analogous. In both cases the people were eager when they believed the bill to be in danger, and quiet when they believed it to be in security. During the three or four weeks which followed the promulgation of the Ministerial plan, all was joy, and gratitude, and vigorous exertion. Everywhere meetings were held: everywhere resolutions were passed: from every quarter were sent up petitions to this House, and addresses to the Throne: and then the nation, having given vent to its first feelings of delight, having clearly and strongly expressed its opinions, having seen the principle of the bill adopted by the House of Commons on the second reading, became composed, and awaited the result with a tranquillity which the Opposition mistook for indifference. All at once the aspect of affairs changed. General Gascoyne's amendment was carried: the bill was again in danger: exertions were again necessary. Then was it well seen whether the calmness of the public mind was any indication of indifference. The depth and sincerity of the prevailing sentiments were proved, not by mere talking, but by actions, by votes, by sacrifices. Intimidation was defied: expenses were rejected: old ties were broken: the people struggled manfully: they triumphed gloriously: they placed the bill in perfect security, as far as this House was concerned; and they returned to their repose. They are now, as they were on the eve of General Gascoyne's motion, awaiting the issue of the deliberations of Parliament, without any indecent show of violence, but with anxious interest and immovable resolution. And because

[1] Sir Richard Vyvyan.

they are not exhibiting that noisy and rapturous enthusiasm which is in its own nature transient, because they are not as much excited as on the day when the plan of the Government was first made known to them, or on the day when the late Parliament was dissolved, because they do not go on week after week, hallooing and holding meetings, and marching about with flags, and making bonfires, and illuminating their houses, we are again told that there is a reaction. To such a degree can men be deceived by their wishes, in spite of their own recent experience. Sir, there is no reaction; and there will be no reaction. All that has been said on this subject convinces me only that those who are now, for the second time, raising this cry, know nothing of the crisis in which they are called on to act, or of the nation which they aspire to govern. All their opinions respecting this bill are founded on one great error. They imagine that the public feeling concerning Reform is a mere whim which sprang up suddenly out of nothing, and which will as suddenly vanish into nothing. They, therefore, confidently expect a reaction. They are always looking out for a reaction. Everything that they see, or that they hear, they construe into a sign of the approach of this reaction. They resemble the man in Horace, who lies on the bank of the river, expecting that it will every moment pass by and leave him a clear passage, not knowing the depth and abundance of the fountain which feeds it, not knowing that it flows, and will flow on for ever. They have found out a hundred ingenious devices by which they deceive themselves. Sometimes they tell us that the public feeling about Reform was caused by the events which took place at Paris about fourteen months ago; though every observant and impartial man knows, that the excitement which the late French revolution produced in England was not the cause but the effect of that progress which liberal opinions had made amongst us. Sometimes they tell us that we should not have been troubled with any complaints on the subject of the Representation, if the House of Commons had agreed to a certain motion, made in the Session of 1830, for inquiry into the causes of the public distress. I remember nothing about that motion, except that it gave rise to the dullest debate ever known; and the country, I am firmly convinced, cared not one straw about it. But is it not strange that men of real ability can deceive themselves so grossly, as to think that any change in the government of a foreign nation, or the rejection of any single motion, however popular, could all at once raise up a great, rich, enlightened nation, against its ancient institutions? Could such small drops have produced an overflowing, if the vessel had not already been filled to the very brim? These explanations are incredible, and if they were credible, would be anything but consolatory. If it were really true that the English people had taken a sudden aversion to a representative system which they had always loved and admired, because a single division in Parliament had gone against their wishes, or because, in a foreign country, in circumstances bearing not the faintest analogy to those in which we are placed, a change of dynasty had happened, what hope could we have for such a nation of madmen? How could we expect that the present form of government, or any form of government, would be durable amongst them?

Sir, the public feeling concerning Reform is of no such recent origin, and springs from no such frivolous causes. Its first faint commencement may be traced far, very far, back in our history. During seventy years that feeling has had a great influence on the public mind. Through the first thirty years of the reign of George the Third, it was gradually increasing. The great leaders of the two parties in the State were favourable to Reform. Plans of reform were supported by large and most respectable minorities in the House of Commons. The French Revolution, filling the higher and middle classes with an extreme dread of change, and the war calling away the public attention from internal to external politics, threw the question back; but the people never lost sight of it. Peace came, and they were at leisure to think of domestic improvements. Distress came, and they suspected, as was natural, that their distress was the effect of unfaithful stewardship and unskilful legislation. An opinion favourable to Parliamentary Reform grew up rapidly, and became strong among the middle classes. But one tie, one strong tie, still bound those classes to the Tory party. I mean the Catholic Question. It is impossible to deny that, on that subject, a large proportion, a majority, I fear, of the middle class of Englishmen, conscientiously held opinions opposed to those which I have always entertained, and were disposed to sacrifice every other consideration to what they regarded as a religious duty. Thus the Catholic Question hid, so to speak, the question of Parliamentary Reform. The feeling in favour of Parliamentary Reform grew, but it grew in the shade. Every man, I think, must have observed the progress of that feeling in his own social circle. But few Reform meetings were held, and few petitions in favour of Reform presented. At length the Catholics were emancipated; the solitary link of sympathy which attached the people to the Tories was broken; the cry of "No Popery" could no longer be opposed to the cry of "Reform." That which, in the opinion of the two great parties in Parliament, and of a vast portion of the community, had been the first question, suddenly disappeared; and the question of Parliamentary Reform took the first place. Then was put forth all the strength which had been growing in silence and obscurity. Then it appeared that Reform had on its side a coalition of interests and opinions unprecedented in our history, all the liberality and intelligence which had supported the Catholic claims, and all the clamour which had opposed them.

This, I believe, is the true history of that public feeling on the subject of Reform which has been ascribed to causes quite inadequate to the production of such an effect. If ever there was in the history of mankind a national sentiment which was the very opposite of a caprice, with which accident had nothing to do, which was produced by the slow, steady, certain progress of the human mind, it is the sentiment of the English people on the subject of Reform. Accidental circumstances may have brought that feeling to maturity in a particular year, or a particular month. That point I will not dispute; for it is not worth disputing. But those accidental circumstances have brought on Reform, only as the circumstance that, at a particular time, indulgences were offered for sale in a particular town in Saxony, brought on the great separation from the Church of Rome. In both cases the public mind was prepared to move on the slightest impulse.

Thinking thus of the public opinion concerning Reform, being convinced that this opinion is the mature product of time and of discussion, I expect no reaction. I no more expect to see my countrymen again content with the mere semblance of a Representation, than to see them again drowning witches or burning heretics, trying causes by red hot ploughshares, or offering up human sacrifices to wicker idols. I no more expect a reaction in favour of Gatton and Old Sarum, than a reaction in favour of Thor and Odin. I should think such a reaction almost as much a miracle, as that the shadow should go back upon the dial. Revolutions produced by violence are often followed by reactions; the victories of reason once gained, are gained for eternity.

In fact, if there be, in the present aspect of public affairs, any sign peculiarly full of evil omen to the opponents of Reform, it is that very calmness of the public mind on which they found their expectation of success. They think that it is the calmness of indifference. It is the calmness of confident hope; and in proportion to the confidence of hope will be the bitterness of disappointment. Disappointment, indeed, I do not anticipate. That we are certain of success in this House is now acknowledged; and our opponents have, in consequence, during the whole of this Session, and particularly during the present debate, addressed their arguments and exhortations rather to the Lords than to the assembly of which they are themselves Members. Their principal argument has always been, that the bill will destroy the peerage. The honorable and learned Member for Rye has, in plain terms, called on the Barons of England to save their order from demo-cratic encroachments, by rejecting this measure. All these argu-ments, all these appeals, being interpreted, mean this: "Proclaim to your countrymen that you have no common interests with them, no common sympathies with them; that you can be powerful only by their weakness, and exalted only by their degradation; that the corruption which disgusts them, and the oppression against which their spirit rises up, are indispensable to your authority; that the freedom and purity of election are incom-patible with the very existence of your House. Give them clearly to understand that your power rests, not, as they have hitherto imagined, on their rational convictions, or on their habitual venera-tion, or on your own great property, but on a system fertile of political evils, fertile also of low iniquities of which ordinary justice takes cognisance. Bind up, in inseparable union, the privileges of your estate with the grievances of ours: resolve to stand or fall with abuses visibly marked out for destruction: tell the people that they are attacking you in attacking the three holes in the wall,[1] and that they shall never get rid of the three holes in the wall till they have got rid of you; that a hereditary peerage, and a representative assembly, can coexist only in name, and that, if they will have a real House of Peers, they must be content with a mock House of Commons." This, I say, is the advice given to the Lords by those who call themselves the friends of aristocracy. That advice so pernicious will not be followed, I am well assured; yet I cannot but listen to it with uneasiness. I cannot but wonder that it should proceed from the lips of men who are constantly lecturing us on the duty of consulting history and experience. Have they never heard what effects counsels like their own, when too faithfully followed, have produced? Have they never visited that neighbouring country, which still presents to the eye, even of a passing stranger, the signs of a great dissolution and renovation of society? Have they never walked by those stately mansions, now sinking into decay, and portioned out into lodging rooms, which line the silent streets of the Faubourg St. Germain? Have

---

[1] [At Midhurst the sites of the burgage tenement (which carried votes) were marked by inscribed stones sunk in the wall.]

they never seen the ruins of those castles whose terraces and gardens overhang the Loire? Have they never heard that from those magnificent hotels, from those ancient castles, an aristocracy as splendid, as brave, as proud, as accomplished as ever Europe saw, was driven forth to exile and beggary, to implore the charity of hostile Governments and hostile creeds, to cut wood in the back settlements of America, or to teach French in the schoolrooms of London? And why were those haughty nobles destroyed with that utter destruction? Why were they scattered over the face of the earth, their titles abolished, their escutcheons defaced, their parks wasted, their palaces dismantled, their heritage given to strangers? Because they had no sympathy with the people, no discernment of the signs of their time; because, in the pride and narrowness of their hearts, they called those whose warnings might have saved them theorists and speculators; because they refused all concession till the time had arrived when no concession would avail. I have no apprehension that such a fate awaits the nobles of England. I draw no parallel between our aristocracy and that of France. Those who represent the peerage as a class whose power is incompatible with the just influence of the people in the State, draw that parallel, and not I. They do all in their power to place the Lords and Commons of England in that position with respect to each other in which the French gentry stood with respect to the Third Estate. But I am convinced that these advisers will not succeed. We see, with pride and delight, among the friends of the people, the Talbots, the Cavendishes, the princely house of Howard. Foremost among those who have entitled themselves, by their exertions in this House, to the lasting gratitude of their countrymen, we see the descendants of Marlborough, of Russell, and of Derby. I hope, and firmly believe, that the Lords will see what their interest and their honor require. I hope, and firmly believe, that they will act in such a manner as to entitle themselves to the esteem and affection of the people. But if not, let not the enemies of Reform imagine that their reign is straightway to recommence, or that they have obtained anything more than a short and uneasy respite. We are bound to respect the constitutional rights of the Peers; but we are bound also not to forget our own. We, too, have our privileges: we, too, are an estate of the realm. A House of Commons strong in the love and confidence of the people, a House of Commons which has nothing to fear from a dissolution, is something in the government. Some persons, I well know, indulge a hope that the rejection of the bill will at once restore the domination of that party which fled from power last November, leaving everything abroad and everything at home in confusion; leaving the European system, which it had built up at a vast cost of blood and treasure, falling to pieces in every direction; leaving the dynasties which it had restored, hastening into exile; leaving the nations which it had joined together, breaking away from each other; leaving the fundholders in dismay; leaving the peasantry in insurrection; leaving the most fertile counties lighted up with the fires of incendiaries; leaving the capital in such a state, that a royal procession could not safely pass through it. Dark and terrible, beyond any season within my remembrance of political affairs, was the day of their flight. Far darker and far more terrible will be the day of their return. They will return in opposition to the whole British nation, united as it was never before united on any internal question; united as firmly as when the Armada was sailing up the channel; united as firmly as when Bonaparte pitched his camp on the cliffs of Boulogne. They will return pledged to defend evils which the people are resolved to destroy. They will return to a situation in which they can stand only by crushing and trampling down public opinion, and from which, if they fall, they may, in their fall, drag down with them the whole frame of society. Against such evils, should such evils appear to threaten the country, it will be our privilege and our duty to warn our gracious and beloved Sovereign. It will be our privilege and our duty to convey the wishes of a loyal people to the throne of a patriot king. At such a crisis the proper place for the House of Commons is in front of the nation; and in that place this House will assuredly be found. Whatever prejudice or weakness may do elsewhere to ruin the empire, here, I trust, will not be wanting the wisdom, the virtue, and the energy that may save it.

## GOVERNMENT OF INDIA

A SPEECH DELIVERED IN THE HOUSE OF COMMONS ON THE 10TH OF JULY, 1833

On Wednesday, the tenth of July, 1833, Mr. Charles Grant, President of the Board of Control, moved that the Bill for effecting an arrangement with the India Company, and for the better government of His Majesty's Indian territories, should be read a second time. The motion was carried without a division, but not without a long debate, in the course of which the following Speech was made.

HAVING, while this bill was in preparation, enjoyed the fullest and kindest confidence of my right honorable friend, the President of the Board of Control, agreeing with him completely in all those views which on a former occasion he so luminously and eloquently developed, having shared his anxieties, and feeling that in some degree I share his responsibility, I am naturally desirous to obtain the attention of the House while I attempt to defend the principles of the proposed arrangement. I wish that I could promise to be very brief; but the subject is so extensive that I will only promise to condense what I have to say as much as I can.

I rejoice, Sir, that I am completely dispensed, by the turn which our debates have taken, from the necessity of saying anything in favour of one part of our plan, the opening of the China trade. No voice, I believe, has yet been raised here in support of the monopoly. On that subject all public men of all parties seem to be agreed. The resolution proposed by the Ministers has received the unanimous assent of both Houses, and the approbation of the whole kingdom. I will not, therefore, Sir, detain you by vindicating what no gentleman has yet ventured to attack, but will proceed to call your attention to those effects which this great commercial revolution necessarily produced on the system of Indian government and finance.

The China trade is to be opened. Reason requires this. Public opinion requires it. The Government of the Duke of Wellington felt the necessity as strongly as the Government of Lord Grey. No Minister, Whig or Tory, could have been found to propose a renewal of the monopoly. No parliament, reformed or unreformed, would have listened to such a proposition. But though the opening of the trade was a matter concerning which the public had long made up its mind, the political consequences which must necessarily follow from the opening of the trade seem to me to be even now little understood. The language which I have heard in almost every circle where the subject was discussed was this: "Take away the monopoly, and leave the government of India to the Company:" a very short and convenient way of settling one of the most complicated questions that ever a legislature had to consider. The honorable Member for Sheffield,[1] though not disposed to retain the Company as an organ of Government, has repeatedly used language which proves that he shares in the general misconception. The fact is that the abolition of the monopoly rendered it absolutely necessary to make a fundamental change in the constitution of that great Corporation.

The Company had united in itself two characters, the character of trader and the character of sovereign. Between the trader and the sovereign there was a long and complicated account, almost every item of which furnished matter for litigation. While the monopoly continued, indeed, litigation was averted. The effect of the monopoly was, to satisfy the claims both of commerce and of territory, at the expense of a third party, the English people; to secure at once funds for the dividend of the stockholder and funds for the government of the Indian Empire, by means of a heavy tax on the tea consumed in this country. But when the third party would no longer bear this charge, all the great financial questions which had, at the cost of that third party, been kept in abeyance, were opened in an instant. The connection between the Company in its mercantile capacity, and the same Company in its political capacity, was dissolved. Even if the Company were permitted, as has been suggested, to govern India and at the same time to trade with China, no advances would be made from the profits of its Chinese trade for the support of its Indian government. It was in consideration of the exclusive privilege that the Company had hitherto been required to make those advances; it was by the exclusive privilege that the Company had been enabled to make them. When that privilege was taken away, it would be unreasonable in the Legislature to impose such an obligation, and impossible for the Company to fulfil it. The whole system of loans from commerce to territory, and repayments from territory to commerce, must cease. Each party must rest altogether on its own resources. It was therefore absolutely necessary to ascertain what resources each party possessed, to bring the long and intricate account between them to a close, and to assign to each a fair portion of assets and liabilities. There was vast property. How much of that property was applicable to purposes of state? How much was applicable to a dividend? There were debts to the amount of many millions. Which of these were the debts of the government that ruled at Calcutta? Which of the great mercantile house that bought tea at Canton? Were the creditors to look to the land revenues of India for their money? Or were they entitled to put executions into the warehouses behind Bishopsgate Street?

There were two ways of settling these questions; adjudication and compromise. The difficulties of adjudication were great; I think insuperable. Whatever acuteness and diligence could do has been done. One person in particular, whose talents and industry peculiarly fitted him for such investigations, and of whom I can never think without regret, Mr. Hyde Villiers,[1] devoted himself to the examination with an ardour and a perseverance

[1] [1801–32, a Cambridge friend of Macaulay's, became in 1832 Secretary to the Board of Control (India).]

which, I believe, shortened a life most valuable to his country and to his friends. The assistance of the most skilful accountants has been called in. But the difficulties are such as no accountant, however skilful, could possibly remove. The difficulties are not arithmetical, but political. They arise from the constitution of the Company, from the long and intimate union of the commercial and imperial characters in one body. Suppose that the treasurer of a charity were to mix up the money which he receives on account of the charity with his own private rents and dividends, to pay the whole into his bank to his own private account, to draw it out again by cheques in exactly the same form when he wanted it for his private expenses, and when he wanted it for the purposes of his public trust. Suppose that he were to continue to act thus till he was himself ignorant whether he were in advance or in arrear; and suppose that many years after his death a question were to arise whether his estate were in debt to the charity or the charity in debt to his estate. Such is the question which is now before us, with this important difference; that the accounts of an individual could not be in such a state unless he had been guilty of fraud, or of that gross negligence which is scarcely less culpable than fraud, and that the accounts of the Company were brought into this state by circumstances of a very peculiar kind, by circumstances unparalleled in the history of the world.

It is a mistake to suppose that the Company was a merely commercial body till the middle of the last century. Commerce was its chief object; but in order to enable it to pursue that object, it had been, like the other Companies which were its rivals, like the Dutch India Company, like the French India Company, invested from a very early period with political functions. More than a hundred and twenty years ago, the Company was in miniature precisely what it now is. It was intrusted with the very highest prerogatives of sovereignty. It had its forts, and its white captains, and its black sepoys; it had its civil and criminal tribunals; it was authorised to proclaim martial law; it sent ambassadors to the native governments, and concluded treaties with them; it was Zemindar of several districts, and within those districts, like other Zemindars of the first class, it exercised the powers of a sovereign, even to the infliction of capital punishment on the Hindoos within its jurisdiction. It is incorrect, therefore, to say, that the Company was at first a mere trader, and has since become a sovereign. It was at first a great trader and a petty prince. The political functions at first attracted little notice, because they were merely auxiliary to the commercial functions. By degrees, however, the political functions became more and more important. The Zemindar became a great nabob, became sovereign of all India; the two hundred sepoys became two hundred thousand. This change was gradually wrought, and was not immediately comprehended. It was natural that, while the political functions of the Company were merely auxiliary to its commerce, the political accounts should have been mixed up with the commercial accounts. It was equally natural that this mode of keeping accounts, having once been established, should have remained unaltered; and the more so, as the change in the situation of the Company, though rapid, was not sudden. It is impossible to name any one day, or any one year, as the day or the year when the Company became a great potentate. It has been the fashion indeed to fix on the year 1765, the year in which the Mogul issued a commission authorising the Company to administer the revenues of Bengal, Bahar, and Orissa, as the precise date of the accession of this singular body to sovereignty. I am utterly at a loss to understand why this epoch should be selected. Long before 1765 the Company had the reality of political power. Long before that year, they made a nabob of Arcot; they made and unmade nabobs of Bengal; they humbled the Vizier of Oude; they braved the Emperor of Hindostan himself; more than half the revenues of Bengal were under one pretence or another administered by them. And after the grant, the Company was not, in form and name, an independent power. It was merely a minister of the Court of Delhi. Its coinage bore the name of Shah Alum. The inscription which, down to the time of the Marquess of Hastings, appeared on the seal of the Governor General, declared that great functionary to be the slave of the Mogul. Even to this day we have never formally deposed the king of Delhi. The Company contents itself with being Mayor of the Palace, while the *Roi Fainéant* is suffered to play at being a sovereign. In fact, it was considered, both by Lord Clive and by Warren Hastings, as a point of policy to leave the character of the Company thus undefined, in order that the English might treat the princes in whose names they governed as realities or nonentities, just as might be most convenient.

Thus the transformation of the Company from a trading body, which possessed some sovereign prerogatives for the purposes of trade, into a sovereign body, the trade of which was auxiliary to its sovereignty, was effected by degrees and under disguise. It is not strange, therefore, that the mercantile and political transactions of this great corporation should be entangled together in inextricable complication. The commercial investments have been purchased out of the revenues of the empire. The expenses of war and government have been defrayed out of the profits of the trade. Commerce and territory have contributed to the improvement of the same spot of land, to the repairs of the same building. Securities have been given in precisely the same form, for money which has been borrowed for purposes of State, and for money which has been borrowed for purposes of traffic. It is easy, indeed,—and this is a circumstance which has, I think, misled some gentlemen,—it is easy to see what part of the assets of the Company appears in a commercial form, and what part appears in a political or territorial form. But this is not the question. Assets which are commercial in form may be territorial as respects the right of property; assets which are territorial in form may be commercial as respects the right of property. A chest of tea is not necessarily commercial property; it may have been bought out of the territorial revenue. A fort is not necessarily territorial property; it may stand on ground which the Company bought a hundred years ago out of their commercial profits. Adjudication, if by adjudication be meant decision according to some known rule of law, was out of the question. To leave matters like these to be determined by the ordinary maxims of our civil jurisprudence would have been the height of absurdity and injustice. For example, the home bond debt of the Company, it is believed, was incurred partly for political and partly for commercial purposes. But there is no evidence which would enable us to assign to each branch its proper share. The bonds all run in the same form; and a court of justice would, therefore, of course, either lay the whole burthen on the proprietors, or lay the whole on the territory. We have legal opinions, very respectable legal opinions, to the effect, that in strictness of law the territory is not responsible, and that the commercial assets are responsible for every farthing of the debts which were incurred for the government and defence of India. But though this may be, and I believe is, law, it is, I am sure, neither reason nor justice. On the other hand, it is urged by the advocates of the Company, that some valuable portions of the territory are the property of that body in its commercial capacity; that Calcutta, for example, is the private estate of the Company; that the Company holds the island of Bombay, in free and common socage, as of the Manor of East Greenwich. I will not pronounce any opinion on these points. I have considered them enough to see that there is quite difficulty enough in them to exercise all the ingenuity of all the lawyers in the kingdom for twenty years. But the fact is, Sir, that the municipal law was not made for controversies of this description. The existence of such a body as this gigantic corporation, this political monster of two natures, subject in one hemisphere, sovereign in another, had never been contemplated by the legislators or judges of former ages. Nothing but grotesque absurdity and atrocious injustice could have been the effect, if the claims and liabilities of such a body had been settled according to the rules of Westminster Hall, if the maxims of conveyancers had been applied to the titles by which flourishing cities and provinces are held, or the maxims of the law merchant to those promissory notes which are the securities for a great National Debt, raised for the purpose of exterminating the Pindarrees[1] and humbling the Burmese.

It was, as I have said, absolutely impossible to bring the question between commerce and territory to a satisfactory adjudication; and I must add that, even if the difficulties which I have mentioned could have been surmounted, even if there had been reason to hope that a satisfactory adjudication could have been obtained, I should still have wished to avoid that course. I think it desirable that the Company should continue to have a share in the government of India; and it would evidently have been impossible, pending a litigation between commerce and territory, to leave any political power to the Company. It would clearly have been the duty of those who were charged with the superintendence of India, to be the patrons of India throughout that momentous litigation, to scrutinise with the utmost severity every claim which might be made on the Indian revenues, and to oppose, with energy and perseverance, every such claim, unless its justice were manifest. If the Company was to be engaged in a suit for many millions, in a suit which might last for many years, against the Indian territory, could we entrust the Company with the government of that territory? Could we put the plaintiff in the situation of *prochain ami* of the defendant? Could we appoint governors who would have had an interest opposed in the most direct manner to the interest of the governed, whose stock would have been raised in value by every decision which added to the burthens of their subjects, and depressed by every decision which diminished those burthens? It would be absurd to suppose that they would efficiently defend our Indian Empire against the claims which they were themselves bringing against it; and it would be equally absurd to give the government of the Indian Empire to those who could not be trusted to defend its interests.

Seeing, then, that it was most difficult, if not wholly impossible,

[1] [Pindaris: mounted freebooters of Central India, crushed by Lord Hastings 1816–18; the Burma Campaign was in 1825–6.]

to resort to adjudication between commerce and territory, seeing that, if recourse were had to adjudication, it would be necessary to make a complete revolution in the whole constitution of India, the Government has proposed a compromise. That compromise, with some modifications which did not in the slightest degree affect its principle, and which, while they gave satisfaction to the Company, will eventually lay no additional burthen on the territory, has been accepted. It has, like all other compromises, been loudly censured by violent partisans on both sides. It has been represented by some as far too favorable to the Company, and by others as most unjust to the Company. Sir, I own that we cannot prove that either of these accusations is unfounded. It is of the very essence of our case that we should not be able to show that we have assigned, either to commerce or to territory, its precise due. For our principal reason for recommending a compromise was our full conviction that it was absolutely impossible to ascertain with precision what was due to commerce and what was due to territory. It is not strange that some people should accuse us of robbing the Company, and others of conferring a vast boon on the Company, at the expense of India: for we have proposed a middle course, on the very ground that there was a chance of a result much more favorable to the Company than our arrangement, and a chance also of a result much less favorable. If the questions pending between the Company and India had been decided as the ardent supporters of the Company predicted, India would, if I calculate rightly, have paid eleven millions more than she will now have to pay. If those questions had been decided as some violent enemies of the Company predicted, that great body would have been utterly ruined. The very meaning of compromise is that each party gives up his chance of complete success, in order to be secured against the chance of utter failure. And, as men of sanguine minds always overrate the chances in their own favour, every fair compromise is sure to be severely censured on both sides. I conceive that, in a case so dark and complicated as this, the compromise which we recommend is sufficiently vindicated, if it cannot be proved to be unfair. We are not bound to prove it to be fair. For it would have been unnecessary for us to resort to compromise at all, if we had been in possession of evidence which would have enabled us to pronounce, with certainty, what claims were fair and what were unfair. It seems to me that we have acted with due consideration for every party. The dividend which we give to the proprietors is precisely the same dividend which they have been receiving during forty years, and which they have expected to receive permanently. The price of their stock bears at present the same proportion to the price of other stock which it bore four or five years ago, before the anxiety and excitement which the late negotiations naturally produced had begun to operate. As to the territory on the other hand, it is true that, if the assets which are now in a commercial form should not produce a fund sufficient to pay the debts and dividend of the Company, the territory must stand to the loss and pay the difference. But in return for taking this risk, the territory obtains an immediate release from claims to the amount of many millions. I certainly do not believe that all those claims could have been substantiated; but I know that very able men think differently. And, if only one-fourth of the sum demanded had been awarded to the Company, India would have lost more than the largest sum which, as it seems to me, she can possibly lose under the proposed arrangement.

In a pecuniary point of view, therefore, I conceive that we can defend the measure as it affects the territory. But to the territory the pecuniary question is of secondary importance. If we have made a good pecuniary bargain for India, but a bad political bargain, if we have saved three or four millions to the finances of that country, and given to it, at the same time, pernicious institutions, we shall indeed have been practising a most ruinous parsimony. If, on the other hand, it shall be found that we have added fifty or a hundred thousand pounds a-year to the expenditure of an empire which yields a revenue of twenty millions, but that we have at the same time secured to that empire, as far as in us lies, the blessings of good government, we shall have no reason to be ashamed of our profusion. I hope and believe that India will have to pay nothing. But on the most unfavorable supposition that can be made, she will not have to pay so much to the Company as she now pays annually to a single state pageant, to the titular Nabob of Bengal, for example, or the titular King of Delhi. What she pays to these nominal princes, who, while they did anything, did mischief, and who now do nothing, she may well consent to pay to her real rulers, if she receives from them, in return, efficient protection and good legislation.

We come then to the great question. Is it desirable to retain the Company as an organ of government for India? I think that it is desirable. The question is, I acknowledge, beset with difficulties. We have to solve one of the hardest problems in politics. We are trying to make brick without straw, to bring a clean thing out of an unclean, to give a good government to a people to whom we cannot give a free government. In this country, in any neighbouring country, it is easy to frame securities against oppression. In Europe, you have the materials of good government everywhere ready to your hands. The people are everywhere perfectly competent to hold some share, not in every country an equal share, but some share, of political power. If the question were, What is the best mode of securing good government in Europe? the merest smatterer in politics would answer, representative institutions. In India you cannot have representative institutions. Of all the innumerable speculators who have offered their suggestions on Indian politics, not a single one, as far as I know, however democratical his opinions may be, has ever maintained the possibility of giving, at the present time, such institutions to India. One gentleman, extremely well acquainted with the affairs of our Eastern Empire, a most valuable servant of the Company, and the author of a History of India, which, though certainly not free from faults, is, I think, on the whole, the greatest historical work which has appeared in our language since that of Gibbon, I mean Mr. Mill, was examined on this point. That gentleman is well known to be a very bold and uncompromising politician. He has written strongly, far too strongly I think, in favour of pure democracy. He has gone so far as to maintain that no nation which has not a representative legislature, chosen by universal suffrage, enjoys security against oppression. But when he was asked before the Committee of last year, whether he thought representative government practicable in India, his answer was, "utterly out of the question." This, then, is the state in which we are. We have to frame a good government for a country into which, by universal acknowledgment, we cannot introduce those institutions which all our habits, which all the reasonings of European philosophers, which all the history of our own part of the world would lead us to consider as the one great security for good government. We have to engraft on despotism those blessings which are the natural fruits of liberty. In these circumstances, Sir, it behoves us to be cautious, even to the verge of timidity. The light of political science and of history are withdrawn: we are walking in darkness: we do not distinctly see whither we are going. It is the wisdom of a man, so situated, to feel his way, and not to plant his foot till he is well assured that the ground before him is firm.

Some things, however, in the midst of this obscurity, I can see with clearness. I can see, for example, that it is desirable that the authority exercised in this country over the Indian government should be divided between two bodies, between a minister or a board appointed by the Crown, and some other body independent of the Crown. If India is to be a dependency of England, to be at war with our enemies, to be at peace with our allies, to be protected by the English navy from maritime aggression, to have a portion of the English army mixed with its sepoys, it plainly follows that the King, to whom the Constitution gives the direction of foreign affairs, and the command of the military and naval forces, ought to have a share in the direction of the Indian government. Yet, on the other hand, that a revenue of twenty millions a year, an army of two hundred thousand men, a civil service abounding with lucrative situations, should be left to the disposal of the Crown without any check whatever, is what no Minister, I conceive, would venture to propose. This House is indeed the check provided by the Constitution on the abuse of the royal prerogative. But that this House is, or is likely ever to be, an efficient check on abuses practised in India, I altogether deny. We have, as I believe we all feel, quite business enough. If we were to undertake the task of looking into Indian affairs as we look into British affairs, if we were to have Indian budgets and Indian estimates, if we were to go into the Indian currency question and the Indian Bank Charter, if to our disputes about Belgium and Holland, Don Pedro and Don Miguel, were to be added disputes about the debts of the Guicowar and the disorders of Mysore, the ex-king of the Afghans and the Maharajah Runjeet Sing; if we were to have one night occupied by the embezzlements of the Benares mint, and another by the panic in the Calcutta money market; if the questions of Suttee or no Suttee, Pilgrim tax or no Pilgrim tax, Ryotwary or Zemindary, half Batta or whole Batta, were to be debated at the same length at which we have debated Church reform and the assessed taxes, twenty-four hours a day and three hundred and sixty-five days a year would be too short a time for the discharge of our duties. The House, it is plain, has not the necessary time to settle these matters; nor has it the necessary knowledge; nor has it the motives to acquire that knowledge. The late change in its constitution has made it, I believe, a much more faithful representative of the English people. But it is as far as ever from being a representative of the Indian people. A broken head in Cold Bath Fields[1] produces a greater sensation among us than three pitched battles in India. A few weeks ago we had to decide on a claim[2] brought by an individual against the revenues of India.

---

[1] [A Liberty or Death meeting on May 12th this year. A policeman was killed and the jury found it Justifiable Homicide.]

[2] [Hutchinson's Claim Bill, against the Rajah of Travancore, lost on second reading. A pepper speculation.]

If it had been an English question the walls would scarcely have held the Members who would have flocked to the division. It was an Indian question; and we could scarcely, by dint of supplication, make a House. Even when my right honorable friend, the President of the Board of Control, gave his able and interesting explanation of the plan which he intended to propose for the government of a hundred millions of human beings, the attendance was not so large as I have often seen it on a turnpike bill or a railroad bill.

I then take these things as proved, that the Crown must have a certain authority over India, that there must be an efficient check on the authority of the Crown, and that the House of Commons cannot be that efficient check. We must then find some other body to perform that important office. We have such a body, the Company. Shall we discard it?

It is true that the power of the Company is an anomaly in politics. It is strange, very strange, that a joint stock society of traders, a society, the shares of which are daily passed from hand to hand, a society, the component parts of which are perpetually changing, a society, which, judging *a priori* from its constitution, we should have said was as little fitted for imperial functions as the Merchant Tailors' Company or the New River Company, should be intrusted with the sovereignty of a larger population, the disposal of a larger clear revenue, the command of a larger army, than are under the direct management of the Executive Government of the United Kingdom. But what constitution can we give to our Indian Empire which shall not be strange, which shall not be anomalous? That Empire is itself the strangest of all political anomalies. That a handful of adventurers from an island in the Atlantic should have subjugated a vast country divided from the place of their birth by half the globe; a country which at no very distant period was merely the subject of fable to the nations of Europe; a country never before violated by the most renowned of Western Conquerors; a country which Trajan never entered; a country lying beyond the point where the phalanx of Alexander refused to proceed; that we should govern a territory ten thousand miles from us, a territory larger and more populous than France, Spain, Italy, and Germany put together, a territory, the present clear revenue of which exceeds the present clear revenue of any state in the world, France excepted; a territory, inhabited by men differing from us in race, colour, language, manners, morals, religion; these are prodigies to which the world has seen nothing similar. Reason is confounded. We interrogate the past in vain.

General rules are useless where the whole is one vast exception. The Company is an anomaly; but it is part of a system where everything is anomaly. It is the strangest of all governments; but it is designed for the strangest of all Empires.

If we discard the Company, we must find a substitute: and, take what substitute we may, we shall find ourselves unable to give any reason for believing that the body which we have put in the room of the Company is likely to acquit itself of its duties better than the Company. Commissioners appointed by the King during pleasure would be no check on the Crown; Commissioners appointed by the King or by Parliament for life would always be appointed by the political party which might be uppermost, and if a change of administration took place, would harass the new Government with the most vexatious opposition. The plan suggested by the right honorable Gentleman, the Member for Montgomeryshire,[1] is I think the very worst that I have ever heard. He would have Directors nominated every four years by the Crown. Is it not plain that these Directors would always be appointed from among the supporters of the Ministry for the time being; that their situations would depend on the permanence of that Ministry; that therefore all their power and patronage would be employed for the purpose of propping that Ministry, and, in case of a change, for the purpose of molesting those who might succeed to power; that they would be subservient while their friends were in, and factious when their friends were out? How would Lord Grey's Ministry have been situated if the whole body of Directors had been nominated by the Duke of Wellington in 1830? I mean no imputation on the Duke of Wellington. If the present Ministers had to nominate Directors for four years, they would, I have no doubt, nominate men who would give no small trouble to the Duke of Wellington if he were to return to office. What we want is a body independent of the Government, and no more than independent, not a tool of the Treasury, not a tool of the opposition. No new plan which I have heard proposed would give us such a body. The Company, strange as its constitution may be, is such a body. It is, as a corporation, neither Whig nor Tory, neither high-church nor low-church. It cannot be charged with having been for or against the Catholic Bill, for or against the Reform Bill. It has constantly acted with a view, not to English politics, but to Indian politics. We have seen the country convulsed by faction. We have seen Ministers driven from office by this House, Parliament dissolved in anger, general elections

[1] Mr. Charles Wynn.

of unprecedented turbulence, debates of unprecedented interest. We have seen the two branches of the Legislature placed in direct opposition to each other. We have seen the advisers of the Crown dismissed one day, and brought back the next day on the shoulders of the people. And amidst all these agitating events the Company has preserved strict and unsuspected neutrality. This is, I think, an inestimable advantage; and it is an advantage which we must altogether forego, if we consent to adopt any of the schemes which I have heard proposed on the other side of the House.

We must judge of the Indian government, as of all other governments, by its practical effects. According to the honorable Member for Sheffield, India is ill governed; and the whole fault is with the Company. Innumerable accusations, great and small, are brought by him against the Directors. They are fond of war: they are fond of dominion: the taxation is burthensome: the laws are undigested: the roads are rough: the post goes on foot: and for everything the Company is answerable. From the dethronement of the Mogul princes to the mishaps of Sir Charles Metcalfe's courier, every disaster that has taken place in the East during sixty years is laid to the charge of this Corporation. And the inference is, that all the power which they possess ought to be taken out of their hands, and transferred at once to the Crown.

Now, Sir, it seems to me that, for all the evils which the honorable Gentleman has so pathetically recounted, the Ministers of the Crown are as much to blame as the Company; nay, much more so: for the Board of Control could, without the consent of the Directors, have redressed those evils; and the Directors most certainly could not have redressed them without the consent of the Board of Control. Take the case of that frightful grievance which seems to have made the deepest impression on the mind of the honorable Gentleman, the slowness of the mail. Why, Sir, if my right honorable friend, the President of our Board, thought fit, he might direct me to write to the Court and require them to frame a dispatch on that subject. If the Court disobeyed, he might himself frame a dispatch ordering Lord William Bentinck to put the dawks all over Bengal on horseback. If the Court refused to send out this dispatch, the Board could apply to the King's Bench for a Mandamus. If, on the other hand, the Directors wished to accelerate the journeys of the mail, and the Board were adverse to the project, the Directors could do nothing at all. For all measures of internal policy the servants of the King are at least as deeply responsible as the Company. For all measures of foreign policy the servants of the King, and they alone, are responsible.

I was surprised to hear the honorable Gentleman accuse the Directors of insatiable ambition and rapacity, when he must know that no act of aggression on any native state can be committed by the Company without the sanction of the Board, and that, in fact, the Board has repeatedly approved of warlike measures, which were strenuously opposed by the Company. He must know, in particular, that, during the energetic and splendid administration of the Marquess Wellesley, the Company was all for peace, and the Board all for conquest. If a line of conduct which the honorable Gentleman thinks unjustifiable has been followed by the Ministers of the Crown in spite of the remonstrances of the Directors, this is surely a strange reason for turning off the Directors, and giving the whole power unchecked to the Crown.

The honorable Member tells us that India, under the present system, is not so rich and flourishing as she was two hundred years ago. Really, Sir, I doubt whether we are in possession of sufficient data to enable us to form a judgment on that point. But the matter is of little importance. We ought to compare India under our Government, not with India under Acbar and his immediate successors, but with India as we found it. The calamities through which that country passed during the interval between the fall of the Mogul power and the establishment of the English supremacy were sufficient to throw the people back whole centuries. It would surely be unjust to say, that Alfred was a bad king because Britain, under his government, was not so rich or so civilised as in the time of the Romans.

In what state, then, did we find India? And what have we made India? We found society throughout that vast country in a state to which history scarcely furnishes a parallel. The nearest parallel would, perhaps, be the state of Europe during the fifth century. The Mogul empire in the time of the successors of Aurungzebe, like the Roman empire in the time of the successors of Theodosius, was sinking under the vices of a bad internal administration, and under the assaults of barbarous invaders. At Delhi, as at Ravenna, there was a mock sovereign, immured in a gorgeous state prison. He was suffered to indulge in every sensual pleasure. He was adored with servile prostrations. He assumed and bestowed the most magnificent titles. But, in fact, he was a mere puppet in the hands of some ambitious subject. While the Honorii and Augustuli of the East, surrounded by their fawning eunuchs, revelled and dozed without knowing or caring what might pass beyond the walls of their palace gardens, the provinces had ceased to respect a government which could neither punish nor protect them. Society was a chaos. Its restless and shifting elements formed themselves every moment into some new combination, which the next moment dissolved. In the course of a single generation a hundred dynasties grew up, flourished, decayed, were extinguished, were forgotten. Every adventurer who could muster a troop of horse might aspire to a throne. Every palace was every year the scene of conspiracies, treasons, revolutions, parricides. Meanwhile a rapid succession of Alarics and Attilas passed over the defenceless empire. A Persian invader penetrated to Delhi, and carried back in triumph the most precious treasures of the House of Tamerlane. The Afghan soon followed, by the same track, to glean whatever the Persian had spared. The Jauts established themselves on the Jumna. The Seiks devasted Lahore. Every part of India, from Tanjore to the Himalayas, was laid under contribution by the Mahrattas. The people were ground down to the dust by the oppressor without and the oppressor within, by the robber from whom the Nabob was unable to protect them, by the Nabob who took whatever the robber had left to them. All the evils of despotism, and all the evils of anarchy, pressed at once on that miserable race. They knew nothing of government but its exactions. Desolation was in their imperial cities, and famine all along the banks of their broad and redundant rivers. It seemed that a few more years would suffice to efface all traces of the opulence and civilisation of an earlier age.

Such was the state of India when the Company began to take part in the disputes of its ephemeral sovereigns. About eighty years have elapsed since we appeared as auxiliaries in a contest between two rival families for the sovereignty of a small corner of the Peninsula. From that moment commenced a great, a stupendous process, the reconstruction of a decomposed society. Two generations have passed away; and the process is complete. The scattered fragments of the empire of Aurungzebe have been united in an empire stronger and more closely knit together than that which Aurungzebe ruled. The power of the new sovereigns penetrates their dominions more completely, and is far more implicitly obeyed, than was that of the proudest princes of the Mogul dynasty.

It is true, that the early history of this great revolution is chequered with guilt and shame. It is true that the founders of our Indian empire too often abused the strength which they derived from superior energy and superior knowledge. It is true that, with some of the highest qualities of the race from which they sprang, they combined some of the worst defects of the race over which they ruled. How should it have been otherwise? Born in humble stations, accustomed to earn a slender maintenance by obscure industry, they found themselves transformed in a few months from clerks drudging over desks, or captains in marching regiments, into statesmen and generals, with armies at their command, with the revenues of kingdoms at their disposal, with power to make and depose sovereigns at their pleasure. They were what it was natural that men should be who had been raised by so rapid an ascent to so dizzy an eminence, profuse and rapacious, imperious and corrupt.

It is true, then, that there was too much foundation for the representations of those satirists and dramatists who held up the character of the English Nabob to the derision and hatred of a former generation. It is true that some disgraceful intrigues, some unjust and cruel wars, some instances of odious perfidy and avarice stain the annals of our Eastern empire. It is true that the duties of government and legislation were long wholly neglected or carelessly performed. It is true that when the conquerors at length began to apply themselves in earnest to the discharge of their high functions, they committed the errors natural to rulers who were but imperfectly acquainted with the language and manners of their subjects. It is true that some plans, which were dictated by the purest and most benevolent feelings, have not been attended by the desired success. It is true that India suffers to this day from a heavy burthen of taxation and from a defective system of law. It is true, I fear, that in those states which are connected with us by subsidiary alliance, all the evils of oriental despotism have too frequently shown themselves in their most loathsome and destructive form.

All this is true. Yet in the history and in the present state of our Indian empire I see ample reason for exultation and for a good hope.

I see that we have established order where we found confusion. I see that the petty dynasties which were generated by the corruption of the great Mahometan empire, and which, a century ago, kept all India in constant agitation, have been quelled by one overwhelming power. I see that the predatory tribes which, in the middle of the last century, passed annually over the harvests of India with the destructive rapidity of a hurricane, have quailed before the valour of a braver and sterner race, have been vanquished, scattered, hunted to their strongholds, and either extirpated by the English sword, or compelled to exchange the pursuits of rapine for those of industry.

I look back for many years; and I see scarcely a trace of the vices which blemished the splendid fame of the first conquerors of Bengal. I see peace studiously preserved. I see faith inviolably maintained towards feeble and dependent states. I see confidence gradually infused into the minds of suspicious neighbours. I see the horrors of war mitigated by the chivalrous and Christian spirit of Europe. I see examples of moderation and clemency such as I should seek in vain in the annals of any other victorious and dominant nation. I see captive tyrants, whose treachery and cruelty might have excused a severe retribution, living in security, comfort, and dignity, under the protection of the government which they laboured to destroy.

I see a large body of civil and military functionaries resembling in nothing but capacity and valour those adventurers who, seventy years ago, came hither, laden with wealth and infamy, to parade before our fathers the plundered treasures of Bengal and Tanjore. I reflect with pride that to the doubtful splendour which surrounds the memory of Hastings and of Clive, we can oppose the spotless glory of Elphinstone and Munro.[1] I contemplate with reverence and delight the honorable poverty which is the evidence of rectitude firmly maintained amidst strong temptations. I rejoice to see my countrymen, after ruling millions of subjects, after commanding victorious armies, after dictating terms of peace at the gates of hostile capitals, after administering the revenues of great provinces, after judging the causes of wealthy Zemindars, after residing at the Courts of tributary Kings, return to their native land with no more than a decent competence.

I see a government anxiously bent on the public good. Even in its errors I recognise a paternal feeling towards the great people committed to its charge. I see toleration strictly maintained: yet I see bloody and degrading superstitions gradually losing their power. I see the morality, the philosophy, the taste of Europe, beginning to produce a salutary effect on the hearts and understandings of our subjects. I see the public mind of India, that public mind which we found debased and contracted by the worst forms of political and religious tyranny, expanding itself to just and noble views of the ends of government and of the social duties of man.

I see evils: but I see the government actively employed in the work of remedying those evils. The taxation is heavy; but the work of retrenchment is unsparingly pursued. The mischiefs arising from the system of subsidiary alliance are great: but the rulers of India are fully aware of those mischiefs, and are engaged

[1] [Governors of Bombay and Madras.]

M—23

in guarding against them. Wherever they now interfere for the purpose of supporting a native government, they interfere also for the purpose of reforming it.

Seeing these things, then, am I prepared to discard the Company as an organ of government? I am not. Assuredly I will never shrink from innovation where I see reason to believe that innovation will be improvement. That the present Government does not shrink from innovations which it considers as improvements the bill now before the House sufficiently shows. But surely the burthen of the proof lies on the innovators. They are bound to show that there is a fair probability of obtaining some advantage before they call upon us to take up the foundations of the Indian government. I have no superstitious veneration for the Court of Directors or the Court of Proprietors. Find me a better Council: find me a better constituent body: and I am ready for a change. But of all the substitutes for the Company which have hitherto been suggested, not one has been proved to be better than the Company; and most of them I could, I think, easily prove to be worse. Circumstances might force us to hazard a change. If the Company were to refuse to accept of the government unless we would grant pecuniary terms which I thought extravagant, or unless we gave up the clauses in this bill which permit Europeans to hold landed property and natives to hold office, I would take them at their word. But I will not discard them in the mere rage of experiment.

Do I call the government of India a perfect government? Very far from it. No nation can be perfectly well governed till it is competent to govern itself. I compare the Indian government with other governments of the same class, with despotisms, with military despotisms, with foreign military despotisms; and I find none that approaches it in excellence. I compare it with the government of the Roman provinces, with the government of the Spanish colonies; and I am proud of my country and my age. Here are a hundred millions of people under the absolute rule of a few strangers, differing from them physically, differing from them morally, mere Mamelukes, not born in the country which they rule, not meaning to lay their bones in it. If you require me to make this government as good as that of England, France, or the United States of America, I own frankly that I can do no such thing. Reasoning *a priori*, I should have come to the conclusion that such a government must be a horrible tyranny. It is a source of constant amazement to me that it is so good as I find it to be. I will not, therefore, in a case in which I have neither principles nor precedents to guide me, pull down the existing system on account of its theoretical defects. For I know that any system which I could put in its place would be equally condemned by theory, while it would not be equally sanctioned by experience.

Some change in the constitution of the Company was, as I have shown, rendered inevitable by the opening of the China Trade; and it was the duty of the Government to take care that the change should not be prejudicial to India. There were many ways in which the compromise between commerce and territory might have been effected. We might have taken the assets, and paid a sum down, leaving the Company to invest that sum as they chose. We might have offered English security with a lower interest. We might have taken the course which the late ministers designed to take. They would have left the Company in possession of the means of carrying on its trade in competition with private merchants. My firm belief is that, if this course had been taken, the Company must, in a very few years, have abandoned the trade, or the trade would have ruined the Company. It was not, however, solely or principally by regard for the interest of the Company, or of English merchants generally, that the Government was guided on this occasion. The course which appeared to us the most likely to promote the interests of our Eastern Empire was to make the proprietors of India stock creditors of the Indian territory. Their interest will thus be in a great measure the same with the interest of the people whom they are to rule. Their income will depend on the revenues of their empire. The revenues of their empire will depend on the manner in which the affairs of that empire are administered. We furnish them with the strongest motives to watch over the interests of the cultivator and the trader, to maintain peace, to carry on with vigour the work of retrenchment, to detect and punish extortion and corruption. Though they live at a distance from India, though few of them have ever seen or may ever see the people whom they rule, they will have a great stake in the happiness of their subjects. If their misgovernment should produce disorder in the finances, they will themselves feel the effects of that disorder in their own household expenses. I believe this to be, next to a representative constitution, the constitution which is the best security for good government. A representative constitution India cannot at present have. And we have therefore, I think, given her the best constitution of which she is capable.

One word as to the new arrangement which we propose with respect to the patronage. It is intended to introduce the principle of competition in the disposal of writerships; and from this change

I cannot but anticipate the happiest results. The civil servants of the Company are undoubtedly a highly respectable body of men; and in that body, as in every large body, there are some persons of very eminent ability. I rejoice most cordially to see this. I rejoice to see that the standard of morality is so high in England, that intelligence is so generally diffused through England, that young persons who are taken from the mass of society, by favour and not by merit, and who are therefore only fair samples of the mass, should, when placed in situations of high importance, be so seldom found wanting. But it is not the less true that India is entitled to the service of the best talents which England can spare. That the average of intelligence and virtue is very high in this country is matter for honest exultation. But it is no reason for employing average men where you can obtain superior men. Consider too, Sir, how rapidly the public mind of India is advancing, how much attention is already paid by the higher classes of the natives to those intellectual pursuits on the cultivation of which the superiority of the European race to the rest of mankind principally depends. Surely, in such circumstances, from motives of selfish policy, if from no higher motive, we ought to fill the magistracies of our Eastern Empire with men who may do honor to their country, with men who may represent the best part of the English nation. This, Sir, is our object; and we believe that by the plan which is now proposed this object will be attained. It is proposed that for every vacancy in the civil service four candidates shall be named, and the best candidate selected by examination. We conceive that, under this system, the persons sent out will be young men above par, young men superior either in talents or in diligence to the mass. It is said, I know, that examinations in Latin, in Greek, and in mathematics, are no tests of what men will prove to be in life. I am perfectly aware that they are not infallible tests: but that they are tests I confidently maintain. Look at every walk of life, at this House, at the other House, at the Bar, at the Bench, at the Church, and see whether it be not true that those who attain high distinction in the world were generally men who were distinguished in their academic career. Indeed, Sir, this objection would prove far too much even for those who use it. It would prove that there is no use at all in education. Why should we put boys out of their way? Why should we force a lad, who would much rather fly a kite or trundle a hoop, to learn his Latin Grammar? Why should we keep a young man to his Thucydides or his Laplace, when he would much rather be shooting? Education would be mere useless torture, if, at two or three and twenty, a man who had neglected his studies were exactly on a par with a man who had applied himself to them, exactly as likely to perform all the offices of public life with credit to himself and with advantage to society. Whether the English system of education be good or bad is not now the question. Perhaps I may think that too much time is given to the ancient languages and to the abstract sciences. But what then? Whatever be the languages, whatever be the sciences, which it is, in any age or country, the fashion to teach, the persons who become the greatest proficients in those languages and those sciences will generally be the flower of the youth, the most acute, the most industrious, the most ambitious of honorable distinctions. If the Ptolemaic system were taught at Cambridge instead of the Newtonian, the senior wrangler would nevertheless be in general a superior man to the wooden spoon. If, instead of learning Greek, we learned the Cherokee, the man who understood the Cherokee best, who made the most correct and melodious Cherokee verses, who comprehended most accurately the effect of the Cherokee particles, would generally be a superior man to him who was destitute of these accomplishments. If astrology were taught at our Universities, the young man who cast nativities best would generally turn out a superior man. If alchymy were taught, the young man who showed most activity in the pursuit of the philosopher's stone would generally turn out a superior man.

I will only add one other observation on this subject. Although I am inclined to think that too exclusive an attention is paid in the education of young English gentlemen to the dead languages, I conceive that when you are choosing men to fill situations for which the very first and most indispensable qualification is familiarity with foreign languages, it would be difficult to find a better test of their fitness than their classical acquirements.

Some persons have expressed doubts as to the possibility of procuring fair examinations. I am quite sure that no person who has been either at Cambridge or at Oxford can entertain such doubts. I feel, indeed, that I ought to apologise for even noticing an objection so frivolous.

Next to the opening of the China Trade, Sir, the change most eagerly demanded by the English people was, that the restrictions on the admission of Europeans to India should be removed. In this change there are undoubtedly very great advantages. The chief advantage is, I think, the improvement which the minds of our native subjects may be expected to derive from free intercourse with a people far advanced beyond themselves in intellectual cultivation. I cannot deny, however, that the advantages are attended with some danger.

The danger is that the new comers, belonging to the ruling nation, resembling in colour, in language, in manners, those who hold supreme military and political power, and differing in all these respects from the great mass of the population, may consider themselves as a superior class, and may trample on the indigenous race. Hitherto there have been strong restraints on Europeans resident in India. Licences were not easily obtained. Those residents who were in the service of the Company had obvious motives for conducting themselves with propriety. If they incurred the serious displeasure of the Government, their hopes of promotion were blighted. Even those who were not in the public service were subject to the formidable power which the Government possessed of banishing them at its pleasure.

The licence of the Government will now no longer be necessary to persons who desire to reside in the settled provinces of India. The power of arbitrary deportation is withdrawn. Unless, therefore, we mean to leave the natives exposed to the tyranny and insolence of every profligate adventurer who may visit the East, we must place the European under the same power which legislates for the Hindoo. No man loves political freedom more than I. But a privilege enjoyed by a few individuals, in the midst of a vast population who do not enjoy it, ought not to be called freedom. It is tyranny. In the West Indies I have not the least doubt that the existence of the Trial by Jury and of Legislative Assemblies has tended to make the condition of the slaves worse than it would otherwise have been. Or, to go to India itself for an instance, though I fully believe that a mild penal code is better than a severe penal code, the worst of all systems was surely that of having a mild code for the Brahmins, who sprang from the head of the Creator, while there was a severe code for the Sudras, who sprang from his feet. India has suffered enough already from the distinction of castes, and from the deeply rooted prejudices which that distinction has engendered. God forbid that we should inflict on her the curse of a new caste, that we should send her a new breed of Brahmins, authorised to treat all the native population as Parias!

With a view to the prevention of this evil, we propose to give to the Supreme Government the power of legislating for Europeans as well as for natives. We propose that the regulations of the Government shall bind the King's Court as they bind all other courts, and that registration by the Judges of the King's Courts shall no longer be necessary to give validity to those regulations within the towns of Calcutta, Madras, and Bombay.

I could scarcely, Sir, believe my ears when I heard this part of our plan condemned in another place. I should have thought that it would have been received with peculiar favour in that quarter where it has met with the most severe condemnation. What, at present, is the case? If the Supreme Court and the Government differ on a question of jurisdiction, or on a question of legislation within the towns which are the seats of Government, there is absolutely no umpire but the Imperial Parliament. The device of putting one wild elephant between two tame elephants was ingenious; but it may not always be practicable. Suppose a tame elephant between two wild elephants, or suppose that the whole herd should run wild together. The thing is not without example. And is it not most unjust and ridiculous that, on one side of a ditch, the edict of the Governor General should have the force of law, and that on the other side it should be of no effect unless registered by the Judges of the Supreme Court? If the registration be a security for good legislation, we are bound to give that security to all classes of our subjects. If the registration be not a security for good legislation, why give it to any? Is the system good? Extend it. Is it bad? Abolish it. But in the name of common sense do not leave it as it is. It is as absurd as our old law of sanctuary. The law which authorises imprisonment for debt may be good or bad. But no man in his senses can approve of the ancient system under which a debtor who might be arrested in Fleet Street was safe as soon as he had scampered into Whitefriars. Just in the same way, doubts may fairly be entertained about the expediency of allowing four or five persons to make laws for India; but to allow them to make laws for all India without the Mahratta ditch, and to except Calcutta, is the height of absurdity.

I say, therefore, that either you must enlarge the power of the Supreme Court, and give it a general veto on laws, or you must enlarge the power of the Government, and make its regulations binding on all Courts without distinction. The former course no person has ventured to propose. To the latter course objections have been made; but objections which to me, I must own, seem altogether frivolous.

It is acknowledged that of late years inconvenience has arisen from the relation in which the Supreme Court stands to the Government. But, it is said, that Court was originally instituted for the protection of natives against Europeans. The wise course would therefore be to restore its original character.

Now, Sir, the fact is, that the Supreme Court has never been so mischievous as during the first ten years of its power, or so respectable as it has lately been. Everybody who knows anything of its early history knows, that, during a considerable time, it was the terror of Bengal, the scourge of the native population, the screen of European delinquents, a convenient tool of the Government for all purposes of evil, an insurmountable obstacle to the Government in all undertakings for the public good; that its proceedings were made up of pedantry, cruelty, and corruption; that its disputes with the Government were at one time on the point of breaking up the whole fabric of society; and that a convulsion was averted only by the dexterous policy of Warren Hastings, who at last bought off the opposition of the Chief Justice for eight thousand pounds a year. It is notorious that, while the Supreme Court opposed Hastings in all his best measures, it was a thoroughgoing accomplice in his worst; that it took part in the most scandalous of those proceedings which, fifty years ago, roused the indignation of Parliament and of the country; that it assisted in the spoliation of the princesses of Oude; that it passed sentence of death on Nuncomar. And this is the Court which we are to restore from its present state of degeneracy to its original purity. This is the protection which we are to give to the natives against the Europeans. Sir, so far is it from being true that the character of the Supreme Court has deteriorated, that it has, perhaps, improved more than any other institution in India. But the evil lies deep in the nature of the institution itself. The Judges have in our time deserved the greatest respect. Their judgment and integrity have done much to mitigate the vices of the system. The worst charge that can be brought against any of them is that of pertinacity, disinterested, conscientious pertinacity, in error. The real evil is the state of the law. You have two supreme powers in India. There is no arbitrator except a Legislature fifteen thousand miles off. Such a system is on the face of it an absurdity in politics. My wonder is, not that this system has several times been on the point of producing fatal consequences to the peace and resources of India;—those, I think, are the words in which Warren Hastings described the effect of the contest between his Government and the Judges;—but that it has not actually produced such consequences. The most distinguished members of the Indian Government, the most distinguished Judges of the Supreme Court, call upon you to reform this system. Sir Charles Metcalfe, Sir Charles Grey, represent with equal urgency the expediency of having one single paramount council armed with legislative power. The admission of Europeans to India renders it absolutely necessary not to delay our decision. The effect of that admission would be to raise a hundred questions, to produce a hundred contests between the Council and the judicature. The Government would be paralysed at the precise moment at which all its energy was required. While the two equal powers were acting in opposite directions, the whole machine of the state would stand still. The Europeans would be uncontrolled. The natives would be unprotected. The consequences I will not pretend to foresee. Everything beyond is darkness and confusion.

Having given to the Government supreme legislative power, we next propose to give to it for a time the assistance of a Commission for the purpose of digesting and reforming the laws of India, so that those laws may, as soon as possible, be formed into a code. Gentlemen of whom I wish to speak with the highest respect have expressed a doubt whether India be at present in a fit state to receive a benefit which is not yet enjoyed by this free and highly civilised country. Sir, I can allow to this argument very little weight beyond that which it derives from the personal authority of those who use it. For in the first place, our freedom and our high civilisation make this improvement, desirable as it must always be, less indispensably necessary to us than to our Indian subjects; and in the next place our freedom and civilisation, I fear, make it far more difficult for us to obtain this benefit for ourselves than to bestow it on them.

I believe that no country ever stood so much in need of a code of laws as India; and I believe also that there never was a country in which the want might so easily be supplied. I said that there were many points of analogy between the state of that country after the fall of the Mogul power, and the state of Europe after the fall of the Roman empire. In one respect the analogy is very striking. As there were in Europe then, so there are in India now, several systems of law widely differing from each other, but coexisting and coequal. The indigenous population has its own laws. Each of the successive races of conquerors has brought with it its own peculiar jurisprudence: the Mussulman his Koran and the innumerable commentators on the Koran; the Englishman his Statute Book and his Term Reports. As there were established in Italy, at one and the same time, the Roman law, the Lombard law, the Ripuarian law, the Bavarian law, and the Salic law, so we have now in our Eastern empire Hindoo law, Mahometan law, Parsee law, English law, perpetually mingling with each other and disturbing each other, varying with the person, varying

M—23*

with the place. In one and the same cause the process and pleadings are in the fashion of one nation, the judgment is according to the laws of another. An issue is evolved according to the rules of Westminster, and decided according to those of Benares. The only Mahometan book in the nature of a code is the Koran; the only Hindoo book the Institutes. Every body who knows those books knows that they provide for a very small part of the cases which must arise in every community. All beyond them is comment and tradition. Our regulations in civil matters do not define rights, but merely establish remedies. If a point of Hindoo law arises, the Judge calls on the Pundit for an opinion. If a point of Mahometan law arises, the Judge applies to the Cauzee. What the integrity of these functionaries is, we may learn from Sir William Jones. That eminent man declared that he could not answer it to his conscience to decide any point of law on the faith of a Hindoo expositor. Sir Thomas Strange confirms this declaration. Even if there were no suspicion of corruption on the part of the interpreters of the law, the science which they profess is in such a state of confusion that no reliance can be placed on their answers. Sir Francis Macnaghten tells us, that it is a delusion to fancy that there is any known and fixed law under which the Hindoo people live; that texts may be produced on any side of any question; that expositors equal in authority perpetually contradict each other; that the obsolete law is perpetually confounded with the law actually in force, and that the first lesson to be impressed on a functionary who has to administer Hindoo law is that it is vain to think of extracting certainty from the books of the jurist. The consequence is that in practice the decisions of the tribunals are altogether arbitrary. What is administered is not law, but a kind of rude and capricious equity. I asked an able and excellent judge lately returned from India how one of our Zillah Courts[1] would decide several legal questions of great importance, questions not involving considerations of religion or of caste, mere questions of commercial law. He told me, that it was a mere lottery. He knew how he should himself decide them. But he knew nothing more. I asked a most distinguished civil servant of the Company, with reference to the clause in this Bill on the subject of slavery, whether at present, if a dancing girl ran away from her master, the judge would force her to go back. "Some judges," he said, "send a girl back. Others set her at liberty. The whole is a mere matter of chance. Everything depends on the temper of the individual judge."

[1] [An administrative district: the jurisdiction of a collector.]

Even in this country, we have had complaints of judge-made law; even in this country, where the standard of morality is higher than in almost any other part of the world; where, during several generations, not one depositary of our legal traditions has incurred the suspicion of personal corruption; where there are popular institutions; where every decision is watched by a shrewd and learned audience; where there is an intelligent and observant public; where every remarkable case is fully reported in a hundred newspapers; where, in short, there is everything which can mitigate the evils of such a system. But judge-made law, where there is an absolute government and a lax morality, where there is no bar and no public, is a curse and a scandal not to be endured. It is time that the magistrate should know what law he is to administer, and the subject should know under what law he is to live. We do not mean that all the people of India should live under the same law: far from it: there is not a word in the bill, there was not a word in my right honorable friend's speech, susceptible of such an interpretation. We know how desirable that object is; but we also know that it is unattainable. We know that respect must be paid to feelings generated by differences of religion, of nation, and of caste. Much, I am persuaded, may be done to assimilate the different systems of law without wounding those feelings. But, whether we assimilate those systems or not, let us ascertain them; let us digest them. We propose no rash innovation; we wish to give no shock to the prejudices of any part of our subjects. Our principle is simply this; uniformity where you can have it; diversity where you must have it; but in all cases certainty.

As I believe that India stands more in need of a code[1] than any other country in the world, I believe also that there is no country on which that great benefit can more easily be conferred. A code is almost the only blessing, perhaps it is the only blessing, which absolute governments are better fitted to confer on a nation than popular governments. The work of digesting a vast and artificial system of unwritten jurisprudence is far more easily performed, and far better performed, by few minds than by many, by a Napoleon than by a Chamber of Deputies and a Chamber of Peers, by a government like that of Prussia or Denmark than by a government like that of England. A quiet knot of two or three veteran jurists is an infinitely better machinery for such a purpose than a large popular assembly divided, as such assemblies almost always are, into adverse factions. This seems to me, therefore, to be pre-

[1] [The code was mainly drafted by Macaulay himself as Legal Member of the Council 1834-8.]

cisely that point of time at which the advantage of a complete written code of laws may most easily be conferred on India. It is a work which cannot be well performed in an age of barbarism, which cannot without great difficulty be performed in an age of freedom. It is a work which especially belongs to a government like that of India, to an enlightened and paternal despotism.

I have detained the House so long, Sir, that I will defer what I had to say on some parts of this measure, important parts, indeed, but far less important, as I think, than those to which I have adverted, till we are in Committee. There is, however, one part of the bill on which, after what has recently passed elsewhere, I feel myself irresistibly impelled to say a few words. I allude to that wise, that benevolent, that noble clause, which enacts that no native of our Indian empire shall, by reason of his colour, his descent, or his religion, be incapable of holding office. At the risk of being called by that nickname which is regarded as the most opprobrious of all nicknames by men of selfish hearts and contracted minds, at the risk of being called a philosopher,[1] I must say that, to the last day of my life, I shall be proud of having been one of those who assisted in the framing of the bill which contains that clause. We are told that the time can never come when the natives of India can be admitted to high civil and military office. We are told that this is the condition on which we hold our power. We are told, that we are bound to confer on our subjects every benefit—which they are capable of enjoying?—no; —which it is in our power to confer on them?—no;—but which we can confer on them without hazard to the perpetuity of our own domination. Against that proposition I solemnly protest as inconsistent alike with sound policy and sound morality.

I am far, very far, from wishing to proceed hastily in this most delicate matter. I feel that, for the good of India itself, the admission of natives to high office must be effected by slow degrees. But that, when the fulness of time is come, when the interest of India requires the change, we ought to refuse to make that change lest we should endanger our own power, this is a doctrine of which I cannot think without indignation. Governments, like men, may buy existence too dear. "Propter vitam vivendi perdere causas," is a despicable policy both in individuals and in states. In the present case, such a policy would be not only despicable, but absurd. The mere extent of empire is not necessarily an advantage.

[1] [This echoes Canning's defence of Huskisson in 1826. "Why is it to be supposed that to apply the refinement of philosophy to the affairs of common life indicates obduracy of feeling or obtuseness of sensibility?"]

To many governments it has been cumbersome; to some it has been fatal. It will be allowed by every statesman of our time that the prosperity of a community is made up of the prosperity of those who compose the community, and that it is the most childish ambition to covet dominion which adds to no man's comfort or security. To the great trading nation, to the great manufacturing nation, no progress which any portion of the human race can make in knowledge, in taste for the conveniences of life, or in the wealth by which those conveniences are produced, can be matter of indifference. It is scarcely possible to calculate the benefits which we might derive from the diffusion of European civilisation among the vast population of the East. It would be, on the most selfish view of the case, far better for us that the people of India were well governed and independent of us, than ill governed and subject to us; that they were ruled by their own kings, but wearing our broadcloth, and working with our cutlery, than that they were performing their salams to English collectors and English magistrates, but were too ignorant to value, or too poor to buy, English manufactures. To trade with civilised men is infinitely more profitable than to govern savages. That would, indeed, be a doting wisdom, which, in order that India might remain a dependency, would make it an useless and costly dependency, which would keep a hundred millions of men from being our customers in order that they might continue to be our slaves.

It was, as Bernier tells us, the practice of the miserable tyrants whom he found in India, when they dreaded the capacity and spirit of some distinguished subject, and yet could not venture to murder him, to administer to him a daily dose of the pousta, a preparation of opium, the effect of which was in a few months to destroy all the bodily and mental powers of the wretch who was drugged with it, and to turn him into a helpless idiot. The detestable artifice, more horrible than assassination itself, was worthy of those who employed it. It is no model for the English nation. We shall never consent to administer the pousta to a whole community, to stupify and paralyse a great people whom God has committed to our charge, for the wretched purpose of rendering them more amenable to our control. What is power worth if it is founded on vice, on ignorance, and on misery; if we can hold it only by violating the most sacred duties which as governors we owe to the governed, and which, as a people blessed with far more than an ordinary measure of political liberty and of intellectual light, we owe to a race debased by three thousand years of despotism and priest-craft? We are free, we are civilised, to little purpose, if we grudge to any portion of the human race an equal measure of freedom and civilisation.

Are we to keep the people of India ignorant in order that we may keep them submissive? Or do we think that we can give them knowledge without awakening ambition? Or do we mean to awaken ambition and to provide it with no legitimate vent? Who will answer any of these questions in the affirmative? Yet one of them must be answered in the affirmative, by every person who maintains that we ought permanently to exclude the natives from high office. I have no fears. The path of duty is plain before us: and it is also the path of wisdom, of national prosperity, of national honor.

The destinies of our Indian empire are covered with thick darkness. It is difficult to form any conjecture as to the fate reserved for a state which resembles no other in history, and which forms by itself a separate class of political phenomena. The laws which regulate its growth and its decay are still unknown to us. It may be that the public mind of India may expand under our system till it has outgrown that system; that by good government we may educate our subjects into a capacity for better government; that, having become instructed in European knowledge, they may, in some future age, demand European institutions. Whether such a day will ever come I know not. But never will I attempt to avert or to retard it. Whenever it comes, it will be the proudest day in English history. To have found a great people sunk in the lowest depths of slavery and superstition, to have so ruled them as to have made them desirous and capable of all the privileges of citizens, would indeed be a title to glory all our own. The sceptre may pass away from us. Unforeseen accidents may derange our most profound schemes of policy. Victory may be inconstant to our arms. But there are triumphs which are followed by no reverse. There is an empire exempt from all natural causes of decay. Those triumphs are the pacific triumphs of reason over barbarism; that empire is the imperishable empire of our arts and our morals, our literature and our laws.

# INDIAN EDUCATION

MINUTE OF THE 2ND OF FEBRUARY, 1835

[On his arrival in India, as a Member of the Supreme Council, Macaulay was appointed President of the Committee of Public Instruction, which he found irreconcilably split into two factions: the orientalists and those who wanted to teach the Indians Western learning. He addressed this minute to the Governor General, Lord Bentinck, who, on 7 March, pronounced in favour of "the promotion of European literature and science among the natives of India."]

As it seems to be the opinion of some of the gentlemen who compose the Committee of Public Instruction, that the course which they have hitherto pursued was strictly prescribed by the British Parliament in 1813, and as, if that opinion be correct, a legislative act will be necessary to warrant a change, I have thought it right to refrain from taking any part in the preparation of the adverse statements which are now before us, and to reserve what I had to say on the subject till it should come before me as a member of the Council of India.

It does not appear to me that the Act of Parliament can, by any art of construction, be made to bear the meaning which has been assigned to it. It contains nothing about the particular languages or sciences which are to be studied. A sum is set apart "for the revival and promotion of literature and the encouragement of the learned natives of India, and for the introduction and promotion of a knowledge of the sciences among the inhabitants of the British territories." It is argued, or rather taken for granted, that by literature, the Parliament can have meant only Arabic and Sanscrit literature, that they never would have given the honorable appellation of "a learned native" to a native who was familiar with the poetry of Milton, the Metaphysics of Locke, and the Physics of Newton; but that they meant to designate by that name only such persons as might have studied in the sacred books of the Hindoos all the uses of cusa-grass, and all the mysteries of absorption into the Deity. This does not appear to be a very satisfactory interpretation. To take a parallel case; suppose that the Pacha of Egypt, a country once superior in knowledge to the nations of Europe, but now sunk far below them, were to appropriate a sum for the purpose of "reviving and promoting literature, and encouraging learned natives of Egypt," would anybody infer that he meant the youth of his pachalic to give years to the study of hieroglyphics, to search into all the doctrines disguised under the fable of Osiris, and to ascertain with all possible accuracy the ritual with which cats and onions were anciently adored? Would he be justly charged with inconsistency, if, instead of employing his young subjects in deciphering obelisks, he were to order them to be instructed in the English and French languages, and in all the sciences to which those languages are the chief keys?

The words on which the supporters of the old system rely do not bear them out, and other words follow which seem to be quite decisive on the other side. This lac of rupees is set apart, not only for "reviving literature in India," the phrase on which their whole interpretation is founded, but also for "the introduction and promotion of a knowledge of the sciences among the inhabitants of the British territories,"—words which are alone sufficient to authorise all the changes for which I contend.

If the Council agree in my construction, no legislative Act will be necessary. If they differ from me, I will prepare a short Act rescinding that clause of the Charter of 1813, from which the difficulty arises.

The argument which I have been considering, affects only the form of proceeding. But the admirers of the Oriental system of education have used another argument, which, if we admit it to be valid, is decisive against all change. They conceive that the public faith is pledged to the present system, and that to alter the appropriation of any of the funds which have hitherto been spent in encouraging the study of Arabic and Sanscrit, would be downright spoliation. It is not easy to understand by what process of reasoning they can have arrived at this conclusion. The grants which are made from the public purse for the encouragement of literature differed in no respect from the grants which are made from the same purse for other objects of real or supposed utility. We found a sanatarium on a spot which we suppose to be healthy. Do we thereby pledge ourselves to keep a sanatarium there, if the result should not answer our expectation? We commence the erection of a pier. Is it a violation of the public faith to stop the works, if we afterwards see reason to believe that the building will be useless? The rights of property are undoubtedly sacred. But nothing endangers those rights so much as the practice, now unhappily too common, of attributing them to things to which they do not belong. Those who would impart to abuses the sanctity of property are in truth imparting to the institution of property the unpopularity and the fragility of abuses. If the Government has given to any person a formal assurance; nay, if the Government has excited in any person's mind a reasonable expectation that he shall receive a certain income as a teacher or a learner of Sanscrit or Arabic, I would respect that person's pecuniary interests—I would rather err on the side of liberality to individuals than suffer the public faith to be called in question. But to talk of a Government pledging itself to teach certain languages and certain sciences, though those languages may become useless, though those sciences may be exploded, seems to me quite unmeaning. There is not a single word in any public instructions, from which it can be inferred that the Indian Government ever intended to give any pledge on this subject, or ever considered the destination of these funds as unalterably fixed. But had it been otherwise, I should have denied the competence of our predecessors to bind us by any pledge on such a subject. Suppose that a Government had in the last century enacted in the most solemn manner that all its subjects should, to the end of time, be inoculated for the small-pox: would that Government be bound to persist in the practice after Jenner's discovery? These promises, of which nobody claims the performance, and from which nobody can grant a release; these vested rights, which vest in nobody; this property without proprietors; this robbery, which makes nobody poorer, may be comprehended by persons of higher faculties than mine.— I consider this plea merely as a set form of words, regularly used both in England and in India, in defence of every abuse for which no other plea can be set up.

I hold this lac of rupees to be quite at the disposal of the Governor General in Council, for the purpose of promoting learning in India, in any way which may be thought most advisable. I hold his Lordship to be quite as free to direct that it shall no longer be employed in encouraging Arabic and Sanscrit, as he is to direct that the reward for killing tigers in Mysore shall be diminished, or that no more public money shall be expended on the chanting at the cathedral.

We now come to the gist of the matter. We have a fund to be employed as Government shall direct for the intellectual improvement of the people of this country. The simple question is, what is the most useful way of employing it?

All parties seem to be agreed on one point, that the dialects commonly spoken among the natives of this part of India, contain neither literary nor scientific information, and are, moreover, so poor and rude that, until they are enriched from some other quarter, it will not be easy to translate any valuable work into them. It seems to be admitted on all sides, that the intellectual improvement of those classes of the people who have the means of pursuing higher studies can at present be effected only by means of some language not vernacular amongst them.

What then shall that language be? One-half of the Committee maintain that it should be the English. The other half strongly recommend the Arabic and Sanscrit. The whole question seems to me to be, which language is the best worth knowing?

I have no knowledge of either Sanscrit or Arabic.—But I have done what I could to form a correct estimate of their value. I have read translations of the most celebrated Arabic and Sanscrit works. I have conversed both here and at home with men distinguished by their proficiency in the Eastern tongues. I am quite ready to take the Oriental learning at the valuation of the Orientalists themselves. I have never found one among them who could deny that a single shelf of a good European library was worth the whole native literature of India and Arabia. The intrinsic superiority of the Western literature is, indeed, fully admitted by those members of the Committee who support the Oriental plan of education.

It will hardly be disputed, I suppose, that the department of literature in which the Eastern writers stand highest is poetry. And I certainly never met with any Orientalist who ventured to maintain that the Arabic and Sanscrit poetry could be compared to that of the great European nations. But when we pass from works of imagination to works in which facts are recorded, and general principles investigated, the superiority of the Europeans becomes absolutely immeasurable. It is, I believe, no exaggeration to say, that all the historical information which has been collected from all the books written in the Sanscrit language is less valuable than what may be found in the most paltry abridgments used at preparatory schools in England. In every branch of physical or moral philosophy, the relative position of the two nations is nearly the same.

How, then, stands the case? We have to educate a people who cannot at present be educated by means of their mother-tongue. We must teach them some foreign language. The claims of our own language it is hardly necessary to recapitulate. It stands preeminent even among the languages of the west. It abounds with works of imagination not inferior to the noblest which Greece has bequeathed to us; with models of every species of eloquence; with historical compositions, which, considered merely as narratives, have seldom been surpassed, and which, considered as vehicles of ethical and political instruction, have never been equalled; with just and lively representations of human life and human nature; with the most profound speculations on metaphysics, morals, government, jurisprudence, and trade; with full and correct information respecting every experimental science which tends to preserve the health, to increase the comfort, or to expand the intellect of man. Whoever knows that language has ready access to all the vast intellectual wealth, which all the wisest nations of the earth have created and hoarded in the course of ninety generations. It may safely be said, that the literature now extant in that language is of far greater value than all the literature which three hundred years ago was extant in all the languages of the world together. Nor is this all. In India, English is the language spoken by the ruling class. It is spoken by the higher class of natives at the seats of Government. It is likely to become the language of commerce throughout the seas of the East. It is the language of two great European communities which are rising, the one in the south of Africa, the other in Australasia; communities which are every year becoming more important, and more closely connected with our Indian empire. Whether we look at the intrinsic value of our literature, or at the particular situation of this country, we shall see the strongest reason to think that, of all foreign tongues, the English tongue is that which would be the most useful to our native subjects.

The question now before us is simply whether, when it is in our power to teach this language, we shall teach languages in which, by universal confession, there are no books on any subject which deserve to be compared to our own; whether, when we can teach European science, we shall teach systems which, by universal confession, whenever they differ from those of Europe, differ for the worse; and whether, when we can patronise sound Philosophy and true History, we shall countenance, at the public expense, medical doctrines, which would disgrace an English farrier,—Astronomy, which would move laughter in girls at an English boarding school,—History, abounding with kings thirty feet high, and reigns thirty thousand years long,—and Geography, made up of seas of treacle and seas of butter.

We are not without experience to guide us. History furnishes several analogous cases, and they all teach the same lesson. There are in modern times, to go no further, two memorable instances of a great impulse given to the mind of a whole society,—of prejudices overthrown,—of knowledge diffused,—of taste purified,—of arts and sciences planted in countries which had recently been ignorant and barbarous.

The first instance to which I refer, is the great revival of letters among the Western nations at the close of the fifteenth and the beginning of the sixteenth century. At that time almost every thing that was worth reading was contained in the writings of the ancient Greeks and Romans. Had our ancestors acted as the Committee of Public Instruction has hitherto acted; had they neglected the language of Cicero and Tacitus; had they confined their attention to the old dialects of our own island; had they printed nothing and taught nothing at the universities but Chronicles in Anglo-Saxon, and Romances in Norman-French, would England have been what she now is? What the Greek and Latin were to the contemporaries of More and Ascham, our tongue is to the people of India. The literature of England is now more valuable than that of classical antiquity. I doubt whether the Sanscrit literature be as valuable as that of our Saxon and Norman progenitors. In some departments,—in History, for example, I am certain that it is much less so.

Another instance may be said to be still before our eyes. Within the last hundred and twenty years, a nation which has previously been in a state as barbarous as that in which our ancestors were before the crusades, has gradually emerged from the ignorance in which it was sunk, and has taken its place among civilized communities.—I speak of Russia. There is now in that country a large educated class, abounding with persons fit to serve the state in the highest functions, and in no wise inferior to the most accomplished men who adorn the best circles of Paris and London. There is reason to hope that this vast empire, which in the time of our grandfathers was probably behind the Punjab, may, in the time of our grandchildren, be pressing close on France and Britain in the career of improvement. And how was this change effected? Not by flattering national prejudices: not by feeding the mind of the young Muscovite with the old women's stories which his rude fathers had believed: not by filling his head with lying legends about St. Nicholas: not by encouraging him to study the great question, whether the world was or was not created on the 13th of September: not by calling him "a learned native," when he has mastered all these points of knowledge: but by teaching him those foreign languages in which the greatest mass of information had been laid up, and thus putting all that information within his reach. The languages of Western Europe civilized Russia. I cannot doubt that they will do for the Hindoo what they have done for the Tartar.

And what are the arguments against that course which seems to be alike recommended by theory and by experience? It is said that we ought to secure the co-operation of the native public, and that we can do this only by teaching Sanscrit and Arabic.

I can by no means admit that when a nation of high intellectual attainments undertakes to superintend the education of a nation comparatively ignorant, the learners are absolutely to prescribe the course which is to be taken by the teachers. It is not necessary, however, to say any thing on this subject. For it is proved by unanswerable evidence that we are not at present securing the co-operation of the natives. It would be bad enough to consult their intellectual taste at the expense of their intellectual health. But we are consulting neither,—we are withholding from them the learning for which they are craving, we are forcing on them the mock-learning which they nauseate.

This is proved by the fact that we are forced to pay our Arabic and Sanscrit students, while those who learn English are willing to pay us. All the declamations in the world about the love and reverence of the natives for their sacred dialects will never, in the mind of any impartial person, outweigh the undisputed fact, that we cannot find, in all our vast empire, a single student who will let us teach him those dialects unless we will pay him.

I have now before me the accounts of the Madrassa for one month,—the month of December, 1833. The Arabic students appear to have been seventy-seven in number. All receive stipends from the public. The whole amount paid to them is above 500 rupees a month. On the other side of the account stands the following item: Deduct amount realized from the out-students of English for the months of May, June and July last, 103 rupees.

I have been told that it is merely from want of local experience that I am surprised at these phenomena, and that it is not the fashion for students in India to study at their own charges. This only confirms me in my opinion. Nothing is more certain than that it never can in any part of the world be necessary to pay men for doing what they think pleasant and profitable. India is no exception to this rule. The people of India do not require to be paid for eating rice when they are hungry, or for wearing woollen cloth in the cold season. To come nearer to the case before us, the children who learn their letters and a little elementary Arithmetic from the village school-master are not paid by him. He is paid for teaching them. Why then is it necessary to pay people to learn Sanscrit and Arabic? Evidently because it is universally felt that the Sanscrit and Arabic are languages, the knowledge of which does not compensate for the trouble of acquiring them. On all such subjects the state of the market is the decisive test.

Other evidence is not wanting, if other evidence were required. A petition was presented last year to the Committee by several ex-students of the Sanscrit College. The petitioners stated that they had studied in the college ten or twelve years; that they had made themselves acquainted with Hindoo literature and science; that they had received certificates of proficiency: and what is the fruit of all this! "Notwithstanding such testimonials," they say, "we have but little prospect of bettering our condition without the kind assistance of your Honorable Committee, the indifference with which we are generally looked upon by our countrymen leaving no hope of encouragement and assistance from them." They therefore beg that they may be recommended to the Governor General for places under the Government, not places of high dignity or emolument, but such as may just enable them to exist. "We want means," they say, "for a decent living, and for our progressive improvement, which, however, we cannot obtain without the assistance of Government, by whom we have been educated and maintained from childhood." They conclude by representing, very pathetically, that they are sure that it was never the intention of Government, after behaving so liberally to them during their education, to abandon them to destitution and neglect.

I have been used to see petitions to Government for compensation. All these petitions, even the most unreasonable of them, proceeded on the supposition that some loss had been sustained—that some wrong had been inflicted. These are surely the first petitioners who ever demanded compensation for having been educated gratis,—for having been supported by the public during twelve years, and then sent forth into the world well furnished with literature and science. They represent their education as an injury which gives them a claim on the Government for redress, as an injury for which the stipends paid to them during the infliction were a very inadequate compensation. And I doubt not that they are in the right. They have wasted the best years of life in learning what procures for them neither bread nor respect. Surely we might, with advantage, have saved the cost of making these persons useless and miserable; surely, men may be brought up to be burdens to the public and objects of contempt to their neighbours at a somewhat smaller charge to the state. But such is our policy. We do not even stand neuter in the contest between truth and falsehood. We are not content to leave the natives to the influence of their own hereditary prejudices. To the natural difficulties which obstruct the progress of sound science in the East, we add fresh difficulties of our own making. Bounties and premiums, such as ought not to be given even for the propagation of truth, we lavish on false taste and false philosophy.

By acting thus we create the very evil which we fear. We are making that opposition which we do not find. What we spend on the Arabic and Sanscrit colleges is not merely a dead loss to the cause of truth; it is bounty-money paid to raise up champions of error. It goes to form a nest, not merely of helpless place-hunters, but of bigots prompted alike by passion and by interest to raise a cry against every useful scheme of education. If there should be any opposition among the natives to the change which I recommend, that opposition will be the effect of our own system. It will be headed by persons supported by our stipends and trained in our colleges. The longer we persevere in our present course, the more formidable will that opposition be. It will be every year reinforced by recruits whom we are paying. From the native society left to itself, we have no difficulties to apprehend; all the murmuring will come from that oriental interest which we have, by artificial means, called into being, and nursed into strength.

There is yet another fact, which is alone sufficient to prove that the feeling of the native public, when left to itself, is not such as the supporters of the old system represent it to be. The Committee have thought fit to lay out above a lac of rupees in printing Arabic and Sanscrit books. Those books find no purchasers. It is very rarely that a single copy is disposed of. Twenty-three thousand volumes, most of them folios and quartos, fill the libraries, or rather the lumber-rooms, of this body. The Committee contrive to get rid of some portion of their vast stock of oriental literature by giving books away. But they cannot give so fast as they print. About twenty thousand rupees a year are spent in adding fresh masses of waste paper to a hoard which, I should think, is already sufficiently ample. During the last three years, about sixty thousand rupees have been expended in this manner. The sale of Arabic and Sanscrit books, during those three years, has not yielded quite one thousand rupees. In the mean time the School-book Society is selling seven or eight thousand English volumes every year, and not only pays the expenses of printing, but realises a profit of 20 per cent. on its outlay.

The fact that the Hindoo law is to be learned chiefly from Sanscrit books, and the Mahomedan law from Arabic books, has been much insisted on, but seems not to bear at all on the question. We are commanded by Parliament to ascertain and digest the laws of India. The assistance of a law Commission has been given to us for that purpose. As soon as the code is promulgated, the Shasster and the Hedaya will be useless to a Moonsiff or Sudder Ameen. I hope and trust that before the boys who are now entering at the Madrassa and the Sanscrit college have completed their studies, this great work will be finished. It would be manifestly absurd to educate the rising generation with a view to a state of things which we mean to alter before they reach manhood.

But there is yet another argument which seems even more untenable. It is said that the Sanscrit and Arabic are the languages in which the sacred books of a hundred millions of people are written, and that they are, on that account, entitled to peculiar encouragement. Assuredly it is the duty of the British Government in India to be not only tolerant, but neutral on all religious questions. But to encourage the study of a literature admitted to be of small intrinsic value, only because that literature inculcates the most serious errors on the most important subjects, is a course hardly reconcileable with reason, with morality, or even with that very neutrality which ought, as we all agree, to be sacredly preserved. It is confessed that a language is barren of useful knowledge. We are to teach it because it is fruitful of monstrous superstitions. We are to teach false History, false Astronomy, false Medicine, because we find them in company with a false religion. We abstain, and I trust shall always abstain, from giving any public encouragement to those who are engaged in the work of converting natives to Christianity. And while we act thus, can we reasonably and decently bribe men out of the revenues of the state to waste their youth in learning how they are to purify themselves after touching an ass, or what text of the Vedas they are to repeat to expiate the crime of killing a goat?

It is taken for granted by the advocates of Oriental learning, that no native of this country can possibly attain more than a mere smattering of English. They do not attempt to prove this; but they perpetually insinuate it. They designate the education which their opponents recommend as a mere spelling book education. They assume it as undeniable, that the question is between a profound knowledge of Hindoo and Arabian literature and science on the one side, and a superficial knowledge of the rudiments of English on the other. This is not merely an assumption, but an assumption contrary to all reason and experience. We know that foreigners of all nations do learn our language sufficiently to have access to all the most abstruse knowledge which it contains, sufficiently to relish even the more delicate graces of our most idiomatic writers. There are in this very town natives who are quite competent to discuss political or scientific questions with fluency and precision in the English language. I have heard the very question on which I am now writing discussed by native gentlemen with a liberality and an intelligence which would do credit to any member of the Committee of Public Instruction. Indeed it is unusual to find, even in the literary circles of the continent, any foreigner who can express himself in English with so much facility and correctness as we find in many Hindoos. Nobody, I suppose, will contend that English is so difficult to a Hindoo as Greek to an Englishman. Yet an intelligent English youth, in a much smaller number of years than our unfortunate pupils pass at the Sanscrit college, becomes able to read, to enjoy, and even to imitate, not unhappily, the compositions of the best Greek Authors. Less than half the time which enables an English youth to read Herodotus and Sophocles, ought to enable a Hindoo to read Hume and Milton.

To sum up what I have said, I think it clear that we are not fettered by the Act of Parliament of 1813; that we are not fettered by any pledge expressed or implied; that we are free to employ our funds as we choose; that we ought to employ them in teaching what is best worth knowing; that English is better worth knowing than Sanscrit or Arabic; that the natives are desirous to be taught English, and are not desirous to be taught Sanscrit or Arabic; that neither as the languages of law, nor as the languages of religion, have the Sanscrit and Arabic any peculiar claim to our engagement; that it is possible to make natives of this country thoroughly good English scholars, and that to this end our efforts ought to be directed.

In one point I fully agree with the gentlemen to whose general views I am opposed. I feel with them, that it is impossible for us, with our limited means, to attempt to educate the body of the people. We must at present do our best to form a class who may be interpreters between us and the millions whom we govern; a class of persons, Indian in blood and colour, but English in taste, in opinions, in morals, and in intellect. To that class we may leave it to refine the vernacular dialects of the country, to enrich those dialects with terms of science borrowed from the Western nomenclature, and to render them by degrees fit vehicles for conveying knowledge to the great mass of the population.

I would strictly respect all existing interests. I would deal even generously with all individuals who have had fair reason to expect a pecuniary provision. But I would strike at the root of the bad system which has hitherto been fostered by us. I would at once stop the printing of Arabic and Sanscrit books, I would abolish the Madrassa and the Sanscrit college at Calcutta. Benares is the great seat of Brahmanical learning; Delhi, of Arabic learning. If we retain the Sanscrit college at Benares and the Mahometan college at Delhi, we do enough, and much more than enough in my opinion, for the Eastern languages. If the Benares and Delhi colleges should be retained, I would at least recommend that no stipends shall be given to any students who may hereafter repair thither, but that the people shall be left to make their own choice between the rival systems of education without being bribed by us to learn what they have no desire to know. The funds which would thus be placed at our disposal would enable us to give larger encouragement to the Hindoo college at Calcutta, and to establish in the principal cities throughout the Presidencies of Fort William and Agra schools in which the English language might be well and thoroughly taught.

If the decision of his Lordship in Council should be such as I anticipate, I shall enter on the performance of my duties with the greatest zeal and alacrity. If, on the other hand, it be the opinion of the Government that the present system ought to remain unchanged, I beg that I may be permitted to retire from the chair of the Committee. I feel that I could not be of the smallest use there—I feel, also, that I should be lending my countenance to what I firmly believe to be a mere delusion. I believe that the present system tends, not to accelerate the progress of truth, but to delay the natural death of expiring errors. I conceive that we have at present no right to the respectable name of a Board of Public Instruction. We are a Board for wasting public money, for printing books which are of less value than the paper on which they are printed was while it was blank; for giving artificial encouragement to absurd history, absurd metaphysics, absurd physics, absurd theology; for raising up a breed of scholars who find their scholarship an encumbrance and a blemish, who live on the public while they are receiving their education, and whose education is so utterly useless to them that when they have received it they must either starve or live on the public all the rest of their lives. Entertaining these opinions, I am naturally desirous to decline all share in the responsibility of a body, which unless it alters its whole mode of proceeding, I must consider not merely as useless, but as positively noxious.

# COPYRIGHT. I

A SPEECH DELIVERED IN THE HOUSE OF COMMONS ON THE
5TH OF FEBRUARY, 1841

On the twenty-ninth of January, 1841, Mr. Serjeant Talfourd[1] obtained leave to bring in a bill to amend the law of copyright. The object of this bill was to extend the term of copyright in a book to sixty years, reckoned from the death of the writer.

On the fifth of February Mr. Serjeant Talfourd moved that the bill should be read a second time. In reply to him the following Speech was made. The bill was rejected by 45 votes to 38.

[*Note:* The law and its amendment may be summarised thus:
  *Existing law:* Copyright for life *or* 28 years, whichever longer.
  *Talfourd:* Copyright for life *and* 60 years.
  *Mahon:* Copyright for life *and* 25 years.
  *Macaulay:* Copyright for life *or* 42 years, whichever longer.]

THOUGH, Sir, it is in some sense agreeable to approach a subject with which political animosities have nothing to do, I offer myself to your notice with some reluctance. It is painful to me to take a course which may possibly be misunderstood or misrepresented as unfriendly to the interests of literature and literary men. It is painful to me, I will add, to oppose my honorable and learned friend on a question which he has taken up from the purest motives, and which he regards with a parental interest. These feelings have hitherto kept me silent when the law of copyright has been under discussion. But as I am, on full consideration, satisfied that the measure before us will, if adopted, inflict grievous injury on the public, without conferring any compensating advantage on men of letters, I think it my duty to avow that opinion and to defend it.

The first thing to be done, Sir, is to settle on what principles the question is to be argued. Are we free to legislate for the public good, or are we not? Is this a question of expediency, or is it a question of right? Many of those who have written and petitioned against the existing state of things treat the question as one of right. The law of nature, according to them, gives to every man a sacred and indefeasible property in his own ideas, in the fruits of his own reason and imagination. The legislature has indeed the power to take away this property, just as it has the power to

---

[1] [Talfourd's first Copyright Bill was introduced in 1837 and was rewarded with the dedication of *Pickwick*. In 1841 he unsuccessfully defended Moxon for publishing a blasphemous libel, *Queen Mab*.]

pass an act of attainder for cutting off an innocent man's head without a trial. But, as such an act of attainder would be legal murder, so would an act invading the right of an author to his copy be, according to these gentlemen, legal robbery.

Now, Sir, if this be so, let justice be done, cost what it may. I am not prepared like my honorable and learned friend, to agree to a compromise between right and expediency, and to commit an injustice for the public convenience. But I must say, that his theory soars far beyond the reach of my faculties. It is not necessary to go, on the present occasion, into a metaphysical inquiry about the origin of the right of property; and certainly nothing but the strongest necessity would lead me to discuss a subject so likely to be distasteful to the House. I agree, I own, with Paley in thinking that property is the creature of the law, and that the law which creates property can be defended only on this ground, that it is a law beneficial to mankind. But it is unnecessary to debate that point. For, even if I believed in a natural right of property, independent of utility and anterior to legislation, I should still deny that this right could survive the original proprietor. Few, I apprehend, even of those who have studied in the most mystical and sentimental schools of moral philosophy, will be disposed to maintain that there is a natural law of succession older and of higher authority than any human code. If there be, it is quite certain that we have abuses to reform much more serious than any connected with the question of copyright. For this natural law can be only one; and the modes of succession in the Queen's dominions are twenty. To go no further than England, land generally descends to the eldest son. In Kent the sons share and share alike. In many districts the youngest takes the whole. Formerly a portion of a man's personal property was secured to his family; and it was only of the residue that he could dispose by will. Now he can dispose of the whole by will: but you limited his power, a few years ago, by enacting that the will should not be valid unless there were two witnesses. If a man dies intestate, his personal property generally goes according to the statute of distributions; but there are local customs which modify that statute. Now which of all these systems is conformed to the eternal standard of right? Is it primogeniture, or gavelkind, or borough English? Are wills *jure divino*? Are the two witnesses *jure divino*? Might not the *pars rationabilis* of our old law have a fair claim to be regarded as of celestial institution? Was the statute of distributions enacted in Heaven long before it was adopted by Parliament? Or is it to Custom of York, or to Custom of London, that this preeminence belongs? Surely, Sir, even those who hold that there is a natural right of property must admit that rules prescribing the manner in which the effects of deceased persons shall be distributed are purely arbitrary, and originate altogether in the will of the legislature. If so, Sir, there is no controversy between my honorable and learned friend and myself as to the principles on which this question is to be argued. For the existing law gives an author copyright during his natural life; nor do I propose to invade that privilege, which I should, on the contrary, be prepared to defend strenuously against any assailant. The only point in issue between us is, how long after an author's death the State shall recognise a copyright in his representatives and assigns; and it can, I think, hardly be disputed by any rational man that this is a point which the legislature is free to determine in the way which may appear to be most conducive to the general good.

We may now, therefore, I think, descend from these high regions, where we are in danger of being lost in the clouds, to firm ground and clear light. Let us look at this question like legislators, and after fairly balancing conveniences and inconveniences, pronounce between the existing law of copyright and the law now proposed to us. The question of copyright, Sir, like most questions of civil prudence, is neither black nor white, but grey. The system of copyright has great advantages and great disadvantages; and it is our business to ascertain what these are, and then to make an arrangement under which the advantages may be as far as possible secured, and the disadvantages as far as possible excluded. The charge which I bring against my honorable and learned friend's bill is this, that it leaves the advantages nearly what they are at present, and increases the disadvantages at least four fold.

The advantages arising from a system of copyright are obvious. It is desirable that we should have a supply of good books: we cannot have such a supply unless men of letters are liberally remunerated; and the least objectionable way of remunerating them is by means of copyright. You cannot depend for literary instruction and amusement on the leisure of men occupied in the pursuits of active life. Such men may occasionally produce compositions of great merit. But you must not look to such men for works which require deep meditation and long research. Works of that kind you can expect only from persons who make literature the business of their lives. Of these persons few will be found among the rich and the noble. The rich and the noble are not impelled to intellectual exertion by necessity. They may be impelled to intellectual exertion by the desire of distinguishing themselves, or by the desire of benefiting the community. But it is generally within these walls that they seek to signalise themselves and to serve their fellow creatures. Both their ambition and their public spirit, in a country like this, naturally take a political turn. It is then on men whose profession is literature, and whose private means are not ample, that you must rely for a supply of valuable books. Such men must be remunerated for their literary labour. And there are only two ways in which they can be remunerated. One of those ways is patronage; the other is copyright.

There have been times in which men of letters looked, not to the public, but to the government, or to a few great men, for the reward of their exertions. It was thus in the time of Mæcenas and Pollio at Rome, of the Medici at Florence, of Lewis the Fourteenth in France, of Lord Halifax and Lord Oxford in this country. Now, Sir, I well know that there are cases in which it is fit and graceful, nay, in which it is a sacred duty to reward the merits or to relieve the distresses of men of genius by the exercise of this species of liberality. But these cases are exceptions. I can conceive no system more fatal to the integrity and independence of literary men than one under which they should be taught to look for their daily bread to the favour of ministers and nobles. I can conceive no system more certain to turn those minds which are formed by nature to be the blessings and ornaments of our species into public scandals and pests.

We have, then, only one resource left. We must betake ourselves to copyright, be the inconveniences of copyright what they may. Those inconveniences, in truth, are neither few nor small. Copyright is monopoly, and produces all the effects which the general voice of mankind attributes to monopoly. My honorable and learned friend talks very contemptuously of those who are led away by the theory that monopoly makes things dear. That monopoly makes things dear is certainly a theory, as all the great truths which have been established by the experience of all ages and nations, and which are taken for granted in all reasonings, may be said to be theories. It is a theory in the same sense in which it is a theory, that day and night follow each other, that lead is heavier than water, that bread nourishes, that arsenic poisons, that alcohol intoxicates. If, as my honorable and learned friend seems to think, the whole world is in the wrong on this point, if the real effect of monopoly is to make articles good and cheap, why does he stop short in his career of change? Why does he limit the operation of so salutary a principle to sixty years? Why does he consent to anything short of a perpetuity? He told us that in consenting to anything short of a perpetuity he was making a compromise between extreme right and expediency. But if his opinion about monopoly be correct, extreme right and expediency would coincide. Or rather why should we not restore the monopoly of the East India trade to the East India Company? Why should we not revive all those old monopolies which, in Elizabeth's reign, galled our fathers so severely that, maddened by intolerable wrong, they opposed to their sovereign a resistance before which her haughty spirit quailed for the first and for the last time? Was it the cheapness and excellence of commodities that then so violently stirred the indignation of the English people? I believe, Sir, that I may safely take it for granted that the effect of monopoly generally is to make articles scarce, to make them dear, and to make them bad. And I may with equal safety challenge my honorable friend to find out any distinction between copyright and other privileges of the same kind; any reason why a monopoly of books should produce an effect directly the reverse of that which was produced by the East India Company's monopoly of tea, or by Lord Essex's monopoly of sweet wines. Thus, then, stands the case. It is good that authors should be remunerated; and the least exceptionable way of remunerating them is by a monopoly. Yet monopoly is an evil. For the sake of the good we must submit to the evil; but the evil ought not to last a day longer than is necessary for the purpose of securing the good.

Now, I will not affirm, that the existing law is perfect, that it exactly hits the point at which the monopoly ought to cease; but this I confidently say, that the existing law is very much nearer that point than the law proposed by my honorable and learned friend. For consider this; the evil effects of the monopoly are proportioned to the length of its duration. But the good effects for the sake of which we bear with the evil effects are by no means proportioned to the length of its duration. A monopoly of sixty years produces twice as much evil as a monopoly of thirty years, and thrice as much evil as a monopoly of twenty years. But it is by no means the fact that a posthumous monopoly of sixty years gives to an author thrice as much pleasure and thrice as strong a motive as a posthumous monopoly of twenty years. On the contrary, the difference is so small as to be hardly perceptible. We all know how faintly we are affected by the prospect of very distant advantages, even when they are advantages which we may reasonably hope that we shall ourselves enjoy. But an advantage that is to be enjoyed more than half a century after we are dead, by somebody, we know not by whom, perhaps by somebody unborn, by somebody utterly unconnected with us, is really no motive at all to action. It is very probable, that in the course of some generations, land in the unexplored and unmapped heart of the Australasian continent, will be very valuable. But there is none of us who would lay down five pounds for a whole province in the heart of the Australasian continent. We know, that neither we, nor anybody for whom we care, will ever receive a farthing of rent from such a province. And a man is very little moved by the thought that in the year 2000 or 2100, somebody who claims through him will employ more shepherds than Prince Esterhazy, and will have the finest house and gallery of pictures at Victoria or Sydney. Now, this is the sort of boon which my honorable and learned friend holds out to authors. Considered as a boon to them, it is a mere nullity; but, considered as an impost on the public, it is no nullity, but a very serious and pernicious reality. I will take an example. Dr. Johnson died fifty-six years ago. If the law were what my honorable and learned friend wishes to make it, somebody would now have the monopoly of Dr. Johnson's works. Who that somebody would be it is impossible to say; but we may venture to guess. I guess, then, that it would have been some bookseller, who was the assign of another bookseller, who was the grandson of a third bookseller, who had bought the copyright from Black Frank, the Doctor's servant and residuary legatee, in 1785 or 1786. Now, would the knowledge that this copyright would exist in 1841 have been a source of gratification to Johnson? Would it have stimulated his exertions? Would it have once drawn him out of his bed before noon? Would it have once cheered him under a fit of the spleen? Would it have induced him to give us one more allegory, one more life of a poet, one more imitation of Juvenal? I firmly believe not. I firmly believe that a hundred years ago, when he was writing our debates for the Gentleman's Magazine, he would very much rather have had twopence to buy a plate of shin of beef at a cook's shop underground. Considered as a reward to him, the difference between a twenty years' term and a sixty years' term of posthumous copyright would have been nothing or next to nothing. But is the difference nothing to us? I can buy Rasselas for sixpence; I might have had to give five shillings for it. I can buy the Dictionary, the entire genuine Dictionary, for two guineas, perhaps for less; I might have had to give five or six guineas for it. Do I grudge this to a man like Dr. Johnson? Not at all. Show me that the prospect of this boon roused him to any vigorous effort, or sustained his spirits under depressing circumstances, and I am quite willing to pay the price of such an object, heavy as that price is. But what I do complain of is that my circumstances are to be worse, and Johnson's none the better; that I am to give five pounds for what to him was not worth a farthing.

The principle of copyright is this. It is a tax on readers for the purpose of giving a bounty to writers. The tax is an exceedingly bad one; it is a tax on one of the most innocent and most salutary of human pleasures; and never let us forget, that a tax on innocent pleasures is a premium on vicious pleasures. I admit, however, the necessity of giving a bounty to genius and learning. In order to give such a bounty, I willingly submit even to this severe and burdensome tax. Nay, I am ready to increase the tax, if it can be shown that by so doing I should proportionally increase the bounty. My complaint is, that my honorable and learned friend doubles, triples, quadruples, the tax, and makes scarcely any perceptible addition to the bounty. Why, Sir, what is the additional amount of taxation which would have been levied on the public for Dr. Johnson's works alone, if my honorable and learned friend's bill had been the law of the land? I have not data sufficient to form an opinion. But I am confident that the taxation on his Dictionary alone would have amounted to many thousands of pounds. In reckoning the whole additional sum which the holders of his copyrights would have taken out of the pockets of the public during the last half century at twenty thousand pounds, I feel satisfied that I very greatly underrate it. Now, I again say that I think it but fair that we should pay twenty thousand pounds in consideration of twenty thousand pounds' worth of pleasure and encouragement received by Dr. Johnson. But I think it very hard that we should pay twenty thousand pounds for what he would not have valued at five shillings.

My honorable and learned friend dwells on the claims of the posterity of great writers. Undoubtedly, Sir, it would be very pleasing to see a descendant of Shakespeare living in opulence on the fruits of his great ancestor's genius. A house maintained in splendour by such a patrimony would be a more interesting and striking object than Blenheim is to us, or than Strathfieldsaye will be to our children. But, unhappily, it is scarcely possible that, under any system, such a thing can come to pass. My honorable and learned friend does not propose that copyright shall descend to the eldest son, or shall be bound up by irrevocable entail. It is to be merely personal property. It is therefore highly improbable that it will descend during sixty years or half that term from parent to child. The chance is that more people than one will have an interest in it. They will in all probability sell it and divide the proceeds. The price which a bookseller will give for it will bear no proportion to the sum which he will afterwards draw from the public, if his speculation proves successful. He will give little, if any thing, more for a term of sixty years than for a term of thirty or five and twenty. The present value of a distant advantage is always small; but when there is great room to doubt whether a distant advantage will be any advantage at all, the present value sinks to almost nothing. Such is the inconstancy of the public taste that no sensible man will venture to pronounce, with confidence, what the sale of any book published in our days will be in the years between 1890 and 1900. The whole fashion of thinking and writing has often undergone a change in a much shorter period than that to which my honorable and learned friend would extend posthumous copyright. What would have been considered the best literary property in the earliest part of Charles the Second's reign? I imagine Cowley's poems. Overleap sixty years, and you are in the generation of which Pope asked, "who now reads Cowley?" What works were ever expected with more impatience by the public than those of Lord Bolingbroke, which appeared, I think, in 1754. In 1814, no bookseller would have thanked you for the copyright of them all, if you had offered it to him for nothing. What would Paternoster Row give now for the copyright of Hayley's Triumphs of Temper, so much admired within the memory of many people still living? I say, therefore, that, from the very nature of literary property, it will almost always pass away from an author's family; and I say, that the price given for it to the family will bear a very small proportion to the tax which the purchaser, if his speculation turns out well, will in the course of a long series of years levy on the public.

If, Sir, I wished to find a strong and perfect illustration of the effects which I anticipate from long copyright, I should select,—my honorable and learned friend will be surprised,—I should select the case of Milton's granddaughter. As often as this bill has been under discussion, the fate of Milton's granddaughter has been brought forward by the advocates of monopoly. My honorable and learned friend has repeatedly told the story with great eloquence and effect. He has dilated on the sufferings, on the abject poverty, of this illfated woman, the last of an illustrious race. He tells us that, in the extremity of her distress, Garrick gave her a benefit, that Johnson wrote a prologue, and that the public contributed some hundreds of pounds. Was it fit, he asks, that she should receive, in this eleemosynary form, a small portion of what was in truth a debt? Why, he asks, instead of obtaining a pittance from charity, did she not live in comfort and luxury on the proceeds of the sale of her ancestor's works? But, Sir, will my honorable and learned friend tell me that this event, which he has so often and so pathetically described, was caused by the shortness of the term of copyright? Why, at that time, the duration of copyright was longer than even he, at present, proposes to make it. The monopoly lasted not sixty years, but for ever. At the time at which Milton's granddaughter asked charity, Milton's works were the exclusive property of a bookseller. Within a few months of the day on which the benefit was given at Garrick's theatre, the holder of the copyright of Paradise Lost,—I think it was Tonson, —applied to the Court of Chancery for an injunction against a bookseller, who had published a cheap edition of the great epic poem, and obtained the injunction. The representation of Comus was, if I remember rightly, in 1750; the injunction in 1752. Here, then, is a perfect illustration of the effect of long copyright. Milton's works are the property of a single publisher. Everybody who wants them must buy them at Tonson's shop, and at Tonson's price. Whoever attempts to undersell Tonson is harassed with legal proceedings. Thousands who would gladly possess a copy of Paradise Lost, must forego that great enjoyment. And what, in the meantime, is the situation of the only person for whom we can suppose that the author, protected at such a cost to the public, was at all interested? She is reduced to utter destitution. Milton's works are under a monopoly. Milton's granddaughter is starving. The reader is pillaged; but the writer's family is not enriched. Society is taxed doubly. It has to give an exorbitant price for the poems; and it has at the same time to give alms to the only surviving descendant of the poet.

But this is not all. I think it right, Sir, to call the attention of the House to an evil which is perhaps more to be apprehended when an author's copyright remains in the hands of his family, than when it is transferred to booksellers. I seriously fear that, if such a measure as this should be adopted, many valuable works will be either totally suppressed or grievously mutilated. I can prove that this danger is not chimerical; and I am quite certain that, if the danger be real, the safeguards which my honorable and learned friend has devised are altogether nugatory. That the danger is not chimerical may easily be shown. Most of us, I am sure, have known persons who, very erroneously as I think, but from the best motives, would not choose to reprint Fielding's novels, or Gibbon's History of the Decline and Fall of the Roman Empire. Some gentlemen may perhaps be of opinion, that it would be as well if Tom Jones and Gibbon's History were never reprinted. I will not, then, dwell on these or similar cases. I will take cases respecting which it is not likely that there will be any difference of opinion here; cases, too, in which the danger of which I now speak is not matter of supposition, but matter of fact. Take Richardson's novels. Whatever I may, on the present occasion, think of my honorable and learned friend's judgment as a legislator, I must always respect his judgment as a critic. He will, I am sure, say that Richardson's novels are among the most valuable, among the most original works in our language. No writings have done more to raise the fame of English genius in foreign countries. No writings are more deeply pathetic. No writings, those of Shakespeare excepted, show more profound knowledge of the human heart. As to their moral tendency, I can cite the most respectable testimony. Dr. Johnson describes Richardson as one who had taught the passions to move at the command of virtue. My dear and honored friend, Mr. Wilberforce, in his celebrated religious treatise, when speaking of the unchristian tendency of the fashionable novels of the eighteenth century, distinctly excepts Richardson from the censure. Another excellent person whom I can never mention without respect and kindness, Mrs. Hannah More, often declared in conversation, and has declared in one of her published poems, that she first learned from the writings of Richardson those principles of piety by which her life was guided. I may safely say that books celebrated as works of art through the whole civilised world, and praised for their moral tendency by Dr. Johnson, by Mr. Wilberforce, by Mrs. Hannah More, ought not to be suppressed. Sir, it is my firm belief, that if the law had been what my honorable and learned friend proposes to make it, they would have been suppressed. I remember Richardson's grandson well; he was a clergyman in the city of London; he was a most upright and excellent man; but he had conceived a strong prejudice against works of fiction. He thought all novel-reading not only frivolous but sinful. He said,—this I state on the authority of one of his clerical brethren who is now a bishop,—he said that he had never thought it right to read one of his grandfather's books. Suppose, Sir, that the law had been what my honorable and learned friend would make it. Suppose that the copyright of Richardson's novels had descended, as might well have been the case, to this gentleman. I firmly believe, that he would have thought it sinful to give them a wide circulation. I firmly believe, that he would not for a hundred thousand pounds have deliberately done what he thought sinful. He would not have reprinted them. And what protection does my honorable and learned friend give to the public in such a case? Why, Sir, what he proposes is this: if a book is not reprinted during five years, any person who wishes to reprint it may give notice in the London Gazette: the advertisement must be repeated three times: a year must elapse; and then, if the proprietor of the copyright does not put forth a new edition, he loses his exclusive privilege. Now, what protection is this to the public? What is a new edition? Does the law define the number of copies that make an edition? Does it limit the price of a copy? Are twelve copies on large paper, charged at thirty guineas each, an edition? It has been usual, when monopolies have been granted, to prescribe numbers and to limit prices. But I do not find that my honorable and learned friend proposes to do so in the present case. And, without some such provision the security which he offers is manifestly illusory. It is my conviction that, under such a system as that which he recommends to us, a copy of Clarissa would have been as rare as an Aldus or a Caxton.

I will give another instance. One of the most instructive, interesting, and delightful books in our language is Boswell's Life of Johnson. Now it is well known that Boswell's eldest son considered this book, considered the whole relation of Boswell to Johnson, as a blot in the escutcheon of the family. He thought, not perhaps altogether without reason, that his father had exhibited himself in a ludicrous and degrading light. And thus he became so sore and irritable that at last he could not bear to hear the Life of Johnson mentioned. Suppose that the law had been what my honorable and learned friend wishes to make it. Suppose that the copyright of Boswell's Life of Johnson had belonged, as it well might, during sixty years, to Boswell's eldest son. What would have been the consequence? An unadulterated copy of the finest biographical work in the world would have been as scarce as the first edition of Camden's Britannia.

These are strong cases. I have shown you that, if the law had been what you are now going to make it, the finest prose work of fiction in the language, the finest biographical work in the language, would very probably have been suppressed. But I have stated my case weakly. The books which I have mentioned are singularly inoffensive books, books not touching on any of those questions which drive even wise men beyond the bounds of wisdom. There are books of a very different kind, books which are the rallying points of great political and religious parties. What is likely to happen if the copyright of one of these books should by descent or transfer come into the possession of some hostile zealot? I will take a single instance. It is only fifty years since John Wesley died; and all his works, if the law had been what my honorable and learned friend wishes to make it, would now have been the property of some person or other. The sect founded by Wesley is the most numerous, the wealthiest, the most powerful, the most zealous of sects. In every parliamentary election it is a matter of the greatest importance to obtain the support of the Wesleyan Methodists. Their numerical strength is reckoned by hundreds of thousands. They hold the memory of their founder in the greatest reverence; and not without reason, for he was unquestionably a great and good man. To his authority they constantly appeal. His works are in their eyes of the highest value. His doctrinal writings they regard as containing the best system of theology ever deduced from Scripture. His journals, interesting even to the common reader, are peculiarly interesting to the Methodist: for they contain the whole history of that singular polity which, weak and despised in its beginning, is now, after the lapse of a century, so strong, so flourishing, and so formidable. The hymns to which he gave his Imprimatur are a most important part of the public worship of his followers. Now, suppose that the copyright of these works should belong to some person who holds the memory of Wesley and the doctrines and discipline of the Methodists in abhorrence. There are many such persons. The Ecclesiastical Courts are at this very time sitting on the case of a clergyman of the Established Church who refused Christian burial to a child baptized by a Methodist preacher. I took up the other day a work which is considered as among the most respectable organs of a large and growing party in the Church of England, and there I saw John Wesley designated as a forsworn priest. Suppose that the works of Wesley were suppressed. Why, Sir, such a grievance would be enough to shake the foundations of Government. Let gentlemen who are attached to the Church reflect for a moment what their feelings would be if the Book of Common Prayer were not to be reprinted for thirty or forty years, if the price of a Book of Common Prayer were run up to five or ten guineas. And then let them determine whether they will pass a law under which it is possible, under which it is probable, that so intolerable a wrong may be done to some sect consisting perhaps of half a million of persons.

I am so sensible, Sir, of the kindness with which the House has listened to me, that I will not detain you longer. I will only say this, that if the measure before us should pass, and should produce one tenth part of the evil which it is calculated to produce, and which I fully expect it to produce, there will soon be a remedy, though of a very objectionable kind. Just as the absurd acts which prohibited the sale of game were virtually repealed by the poacher, just as many absurd revenue acts have been virtually repealed by the smuggler, so will this law be virtually repealed by piratical booksellers. At present the holder of copyright has the public feeling on his side. Those who invade copyright are regarded as knaves who take the bread out of the mouths of deserving men. Every body is well pleased to see them restrained by the law, and compelled to refund their illgotten gains. No tradesmen of good repute will have anything to do with such disgraceful transactions. Pass this law: and that feeling is at an end. Men very different from the present race of piratical booksellers will soon infringe this intolerable monopoly. Great masses of capital will be constantly employed in the violation of the law. Every art will be employed to evade legal pursuit; and the whole nation will be in the plot. On which side indeed should the public sympathy be when the question is whether some book as popular as Robinson Crusoe, or the Pilgrim's Progress, shall be in every cottage, or whether it shall be confined to the libraries of the rich, for the advantage of the greatgrandson of a bookseller who, a hundred years before, drove a hard bargain for the copyright with the author when in great distress? Remember too that, when once it ceases to be considered as wrong and discreditable to invade literary property, no person can say where the invasion will stop. The public seldom make nice distinctions. The wholesome copyright which now exists will share in the disgrace and danger of the new copyright which you are about to create. And you will find that, in attempting to impose unreasonable restraints on the reprinting of the works of the dead, you have, to a great extent, annulled those restraints which now prevent men from pillaging and defrauding the living. If I saw, Sir, any probability that this bill could be so amended in the Committee that my objections might be removed, I would not divide the House in this stage. But I am so fully convinced that no alteration which would not seem insupportable to my honorable and learned friend, could render his measure supportable to me, that I must move, though with regret, that this bill be read a second time this day six months.

# COPYRIGHT. II

A SPEECH DELIVERED IN A COMMITTEE OF THE HOUSE OF COMMONS
ON THE 6TH OF APRIL, 1842

On the third of March, 1842, Lord Mahon obtained permission to bring
in a bill to amend the Law of Copyright. This bill extended the term of
Copyright in a book to twenty-five years, reckoned from the death of
the author.

On the sixth of April the House went into Committee on the bill, and
Mr. Greene took the Chair. Several divisions took place, of which the
result was that the plan suggested in the following Speech was, with
some modifications, adopted.

MR. GREENE,

I have been amused and gratified by the remarks which my
noble friend[1] has made on the arguments by which I prevailed
on the last House of Commons to reject the bill introduced by a
very able and accomplished man, Mr. Serjeant Talfourd. My
noble friend has done me a high and rare honor. For this is, I
believe, the first occasion on which a speech made in one Parlia-
mant has been answered in another. I should not find it difficult
to vindicate the soundness of the reasons which I formerly urged,
to set them in a clearer light, and to fortify them by additional facts.
But it seems to me that we had better discuss the bill which is
now on our table than the bill which was there fourteen months
ago. Glad I am to find that there is a very wide difference between
the two bills, and that my noble friend, though he has tried to
refute my arguments, has acted as if he had been convinced by
them. I objected to the term of sixty years as far too long. My
noble friend has cut that term down to twenty-five years. I warned
the House that, under the provisions of Mr. Serjeant Talfourd's
bill, valuable works might not improbably be suppressed by the
representatives of authors. My noble friend has prepared a clause
which, as he thinks, will guard against that danger. I will not
therefore waste the time of the Committee by debating points
which he has conceded, but will proceed at once to the proper
business of this evening.

Sir, I have no objection to the principle of my noble friend's
bill. Indeed, I had no objection to the principle of the bill of last
year. I have long thought that the term of copyright ought to be
extended. When Mr. Serjeant Talfourd moved for leave to bring
in his bill, I did not oppose the motion. Indeed, I meant to vote

[1] Lord Mahon.

for the second reading, and to reserve what I had to say for the Committee. But the learned Serjeant left me no choice. He, in strong language, begged that nobody who was disposed to reduce the term of sixty years would divide with him. "Do not," he said, "give me your support if all that you mean to grant to men of letters is a miserable addition of fourteen or fifteen years to the present term. I do not wish for such support. I despise it." Not wishing to obtrude on the learned Serjeant a support which he despised, I had no course left but to take the sense of the House on the second reading. The circumstances are now different. My noble friend's bill is not at present a good bill; but it may be improved into a very good bill; nor will he, I am persuaded, withdraw it if it should be so improved. He and I have the same object in view; but we differ as to the best mode of attaining that object. We are equally desirious to extend the protection now enjoyed by writers. In what way it may be extended with most benefit to them and with least inconvenience to the public, is the question.

The present state of the law is this. The author of a work has a certain copyright in that work for a term of twenty-eight years. If he should live more than twenty-eight years after the publication of the work, he retains the copyright to the end of his life.

My noble friend does not propose to make any addition to the term of twenty-eight years. But he proposes that the copyright shall last twenty-five years after the author's death. Thus my noble friend makes no addition to that term which is certain, but makes a very large addition to that term which is uncertain.

My plan is different. I would make no addition to the uncertain term; but I would make a large addition to the certain term. I propose to add fourteen years to the twenty-eight years which the law now allows to an author. His copyright will, in this way, last till his death, or till the expiration of forty-two years, whichever shall first happen. And I think that I shall be able to prove to the satisfaction of the Committee that my plan will be more beneficial to literature and to literary men than the plan of my noble friend.

It must surely, Sir, be admitted that the protection which we give to books ought to be distributed as evenly as possible, that every book should have a fair share of that protection, and no book more than a fair share. It would evidently be absurd to put tickets into a wheel, with different numbers marked upon them, and to make writers draw, one a term of twenty-eight years, another a term of fifty, another a term of ninety. And yet this sort of lottery is what my noble friend proposes to establish. I know that we cannot altogether exclude chance. You have two terms of copy-

M—24*

right; one certain, the other uncertain; and we cannot, I admit, get rid of the uncertain term. It is proper, no doubt, that an author's copyright should last during his life. But, Sir, though we cannot altogether exclude chance, we can very much diminish the share which chance must have in distributing the recompense which we wish to give to genius and learning. By every addition which we make to the certain term we diminish the influence of chance; by every addition which we make to the uncertain term we increase the influence of chance. I shall make myself best understood by putting cases. Take two eminent female writers, who died within our own memory, Madame D'Arblay and Miss Austen. As the law now stands, Miss Austen's charming novels would have only from twenty-eight to thirty-three years of copyright. For that extraordinary woman died young: she died before her genius was fully appreciated by the world. Madame D'Arblay outlived the whole generation to which she belonged. The copyright of her celebrated novel, Evelina, lasted, under the present law, sixty-two years. Surely this inequality is sufficiently great, sixty-two years of copyright for Evelina, only twenty-eight for Persuasion. But to my noble friend this inequality seems not great enough. He proposes to add twenty-five years to Madame D'Arblay's term, and not a single day to Miss Austen's term. He would give to Persuasion a copyright of only twenty-eight years, as at present, and to Evelina a copyright more than three times as long, a copyright of eighty-seven years. Now, is this reasonable? See, on the other hand, the operation of my plan. I make no addition at all to Madame D'Arblay's term of sixty-two years, which is, in my opinion, quite long enough; but I extend Miss Austen's term to forty-two years, which is, in my opinion, not too much. You see, Sir, that at present chance has too much sway in this matter; that at present the protection which the state gives to letters is very unequally given. You see that if my noble friend's plan be adopted, more will be left to chance than under the present system, and you will have such inequalities as are unknown under the present system. You see also that, under the system which I recommend, we shall have, not perfect certainty, not perfect equality, but much less uncertainty and inequality than at present.

But this is not all. My noble friend's plan is not merely to institute a lottery in which some writers will draw prizes and some will draw blanks. It is much worse than this. His lottery is so contrived that, in the vast majority of cases, the blanks will fall to the best books, and the prizes to books of inferior merit.

Take Shakspeare. My noble friend gives a longer protection than I should give to Love's Labour's Lost, and Pericles, Prince of Tyre; but he gives a shorter protection than I should give to Othello and Macbeth.

Take Milton. Milton died in 1674. The copyrights of Milton's great works would, according to my noble friend's plan, expire in 1699. Comus appeared in 1634, the Paradise Lost in 1668. To Comus, then, my noble friend would give sixty-five years of copyright, and to the Paradise Lost only thirty-one years. Is that reasonable? Comus is a noble poem: but who would rank it with the Paradise Lost? My plan would give forty-two years both to the Paradise Lost and to Comus.

Let us pass on from Milton to Dryden. My noble friend would give more than sixty years of copyright to Dryden's worst works; to the encomiastic verses on Oliver Cromwell, to the Wild Gallant, to the Rival Ladies, to other wretched pieces as bad as anything written by Flecknoe or Settle: but for Theodore and Honoria, for Tancred and Sigismunda, for Cimon and Iphigenia, for Palamon and Arcite, for Alexander's Feast, my noble friend thinks a copyright of twenty-eight years sufficient. Of all Pope's works, that to which my noble friend would give the largest measure of protection is the volume of Pastorals, remarkable only as the production of a boy. Johnson's first work was a Translation of a Book of Travels in Abyssinia, published in 1735. It was so poorly executed that in his later years he did not like to hear it mentioned. Boswell once picked up a copy of it, and told his friend that he had done so. "Do not talk about it," said Johnson: "it is a thing to be forgotten." To this performance my noble friend would give protection during the enormous term of seventy-five years. To the Lives of the Poets he would give protection during about thirty years. Well; take Henry Fielding; it matters not whom I take, but take Fielding. His early works are read only by the curious, and would not be read even by the curious, but for the fame which he acquired in the later part of his life by works of a very different kind. What is the value of the Temple Beau, of the Intriguing Chambermaid, of half a dozen other plays of which few gentlemen have even heard the names? Yet to these worthless pieces my noble friend would give a term of copyright longer by more than twenty years than that which he would give to Tom Jones and Amelia.

Go on to Burke. His little tract, entitled The Vindication of Natural Society, is certainly not without merit; but it would not be remembered in our days if it did not bear the name of Burke. To this tract my noble friend would give a copyright of near seventy years. But to the great work on the French Revolution, to the Appeal from the New to the Old Whigs, to the letters on the Regicide Peace, he would give a copyright of thirty years or little more.

And, Sir, observe that I am not selecting here and there extraordinary instances in order to make up the semblance of a case. I am taking the greatest names of our literature in chronological order. Go to other nations; go to remote ages; you will still find the general rule the same. There was no copyright at Athens or Rome; but the history of the Greek and Latin literature illustrates my argument quite as well as if copyright had existed in ancient times. Of all the plays of Sophocles, the one to which the plan of my noble friend would have given the most scanty recompence would have been that wonderful masterpiece, the Œdipus at Colonos. Who would class together the Speech of Demosthenes against his Guardians, and the Speech for the Crown? My noble friend, indeed, would not class them together. For to the Speech against the Guardians he would give a copyright of near seventy years; and to the incomparable Speech for the Crown a copyright of less than half that length. Go to Rome. My noble friend would give more than twice as long a term to Cicero's juvenile declamation in defence of Roscius Amerinus as to the Second Philippic. Go to France; my noble friend would give a far longer term to Racine's Frères Ennemis than to Athalie, and to Molière's Étourdi than to Tartuffe. Go to Spain. My noble friend would give a longer term to forgotten works of Cervantes, works which nobody now reads, than to Don Quixote. Go to Germany. According to my noble friend's plan, of all the works of Schiller the Robbers would be the most favoured: of all the works of Goethe, the Sorrows of Werter would be the most favoured. I thank the Committee for listening so kindly to this long enumeration. Gentlemen will perceive, I am sure, that it is not from pedantry that I mention the names of so many books and authors. But just as, in our debates on civil affairs, we constantly draw illustrations from civil history, we must, in a debate about literary property, draw our illustrations from literary history. Now, Sir, I have, I think, shown from literary history that the effect of my noble friend's plan would be to give to crude and imperfect works, to third-rate and fourth-rate works, a great advantage over the highest productions of genius. It is impossible to account for the facts which I have laid before you by attributing them to mere accident. Their number is too great, their character too uniform. We must seek for some other explanation; and we shall easily find one

It is the law of our nature that the mind shall attain its full power by slow degrees; and this is especially true of the most vigorous minds. Young men, no doubt, have often produced works of great merit; but it would be impossible to name any writer of the first order whose juvenile performances were his best. That all the most valuable books of history, of philology, of physical and metaphysical science, of divinity, of political economy, have been produced by men of mature years will hardly be disputed. The case may not be quite so clear as respects works of the imagination. And yet I know no work of the imagination of the very highest class that was ever, in any age or country, produced by a man under thirty-five. Whatever powers a youth may have received from nature, it is impossible that his taste and judgment can be ripe, that his mind can be richly stored with images, that he can have observed the vicissitudes of life, that he can have studied the nicer shades of character. How, as Marmontel very sensibly said, is a person to paint portraits who has never seen faces? On the whole I believe that I may, without fear of contradiction, affirm this, that of the good books now extant in the world more than nineteen-twentieths were published after the writers had attained the age of forty. If this be so, it is evident that the plan of my noble friend is framed on a vicious principle. For, while he gives to juvenile productions a very much larger protection than they now enjoy, he does comparatively little for the works of men in the full maturity of their powers, and absolutely nothing for any work which is published during the last three years of the life of the writer. For, by the existing law, the copyright of such a work lasts twenty-eight years from the publication; and my noble friend gives only twenty-five years to be reckoned from the writer's death.

What I recommend is that the certain term, reckoned from the date of publication, shall be forty-two years instead of twenty-eight years. In this arrangement there is no uncertainty, no inequality. The advantage which I propose to give will be the same to every book. No work will have so long a copyright as my noble friend gives to some books, or so short a copyright as he gives to others. No copyright will last ninety years. No copyright will end in twenty-eight years. To every book published in the course of the last seventeen years of a writer's life I give a longer term of copyright than my noble friend gives; and I am confident that no person versed in literary history will deny this,—that in general the most valuable works of an author are published in the course of the last seventeen years of his life. I will rapidly enumerate a few, and but a few, of the great works of English writers to which my plan is more favorable than my noble friend's plan. To Lear, to Macbeth, to Othello, to the Fairy Queen, to the Paradise Lost, to Bacon's Novum Organum and De Augmentis, to Locke's Essay on the Human Understanding, to Clarendon's History, to Hume's History, to Gibbon's History, to Smith's Wealth of Nations, to Addison's Spectators, to almost all the great works of Burke, to Clarissa and Sir Charles Grandison, to Joseph Andrews, Tom Jones and Amelia, and, with the single exception of Waverley, to all the novels of Sir Walter Scott, I give a longer term of copyright than my noble friend gives. Can he match that list? Does not that list contain what England has produced greatest in many various ways, poetry, philosophy, history, eloquence, wit, skilful portraiture of life and manners? I confidently therefore call on the Committee to take my plan in preference to the plan of my noble friend. I have shown that the protection which he proposes to give to letters is unequal, and unequal in the worst way. I have shown that his plan is to give protection to books in inverse proportion to their merit. I shall move when we come to the third clause of the bill to omit the words "twenty-five years," and in a subsequent part of the same clause I shall move to substitute for the words "twenty-eight years" the words "forty-two years." I earnestly hope that the Committee will adopt these amendments; and I feel the firmest conviction that my noble friend's bill, so amended, will confer a great boon on men of letters with the smallest possible inconvenience to the public.

## MAYNOOTH

### A SPEECH DELIVERED IN THE HOUSE OF COMMONS ON THE 14TH OF APRIL, 1845

On Saturday the eleventh of April, 1845, Sir Robert Peel moved the second reading of the Maynooth College Bill. After a debate of six nights the motion was carried by 323 votes to 176. On the second night the following Speech was made.

I DO not mean, Sir, to follow the honorable gentleman who has just sate down into a discussion on an amendment which is not now before us. When my honorable friend the Member for Sheffield shall think it expedient to make a motion on that important subject to which he has repeatedly called the attention of the House, I may, perhaps, ask to be heard. At present I shall content myself with explaining the reasons which convince me that it is my duty to vote for the second reading of this bill; and I cannot, I think, better explain those reasons than by passing in review, as rapidly as I can, the chief objections which have been made to the bill here and elsewhere.

The objectors, Sir, may be divided into three classes. The first class consists of those persons who object, not to the principle of the grant to Maynooth College, but merely to the amount. The second class consists of persons who object on principle to all grants made to a church which they regard as corrupt. The third class consists of persons who object on principle to all grants made to churches, whether corrupt or pure.

Now, Sir, of these three classes the first is evidently that which takes the most untenable ground. How any person can think that Maynooth College ought to be supported by public money, and yet can think this bill too bad to be suffered to go into Committee, I do not well understand. I am forced however to believe that there are many such persons. For I cannot but remember that the old annual vote attracted scarcely any notice; and I see that this bill has produced violent excitement. I cannot but remember that the old annual vote used to pass with very few dissentients; and I see that great numbers of gentlemen, who never were among those dissentients, have crowded down to the House in order to divide against this bill. It is indeed certain that a large proportion, I believe a majority, of those members who cannot, as they assure us, conscientiously support the plan proposed by the right honorable Baronet at the head of the Government, would without the smallest scruple have supported him if he had in this, as in former years, asked us to give nine thousand pounds for twelve months. So it is: yet I cannot help wondering that it should be so. For how can any human ingenuity turn a question between nine thousand pounds and twenty-six thousand pounds, or between twelve months and an indefinite number of months, into a question of principle. Observe: I am not now answering those who maintain that nothing ought to be given out of the public purse to a corrupt church; nor am I now answering those who maintain that nothing ought to be given out of the public purse to any church whatever. They, I admit, oppose this bill on principle. I perfectly understand, though I do not myself hold, the opinion of the zealous voluntary who says, "Whether the Roman Catholic Church teaches truth or error, she ought to have no assistance from the State." I also perfectly understand, though I do not myself hold, the opinion of the zealous Protestant who says,

"The Roman Catholic Church teaches error, and therefore ought to have no assistance from the State." But I cannot understand the reasoning of the man who says, "In spite of the errors of the Roman Catholic Church, I think that she ought to have some assistance from the State; but I am bound to mark my abhorrence of her errors by doling out to her a miserable pittance. Her tenets are so absurd and noxious that I will pay the professor who teaches them wages less than I should offer to my groom. Her rites are so superstitious that I will take care that they shall be performed in a chapel with a leaky roof and a dirty floor. By all means let us keep her a college, provided only that it be a shabby one. Let us support those who are intended to teach her doctrines and to administer her sacraments to the next generation, provided only that every future priest shall cost us less than a foot soldier. Let us board her young theologians; but let their larder be so scantily supplied that they may be compelled to break up before the regular vacation from mere want of food. Let us lodge them; but let their lodging be one in which they may be packed like pigs in a stye, and be punished for their heterodoxy by feeling the snow and the wind through the broken panes." Is it possible to conceive anything more absurd or more disgraceful? Can anything be clearer than this, that whatever it is lawful to do it is lawful to do well. If it be right that we should keep up this college at all, it must be right that we should keep it up respectably. Our national dignity is concerned. For this institution, whether good or bad, is, beyond all dispute, a very important institution. Its office is to form the character of those who are to form the character of millions. Whether we ought to extend any patronage to such an institution is a question about which wise and honest men may differ. But that, if we do extend our patronage to such an institution, our patronage ought to be worthy of the object, and worthy of the greatness of our country, is a proposition from which I am astonished to hear any person dissent.

It is, I must say, with a peculiarly bad grace that one of the members for the University to which I have the honor to belong,[1] a gentleman who never thought himself bound to say a word or to give a vote against the grant of nine thousand pounds, now vehemently opposes the grant of twenty-six thousand pounds as exorbitant. When I consider how munificently the colleges of Cambridge and Oxford are endowed, and with what pomp religion and learning are there surrounded; when I call to mind the long

[1] The Honorable Charles Law, member for the University of Cambridge.

streets of palaces, the towers and oriels, the venerable cloisters, the trim gardens, the organs, the altar pieces, the solemn light of the stained windows, the libraries, the museums, the galleries of painting and sculpture; when I call to mind also the physical comforts which are provided both for instructors and for pupils; when I reflect that the very sizars and servitors are far better lodged and fed than those students who are to be, a few years hence, the priests and bishops of the Irish people; when I think of the spacious and stately mansions of the heads of houses, of the commodious chambers of the fellows and scholars, of the refectories, the combination rooms, the bowling greens, the stabling, of the state and luxury of the great feast days, of the piles of old plate on the tables, of the savoury steam of the kitchens, of the multitudes of geese and capons which turn at once on the spits, of the oceans of excellent ale in the butteries; and when I remember from whom all this splendour and plenty is derived; when I remember what was the faith of Edward the Third and of Henry the Sixth, of Margaret of Anjou and Margaret of Richmond, of William of Wykeham and William of Waynefleet, of Archbishop Chicheley and Cardinal Wolsey; when I remember what we have taken from the Roman Catholics, King's College, New College, Christ Church, my own Trinity; and when I look at the miserable Dotheboys Hall[1] which we have given them in exchange, I feel, I must own, less proud than I could wish of being a Protestant and a Cambridge man.

Some gentlemen, it is true, have made an attempt to show that there is a distinction of principle between the old grant which they have always supported and the larger grant which they are determined to oppose. But never was attempt more unsuccessful. They say that, at the time of the Union, we entered into an implied contract with Ireland to keep up this college. We are therefore, they argue, bound by public faith to continue the old grant; but we are not bound to make any addition to that grant. Now, Sir, on this point, though on no other, I do most cordially agree with those petitioners who have, on this occasion, covered your table with such huge bales of spoiled paper and parchment. I deny the existence of any such contract. I think myself perfectly free to vote for the abolition of this college, if I am satisfied that it is a pernicious institution; as free as I am to vote against any item of the ordnance estimates; as free as I am to vote for a reduction of the number of marines. It is strange, too, that those who appeal to this imaginary contract should not perceive that, even if their fiction be admitted as true, it will by no means get them out of their

[1] [*Nicholas Nickleby* appeared in 1838.]

difficulty. Tell us plainly what are the precise terms of the contract which you suppose Great Britain to have made with Ireland about this college. Whatever the terms be, they will not serve your purpose. Was the contract this, that the Imperial Parliament would do for the college what the Irish Parliament had been used to do? Or was the contract this, that the Imperial Parliament would keep the college in a respectable and efficient state? If the former was the contract, nine thousand pounds would be too much. If the latter was the contract, you will not, I am confident, be able to prove that twenty-six thousand pounds is too little.

I have now, I think, said quite as much as need be said in answer to those who maintain that we ought to give support to this college, but that the support ought to be niggardly and precarious. I now come to another and a much more formidable class of objectors. Their objections may be simply stated thus. No man can justifiably, either as an individual or as a trustee for the public, contribute to the dissemination of religious error. But the Church of Rome teaches religious error. Therefore we cannot justifiably contribute to the support of an institution of which the object is the dissemination of the doctrines of the Church of Rome. Now, Sir, I deny the major of this syllogism. I think that there are occasions on which we are bound to contribute to the dissemination of doctrines with which errors are inseparably intermingled. Let me be clearly understood. The question is not whether we should teach truth or teach error, but whether we should teach truth adulterated with error, or teach no truth at all. The constitution of the human mind is such that it is impossible to provide any machinery for the dissemination of truth which shall not, with the truth, disseminate some error. Even those rays which come down to us from the great source of light, pure as they are in themselves, no sooner enter that gross and dark atmosphere in which we dwell than they are so much refracted, discoloured, and obscured, that they too often lead us astray. It will be generally admitted that, if religious truth can be anywhere found untainted by error, it is in the Scriptures. Yet is there actually on the face of the globe a single copy of the Scriptures of which it can be said that it contains truth absolutely untainted with error? Is there any manuscript, any edition of the Old or New Testament in the original tongues, which any scholar will pronounce faultless? But to the vast majority of Christians the original tongues are and always must be unintelligible. With the exception of perhaps one man in ten thousand, we must be content with translations. And is there any translation in which there are not numerous mistakes?

Are there not numerous mistakes even in our own authorised version, executed as that version was with painful diligence and care, by very able men and under very splendid patronage? Of course mistakes must be still more numerous in those translations which pious men have lately made into Bengalee, Hindostanee, Tamul, Canarese, and other Oriental tongues. I admire the zeal, the industry, the energy of those who, in spite of difficulties which to ordinary minds would seem insurmountable, accomplished that arduous work. I applaud those benevolent societies which munificently encouraged that work. But I have been assured by good judges that the translations have many faults. And how should it have been otherwise? How should an Englishman produce a faultless translation from the Hebrew into the Cingalese? I say, therefore, that even the Scriptures, in every form in which men actually possess them, contain a certain portion of error. And, if this be so, how can you look for pure undefecated truth in any other composition? You contribute, without any scruple, to the printing of religious tracts, to the establishing of Sunday Schools, to the sending forth of missionaries. But are your tracts perfect? Are your schoolmasters infallible? Are your missionaries inspired? Look at the two churches which are established in this island. Will you say that they both teach truth without any mixture of error? That is impossible. For they teach different doctrines on more than one important subject. It is plain, therefore, that if, as you tell us, it be a sin in a state to patronise an institution which teaches religious error, either the Church of England or the Church of Scotland ought to be abolished. But will anybody even venture to affirm that either of those churches teaches truth without any mixture of error? Have there not long been in the Church of Scotland two very different schools of theology? During many years, Dr. Robertson, the head of the moderate party, and Dr. Erskine, the head of the Calvinistic party, preached under the same roof, one in the morning, the other in the evening. They preached two different religions, so different that the followers of Robertson thought the followers of Erskine fanatics, and the followers of Erskine thought the followers of Robertson Arians or worse. And is there no mixure of error in the doctrine taught by the clergy of the Church of England? Is not the whole country at this moment convulsed by disputes as to what the doctrine of the Church on some important subjects really is? I shall not take on myself to say who is right and who is wrong. But this I say with confidence, that, whether the Tractarians or the Evangelicals be in the right, many hundreds of those divines who every Sunday occupy the pulpits of our parish churches must be very much in the wrong.

Now, Sir, I see that many highly respectable persons, who think it a sin to contribute to the teaching of error at Maynooth College, think it not merely lawful, but a sacred duty, to contribute to the teaching of error in the other cases which I have mentioned. They know that our version of the Bible contains some error. Yet they subscribe to the Bible Society. They know that the Serampore translations contain a still greater quantity of error. Yet they give largely towards the printing and circulating of those translations. My honorable friend the Member for the University of Oxford will not deny that there is among the clergy of the Church of England a Puritan party, and also an Antipuritan party, and that one of these parties must teach some error. Yet he is constantly urging us to grant to this Church an additional endowment of I know not how many hundreds of thousands of pounds. He would doubtless defend himself by saying that nothing on earth is perfect; that the purest religious society must consist of human beings, and must have those defects which arise from human infirmities; and that the truths held by the established clergy, though not altogether unalloyed with error, are so precious, that it is better that they should be imparted to the people with the alloy than that they should not be imparted at all. Just so say I. I am sorry that we cannot teach pure truth to the Irish people. But I think it better that they should have important and salutary truth, polluted by some error, than that they should remain altogether uninstructed. I heartily wish that they were Protestants. But I had rather that they should be Roman Catholics than that they should have no religion at all. Would you, says one gentleman, teach the people to worship Jugernaut or Kalee? Certainly not. My argument leads to no such conclusion. The worship of Jugernaut and Kalee is a curse to mankind. It is much better that people should be without any religion than that they should believe in a religion which enjoins prostitution, suicide, robbery, assassination. But will any Protestant deny that it is better that the Irish should be Roman Catholics than that they should live and die like the beasts of the field, indulge their appetites without any religious restraint, suffer want and calamity without any religious consolation, and go to their graves without any religious hope? These considerations entirely satisfy my mind. Of course I would not propagate error for its own sake. To do so would be not merely wicked, but diabolical. But, in order that I may be able to propagate truth, I consent to propagate that portion of error which adheres to truth, and which cannot be separated from truth. I wish Christianity to have a great influence on the peasantry of Ireland. I see no probability that Christianity will have that influence except in one form. That form I consider as very corrupt. Nevertheless, the good seems to me greatly to predominate over the evil; and therefore, being unable to get the good alone, I am content to take the good and the evil together.

I now come to the third class of our opponents. I mean those who take their stand on the voluntary principle. I will not, on this occasion, inquire whether they are right in thinking that governments ought not to contribute to the support of any religion, true or false. For it seems to me that, even if I were to admit that the general rule is correctly laid down by them, the present case would be an exception to that rule. The question on which I am about to vote is not whether the State shall or shall not give any support to religion in Ireland. The State does give such support, and will continue to give such support, whatever may be the issue of this debate. The only point which we have now to decide is whether, while such support is given, it shall be given exclusively to the religion of the minority. Here is an island with a population of near eight millions, and with a wealthy established church, the members of which are little more than eight hundred thousand. There is an archbishop with ten thousand a year. If I recollect rightly, seventy thousand pounds are divided among twelve prelates. At the same time the Protestant dissenters in the north of Ireland receive, in another form, support from the State. But the great majority of the population, the poorest part of the population, the part of the population which is most in need of assistance, the part of the population which holds that faith for the propagation of which the tithes were originally set apart, and the church lands originally given, is left to maintain its own priests. Now is not this a case which stands quite by itself? And may not even those who hold the general proposition, that every man ought to pay his own spiritual pastor, yet vote, without any inconsistency, for this bill? I was astonished to hear the honorable Member for Shrewsbury[1] tell us that, if we make this grant, it will be impossible for us to resist the claims of any dissenting sect. He particularly mentioned the Wesleyan Methodists. Are the cases analogous? Is there the slightest resemblance between them? Let the honorable gentleman show me that of the sixteen millions of people who inhabit England thirteen millions are Wesleyan Methodists. Let him show me that the members of the Established Church in

[1] Mr. Disraeli.

England are only one tenth of the population. Let him show me that English dissenters who are not Wesleyan Methodists receive a Regium Donum. Let him show me that immense estates bequeathed to John Wesley for the propagation of Methodism have, by Act of Parliament, been taken from the Methodists and given to the Church. If he can show me this, I promise him that, whenever the Wesleyan Methodists shall ask for twenty-six thousand pounds a year to educate their ministers, I shall be prepared to grant their request. But neither the case of the Methodists, nor any other case which can be mentioned, resembles the case with which we have to do. Look round Europe, round the world, for a parallel; and you will look in vain. Indeed the state of things which exists in Ireland never could have existed had not Ireland been closely connected with a country, which possessed a great superiority of power, and which abused that superiority. The burden which we are now, I hope, about to lay on ourselves is but a small penalty for a great injustice. Were I a staunch voluntary, I should still feel that, while the church of eight hundred thousand people retains its great endowments, I should not be justified in refusing this small boon to the church of eight millions.

To sum up shortly what I have said; it is clear to me in the first place that, if we have no religious scruple about granting to this College nine thousand pounds for one year, we ought to have no religious scruple about granting twenty-six thousand pounds a year for an indefinite term.

Secondly, it seems to me that those persons who tell us that we ought never in any circumstances to contribute to the propagation of error do in fact lay down a rule which would altogether interdict the propagation of truth.

Thirdly, it seems to me that, even on the hypothesis that the voluntary principle is the sound principle, the present case is an excepted case, to which it would be unjust and unwise to apply that principle.

So much, Sir, as to this bill: and now let me add a few words about those by whom it has been framed and introduced. We were exhorted, on the first night of this debate, to vote against the bill, without inquiring into its merits, on the ground that, good or bad, it was proposed by men who could not honestly and honorably propose it. A similar appeal has been made to us this evening. In these circumstances, Sir, I must, not I hope from party spirit, not, I am sure, from personal animosity, but from a regard for the public interest, which must be injuriously affected by everything which tends to lower the character of public men, say plainly what I think of the conduct of Her Majesty's Ministers. Undoubtedly it is of the highest importance that we should legislate well. But it is also of the highest importance that those who govern us should have, and should be known to have, fixed principles, and should be guided by those principles both in office and in opposition. It is of the highest importance that the world should not be under the impression that a statesman is a person who, when he is out, will profess and promise anything in order to get in, and who, when he is in, will forget all that he professed and promised when he was out. I need not, I suppose, waste time in proving that a law may be in itself an exceedingly good law, and yet that it may be a law which, when viewed in connection with the former conduct of those who proposed it, may prove them to be undeserving of the confidence of their country. When this is the case, our course is clear. We ought to distinguish between the law and its authors. The law we ought, on account of its intrinsic merits, to support. Of the authors of the law, it may be our duty to speak in terms of censure.

In such terms I feel it to be my duty to speak of Her Majesty's present advisers. I have no personal hostility to any of them; and that political hostility which I do not disavow has never prevented me from doing justice to their abilities and virtues. I have always admitted, and I now most willingly admit, that the right honorable Baronet at the head of the Government possesses many of the qualities of an excellent minister, eminent talents for debate, eminent talents for business, great experience, great information, great skill in the management of this House. I will go further, and say that I give him full credit for a sincere desire to promote the welfare of his country. Nevertheless, it is impossible for me to deny that there is too much ground for the reproaches of those who, having, in spite of a bitter experience, a second time trusted him, now find themselves a second time deluded. I cannot but see that it has been too much his practice, when in opposition, to make use of passions with which he has not the slightest sympathy, and of prejudices which he regards with profound contempt. As soon as he is in power a change takes place. The instruments which have done his work are flung aside. The ladder by which he has climbed is kicked down. I am forced to say that the right honorable Baronet acts thus habitually and on system. The instance before us is not a solitary instance. I do not wish to dwell on the events which took place seventeen or eighteen years ago, on the language which the right honorable Baronet held about the Catholic question when he was out of power in 1827, and on the change which twelve months of power produced. I will only say that one such change was quite enough for one life. Again the right honorable Baronet was in opposition; and again he employed his old tactics. I will not minutely relate the history of the manœuvres by which the Whig Government was overthrown. It is enough to say that many powerful interests were united against that Government under the leading of the right honorable Baronet, and that of those interests there is not one which is not now disappointed and complaining. To confine my remarks to the subject immediately before us,—can any man deny that, of all the many cries which were raised against the late administration, that which most strongly stirred the public mind was the cry of No Popery? Is there a single gentleman in the House who doubts that, if, four years ago, my noble friend the Member for the City of London had proposed this bill, he would have been withstood by every member of the present Cabinet? Four years ago, Sir, we were discussing a very different bill. The party which was then in opposition, and which is now in place, was attempting to force through Parliament a law, which bore indeed a specious name, but of which the effect would have been to disfranchise the Roman Catholic electors of Ireland by tens of thousands. It was in vain that we argued, that we protested, that we asked for the delay of a single session, for delay till an inquiry could be made, for delay till a Committee should report. We were told that the case was one of extreme urgency, that every hour was precious, that the House must, without loss of time, be purged of the minions of Popery. These arts succeeded. A change of administration took place. The right honorable Baronet came into power. He has now been near four years in power. He has had a Parliament which would, beyond all doubt, have passed eagerly and gladly that Registration Bill which he and his colleagues had pretended that they thought indispensable to the welfare of the State. And where is that bill now? Flung away; condemned by its own authors; pronounced by them to be so oppressive, so inconsistent with all the principles of representative Government, that, though they had vehemently supported it when they were on your left hand, they could not think of proposing it from the Treasury Bench. And what substitute does the honorable Baronet give his followers to console them for the loss of their favourite Registration Bill? Even this bill for the endowment of Maynooth College. Was such a feat of legerdemain ever seen? And can we wonder that the eager, honest, hotheaded Protestants, who raised you to power in the confident hope that you would curtail the privileges of the Roman

Catholics, should stare and grumble when you propose to give public money to the Roman Catholics? Can we wonder that, from one end of the country to the other, everything should be ferment and uproar, that petitions should, night after night, whiten all our benches like a snowstorm? Can we wonder that the people out of doors should be exasperated by seeing the very men who, when we were in office, voted against the old grant to Maynooth, now pushed and pulled into the House by your whippers-in to vote for an increased grant? The natural consequences follow. All those fierce spirits, whom you hallooed on to harass us, now turn round and begin to worry you. The Orangeman raises his war-whoop: Exeter Hall sets up its bray: Mr. Macneile[1] shudders to see more costly cheer than ever provided for the priests of Baal at the table of the Queen; and the Protestant Operatives of Dublin call for impeachments in exceedingly bad English. But what did you expect? Did you think, when, to serve your turn, you called the Devil up, that it was as easy to lay him as to raise him? Did you think, when you went on, session after session, thwarting and reviling those whom you knew to be in the right, and flattering all the worst passions of those whom you knew to be in the wrong, that the day of reckoning would never come? It has come. There you sit, doing penance for the disingenuousness of years. If it be not so, stand up manfully, and clear your fame before the House and the country. Show us that some steady principle has guided your conduct with respect to Irish affairs? Show us how if you are honest in 1845, you can have been honest in 1841. Explain to us why, after having goaded Ireland to madness for the purpose of ingratiating yourselves with the English, you are now setting England on fire for the purpose of ingratiating yourselves with the Irish. Give us some reason which shall prove that the policy which you are following, as Ministers, is entitled to support, and which shall not equally prove you to have been the most factious and unprincipled opposition that ever this country saw.

But, Sir, am I, because I think thus of the conduct of Her Majesty's Ministers, to take the counsel of the honorable Member for Shrewsbury and to vote against their bill? Not so. I know well that the fate of this bill and the fate of the administration are in our hands. But far be it from us to imitate the arts by which we were overthrown. The spectacle exhibited on the bench opposite will do quite mischief enough. That mischief will not be lessened, but doubled, if there should be an answering display

[1] [Hugh McNeile finally became Dean of Ripon on the recommendation of Disraeli (1868), overriding the Queen's doubts.]

of inconsistency on this side of the House. If this bill, having been introduced by Tories, shall be rejected by Whigs, both the great parties in the State will be alike discredited. There will be one vast shipwreck of all the public character in the country. Therefore, making up my mind to sacrifices which are not unattended with pain, and repressing some feelings which stir strongly within me, I have determined to give my strenuous support to this bill. Yes, Sir, to this bill, and to every bill which shall seem to me likely to promote the real Union of Great Britain and Ireland, I will give my support, regardless of obloquy, regardless of the risk which I may run of losing my seat in Parliament. For such obloquy I have learned to consider as true glory; and as to my seat, I am determined that it never shall be held by an ignominious tenure; and I am sure that it can never be lost in a more honorable cause.

## THE TEN HOURS BILL

A SPEECH DELIVERED IN THE HOUSE OF COMMONS ON THE 22ND OF MAY, 1846

On the twenty-ninth of April, 1846, Mr. Fielden, Member for Oldham, moved the second reading of a bill for limiting the labour of young persons in factories to ten hours a day. The debate was adjourned, and was repeatedly resumed at long intervals. At length on the twenty-second of May the bill was rejected by 203 votes to 193.[1] On that day the following Speech was made.

IT is impossible, Sir, that I can remain silent after the appeal which has been made to me in so pointed a manner by my honorable friend the Member for Sheffield.[2] And, even if that appeal had not been made to me, I should have been very desirous to have an opportunity of explaining the grounds on which I shall vote for the second reading of this bill.

It is, I hope, unnecessary for me to assure my honorable friend that I utterly disapprove of those aspersions which have, both in this House and out of it, been thrown on the owners of factories. For that valuable class of men I have no feeling but respect and good will. I am convinced that with their interests the interests of the whole community, and especially of the labouring classes, are inseparably bound up. I can also with perfect sincerity declare that the vote which I shall give to-night will not be a factious vote. In no circumstances indeed should I think that the laws

[1] [The bill was carried in 1847.]     [2] Mr. Ward.

of political hostility warranted me in treating this question as a party question. But at the present moment I would much rather strengthen than weaken the hands of Her Majesty's Ministers.[1] It is by no means pleasant to me to be under the necessity of opposing them. I assure them, I assure my friends on this side of the House with whom I am so unfortunate as to differ, and especially my honorable friend the Member for Sheffield who spoke, I must say, in rather too plaintive a tone, that I have no desire to obtain credit for humanity at their expense. I fully believe that their feeling towards the labouring people is quite as kind as mine. There is no difference between us as to ends; there is an honest difference of opinion as to means: and we surely ought to be able to discuss the points on which we differ without one angry emotion or one acrimonious word.

The details of the bill, Sir, will be more conveniently and more regularly discussed when we consider it in Committee. Our business at present is with the principle: and the principle, we are told by many gentlemen of great authority, is unsound. In their opinion, neither this bill, nor any other bill regulating the hours of labour, can be defended. This, they say, is one of those matters about which we ought not to legislate at all; one of those matters which settle themselves far better than any government can settle them. Now it is most important that this point should be fully cleared up. We certainly ought not to usurp functions which do not properly belong to us: but, on the other hand, we ought not to abdicate functions which do properly belong to us. I hardly know which is the greater pest to society, a paternal government, that is to say a prying, meddlesome government, which intrudes itself into every part of human life, and which thinks that it can do everything for everybody better than anybody can do anything for himself; or a careless, lounging government, which suffers grievances, such as it could at once remove, to grow and multiply, and which to all complaint and remonstrance has only one answer: "We must let things alone: we must let things take their course: we must let things find their level." There is no more important problem in politics than to ascertain the just mean between these two most pernicious extremes, to draw correctly the line which divides those cases in which it is the duty of the State to interfere from those cases in which it is the duty of the State to abstain from interference. In old times the besetting sin of rulers was undoubtedly an inordinate disposition to meddle. The lawgiver

[1] [Because the bill repealing the Corn Laws was at that moment before the Lords.]

was always telling people how to keep their shops, how to till their fields, how to educate their children, how many dishes to have on their tables, how much a yard to give for the cloth which made their coats. He was always trying to remedy some evil which did not properly fall within his province; and the consequence was that he increased the evils which he attempted to remedy. He was so much shocked by the distress inseparable from scarcity that he made statutes against forestalling and regrating, and so turned the scarcity into a famine. He was so much shocked by the cunning and hardheartedness of moneylenders that he made laws against usury; and the consequence was that the borrower, who, if he had been left unprotected, would have got money at ten per cent., could hardly, when protected, get it at fifteen per cent. Some eminent political philosophers of the last century exposed with great ability the folly of such legislation, and, by doing so, rendered a great service to mankind. There has been a reaction, a reaction which has doubtless produced much good, but which, like most reactions, has not been without evils and dangers. Our statesmen cannot now be accused of being busybodies. But I am afraid that there is, even in some of the ablest and most upright among them, a tendency to the opposite fault. I will give an instance of what I mean. Fifteen years ago it became evident that railroads would soon, in every part of the kingdom, supersede to a great extent the old highways. The tracing of the new routes which were to join all the chief cities, ports, and naval arsenals of the island was a matter of the highest national importance. But, unfortunately, those who should have acted for the nation refused to interfere. Consequently, numerous questions which were really public, questions which concerned the public convenience, the public prosperity, the public security, were treated as private questions. That the whole society was interested in having a good system of internal communication seemed to be forgotten. The speculator who wanted a large dividend on his shares, the landowner who wanted a large price for his acres, obtained a full hearing. But nobody applied to be heard on behalf of the community. The effects of that great error we feel, and we shall not soon cease to feel. Unless I am greatly mistaken, we are in danger of committing to-night an error of the same kind. The honorable Member for Montrose[1] and my honorable friend the Member for Sheffield think that the question before us is merely a question between the old and the new theories of commerce. They cannot understand how any friend of free trade can wish the

[1] Mr. Hume.

Legislature to interfere between the capitalist and the labourer. They say, "You do not make a law to settle the price of gloves, or the texture of gloves, or the length of credit which the glover shall give. You leave it to him to determine whether he will charge high or low prices, whether he will use strong or flimsy materials, whether he will trust or insist on ready money. You acknowledge that these are matters which he ought to be left to settle with his customers, and that we ought not to interfere. It is possible that he may manage his shop ill. But it is certain that we shall manage it ill. On the same grounds on which you leave the seller of gloves and the buyer of gloves to make their own contract, you ought to leave the seller of labour and the buyer of labour to make their own contract."

I have a great respect, Sir, for those who reason thus: but I cannot see this matter in the light in which it appears to them; and, though I may distrust my own judgment, I must be guided by it. I am, I believe, as strongly attached as any member of this House to the principle of free trade, rightly understood. Trade, considered merely as trade, considered merely with reference to the pecuniary interest of the contracting parties, can hardly be too free. But there is a great deal of trade which cannot be considered merely as trade, and which affects higher than pecuniary interests. And to say that Government never ought to regulate such trade is a monstrous proposition, a proposition at which Adam Smith would have stood aghast. We impose some restrictions on trade for purposes of police. Thus, we do not suffer everybody who has a cab and a horse to ply for passengers in the streets of London. We do not leave the fare to be determined by the supply and the demand. We do not permit a driver to extort a guinea for going half a mile on a rainy day when there is no other vehicle on the stand. We impose some restrictions on trade for the sake of revenue. Thus, we forbid a farmer to cultivate tobacco on his own ground. We impose some restrictions on trade for the sake of national defence. Thus we compel a man who would rather be ploughing or weaving to go into the militia; and we fix the amount of pay which he shall receive without asking his consent. Nor is there in all this anything inconsistent with the soundest political economy. For the science of political economy teaches us only that we ought not on commercial grounds to interfere with the liberty of commerce; and we, in the cases which I have put, interfere with the liberty of commerce on higher than commercial grounds.

And now, Sir, to come closer to the case with which we have to deal, I say, first, that where the health of the community is concerned, it may be the duty of the State to interfere with the contracts of individuals; and to this proposition I am quite sure that Her Majesty's Government will cordially assent. I have just read a very interesting report signed by two members of that Government, the Duke of Buccleuch, and the noble earl who was lately Chief Commissioner of the Woods and Forests, and who is now Secretary for Ireland[1]; and, since that report was laid before the House, the noble earl himself has, with the sanction of the Cabinet, brought in a bill for the protection of the public health. By this bill it is provided that no man shall be permitted to build a house on his own land in any great town without giving notice to certain Commissioners. No man is to sink a cellar without the consent of these Commissioners. The house must not be of less than a prescribed width. No new house must be built without a drain. If an old house has no drain, the Commissioners may order the owner to make a drain. If he refuses, they make a drain for him, and send him in the bill. They may order him to whitewash his house. If he refuses, they may send people with pails and brushes to whitewash it for him, at his charge. Now, suppose that some proprietor of houses at Leeds or Manchester were to expostulate with the Government in the language in which the Government has expostulated with the supporters of this bill for the regulation of factories. Suppose that he were to say to the noble earl, "Your lordship professes to be a friend to free trade. Your lordship's doctrine is that everybody ought to be at liberty to buy cheap and to sell dear. Why then may not I run up a house as cheap as I can, and let my rooms as dear as I can? Your lordship does not like houses without drains. Do not take one of mine then. You think my bedrooms filthy. Nobody forces you to sleep in them. Use your own liberty: but do not restrain that of your neighbours. I can find many a family willing to pay a shilling a week for leave to live in what you call a hovel. And why am not I to take the shilling which they are willing to give me? And why are not they to have such shelter as, for that shilling, I can afford them? Why did you send a man without my consent to clean my house, and then force me to pay for what I never ordered? My tenants thought the house clean enough for them; or they would not have been my tenants: and, if they and I were satisfied, why did you, in direct defiance of all the principles of free trade, interfere between us?" This reasoning, Sir, is exactly of a piece with the reasoning of the honorable Member for Montrose, and of my

[1] The Earl of Lincoln.

honorable friend the Member for Sheffield. If the noble earl will allow me to make a defence for him, I believe that he would answer the objection thus: "I hold," he would say, "the sound doctrine of free trade. But your doctrine of free trade is an exaggeration, a caricature of the sound doctrine; and by exhibiting such caricature you bring discredit on the sound doctrine. We should have nothing to do with the contracts between you and your tenants, if those contracts affected only pecuniary interests. But higher than pecuniary interests are at stake. It concerns the commonwealth that the great body of the people should not live in a way which makes life wretched and short, which enfeebles the body and pollutes the mind. If, by living in houses which resemble hogstyes, great numbers of our countrymen have contracted the tastes of hogs, if they have become so familiar with filth and stench and contagion, that they burrow without reluctance in holes which would turn the stomach of any man of cleanly habits, that is only an additional proof that we have too long neglected our duties, and an additional reason for our now performing them."

Secondly, I say that where the public morality is concerned it may be the duty of the State to interfere with the contracts of individuals. Take the traffic in licentious books and pictures. Will anybody deny that the State may, with propriety, interdict that traffic? Or take the case of lotteries. I have, we will suppose, an estate for which I wish to get twenty thousand pounds. I announce my intention to issue a thousand tickets at twenty pounds each. The holder of the number which is first drawn is to have the estate. But the magistrate interferes; the contract between me and the purchasers of my tickets is annulled; and I am forced to pay a heavy penalty for having made such a contract. I appeal to the principle of free trade, as expounded by the honorable gentlemen the Members for Montrose and Sheffield. I say to you, the legislators who have restricted my liberty, "What business have you to interfere between a buyer and a seller? If you think the speculation a bad one, do not take tickets. But do not interdict other people from judging for themselves." Surely you would answer, "You would be right if this were a mere question of trade: but it is a question of morality. We prohibit you from disposing of your property in this particular mode, because it is a mode which tends to encourage a most pernicious habit of mind, a habit of mind incompatible with all the qualities on which the well being of individuals and of nations depends."

It must then, I think, be admitted that, where health is concerned, and where morality is concerned, the State is justified in interfering with the contracts of individuals. And, if this be admitted, it follows that the case with which we now have to do is a case for interference.

Will it be denied that the health of a large part of the rising generation may be seriously affected by the contracts which this bill is intended to regulate? Can any man who has read the evidence which is before us, can any man who has ever observed young people, can any man who remembers his own sensations when he was young, doubt that twelve hours a day of labour in a factory is too much for a lad of thirteen?

Or will it be denied that this is a question in which public morality is concerned? Can any one doubt,—none, I am sure, of my friends around me doubts,—that education is a matter of the highest importance to the virtue and happiness of a people? Now we know that there can be no education without leisure. It is evident that, after deducting from the day twelve hours for labour in a factory, and the additional hours necessary for exercise, refreshment, and repose, there will not remain time enough for education.

I have now, I think, shown that this bill is not in principle objectionable; and yet I have not touched the strongest part of our case. I hold that, where public health is concerned, and where public morality is concerned, the State may be justified in regulating even the contracts of adults. But we propose to regulate only the contracts of infants. Now was there ever a civilised society in which the contracts of infants were not under some regulation? Is there a single member of this House who will say that a wealthy minor of thirteen ought to be at perfect liberty to execute a conveyance of his estate, or to give a bond for fifty thousand pounds? If anybody were so absurd as to say, "What has the Legislature to do with the matter? Why cannot you leave trade free? Why do you pretend to understand the boy's interest better than he understands it?"—you would answer; "When he grows up, he may squander his fortune away if he likes: but at present the State is his guardian; and he shall not ruin himself till he is old enough to know what he is about." The minors whom we wish to protect have not indeed large property to throw away: but they are not the less our wards. Their only inheritance, the only fund to which they must look for their subsistence through life, is the sound mind in the sound body. And is it not our duty to prevent them from wasting that most precious wealth before they know its value?

But, it is said, this bill, though it directly limits only the labour of infants, will, by an indirect operation, limit also the labour of adults. Now, Sir, though I am not prepared to vote for a bill directly limiting the labour of adults, I will plainly say that I do not think that the limitation of the labour of adults would necessarily produce all those frightful consequences which we have heard predicted. You cheer me in very triumphant tones, as if I had uttered some monstrous paradox. Pray, does it not occur to any of you that the labour of adults is now limited in this country? Are you not aware that you are living in a society in which the labour of adults is limited to six days in seven? It is you, not I, who maintain a paradox opposed to the opinions and the practices of all nations and ages. Did you ever hear of a single civilised State since the beginning of the world in which a certain portion of time was not set apart for the rest and recreation of adults by public authority? In general, this arrangement has been sanctioned by religion. The Egyptians, the Jews, the Greeks, the Romans, had their holidays: the Hindoo has his holidays: the Mussulman has his holidays: there are holidays in the Greek Church, holidays in the Church of Rome, holidays in the Church of England. Is it not amusing to hear a gentleman pronounce with confidence that any legislation which limits the labour of adults must produce consequences fatal to society, without once reflecting that in the society in which he lives, and in every other society that exists, or ever has existed, there has been such legislation without any evil consequence? It is true that a Puritan Government in England, and an Atheistical Government in France, abolished the old holidays as superstitious. But those governments felt it to be absolutely necessary to institute new holidays. Civil festivals were substituted for religious festivals. You will find among the ordinances of the Long Parliament a law providing that, in exchange for the days of rest and amusement which the people had been used to enjoy at Easter, Whitsuntide, and Christmas, the second Tuesday of every month should be given to the working man, and that any apprentice who was forced to work on the second Tuesday of any month might have his master up before a magistrate. The French Jacobins decreed that the Sunday should no longer be a day of rest; but they instituted another day of rest, the Decade. They swept away the holidays of the Roman Catholic Church; but they instituted another set of holidays, the Sansculottides, one sacred to Genius, one to Industry, one to Opinion, and so on. I say, therefore, that the practice of limiting by law the time of the labour of adults is

M—25

so far from being, as some gentlemen seem to think, an unheard of and monstrous practice, that it is a practice as universal as cookery, as the wearing of clothes, as the use of domestic animals.

And has this practice been proved by experience to be pernicious? Let us take the instance with which we are most familiar. Let us inquire what has been the effect of those laws which, in our own country, limit the labour of adults to six days in every seven. It is quite unnecessary to discuss the question whether Christians be or be not bound by a divine command to observe the Sunday. For it is evident that, whether our weekly holiday be of divine or of human institution, the effect on the temporal interests of society will be exactly the same. Now, is there a single argument in the whole Speech of my honorable friend the Member for Sheffield which does not tell just as strongly against the laws which enjoin the observance of the Sunday as against the bill on our table? Surely, if his reasoning is good for hours, it must be equally good for days.

He says, "If this limitation be good for the working people, rely on it that they will find it out, and that they will themselves establish it without any law." Why not reason in the same way about the Sunday? Why not say, "If it be a good thing for the people of London to shut their shops one day in seven, they will find it out, and will shut their shops without a law?" Sir, the answer is obvious. I have no doubt that, if you were to poll the shopkeepers of London, you would find an immense majority, probably a hundred to one, in favour of closing shops on the Sunday; and yet it is absolutely necessary to give to the wish of the majority the sanction of a law; for, if there were no such law, the minority, by opening their shops, would soon force the majority to do the same.

But, says my honorable friend, you cannot limit the labour of adults unless you fix wages. This proposition he lays down repeatedly, assures us that it is incontrovertible, and indeed seems to think it self-evident; for he has not taken the trouble to prove it. Sir, my answer shall be very short. We have, during many centuries, limited the labour of adults to six days in seven; and yet we have not fixed the rate of wages.

But, it is said, you cannot legislate for all trades; and therefore you had better not legislate for any. Look at the poor sempstress. She works far longer and harder than the factory child. She sometimes plies her needle fifteen, sixteen hours in the twenty-four. See how the housemaid works, up at six every morning, and toiling up stairs and down stairs till near midnight. You own that you cannot do anything for the sempstress and the house-maid. Why then trouble yourself about the factory child? Take care that by protecting one class you do not aggravate the hardships endured by the classes which you cannot protect. Why, Sir, might not all this be said, word for word, against the laws which enjoin the observance of the Sunday? There are classes of people whom you cannot prevent from working on the Sunday. There are classes of people whom, if you could, you ought not to prevent from working on the Sunday. Take the sempstress, of whom so much has been said. You cannot keep her from sewing and hemming all Sunday in her garret. But you do not think that a reason for suffering Covent Garden Market, and Leadenhall Market, and Smithfield Market, and all the shops from Mile End to Hyde Park to be open all Sunday. Nay, these factories about which we are debating,—does anybody propose that they shall be allowed to work all Sunday? See then how inconsistent you are. You think it unjust to limit the labour of the factory child to ten hours a day, because you cannot limit the labour of the sempstress. And yet you see no injustice in limiting the labour of the factory child, aye, and of the factory man, to six days in the week, though you cannot limit the labour of the sempstress.

But, you say, by protecting one class we shall aggravate the sufferings of all the classes which we cannot protect. You say this; but you do not prove it; and all experience proves the contrary. We interfere on the Sunday to close the shops. We do not interfere with the labour of the housemaid. But are the house-maids of London more severely worked on the Sunday than on other days? The fact notoriously is the reverse. For your legislation keeps the public feeling in a right state, and thus protects indirectly those whom it cannot protect directly.

Will my honorable friend the Member for Sheffield maintain that the law which limits the number of working days has been injurious to the working population? I am certain that he will not. How then can he expect me to believe that a law which limits the number of working hours must necessarily be injurious to the working population? Yet he and those who agree with him seem to wonder at our dulness because we do not at once admit the truth of the doctrine which they propound on this subject. They reason thus. We cannot reduce the number of hours of labour in factories without reducing the amount of production. We cannot reduce the amount of production without reducing the remuneration of the labourer. Meanwhile, foreigners, who are at liberty to work till they drop down dead at their looms, will soon beat us out of all the markets of the world. Wages will go down fast. The condition of our working people will be far worse than it is; and our unwise interference will, like the unwise interference of our ancestors with the dealings of the corn factor and the money lender, increase the distress of the very class which we wish to relieve.

Now, Sir, I fully admit that there might be such a limitation of the hours of labour as would produce the evil consequences with which we are threatened: and this, no doubt, is a very good reason for legislating with great caution, for feeling our way, for looking well to all the details of this bill. But it is certainly not true that every limitation of the hours of labour must produce these consequences. And I am, I must say, surprised when I hear men of eminent ability and knowledge lay down the proposition that a diminution of the time of labour must be followed by a diminution of the wages of labour, as a proposition universally true, as a proposition capable of being strictly demonstrated, as a proposition about which there can be no more doubt than about any theorem in Euclid. Sir, I deny the truth of the proposition; and for this plain reason. We have already, by law, greatly reduced the time of labour in the factories. Thirty years ago, the late Sir Robert Peel[1] told the House that it was a common practice to make children of eight years of age toil in mills fifteen hours a day. A law has since been made which prohibits persons under eighteen years of age from working in mills more than twelve hours a day. That law was opposed on exactly the same grounds on which the bill before us is opposed. Parliament was told then, as it is told now, that with the time of labour the quantity of production would decrease, that with the quantity of production the wages would decrease, that our manufacturers would be unable to contend with foreign manufacturers, and that the condition of the labouring population instead of being made better by the interference of the Legislature would be made worse. Read over those debates; and you may imagine that you are reading the debate of this evening. Parliament disregarded these prophecies. The time of labour was limited. Have wages fallen? Has the cotton trade left Manchester for France or Germany? Has the condition of the working people become more miserable? Is it not universally acknowledged that the evils which were so confidently predicted have not come to pass? Let me be understood. I am not arguing that, because a law which reduced the hours of daily labour from fifteen to twelve did not reduce wages, a law reducing those hours

[1] [The first Factory Act was introduced by Peel's father in 1802.]

from twelve to ten or eleven cannot possibly reduce wages. That would be very inconclusive reasoning. What I say is this, that, since a law which reduced the hours of daily labour from fifteen to twelve has not reduced wages, the proposition that every reduction of the hours of labour must necessarily reduce wages is a false proposition. There is evidently some flaw in that demonstration which my honorable friend thinks so complete; and what the flaw is we may perhaps discover if we look at the analogous case to which I have so often referred.

Sir, exactly three hundred years ago, great religious changes were taking place in England. Much was said and written, in that inquiring and innovating age, about the question whether Christians were under a religious obligation to rest from labour on one day in the week; and it is well known that the chief Reformers, both here and on the continent, denied the existence of any such obligation. Suppose then that, in 1546, Parliament had made a law that there should thenceforth be no distinction between the Sunday and any other day. Now, Sir, our opponents, if they are consistent with themselves, must hold that such a law would have immensely increased the wealth of the country and the remuneration of the working man. What an effect, if their principles be sound, must have been produced by the addition of one sixth to the time of labour! What an increase of production! What a rise of wages! How utterly unable must the foreign artisan, who still had his days of festivity and of repose, have found himself to maintain a competition with a people whose shops were open, whose markets were crowded, whose spades, and axes, and planes, and hods, and anvils, and looms were at work from morning till night on three hundred and sixty-five days a year! The Sundays of three hundred years make up fifty years of our working days. We know what the industry of fifty years can do. We know what marvels the industry of the last fifty years has wrought. The arguments of my honorable friend irresistibly lead us to this conclusion, that if, during the last three centuries, the Sunday had not been observed as a day of rest, we should have been a far richer, a far more highly civilised people than we now are, and that the labouring class especially would have been far better off than at present. But does he, does any Member of the House, seriously believe that this would have been the case? For my own part, I have not the smallest doubt that, if we and our ancestors had, during the last three centuries, worked just as hard on the Sundays as on the week days, we should have been at this moment a poorer people and a less civilised people than we are; that there would have been less production than there has been, that the wages of the labourer would have been lower than they are, and that some other nation would have been now making cotton stuffs and woollen stuffs and cutlery for the whole world.

Of course, Sir, I do not mean to say that a man will not produce more in a week by working seven days than by working six days. But I very much doubt whether, at the end of a year, he will generally have produced more by working seven days a week than by working six days a week; and I firmly believe that, at the end of twenty years, he will have produced much less by working seven days a week than by working six days a week. In the same manner I do not deny that a factory child will produce more, in a single day, by working twelve hours than by working ten hours, and by working fifteen hours than by working twelve hours. But I do deny that a great society in which children work fifteen, or even twelve hours a day, will, in the lifetime of a generation, produce as much as if those children had worked less. If we consider man merely in a commercial point of view, if we consider him merely as a machine for the production of worsted and calico, let us not forget what a piece of mechanism he is, how fearfully and wonderfully made. We do not treat a fine horse or a sagacious dog exactly as we treat a spinning jenny. Nor will any slaveholder, who has sense enough to know his own interest, treat his human chattels exactly as he treats his horses and his dogs. And would you treat the free labourer of England like a mere wheel or pulley? Rely on it that intense labour, beginning too early in life, continued too long every day, stunting the growth of the body, stunting the growth of the mind, leaving no time for healthful exercise, leaving no time for intellectual culture, must impair all those high qualities which have made our country great. Your overworked boys will become a feeble and ignoble race of men, the parents of a more feeble and more ignoble progeny; nor will it be long before the deterioration of the labourer will injuriously affect those very interests to which his physical and moral energies have been sacrificed. On the other hand, a day of rest recurring in every week, two or three hours of leisure, exercise, innocent amusement or useful study, recurring every day, must improve the whole man, physically, morally, intellectually; and the improvement of the man will improve all that the man produces. Why is it, Sir, that the Hindoo cotton manufacturer[1], close to whose door

[1] [In Chapter III of his History, Macaulay records that in 1680, Mr. Bassett, M.P. for Barnstaple, pointed out that the English workman at a shilling a day could not compete with the Bengalee at a copper piece.]

the cotton grows, cannot, in the bazaar of his own town, maintain a competition with the English cotton manufacturer, who has to send thousands of miles for the raw material, and who has then to send the wrought material thousands of miles to market? You will say that it is owing to the excellence of our machinery. And to what is the excellence of our machinery owing? How many of the improvements which have been made in our machinery do we owe to the ingenuity and patient thought of working men? Adam Smith tells us in the first chapter of his great work, that you can hardly go to a factory without seeing some very pretty machine, —that is his expression,—devised by some labouring man. Hargraves, the inventor of the spinning jenny, was a common artisan. Crompton, the inventor of the mule jenny, was a working man. How many hours of the labour of children would do so much for our manufacturers as one of these improvements has done? And in what sort of society are such improvements most likely to be made? Surely in a society in which the faculties of the working people are developed by education. How long will you wait before any negro, working under the lash in Louisiana, will contrive a better machinery for squeezing the sugar canes? My honorable friend seems to me, in all his reasonings about the commercial prosperity of nations, to overlook entirely the chief cause on which that prosperity depends. What is it, Sir, that makes the great difference between country and country? Not the exuberance of soil; not the mildness of climate; not mines, nor havens, nor rivers. These things are indeed valuable when put to their proper use by human intelligence: but human intelligence can do much without them; and they without human intelligence can do nothing. They exist in the highest degree in regions of which the inhabitants are few, and squalid, and barbarous, and naked, and starving; while on sterile rocks, amidst unwholesome marshes, and under inclement skies, may be found immense populations, well fed, well lodged, well clad, well governed. Nature meant Egypt and Sicily to be the gardens of the world. They once were so. Is it anything in the earth or in the air that makes Scotland more prosperous than Egypt, that makes Holland more prosperous than Sicily? No; it was the Scotchman that made Scotland: it was the Dutchman that made Holland. Look at North America. Two centuries ago the sites on which now arise mills, and hotels, and banks, and colleges, and churches, and the Senate Houses of flourishing commonwealths, were deserts abandoned to the panther and the bear. What has made the change? Was it the rich mould, or the redundant rivers? No:

the prairies were as fertile, the Ohio and the Hudson were as broad and as full then as now. Was the improvement the effect of some great transfer of capital from the old world to the new? No: the emigrants generally carried out with them no more than a pittance; but they carried out the English heart, and head, and arm; and the English heart and head and arm turned the wilderness into cornfield and orchard, and the huge trees of the primeval forest into cities and fleets. Man, man is the great instrument that produces wealth. The natural difference between Campania and Spitzbergen is trifling when compared with the difference between a country inhabited by men full of bodily and mental vigour, and a country inhabited by men sunk in bodily and mental decrepitude. Therefore it is that we are not poorer but richer, because we have, through many ages, rested from our labour one day in seven. That day is not lost. While industry is suspended, while the plough lies in the furrow, while the Exchange is silent, while no smoke ascends from the factory, a process is going on quite as important to the wealth of nations as any process which is performed on more busy days. Man, the machine of machines, the machine compared with which all the contrivances of the Watts and the Arkwrights are worthless, is repairing and winding up, so that he returns to his labours on the Monday with clearer intellect, with livelier spirits, with renewed corporal vigour. Never will I believe that what makes a population stronger, and healthier, and wiser, and better, can ultimately make it poorer. You try to frighten us by telling us that, in some German factories, the young work seventeen hours in the twenty-four, that they work so hard that among thousands there is not one who grows to such a stature that he can be admitted into the army; and you ask whether, if we pass this bill, we can possibly hold our own against such competition as this? Sir, I laugh at the thought of such competition. If ever we are forced to yield the foremost place among commercial nations, we shall yield it, not to a race of degenerate dwarfs, but to some people preeminently vigorous in body and in mind.

For these reasons, Sir, I approve of the principle of this bill, and shall, without hesitation, vote for the second reading. To what extent we ought to reduce the hours of labour is a question of more difficulty. I think that we are in the situation of a physician who has satisfied himself that there is a disease, and that there is a specific medicine for the disease, but who is not certain what quantity of that medicine the patient's constitution will bear. Such a physician would probably administer his remedy by small doses, and carefully watch its operation. I cannot help thinking that, by at once reducing the hours of labour from twelve to ten, we should hazard too much. The change is great, and ought to be cautiously and gradually made. Suppose that there should be an immediate fall of wages, which is not impossible. Might there not be a violent reaction? Might not the public take up a notion that our legislation had been erroneous in principle, though, in truth, our error would have been an error, not of principle, but merely of degree? Might not Parliament be induced to retrace its steps? Might we not find it difficult to maintain even the present limitation? The wisest course would, in my opinion, be to reduce the hours of labour from twelve to eleven, to observe the effect of that experiment, and if, as I hope and believe, the result should be satisfactory, then to make a further reduction from eleven to ten. This is a question, however, which will be with more advantage considered when we are in Committee.

One word, Sir, before I sit down, in answer to my noble friend near me.[1] He seems to think that this bill is ill timed. I own that I cannot agree with him. We carried up on Monday last to the bar of the Lords a bill which will remove the most hateful and pernicious restriction that ever was laid on trade. Nothing can be more proper than to apply, in the same week, a remedy to a great evil of a directly opposite kind. As lawgivers, we have two great faults to confess and to repair. We have done that which we ought not to have done. We have left undone that which we ought to have done. We have regulated that which we should have left to regulate itself. We have left unregulated that which we were bound to regulate. We have given to some branches of industry a protection which has proved their bane. We have withheld from public health and public morals the protection which was their due. We have prevented the labourer from buying his loaf where he could get it cheapest; but we have not prevented him from ruining his body and mind by premature and immoderate toil. I hope that we have seen the last both of a vicious system of interference and of a vicious system of non-interference, and that our poorer countrymen will no longer have reason to attribute their sufferings either to our meddling or to our neglect.

[1] Lord Morpeth.

# EDUCATION

A SPEECH DELIVERED IN THE HOUSE OF COMMONS ON THE 19TH OF APRIL, 1847

In the year 1847 the Government asked from the House of Commons a grant of one hundred thousand pounds for the education of the people. On the nineteenth of April, Lord John Russell, having explained the reasons for this application, moved the order of the day for a Committee of Supply. Mr. Thomas Duncombe, Member for Finsbury, moved the following amendment:

"That previous to any grant of public money being assented to by this House, for the purpose of carrying out the scheme of national education, as developed in the Minutes of the Committee of Council on Education in August and December last, which minutes have been presented to both Houses of Parliament by command of Her Majesty, a select Committee be appointed to inquire into the justice and expediency of such a scheme, and its probable annual cost; also to inquire whether the regulations attached thereto do not unduly increase the influence of the Crown, invade the constitutional functions of Parliament, and interfere with the religious convictions and civil rights of Her Majesty's subjects."

In opposition to this amendment, the following speech was made. After a debate of three nights, Mr. Thomas Duncombe obtained permission to withdraw the latter part of his amendment. The first part was put, and negatived by 372 votes to 47.

You will not wonder, Sir, that I am desirous to catch your eye this evening. The first duty which I performed, as a Member of the Committee of Council[1] which is charged with the superintendence of public instruction, was to give my hearty assent to the plan which the honorable Member for Finsbury calls on the House to condemn. I am one of those who have been accused in every part of the kingdom, and who are now accused in Parliament, of aiming, under specious pretences, a blow at the civil and religious liberties of the people. It is natural therefore that I should seize the earliest opportunity of vindicating myself from so grave a charge.

The honorable Member for Finsbury must excuse me if, in the remarks which I have to offer to the House, I should not follow very closely the order of his speech. The truth is that a mere answer to his speech would be no defence of myself or of my colleagues. I am surprised, I own, that a man of his acuteness

[1] [Macaulay was Paymaster-General (a sinecure office) in Lord John Russell's administration 1846–7; he was then defeated at the General Election and retired from active public life.]

778

and ability should, on such an occasion, have made such a speech. The country is excited from one end to the other by a great question of principle. On that question the Government has taken one side. The honorable Member stands forth as the chosen and trusted champion of a great party which takes the other side. We expected to hear from him a full exposition of the views of those in whose name he speaks. But, to our astonishment, he has scarcely even alluded to the controversy which has divided the whole nation. He has entertained us with sarcasms and personal anecdotes: he has talked much about matters of mere detail: but I must say that, after listening with close attention to all that he has said, I am quite unable to discover whether, on the only important point which is in issue, he agrees with us or with that large and active body of Nonconformists which is diametrically opposed to us. He has sate down without dropping one word from which it is possible to discover whether he thinks that education is or that it is not a matter with which the State ought to interfere. Yet that is the question about which the whole nation has, during several weeks, been writing, reading, speaking, hearing, thinking, petitioning, and on which it is now the duty of Parliament to pronounce a decision. That question once settled, there will be, I believe, very little room for dispute. If it be not competent to the State to interfere with the education of the people, the mode of interference recommended by the Committee of Council must of course be condemned. If it be the right and the duty of the State to make provision for the education of the people, the objections made to our plan will, in a very few words, be shown to be frivolous.

I shall take a course very different from that which has been taken by the honorable gentleman. I shall in the clearest manner profess my opinion on that great question of principle which he has studiously evaded; and for my opinion I shall give what seem to me to be unanswerable reasons.

I believe, Sir, that it is the right and the duty of the State to provide means of education for the common people. This proposition seems to me to be implied in every definition that has ever yet been given of the functions of a government. About the extent of those functions there has been much difference of opinion among ingenious men. There are some who hold that it is the business of a government to meddle with every part of the system of human life, to regulate trade by bounties and prohibitions, to regulate expenditure by sumptuary laws, to regulate literature by a censorship, to regulate religion by an inquisition. Others go to the opposite extreme, and assign to Government a very narrow sphere of action. But the very narrowest sphere that ever was assigned to governments by any school of political philosophy is quite wide enough for my purpose. On one point all the disputants are agreed. They unanimously acknowledge that it is the duty of every government to take order for giving security to the persons and property of the members of the community.

This being admitted, can it be denied that the education of the common people is a most effectual means of securing our persons and our property? Let Adam Smith answer that question for me. His authority, always high, is, on this subject, entitled to peculiar respect, because he extremely disliked busy, prying, interfering governments. He was for leaving literature, arts, sciences, to take care of themselves. He was not friendly to ecclesiastical establishments. He was of opinion, that the State ought not to meddle with the education of the rich. But he has expressly told us that a distinction is to be made, particularly in a commercial and highly civilised society, between the education of the rich and the education of the poor. The education of the poor, he says, is a matter which deeply concerns the commonwealth. Just as the magistrate ought to interfere for the purpose of preventing the leprosy from spreading among the people, he ought to interfere for the purpose of stopping the progress of the moral distempers which are inseparable from ignorance. Nor can this duty be neglected without danger to the public peace. If you leave the multitude uninstructed, there is serious risk that religious animosities may produce the most dreadful disorders. The most dreadful disorders! Those are Adam Smith's own words; and prophetic words they were. Scarcely had he given this warning to our rulers when his prediction was fulfilled in a manner never to be forgotten. I speak of the No Popery riots of 1780. I do not know that I could find in all history a stronger proof of the proposition, that the ignorance of the common people makes the property, the limbs, the lives of all classes insecure. Without the shadow of a grievance, at the summons of a madman, a hundred thousand people rise in insurrection. During a whole week, there is anarchy in the greatest and wealthiest of European cities. The parliament is besieged. Your predecessor sits trembling in his chair, and expects every moment to see the door beaten in by the ruffians whose roar he hears all round the house. The peers are pulled out of their coaches. The bishops in their lawn are forced to fly over the tiles. The chapels of foreign ambassadors, buildings made sacred by the law of nations, are destroyed. The house of the Chief Justice is demolished. The little children of the Prime Minister are taken out of their beds and laid in their night clothes on the table of the Horse Guards, the only safe asylum from the fury of the rabble. The prisons are opened. Highwaymen, housebreakers, murderers, come forth to swell the mob by which they have been set free. Thirty-six fires are blazing at once in London. Then comes the retribution. Count up all the wretches who were shot, who were hanged, who were crushed, who drank themselves to death at the rivers of gin which ran down Holborn Hill; and you will find that battles have been lost and won with a smaller sacrifice of life. And what was the cause of this calamity, a calamity which, in the history of London ranks with the great plague and the great fire? The cause was the ignorance of a population which had been suffered, in the neighbourhood of palaces, theatres, temples, to grow up as rude and stupid as any tribe of tattooed cannibals in New Zealand, I might say as any drove of beasts in Smithfield Market.

The instance is striking: but it is not solitary. To the same cause are to be ascribed the riots of Nottingham, the sack of Bristol, all the outrages of Ludd, and Swing, and Rebecca, beautiful and costly machinery broken to pieces in Yorkshire, barns and haystacks blazing in Kent, fences and buildings pulled down in Wales. Could such things have been done in a country in which the mind of the labourer had been opened by education, in which he had been taught to find pleasure in the exercise of his intellect, taught to revere his Maker, taught to respect legitimate authority, and taught at the same time to seek the redress of real wrongs by peaceful and constitutional means?

This then is my argument. It is the duty of Government to protect our persons and property from danger. The gross ignorance of the common people is a principal cause of danger to our persons and property. Therefore, it is the duty of the Government to take care that the common people shall not be grossly ignorant.

And what is the alternative? It is universally allowed that, by some means, Government must protect our persons and property. If you take away education, what means do you leave? You leave means such as only necessity can justify, means which inflict a fearful amount of pain, not only on the guilty, but on the innocent who are connected with the guilty. You leave guns and bayonets, stocks and whipping-posts, treadmills, solitary cells, penal colonies, gibbets. See then how the case stands. Here is an end which, as we all agree, governments are bound to attain. There are only two ways of attaining it. One of those ways is by making men better, and wiser, and happier. The other way is by making them infamous and miserable. Can it be doubted which way we ought to prefer? Is it not strange, is it not almost incredible, that pious and benevolent men should gravely propound the doctrine that the magistrate is bound to punish and at the same time bound not to teach? To me it seems quite clear that whoever has a right to hang has a right to educate. Can we think without shame and remorse that more than half of those wretches who have been tied up at Newgate in our time might have been living happily, that more than half of those who are now in our gaols might have been enjoying liberty and using that liberty well, that such a hell on earth as Norfolk Island need never have existed, if we had expended in training honest men but a small part of what we have expended in hunting and torturing rogues.

I would earnestly entreat every gentleman to look at a report which is contained in the Appendix to the First Volume of the Minutes of the Committee of Council. I speak of the report made by Mr. Seymour Tremenheare on the state of that part of Monmouthshire which is inhabited by a population chiefly employed in mining. He found that, in this district, towards the close of 1839, out of eleven thousand children who were of an age to attend school, eight thousand never went to any school at all, and that most of the remaining three thousand might almost as well have gone to no school as to the squalid hovels in which men who ought themselves to have been learners pretended to teach. In general these men had only one qualification for their employment; and that was their utter unfitness for every other employment. They were disabled miners, or broken hucksters. In their schools all was stench, and noise, and confusion. Now and then the clamour of the boys was silenced for two minutes by the furious menaces of the master; but it soon broke out again. The instruction given was of the lowest kind. Not one school in ten was provided with a single map. This is the way in which you suffered the minds of a great population to be formed. And now for the effects of your negligence. The barbarian inhabitants of this region rise in an insane rebellion against the Government. They come pouring down their valleys to Newport. They fire on the Queen's troops. They wound a magistrate. The soldiers fire in return; and too many of these wretched men pay with their lives the penalty of their crime. But is the crime theirs alone? Is it strange that they should listen to the only teaching that they had? How can you, who took no pains to instruct them, blame them for giving ear to the demagogue who took pains to delude them? We put them down, of course. We punished them. We had no choice. Order must be maintained; property must be protected; and, since we had omitted to take the best way of keeping these people quiet, we were under the necessity of keeping them quiet by the dread of the sword and the halter. But could any necessity be more cruel? And which of us would run the risk of being placed under such necessity a second time?

I say, therefore, that the education of the people is not only a means, but the best means, of attaining that which all allow to be a chief end of government; and, if this be so, it passes my faculties to understand how any man can gravely contend that Government has nothing to do with the education of the people.

My confidence in my opinion is strengthened when I recollect that I hold that opinion in common with all the greatest lawgivers, statesmen, and political philosophers of all nations and ages, with all the most illustrious champions of civil and spiritual freedom, and especially with those men whose names were once held in the highest veneration by the Protestant Dissenters of England. I might cite many of the most venerable names of the old world; but I would rather cite the example of that country which the supporters of the Voluntary system here are always recommending to us as a pattern. Go back to the days when the little society which has expanded into the opulent and enlightened commonwealth of Massachusetts began to exist. Our modern Dissenters will scarcely, I think, venture to speak contumeliously of those Puritans whose spirit Laud and his High Commission Court could not subdue, of those Puritans who were willing to leave home and kindred, and all the comforts and refinements of civilised life, to cross the ocean, to fix their abode in forests among wild beasts and wild men, rather than commit the sin of performing, in the House of God, one gesture which they believed to be displeasing to Him. Did those brave exiles think it inconsistent with civil or religious freedom that the State should take charge of the education of the people? No, Sir; one of the earliest laws enacted by the Puritan colonists was that every township, as soon as the Lord had increased it to the number of fifty houses, should appoint one to teach all children to write and read, and that every township of a hundred houses should set up a grammar school. Nor have the descendants of those who made this law ever ceased to hold that the public authorities were bound to provide the means of public instruction. Nor is this doctrine confined to New England. "Educate the people" was the first admonition addressed by Penn to the colony which he founded. "Educate the people" was the legacy of Washington to the nation which he had saved. "Educate the people" was the unceasing exhortation of Jefferson; and I quote Jefferson with peculiar pleasure, because, of all the eminent men that have ever lived, Adam Smith himself not excepted, Jefferson was the one who most abhorred everything like meddling on the part of governments. Yet the chief business of his later years was to establish a good system of State education in Virginia.

And, against such authority as this, what have you who take the other side to show? Can you mention a single great philosopher, a single man distinguished by his zeal for liberty, humanity, and truth, who, from the beginning of the world down to the time of this present Parliament, ever held your doctrines? You can oppose to the unanimous voice of all the wise and good, of all ages, and of both hemispheres, nothing but a clamour which was first heard a few months ago, a clamour in which you cannot join without condemning, not only all whose memory you profess to hold in reverence, but even your former selves.

This new theory of politics has at least the merit of originality. It may be fairly stated thus. All men have hitherto been utterly in the wrong as to the nature and objects of civil government. The great truth, hidden from every preceding generation, and at length revealed, in the year 1846, to some highly respectable ministers and elders of dissenting congregations, is this. Government is simply a great hangman. Government ought to do nothing except by harsh and degrading means. The one business of Government is to handcuff, and lock up, and scourge, and shoot, and stab, and strangle. It is odious tyranny in a government to attempt to prevent crime by informing the understanding and elevating the moral feeling of a people. A statesman may see hamlets turned, in the course of one generation, into great seaport towns and manufacturing towns. He may know that on the character of the vast population which is collected in those wonderful towns, depends the prosperity, the peace, the very existence of society. But he must not think of forming that character. He is an enemy of public liberty if he attempts to prevent those hundreds of thousands of his countrymen from becoming mere Yahoos. He may, indeed, build barrack after barrack to overawe them. If they break out into insurrection, he may send cavalry to sabre them: he may mow them down with grape shot: he may hang them, draw them, quarter them, anything but teach them. He may see, and may shudder as he sees, throughout large rural districts, millions of infants growing up from infancy to manhood as ignorant, as mere slaves of sensual appetite, as the beasts that perish. No matter. He is a traitor to the cause of civil and religious freedom if he does not look on with folded arms, while absurd hopes and evil passions ripen in that rank soil. He must wait for the day of his harvest. He must wait till the Jaquerie comes, till farm houses are burning, till threshing machines are broken in pieces; and then begins his business, which is simply to send one poor ignorant savage to the county gaol, and another to the antipodes, and a third to the gallows.

Such, Sir, is the new theory of government which was first propounded, in the year 1846, by some men of high note among the Nonconformists of England. It is difficult to understand how men of excellent abilities and excellent intentions,—and there are, I readily admit, such men among those who hold this theory,— can have fallen into so absurd and pernicious an error. One explanation only occurs to me. This is, I am inclined to believe, an instance of the operation of the great law of reaction. We have just come victorious out of a long and fierce contest for the liberty of trade. While that contest was undecided, much was said and written about the advantages of free competition, and about the danger of suffering the State to regulate matters which should be left to individuals. There has consequently arisen in the minds of persons who are led by words, and who are little in the habit of making distinctions, a disposition to apply to political questions and moral questions principles which are sound only when applied to commercial questions. These people, not content with having forced the Government to surrender a province wrongfully usurped, now wish to wrest from the Government a domain held by a right which was never before questioned, and which cannot be questioned with the smallest show of reason. "If," they say, "free competition is a good thing in trade, it must surely be a good thing in education. The supply of other commodities, of sugar, for example, is left to adjust itself to the demand; and the consequence is, that we are better supplied with sugar than if the Government undertook to supply us. Why then should we doubt that the supply of instruction will, without the intervention of the Government, be found equal to the demand?"

Never was there a more false analogy. Whether a man is well supplied with sugar is a matter which concerns himself alone. But whether he is well supplied with instruction is a matter which concerns his neighbours and the State. If he cannot afford to pay for sugar, he must go without sugar. But it is by no means fit that, because he cannot afford to pay for education, he should go without education. Between the rich and their instructors there may, as Adam Smith says, be free trade. The supply of music masters and Italian masters may be left to adjust itself to the demand. But what is to become of the millions who are too poor to procure without assistance the services of a decent schoolmaster? We have indeed heard it said that even these millions will be supplied with teachers by the free competition of benevolent individuals who will vie with each other in rendering this service to mankind. No doubt there are many benevolent individuals who spend their time and money most laudably in setting up and supporting schools; and you may say, if you please, that there is, among these respectable persons, a competition to do good. But do not be imposed upon by words. Do not believe that this competition resembles the competition which is produced by the desire of wealth and by the fear of ruin. There is a great difference, be assured, between the rivalry of philanthropists and the rivalry of grocers. The grocer knows that, if his wares are worse than those of other grocers, he shall soon go before the Bankrupt Court, and his wife and children will have no refuge but the workhouse: he knows that, if his shop obtains an honorable celebrity, he shall be able to set up a carriage and buy a villa: and this knowledge impels him to exertions compared with which the exertions of even very charitable people to serve the poor are but languid. It would be strange infatuation indeed to legislate on the supposition that a man cares for his fellow creatures as much as he cares for himself.

Unless, Sir, I greatly deceive myself, those arguments, which show that the Government ought not to leave to private people the task of providing for the national defence, will equally show that the Government ought not to leave to private people the task of providing for national education. On this subject, Mr. Hume has laid down the general law with admirable good sense and perspicuity. I mean David Hume, not the Member for Montrose, though that honorable gentleman will, I am confident, assent to the doctrine propounded by his illustrious namesake. David Hume, Sir, justly says that most of the arts and trades which exist in the world produce so much advantage and pleasure to individuals, that the magistrate may safely leave it to individuals to encourage those arts and trades. But he adds that there are callings which, though they are highly useful, nay, absolutely necessary to society, yet do not administer to the peculiar pleasure or profit of any individual. The military calling is an instance. Here, says Hume, the government must interfere. It must take on itself to regulate these callings, and to stimulate the industry of the persons who follow these callings by pecuniary and honorary rewards.

Now, Sir, it seems to me that, on the same principle on which Government ought to superintend and to reward the soldier, Government ought to superintend and to reward the schoolmaster. I mean, of course, the schoolmaster of the common people. That his calling is useful, that his calling is necessary, will hardly be denied. Yet it is clear that his services will not be adequately remunerated if he is left to be remunerated by those whom he teaches, or by the voluntary contributions of the charitable. Is this disputed? Look at the facts. You tell us that schools will multiply and flourish exceedingly, if the Government will only abstain from interfering with them. Has not the Government long abstained from interfering with them? Has not everything been left, through many years, to individual exertion? If it were true that education, like trade, thrives most where the magistrate meddles least, the common people of England would now be the best educated in the world. Our schools would be model schools. Every one would have a well chosen little library, excellent maps, a small but neat apparatus for experiments in natural philosophy. A grown person unable to read and write would be pointed at like Giant O'Brien or the Polish Count. Our schoolmasters would be as eminently expert in all that relates to teaching as our cutlers, our cottonspinners, our engineers are allowed to be in their respective callings. They would, as a class, be held in high consideration; and their gains would be such that it would be easy to find men of respectable character and attainments to fill up vacancies.

Now, is this the case? Look at the charges of the judges, at the resolutions of the grand juries, at the reports of public officers, at the reports of voluntary associations. All tell the same sad and ignominious story. Take the reports of the Inspectors of Prisons. In the House of Correction at Hertford, of seven hundred prisoners one half could not read at all; only eight could read and write well. Of eight thousand prisoners who had passed through Maidstone gaol only fifty could read and write well. In Coldbath Fields Prison, the proportion that could read and write well seems to have been still smaller. Turn from the registers of prisoners to the registers of marriages. You will find that about a hundred and thirty thousand couples were married in the year 1844. More than forty thousand of the bridegrooms and more than sixty thousand of the brides did not sign their names, but made their marks. Nearly one third of the men and nearly one half of the women, who are in the prime of life, who are to be the parents of the Englishmen of the next generation, who are to bear a chief part in forming the minds of the Englishmen of the next generation,

cannot write their own names. Remember, too, that, though
people who cannot write their own names must be grossly ignorant,
people may write their own names and yet have very little knowledge. Tens of thousands who were able to write their names
had in all probability received only the wretched education of a
common day school. We know what such a school too often is;
a room crusted with filth, without light, without air, with a heap
of fuel in one corner and a brood of chickens in another; the
only machinery of instruction a dogeared spellingbook and a
broken slate; the masters the refuse of all other callings, discarded
footmen, ruined pedlars, men who cannot work a sum in the rule
of three, men who cannot write a common letter without blunders,
men who do not know whether the earth is a sphere or a cube, men
who do not know whether Jerusalem is in Asia or America. And
to such men, men to whom none of us would entrust the key of
his cellar, we have entrusted the mind of the rising generation,
and, with the mind of the rising generation, the freedom, the
happiness, the glory of our country.

Do you question the accuracy of this description? I will produce evidence to which I am sure that you will not venture to
take an exception. Every gentleman here knows, I suppose, how
important a place the Congregational Union holds among the
Nonconformists, and how prominent a part Mr. Edward Baines
has taken in opposition to State education. A Committee of the
Congregational Union drew up last year a report on the subject
of education. That report was received by the Union; and the
person who moved that it should be received was Mr. Edward
Baines. That report contains the following passage: "If it were
necessary to disclose facts to such an assembly as this, as to the
ignorance and debasement of the neglected portions of our population in towns and rural districts, both adults and juvenile, it
could easily be done. Private information communicated to the
Board, personal observation and investigation of the various
localities, with the published documents of the Registrar General,
and the reports of the state of prisons in England and Wales,
published by order of the House of Commons, would furnish
enough to make us modest in speaking of what has been done for
the humbler classes, and make us ashamed that the sons of the
soil of England should have been so long neglected, and should
present to the enlightened traveller from other shores such a sad
spectacle of neglected cultivation, lost mental power, and spiritual
degradation." Nothing can be more just. All the information
which I have been able to obtain bears out the statements of the

Congregational Union. I do believe that the ignorance and degradation of a large part of the community to which we belong ought to make us ashamed of ourselves. I do believe that an enlightened traveller from New York, from Geneva, or from Berlin, would be shocked to see so much barbarism in the close neighbourhood of so much wealth and civilisation. But is it not strange that the very gentlemen who tell us in such emphatic language that the people are shamefully ill educated, should yet persist in telling us that under a system of free competition the people are certain to be excellently educated? Only this morning the opponents of our plan circulated a paper in which they confidently predict that free competition will do all that is necessary, if we will only wait with patience. Wait with patience! Why, we have been waiting ever since the Heptarchy. How much longer are we to wait! Till the year 2847? Or till the year 3847? That the experiment has as yet failed you do not deny. And why should it have failed? Has it been tried in unfavourable circumstances? Not so; it has been tried in the richest, and in the freest, and in the most charitable country in all Europe. Has it been tried on too small a scale? Not so: millions have been subjected to it. Has it been tried during too short a time? Not so: it has been going on during ages. The cause of the failure then is plain. Our whole system has been unsound. We have applied the principle of free competition to a case to which that principle is not applicable.

But, Sir, if the state of the southern part of our island has furnished me with one strong argument, the state of the northern part furnishes me with another argument, which is, if possible, still more decisive. A hundred and fifty years ago England was one of the best governed and most prosperous countries in the world: Scotland was perhaps the rudest and poorest country that could lay any claim to civilisation. The name of Scotchman was then uttered in this part of the island with contempt. The ablest Scotch statesmen contemplated the degraded state of their poorer countrymen with a feeling approaching to despair. It is well known that Fletcher of Saltoun, a brave and accomplished man, a man who had drawn his sword for liberty, who had suffered proscription and exile for liberty, was so much disgusted and dismayed by the misery, the ignorance, the idleness, the lawlessness of the common people, that he proposed to make many thousands of them slaves. Nothing, he thought, but the discipline which kept order and inforced exertion among the negroes of a sugar colony, nothing but the lash and the stocks, could reclaim the vagabonds who infested every part of Scotland from their indolent and predatory habits, and compel them to support themselves by steady labour. He therefore, soon after the Revolution, published a pamphlet, in which he earnestly, and, as I believe, from the mere impulse of humanity and patriotism, recommended to the Estates of the Realm this sharp remedy, which alone, as he conceived, could remove the evil. Within a few months after the publication of that pamphlet a very different remedy was applied. The Parliament which sate at Edinburgh passed an act for the establishment of parochial schools. What followed? An improvement such as the world had never seen took place in the moral and intellectual character of the people. Soon, in spite of the rigour of the climate, in spite of the sterility of the earth, Scotland became a country which had no reason to envy the fairest portions of the globe. Wherever the Scotchman went,—and there were few parts of the world to which he did not go,—he carried his superiority with him. If he was admitted into a public office, he worked his way up to the highest post. If he got employment in a brewery or a factory, he was soon the foreman. If he took a shop, his trade was the best in the street. If he enlisted in the army, he became a colour-serjeant. If he went to a colony, he was the most thriving planter there. The Scotchman of the seventeenth century had been spoken of in London as we speak of the Esquimaux. The Scotchman of the eighteenth century was an object, not of scorn, but of envy. The cry was that, wherever he came, he got more than his share; that, mixed with Englishmen or mixed with Irishmen, he rose to the top as surely as oil rises to the top of water. And what had produced this great revolution? The Scotch air was still as cold, the Scotch rocks were still as bare as ever. All the natural qualities of the Scotchman were still what they had been when learned and benevolent men advised that he should be flogged, like a beast of burden, to his daily task. But the State had given him an education. That education was not, it is true, in all respects what it should have been. But, such as it was, it had done more for the bleak and dreary shores of the Forth and the Clyde than the richest of soils and the most genial of climates had done for Capua and Tarentum. Is there one member of this House, however strongly he may hold the doctrine that the Government ought not to interfere with the education of the people, who will stand up and say that, in his opinion, the Scotch would now have been a happier and a more enlightened people if they had been left, during the last five generations, to find instruction for themselves?

I say then, Sir, that, if the science of Government be an experimental science, this question is decided. We are in a condition to perform the inductive process according to the rules laid down in the Novum Organum. We have two nations closely connected, inhabiting the same island, sprung from the same blood, speaking the same language, governed by the same Sovereign and the same Legislature, holding essentially the same religious faith, having the same allies and the same enemies. Of these two nations one was, a hundred and fifty years ago, as respects opulence and civilisation, in the highest rank among European communities, the other in the lowest rank. The opulent and highly civilised nation leaves the education of the people to free competition. In the poor and half barbarous nation the education of the people is undertaken by the State. The result is that the first are last and the last first. The common people of Scotland,—it is vain to disguise the truth,—have passed the common people of England. Free competition, tried with every advantage, has produced effects of which, as the Congregational Union tell us, we ought to be ashamed, and which must lower us in the opinion of every intelligent foreigner. State education, tried under every disadvantage, has produced an improvement to which it would be difficult to find a parallel in any age or country. Such an experiment as this would be regarded as conclusive in surgery or chemistry, and ought, I think, to be regarded as equally conclusive in politics.

These, Sir, are the reasons which have satisfied me that it is the duty of the State to educate the people. Being firmly convinced of that truth, I shall not shrink from proclaiming it here and elsewhere, in defiance of the loudest clamour that agitators can raise. The remainder of my task is easy. For, if the great principle for which I have been contending is admitted, the objections which have been made to the details of our plan will vanish fast. I will deal with those objections in the order in which they stand in the amendment moved by the honorable member for Finsbury.

First among his objections he places the cost. Surely, Sir, no person who admits that it is our duty to train the minds of the rising generation can think a hundred thousand pounds too large a sum for that purpose. If we look at the matter in the lowest point of view, if we consider human beings merely as producers of wealth, the difference between an intelligent and a stupid population, estimated in pounds, shillings, and pence, exceeds a hundredfold the proposed outlay. Nor is this all. For every pound that you have saved in education, you will spend five in prosecutions, in prisons, in penal settlements. I cannot believe that the

House, having never grudged anything that was asked for the purpose of maintaining order and protecting property by means of pain and fear, will begin to be niggardly as soon as it is proposed to effect the same objects by making the people wiser and better.

The next objection made by the honorable member to our plan is that it will increase the influence of the Crown. This sum of a hundred thousand pounds may, he apprehends, be employed in corruption and jobbing. Those schoolmasters who vote for ministerial candidates will obtain a share of the grant: those schoolmasters who vote for opponents of the ministry will apply for assistance in vain. Sir, the honorable member never would have made this objection if he had taken the trouble to understand the minutes which he has condemned. We propose to place this part of the public expenditure under checks which must make such abuses as the honorable Member anticipates morally impossible. Not only will there be those ordinary checks which are thought sufficient to prevent the misapplication of the many millions annually granted for the army, the navy, the ordance, the civil government: not only must the Ministers of the Crown come every year to this House for a vote, and be prepared to render an account of the manner in which they have laid out what had been voted in the preceding year; but, when they have satisfied the House, when they have got their vote, they will still be unable to distribute the money at their discretion. Whatever they may do for any schoolmaster must be done in concert with those persons who, in the district where the schoolmaster lives, take an interest in education, and contribute out of their private means to the expense of education. When the honorable gentleman is afraid that we shall corrupt the schoolmasters, he forgets, first, that we do not appoint the schoolmasters; secondly, that we cannot dismiss the schoolmasters; thirdly, that managers who are altogether independent of us can, without our consent, dismiss the schoolmasters; and fourthly that without the recommendation of those managers we can give nothing to the schoolmasters. Observe, too, that such a recommendation will not be one of those recommendations which goodnatured easy people are too apt to give to everybody who asks; nor will it at all resemble those recommendations which the Secretary of the Treasury is in the habit of receiving. For every pound which we pay on the recommendation of the managers, the managers themselves must pay two pounds. They must also provide the schoolmaster with a house out of their own funds before they can obtain for him a grant from the public funds.

What chance of jobbing is there here? It is common enough, no doubt, for a Member of Parliament who votes with Government to ask that one of those who zealously supported him at the last election may have a place in the Excise or the Customs. But such a member would soon cease to solicit if the answer were, "Your friend shall have a place of fifty pounds a year, if you will give him a house and settle on him an income of a hundred a year." What chance then, I again ask, is there of jobbing? What, say some of the dissenters of Leeds, is to prevent a Tory Government, a High Church Government, from using this parliamentary grant to corrupt the schoolmasters of our borough, and to induce them to use all their influence in favour of a Tory and High Church candidate? Why, Sir, the dissenters of Leeds themselves have the power to prevent it. Let them subscribe to the schools: let them take a share in the management of the schools: let them refuse to recommend to the Committee of Council any schoolmaster whom they suspect of having voted at any election from corrupt motives: and the thing is done. Our plan, in truth, is made up of checks. My only doubt is whether the checks may not be found too numerous and too stringent. On our general conduct there is the ordinary check, the parliamentary check. And, as respects those minute details which it is impossible that this House can investigate, we shall be checked, in every town and in every rural district, by boards consisting of independent men zealous in the cause of education.

The truth is, Sir, that those who clamour most loudly against our plan, have never thought of ascertaining what it is. I see that a gentleman, who ought to have known better, has not been ashamed publicly to tell the world that our plan will cost the nation two millions a year, and will paralyse all the exertions of individuals to educate the people. These two assertions are uttered in one breath. And yet, if he who made them had read our minutes before he railed at them, he would have seen that his predictions are contradictory; that they cannot both be fulfilled; that, if individuals do not exert themselves, the country will have to pay nothing; and that, if the country has to pay two millions, it will be because individuals have exerted themselves with such wonderful, such incredible, vigour, as to raise four millions by voluntary contributions.

The next objection made by the honorable Member for Finsbury is that we have acted unconstitutionally, and have incroached on the functions of Parliament. The Committee of Council he seems to consider as an unlawful assembly. He calls it sometimes a self elected body and sometimes a self appointed body. Sir, these are words without meaning. The Committee is no more a self elected body than the Board of Trade. It is a body appointed by the Queen; and in appointing it Her Majesty has exercised, under the advice of her responsible Ministers, a prerogative as old as the monarchy. But, says the honorable member, the constitutional course would have been to apply for an Act of Parliament. On what ground? Nothing but an Act of Parliament can legalise that which is illegal. But whoever heard of an Act of Parliament to legalise what was already beyond all dispute legal? Of course, if we wished to send aliens out of the country, or to detain disaffected persons in custody without bringing them to trial, we must obtain an Act of Parliament empowering us to do so. But why should we ask for an Act of Parliament to empower us to do what anybody may do, what the honorable Member for Finsbury may do? Is there any doubt that he or anybody else may subscribe to a school, give a stipend to a monitor, or settle a retiring pension on a preceptor who has done good service? What any of the Queen's subjects may do the Queen may do. Suppose that her privy purse were so large that she could afford to employ a hundred thousand pounds in this beneficent manner; would an Act of Parliament be necessary to enable her to do so? Every part of our plan may lawfully be carried into execution by any person, Sovereign or subject, who has the inclination and the money. We have not the money; and for the money we come, in a strictly constitutional manner, to the House of Commons. The course which we have taken is in conformity with all precedent, as well as with all principle. There are military schools. No Act of Parliament was necessary to authorise the establishing of such schools. All that was necessary was a grant of money to defray the charge. When I was Secretary at War it was my duty to bring under Her Majesty's notice the situation of the female children of her soldiers. Many such children accompanied every regiment, and their education was grievously neglected. Her Majesty was graciously pleased to sign a warrant by which a girls' school was attached to each corps. No Act of Parliament was necessary. For to set up a school where girls might be taught to read, and write, and sew, and cook, was perfectly legal already. I might have set it up myself, if I had been rich enough. All that I had to ask from Parliament was the money. But I ought to beg pardon for arguing a point so clear.

The next objection to our plans is that they interfere with the religious convictions of Her Majesty's subjects. It has been sometimes insinuated, but it has never been proved, that the Committee of Council has shown undue favour to the Established Church.

Sir, I have carefully read and considered the minutes; and I wish that every man who has exerted his eloquence against them had done the same. I say that I have carefully read and considered them, and that they seem to me to have been drawn up with exemplary impartiality. The benefits which we offer we offer to people of all religious persuasions alike. The dissenting managers of schools will have equal authority with the managers who belong to the Church. A boy who goes to meeting will be just as eligible to be a monitor, and will receive just as large a stipend, as if he went to the cathedral. The schoolmaster who is a nonconformist and the schoolmaster who is a conformist will enjoy the same emoluments, and will, after the same term of service, obtain, on the same conditions, the same retiring pension. I wish that some gentleman would, instead of using vague phrases about religious liberty and the rights of conscience, answer this plain question. Suppose that in one of our large towns there are four schools, a school connected with the Church, a school connected with the Independents, a Baptist school, and a Wesleyan school; what encouragement, pecuniary or honorary, will, by our plan, be given to the school connected with the Church, and withheld from any of the other three schools? Is it not indeed plain that, if by neglect or maladministration the Church school should get into a bad state, while the dissenting schools flourish, the dissenting schools will receive public money and the Church school will receive none?

It is true, I admit, that, in rural districts which are too poor to support more than one school, the religious community to which the majority belongs will have an advantage over other religious communities. But this is not our fault. If we are as impartial as it is possible to be, you surely do not expect more. If there should be a parish containing nine hundred churchmen and a hundred dissenters, if there should, in that parish, be a school connected with the Church, if the dissenters in that parish should be too poor to set up another school, undoubtedly the school connected with the Church will, in that parish, get all that we give; and the dissenters will get nothing. But observe that there is no partiality to the Church, as the Church, in this arrangement. The churchmen get public money, not because they are churchmen, but because they are the majority. The dissenters get nothing, not because they are dissenters, but because they are a small minority. There are districts where the case will be reversed, where there will be dissenting schools, and no Church schools. In such cases the dissenters will get what we have to give, and the churchmen will get nothing.

But, Sir, I ought not to say that a churchman gets nothing by a system which gives a good education to dissenters, or that a dissenter gets nothing by a system which gives a good education to churchmen. We are not, I hope, so much conformists, or so much nonconformists, as to forget that we are Englishmen and Christians. We all, Churchmen, Presbyterians, Independents, Baptists, Methodists, have an interest in this, that the great body of the people should be rescued from ignorance and barbarism. I mentioned Lord George Gordon's mob. That mob began, it is true, with the Roman Catholics: but, long before the tumults were over, there was not a respectable Protestant in London who was not in fear for his house, for his limbs, for his life, for the lives of those who were dearest to him. The honorable Member for Finsbury says that we call on men to pay for an education from which they derive no benefit. I deny that there is one honest and industrious man in the country who derives no benefit from living among honest and industrious neighbours rather than among rioters and vagabonds. This matter is as much a matter of common concern as the defence of our coast. Suppose that I were to say, "Why do you tax me to fortify Portsmouth? If the people of Portsmouth think that they cannot be safe without bastions and ravelins, let the people of Portsmouth pay the engineers and masons. Why am I to bear the charge of works from which I derive no advantage?" You would answer, and most justly, that there is no man in the island who does not derive advantage from these works, whether he resides within them or not. And, as every man, in whatever part of the island he may live, is bound to contribute to the support of those arsenals which are necessary for our common security, so is every man, to whatever sect he may belong, bound to contribute to the support of those schools on which, not less than on our arsenals, our common security depends.

I now come to the last words of the amendment. The honorable Member for Finsbury is apprehensive that our plan may interfere with the civil rights of Her Majesty's subjects. How a man's civil rights can be prejudiced by his learning to read and write, to multiply and divide, or even by his obtaining some knowledge of history and geography, I do not very well apprehend. One thing is clear, that persons sunk in that ignorance in which, as we are assured by the Congregational Union, great numbers of our countrymen are sunk, can be free only in name. It is hardly necessary for us to appoint a Select Committee for the purpose of inquiring whether knowledge be the ally or the enemy of liberty. He is, I must say, but a shortsighted friend of the common people who is eager to bestow on them a franchise which would make them allpowerful, and yet would withhold from them that instruction without which their power must be a curse to themselves and to the State.

This, Sir, is my defence. From the clamour of our accusers I appeal with confidence to the country to which we must, in no long time, render an account of our stewardship. I appeal with still more confidence to future generations, which, while enjoying all the blessings of an impartial and efficient system of public instruction, will find it difficult to believe that the authors of that system should have had to struggle with a vehement and pertinacious opposition, and still more difficult to believe that such an opposition was offered in the name of civil and religious freedom.

# THE EXAMINATION OF EDWARD OXFORD
## BY THE PRIVY COUNCIL

In the Library of Trinity College, Cambridge, are eleven volumes of Macaulay's journals. Sir George Otto Trevelyan quotes a large number of extracts in his *Life and Letters of Lord Macaulay*, but they have never been published in full. In the volume which runs from 20 October 1838 to 3 May 1849 (press-mark: 0.15.1) are five loose four-page foolscap sheets containing a journal for 10 and 11 June 1840. The following extract consists of sheets 2, 3 and 4.

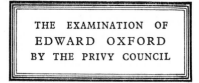

WEDNESDAY June 10. cont^d—Left the stupidest of all Committees at four PM—looked into the House—benches thin—nothing to do—home—read—dressed—to Lord Holland's—sent in Carlisle's Embassy to My Lady—went to My Lord in the Library—no Cabinet Minister but Clarendon yet come—I found them both in great agitation. The Queen had been fired at scarce an hour before on her way along Constitution Hill—The other Ministers dropped in, one by one, full of the story—The particulars not fully known—But she is perfectly safe—I went to Lady H's dressing-room at her summons to be thanked for the book— Clarendon came too—Luttrell and Miss Fox were drinking tea there—-We told her of the attempt at assassination. She and every body greatly shocked—To dinner—Melbourne and Normanby not yet arrived. They came before dinner was over. The Queen well and cheerful. Much talk as to the course to be pursued. I went to the library and looked out half a dozen precedents just in point—Margaret Nicholson—Hadfield—Despard—Settled to have a Privy Council to morrow, nothing unforeseen preventing, and to examine this young ruffian—Nothing is yet known of him but that his name is Edward Oxford . . .

Thursday June 11.—1840—Read Capefigue—thought over Irish Reg^n Question and looked over my papers—Quite ready for debate on the principle if such a debate should come on; but I hardly expected it. Walked with Hannah Fanny & Baba in St James's Park—put down my name at Prince Albert's—To my office—Summons to Privy Council at two—Went to the Home Office. A singular scene—Great number of curious people about— great signs of anxiety. All the Cabinet Ministers but L^d Holland were present—The Under Sec^y for the Home Department—The Attorney General and Maule Solicitor for the Treasury. On the table lay in a heap the effects discovered in a box at the Prisoner's lodging—very singular and mysterious they were. There were two pistol cases which had evidently held the pistols which he fired at the Queen—One of the pistol-cases bore the letters E.R. What could that mean except Ernest Rex?—And yet how monstrously improbable!—There were three letters and another paper, all I think in one hand—The letters were signed Smith—an assumed name I suspect, and were dated from Young England. One of the letters spoke of the great news from Hanover. Another complimented Mr Oxford on his beautiful speaking at the Society. "We heard" says the writer "knocking at our door the other night. We put the crape on our faces, & made our swords and pistols ready. Some of us held the papers ready to be thrown into the fire. Others were prepared to burn the house. But it turned out to be nothing." "Lieutenant Mars," it was also said, "introduced to the society a fine tall gentlemanlike man whose name had not transpired, but who was supposed to be an Officer in the army."—

The fourth paper purported to contain the rules of a most extraordinary society to which this wretched boy appears to have belonged—They were to this effect—Every member to have a sword, two pistols and a rifle—No member to leave town for more than a month without communicating with the Society. Disguises to be provided for such members as should be sent abroad or into the country on business. The disguises to be sometimes those of merchants—sometimes of labourers sometimes of gentlemen. Every member who could raise 100 men to be a Captain. None to be admitted without an oath of allegiance to the cause. Fictitious names provided for all the officers. There was President Gowrie—an allusion, I imagine, to the famous conspiracy—then a set of the most absurd names for different dignitaries—Justinian—Aloman—Caloman—Ernest—Frederic—Godfrey, Gregory, Albany, Mars, Neptune, Hannibal, Oxonian, Milton. Then regulations of costume—who was to have three red bows and who two red bows. The crape veil of the assassin lay on the table and had two red bows—the badge of a captain in their hierarchy. I ought to say that the rules as well as the letters were ill spelt—and, I should say in foreign spelling. Master for example was spelt *mastre*—not an English blunder. There was something German too about the choice of names. The box had also contained the crape veil which I have mentioned—a sabre—a wretched thing brass-handled—a few books.—A testament was one—The others were a geographical dictionary and a pocket book which had contained the manuscript before mentioned.—I had doubted whether Oxford was not a *nom de guerre* like Oxonian. But in the first page of the Testament I found *given by Somebody to Mrs Hannah Oxford*. At last the prisoner was brought in. He looked young—

about seventeen—was short and slightly made—dark complexion
—and not exactly ugly—but with a singularly odious countenance
—Perhaps I fancied so, knowing what he had done. Yet I really
believe that I should have thought so if I had never heard any
thing about him. His face was constantly twitching—sometimes
into a sneer—sometimes into a sort of attempt at a grin perfectly
hideous. He stood with folded arms, resolutely enough, but a
little theatrically. One of his legs shook violently. That, and the
working of his face which seemed to try to express scorn, were the
only marks of feeling which he gave, except for one moment
which I will mention hereafter. Lord Normanby took the lead, as
belonged to his place, and with great—perhaps immoderate
severity—addressed the prisoner. I say immoderate not because
I think that rudeness or severity ought to have been shewn; but
because the greatest solemnity and gravity consistent with
humanity would have best befitted the occasion. The witnesses
were called in, & the Attorney conducted the examination. The
prisoner—like most ignorant foolish people whom I have seen in
his situation, appeared to think only of catching out the witnesses
in trifling contradictions immaterial to the question while he owned,
every time that he opened his lips, more than enough to hang him.
He gloried in puzzling one of them as to whether he held the
pistol, the second time of firing in his left hand or in his right—
"Do you know which is your right hand & which your left." and
such other foolish questions. But he was most affronting to Lord
Colchester—He called him Lord Tom Noodle, & so forth—The
evidence all hung together with discrepancies as slight as I ever
knew in such a case. There were three if not four distinct eye
witnesses to the crime. The property found in the prisoner's
box was identified—His brother in law with whom he lived was
called in—Then and only then the fellow who during the rest of
the examination behaved with hardened depravity shewed signs
of feeling. He turned away from his brother-in-law, looked much
agitated and declined to cross-examine. When the evidence had
been gone through and he was called on to offer any thing that
might be of use to him always under caution, he stepped forward,
talked of the variations of the witnesses one of whom called a
distance ten yards which another called twenty yards, and one of
who had said that he fired with his right hand when another said
that he had fired with his left—He then—as if to prevent these
variations supposing them material from doing him the smallest
good, said in the most audacious manner that he had fired twice,
that at the first fire Prince Albert sprang up and seemed ready to

jump out of the carriage—but thought better of it, and so forth. As to his motive he declined saying any thing—We of course committed him. And now what do you think of this strange affair? I do not suspect [the King of Hanover. I do not even think —in spite of some appearances][1] that the Orange party, here through even its lowest and vilest members is concerned in this crime. On the other hand I think that Chartism has nothing to do with it. It is at the same time clear that the fellow is not alone —that he belongs to a villainous association. Of what nature? I am writing in the dark. But what seems tolerably clear is that it is an association under foreign management. It has altogether a foreign—decidedly a German air.—The orthography of the Secretary is foreign—the names and the general taste is foreign. The allusion to Hanover and the ER are very remarkable. The name Ernest in the list of fictitious appellations I do not think so much of. It is only one of several common German names. But, as at present advised, I suspect that a plot originating in Hanover has been formed for the assassination of the Queen—that German agents are at the head of the design—that they have played off on this young villain, who seems to be of the genuine Ravaillac breed, some delusion which has infatuated him. I should not wonder if they had worked him up by democratic stimulants for a purpose by no means democratic. The King of Hanover cannot be implicated, one would think—But he may have German dependants who would do anything to place him on the English throne. Of one thing I am perfectly satisfied—that the wretch is no more mad than I am. There must be no weak indulgence in such a case.[2]

[1] [Crossed out.]

[2] [Oxford was found "Not guilty, on the ground of insanity," on 10 July 1840, and was sentenced to be confined during Her Majesty's pleasure.]

# POETRY

*Lays of Ancient Rome* was first published by Longman in 1842. Macaulay made a few small corrections in the third edition of 1843, and this text has been used for *Horatius* and *The Battle of the Lake Regillus*. In 1848 a "new edition" of the *Lays* appeared which also included *Ivry* and *The Armada* and provides the text for these two poems. *Ivry* had already been printed, but without the sixth stanza, as the second of two *Songs of the Huguenots* in *Knight's Quarterly Magazine* for January–April 1824. *The Armada* had appeared in *Friendship's Offering* in 1832. *The Marriage of Tirzah and Ahirad*, *The Last Buccaneer*, and *Epitaph on a Jacobite* are here printed from the posthumous *Miscellaneous Writings*, published by Longman in 1860.

Macaulay handed the manuscript of the *Epitaph* to his friend Stanhope across the table at a meeting of the Trustees of the British Museum. It is preserved at Chevening.

## POETRY

# LAYS OF ANCIENT ROME

## HORATIUS

### A LAY
MADE ABOUT THE YEAR OF THE CITY CCCLX

#### I

LARS PORSENA of Clusium
　By the Nine Gods he swore
That the great house of Tarquin
　Should suffer wrong no more.
By the Nine Gods he swore it,
　And named a trysting day,
And bade his messengers ride forth,
East and west and south and north,
　To summon his array.

#### 2

East and west and south and north
　The messengers ride fast,
And tower and town and cottage
　Have heard the trumpet's blast.
Shame on the false Etruscan
　Who lingers in his home,
When Porsena of Clusium
　Is on the march for Rome.

#### 3

The horsemen and the footmen
　Are pouring in amain
From many a stately market-place;
　From many a fruitful plain;
From many a lonely hamlet,
　Which, hid by beech and pine,
Like an eagle's nest, hangs on the crest
　Of purple Apennine;

### 4

From lordly Volaterræ,
　Where scowls the far-famed hold
Piled by the hands of giants
　For godlike kings of old;
From seagirt Populonia,
　Whose sentinels descry
Sardinia's snowy mountain-tops
　Fringing the southern sky;

### 5

From the proud mart of Pisæ,
　Queen of the western waves,
Where ride Massilia's triremes
　Heavy with fair-haired slaves;
From where sweet Clanis wanders
　Through corn and vines and flowers;
From where Cortona lifts to heaven
　Her diadem of towers.

### 6

Tall are the oaks whose acorns
　Drop in dark Auser's rill;
Fat are the stags that champ the boughs
　Of the Ciminian hill;
Beyond all streams Clitumnus
　Is to the herdsman dear;
Best of all pools the fowler loves
　The great Volsinian mere.

### 7

But now no stroke of woodman
　Is heard by Auser's rill;
No hunter tracks the stag's green path
　Up the Ciminian hill;
Unwatched along Clitumnus
　Grazes the milk-white steer;
Unharmed the water fowl may dip
　In the Volsinian mere.

### 8

The harvests of Arretium,
　This year, old men shall reap;

This year, young boys in Umbro
  Shall plunge the struggling sheep;
And in the vats of Luna,
  This year, the must shall foam
Round the white feet of laughing girls,
  Whose sires have marched to Rome.


9

There be thirty chosen prophets,
  The wisest of the land,
Who always by Lars Porsena
  Both morn and evening stand:
Evening and morn the Thirty
  Have turned the verses o'er,
Traced from the right on linen white
  By mighty seers of yore.


10

And with one voice the Thirty
  Have their glad answer given:
"Go forth, go forth, Lars Porsena;
  Go forth, beloved of Heaven;
Go, and return in glory
  To Clusium's royal dome;
And hang round Nurscia's altars
  The golden shields of Rome."


11

And now hath every city
  Sent up her tale of men;
The foot are fourscore thousand,
  The horse are thousands ten.
Before the gates of Sutrium
  Is met the great array.
A proud man was Lars Porsena
  Upon the trysting day.


12

For all the Etruscan armies
  Were ranged beneath his eye,
And many a banished Roman,
  And many a stout ally;

And with a mighty following
　To join the muster came
The Tusculan Mamilius,
　Prince of the Latian name.

### 13

But by the yellow Tiber
　Was tumult and affright:
From all the spacious champaign
　To Rome men took their flight.
A mile around the city,
　The throng stopped up the ways;
A fearful sight it was to see
　Through two long nights and days.

### 14

For aged folk on crutches,
　And women great with child,
And mothers sobbing over babes
　That clung to them and smiled,
And sick men borne in litters
　High on the necks of slaves,
And troops of sun-burned husbandmen
　With reaping-hooks and staves.

### 15

And droves of mules and asses
　Laden with skins of wine,
And endless flocks of goats and sheep,
　And endless herds of kine,
And endless trains of waggons
　That creaked beneath the weight
Of corn-sacks and of household goods,
　Choked every roaring gate.

### 16

Now, from the rock Tarpeian,
　Could the wan burghers spy
The line of blazing villages
　Red in the midnight sky.
The Fathers of the City,
　They sat all night and day,
For every hour some horseman came
　With tidings of dismay.

### 17

To eastward and to westward
  Have spread the Tuscan bands;
Nor house, nor fence, nor dovecote
  In Crustumerium stands.
Verbenna down to Ostia
  Hath wasted all the plain;
Astur hath stormed Janiculum,
  And the stout guards are slain.

### 18

I wis, in all the Senate,
  There was no heart so bold,
But sore it ached, and fast it beat,
  When that ill news was told.
Forthwith up rose the Consul,
  Up rose the Fathers all;
In haste they girded up their gowns,
  And hied them to the wall.

### 19

They held a council standing
  Before the River-Gate;
Short time was there, ye well may guess,
  For musing or debate.
Out spake the Consul roundly:
  "The bridge must straight go down;
For, since Janiculum is lost,
  Nought else can save the town."

### 20

Just then a scout came flying,
  All wild with haste and fear:
"To arms! to arms! Sir Consul;
  Lars Porsena is here."
On the low hills to westward
  The Consul fixed his eye,
And saw the swarthy storm of dust
  Rise fast along the sky.

### 21

And nearer fast and nearer
  Doth the red whirlwind come;

And louder still and still more loud,
From underneath that rolling cloud,
Is heard the trumpet's war-note proud,
    The trampling, and the hum.
And plainly and more plainly
    Now through the gloom appears,
Far to left and far to right,
In broken gleams of dark-blue light,
The long array of helmets bright,
    The long array of spears.


22

And plainly and more plainly,
    Above that glimmering line,
Now might ye see the banners
    Of twelve fair cities shine;
But the banner of proud Clusium
    Was highest of them all,
The terror of the Umbrian,
    The terror of the Gaul.


23

And plainly and more plainly
    Now might the burghers know,
By port and vest, by horse and crest,
    Each warlike Lucumo.
There Cilnius of Arretium
    On his fleet roan was seen;
And Astur of the four-fold shield,
Girt with the brand none else may wield,
Tolumnius with the belt of gold,
And dark Verbenna from the hold
    By reedy Thrasymene.


24

Fast by the royal standard,
    O'erlooking all the war,
Lars Porsena of Clusium
    Sate in his ivory car.
By the right wheel rode Mamilius,
    Prince of the Latian name;
And by the left false Sextus,
    That wrought the deed of shame.

### 25

But when the face of Sextus
  Was seen among the foes,
A yell that rent the firmament
  From all the town arose.
On the house-tops was no woman
  But spat towards him and hissed;
No child but screamed out curses,
  And shook its little fist.

### 26

But the Consul's brow was sad,
  And the Consul's speech was low,
And darkly looked he at the wall,
  And darkly at the foe.
"Their van will be upon us
  Before the bridge goes down;
And if they once may win the bridge,
  What hope to save the town?"

### 27

Then out spake brave Horatius,
  The Captain of the gate:
"To every man upon this earth
  Death cometh soon or late.
And how can man die better
  Than facing fearful odds,
For the ashes of his father
  And the temples of his Gods,

### 28

"And for the tender mother
  Who dandled him to rest,
And for the wife who nurses
  His baby at her breast,
And for the holy maidens
  Who feed the eternal flame,
To save them from false Sextus
  That wrought the deed of shame?

### 29

"Hew down the bridge, Sir Consul,
  With all the speed ye may;

I, with two more to help me,
  Will hold the foe in play.
In yon strait path a thousand
  May well be stopped by three.
Now who will stand on either hand,
  And keep the bridge with me?"

### 30

Then out spake Spurius Lartius;
  A Ramnian proud was he:
"Lo, I will stand at thy right hand,
  And keep the bridge with thee."
And out spake strong Herminius;
  Of Titian blood was he:
"I will abide on thy left side,
  And keep the bridge with thee."

### 31

"Horatius," quoth the Consul,
  "As thou sayest, so let it be."
And straight against that great array
  Forth went the dauntless Three.
For Romans in Rome's quarrel
  Spared neither land nor gold,
Nor son nor wife, nor limb nor life,
  In the brave days of old.

### 32

Then none was for a party;
  Then all were for the state;
Then the great man helped the poor,
  And the poor man loved the great:
Then lands were fairly portioned;
  Then spoils were fairly sold:
The Romans were like brothers
  In the brave days of old.

### 33

Now Roman is to Roman
  More hateful than a foe,
And the Tribunes beard the high,
  And the Fathers grind the low.

As we wax hot in faction,
  In battle we wax cold:
Wherefore men fight not as they fought
  In the brave days of old.


34

Now while the Three were tightening
  Their harness on their backs,
The Consul was the foremost man
  To take in hand an axe:
And Fathers mixed with Commons
  Seized hatchet, bar, and crow,
And smote upon the planks above,
  And loosed the props below.


35

Meanwhile the Tuscan army,
  Right glorious to behold,
Came flashing back the noonday light,
Rank behind rank, like surges bright
  Of a broad sea of gold.
Four hundred trumpets sounded
  A peal of warlike glee,
As that great host, with measured tread,
And spears advanced, and ensigns spread,
Rolled slowly towards the bridge's head,
  Where stood the dauntless Three.


36

The Three stood calm and silent
  And looked upon the foes,
And a great shout of laughter
  From all the vanguard rose:
And forth three chiefs came spurring
  Before that deep array;
To earth they sprang, their swords they drew,
And lifted high their shields, and flew
  To win the narrow way;


37

Aunus from green Tifernum,
  Lord of the Hill of Vines;

And Seius, whose eight hundred slaves
  Sicken in Ilva's mines;
And Picus, long to Clusium
  Vassal in peace and war,
Who led to fight his Umbrian powers
From that grey crag where, girt with towers,
The fortress of Nequinum lowers
  O'er the pale waves of Nar.


### 38

Stout Lartius hurled down Aunus
  Into the stream beneath:
Herminius struck at Seius,
  And clove him to the teeth:
At Picus brave Horatius
  Darted one fiery thrust;
And the proud Umbrian's gilded arms
  Clashed in the bloody dust.


### 39

Then Ocnus of Falerii
  Rushed on the Roman Three;
And Lausulus of Urgo,
  The rover of the sea;
And Aruns of Volsinium,
  Who slew the great wild boar,
The great wild boar that had his den
Amidst the reeds of Cosa's fen,
And wasted fields, and slaughtered men,
  Along Albinia's shore.


### 40

Herminius smote down Aruns:
  Lartius laid Ocnus low:
Right to the heart of Lausulus
  Horatius sent a blow.
"Lie there," he cried, "fell pirate!
  No more, aghast and pale,
From Ostia's walls the crowd shall mark
The track of thy destroying bark.
No more Campania's hinds shall fly
To woods and caverns when they spy
  Thy thrice accursed sail."

41

But now no sound of laughter
  Was heard amongst the foes.
A wild and wrathful clamour
  From all the vanguard rose.
Six spears' lengths from the entrance
  Halted that deep array,
And for a space no man came forth
  To win the narrow way.

42

But hark! the cry is Astur:
  And lo! the ranks divide;
And the great Lord of Luna
  Comes with his stately stride.
Upon his ample shoulders
  Clangs loud the four-fold shield,
And in his hand he shakes the brand
  Which none but he can wield.

43

He smiled on those bold Romans
  A smile serene and high;
He eyed the flinching Tuscans,
  And scorn was in his eye.
Quoth he, "The she-wolf's litter
  Stand savagely at bay:
But will ye dare to follow,
  If Astur clears the way?"

44

Then, whirling up his broadsword
  With both hands to the height,
He rushed against Horatius,
  And smote with all his might.
With shield and blade Horatius
  Right deftly turned the blow.
The blow, though turned, came yet too nigh;
It missed his helm, but gashed his thigh:
The Tuscans raised a joyful cry
  To see the red blood flow.

### 45

He reeled, and on Herminius
  He leaned one breathing-space;
Then, like a wild cat mad with wounds,
  Sprang right at Astur's face.
Through teeth, and skull, and helmet,
  So fierce a thrust he sped,
The good sword stood a hand-breadth out
  Behind the Tuscan's head.

### 46

And the great Lord of Luna
  Fell at that deadly stroke,
As falls on Mount Alvernus
  A thunder-smitten oak.
Far o'er the crashing forest
  The giant arms lie spread;
And the pale augurs, muttering low,
  Gaze on the blasted head.

### 47

On Astur's throat Horatius
  Right firmly pressed his heel,
And thrice and four times tugged amain,
  Ere he wrenched out the steel.
"And see," he cried, "the welcome,
  Fair guests, that waits you here!
What noble Lucumo comes next
  To taste our Roman cheer?"

### 48

But at his haughty challenge
  A sullen murmur ran,
Mingled of wrath, and shame, and dread,
  Along that glittering van.
There lacked not men of prowess,
  Nor men of lordly race;
For all Etruria's noblest
  Were round the fatal place.

### 49

But all Etruria's noblest
  Felt their hearts sink to see

On the earth the bloody corpses,
   In the path the dauntless Three:
And, from the ghastly entrance
   Where those bold Romans stood,
All shrank, like boys who unaware,
Ranging the woods to start a hare,
Come to the mouth of the dark lair
Where, growling low, a fierce old bear
   Lies amidst bones and blood.


50

Was none who would be foremost
   To lead such dire attack;
But those behind cried "Forward!"
   And those before cried "Back!"
And backward now and forward
   Wavers the deep array;
And on the tossing sea of steel,
To and fro the standards reel;
And the victorious trumpet-peal
   Dies fitfully away.


51

Yet one man for one moment
   Strode out before the crowd;
Well known was he to all the Three,
   And they gave him greeting loud.
"Now welcome, welcome, Sextus!
   Now welcome to thy home!
Why dost thou stay, and turn away?
   Here lies the road to Rome."


52

Thrice looked he at the city;
   Thrice looked he at the dead;
And thrice came on in fury,
   And thrice turned back in dread:
And, white with fear and hatred,
   Scowled at the narrow way
Where, wallowing in a pool of blood,
   The bravest Tuscans lay.

### 53

But meanwhile axe and lever
　　Have manfully been plied;
And now the bridge hangs tottering
　　Above the boiling tide.
"Come back, come back, Horatius!"
　　Loud cried the Fathers all.
"Back, Lartius! back, Herminius!
　　Back, ere the ruin fall!"

### 54

Back darted Spurius Lartius;
　　Herminius darted back:
And, as they passed, beneath their feet
　　They felt the timbers crack.
But when they turned their faces,
　　And on the farther shore
Saw brave Horatius stand alone,
　　They would have crossed once more.

### 55

But with a crash like thunder
　　Fell every loosened beam,
And, like a dam, the mighty wreck
　　Lay right athwart the stream:
And a long shout of triumph
　　Rose from the walls of Rome,
As to the highest turret-tops
　　Was splashed the yellow foam.

### 56

And, like a horse unbroken
　　When first he feels the rein,
The furious river struggled hard,
　　And tossed his tawny mane;
And burst the curb, and bounded,
　　Rejoicing to be free;
And whirling down, in fierce career,
Battlement, and plank, and pier,
　　Rushed headlong to the sea.

### 57

Alone stood brave Horatius,
　　But constant still in mind;

Thrice thirty thousand foes before,
   And the broad flood behind.
"Down with him!" cried false Sextus,
   With a smile on his pale face.
"Now yield thee," cried Lars Porsena,
   "Now yield thee to our grace."

### 58

Round turned he, as not deigning
   Those craven ranks to see;
Nought spake he to Lars Porsena,
   To Sextus nought spake he;
But he saw on Palatinus
   The white porch of his home;
And he spake to the noble river
   That rolls by the towers of Rome.

### 59

"Oh, Tiber! father Tiber!
   To whom the Romans pray,
A Roman's life, a Roman's arms,
   Take thou in charge this day!"
So he spake, and speaking sheathed
   The good sword by his side,
And with his harness on his back,
   Plunged headlong in the tide.

### 60

No sound of joy or sorrow
   Was heard from either bank;
But friends and foes in dumb surprise,
With parted lips and straining eyes,
   Stood gazing where he sank;
And when above the surges
   They saw his crest appear,
All Rome sent forth a rapturous cry,
And even the ranks of Tuscany
   Could scarce forbear to cheer.

### 61

But fiercely ran the current,
   Swollen high by months of rain:
And fast his blood was flowing;
   And he was sore in pain,

And heavy with his armour,
  And spent with changing blows:
And oft they thought him sinking,
  But still again he rose.

### 62

Never, I ween, did swimmer,
  In such an evil case,
Struggle through such a raging flood
  Safe to the landing place:
But his limbs were borne up bravely
  By the brave heart within,
And our good father Tiber
  Bare bravely up his chin.

### 63

"Curse on him!" quoth false Sextus;
  "Will not the villain drown?
But for this stay, ere close of day
  We should have sacked the town!"
"Heaven help him!" quoth Lars Porsena,
  "And bring him safe to shore;
For such a gallant feat of arms
  Was never seen before."

### 64

And now he feels the bottom;
  Now on dry earth he stands;
Now round him throng the Fathers
  To press his gory hands;
And now with shouts and clapping,
  And noise of weeping loud,
He enters through the River-Gate,
  Borne by the joyous crowd.

### 65

They gave him of the corn-land,
  That was of public right,
As much as two strong oxen
  Could plough from morn till night;
And they made a molten image,
  And set it up on high,
And there it stands unto this day
  To witness if I lie.

### 66

It stands in the Comitium,
  Plain for all folk to see;
Horatius in his harness,
  Halting upon one knee:
And underneath is written,
  In letters all of gold,
How valiantly he kept the bridge
  In the brave days of old.

### 67

And still his name sounds stirring
  Unto the men of Rome,
As the trumpet-blast that cries to them
  To charge the Volscian home;
And wives still pray to Juno
  For boys with hearts as bold
As his who kept the bridge so well
  In the brave days of old.

### 68

And in the nights of winter,
  When the cold north winds blow,
And the long howling of the wolves
  Is heard amidst the snow;
When round the lonely cottage
  Roars loud the tempest's din,
And the good logs of Algidus
  Roar louder yet within;

### 69

When the oldest cask is opened,
  And the largest lamp is lit,
When the chestnuts glow in the embers,
  And the kid turns on the spit;
When young and old in circle
  Around the firebrands close;
When the girls are weaving baskets,
  And the lads are shaping bows;

### 70

When the goodman mends his armour,
  And trims his helmet's plume;

When the goodwife's shuttle merrily
  Goes flashing through the loom;
With weeping and with laughter
  Still is the story told,
How well Horatius kept the bridge
  In the brave days of old.


## THE BATTLE OF THE LAKE REGILLUS

A LAY SUNG AT THE FEAST OF CASTOR AND POLLUX
ON THE IDES OF QUINTILIS, IN THE YEAR OF THE CITY CCCCLI

### 1

Ho, trumpets, sound a war-note!
  Ho, lictors, clear the way!
The Knights will ride, in all their pride,
  Along the streets to-day.
To-day the doors and windows
  Are hung with garlands all,
From Castor in the Forum,
  To Mars without the wall.
Each Knight is robed in purple,
  With olive each is crown'd;
A gallant war-horse under each
  Paws haughtily the ground.
While flows the Yellow River,
  While stands the Sacred Hill,
The proud Ides of Quintilis
  Shall have such honour still.
Gay are the Martian Kalends:
  December's Nones are gay:
But the proud Ides, when the squadron rides,
  Shall be Rome's whitest day.

### 2

Unto the Great Twin Brethren
  We keep this solemn feast.
Swift, swift, the Great Twin Brethren
  Came spurring from the east.
They came o'er wild Parthenius
  Tossing in waves of pine,
O'er Cirrha's dome, o'er Adria's foam,
  O'er purple Apennine.

From where with flutes and dances
  Their ancient mansion rings,
In lordly Lacedæmon,
  The City of two kings,
To where, by Lake Regillus,
  Under the Porcian height,
All in the lands of Tusculum,
  Was fought the glorious fight.

### 3

Now on the place of slaughter
  Are cots and sheepfolds seen,
And rows of vines, and fields of wheat,
  And apple-orchards green:
The swine crush the big acorns
  That fall from Corne's oaks.
Upon the turf by the Fair Fount
  The reaper's pottage smokes.
The fisher baits his angle;
  The hunter twangs his bow;
Little they think on those strong limbs
  That moulder deep below.
Little they think how sternly
  That day the trumpets pealed;
How in the slippery swamp of blood
  Warrior and war-horse reeled;
How wolves came with fierce gallop,
  And crows on eager wings,
To tear the flesh of captains,
  And peck the eyes of kings;
How thick the dead lay scattered
  Under the Porcian height;
How through the gates of Tusculum
  Raved the wild stream of flight;
And how the Lake Regillus
  Bubbled with crimson foam,
What time the Thirty Cities
  Came forth to war with Rome.

### 4

But, Roman, when thou standest
  Upon that holy ground,
Look thou with heed on the dark rock
  That girds the dark lake round.

So shalt thou see a hoof-mark
   Stamped deep into the flint:
It was no hoof of mortal steed
   That made so strange a dint:
There to the Great Twin Brethren
   Vow thou thy vows, and pray
That they, in tempest and in fight,
   Will keep thy head alway.

### 5

Since last the Great Twin Brethren
   Of mortal eyes were seen,
Have years gone by an hundred
   And fourscore and thirteen.
That summer a Virginius
   Was Consul first in place;
The second was stout Aulus,
   Of the Posthumian race.
The Herald of the Latines
   From Gabii came in state:
The Herald of the Latines
   Passed through Rome's Eastern Gate:
The Herald of the Latines
   Did in our Forum stand;
And there he did his office,
   A sceptre in his hand.

### 6

"Hear, Senators and people
   Of the good town of Rome:
The Thirty Cities charge you
   To bring the Tarquins home:
And if ye still be stubborn,
   To work the Tarquins wrong,
The Thirty Cities warn you,
   Look that your walls be strong."

### 7

Then spake the Consul Aulus,
   He spake a bitter jest:
"Once the jays sent a message
   Unto the eagle's nest:—
Now yield thou up thine eyrie
   Unto the carrion-kite,

Or come forth valiantly, and face
   The jays in deadly fight.—
Forth looked in wrath the eagle;
   And carrion-kite and jay,
Soon as they saw his beak and claw,
   Fled screaming far away."


8

The Herald of the Latines
   Hath hied him back in state:
The Fathers of the City
   Are met in high debate.
Then spake the elder Consul,
   An ancient man and wise:
"Now hearken, Conscript Fathers,
   To that which I advise.
In seasons of great peril
   'Tis good that one bear sway;
Then choose we a Dictator,
   Whom all men shall obey.
Camerium knows how deeply
   The sword of Aulus bites;
And all our city calls him
   The man of seventy fights.
Then let him be Dictator
   For six months and no more,
And have a Master of the Knights,
   And axes twenty-four."


9

So Aulus was Dictator,
   The man of seventy fights;
He made Æbutius Elva
   His Master of the Knights.
On the third morn thereafter,
   At dawning of the day,
Did Aulus and Æbutius
   Set forth with their array.
Sempronius Atratinus
   Was left in charge at home
With boys, and with grey-headed men,
   To keep the walls of Rome.

Hard by the Lake Regillus
　　Our camp was pitched at night:
Eastward a mile the Latines lay,
　　Under the Porcian height.
Far over hill and valley
　　Their mighty host was spread;
And with their thousand watch-fires
　　The midnight sky was red.

10

Up rose the golden morning
　　Over the Porcian height,
The proud Ides of Quintilis
　　Marked evermore with white.
Not without secret trouble
　　Our bravest saw the foes,
For girt by threescore thousand spears,
　　The thirty standards rose.
From every warlike city
　　That boasts the Latian name,
Foredoomed to dogs and vultures,
　　That gallant army came;
From Setia's purple vineyards,
　　From Norba's ancient wall,
From the white streets of Tusculum,
　　The proudest town of all;
From where the Witch's Fortress
　　O'erhangs the dark-blue seas,
From the still glassy lake that sleeps
　　Beneath Aricia's trees—
Those trees in whose dim shadow
　　The ghastly priest doth reign,
The priest who slew the slayer,
　　And shall himself be slain;—
From the drear banks of Ufens,
　　Where flights of marsh-fowl play,
And buffaloes lie wallowing
　　Through the hot summer's day;
From the gigantic watch-towers,
　　No work of earthly men,
Whence Cora's sentinels o'erlook
　　The never-ending fen;

From the Laurentian jungle,
  The wild hog's reedy home;
From the green steeps whence Anio leaps
  In floods of snow-white foam.

### 11

Aricia, Cora, Norba,
  Velitræ, with the might
Of Setia and of Tusculum,
  Were marshalled on their right:
Their leader was Mamilius,
  Prince of the Latian name;
Upon his head a helmet
  Of red gold shone like flame:
High on a gallant charger
  Of dark-grey hue he rode;
Over his gilded armour
  A vest of purple flowed,
Woven in the land of sunrise
  By Syria's dark-browed daughters,
And by the sails of Carthage brought
  Far o'er the southern waters.

### 12

Lavinium and Laurentum
  Had on the left their post,
With all the banners of the marsh,
  And banners of the coast.
Their leader was false Sextus,
  That wrought the deed of shame:
With restless pace and haggard face,
  To his last field he came.
Men said he saw strange visions,
  Which none beside might see;
And that strange sounds were in his ears,
  Which none might hear but he.
A woman fair and stately,
  But pale as are the dead,
Oft through the watches of the night
  Sate spinning by his bed.
And as she plied the distaff,
  In a sweet voice and low,
She sang of great old houses,
  And fights fought long ago.

So spun she, and so sang she,
    Until the east was grey;
Then pointed to her bleeding breast,
    And shrieked, and fled away.


### 13

But in the centre thickest
    Were ranged the shields of foes,
And from the centre loudest
    The cry of battle rose.
There Tibur marched and Pedum
    Beneath proud Tarquin's rule,
And Ferentinum of the rock,
    And Gabii of the pool.
There rode the Volscian succours:
    There, in a dark stern ring,
The Roman exiles gathered close
    Around the ancient king.
Though white as Mount Soracte,
    When winter nights are long,
His beard flowed down o'er mail and belt,
    His heart and hand were strong:
Under his hoary eye-brows
    Still flashed forth quenchless rage:
And, if the lance shook in his gripe,
    'Twas more with hate than age.
Close at his side was Titus
    On an Apulian steed,
Titus, the youngest Tarquin,
    Too good for such a breed.


### 14

Now on each side the leaders
    Gave signal for the charge;
And on each side the footmen
    Strode on with lance and targe;
And on each side the horsemen
    Struck their spurs deep in gore,
And front to front the armies
    Met with a mighty roar:
And under that great battle
    The earth with blood was red;

And, like the Pomptine fog at morn,
  The dust hung overhead;
And louder still and louder,
  Rose from the darkened field
The braying of the war-horns,
  The clang of sword and shield,
The rush of squadrons sweeping
  Like whirlwinds o'er the plain,
The shouting of the slayers,
  And screeching of the slain.

### 15

False Sextus rode out foremost:
  His look was high and bold;
His corslet was of bison's hide,
  Plated with steel and gold.
As glares the famished eagle
  From the Digentian rock,
On a choice lamb that bounds alone
  Before Bandusia's flock,
Herminius glared on Sextus,
  And came with eagle speed;
Herminius on black Auster,
  Brave champion on brave steed;
In his right hand the broadsword
  That kept the bridge so well,
And on his helm the crown he won
  When proud Fidenæ fell.
Woe to the maid whose lover
  Shall cross his path to-day!
False Sextus saw, and trembled,
  And turned, and fled away.
As turns, as flies, the woodman
  In the Calabrian brake,
When through the reeds gleams the round eye
  Of that fell painted snake;
So turned, so fled, false Sextus,
  And hid him in the rear,
Behind the dark Lavinian ranks,
  Bristling with crest and spear.

### 16

Then far to north Æbutius,
  The Master of the Knights,

Gave Tubero of Norba
　　To feed the Porcian kites.
Next under those red horse-hoofs
　　Flaccus of Setia lay;
Better had he been pruning
　　Among his elms that day.
Mamilius saw the slaughter,
　　And tossed his golden crest,
And towards the Master of the Knights
　　Through the thick battle pressed.
Æbutius smote Mamilius
　　So fiercely on the shield,
That the great lord of Tusculum
　　Well nigh rolled on the field.
Mamilius smote Æbutius,
　　With a good aim and true,
Just where the neck and shoulder join,
　　And pierced him through and through;
And brave Æbutius Elva
　　Fell swooning to the ground:
But a thick wall of bucklers
　　Encompassed him around.
His clients from the battle
　　Bare him some little space;
And filled a helm from the dark lake,
　　And bathed his brow and face;
And when at last he opened
　　His swimming eyes to light,
Men say, the earliest word he spake
　　Was, "Friends, how goes the fight?"


17

But meanwhile in the centre
　　Great deeds of arms were wrought;
There Aulus the Dictator,
　　And there Valerius fought.
Aulus, with his good broadsword,
　　A bloody passage cleared
To where, amidst the thickest foes,
　　He saw the long white beard.
Flat lighted that good broadsword
　　Upon proud Tarquin's head.

He dropped the lance: he dropped the reins:
　　He fell as fall the dead.
Down Aulus springs to slay him,
　　With eyes like coals of fire;
But faster Titus hath sprung down,
　　And hath bestrode his sire.
Latian captains, Roman knights,
　　Fast down to earth they spring,
And hand to hand they fight on foot
　　Around the ancient king.
First Titus gave tall Cæso
　　A death wound in the face;
Tall Cæso was the bravest man
　　Of the brave Fabian race:
Aulus slew Rex of Gabii,
　　The priest of Juno's shrine:
Valerius smote down Julius,
　　Of Rome's great Julian line;
Julius, who left his mansion
　　High on the Velian hill,
And through all turns of weal and woe
　　Followed proud Tarquin still.
Now right across proud Tarquin
　　A corpse was Julius laid;
And Titus groaned with rage and grief,
　　And at Valerius made.
Valerius struck at Titus,
　　And lopped off half his crest;
But Titus stabbed Valerius
　　A span deep in the breast.
Like a mast snapped by the tempest,
　　Valerius reeled and fell.
Ah! woe is me for the good house
　　That loves the people well!
Then shouted loud the Latines;
　　And with one rush they bore
The struggling Romans backward
　　Three lances' length and more:
And up they took proud Tarquin,
　　And laid him on a shield,
And four strong yeomen bare him,
　　Still senseless, from the field.

18

But fiercer grew the fighting
   Around Valerius dead;
For Titus dragged him by the foot,
   And Aulus by the head.
"On, Latines, on!" quoth Titus,
   "See how the rebels fly!"
"Romans, stand firm!" quoth Aulus,
   "And win this fight or die!
They must not give Valerius
   To raven and to kite;
For aye Valerius loathed the wrong,
   And aye upheld the right:
And for your wives and babies
   In the front rank he fell.
Now play the men for the good house
   That loves the people well!"

19

Then tenfold round the body
   The roar of battle rose,
Like the roar of a burning forest,
   When a strong northwind blows.
Now backward, and now forward,
   Rocked furiously the fray,
Till none could see Valerius,
   And none wist where he lay.
For shivered arms and ensigns
   Were heaped there in a mound,
And corpses stiff, and dying men
   That writhed and gnawed the ground;
And wounded horses kicking,
   And snorting purple foam:
Right well did such a couch befit
   A Consular of Rome.

20

But north looked the Dictator;
   North looked he long and hard;
And spake to Caius Cossus,
   The Captain of his Guard:

"Caius, of all the Romans
    Thou hast the keenest sight;
Say, what through yonder storm of dust
    Comes from the Latian right?"

### 21

Then answered Caius Cossus:
    "I see an evil sight;
The banner of proud Tusculum
    Comes from the Latian right;
I see the plumed horsemen;
    And far before the rest
I see the dark-grey charger,
    I see the purple vest;
I see the golden helmet
    That shines far off like flame;
So ever rides Mamilius,
    Prince of the Latian name."

### 22

"Now hearken, Caius Cossus:
    Spring on thy horse's back;
Ride as the wolves of Apennine
    Were all upon thy track!
Haste to our southward battle;
    And never draw thy rein
Until thou find Herminius,
    And bid him come amain."

### 23

So Aulus spake, and turned him
    Again to that fierce strife;
And Caius Cossus mounted,
    And rode for death and life.
Loud clanged beneath his horse-hoofs
    The helmets of the dead,
And many a curdling pool of blood
    Splashed him from heel to head.
So came he far to southward,
    Where fought the Roman host,
Against the banners of the marsh
    And banners of the coast.

Like corn before the sickle
    The stout Lavinians fell,
Beneath the edge of the true sword
    That kept the bridge so well.

### 24

"Herminius! Aulus greets thee;
    He bids thee come with speed,
To help our central battle;
    For sore is there our need.
There wars the youngest Tarquin,
    And there the Crest of Flame,
The Tusculan Mamilius,
    Prince of the Latian name.
Valerius hath fallen fighting
    In front of our array;
And Aulus of the seventy fields
    Alone upholds the day."

### 25

Herminius beat his bosom;
    But never a word he spake.
He clapped his hand on Auster's mane;
    He gave the reins a shake,
Away, away, went Auster,
    Like an arrow from the bow:
Black Auster was the fleetest steed
    From Aufidus to Po.

### 26

Right glad were all the Romans
    Who, in that hour of dread,
Against great odds bare up the war
    Around Valerius dead,
When from the south the cheering
    Rose with a mighty swell;
"Herminius comes, Herminius,
    Who kept the bridge so well!"

### 27

Mamilius spied Herminius,
    And dashed across the way.
"Herminius! I have sought thee
    Through many a bloody day.

One of us two, Herminius,
　　Shall never more go home.
I will lay on for Tusculum,
　　And lay thou on for Rome!"

### 28

All round them paused the battle,
　　While met in mortal fray
The Roman and the Tusculan,
　　The horses black and grey.
Herminius smote Mamilius
　　Through breast-plate and through breast;
And fast flowed out the purple blood
　　Over the purple vest.
Mamilius smote Herminius
　　Through head-piece and through head;
And side by side those chiefs of pride
　　Together fell down dead.
Down fell they dead together
　　In a great lake of gore;
And still stood all who saw them fall
　　While men might count a score.

### 29

Fast, fast, with heels wild spurning,
　　The dark-grey charger fled:
He burst through ranks of fighting men;
　　He sprang o'er heaps of dead.
His bridle far out-streaming,
　　His flanks all blood and foam,
He sought the southern mountains,
　　The mountains of his home.
The pass was steep and rugged,
　　The wolves they howled and whined;
But he ran like a whirlwind up the pass,
　　And he left the wolves behind.
Through many a startled hamlet
　　Thundered his flying feet:
He rushed through the gate of Tusculum,
　　He rushed up the long white street;
He rushed by tower and temple,
　　And paused not from his race
Till he stood before his master's door
　　In the stately market-place.

And straightway round him gathered
   A pale and trembling crowd,
And when they knew him, cries of rage
   Brake forth, and wailing loud:
And women rent their tresses
   For their great prince's fall;
And old men girt on their old swords,
   And went to man the wall.


30

But, like a graven image,
   Black Auster kept his place,
And ever wistfully he looked
   Into his master's face.
The raven-mane that daily,
   With pats and fond caresses,
The young Herminia washed and combed,
   And twined in even tresses,
And decked with coloured ribands
   From her own gay attire,
Hung sadly o'er her father's corpse
   In carnage and in mire.
Forth with a shout sprang Titus,
   And seized black Auster's rein.
Then Aulus sware a fearful oath,
   And ran at him amain.
"The furies of thy brother
   With me and mine abide,
If one of your accursed house
   Upon black Auster ride!"
As on an Alpine watch-tower
   From heaven comes down the flame,
Full on the neck of Titus
   The blade of Aulus came:
And out the red blood spouted,
   In a wide arch and tall,
As spouts a fountain in the court
   Of some rich Capuan's hall.
The knees of all the Latines
   Were loosened with dismay
When dead, on dead Herminius,
   The bravest Tarquin lay.

### 31

And Aulus the Dictator
   Stroked Auster's raven mane,
With heed he looked unto the girths,
   With heed unto the rein.
"Now bear me well, black Auster,
   Into yon thick array;
And thou and I will have revenge
   For thy good lord this day."

### 32

So spake he; and was buckling
   Tighter black Auster's band,
When he was aware of a princely pair
   That rode at his right hand.
So like they were, no mortal
   Might one from other know:
White as snow their armour was:
   Their steeds were white as snow.
Never on earthly anvil
   Did such rare armour gleam;
And never did such gallant steeds
   Drink of an earthly stream.

### 33

And all who saw them trembled,
   And pale grew every cheek;
And Aulus the Dictator
   Scarce gathered voice to speak.
"Say by what name men call you?
   What city is your home?
And wherefore ride ye in such guise
   Before the ranks of Rome?"

### 34

"By many names men call us;
   In many lands we dwell:
Well Samothracia knows us;
   Cyrene knows us well.
Our house in gay Tarentum
   Is hung each morn with flowers:
High o'er the masts of Syracuse
   Our marble portal towers:

But by the proud Eurotas
  Is our dear native home;
And for the right we come to fight
  Before the ranks of Rome."


### 35

So answered those strange horsemen,
  And each couched low his spear;
And forthwith all the ranks of Rome
  Were bold, and of good cheer:
And on the thirty armies
  Came wonder and affright,
And Ardea wavered on the left,
  And Cora on the right.
"Rome to the charge!" cried Aulus;
  "The foe begins to yield!
Charge for the hearth of Vesta!
  Charge for the Golden Shield!
Let no man stop to plunder,
  But slay, and slay, and slay;
The Gods who live for ever
  Are on our side to-day."


### 36

Then the fierce trumpet-flourish
  From earth to heaven arose,
The kites know well the long stern swell
  That bids the Romans close.
Then the good sword of Aulus
  Was lifted up to slay:
Then, like a crag down Apennine,
  Rushed Auster through the fray.
But under those strange horsemen
  Still thicker lay the slain;
And after those strange horses
  Black Auster toiled in vain.
Behind them Rome's long battle
  Came rolling on the foe,
Ensigns dancing wild above,
  Blades all in line below.
So comes the Po in flood-time
  Upon the Celtic plain:

So comes the squall, blacker than night,
　Upon the Adrian main.
Now, by our Sire Quirinus,
　It was a goodly sight
To see the thirty standards
　Swept down the tide of flight.
So flies the spray of Adria
　When the black squall doth blow;
So corn-sheaves in the flood-time
　Spin down the whirling Po.
False Sextus to the mountains
　Turned first his horse's head;
And fast fled Ferentinum,
　And fast Lanuvium fled.
The horsemen of Nomentum
　Spurred hard out of the fray;
The footmen of Velitræ
　Threw shield and spear away.
And underfoot was trampled,
　Amidst the mud and gore,
The banner of proud Tusculum,
　That never stooped before:
And down went Flavius Faustus,
　Who led his stately ranks
From where the apple blossoms wave
　On Anio's echoing banks,
And Tullus of Arpinum,
　Chief of the Volscian aids,
And Metius with the long fair curls,
　The love of Anxur's maids,
And the white head of Vulso,
　The great Arician seer,
And Nepos of Laurentum,
　The hunter of the deer;
And in the back false Sextus
　Felt the good Roman steel,
And wriggling in the dust he died,
　Like a worm beneath the wheel:
And fliers and pursuers
　Were mingled in a mass;
And far away the battle
　Went roaring through the pass.

M—27*

### 37

Sempronius  Atratinus
  Sate in the Eastern Gate.
Beside him were three Fathers,
  Each in his chair of state;
Fabius, whose nine stout grandsons
  That day were in the field,
And Manlius, eldest of the Twelve
  Who keep the Golden Shield;
And Sergius, the High Pontiff,
  For wisdom far renowned;
In all Etruria's colleges
  Was no such Pontiff found.
And all around the portal,
  And high above the wall,
Stood a great throng of people,
  But sad and silent all;
Young lads, and stooping elders
  That might not bear the mail,
Matrons with lips that quivered,
  And maids with faces pale.
Since the first gleam of day-light,
  Sempronius had not ceased
To listen for the rushing
  Of horse-hoofs from the east.
The mist of eve was rising,
  The sun was hastening down,
When he was aware of a princely pair
  Fast pricking towards the town.
So like they were, man never
  Saw twins so like before;
Red with gore their armour was,
  Their steeds were red with gore.

### 38

"Hail to the great Asylum!
  Hail to the hill-tops seven!
Hail to the fire that burns for aye,
  And the shield that fell from heaven!
This day, by Lake Regillus,
  Under the Porcian height,
All in the lands of Tusculum
  Was fought a glorious fight.

To-morrow your Dictator
  Shall bring in triumph home
The spoils of thirty cities
  To deck the shrines of Rome!"


### 39

Then burst from that great concourse
  A shout that shook the towers,
And some ran north, and some ran south,
  Crying, "The day is ours!"
But on rode these strange horsemen,
  With slow and lordly pace;
And none who saw their bearing
  Durst ask their name or race.
On rode they to the Forum,
  While laurel-boughs and flowers,
From house-tops and from windows,
  Fell on their crests in showers.
When they drew nigh to Vesta,
  They vaulted down amain,
And washed their horses in the well
  That springs by Vesta's fane.
And straight again they mounted,
  And rode to Vesta's door;
Then, like a blast, away they passed,
  And no man saw them more.


### 40

And all the people trembled,
  And pale grew every cheek;
And Sergius the High Pontiff
  Alone found voice to speak:
"The Gods who live for ever
  Have fought for Rome to-day!
These be the Great Twin Brethren
  To whom the Dorians pray.
Back comes the Chief in triumph,
  Who, in the hour of fight,
Hath seen the Great Twin Brethren
  In harness on his right.
Safe comes the ship to haven,
  Through billows and through gales,

If once the Great Twin Brethren
　　Sit shining on the sails.
Wherefore they washed their horses
　　In Vesta's holy well,
Wherefore they rode to Vesta's door,
　　I know, but may not tell.
Here, hard by Vesta's temple,
　　Build we a stately dome
Unto the Great Twin Brethren
　　Who fought so well for Rome.
And when the months returning
　　Bring back this day of fight,
The proud Ides of Quintilis,
　　Marked evermore with white,
Unto the Great Twin Brethren
　　Let all the people throng,
With chaplets and with offerings,
　　With music and with song;
And let the doors and windows
　　Be hung with garlands all,
And let the Knights be summoned
　　To Mars without the wall:
Thence let them ride in purple
　　With joyous trumpet-sound,
Each mounted on his war-horse,
　　And each with olive crowned;
And pass in solemn order
　　Before the sacred dome,
Where dwell the Great Twin Brethren
　　Who fought so well for Rome."

# MISCELLANEOUS POEMS

## IVRY

### A SONG OF THE HUGUENOTS

Now glory to the Lord of Hosts, from whom all glories are!
And glory to our Sovereign Liege, King Henry of Navarre!
Now let there be the merry sound of music and of dance,
Through thy corn-fields green, and sunny vines, oh pleasant land
    of France!
And thou, Rochelle, our own Rochelle, proud city of the waters,
Again let rapture light the eyes of all thy mourning daughters.
As thou wert constant in our ills, be joyous in our joy,
For cold, and stiff, and still are they who wrought thy walls annoy.
Hurrah! Hurrah! a single field hath turned the chance of war,
Hurrah! Hurrah! for Ivry, and Henry of Navarre.


Oh! how our hearts were beating, when, at the dawn of day,
We saw the army of the League drawn out in long array;
With all its priest-led citizens, and all its rebel peers,
And Appenzel's stout infantry, and Egmont's Flemish spears.
There rode the brood of false Lorraine, the curses of our land;
And dark Mayenne was in the midst, a truncheon in his hand:
And, as we looked on them, we thought of Seine's empurpled
    flood,
And good Coligni's hoary hair all dabbled with his blood;
And we cried unto the living God, who rules the fate of war,
To fight for his own holy name, and Henry of Navarre.


The King is come to marshal us, in all his armour drest,
And he has bound a snow-white plume upon his gallant crest.
He looked upon his people, and a tear was in his eye;
He looked upon the traitors, and his glance was stern and high.
Right graciously he smiled on us, as rolled from wing to wing,
Down all our line, a deafening shout, "God save our Lord the
    King."
"An if my standard-bearer fall, as fall full well he may,
For never saw I promise yet of such a bloody fray,
Press where ye see my white plume shine, amidst the ranks of war,
And be your oriflamme to-day the helmet of Navarre."

Hurrah! the foes are moving. Hark to the mingled din,
Of fife, and steed, and trump, and drum, and roaring culverin.
The fiery Duke is pricking fast across Saint André's plain,
With all the hireling chivalry of Guelders and Almayne.
Now by the lips of those ye love, fair gentlemen of France,
Charge for the golden lilies,—upon them with the lance.
A thousand spurs are striking deep, a thousand spears in rest,
A thousand knights are pressing close behind the snow-white crest;
And in they burst, and on they rushed, while, like a guiding star,
Amidst the thickest carnage blazed the helmet of Navarre.

Now, God be praised, the day is ours. Mayenne hath turned
    his rein.
D'Aumale hath cried for quarter. The Flemish count is slain.
Their ranks are breaking like thin clouds before a Biscay gale;
The field is heaped with bleeding steeds, and flags, and cloven
    mail.
And then we thought on vengeance, and, all along our van,
"Remember Saint Bartholomew," was passed from man to man.
But out spake gentle Henry, "No Frenchman is my foe:
Down, down, with every foreigner, but let your brethren go."
Oh! was there ever such a knight, in friendship or in war,
As our Sovereign Lord, King Henry, the soldier of Navarre?

Right well fought all the Frenchmen who fought for France to-day;
And many a lordly banner God gave them for a prey.
But we of the religion have borne us best in fight;
And the good Lord of Rosny hath ta'en the cornet white.
Our own true Maximilian the cornet white hath ta'en,
The cornet white with crosses black, the flag of false Lorraine.
Up with it high; unfurl it wide; that all the host may know
How God hath humbled the proud house which wrought his
    church such woe.
Then on the ground, while trumpets sound their loudest point
    of war,
Fling the red shreds, a footcloth meet for Henry of Navarre.

Ho! maidens of Vienna; Ho! matrons of Lucerne;
Weep, weep, and rend your hair for those who never shall return.
Ho! Philip, send, for charity, thy Mexican pistoles,
That Antwerp monks may sing a mass for thy poor spearmen's
    souls.

Ho! gallant nobles of the League, look that your arms be bright;
Ho! burghers of Saint Genevieve, keep watch and ward to-night.
For our God hath crushed the tyrant, our God hath raised the
    slave,
And mocked the counsel of the wise, and the valour of the brave.
Then glory to his holy name, from whom all glories are;
And glory to our Sovereign Lord, King Henry of Navarre.


# THE MARRIAGE OF TIRZAH AND AHIRAD

### GENESIS VI. 3

It is the dead of night:
  Yet more than noonday light
Beams far and wide from many a gorgeous hall.
  Unnumbered harps are tinkling,
  Unnumbered lamps are twinkling,
In the great city of the fourfold wall.
  By the brazen castle's moat,
  The sentry hums a livelier note.
  The ship-boy chaunts a shriller lay
  From the galleys in the bay.
  Shout, and laugh, and hurrying feet
  Sound from mart and square and street,
  From the breezy laurel shades,
  From the granite colonnades,
  From the golden statue's base,
  From the stately market-place,
  Where, upreared by captive hands,
  The great Tower of Triumph stands,
  All its pillars in a blaze
  With the many-coloured rays,
  Which lanthorns of ten thousand dyes
  Shed on ten thousand panoplies.
    But closest is the throng,
    And loudest is the song,
In that sweet garden by the river's side,
  The abyss of myrtle bowers,
  The wilderness of flowers,
Where Cain hath built the palace of his pride.
  Such palace ne'er shall be again
  Among the dwindling race of men.

From all its threescore gates the light
  Of gold and steel afar was thrown;
Two hundred cubits rose in height
  The outer wall of polished stone.
  On the top was ample space
  For a gallant chariot race.
  Near either parapet a bed
  Of the richest mould was spread,
Where amidst flowers of every scent and hue
Rich orange trees, and palms, and giant cedars grew.


  In the mansion's public court
  All is revel, song, and sport;
For there, till morn shall tint the east,
Menials and guards prolong the feast.
The boards with painted vessels shine;
The marble cisterns foam with wine.
A hundred dancing girls are there
With zoneless waists and streaming hair;
And countless eyes with ardour gaze,
  And countless hands the measure beat,
As mix and part in amorous maze
  Those floating arms and bounding feet.
But none of all the race of Cain,
  Save those whom he hath deigned to grace
With yellow robe and sapphire chain,
  May pass beyond that outer space.
  For now within the painted hall
  The Firstborn keeps high festival.
Before the glittering valves all night
  Their post the chosen captains hold.
Above the portal's stately height
  The legend flames in lamps of gold:
  "In life united and in death
  "May Tirzah and Ahirad be,
  The bravest he of all the sons of Seth,
  Of all the house of Cain the loveliest she."


  Through all the climates of the earth
  This night is given to festal mirth.
  The long continued war is ended.
  The long divided lines are blended.

Ahirad's bow shall now no more
Make fat the wolves with kindred gore.
The vultures shall expect in vain
Their banquet from the sword of Cain.
Without a guard the herds and flocks
Along the frontier moors and rocks
   From eve to morn may roam;
Nor shriek, nor shout, nor reddened sky,
Shall warn the startled hind to fly
   From his beloved home.
Nor to the pier shall burghers crowd
   With straining necks and faces pale,
And think that in each flitting cloud
   They see a hostile sail.
The peasant without fear shall guide
Down smooth canal or river wide
   His painted bark of cane,
Fraught, for some proud bazaar's arcades,
With chestnuts from his native shades,
   And wine, and milk, and grain.
Search round the peopled globe to-night,
   Explore each continent and isle,
There is no door without a light,
   No face without a smile.
The noblest chiefs of either race,
   From north and south, from west and east,
Crowd to the painted hall to grace
   The pomp of that atoning feast.
With widening eyes and labouring breath
Stand the fair-haired sons of Seth,
As bursts upon their dazzled sight
The endless avenue of light,
The bowers of tulip, rose, and palm,
The thousand cressets fed with balm,
The silken vests, the boards piled high
With amber, gold, and ivory,
The crystal founts whence sparkling flow
The richest wines o'er beds of snow,
The walls where blaze in living dyes
The king's three hundred victories.
The heralds point the fitting seat
To every guest in order meet,
And place the highest in degree

Nearest th' imperial canopy.
Beneath its broad and gorgeous fold,
With naked swords and shields of gold,
Stood the seven princes of the tribes of Nod.
Upon an ermine carpet lay
Two tiger cubs in furious play,
Beneath the emerald throne where sat the signed of God.

Over that ample forehead white
    The thousandth year returneth.
Still, on its commanding height,
With a fierce and blood-red light,
    The fiery token burneth.
Wheresoe'er that mystic star
Blazeth in the van of war,
    Back recoil before its ray
Shield and banner, bow and spear,
    Maddened horses break away
From the trembling charioteer.
    The fear of that stern king doth lie
    On all that live beneath the sky;
All shrink before the mark of his despair,
The seal of that great curse which he alone can bear.

Blazing in pearls and diamonds' sheen,
    Tirzah, the young Ahirad's bride,
Of humankind the destined queen,
    Sits by her great forefather's side.
The jetty curls, the forehead high,
    The swanlike neck, the eagle face,
The glowing cheek, the rich dark eye,
    Proclaim her of the elder race.
With flowing locks of auburn hue,
And features smooth, and eye of blue,
    Timid in love as brave in arms,
The gentle heir of Seth askance
Snatches a bashful, ardent glance
    At her majestic charms;
Blest when across that brow high musing flashes
    A deeper tint of rose,
Thrice blest when from beneath the silken lashes
    Of her proud eye she throws
The smile of blended fondness and disdain
Which marks the daughters of the house of Cain.

All hearts are light around the hall
Save his who is the lord of all.
The painted roofs, the attendant train,
The lights, the banquet, all are vain.
He sees them not.  His fancy strays
To other scenes and other days.
A cot by a lone forest's edge,
   A fountain murmuring through the trees,
A garden with a wild flower hedge,
   Whence sounds the music of the bees,
A little flock of sheep at rest
Upon a mountain's swarthy breast.
On his rude spade he seems to lean
   Beside the well remembered stone,
Rejoicing o'er the promise green
   Of the first harvest man hath sown.
   He sees his mother's tears;
   His father's voice he hears,
Kind as when first it praised his youthful skill.
   And soon a seraph-child,
   In boyish rapture wild,
With a light crook comes bounding from the hill,
   Kisses his hands, and strokes his face,
   And nestles close in his embrace.
   In his adamantine eye
   None might discern his agony;
But they who had grown hoary next his side,
   And read his stern dark face with deepest skill,
Could trace strange meanings in that lip of pride,
   Which for one moment quivered and was still.
No time for them to mark or him to feel
   Those inward stings; for clarion, flute, and lyre,
   And the rich voices of a countless quire,
Burst on the ear in one triumphant peal.
In breathless transport sits the admiring throng,
As sink and swell the notes of Jubal's lofty song.


"Sound the timbrel, strike the lyre,
  Wake the trumpet's blast of fire,
   Till the gilded arches ring.
  Empire, victory, and fame,
  Be ascribed unto the name

Of our father and our king.
Of the deeds which he hath done,
Of the spoils which he hath won,
    Let his grateful children sing.

"When the deadly fight was fought,
When the great revenge was wrought,
When on the slaughtered victims lay
The minion stiff and cold as they,
Doomed to exile, sealed with flame,
From the west the wanderer came.
Six score years and six he strayed
A hunter through the forest shade.
The lion's shaggy jaws he tore,
To earth he smote the foaming boar,
He crushed the dragon's fiery crest,
And scaled the condor's dizzy nest;
Till hardy sons and daughters fair
Increased around his woodland lair.
Then his victorious bow unstrung
On the great bison's horn he hung.
Giraffe and elk he left to hold
    The wilderness of boughs in peace,
And trained his youth to pen the fold,
    To press the cream, and weave the fleece.
As shrunk the streamlet in its bed,
    As black and scant the herbage grew,
O'er endless plains his flocks he led
    Still to new brooks and pastures new.
So strayed he till the white pavilions
Of his camp were told by millions,
Till his children's households seven
Were numerous as the stars of heaven.
Then he bade us rove no more;
    And in the place that pleased him best,
On the great river's fertile shore,
    He fixed the city of his rest.
He taught us then to bind the sheaves,
    To strain the palm's delicious milk,
And from the dark green mulberry leaves
    To cull the filmy silk.
Then first from straw-built mansions roamed
    O'er flower-beds trim the skilful bees;

Then first the purple wine vats foamed
  Around the laughing peasant's knees;
And olive-yards, and orchards green,
O'er all the hills of Nod were seen.

"Of our father and our king
  Let his grateful children sing.
From him our race its being draws,
His are our arts, and his our laws.
Like himself he bade us be,
Proud, and brave, and fierce, and free.
True, through every turn of fate,
In our friendship and our hate.
Calm to watch, yet prompt to dare;
Quick to feel, yet firm to bear;
Only timid, only weak,
Before sweet woman's eye and cheek.
We will not serve, we will not know,
The God who is our father's foe.
In our proud cities to his name
No temples rise, no altars flame.
Our flocks of sheep, our groves of spice,
To him afford no sacrifice.
Enough that once the House of Cain
Hath courted with oblation vain
    The sullen power above.
Henceforth we bear the yoke no more;
The only gods whom we adore
    Are glory, vengeance, love.

"Of our father and our king
  Let his grateful children sing.
What eye of living thing may brook
On his blazing brow to look?
What might of living thing may stand
Against the strength of his right hand?
First he led his armies forth
Against the Mammoths of the north,
What time they wasted in their pride
Pasture and vineyard far and wide.
Then the White River's icy flood
Was thawed with fire and dyed with blood.

And heard for many a league the sound
Of the pine forests blazing round,
And the death-howl and trampling din
Of the gigantic herd within.
From the surging sea of flame
Forth the tortured monsters came;
As of breakers on the shore
Was their onset and their roar;
As the cedar-trees of God
Stood the stately ranks of Nod.
One long night and one short day
The sword was lifted up to slay.
    Then marched the firstborn and his sons
O'er the white ashes of the wood,
And counted of that savage brood
    Nine times nine thousand skeletons.

"On the snow with carnage red
The wood is piled, the skins are spread.
A thousand fires illume the sky;
Round each a hundred warriors lie.
But, long ere half the night was spent,
Forth thundered from the golden tent
    The rousing voice of Cain.
A thousand trumps in answer rang,
And fast to arms the warriors sprang
    O'er all the frozen plain.
A herald from the wealthy bay
Hath come with tidings of dismay.
From the western ocean's coast
Seth hath led a countless host,
And vows to slay with fire and sword
All who call not on the Lord.
His archers hold the mountain forts;
His light armed ships blockade the ports;
    His horsemen tread the harvest down.
On twelve proud bridges he hath passed
The river dark with many a mast,
And pitched his mighty camp at last
    Before the imperial town.

"On the south and on the west,
Closely was the city prest.

Before us lay the hostile powers.
The breach was wide between the towers.
Pulse and meal within were sold
For a double weight of gold.
Our mighty father had gone forth
Two hundred marches to the north.
Yet in that extreme of ill
We stoutly kept his city still;
And swore beneath his royal wall,
Like his true sons, to fight and fall.


"Hark, hark, to gong and horn,
Clarion, and fife, and drum,
The morn, the fortieth morn,
Fixed for the great assault is come.
Between the camp and city spreads
A waving sea of helmed heads.
From the royal car of Seth
Was hung the blood-red flag of death:
At sight of that thrice-hallowed sign
Wide flew at once each banner's fold:
The captains clashed their arms of gold;
The war cry of Elohim rolled
Far down their endless line.
On the northern hills afar
Pealed an answering note of war.
Soon the dust in whirlwinds driven,
Rushed across the northern heaven.
Beneath its shroud came thick and loud
The tramp as of a countless crowd;
And at intervals were seen
Lance and hauberk glancing sheen;
And at intervals were heard
Charger's neigh and battle word.


"Oh what a rapturous cry
From all the city's thousand spires arose,
With what a look the hollow eye
Of the lean watchman glared upon the foes,
With what a yell of joy the mother pressed
The moaning baby to her withered breast,

When through the swarthy cloud that veiled the plain
Burst on his children's sight the flaming brow of Cain!"

There paused perforce that noble song;
For from all the joyous throng,
Burst forth a rapturous shout which drowned
Singer's voice and trumpet's sound.
Thrice that stormy clamour fell,
Thrice rose again with mightier swell.
The last and loudest roar of all
Had died along the painted wall.
The crowd was hushed; the minstrel train
Prepared to strike the chords again;
When on each ear distinctly smote
A low and wild and wailing note.
It moans again.  In mute amaze
Menials, and guests, and harpers gaze.
They look above, beneath, around,
No shape doth own that mournful sound.
It comes not from the tuneful quire;
    It comes not from the feasting peers;
There is no tone of earthly lyre
    So soft, so sad, so full of tears.
Then a strange horror came on all
Who sate at that high festival.
The far famed harp, the harp of gold,
Dropped from Jubal's trembling hold.
Frantic with dismay the bride
Clung to her Ahirad's side.
And the corpse-like hue of dread
Ahirad's haughty face o'erspread.
Yet not even in that agony of awe
    Did the young leader of the fair-haired race
From Tirzah's shuddering grasp his hand withdraw
    Or turn his eyes from Tirzah's livid face.
        The tigers to their lord retreat,
        And crouch and whine beneath his feet.
    Prone sink to earth the golden shielded seven.
        All hearts are cowed save his alone
        Who sits upon the emerald throne;
    For he hath heard Elohim speak from heaven.
        Still thunders in his ear the peal;
        Still blazes on his front the seal:

And on the soul of the proud king
No terror of created thing
From sky, or earth, or hell, hath power
Since that unutterable hour.

He rose to speak, but paused, and listening stood,
Not daunted, but in sad and curious mood,
    With knitted brow, and searching eye of fire.
A deathlike silence sank on all around,
And through the boundless space was heard no
        sound,
    Save the soft tones of that mysterious lyre.
    Broken, faint, and low,
    At first the numbers flow.
Louder, deeper, quicker, still
    Into one fierce peal they swell,
And the echoing palace fill
    With a strange funereal yell.
A voice comes forth. But what, or where?
On the earth, or in the air?
Like the midnight winds that blow
Round a lone cottage in the snow,
With howling swell and sighing fall,
It wails along the trophied hall.
In such a wild and dreary moan
    The watches of the Seraphim
    Poured out all night their plaintive hymn
Before the eternal throne.
Then, when from many a heavenly eye
    Drops as of earthly pity fell
For her who had aspired too high,
    For him who loved too well.
When, stunned by grief, the gentle pair
From the nuptial garden fair,
Linked in a sorrowful caress,
Strayed through the untrodden wilderness:
And close behind their footsteps came
The desolating sword of flame,
And drooped the cedared alley's pride,
And fountains shrank, and roses died.

"Rejoice, oh Son of God, rejoice,"
Sang that melancholy voice,

"Rejoice, the maid is fair to see;
  The bower is decked for her and thee;
  The ivory lamps around it throw
  A soft and pure and mellow glow.
  Where'er the chastened lustre falls
  On roof or cornice, floor or walls,
  Woven of pink and rose appear
  Such words as love delights to hear.
The breath of myrrh, the lute's soft sound,
Float through the moonlight galleries round.
O'er beds of violet and through groves of spice,
  Lead thy proud bride into the nuptial bower;
For thou hast bought her with a fearful price,
  And she hath dowered thee with a fearful dower.
  The price is life. The dower is death.
    Accursed loss! Accursed gain!
  For her thou givest the blessedness of Seth,
    And to thine arms she brings the curse of Cain.
  Round the dark curtains of the fiery throne
    Pauses awhile the voice of sacred song:
  From all the angelic ranks goes forth a groan,
    'How long, O Lord, how long?
The still small voice makes answer, 'Wait and see,
Oh sons of glory, what the end shall be.'


"But, in the outer darkness of the place
Where God hath shown his power without his grace,
  Is laughter and the sound of glad acclaim,
    Loud as when, on wings of fire,
    Fulfilled of his malign desire,
  From Paradise the conquering serpent came.
The giant ruler of the morning star
    From off his fiery bed
    Lifts high his stately head,
Which Michael's sword hath marked with many a
      scar.
    At his voice the pit of hell
    Answers with a joyous yell,
    And flings her dusky portals wide
    For the bridegroom and the bride.


  "But louder still shall be the din
  In the halls of Death and Sin,

When the full measure runneth o'er,
When mercy can endure no more,
When he who vainly proffers grace,
Comes in his fury to deface
   The fair creation of his hand;
When from the heaven streams down amain
For forty days the sheeted rain;
And from his ancient barriers free,
With a deafening roar the sea
   Comes foaming up the land.
Mother, cast thy babe aside:
Bridegroom, quit thy virgin bride:
Brother, pass thy brother by:
'Tis for life, for life, ye fly.
Along the drear horizon raves
The swift advancing line of waves.
On: on: their frothy crests appear
Each moment nearer and more near.
Urge the dromedary's speed;
Spur to death the reeling steed;
If perchance ye yet may gain
The mountains that o'erhang the plain.


"Oh thou haughty land of Nod,
  Hear the sentence of thy God.
  Thou hast said 'Of all the hills
  Whence, after autumn rains, the rills
    In silver trickle down,
  The fairest is that mountain white
  Which intercepts the morning light
    From Cain's imperial town.
  On its first and gentlest swell
  Are pleasant halls where nobles dwell;
  And marble porticoes are seen
  Peeping through terraced gardens green.
  Above are olives, palms, and vines;
  And higher yet the dark-blue pines;
  And highest on the summit shines
    The crest of everlasting ice.
  Here let the God of Abel own
  That human art hath wonders shown
    Beyond his boasted paradise.'

"Therefore on that proud mountain's crown
Thy few surviving sons and daughters
Shall see their latest sun go down
Upon a boundless waste of waters.
None salutes and none replies;
None heaves a groan or breathes a prayer;
They crouch on earth with tearless eyes,
And clenched hands, and bristling hair.
The rain pours on: no star illumes
The blackness of the roaring sky.
And each successive billow booms
Nigher still and still more nigh.
And now upon the howling blast
The wreaths of spray come thick and fast;
And a great billow by the tempest curled
Falls with a thundering crash; and all is o'er.
And what is left of all this glorious world?
A sky without a beam, a sea without a shore.

"Oh thou fair land, where from their starry home
Cherub and seraph oft delight to roam,
Thou city of the thousand towers,
Thou palace of the golden stairs,
Ye gardens of perennial flowers,
Ye moated gates, ye breezy squares;
Ye parks amidst whose branches high
Oft peers the squirrel's sparkling eye;
Ye vineyards, in whose trellised shade
Pipes many a youth to many a maid;
Ye ports where rides the gallant ship;
Ye marts where wealthy burghers meet;
Ye dark green lanes which know the trip
Of woman's conscious feet;
Ye grassy meads where, when the day is done,
The shepherd pens his fold;
Ye purple moors on which the setting sun
Leaves a rich fringe of gold;
Ye wintry deserts where the larches grow;
Ye mountains on whose everlasting snow
No human foot hath trod;
Many a fathom shall ye sleep
Beneath the grey and endless deep,
In the great day of the revenge of God."

## THE ARMADA

### A FRAGMENT

ATTEND, all ye who list to hear our noble England's praise;
I tell of thrice famous deeds she wrought in ancient days,
When that great fleet invincible against her bore in vain
The richest spoils of Mexico, the stoutest hearts of Spain.

It was about the lovely close of a warm summer day,
There came a gallant merchant-ship full sail to Plymouth Bay;
Her crew hath seen Castile's black fleet, beyond Aurigny's isle,
At earliest twilight, on the waves lie heaving many a mile.
At sunrise she escaped their van, by God's especial grace;
And the tall Pinta, till the noon, had held her close in chase.
Forthwith a guard at every gun was placed along the wall;
The beacon blazed upon the roof of Edgecumbe's lofty hall;
Many a light fishing-bark put out to pry along the coast,
And with loose rein and bloody spur rode inland many a post.
With his white hair unbonneted, the stout old sheriff comes;
Behind him march the halberdiers; before him sound the drums;
His yeomen round the market cross make clear an ample space;
For there behoves him to set up the standard of Her Grace.
And haughtily the trumpets peal, and gaily dance the bells,
As slow upon the labouring wind the royal blazon swells.
Look how the Lion of the sea lifts up his ancient crown,
And underneath his deadly paw treads the gay lilies down.
So stalked he when he turned to flight, on that famed Picard field,
Bohemia's plume, and Genoa's bow, and Cæsar's eagle shield.
So glared he when at Agincourt in wrath he turned to bay,
And crushed and torn beneath his claws the princely hunters lay.
Ho! strike the flagstaff, sir Knight: ho! scatter flowers, fair maids:
Ho! gunners, fire a loud salute: ho! gallants, draw your blades:
Thou sun, shine on her joyously; ye breezes, waft her wide;
Our glorious SEMPER EADEM, the banner of our pride.

The freshening breeze of eve unfurled that banner's massy fold;
The parting gleam of sunshine kissed that haughty scroll of gold;
Night sank upon the dusky beach, and on the purple sea,
Such night in England ne'er had been, nor ne'er again shall be.
From Eddystone to Berwick bounds, from Lynn to Milford Bay,
That time of slumber was as bright and busy as the day;
For swift to east and swift to west the ghastly war-flame spread,

High on St. Michael's Mount it shone: it shone on Beachy Head.
Far on the deep the Spaniard saw, along each southern shire,
Cape beyond cape, in endless range, those twinkling points of fire.
The fisher left his skiff to rock on Tamar's glittering waves:
The rugged miners poured to war from Mendip's sunless caves:
O'er Longleat's towers, o'er Cranbourne's oaks, the fiery herald
   flew:
He roused the shepherds of Stonehenge, the rangers of Beaulieu.
Right sharp and quick the bells all night rang out from Bristol town,
And ere the day three hundred horse had met on Clifton down;
The sentinel on Whitehall gate looked forth into the night,
And saw o'erhanging Richmond Hill the streak of blood-red light.
Then bugle's note and cannon's roar the deathlike silence broke,
And with one start, and with one cry, the royal city woke.
At once on all her stately gates arose the answering fires;
At once the wild alarum clashed from all her reeling spires;
From all the batteries of the Tower pealed loud the voice of fear;
And all the thousand masts of Thames sent back a louder cheer:
And from the furthest wards was heard the rush of hurrying feet,
And the broad streams of pikes and flags rushed down each roaring
   street;
And broader still became the blaze, and louder still the din,
As fast from every village round the horse came spurring in:
And eastward straight from wild Blackheath the warlike errand
   went,
And roused in many an ancient hall the gallant squires of Kent.
Southward from Surrey's pleasant hills flew those bright couriers
   forth;
High on bleak Hampstead's swarthy moor they started for the north;
And on, and on, without a pause, untired they bounded still:
All night from tower to tower they sprang; they sprang from hill
   to hill:
Till the proud peak unfurled the flag o'er Darwin's rocky dales,
Till like volcanoes flared to heaven the stormy hills of Wales,
Till twelve fair counties saw the blaze on Malvern's lonely height,
Till streamed in crimson on the wind the Wrekin's crest of light,
Till broad and fierce the star came forth on Ely's stately fane,
And tower and hamlet rose in arms o'er all the boundless plain;
Till Belvoir's lordly terraces the sign to Lincoln sent,
And Lincoln sped the message on o'er the wide vale of Trent;
Till Skiddaw saw the fire that burned on Gaunt's embattled pile,
And the red glare on Skiddaw roused the burghers of Carlisle.

       *       *       *       *       *       *

## THE LAST BUCCANEER

THE winds were yelling, the waves were swelling,
   The sky was black and drear,
When the crew with eyes of flame brought the ship without
    a name
   Alongside the last Buccaneer.


"Whence flies your sloop full sail before so fierce a gale,
   When all others drive bare on the seas?
Say, come ye from the shore of the holy Salvador,
   Or the gulf of the rich Caribbees?"


"From a shore no search hath found, from a gulf no line can
    sound,
   Without rudder or needle we steer;
Above, below, our bark, dies the sea fowl and the shark,
   As we fly by the last Buccaneer.


"To-night there shall be heard on the rocks of Cape de
    Verde
   A loud crash, and a louder roar;
And to-morrow shall the deep, with a heavy moaning, sweep
   The corpses and wreck to the shore."


The stately ship of Clyde securely now may ride
   In the breath of the citron shades;
And Severn's towering mast securely now flies fast,
   Through the sea of the balmy Trades.


From St. Jago's wealthy port, from Havannah's royal fort,
   The seaman goes forth without fear;
For since that stormy night not a mortal hath had sight
   Of the flag of the last Buccaneer.

## EPITAPH ON A JACOBITE

To my true king I offered free from stain
Courage and faith; vain faith, and courage vain.
For him, I threw lands, honours, wealth, away,
And one dear hope, that was more prized than they.
For him I languished in a foreign clime,
Grey-haired with sorrow in my manhood's prime;
Heard on Lavernia Scargill's whispering trees,
And pined by Arno for my lovelier Tees;
Beheld each night my home in fevered sleep,
Each morning started from the dream to weep;
Till God, who saw me tried too sorely, gave
The resting place I asked, an early grave.
Oh thou, whom chance leads to this nameless stone,
From that proud country which was once mine own,
By those white cliffs I never more must see,
By that dear language which I spake like thee,
Forget all feuds, and shed one English tear
O'er English dust. A broken heart lies here.

Printed in Great Britain
by NOVELLO & COMPANY LIMITED
LONDON W.I